THE KU KLUX KLAN

THE KU KLUX KLAN

A BIBLIOGRAPHY

**Compiled by Lenwood G. Davis and
Janet L. Sims-Wood**

With the assistance of Marsha L. Moore

Foreword by Earl E. Thorpe

GREENWOOD PRESS
Westport, Connecticut • London, England

Acknowledgments

Permission to reprint the following extract is gratefully acknowledged.
"Estimated Membership of the Ku Klux Klan, 1925," page 14, November 2, 1930,
reprinted by permission of *The Washington Post*.

Library of Congress Cataloging in Publication Data

Davis, Lenwood G.
  The Ku Klux Klan.

  Includes index.
  1. Ku Klux Klan—Bibliography. 2. Ku Klux Klan
(1915-   )—Bibliography. I. Sims-Wood, Janet L.,
1945-   . II. Moore, Marsha L. III. Title.
Z1249.K8D38 1984   016.3224'2'0973   83-1709
[E668]
ISBN 0-313-22949-X (lib. bdg.)

Library of Congress Catalog Card Number: 83-1709
ISBN: 0-313-22949-X

First published in 1984

Greenwood Press
A division of Congressional Information Service, Inc.
88 Post Road West, Westport, Connecticut 06881

Printed in the United States of America

10 9 8 7 6 5 4 3 2 1

FOR
ARMENTINE, BONITA AND BILL BANKS,
AND
MARVIN AND HAZEL SIMS

Contents

Foreword

Thoughout American history, periods of intensified racism and ultraconservatism have coincided. This was evident in the 1920s, when, among other things, the administrations of presidents Warren G. Harding, Calvin Coolidge, and Herbert Hoover saw dramatic increases in such things as the resurgence of the Ku Klux Klan, race riots, lynchings, public racist utterances, and a general attack on the rights, privileges, and opportunities of many Americans. The same twin phenomena of intensified racism and ultraconservatism were also evident during the 1880s and 1890s, when many of the Reconstruction era's democratic advances were overthrown and African-Americans were disfranchised and driven from participation in the nation's legislative processes. There are other examples; resurgency of the activities of the malign partnership between intensified racism and ultraconservatism was clearly evident in 1981.

Merl Curti, in the introduction to his volume, *The Growth of American Thought*, describes what roughly may be called a pendulum theory operating in the nation's life and history. He saw an alternating rhythm that swings between more or less liberal and conservative poles. Earlier, Vernon L. Parrington, in his volume, *Main Currents In American Thought*, had depicted an alternating rhythm between poles which he called Hamiltonian and Jeffersonian. Studies such as Charles A. Beard's *An Economic Interpretation Of The Constitution* combine with such a phenomenon as Chief Justice John Marshall's decisions exalting property over human rights to show that much conservatism has been more "rule rather than exception" in American history. African-American scholars have pointed this out, while also emphasizing that for many generations most of their ancestors, comprising one-third of the South's population, were victims of racism in the form of chattel slavery.

During periods of intensified racism and ultraconservatism, the meanest sides of the nation's thought and action are given their fullest expression. This "meanness mania" manifests itself in such forms as greater public and private greed for monetary profits-by-any-means-necessary and intensified attacks on the image, person, and rights of Blacks, labor unions, women, social critics, and others. Organizations and persons on the attack, as the vanguard of the "meanness mania," generally have been on the American scene, but mainly have stayed on the periphery of things until the ultra right wing swing of the pendulum. Then they take center stage and hide their "meanness mania" utterances and actions behind proclamations that they are rescuing civilization from the destructive achievements of the devil-like liberals and progressives and restoring the sacred ways of the Founding Fathers.

In the world of what Sigmund Freud called "the reality principle," everything is dialetical. Thus, when the forward-looking, liberal, progressive, people-oriented forces are dominant in a nation with a two-party system, sooner or later an opportunity presents itself to turn enough voters against those in power. The latter will be blamed for their own mistakes as well as for inherited problems which they have not been able to solve. Propaganda becomes a weapon, and great damage can be done when the greediest, most callous, and meanest side of the national character takes center stage.

Some members of the Ku Klux Klan always have known that their essence is to be part of the "meanness mania," though many other members have not known this. Powerful economic and political operators, who profit handsomely from this total thrust, always have been willing to manipulate and use the Klan.

The forces of progress and real democracy ever must struggle against the "meanness mania." "Eternal vigilance is the price of liberty" must be a motto of all well-meaning Americans, regardless of their race, creed, or color. Frederick Douglass was right when he said: "Those who profess to favor freedom, and yet depreciate agitation, are men who want grain without plowing up the ground. They want rain without thunder and lightning. They want the ocean without the awful roar of its many waters. This struggle may be a moral one; or it may be a physical one; or it may be both moral and physical; but it must be a struggle. Power concedes nothing without a demand."

This bibliography by Lenwood G. Davis, a noted Black historian and internationally known bibliographer, and Janet Sims-Wood, a noted Black librarian, compiler, and bibliographer, is a much-needed reference tool. Needless to say, this work is the most comprehensive bibliography ever compiled on one of the most vicious organizations in the world. The authors have shown that Klan activities are not only seen in the United States but in several foreign countries as well. It is hoped that this work will provide the impetus for more local, state, and federal investigations into Klan activities.

The danger in America comes not from groups like the Moral Majority, but from groups such as the Klan who are in sympathy with them. There is no doubt that this volume by Dr. Davis and Mrs. Sims-Wood will gain importance and stand the test of time as the history and activities of the Ku Klux Klan in the world are more thoroughly analyzed and researched. Only these two resourceful persons could have produced a work of this magnitude. Historians, researchers, scholars, critics, librarians, and others will be indebted to them for years to come.

Earl E. Thorpe

Introduction

This is the first comprehensive bibliography on the Ku Klux Klan since William H. Fisher published *The Invisible Empire: A Bibliography of the Ku Klux Klan* in 1980. Our work, however, differs from his book in that it is larger, with nearly seventy-five percent of the citations coming from newspapers. Fisher devoted little space to newspaper articles or to Klan activities in foreign countries, limiting his treatment of the Klan to selected states. We have included their activities in foreign countries as well as in forty-eight states, making this volume national and international in scope.

The Ku Klux Klan had its origin in Pulaski, Tennessee, in 1866. One of the main objectives of this group was to intimidate the newly freed Blacks in that area. The six men that formed this "club" were former college men, who had been officers in the Civil War. They met in secret, put on disguises, and rode horses at night, engaging in wild pranks and much horseplay, according to Klan history. They declared that there were no plans for violence. They only wanted to instill fear in the Blacks as a means of controlling them: to stop them from voting and participating in the political process.

Although the Civil War had ended only a few months earlier, Southern Whites were "ready" to return society to the status quo. Within two years the Ku Klux Klan had gained statewide attention and had spread to other cities. In April 1867, Klansmen met in Nashville, drew up a constitution, and elected Nathan Bedford Forrest, a former Confederate general, as Grand Wizard. Within a few years the Klan had chapters in most Southern states. Now, the method of control was violence against Blacks: murdering, whipping, hanging, and mutilating. As David M. Chalmers pointed out, "To the White Southerner, the Ku Klux Klan was a law-and-order movement because it was directed at the restoration of the proper order."

It should be pointed out that over the years the Ku Klux Klan has been not only anti-Black, but also anti-Jewish, anti-Catholic, anti-foreign-born, anti-Mexican, and anti-Big Business. Over the years, the Klan never really died; it only declined. In the 1920s and 1930s there was a resurgence of this organization. The Klan declined again in the 1940s and 1950s and was revived in the 1960s. By the late 1960s, with the emergence of the Black Power Movement, the Klan began to fade and continued to decline in the 1970s. As Blacks began to obtain certain laws to protect themselves, Klan activities against Blacks decreased. In the 1970s, Blacks were benefitting from the laws Congress had passed in public accommodations in 1964, the Voting Rights Act of 1965, and the 1968 housing and protection laws. The 1980s saw the revival of the Ku Klux Klan once again with the shoot-out in Greensboro, North Carolina, and, to some degree, the enforcement of "Affirmative Action" laws. William H. Fisher best summarized the Ku Klux Klan when he concluded: "What is unique about the Klan is not that it is a prime example of the intolerance and bigotry that can exist in a society; unfortunately there are more examples of that in our history than one might care to think about. The Klan is unique in the respect that this group is now into its second century of existence. . . ." This means that the Klan has appealed to at least some element in American society for over 100 years, and, despite repeated attempts to remove the Klan from the scene, it has been able to reappear and reestablish itself within the social fabric in some fashion.

This bibliography is divided into eight sections: Chapter 1 deals with major works about the Klan and includes both books and pamphlets. The two latest books are: David M. Chalmers, *Hooded Americanism: The History of the Ku Klux Klan* (1981). This is the second edition of this book, and it includes material on the shoot-out involving the Klan in Greensboro, North Carolina, in 1979. The first edition was published in 1965 and was entitled *Hooded Americanism: The First Century of the Ku Klux Klan 1865-1965*. The most recent book is by Jerry Thompson, *My Life in the Klan: A True Story by the First Investigative Reporter to Infiltrate the Ku Klux Klan* (1982). Chapter 2 lists general works and includes national books in order by state. The latest state history on the Klan is by Larry A. Gerlach entitled *Blazing Crosses in Zion: The Ku Klux Klan in Utah* (1982). Chapter 3 lists dissertations and theses by state and one thesis on Klan activities in Canada. There are also both general dissertations and theses. Chapter 4 includes Ku Klux Klan materials: official documents by men and women of the Klan. Broadsides, poems, novels, and plays are also included in this section. Government documents are cited in Chapter 5. Chapter 6 deals with elected officials' speeches which are listed by state. Chapter 7 consists of articles in the Klan magazine, *The Kourier*, listed by state, in general, and in Europe. Poems and prayers that appeared in this magazine are also included. General works by states and countries round out Chapter 8. Five appendixes and an author index conclude the book.

Any work of this magnitude requires the assistance of many people. It would be nearly impossible to list each and every individual who assisted us. We would, however, like to give special thanks to the following institutions and individuals: The Moorland-Spingarn Research Center at Howard University; Schomburg Center For Research In Black Culture; University of Tennessee Library at Knoxville; Duke University Library at Durham, North Carolina; University of North Carolina at Chapel Hill; Library of Congress; *The Washington Post*; Montclair State College, Upper Montclair, New Jersey; Wake Forest University, Winston Salem, North Carolina; University of Oregon; University of North Carolina at Greensboro; New York City Public Library; Winston Salem State University Library; and the University of Colorado.

We are particularly indebted for the aid given to us by Marsha L. Moore, Janie Miller Harris, Ernest Kaiser, Belinda S. Daniels, Gwendolyn Cogdell, Carrie Hackney, Kathy Jenkins, our typist Pat Lumpkin, and to our families, who supported us throughout this project.

We take full responsibility for all errors and omissions.

THE KU KLUX KLAN

1
Major Works

BOOKS

A SELECTED LIST

1. Alexander, Charles. The Ku Klux Klan In The Southwest. Lexington, KY: University of Kentucky Press, 1965, 288p.

2. Brown, George Alfred. Harold The Klansman. Kansas City, MO.: Western Baptist, 1923, 303p.

3. Chalmers, David. Hooded Americanism; The First Century Of The Ku Klux Klan 1865-1965. Garden City, N.Y.: Doubleday, 1965, 420p.

4. _____. Hooded Americanism: The History Of The Ku Klux Klan. Second Edition. New York: New Viewpoints, 1981, 478p.

5. Cook, Fred J. The Ku Klux Klan: America's Recurring Nightmare. New York: Julian Messner, 1980, 160p.

6. Curry, LeRoy Amos. The Ku Klux Klan Under The Searchlight; An Authoritative, Dignified and Enlightened Discussion Of The American Klan; Revises And Condensed By LeRoy A. Curry, With A Biographical Introduction By Beulah L. Curry; His Wife; A Fair, Candid And Judicial Explanation Of Americanism As Advocated By The Ku Klux Klan And Viewed By An American Citizen. Kansas City, MO.: Printed for the author by the Western Baptist Publishing Co., 1924, 240p.

7. Damer, Eyre. When The Ku Klux Rode. New York: The Neale Publishing Co., 1912, 152p.

8. Davis, Susan Lawrence. Authentic History, Ku Klux Klan, 1865-1877. New York: American Library Service, 1924, 316p.

9.   Frost, Stanley. The Challenge of The Klan. Indiana-
     polis: Bobbs-Merrill Co., 1924. 302pp.

10. Fry, Gladys-Marie. Night Riders [KKK] In Folk History.
     Knoxville: University of Tennessee Press, 1975. 215pp.

11. Fry, Henry Peck. The Modern Ku Klux Klan. Boston, Ma.:
     Small, Maynard & Co., 1922. 259pp. Reprinted in 1969.

12. Fuller, Edgar I. Maelstrom; The Visible Of The Invisi-
     ble Empire: A True History Of The Ku Klux Klan.
     Denver, Colo. Maelstrom Publishing Co., 1925? 200pp.
     Rev. ed. by George La Dura, 1925. 178pp.

13. Gillette, Paul J. and Eugene Tillinger. Inside Ku Klux
     Klan. New York: Pyramid Books, 1965. 160pp.

14. Green, John Paterson. Recollections of the Inhabitants,
     Localities, Superstitions and Ku Klux Outrages of the
     Carolinas, By A "Carpet-Bagger" Who Was Born and Lived
     There. Cleveland, 1880. 205pp.

15. Haas, Ben. K.K.K. San Diego, CA: Regency Books, 1963.
     158pp.

16. Horn, Stanley F. Invisible Empire: The Story of the
     Ku Klux Klan, 1866-1871. Boston: Houghton Mifflin Co.,
     1939. 434pp.

17. Horrible Disclosures. A Full and Authentic Expose of
     The Ku-Klux Klan, From Original Documents of the Order,
     and Other Official Sources. Cincinnati: Padrick &
     Co., 1868. 109pp.

18. Hughes, Llewellyn. In Defense of the Klan. New York,
     1924. 125pp.

19. Jackson, Kenneth T. The Ku Klux Klan in the City,
     1915-1930. New York: Oxford University Press, 1967.
     326pp.

20. Johnsen, Julia E. Ku Klux Klan. New York: H.W.
     Wilson Co., 1923. 105pp.

21. Jones, Winfield. Story of the Ku Klux Klan. Washing-
     ton, D.C.: American Newspaper Syndicate, 1921. 107pp.

22. _____. The True Story of the Ku Klux Klan. Wash-
     ington, D.C.: n.p. 107pp.

23. _____. Knights of the Ku Klux Klan. New York:
     Tocsin Publishers, 1941. 294pp.

24. Kennedy, Stetson. I Rode With The Ku Klux Klan.
     London: Arco Publishers, Limited, 1954. 272pp.

25.   Lester, John C. Ku Klux Klan; Its Origin, Growth and
       Disbandment. Nashville, Tenn. Wheeler, Osborn &
       Duckworth Manufacturing Co., 1884. 117pp.

26.   _____. Ku Klux Klan; Its Origin, Growth and
       Disbandment. St. Clair Shores, MI: Scholarly Press,
       1972. Reprint of 1905 edition. 198pp.

27.   Lowe, David. Ku Klux Klan: The Invisible Empire.
       New York: W.W. Norton, 1967. 128pp.

28.   Mast, Blaine. K.K.K., Friend or Foe: Which? Pitts-
       burgh: Herbick & Held Printing Co., 1924. 115pp.

29.   McIlhany, William H. Klandestine; The Untold Story
       of Delmar Dennis and His Role in the FBI's War
       Against the Ku Klux Klan. New York: Arlington House,
       1975. 255pp.

30.   Mecklin, John Moffatt. The Ku Klux Klan: A Study of
       The American Mind. New York: Harcourt, Brace and
       Co., 1924. 244pp.

31.   Mitchell, Robert Hayes. The Nation's Peril. Twelve
       Years' Experience in the South. Then and Now. The
       Ku Klux Klan, A Complete Exposition of the Order; Its
       Purpose, Plans, Operations, Social and Political
       Significance; the Nation's Salvation. New York:
       Published by the friends of the compiler, 1872.
       144pp.

32.   Monteval, Marion (pseud.). The Klan Inside Out.
       Chicago: The Author, 1924. 170pp.

33.   Randel, William Pierce. The Ku Klux Klan: A Century
       of Infamy. Philadelphia: Chilton Books, 1965. 300pp.

34.   Richardson, William Thomas. Historic Pulaski, Birth-
       place of the Ku Klux Klan, Scene of Execution of Sam
       Davis. Nashville: Methodist Publishing House, 1913.
       108pp.

35.   Sims, Patsy. The Klan Shall Rise Again. New York:
       Stein & Day, 1977. 355pp.

36.   _____. The Klan. New York: Stein & Day, 1978.
       355pp.

37.   Simmons, William Joseph. The Klan Unmasked. Atlanta,
       Ga.: W.F. Thompson Publishing Co., 1923. 289pp.

38.   Stewart, John L. Ku Klux Klan Menace: The Cross
       Against People. Durham, N.C.: The Author, 1980.
       236pp.

39.   Tarrants, Thomas A. The Conversion of A Klansman:
       The Story of A Former Ku Klux Klan Terrorist. Garden
       City, N.Y.: Doubleday, 1979. 130pp.

39a.   Thompson, Jerry. My Life In The Klan: A True Story By
       The First Investigative Reporter To Infiltrate The Ku
       Klux Klan. New York: Putnam, 1982. 320pp.

40.   Trelease, Allen W. White Terror: The Ku Klux Klan
       Conspiracy and Southern Reconstruction. Westport, CT.:
       Greenwood Press, 1971. 557pp.

41.   Tyler, Charles Waller. The K.K.K. New York: Abbey
       Press, 1902. 359pp.

42.   White, Alma. The Ku Klux Klan in Prophecy. Zarephath,
       N.J.: Good Citizen, 1925. 144pp.

43.   _____. Klansmen: Guardians of Liberty. Zarephath,
       N.J.: Good Citizen, 1926. 160pp.

44.   _____. Heroes of the Fiery Cross. Zarephath,
       N.J.: Good Citizen, 1928. 200pp.

PAMPHLETS

A SELECTED LIST

45.　Alexander, Charles C.　Crusade For Conformity:　The
Ku Klux Klan in Texas, 1920-1930.　Houston,? Tex.:
Texas Gulf Coast Historical Association, 1962.　88pp.

46.　Allstorm, Oliver, The Mongrel.　Granite Quarry, N.C.:
Knights of the Ku Klux Klan, 1966.　4pp.

47.　_____.　The Saddest Story Ever Told.　Granite
Quarry, N.C.:　Knights of the Ku Klux Klan, 1966.　1p.

48.　Bair, Fred.　Does the U.S.A. Need the K.K.K.?　Girard,
KA:　Halderman-Julius Co., 1928.　63pp.

49.　Ball, Frank P.　Faults and Virtues of the Ku Klux
Klan.　Brooklyn, N.Y.:　n.p., 1927.　34pp.

50.　Batchelder, M.L., Compiler.　Digest of the Laws of
the Various States Relating to the Ku Klux Klan.
Albany, N.Y.:　New York State Library, Legislative
Reference Section, 1923.

51.　Beard, James Melville.　K.K.K.　Sketches, Humorous
and Didactic, Treating the More Important Events of
the Ku Klux Klan Movement in the South.　With a
Discussion of the Causes Which Gave Rise to it, and
the Social and Political Issues Emanating From It.
Philadelphia:　Claxton, Remsen & Haffelfinger, 1877.
192pp.

52.   Bell, Edward Price. Is the Ku Klux Klan Constructive
       or Destructive? A Debate Between Imperial Wizard
       Evans, Isreal Zangwill, and Others. Girard, KA:
       Halderman-Julius Co., 1924. 60pp.

53.   _____. Creed of the Klansmen: Interviews with
       Dr. H.W. Evans, Imperial Wizard of the Ku Klux Klan;
       Israel Zangwill, the Eminent Jewish Author; One of
       the Chief Legal Advisers of the Klan; Mayor Ora D.
       Davis of Terre Haute; Edward H. Morris, a Leading
       Colored Member of the Chicago Bar; and Frank Johnston,
       Jr., Justice of the Illinois Appellate Court. Chicago,
       Ill.: Daily News, 1924. 29pp.

54.   Bogard, Ben M. Ku Klux Klan Exposed; Inside Facts
       Laid Bare and Explained. Little Rock, Ark.: Parke-
       Harper Printing Co., 1922. 8pp.

55.   Brunson, R.J. Historic Pulaski: Birthplace of the Ku
       Klux Klan, Scene of Execution of Sam Davis. Nash-
       ville, TN: Methodist Publishing Co., 1913.

56.   Burton, Annie Cooper. The Ku Klux Klan. Los Angeles,
       Cal.: W.T. Potter, 1916. 38pp.

57.   Clason, George S., Editor. Catholic, Jew, Ku Klux
       Klan; What They Believe, Where They Conflict.
       Chicago: Nutshell Publishing Co., 1924. 63pp.

58.   Cook, Ezra Asher. Ku Klux Klan Secrets Exposed:
       Attitude Toward Jews, Catholics, Foreigners and
       Masons, Fraudulent Methods Used, Atrocities Committed
       in Name of Order. Chicago: E.A. Cook, 1922. 70pp.

59.   Cooper, John T. "Komments" On the Ku Klux Klan.
       Chocotah, OK: n.p., 19--? 16pp.

60.   Corbin, David T. Argument of Hon. D.T. Corbin in the
       Trial of the Ku Klux, Before the United States Circuit
       Court. November Term 1871, Held in Columbia, South
       Carolina. Washington, D.C.: Chronicle Publishing
       Co., 1872. 33pp.

61.   Dau, William T. Weighted, and Found Wanting: An
       Inquiry Into the Aims and Methods of the Ku Klux Klan.
       Fort Wayne, IN: n.d.

62.   Dennie, Paul. Klan Kriminals. n.p., "Authorized by
       the Constitutional League (Anti Klan)." n.d.

63.   Desmond, James. New Cross Afire in Dixie. Detroit:
       AFL-CIO, 1956. Traces the growth of KKK.

64.   Dever, Lem A. Confessions Of An Imperial Klansman,
       Hot Tar and Feathers. Portland, Oreg.: n.p., 1924.
       48pp.

65. _____. Mask Off! Confessions of an Imperial
Klansman. Vancouver, Wash.: Dever, 1925. 2d Edition,
Revised and Enlarged. 64pp.

66. Dixon, Edward H. The Terrible Mysteries of the Ku
Klux Klan. A Full Expose of the Forms, Objects, and
"Dens" of the Secret Order; With a Complete Descrip-
tion of Their Initiation. From the Confessions of a
Member. By Scalpel, M.D. New York: 1868. 56pp.

67. Estes, George. The Roman Catholic Kingdom, and the
Ku Klux Klan. Portland, Ore.: Empire Publishing Co.,
1923. 32pp.

68. Evans, Hiram W. The Public School Problem in
America... Outlining Fully the Policies and the Pro-
gram of the Knights of Ku Klux Klan Toward the Public
School System. Atlanta, Ga.?: n.p., 1924. 25pp.

69. _____. The Menace of Modern Immigration. Dallas?:
1923? 30pp. Address delivered on "Klan Day" at the
State Fair of Texas in Dallas, October 24, 1923.

70. _____. The Attitude of the Knights of the Ku Klux
Klan Toward the Roman Catholic Hierarchy. Atlanta:
Ku Klux Klan, 1923.

71. _____. The Practice of Klanishness! Imperial
Instructions, Document No. 1. Series AD 1924. AK
LVIII. Atlanta: 1924.

72. _____. America's Menace of the Enemy Within.
Atlanta, Ga., 1926.

73. _____. The Klan of Tomorrow and the Klan Spiritual. Kansas, Mo.: Knights of the Ku Klux Klan,
Inc., 1924. 26pp.

74. _____. Is the Ku Klux Klan Constructive or Des-
tructive? A Debate Between Imperial Wizard Evans,
Israel Zangwill and Others. Girard, Kan.: Halderman-
Julius, 1924. 64pp.

75. _____. Come Now, Let Us Reason Together. Atlanta,
Ga.: n.p., 1924.

76. _____. The Klan Answers... What the Klan Has Done,
What the Klan Must Do, Why the Klan Is Needed, Why We
Are Klansmen. Atlanta: American Printing and Manu-
facturing Co., 1929. 7pp.

77. Fleming, John Stephen. What is Ku Kluxism? Let
Americans Answer - Aliens Only Muddy the Waters.
Birmingham, Ala.: Masonic Weekly Recorder, 1923.
87pp.

78. Flowers, Richmond M. Preliminary Results Of Investi-
     gation of the United Klans of America, Inc., October
     18, 1965. n.p., n.d.

79. Forster, Arnold. Report on the Ku Klux Klan. New
     York: Anti-Defamation League of B'nai B'rith, 1965.
     40pp.

80. Fowler, C. Lewis. The Ku Klux Klan, Its Origin,
     Meaning and Scope of Operation. Atlanta, Ga.: n.p.,
     1922. 60pp.

81. Fuller, Edgar I. The Ku Klux Bubble. Omaha: M.F.
     Jacobs and L.B. Bozell, Compilers, 1923. 79pp.

82. Gannon, William Henry. The G.A.R. vs. the Ku Klux.
     A Few Suggestions Submitted for the Consideration of
     the Business Men and the Working Men of the North.
     Boston: W.F. Brown & Co., 1872. 20pp.

83. Gillette, George A. Dr. Ku Klux Questioned; A Con-
     sideration of Crime Contagion and the Klan Cure.
     Springfield, Mo.: George A. Gillette, Publisher,
     1925. 52pp.

84. Gillette, Paul J. Ku Klux Klan, The Invisible Empire.
     New York: Natlus Publications, 1964. 66pp.

85. Gillis, James M. Ku Klux Klan. New York: Paulist
     Press, 1922. 14pp.

86. Greeley on the Ku Klux. Comments of the New York
     Evening Post on the Speech of Mr. Greeley at Corry,
     Pennsylvania, September 25, 1872. Washington?:
     n.p., 1872. 4pp.

87. Gruening, Martha. Reconstruction and the Ku Klux
     Klan in South Carolina. New York: NAACP, Dept. of
     Publications and Research, n.d.

88. Hager, John F. Lawless Liberty Automatically Becomes
     Tyranny. Kentucky's Message to the Ku Klux Klan; An
     Address Delivered Before the Kentucky Bar Association
     at Covington, Ky., December 15, 1923. n.p., 1924.
     24pp.

89. Haldeman-Julius, Emanuel. K.K.K.; the Kreed of the
     Klansmen, a Symposium by E. Haldeman-Julius and
     Others. Girard, Kan.: Haldeman-Julius Co., 1924.
     64pp.

90. Hodge, Robert E. Rules & Regulations Applicable to
     the Association of South Carolina Klans. n.p., 1957
     10pp.

91.   Horn, Stanley F. A Pictorial Pre-view of Invisible
       Empire: The Story of the Ku Klux Klan, 1866-1871.
       n.p., 1939. 20pp.

92.   Jarvis, Mary (Woodson) (Mrs. T.J. Jarvis). The Con-
       ditions That Led to the Ku Klux Klans. Raleigh, N.C.:
       Capital Printing Co., 1902. 24pp.

93.   _____. The Ku Klux Klans. Raleigh, N.C.: Capital
       Printing Co., 1902. Reprinted in North Carolina
       Booklet, Vol. II, No. 1, May 10, 1902. pp. 1-26.

94.   Jefferson, Charles Edward. Roman Catholicism and the
       Ku Klux Klan. New York, Chicago: Fleming H. Revell
       & Co., 1925. 34pp.

95.   Jones, Winfield. The True Story of the Ku Klux Klan.
       Washington, D.C.: The American Newspaper Syndicate(?),
       1921. 62pp.

96.   _____. Knights of the Ku Klux Klan. New York,
       1941.

97.   Kanorr, W.A. The Ku Klux Klan. New Canaan, CT:
       n.p., ca. 1926.

98.   Kent, Grady R. Flogged By the Ku Klux Klan. Cleve-
       land, Tenn.: White Wing Publishing House, 1942.
       42pp.

99.   Kruszka, Peter P. You Wouldn't Believe It; An Aston-
       ishing Documentary Expose of the "Hooded Empire,"
       Or Impersonators of the "Eyes of the Unknown" - the
       Ku Klux Klan. Chicago: Brafman Publishers, 1939.
       5pp.

100.   Lauginghouse, Joseph J. The Ku Klux Creed. Concord,
       N.C.: Stonewall Jackson Training School. ca. 1911-
       1912. 4pp.

101.   Let the American People Ponder. Ku Klux Diabolism.
       Eleven Pregnant Facts Brought to Light by the Con-
       gressional Investigation Committee. Its Democratic
       Paternity, Its Hellish Features and Party Purpose.
       n.p., 1872.

102.   Mahoney, William James. Some Ideals of the Ku Klux
       Klan. Atlanta, Ga.: Knights of the Ku Klux Klan,
       192?. 8pp.

103.   McKee, George C. The Masked Lady of the White House;
       or, The Ku Klux Klan. A Most Startling Exposure.
       Philadelphia: C.W. Alexander, 1868. 42pp.

104.   Milner, Duncan Chambers. The Original Ku Klux Klan
       and Its Successor, A Paper Read at Stated Meeting of

the Military Order of the Loyal Legion of the United States, Commandery of the State of Illinois, October 6, 1921, by Companion First Lieutenant and Adjutant Duncan C. Milner, 98th Ohio Inf., U.S.V. Chicago: n.p., 1921. 16pp.

105. Morales, Jose A. The Rise and Fall of the Ku Klux Klan; Or, White Supremacy, In Four Acts. New Orleans: Southwestern Literary Society, 1923. 47pp.

106. Morris, William Hugh. Communism vs. Freedom. Tallapoosa, Ga.?: Federated Knights of the Ku Klux Klan, n.d. 4pp.

107. _____. The Klan and White Supremacy. Tallapoosa, Ga.?: Federated Knights of the Ku Klux Klan, 1977. 4pp.

108. New York World. Facts About the Ku Klux Klan as the World Told Them; Hailed By the Press Generally as a Great Public Service. New York: Pulitzer Building. 1921. 16pp.

109. Quant, Ted and John Slaughter. We Won't Go Back! The Rise of the Ku Klux Klan and the Southern Struggle For Equality. Mobile, AL: Southern Equal Rights Congress, 1981. 43pp.

110. Pegram. W.H. A Ku Klux Raid and What Came of it. Historical Papers of the Trinity College Historical Society. Durham, N.C.: Duke University, 1897.

111. Percy, Leroy. Address Made at the Request of the Protestant Anti-Ku Klux Klan Committee of Washington County. New Haven, CT: n.p., 1923.

112. _____. The Machinery of the Ku Klux Klan Has Been Dragged From Its Grave and Revamped For Profit. n.p., 1922. Located at College of Physicians of Philadelphia.

113. Pierson, Rev. Hamilton Wilcox. A Letter to Hon. Charles Summer, With "Statements" of Outrages Upon Freedmen in Georgia, and an Account of My Expulsion From Andersonville, Ga., By the Ku Klux Klan. Washington, D.C.: Chronicle Print, 1870. 28pp.

114. Pollard, Edward A. The Key to the Ku Klux; Individual Report and Revelation of the Condition of the South. n.p., n.p. 18?? 32pp.

115. Rauch, Joseph. The Ku Klux Klan: An Examination of Their Theories of White, Protestant and Native. Louisville, Ky.: n.p., 1923. 31pp.

116.   Recent Activities of the Ku Klux Klan. New York:
       National Association For The Advancement of Colored
       People, 1946. 14pp.

117.   Rogers, Joel Augustus. The Ku Klux Spirit: A Brief
       Outline of the History of the Ku Klux Klan Past and
       Present. New York: Messenger Publishing Co., 1923.
       48pp.

118.   Romine, William Bethel. A Story of the Original Ku
       Klux Klan. Pulaski, TN: Pulaski Citizen, 1924.
       30pp.

119.   Rose, Laura (Martin) (Mrs. S.E.F. Rose). The Ku Klux
       Klan or Invisible Empire. New Orleans, La.: Graham
       Co., 1914. 84pp.

120.   Russo, Pasquale. Ku Klux Klan; Church and Labor.
       Chicago: Pasquale Russo, Publisher, 1923. 59pp.

121.   Sawyer, R.H. Truth About The Invisible Empire.
       Portland, Ore.: Pacific Northwest Domain, 1922.
       16pp.

122.   Shuck, Richard H. Confession of Richard H. Shuck, A
       Member of the Owen and Henry County Marauders, of
       the State of Kentucky. Frankfort, KY: Johnston &
       Barrett, 1877. 35pp.

123.   Simmons, William J. The Practice of Klanishness.
       Atlanta: W.J. Simmons, 1918. 7pp.

124.   _____. The Ku Klux Klan: Yesterday, Today and
       Forever. Atlanta: Ku Klux Klan Press, 1916. 8pp.

125.   _____. The Ku Klux Klan: Yesterday, Today and
       Forever. Atlanta (?): n.p., 193? 12pp.

126.   _____. Imperial Proclamation of the Imperial
       Wizard, Emperor of the Invisible Empire. Knights of
       the Ku Klux Klan. Atlanta: Knights of the Ku Klux
       Klan, 1917.

127.   Sojourner Truth Organization. Fighting The Klan.
       P.O. Box 8493, Chicago, IL: Sojourner Truth Organi-
       zation, 1981. $3.00

128.   Stanton, E.F. "Christ and Other Klansmen;" or, "Lives
       of Love;" the Cream of the Bible Spread Upon Klanism.
       Kansas City, Mo.: Stanton & Harper, 1924. 95pp.

129.   Stevenson, Job E. Ku Klux Klan. Washington: F & J
       Rives & G.A. Bailey, Printers, 1871. 36pp.

130.   _____. Ku-Klux Conspiracy. Washington(?): n.p.
       1872. 8pp.

131.   The Ku Klux Klan; Official, Unofficial and Anti-Klan
        Sources. New York: Andronicus Publishing Co., 1977.

132.   The Martyred Klansman in Which Events Leading Up to
        the Shooting Death of Klansman Thomas Rankin Abbott
        on August 25, 1923, Are Related, Together with a
        Record of the Court Proceedings That Followed.
        Pittsburgh: Patriotic American Publishing Co., 1923.
        91pp.

133.   The Truth About the Niles Riot, November 1, 1924.
        Elyria, Ohio: n.p., 1925. 33pp.

134.   The K.K.K. Katechism; Pertinent Question, Pointed
        and Answers. Columbia, OH: Patriot Publishing Co.,
        1924.

135.   The World. The World Exposes the Ku Klux Klan. New
        York: Press Publishing Co., 1921. 54pp. Series of
        articles published in the World, September 10-27,
        1921.

136.   Tibbets, Luther Calvin. Spirit of the South; or,
        Persecution in the Case of Law, as Administered in
        Virginia. Related by Some Victims Thereof. Also
        its Effects Upon the Nation and its General Govern-
        ment. Washington, D.C.: Published for the trade and
        the people, 1869. 76pp.

137.   Tucker, Howard A. History of Governor Walton's War
        on the Ku Klux Klan. Oklahoma City, OK: Southwest
        Publishing Co., 1923. 67pp.

138.   Venable, James R. The Ku Klux Klan. Stone Mountain,
        GA: National Knights of the Ku Klux Klan, Inc.,
        n.d. 2pp.

139.   Violence, The Ku Klux Klan and The Struggle for
        Equality: An Informational and Instructional Kit.
        Prepared and published by the Connecticut Educational
        Association, The Council on Interracial Books for
        Children, The National Education Association, 1981.
        72pp.

140.   Walls, Dwayne. The Klan: Collapsed and Dormant.
        Nashville, Tenn.: Race Relations Information Center,
        1970. 24pp.

141.   Witcher, Walter. The Unveiling of the Ku Klux Klan;
        Being a Concise and Condensed Analysis of the
        Philosophy of the Ku Klux Klan Together with an
        Exposure of its Intrigues, Conspiracies, and Sham
        Patriotism. Fort Worth, Texas: American Constitu-
        tion League, 1922. 66pp.

142.   Wright, Walter Carl. <u>Religious and Patriotic Ideals of the Ku Klux Klan, Being a Plain, Practical and Thorough Exposition of the Principles, Purposes and Practices of the Ku Klux Klan; a Textbook on Klankraft for the Instruction of Klansmen and the Information of Non-klansmen</u>. Waco, Tx.: Grove Printing Co., 1926. 60pp.

2
General Works
(Books)

A SELECTED LIST

143. Allen, Frederick L. Only Yesterday; An Informal History
Of The Nineteen-Twenties. New York: Harper & Brothers
Publishers, 1931. Some discussion of the growth and
development of the Ku Klux Klan during the 1920's.

144. Allen, James S. Reconstruction; The Battle For Democracy. New York: International Publishers, 1937. Brief
discussion of Ku Klux Klan involvement in politics in
the South during Reconstruction.

145. Anderson, David D., and Robert L. Wright, Editors. The
Dark And Tangled Race In America. Boston: Houghton
Mifflin Company, 1971. Discusses attorney Matt Murphey's
statements concerning his defense of Klansmen accused
of murdering Viola Liuzzo.

146. Angle, Paul M. Bloody Williamson; A Chapter In American Lawlessness. New York: Alfred A. Knopf, 1952. Discusses Ku Klux Klan support of Prohibition.

147. Aptheker, Herbert, Editor. A Documentary History Of
The Negro People In The United States, 1910-1932. Secau-
cus, N.J.: Citadel Press, 1973, Ku Klux Klan - pp. 310-
311, 334, 347, 371, 385, 389, 401, 415, 425, 471, 476,
483-484, 500, 504, 513, 570, 575-576, 669, 694.

148. Barck, Oscar T., Jr., and Nelson M. Blake. Since Nine-
teen Hundred; A History of The United States In Our
Time. 5th edition. New York: Macmillan Co., 1974. Brief
references to anti-Catholic, anti-Jewish activities
during the twentieth century.

149.   Bartley, Numan V. The Rise of Massive Resistance; Race and Politics in the South During the 1950's. Baton Rouge: Louisiana State University Press, 1969. Brief references are made to Ku Klux Klan activities in the South during the 1950's.

150.   Baughman, Lawrence A. Southern Rape Complex; Hundred Year Psychosis. Atlanta, GA: Pendulum Books, 1966. Brief discussion of the Ku Klux Klan and their protection of Southern womanhood.

151.   Benedict, Michael L. The Fruits Of Victory: Alternatives in Restoring the Union, 1865-1877. Philadelphia: J.B. Lippincott Co., 1975. Brief excerpts from the testimony before a federal committee investigating Ku Klux Klan activities in the South during Reconstruction.

152.   Bennett, Lerone, Jr. Black Power U.S.A.: The Human Side of Reconstruction, 1867-1877. Chicago: Johnson Publishing Co., 1967. Brief discussion of the Ku Klux Klan and Radical rule in the South during the Reconstruction era.

153.   Bent, Silas. Newspaper Crusaders; A Neglected Story. New York: McGraw-Hill Book Company, 1939. Various references are made to newspapers report of Ku Klux Klan activities. Special attention is devoted to articles in the New York World.

154.   Billington, Monroe L. The Political South in the Twentieth Century. New York: Charles Scribner's Sons, 1975. Brief discussion of Ku Klux Klan influence in Southern politics during the 1920's.

155.   Billington, Roy Allen. The Protestant Crusade, 1800-1900, A Study of the Origins of American Nativism. New York: MacMillan Company, 1928. Various references are made to the Ku Klux Klan throughout this book.

156.   Blaustein, Albert P. and Robert L. Zangrando, Editors. Civil Rights and the American Negro: A Documentary History. New York: Trident Press, 1968. There is a reprint of the 1871 Ku Klux Klan Act included in this collection.

157.   Bonner, Thomas N. Our Recent Past; American Civilization in the Twentieth Century. Englewood Cliffs, N.J.: Prentice-Hall, 1963. Some discussion of Ku Klux Klan activities in the 1920's. Some attention is devoted to their 1925 march through Washington, D.C.

158.   Booth, Edgar Allen. The Mad Mullah of America. Columbus, Ohio: Boyd Ellison, 1927. The careers of David Curtis Stephenson and Hiram Evans are discussed

by the author, a former Klansman.

159. Braddon, Russell. The Proud American Boy. New York:
      Martin's Press, 1961. This work discusses Klan out-
      rages.

160. Braeman, John, et al., Editors. Change and Continuity
      in Twentieth Century America: The 1920's. Columbus,
      OH: Ohio State University Press, 1968. Some analysis
      of the growth and development of the Ku Klux Klan
      during the 1920's.

161. Brewster, James. Sketches of Southern Mystery, Trea-
      son and Murder. The Secret Political Societies of the
      South, Their Methods and Manners. The Phagedenic
      Caner On Our National Life. Milwaukee: Evening
      Wisconsin Co., 1903.

162. Brink, William and Louis Harris. Black and White, A
      Study of U.S. Racial Attitudes Today. New York:
      Simon and Schuster, 1966, pp. 129-130. Concerns a
      poll of white opinion of the K.K.K.

163. Brisbane, Robert H. The Black Vanguard: Origins of
      the Negro Social Revolution 1900-1960. Valley Forge,
      PA: Judson Press, 1970. Ku Klux Klan, pp. 17, 18,
      19, 72, 73, 96, 108, 123, 124, 141, 214, 224.

164. Brooks, Early L. The Crucifixion of the South.
      Whiteville, N.C.: n.p., 1958. Various references
      are made to the Ku Klux Klan throughout this book.

165. Brown, William Garott. The Lower South in American
      History. New York: Macmillan Co., 1902. Chapter
      Four discusses "The Ku Klux Movement."

166. Burgess, John W. Reconstruction and the Constitution,
      1866-1876. New York: Charles Scribner's Sons, 1902.
      342pp. Vol. 7 See Ku Klux Klan.

167. Butler, Robert A. So They Framed Stephenson.
      Huntington, Ind.: Robert A. Butler, Publisher, 1940.
      A Journalist's theory of innocence, based upon
      Stephenson's own words, which are quoted. This book
      was published by the author.

168. Camejo, Peter. Racism, Revolution, Reaction, 1861-
      1877, The Rise and Fall of Radical Reconstruction.
      New York: Monad Press, 1976, p. 145. Concerns the
      reason for the Klan; pp. 150-151 concerns different
      versions of the Klan.

169. Campbell, Sam H. The Jewish Problem in the United
      States. Atlanta: Ku Klux Klan, 1923. There is a
      Anti-Semitic discourse by a Klan lecturer included
      in this work.

170.   Carlson, John R. Undercover: My Four Years in the
       Nazi Underworld of America. New York: E.P. Dutton
       & Company, 1943. In addition to investigating Nazi
       groups in America the author also investigated the
       Ku Klux Klan and saw a strong connection between the
       groups.

171.   _____. The Plotters. New York: E.P. Dutton &
       Company, 1946. There is a discussion of Ku Klux
       Klan organizations and their activities in various
       states after World War Two.

172.   Carson, Clayborne. In Struggle: SNCC and the Black
       Awakening of the 1960's. Cambridge, Ma: Harvard
       University Press, 1981. Ku Klux Klan, pp. 36, 85,
       254, 255, 282. Author discusses anti-SNCC activities
       by the Ku Klux Klan.

173.   Carter, Hodding. The Angry Scar; The Story of
       Reconstruction. Garden City, N.Y.: Doubleday, 1959,
       pp. 174-196. Deals with Klan history, purpose and
       outrages.

174.   Cash, William J. The Mind of the South. New York:
       Alfred A. Knopf, 1941. Some discussion of the Ku
       Klux Klan and their support of the fundamentalist
       beliefs of the South of the 1920's.

175.   Catholic, Jews, Ku Klux Klan; What They Believe, Where
       They Conflict. Chicago: Nutshell Publishing Company,
       1924.

176.   Chandler, Davidson. Biracial Politics, Conflict and
       Coalition in the Metropolitan South. Baton Rouge,
       La: Louisiana State University Press, 1972, pp. 142-
       180. This is a discussion of the natural alliance of
       Big Business interests and the Ku Klux Klan.

177.   Clark Thomas D. The Emerging South. 2nd ed. New
       York: Oxford University Press, 1968. Brief dis-
       cussion of the Ku Klux Klan's role in the civil
       right struggle in the South during the 1950's and
       1960's.

178.   _____. The South Since Reconstruction. Indiana-
       polis: Bobbs-Merrill Company, 1973. A number of
       reprint works on the Ku Klux Klan are mentioned as
       well as some anti-Klan essays.

179.   _____ and Albert D. Kirwan. The South Since
       Appomattox; A Century of Regional Change. New York:
       Oxford University Press, 1967. The authors discuss
       the growth and development of the Ku Klux Klan
       during Reconstruction, the 1920's and the 1960's.

180.   Coleman, Charles H. Election of Eighteen Sixty
       Eight; The Democratic Effort to Regain Control.

New York: Columbia University Press, 1933. Some
discussion of the Ku Klux Klan's involvement in the
presidential election of 1868.

181.   Conklin, Paul and David Burner. A History of Recent
America. New York: Thomas Y. Crowell Company, 1974.
Some discussion of the revival of Ku Klux Klan ac-
tivities in the South and North in the 1920's.

182.   Cook, James G. The Segregationists. New York:
Appleton-Century-Crofts, 1962. Much attention is
devoted to Ku Klux Klan growth and development after
1954.

183.   Cook, Walter H. Secret Political Societies in the
South During the Period of Reconstruction. Cleveland, OH: Press of the Evangelical Publishing House,
1914. The Ku Klux Klan is discussed as the best
known secret societies during Reconstruction.

184.   Coombs, Norman. The Black Experience in America.
New York: Twayne Publishers, 1972. Some attention
is devoted to the resurgence of the Ku Klux Klan
during the 1920's.

185.   Coughlan, Robert. The Aspirin Age, 1919-1941. New
York: Harper, 1949. See "Konklave in Kokomo."

186.   Cox, Samuel. Three Decades of Federal Legislation,
1855 to 1885. Providence, R.I.: J.A. & R.A. Reid,
Publishers, 1894. A discussion of the Ku Klux Klan
during Reconstruction.

187.   Cronon, Edmund D. Black Moses: The Story of Marcus
Garvey and the Universal Negro Improvement Association. Madison, Wi: University of Wisconsin Press,
1955. The writer discusses Marcus Garvey and his
involvement with the Ku Klux Klan. It has been
alleged that the Klan gave Garvey $5,000.

188.   Crozier, Ethelred W. White Caps and Blue Bills: The
White Caps of Sevier County, A Story of Women &
Kluxers in the Great Smoky Mountains. Knoxville,
Tn: Sevier Publishing and Distributing Co., 1937.
156pp.

189.   Current, Richard N., Editor. Reconstruction, 1865-
1877. Englewood Cliff, N.J.: Prentice-Hall, Inc.,
1965. This work contains reprints of three excerpts
from the Report of the Joint Select Committee to
Inquire into the conditions of Affairs in the Late
Insurrectionary States.

190.   Curry, Richard O., Editor. Radicalism, Racism, and
Party Realignment, The Border States During Reconstruction. Baltimore, Md: Johns Hopkins Press,
1969. There is a brief discussion of Ku Klux Klan

activities in border states.

191.   Dabney, Virginius. Liberalism in the South. Chapel Hill: University of North Carolina Press, 1932. (Reprinted in Thorp, Willard, ed. A Southern Reader. New York: Alfred A. Knopf, 1955). This is a survey of Southern newspapers that opposed the Ku Klux Klan.

192.   Dalrymple, A.V. Liberty Dethroned. Philadelphia: Times Publishing Co., 1923. The author was a federal law-enforcement officer and condemned the activities of the Ku Klux Klan.

193.   Daniel, James W. A Maid of the Foot-Hills, or Missing Links in the Story of Reconstruction. New York: Neale Publishing Co., 1905. This work discusses Ku Klux Klan activities during the Reconstruction.

194.   Davis, Benjamin J. Communist Councilman From Harlem: Autobiographical Notes Written in a Federal Penitentiary. New York: International Publishers, 1969. See Ku Klux Klan, pp. 9, 68, 69, 70-73, 95-96, 129, 150, 155, 158, 161-163.

195.   Davis, Daniel S. Struggle for Freedom; The History of Black Americans. New York: Harcourt, L. Jovanovich, 1972. Brief references are made to the Ku Klux Klan and their activities during the 1860's, 1920's and 1960's.

196.   Davis, David B., Editor. The Fear of Conspiracy; Images of Un-American Subversion from the Revolution to the Present. Ithaca, N.Y.: Cornell University Press, 1971. Much of this data was taken from testimony given during the House Un-American activities Committee's investigation of the Ku Klux Klan.

197.   Davis, Lenwood G. I Have A Dream: The Life and Times of Martin Luther King, Jr. Westport, CT: Greenwood Press, 1973. Ku Klux Klan, pp. 10, 71, 108, 123, 162, 166-167, 184, 214, 240.

198.   _____. A Paul Robeson Reference Guide. Westport, CT: Greenwood Press, 1982. Various references are made to the Ku Klux Klan and their anti-Robeson attitudes throughout this book.

199.   Degler, Carl N. The Other South; Southern Dissenters in the Nineteenth Century. New York: Harper & Row, Publishers, 1974. The writer comments on some southern governors' reactions to halt Ku Klux Klan activities.

200.   Desmond, Humphrey J. Curious Chapters in American
        History. St. Louis: B. Herder Book Co., 1924.
        The writer sees the Ku Klux Klan as one of the
        "curious chapters" in American History.

201.   _____. The A.P.A. Movement: A Sketch. Washing-
        ton: The New Century Press, 1912. An account of an
        anti-Catholic movement by the Ku Klux Klan of the
        late nineteenth century.

202.   Diner, Hasia R. In the Almost Promised Land: Ameri-
        can Jews and Blacks, 1915-1935. Westport, CT:
        Greenwood Press, 1977. Ku Klux Klan, pp. 37, 56,
        74, 96, 97, 114, 153.

203.   Dorman, Michael. We Shall Overcome. New York:
        Delacorte Press, 1964. Ku Klux Klan, pp. 166, 167,
        170, 171, 179, 264, 280, 281, 284, 285, 286, 287,
        327.

204.   Du Bois, W.E. Burghardt. Black Reconstruction: An
        Essay Toward A History of the Past Which Black Folk
        Played in the Attempt to Reconstruct Democracy in
        America, 1860-1880. New York: Russell & Russell,
        1935. The author discusses Ku Klux Klan activities
        during Reconstruction.

205.   Dunning, William A. Reconstruction, Political and
        Economic, 1865-1877. New York, London. Harper &
        Bros., 1907. 387pp. The American nation; a history.
        Edited by A.B. Hart. Vol. XXII, Ku Klux Klan, origin
        and activity, pp. 121-3, 125, 181, 187, Federal
        action, pp. 186-8, 204.

206.   Editors of Freedomways. Paul Robeson: The Great
        Forerunner. New York: Dodd, Mead & Co., 1978. Ku
        Klux Klan, pp. 125, 144, 155, 222, 294, 312.

207.   Evans, Hiram W. The Rising Storm; An Analysis of
        the Growing Conflict Over The Political Dilemma of
        Roman Catholics in America. Atlanta, Ga.: Buckhead
        Publishing Co., 1930. 345pp.

208.   Ezell, John S. The South Since 1865. New York:
        Macmillan Co., 1975. There is a discussion of the
        growth and development of the Ku Klux Klan during
        the Reconstruction era and the 1920's.

209.   Fax, Elton C. Garvey; The Story of a Pioneer Black
        Nationalist. New York: Dodd, Mead & Co., 1972.
        Brief discussion of Marcus Garvey's alleged union
        with the Ku Klux Klan.

210.   Fellman, David. The Constitutional Right of Asso-
        ciation. Chicago: University of Chicago Press,
        1963. Various anti-Klan laws in several states are
        discussed.

211.   Fisher, Paul L. and Ralph L. Lowenstein, Editors.
        Race and the News Media. New York: Anti-Defamation
        League of B'nai Brith, 1967. Ku Klux Klan, pp. 51,
        57, 64, 65, 86, 90, 102, 152.

212.   Fleming, Walter Lynwood, Editor. Documents Relating
        to Reconstruction. Edited by Walter L. Fleming.
        Morgantown, W. Va, 1904. Issued in numbers as West
        Virginia University documents relating to recon-
        struction. Nos. 4-5 and 6-7 published as double
        numbers. Contents - No. 1. The Constitution and
        the ritual of the Knights of the white camelia -
        No. 2. Revised and amended prescript of Ku Klux
        Klan - No. 3. Union league documents - Nos. 4-5.
        Public frauds in South Carolina. The constitution of
        the Council of safety. Local Ku Klux constitution.

213.   Floyd, Nicholas J. Thorns in The Flesh. A Voice of
        Vindication From the South in Answer to "A Fool's
        Errand" and Other Slanders. Philadelphia: Hubbard
        Brothers, 1884. 607pp.

214.   Foner, Philip S., Editor. Paul Robeson Speaks:
        Writings, Speeches, Interviews 1918-1974. New York:
        Brunner/Mazel Publishers, 1978. Ku Klux Klan, pp. 16,
        28, 173, 177, 196, 218, 220, 250, 257, 281, 282, 306,
        309, 391, 394, 395, 412, 434, 489, 529, 583.

215.   Forster, Arnold. A Measure of Freedom. Garden City,
        N.Y.: Doubleday & Company, 1950. Various references
        are made to anti-Jewish attitudes by the Ku Klux Klan
        after World War Two.

216.   _____. The Troublemakers. Garden City, N.Y.:
        Doubleday & Company, 1952. Various references are
        made to anti-Semitism incidences by the Ku Klux Klan.

217.   _____ and Benjamin R. Epstein. The New Anti-
        Semitism. New York: McGraw-Hill Book Company, 1974.
        Various references are made to Ku Klux Klan activities
        since 1954.

218.   Franklin, John Hope. Reconstruction: After the
        Civil War. Chicago, University of Chicago Press,
        1961, pp. 154-175--corrects misconceptions con-
        cerning the Klan and its mission.

219.   Fuller, Edgar I. Nigger in the Woodpile. Washing-
        ton: Lacey, 1967. See Section on Ku Klux Klan.

220.   Gauba, Kanhayalal. Uncle Sham; Being the Strange
        Tale of a Civilization Run Amok. Lahore, India:
        Times Publishing Co., 1929. Various references are
        made to the Ku Klux Klan throughout this book. See
        pp. 35-39.

221.   Gilliam, Dorothy Butler. <u>Paul Robeson: All-American</u>.
       Washington: New Republic Book Co., 1976. Ku Klux
       Klan, pp. 21, 22, 33, 135, 141, 148.

222.   Glock, Charles Y. and Ellen Siegelman, Editors.
       <u>Prejudice, U.S.A</u>. New York: Frederick A Praeger,
       Publishers, 1969. Some discussion is devoted to
       various Ku Klux Klan prejudices during the 1920's.

223.   Goldman, Eric. <u>Rendezvous With Destiny</u>. New York:
       Alfred A. Knopf, 1966, pp. 227-229--reaction of the
       White House to the "Birth of A Nation," Wilson
       congratulates Griffin, Chief Justice White admits
       prior membership.

224.   Goodman, Walter. <u>The Committee; the Extraordinary
       Career of the House Committee on Un-American Acti-
       vities</u>. New York: Farrar, Straus and Giroux, 1968.
       There is a discussion of the Ku Klux Klan and its
       1966 investigation before the HUAC.

225.   Gordon, John J. <u>Unmasked</u>. Brooklyn, N.Y.: J.J.
       Gordon, 1924. 31pp.

226.   Greene, Ward. <u>Star Reports & 34 of Their Stories</u>,
       collected, with notes and an introduction, by Ward
       Greene. New York: Random House, 1948. 402pp. <u>The
       New York World</u> expose of the Ku Klux Klan are among
       the stories discussed.

227.   Gunther, Lenworth, Editor. <u>Black Image; European
       Eyewitness Accounts of Afro-American Life</u>. Port
       Washington, N.Y.: Kennikat Press, 1978. A reprint
       of an interview with Robert Shelton, taken from an
       Australian newspaper is included in this book.

228.   Hamilton, J.G. de Roulhac. <u>History of North Caro-
       lina</u>. Vol. 3, <u>North Carolina Since 1860</u>. Re-
       printed in 1973, The Reprint Company, Spartanburg,
       S.C., p. 136, Alledged benefits of the Klan: pro-
       tected the oppressed, women (white), property, and
       controlled crime; p. 141, The Klan never disturbed
       peace and quiet.

229.   _____. <u>Reconstruction in North Carolina</u>.
       Vol. LVIII, Longmans, Green & Co., Agents, London,
       1914, pp. 572-582 -- concerns attempts to repress
       the Klan in 1870.

230.   Hamilton, Virginia Van Der Veer. <u>Hugo Black: The
       Alabama Years</u>. Baton Rouge, LA: Louisiana State
       University Press, 1972. Author discusses Black's
       brief membership in the Ku Klux Klan.

231.   Haworth, Paul L. <u>Reconstruction and Union, 1865-
       1912</u>. New York: Holt, 1912. A discussion of the

president's plan for reconstruction, the congressional plan, the Ku Klux Klan outrages and the issue the Negro has presented in industry and politics since emancipation.

232.   _____. The U.S. In Our Own Time. New York: Charles Scribner's Sons, 1925, pp. 50-51 -- concerns Klan methodology.

233.   Hayward, Walter S. and Dorothy Adams. The American People, A Popular History of the United States. New York: Sheridan House, 1943, pp. 14-17 -- a sympathetic view of the Klan.

234.   Henry, Robert S. The Story of Reconstruction. Indianapolis: Bobbs-Merrill Co., 1938. There is a brief discussion of the Ku Klux Klan during the Reconstruction Era.

235.   Herbert, Hilary Abner, Editor. Why the Solid South? or, Reconstruction and Its Results. Louisiana, Baltimore: R.H. Woodward & Co., 1890. 452pp. Consult Ku Klux, pp. 192-210.

236.   Higham, John. Strangers in the Land: Patterns of American Nativism, 1860-1925. New Brunswick, N.J.: Rutgers University Press, 1955. The author discusses anti-Jewish and anti-Catholic activities by the Ku Klux Klan during the 1920's.

237.   Hofstadter, Richard. The Age of Reform; From Bryan to F.D.R. New York: Alfred A. Knopf, 1955. Writer discusses the Ku Klux Klan and their role as the protector of the nation's morals.

238.   Hohenberg, John, Editor. The Pulitzer Prize Story. New York: Columbia University Press, 1959. There is a discussion of various newspaper articles that spoke out against the Ku Klux Klan activities over the years.

239.   Howard, Oliver O. Autobiography of Oliver Otis Howard. 2 Vols. New York: Baker & Taylor Co., 1908. The writer was head of the Freedmen's Bureau during Reconstruction. He recollects the Ku Klux Klan opposition toward him and other teachers at Howard University.

240.   Hoyt, Edwin P. Paul Robeson: The American Othello. Cleveland: World Publishing Co., 1967. Ku Klux Klan, pp. 38, 39, 52, 142, 151, 165, 167.

241.   Hudson, Hosea. Black Worker in the Deep South: A Personal Record. New York: International Publishers, 1972. Ku Klux Klan, pp. 33, 34, 79, 84, 85, 86, 87, 88, 89, 90, 91, 92, 100, 102, 126.

242.   Huff, Theodore. A Short Analysis of D.W. Griffith's
        The Birth of A Nation. New York: Museum of Modern
        Art, Film Library, 1961. 69pp.

243.   Huie, William B. Three Lives for Mississippi. New
        York: WCC Books, 1965. The author discusses the
        killing of three civil rights workers, Andrew
        Goodman, James Chaney and Michael Schwerner, who
        were killed by Mississippi Klansmen.

244.   Jackson, Mrs. Helen. Convent Cruelties; or My Life
        in a Convent. 1st ed. Detroit: 1919. Distorted
        account of convent life revealing writer's lack of
        temperamental balance.

245.   Jefferson, Charles E. Five Present-Day Controversies
        New York: Fleming H. Revell Company, 1924. The
        writer discusses "Roman Catholicism and the Ku Klux
        Klan."

246.   Kallen, Horace. Culture and Democracy in the United
        States. New York: Boni and Liveright, 1924.
        Chapter One is entitled "Culture and the Ku Klux
        Klan."

247.   Keesing's Research Report: Race Relations in the
        USA, 1954-1968. New York: Charles Scribner's Sons,
        1970. Ku Klux Klan, membership, pp. 7-8; congres-
        sional investigation, pp. 8-10; murders, 1964, pp.
        184-185; 1965, pp. 161-164; 1966-67, pp. 213-214.

248.   Kennedy, Stetson. Southern Exposure. Garden City,
        N.Y.: Doubleday & Company, Inc., 1946. Author
        discusses Ku Klux Klan activities during the 1930's -
        1940's. There is also a copy of application for
        "citizenship in the Invisible Empire."

249.   Kent, Frank R. The Democratic Party; A History.
        New York: Century Co., 1928. Some reference is
        made to the Ku Klux Klan as an issue in the 1924
        presidential election.

250.   Key, Valdimer O. Southern Politics in State and
        Nation. New York: Random House, 1949. Chapter 9
        is devoted to Ku Klux Klan activities in the South.

251.   Kluger, Richard. Simple Justice: The History of
        Brown v. Board of Education and Black America's
        Struggle For Equality. New York: Alfred A. Knopf,
        1976. Ku Klux Klan, pp. 25, 50, 59, 100, 111, 127,
        141, 210, 223, 224-227, 250, 251, 270, 301, 334, 386,
        527, 592, 762.

252.   Leighton, Isabel, Editor. The Aspirin Age, 1919-1941.
        New York: Simon & Schuster, 1949. There is an ar-
        ticle in this collection by Robert Coughlan entitled
        "Konklave in Kokomo."

253.   Lerner, Gerda, Editor. Black Women In White America:
A Documentary History. New York: Pantheon Books,
1972. See "Ku Klux Klan Terror During Reconstruction," pp. 180-188.

254.   Lerner, Max. Action and Passions; Notes on the
Multiple Revolution of Our Time. New York: Simon
& Schuster, 1949. Some discussion of the growth of
the Ku Klux Klan during William Simmons' reign.

255.   Leuchtenburg, William E., Editor. The Unfinished
Century; America Since 1900. Boston: Little,
Brown and Company, 1973. Author discusses the
growth of the Ku Klux Klan since 1900.

256.   _____. The Perils of Prosperity, 1914-1932.
Chicago: University of Chicago Press, 1958. Various
references are made to the Ku Klux Klan throughout
this book. See pp. 209-213.

257.   Levinger, Lee J. Anti-Semitism in the United States;
Its History and Causes. New York: Bloch Publishing
Co., 1925. A brief discussion of anti-Jewish atti-
tudes by the Ku Klux Klan.

258.   Likins, William M. Patriotism Capitalized; or
Religion Turned Into Gold. Uniontown, PA: Watchman
Publishing Co., 1925. 14pp. Author was a former
Klansman and states that the Ku Klux Klan advocated
Christianity to sell memberships in the "Invisible
Empire."

259.   _____. The Trial of the Serpent. Uniontown, PA:
Watchman Publishing Co., 1928. The author was a
former Klansman and suggests that the Ku Klux Klan
advocated Christianity for profit.

260.   Lindsay, George W. Freedom of Conscience. Extension of Remarks in the House, May 13, 1924. Congressional record, 68th Cong. 1st sess., Vol. 65
No. 129. (Current file): 8921-31, with reference
in part to the Ku Klux Klan.

261.   Lipset, Seymour M. and Earl Raab. The Politics of
Unreason; Right-Wing Extremism in America, 1790-
1970. New York: Harper & Row, Publishers, 1970.
The Ku Klux Klan is included as an extremist group
in this work during the 1920's and the 1960's.

262.   Manchester, William. The Glory and The Dream: A
Narrative History of America, 1932-1972. Boston:
Little, Brown and Company, 1973. A discussion of
Ku Klux Klan opposition to Blacks during the 1960's.

263.   Markmann, Charles Lam. The Noblest Cry: A History
of the American Civil Liberties Union. New York:

St. Martin's Press, 1965. Ku Klux Klan pp. 70, 78,
158, 202, 250, 278, 279, 282, 294, 322.

264.   Martin, Tony. Race First: The Ideological and
        Organizational Struggles of Marcus Garvey and the
        Universal Negro Improvement Association. Westport,
        CT: Greenwood Press, 1976. Ku Klux Klan, pp. 197,
        249, 318, 322, 323, 324, 330, 334n, 344, 345, 346,
        347, 352; discussed at Fourth International Conven-
        tion, 250, 251; Threatened by UNIA, 345; Summit
        conference with Marcus Garvey, 345, 346; and UNIA,
        345, 346, 347.

265.   McGill, Ralph. The South and the Southerner.
        Boston: Little, Brown and Company, 1963. There is
        an historical discussion of the development of the
        Ku Klux Klan between the 1920's and 1950's.

266.   McPherson, James. Ordeal By Fire: The Civil War and
        Reconstruction. New York: Alfred A. Knopf, 1982.
        Ku Klux Klan, 613. Confederate veterans in, 494n,
        543; terrorism in 1868 elections, 537, 543-544;
        persistence of after 1868 elections, 564-565; mili-
        tia campaigns against 565-566; congressional legis-
        lation against, and its enforcement, 566-567; 591;
        as issued in 1872 election, 571.

267.   Mendelsohn, Jack. The Martyrs: Sixteen Who Gave
        Their Lives for Racial Justice. New York: Harper &
        Row, Publishers, 1966. The author discusses the Ku
        Klux Klan and their involvement in the death of
        various Black civil-rights workers in the South
        during the 1960's.

268.   Mitchell, George W. The Question Before Congress;
        A Consideration of the Debates and Final Action by
        Congress Upon Various Phases of the Race Question
        in the United States. Philadelphia: A.M.E. Book
        Concern, 1918. There is some discussion of the
        events surrounding the passage of the 1871 Ku Klux
        Klan Act.

269.   Moore, Edmund A. A Catholic Runs For President;
        The Campaign of 1928. New York: Ronald Press Co.,
        1956. The writer discusses the Ku Klux Klan role
        in the Al Smith's 1928 presidential campaign.

270.   Murray, Robert K. Red Scars: A Study in National
        Hysteria. Minneapolis: University of Minnesota
        Press, 1955. There is a discussion of subversive
        activities by the Ku Klux Klan in the United States.

271.   Muse, Benjamin. Ten Years of Prelude: The Story of
        Integration Since the Supreme Court's 1954 Decision.
        New York: Viking Press, 1964. Writer argues that
        the 1954 Supreme Court decision in the school de-

segregation decision gave impetus to the fading Ku
Klux Klan activities.

272.   Myers, Gustavus. History of Bigotry in the United
        States. New York: Random House, 1943. See Chap-
        ters XX-XIII on the Ku Klux Klan.

273.   Myrdal, Gunnar. An American Dilemma: The Negro
        Problem and Modern Democracy. New York: Harper &
        Brothers, Publishers, 1944. Various references are
        made to Ku Klux Klan activities throughout this
        book.

274.   Nash, Gary B., and Richard Weiss, Editors. The Great
        Fear: Race in the Mind of America. New York: Holt,
        Rinehart and Winston, 1970. There is some dis-
        cussion of the Ku Klux Klan in major urban cities
        during the 1920's.

275.   Oberholtzer, Ellis Paxson. A History of the United
        States Since The Civil War. New York: The Mac-
        millan Company, 1928, pp. 342-350--concerns the
        customs of the Klan, pp. 358-359--concerns the Klan's
        induction of migration.

276.   Odum, Howard W. An American Epoch. New York: Hall,
        1930. See Ku Klux Klan and its influence.

277.   Osofsky, Gilbert. The Burden of Race; A Documentary
        History of Negro-White Relations in America. New
        York: Harper & Row, Publishers, 1967. See "A Visit
        From The Ku Klux Klan," pp. 133-136. Also pp. 264,
        314-317, 429, 479, 497-510.

278.   Ottley, Roi. Black Odyssey: The Story of the Negro
        in America. London: John Murray, 1949, Ku Klux
        Klan, pp. 209, 231-232, 236, 282, 311.

279.   Ovington, Mary. The Walls Came Tumbling Down. New
        York: Harcourt, Brace & Co., 1947. See Ku Klux
        Klan, pp. 128, 177, 200, 201, 242, 264, 295.

280.   Patterson, William L., Editor. We Charge Genocide:
        The Historic Petition to the United Nations for
        Relief From A Crime of the United States Government
        Against the Negro People. New York: International
        Publishers, 1970. See Ku Klux Klan, pp. 4, 15, 17-
        20, 63f, 65f, 78-79, 89f, 104f, 205f, 106f, 107f,
        108f, 109f, 110f, 114f, 118f, 144, 146, 148, 151, 158-
        160, 189-192, 203-215, 223, 225.

281.   Pierce, Neal R. The Deep South States of America:
        People, Politics, and Power in the Seven Deep South
        States. New York: W.W. Norton & Co., 1972. Various
        references are made to activities of the Ku Klux Klan
        in several southern cities during the 1950's and
        1960's.

281a.   Pike, D.W. Secret Societies: Their Origin, History
        & Ultimate Fate. Illustration by Kupfer-Sachs.
        London, Oxford University Press, 1939. The Ku Klux
        Klan is discussed as a secret society that spreads
        violence.

282.   Polk, William Tannahill. Southern Accent: From
        Uncle Remus to Oak Ridge. New York: Morrow, 1953.
        The Ku Klux Klan is discussed as an organization
        that spreads violence. See pp. 161-164.

283.   Powell, Luther I. The Old Cedar School. Troutdale,
        Ore.: George Estes, 1922. "The Ku Klux Klan and
        the Public Schools."

284.   Raum, Green Berry. The Existing Conflict Between
        Republican Government and Southern Oligarchy.
        Washington, D.C.: Charles M. Greene Printing Co.,
        1884. Various references are made to the Ku Klux
        Klan in southern states through the book.

285.   Reimers, David M. White Protestantism and the Negro.
        New York: Oxford University Press, 1965. There is
        a brief discussion of the relationship between the
        Ku Klux Klan and the protestant churches during the
        1920's.

286.   Rhodes, James Ford. History of the United States
        From the Compromise of 1850, to the McKinley-Bryan
        Campaign of 1896. New York: Macmillan Co., 1920.
        See Volume 7 and section on the Ku Klux Klan.

287.   Robeson, Eslanda Goode. Paul Robeson, Negro. New
        York: Harper & Brothers, 1930. Ku Klux Klan,
        pp. 55, 57.

288.   Robeson, Paul. Here I Stand. New York: Othello
        Associates, 1958. Reprinted by Beacon Press in
        1971. Various references are made to Ku Klux Klan.

289.   Rosenstock, Morton. Louis Marshall, Defender of
        Jewish Rights. Detroit: Wayne State University
        Press, 1965. The author discusses anti-Jewish
        activities by the Ku Klux Klan during the 1920's.

290.   Rosenthal, A.M. and Arthur Gelb. One More Victim.
        New York: New American Library, 1967. This work
        discusses a young man of Jewish descent who was a
        member of the Ku Klux Klan and the American Nazi
        Party.

291.   Roy, Ralph L. Apostles of Discord: A Study or Or-
        ganized Bigotry and Disruption on the Fringes of
        Protestantism. Boston: Beacon Press, 1953. The
        writer sees the Ku Klux Klan's activities as a
        facade for unethical practices. There is some dis-

cussion of the religious leaders associated with the
Klan organization. See pp. 118-142.

292.   Seton, Marie. Paul Robeson. London: Dennis Dobson,
1958. Ku Klux Klan, pp. 19, 32, 135, 143, 168, 173,
187, 189, 208, 210, 212.

293.   Severence, Frank H., Editor. Publications of the
Buffalo Historical Society. Buffalo, N.Y.: Buffalo
Historical Society, 1921. There is an article by
Elizabeth M. Howe entitled "A Ku Klux Uniform" in
this collection.

294.   Shannon, David A. Between the Wars: America, 1919-
1941. Boston: Houghton Mifflin Company, 1965. There
are several references to the growth of and development of the Ku Klux Klan during the 1920's.

295.   Siegfried, Andre. America Comes of Age: A French
Analysis. Translated from the French by H.H. Hemming
& Doris Hemming. New York: Harcourt, Brace, 1927. A
Frenchman gives his observations of the Ku Klux Klan.
He discusses their appeal and weaknesses.

296.   Skaggs, William H. The Southern Oligarchy. An
Appeal in Behalf of the Silent Masses of our Country
Against the Despotic Rule of the Few. New York:
Devin-Adair Co., 1924. See Ku Klux Klan.

297.   Sletterdahl, Peter J. The Nightshirt in Politics.
Minneapolis: Ajax Publishing Co., 1926. Bitter
denunciation of the Klan by a former lecturer and
"Imperial Representative."

298.   Snyder, Louis L., and Richard Norris, Editors. A
Treasury of Great Reporting. New York: Simon &
Schuster, 1949. Brief excerpts from the New York
World's expose of the Ku Klux Klan activities. See
pp. 398-404.

299.   Stephenson, Wendell H. and E. Merton Coulter, Editors.
The South During Reconstruction. Vol. 8 of A History
of the South. Baton Rouge, LA: Louisiana State
University Press, 1947. Various references of the
Ku Klux Klan during the Reconstruction era.

300.   Swint, Henry L. The Northern Teacher in the South
1862-1870. New York: Octagon Books, 1967. There
is a brief discussion of the Ku Klux Klan's reaction
against northern school teachers who came South to
help ex-slaves get an education.

301.   Synnestvedt, Sig. The White Response to Black Eman-
cipation; Second-Class Citizenship in the United
States Since Reconstruction. New York: Macmillan
Company, 1972. Writer gives a summary of Ku Klux
Klan activities during Reconstruction.

302. Tannenbaum, Frank. Darker Phases of the South. New
      York: G.P. Putnam's Sons, 1924. See Chapter One,
      "The Ku Klux Klan. Its Social Origin in the South."

303. Taylor, Arnold H. Travail and Triumph: Black Life
      and Culture in the South Since the Civil War. West-
      port, CT: Greenwood Press, 1976. "Ku Klux Klan,"
      pp. 8, 13, 24-30, 223, 249.

304. Tenenbaum, Samuel. Why Men Hate. New York: Beech-
      hurst Press, 1947. The author discusses the finan-
      cial dealings of Klan leaders William Simmon and
      Hiram W. Evans. He also gives an overview of the
      Klan and its activities.

305. Thorpe, Francis Newton. The History of North America.
      Philadelphia. G. Barrie & Sons, 1906. See v. XVI,
      The Ku Klux Klan.

306. Tourgee, Albion Winegar. A Fool's Errand By One of
      the Fools: The Famous Romance of American History.
      The Invisible Empire; A Concise Review of the Epoch
      on Which the Tale is Based... New York: Fords,
      Howard & Hulbert, 1879-80, p. 521. An ex-Klansman
      reveals secrets.

307. Turner, William W. Power on the Right. Berkeley,
      Calif.: Ramparts Press, 1971. There is a brief
      discussion of Ku Klux Klan activities after 1945.

308. Vander Zanden, James W. Race Relations in Transition;
      The Segregation Crisis in the South. New York:
      Random House, 1965. A brief discussion and analysis
      of the Ku Klux Klan during the 1950's.

309. Waterburg, Maris. Seven Years. Illinois, 1890.
      144pp. The author gives her description of the con-
      ditions existing among the freedmen of the South and
      the role the Ku Klux Klan played in terrorizing the
      freedmen.

310. Whalen, William J. Handbook of Secret Organizations.
      Milwaukee: Bruce Publishing Co., 1966, Ku Klux Klan,
      pp. 90-99.

311. Wilhoit, Francis M. The Politics of Massive Re-
      sistance. New York: George Braziller, 1973. The
      writer discusses the Ku Klux Klan since 1954.

312. Williamson, Joel. After Slavery: The Negro in South
      Carolina During Reconstruction, 1861-1877. Chapel
      Hill: University of North Carolina Press, 1965. See
      Ku Klux Klan, pp. 107. Riots as economics, 121, 174;
      in 1868, 260; riots as social and racial struggles,
      261-266; arrests and trials, 266, 334; use by Re-
      publican politicians, 395.

313.   Winter, Paul M. What Price Tolerance. New York:
       All American Book, Lecture and Research Bureau,
       1928. 350pp.

314.   Wish, Harvey, Editor. Reconstruction in the South,
       1865-1877. New York: Farrar, Straus and Giroux,
       1965. Various reprints of Ku Klux Klan documents are
       included in this work.

315.   Woodward, C. Vann. Tom Watson, Agrarian Rebel.
       New York: Macmillan Co., 1938. 518pp. Author
       discusses Watson's relationship and opinion of the
       Ku Klux Klan.

STATES

A SELECTED LIST

1. ALABAMA

316.   Alabama General Assembly, Joint Committee On Outrages.
        Report of Joint Committee On Outrages. Montgomery,
        Al.: J. G. Stokes & Co., 1868, 80pp.

317.   Brauer, Carl M. John F. Kennedy And The Second Recon-
        struction. New York: Columbia University Press, 1977.
        Various references are made to the Ku Klux Klan in the
        1960's and their attempts to prevent the Freedom
        Riders. Some attention is devoted to them inteferring
        in the desegregation of the University of Alabama.

318.   Elovitz, Mark H. A Century Of Jewish Life In Dixie: The
        Birmingham Experience. University: University of Ala-
        bama Press, 1974. A discussion of anti-Jewish attitudes
        in Birmingham, Alabama by the Ku Klux Klan is included
        in this work.

319.   Fleming, Walter Lynwood. The Ku-Klux Testimony Relat-
        ing To Alabama. Montgomery,Al.: 1903.

320.   _____. Civil War and Reconstruction In Alabama. New
        York: Columbia University Press, 1905, 815pp. Consult:
        Index, Ku Klux Klan.

321.   Hamilton, Virginia V. Hugo Black; The Alabama Years.
        Baton Rouge: Louisiana State University Press, 1972.
        Some discussion of Hugo Black and his association with
        the Ku Klux Klan.

322.   McCorvey, Thomas C. "The Invisible Empire." Ala-
        bama Historical Sketches. Edited by George B. John-
        ston. Charlottesville: University of Virginia Press,
        1960. There is an historical discussion of the
        growth and development of the Ku Klux Klan.

323.   Wiggins, Sarah W. The Scalawag in Alabama Politics,
        1865-1881. University: University of Alabama Press,
        1977. There are some references to Alabama's Ku
        Klux Klan activities and their involvement in that
        state's 1870 election.

324.   Wolters, Raymond. The New Negro on Campus: Black
        Colleges Rebellions of the 1920's. Princeton, N.J.:
        Princeton University Press, 1975, 370pp. See
        "Major Moton Defeats the Klan: The Case of The
        Tuskegee Veterans Hospitals," pp. 137-191.

2. ARKANSAS

325.   Bates, Daisy. The Long Shadow of Little Rock; A
        Memoir. New York: David McKay Company, 1962.
        Author was president of Little Rock, Arkansas
        Chapter of the NAACP. She recalls the role of the
        Ku Klux Klan in trying to stop school desegregation
        in Little Rock.

326.   Clayton, Powell. The Aftermath of the Civil War in
        Arkansas. New York: Neale Publishing Co., 1915.
        See Chapter V, Organization and Operation of Ku Klux
        Klan in Arkansas.

327.   Fletcher, John G. Arkansas. Chapel Hill: University
        of North Carolina Press, 1947. The writer comments
        on Governor Powell Clayton's fight to halt Ku Klux Klan
        activities in Arkansas.

328.   Monks, William. A History of Southern Missouri and
        Northern Arkansas; Being An Account of the Early
        Settlements, the Civil War, the Ku-Klux, and Times
        of Peace. West Plain, MO: West Plains Journal Co.,
        1907. 247pp.

3. CALIFORNIA

329.   The Englewood Raiders; A Story of the Cele-
        brated Ku Klux Case at Los Angeles, and Speeches
        to the Jury. Los Angeles: L.L. Bryson, 1923. 71pp.

4. COLORADO

330.   Goldberg, Robert Alan. Hooded Empire: The Ku Klux
        Klan in Colorado. Urbana, Ill: University of
        Chicago Press, 1981. 255pp.

331.   Uchill, Ida L. Pioneers, Peddlers, and Tsadikim.
        Denver: Sage Books, 1957. The author discusses
        Jewish reaction to the presence of the Ku Klux Klan
        in Colorado during the 1920's.

                        5. FLORIDA

332.   Committee For the Defense of Civil Rights in Tampa.
        Terror in Tampa: Ku Klux Klan in Florida. New
        York: Workers Defense League, 1937, 15pp.

333.   McMillen, Neil R. The Citizens' Council: Organized
        Resistance to the Second Reconstruction, 1954-64.
        Urbana: University of Illinois Press, 1971. See
        Section on Ku Klux Klan in Florida, Little Rock as
        its comparison to the Citizens' Council.

334.   Shay, Frank. Judge Lynch; His First Hundred Years.
        New York: Washburn, 1938. There is a discussion of
        the Ku Klux Klan and their influence in politics in
        Tampa, Florida.

335.   Shipp, Bill. Murder At Broad River Bridge: The
        Slaying of Lemuel Penn By Members of the Ku Klux
        Klan. Atlanta: Peachtree Publishers, 1982. 91pp.

336.   Walters, Pat. Down to Now, Reflections on the
        Southern Civil Rights Movement. New York: Pantheon
        Books, 1971. There is a brief discussion of Ku
        Klux Klan activities in St. Augustine, Florida.

                        6. GEORGIA

337.   Black, Earl. Southern Governors and Civil Rights;
        Racial Segregation as a Campaign Issue in the Second
        Reconstruction. Cambridge, Mass.: Harvard Univer-
        sity Press, 1976. Brief discussion of Ku Klux Klan
        role in recent politics in Georgia and other southern
        states.

338.   Kennedy, Stetson. Southern Exposure. Garden City,
        N.Y.: Doubleday & Co., 1946. The author was a Klan
        infiltrator working for the Georgia Attorney-Gene-
        ral.   There are also several Klan documents in this
        work.

339.   Thompson, C. Mildred. Reconstruction in Georgia;
        Economic, Social, Political, 1865-1872. New York:
        Columbia University Press, 1915. There is some
        discussion of the state government to control Ku
        Klux Klan activities in Georgia during Reconstruction.

                        7. ILLINOIS

340.   Illinois General Assembly. Legislative Investigating
        Commission. Ku Klux Klan; A Report to the Illinois

General Assembly. Chicago: The Commission, 1976.
169pp.

8. INDIANA

341.   Busch, Francis X. Guilty or Not Guilty? Indianapolis: Bobbs-Merrill Company, Inc., 1952. There is
a discussion of Indiana Klan leader D.C. Stephenson
and his assault and murder of a woman.

342.   Hodsden, Harry E. Stephenson Was Framed In A Political Conspiracy. La Porte, Indiana: La Porte
Press, 1936. 75pp.

343.   Moore, Powell A. The Calumet Region; Indiana's Last
Frontier. Indianapolis: Indiana Historical Bureau,
1959. Author discusses Ku Klux Klan activities in
Northern Indiana, pp. 457-470, 553-558.

344.   Oberholtzer, Ellis Paxson A History of the United
States Since the Civil War. New York: MacMillan
Co., 1928. Vol. 2, pp. 342-350--concerns the customs
of the Klan, pp. 358-359--concerns the Klan's in-
duction of migration.

345.   Shannon, David A. Twentieth Century America: The
America: The United States Since the 1890's. Vol.
II: The Twenties and Thirties. 4th ed. Chicago:
Rand McNally & Company, 1977. The writer comments
on some of the Ku Klux Klan acticities in southern
states and in Indiana.

9. KANSAS

346.   Clough, Frank C. William Allen White of Emporia.
New York: McGraw-Hill Book Company, 1941. Some
discussion of White and his 1924 campaign for
Governor of Kansas. He ran on an anti-Klan platform.

347.   Hinshaw, David. A Man from Kansas; The Story of
William Allen White. New York: G.P. Putnam's Sons,
1945. The author discusses White's campaigns against
the Kansas Ku Klux Klan.

348.   Johnson, Walter. William Allen White's America.
New York: Henry Holt and Company, 1947. The author
discusses newspaperman White's anti-Klan position
when he was running for Governor of Kansas.

349.   White, Walter. A Man Called White: The Autobiography
of Walter White. New York: Viking Press, 1948.
See Ku Klux Klan, pp. 8, 53-59, 73, 129, 149, 318,
341, 354, 355, 356, 360, 365; at Aiken, South
Carolina, 57-59; and Hugo Black, 178, 179; in Detroit,
224, 225; in North, 56; at Tuskegee Institute, 69-70;
in Walton County, Georgia, 323; and Walter White, 56.

350.   White, William Allen. "Criticism of the Ku Klux
        Klan." Selected Letters of William Allen White,
        1899-1943. Walter Johnson, Editor. New York:
        Henry Holt & Co., 1947, pp. 220-221.

351.   Zornow, William F. Kansas; A History of the Jayhawk
        State. Norman: University of Oklahoma Press, 1957.
        Chapter 18 discusses Ku Klux Klan activities in
        Kansas.

10. LOUISIANA

352.   Cauchey, John W., Editor. Their Majesties the Mob.
        Chicago: University of Chicago Press, 1974. There
        is one section by Robert Duffers entitled "The Ku
        Klux Klan at Work." The author discusses how the
        Klan murdered two men in Mer Rouge, Louisiana.

353.   Ficklen, John Rose. History of Reconstruction in
        Louisiana. Baltimore: Johns Hopkins Press, 1910.
        See Index, Ku Klux Klan.

354.   Meriweather, Elizabeth Avery. The Ku Klux Klan, or
        The Carpet-Bagger in New Orleans. Memphis: Southern
        Baptist Publication Society, 1877. 51pp.

355.   Rogers, John. The Murders of Mer Rouge. St. Louis:
        Security Publishing Co., 1923. Various references
        are made to the Ku Klux Klan throughout the book.

11. MINNESOTA

356.   Mayer, George H. The Political Career of Floyd B.
        Olson. Minneapolis: University of Minnesota Press,
        1951. Ku Klux Klan activities in Minnesota are dis-
        cussed in this work.

·12. MISSISSIPPI

357.   Garner, James W. Reconstruction in Mississippi.
        New York: Macmillan Co., 1901. A brief discussion
        of Ku Klux Klan activities in Mississippi.

358.   Harkey, Ira B. Jr. The Smell of Burning Crosses:
        An Autobiography of A Mississippi Newspaperman.
        Jacksonville, IL: Harris-Wolfe & Co., 1967. 208pp.
        Various references are made to the Ku Klux Klan
        throughout the book.

359.   Lumpkin, Benjamin, Thomas Malone and others. Full
        Report of the Great Ku Klux Trial in the United
        States Circuit Court at Oxford, Miss. Reported by
        David M. Philip. Memphis: W.J. Mansford, 1871.
        100pp.

360.   Mars, Florence. Witness in Philadelphia: A Mississip-
        pi WASP's Account of the 1964 Civil Rights Murders.
        Baton Rouge: Louisiana State University Press, 1977.
        The author testified before a grand jury investiga-
        ting the murder of three civil-rights workers by
        the Ku Klux Klan.

361.   McCord, William. Mississippi: The Long, Hot Summer.
        New York: W.W. Norton & Co., 1965. Author discusses
        Ku Klux Klan activities in Mississippi during the
        1964 summer.

362.   NAACP. Mis For Mississippi and Murder. New York:
        NAACP, 1956. Discusses KKK (pamphlet).

363.   Percy, William A. Lanterns on the Levee; Recollec-
        tions of a Planter's Son. New York: Alfred A.
        Knopf, 1941. The author comments on his father's
        opposition to the Ku Klux Klan's anti-Catholicism in
        the State of Mississippi.

364.   Wells, James M. The Chisolm Massacre: A Picture of
        Home-Rule in Mississippi. Washington: Chisolm
        Monument Association, 1878. An account of "home-
        rule" in Kemper, Mississippi, the Ku Klux Klan and
        its dreadful work of murder and spreading terror
        among the Negroes and progressive whites.

365.   Whitehead, Don. Attack On Terror; The FBI Against
        the Ku Klux Klan in Mississippi. New York: Funk &
        Wagnalls, 1970. 321pp.

13. NEBRASKA

366.   Lief, Alfred. Democracy's (George W.) Norris; The
        Biography of A Lonely Crusade. New York: Stackpole
        Sons, 1939. Chapters 14 and 15 discussed Norris's
        anti-Klan activities when he was a United States
        Senator from Nebraska.

367.   Lowitt, Richard. George W. Norris: The Triumph of
        A Progressive, 1933-1944. Urbana: University of
        Illinois Press, 1978. Author discusses Norris's
        anti-Klan activities when he was a United States
        Senator from Nebraska.

368.   Norris, George W. Fighting Liberal, The Autobio-
        graphy of George W. Norris. New York: Macmillan
        Co., 1945. Chapter 28 discusses his anti-Klan acti-
        vities when he was a United States Senator.

14. NEW YORK

369.   Rubin, Jay. The Ku Klux Klan in Binghamton, New
        York, 1923-1928. Binghamton, N.Y.: Broome County
        Historical Society, 1973. 59pp.

15. NORTH CAROLINA

370.   Badger, Richard C. The Holden-Kirk War! Secret
History of the Holden-Kirk War. Testimony Taken
Before the Legislative Investigating Committee in
April, 1871: Latham, Chairman n.p. 1876. 2pp.

371.   Bermanzohn, Paul C. and Sally A. Bermanzohn. The
True Story of the Greensboro Massacre. Cesar Cauce
Publishing, P.O. Box 389, 39 Bowery, N.Y. 10002,
1982. 254pp. The authors witnessed the murder of
five of their close friends in Greensboro, N.C. by
the Ku Klux Klan and the Nazis.

372.   Bowers, Claude G. The Tragic Era, The Revolution
After Lincoln. Cambridge: Riverside Press, 1929.
pp. 312-326--concerns the Kirk-Holden War, Governor
Holden of N.C. battles the Klan.

373.   Brogden, C.H. Opinion of General C.H. Brogden,
Senator From Wayne and Greene [Counties], on the
Impeachment Trial of William W. Holden, Governor of
North Carolina. Raleigh, N.C.: Sentinel, 1871,
15pp.

374.   Carlton, Luther M. Assassination of J.W. Stephens.
Durham, N.C., 1898. The assasination of John
Walter Stephens by the Ku Klux Klan for having taken
part in politics with the Negroes of North Carolina.

375.   Chafe, William H. Civilities and Civil Rights:
Greensboro, North Carolina, and the Black Struggle
For Freedom. New York: Oxford University Press,
1980. See sections on Ku Klux Klan, pp. 78,95, 184,
194, 224, 226-229, 283.

376.   Dent, Sanders. The Origin and Development of the Ku
Klux Klan. Durham, North Carolina: Duke University?,
1897. pp. 10-27. The origin and development of the
Ku Klux Klan as the result of the social, civil, and
political condition of the South, from the close of
the war to 1869, that involved freed Negroes as
aggressors.

377.   Evans, W. McKee. Ballots and Fence Rails; Reconstruction on the Lower Cape Fear. Chapel Hill:
University of North Carolina Press, 1966. The writer
discusses the Ku Klux Klan activities in the Cape
Fear region of North Carolina before, during and
after the Governor's election of 1870.

378.   Green, John Paterson. Recollections of the Inhabitants, Localities, Superstitions and Ku Klux Outrages
of the Carolinas. Cleveland, OH?: The author, 1880.
205pp.

379.   Gruening, Martha. _Reconstruction and the Ku Klux Klan in North Carolina_. New York: National Association for the Advancement of Colored People, Dept. of Publications and Research, N.D.

380.   Hamilton, J.G. deRoulhac. _Reconstruction in North Carolina_. Vol. LVIII, Longmans, Green & Co., Agents, London, 1914, pp. 572-582--concerns attempts to repress the Klan in 1870.

381.   _____. _History Of North Carolina_. Vol. 3, _North Carolina Since 1860_. Reprinted in 1973, The Reprint Company, Spartanburg, S.C., p. 136, Alledged benefits of the Klan: protected the oppressed, women (white), property, and controlled crime; p. 141, The Klan never disturbed peace and quiet.

382.   Holden, William H. _Third Annual Message of W.W. Holden, Governor of North Carolina_. Raleigh: J.W. Holden, 1870. 286pp. Appendix includes governor's proclamations, correspondence with chief justice and others, and evidence before the Supreme Court of the state, regarding the Ku Klux Klan.

383.   Lefler, Hugh T. _North Carolina History Told by Contemporaries_. Chapel Hill: University of North Carolina Press, 1956. p. 331--concerns the alleged reason for the Klan to organize in North Carolina.

384.   Mitchell, Memory F., Editor. _Messages, Addresses, and Public Papers of Terry Sanford, Governor of North Carolina 1961-1965_. Raleigh, N.C.: North Carolina History Commission, 1966. See Ku Klux Klan, pp. 623-624.

385.   Myerson, Michael. _Nothing Could Be Finer_. New York: International Publishers, 1978. Ku Klux Klan in North Carolina, pp. 5, 6, 11, 12, 14, 17, 18, 19, 29, 44, 55, 56, 66, 69, 92, 100, 108, 229.

386.   Olsen, Otto H. _Carpetbagger's Crusade: The Life of Albion Winegar Tourgee_. Baltimore: Johns Hopkins Press, 1965. Ku Klux Klan, pp. 121, 137: rise of, 147; crimes by and character of, 147-148, 156-169; excuses for, 148-155; opposition to, 153, 159, 160; effect on 1870 elections, 166-167; federal actions against, 184; Tourgee exposes, 184-185; legislature protects, 186-187.

387.   Patton, James W., Editor. _Messages, Addresses, and Public Papers of Luther H. Hodges, Governor of North Carolina 1954-1961_. Raleigh: Council of State, State of North Carolina, 1963. See Ku Klux Klan attack on the Lumbee Indians, Vol. II, pp. 586-588.

388.   Simkins, Francis Butler and Robert Hilliard Woody.
        South Carolina During Reconstruction. Chapel Hills:
        University of North Carolina Press, 1932, pp. 77,
        125--influence of the Klan on the Union League.

389.   Smiley, Wendell W., Compiler. The North Carolina
        Press Views the Ku Klux Klan From 1964 Through 1966.
        Greenville, N.C.: The Author?, 1968. 450pp. A
        collection of photocopied newspaper clippings.

390.   Testimony of the Witnesses in the Preliminary Exami-
        nations of the Lenoir (N.C.) County Prisoners: The
        Secrets of the Ku-Klux Klan, etc., etc. New Berne,
        N.C.: n.p., 1869.

391.   The Ku Klux Klans. Raleigh: Capital Printing Co.,
        1902. 26pp.

392.   Weaver, Charles C. A Ku Klux Klan Raid, and What
        Became of It. Durham, N.C., 1897. 8pp. Discusses
        the last raid of the Ku Klux Klan upon the Negro
        politicians and those who had any connection with
        them before their decline in North Carolina.

393.   Williams, Robert F. Negroes With Guns. New York:
        Marzani & Munsell, 1962. This Black activist
        discusses Blacks in North Carolina shoot-out with
        the Ku Klux Klan in that state.

16. OKLAHOMA

394.   Blake Aldrich. The Ku Klux Klan Kraze; A Trip Through
        the Klavern. Oklahoma City: n.p., 1924. 40pp.
        Lecture by Governor John Walton's secretary, supple-
        mented by excerpts from testimony taken by the mili-
        tary court sitting at Tulsa, Oklahoma, during period
        of martial law imposed on that city.

395.   McBee, William D. The Oklahoma Revolution. Okla-
        homa City: Modern Publishers, 1956. The author, a
        former Speaker of the Oklahoma State House of Repre-
        sentatives, discusses how Governor John C. Walton
        of Oklahoma declared martial law to combat Ku Klux
        Klan forces during the 1920's.

396.   McReynolds, Edwin C. Oklahoma: A History of the
        Sooner State. Norman: University of Oklahoma Press,
        1954. A brief discussion of the Ku Klux Klan's
        activities in Oklahoma during Governor John C.
        Walton's tenure.

397.   Witcher, Walter C. The Reign of Terror in Oklahoma,
        a Detailed Account of the Klan's Barbarous Practices
        and Brutal Outrages Against Individuals; its Control
        Over Judges and Juries and Governor Walton's Heroic
        Fight, Including a General Exposure of Klan Secrets,

Sham and Hypocrisy. Fort Worth, Tex.: W.C. Witcher, 1923. 144pp.

17. OREGON

398.   Sawyer, Reuben H. The Truth About The Invisible Empire, Knights of the Ku Klux Klan. Portland, Oreg.: Northwest Domain, 1922. 16pp.

399.   Turnbull, George S. An Oregon Crusader. Portland, Ore.: Binfords & Mort, Publishers, 1955. The writer discusses newspaperman George Putnam of Oregon editorial campaign against the Ku Klux Klan. The Klan tried to boycott Putnam's (of Oregon) newspaper, but to no avail.

18. PENNSYLVANIA

400.   Loucks, Emerson H. The Ku Klux Klan in Pennsylvania; A Study in Nativism. New York: Telegraph Press, 1936. 213pp.

401.   Mecklin, John Moffatt. The Ku Klux Klan in Pennsylvania. New York: Telegraph Press, 1936.

19. SOUTH CAROLINA

402.   Brawley, Benjamin. Social History of the American History. New York: Macmillan, 1921. pp. 272-278. "Ku Klux Klan" and their involvement in the "Hamburg Massacre" in South Carolina is discussed.

403.   Carson, Clayborne. In Struggle: SNCC and the Black Awakening of the 1960's. Cambridge, Ma: Harvard University Press, 1981. Author discusses Ku Klux Klan activities. See pp. 36, 85, 254, 255, 282.

404.   Lamson, Peggy. The Glorious Failure; Black Congressman Robert Brown Elliott and the Reconstruction in South Carolina. New York: W.W. Norton & Co., 1973. There is a discussion of the Ku Klux Klan trials in 1871 in South Carolina.

405.   Leland, John A. A Voice From South Carolina. Twelve Chapters Before Hampton. Two Chapters After Hampton. With a Journal of a Reputed Ku Klux, and An Appendix. Charleston, S.C.: Walker, Evans & Cogswell, 1879. 231pp.

406.   Quint, Howard H. Profile in Black and White; A Frank Portrait of South Carolina. Washington, D.C.: Public Affairs Press, 1958. The author discusses the Ku Klux Klan in South Carolina and their opposition to desegregation in the 1950's.

407.   Reynolds, John S. Reconstruction in South Carolina, 1865-1877. Columbia, S.C.: State Co., 1905. "The Ku Klux Troubles," pp. 179-217.

408.   Simkins, Francis Butler and Robert Hilliard Woody. South Carolina During Reconstruction. Chapel Hill: University of North Carolina Press, 1932, pp. 77, 125--influence of the Klan on the Union League.

409.   Taylor, Alrutheus A. The Negro in South Carolina During the Reconstruction. Washington, D.C.: Association For the Study of Negro Life and History, 1924. A brief discussion of Ku Klux Klan activities in South Carolina during Klansman's trials in Columbia, S.C. between 1871-1872.

410.   Testimony For The Prosecution in the Case of United States Versus Robert Hayes Mitchell. Cincinnati: Phonographic Institute Co., 1913. This is testimony given in Columbia, South Carolina at the 1871 Ku Klux Klan trial.

411.   Thompson, Henry T. Ousting the Carpetbagger From South Carolina. Columbia, S.C.: R.L. Bryan Co., 1926. There are various references about Ku Klux Klan activities in South Carolina during Reconstruction.

412.   Williams, Alfred T. Hampton and His Red Shirts. Charleston, S.C.: 1935. The author discusses how the Ku Klux Klan was relatively inactive in South Carolina before and during the 1876 election.

20. TENNESSEE

413.   Alexander, Thomas B. Political Reconstruction in Tennessee. Nashville, TN: Vanderbilt University Press, 1950. Brief discussion of the establishment of the Ku Klux Klan in Tennessee.

414.   Furniss, Jim. Tennessee's Klan Kleagle Only 22, But Has He Mass Murder Plan? Atlanta, GA: Southern Regional Council, 1946. 2pp.

415.   Lamon, Lester C. Black Tennesseans, 1900-1930. Knoxville: University of Tennessee Press, 1977. Ku Klux Klan activities are discussed in Tennessee between 1900-1930.

416.   Patton, James W. Unionism and Reconstruction in Tennessee, 1860-1869. Chapel Hill: University of North Carolina Press, 1934. Ku Klux Klan activities in Tennessee during Reconstruction are discussed in this book.

417.   Senter, D.W.C. Special Message of the Governor,
        D.W.C. Senter, in Relation to Mob Violence. Sub-
        mitted February 2, 1870. Nashville: Jones, Purvis
        & Co., 1870. 6pp.

418.   Taylor, Alrutheus A. The Negro in Tennessee, 1865-
        1880. Washington, D.C.: Associated Publishers,
        1941. There is a discussion of Ku Klux Klan acti-
        vities in Tennessee during the Reconstruction period.

419.   Tennessee General Assembly. Senate. Committee On
        Military Affairs. Report of Evidence Taken Before
        the Military Committee In Relation to Outrages Com-
        mited by the Ku Klux Klan In Middle and West Tennes-
        see. Nashville: S.C. Mercer, 1868. 67pp.

420.   Thompson, Jerry. My Life With the Klan: From the
        Pages of the Tennesean. Knoxville: The Tennesean,
        1980. 32pp.

21. TEXAS

421.   Brandfon, Robert L., Editor. The American South in
        the Twentieth Century. New York: Thomas Y. Crowell
        Company, 1967. Two articles are discussed concern-
        ing Miriam Ferguson's election as Governor of Texas
        and her Ku Klux Klan - supported opponent.

422.   Steen, Ralph W. Twentieth Century Texas: An Econo-
        mic and Social History. Austin: Steck Company,
        Publishers, 1942. Brief references are made to the
        Ku Klux Klan.

22. UTAH

423.   Gerlach, Larry R. Blazing Crosses In Zion: The Ku
        Klux Klan In Utah. Logan, Utah: Utah State Uni-
        versity Press, 1982. 270pp.

23. VIRGINIA

424.   Buni, Andrew. Negro in Virginia Politics, 1902-
        1965. Charlottesville: University Press of Vir-
        ginia, 1967. Various references are made to the
        Ku Klux Klan and their involvement in Virginia
        politics during the 1920's and 1960's.

3
Dissertations and Theses

DISSERTATIONS

A SELECTED LIST

1.   ALABAMA

425.   Bell, William D. "The Reconstruction Ku Klux Klan: A
Survey of the Writings on the Klan With a Profile And
Analysis of The Alabama Klan Episode, 1866-1874." Unpublished Ph.D. Dissertation, Louisiana State University
and Agricultural & Mechanical College, 1973, 395pp.

2. ARKANSAS

426.   Alexander, Charles C., Jr.   "Invisible Empire In The
Southwest: The Ku Klux Klan In Texas, Louisiana, Oklahoma, and Arkansas, 1920-1930." Unpublished Ph.D. Dissertation, University of Texas, 1962, 369pp.

3.   CALIFORNIA

427.   Cocoltchos, Christopher N. "The Invisible Government And
The Viable Community: The Ku Klux Klan In Orange County,
California During the 1920's." Unpublished Ph.D. Dissertation, University of California at Los Angeles, 1979,
794pp.

4.   COLORADO

428.   Goldberg, Robert Alan. "Hooded Empire: The Ku Klux Klan
In Colorado, 1921-1932." Unpublished Ph.D. Dissertation,
University of Wisconsin-Midison, 1977, 369pp.

5. GEORGIA

429.   Moseley, Clement C. "Invisible Empire: A History of
the Ku Klux Klan in Twentieth Century Georgia, 1915-
1965." Unpublished Ph.D. Dissertation, University
of Georgia, 1968. 249pp.

6. INDIANA

430.   Cates, Frank M. "The Ku Klux Klan in Indiana Politics: 1920-1925." Unpublished Ph.D. Dissertation,
Indiana University, 1971. 21pp.

431.   Davis, John Augustus. "The Ku Klux Klan in Indiana,
1920-1930: An Historical Study." Unpublished Ph.D.
Dissertation, Northwestern University, 1966. 362pp.

432.   Weaver, Norman F. "The Knights of the Ku Klux Klan
in Wisconsin, Indiana, Ohio, and Michigan." Unpublished Ph.D. Dissertation, University of Wisconsin,
1954. 237pp.

7. LOUISIANA

433.   Alexander, Charles C. Jr. "Invisible Empire in the
Southwest: The Ku Klux Klan in Texas, Louisiana,
Oklahoma, and Arkansas, 1920-1930." Unpublished
Ph.D. Dissertation, University of Texas, 1962.
369pp.

434.   Harrell, Kenneth E. "The Ku Klux Klan in Louisiana,
1920-1930." Unpublished Ph.D. Dissertation, Louisiana State University, 1966. 388pp.

8. MICHIGAN

435.   Weaver, Norman F. "The Knights of the Ku Klux Klan
in Wisconsin, Indiana, Ohio, and Michigan." Unpublished Ph.D. Dissertation, University of Wisconsin,
1954. 237pp.

9. OHIO

436.   Weaver, Norman F. "The Knights of the Ku Klux Klan
in Wisconsin, Indiana, Ohio, and Michigan." Unpublished Ph.D. Dissertation, University of Wisconsin,
1954. 237pp.

10. OKLAHOMA

437.   Alexander, Charles C. "Invisible Empire in the
Southwest: The Ku Klux Klan in Texas, Louisiana,
Oklahoma, and Arkansas, 1920-1930." Unpublished
Ph.D. Dissertation, University of Texas, 1962.
369pp.

438. Clark, Carter B. "A History of the Ku Klux Klan in
      Oklahoma." Unpublished Ph.D. Dissertation, Univer-
      sity of Oklahoma, 1976. 289pp.

11. WISCONSIN

439. Weaver, Norman F. "The Knights of the Ku Klux Klan
      in Wisconsin Indiana, Ohio, and Michigan." Unpub-
      lished Ph.D. Dissertation, University of Wisconsin,
      1954. 237pp.

GENERAL WORKS

440. Avin, Benjamin Herzl. "The Ku Klux Klan, 1915-1925:
      A Study in Religious Intolerance." Unpublished Ph.D.
      Dissertation, Georgetown University, 1952. 203pp.

441. Jackson, Kenneth T. "The Decline of the Ku Klux
      Klan, 1924-1932." Unpublished Ph.D. Dissertation,
      University of Chicago, 1963. 115pp.

442. Jackson, Kenneth Terry. "The Ku Klux Klan in the
      City, 1915-1930." Unpublished Ph.D. Dissertation,
      University of Chicago, 1967. 157pp.

443. Moore, William V. "A Sheet and a Cross: A Symbolic
      Analysis of the Ku Klux Klan." Unpublished Ph.D.
      Dissertation, Tulane University, 1975. 36pp.

444. Swinney, Everette. "Suppressing the Ku Klux Klan:
      The Enforcement of the Reconstruction Amendments,
      1870-1874." Unpublished Ph.D. Dissertation, Univer-
      sity of Texas, 1966. 370pp.

THESES

A SELECTED LIST

1. ALABAMA

445. Scarritt, Charley Wesley. "Grover Hall And The Montgo-
      mery Advertiser." Unpublished Master's Thesis, Univer-
      sity of Missouri, 1950.

446. Snell, William R. "The Ku Klux Klan In Jefferson
      County, Alabama, 1916-1930." Unpublished Master's
      Thesis, Stanford University, 1967

2. CALIFORNIA

447. Von Brauchitsh, Dennis M. "The Ku Klux Klan In Califor-
      nia, 1921 to 1924." Unpublished Master's Thesis, Sacra-
      mento State College, 1967.

448. _____. "The Ku Klux Klan In California, 1921 to
      1924." Unpublished Master's Thesis, California State
      University, 1967.

3. COLORADO

449. Atchison, Carla Joan. "Nativism In Colorado Politics:
      The American Protective Association And The Ku Klux
      Klan." Unpublished Master's Thesis, University of
      Colorado, 1972.

450. Davis, James H. "The Rise of The Ku Klux Klan In Colo-
      rado, 1921-1925." Unpublished Master's Thesis, Univer-
      sity of Denver, 1963.

451. Walrod, Stephen T. "The Ku Klux Klan In Colorado, 1921-
      1926." Unpublished Bachelor of Arts Thesis, Princeton
      University, 1970.

4. INDIANA

452. Weaver, Norman F. "The Ku Klux Klan in Indiana."
Unpublished Master's Thesis, University of Wisconsin,
1947.

5. KANSAS

452a. Jones, Lila Lee. "The Ku Klux Klan In Eastern Kansas
During the 1920's." Unpublished Master's Thesis,
Emporia Kansas State College, 1972.

6. MISSISSIPPI

453. Bradley, Laura Lipsey. "Protestant Churches and the
Ku Klux Klan in Mississippi During the 1920's: Study
of an Unsuccessful Courtship." Unpublished Master's
Thesis, University of Mississippi, 1962.

454. Elders, Audrae T. "The Ku Klux Klan in Mississippi,
1867-1875." Unpublished Master's Thesis, Atlanta
University, 1977.

7. NORTH CAROLINA

455. Fox, Cynthia G. "The Battle of Hayes Pond: The Ku
Klux Klan Versus the Lumbee Indians, Robeson County,
North Carolina, 1958." Unpublished Master's Thesis,
East Carolina University, 1980. 158pp.

456. Lanier, Jerry P. "The Rise and Fall of the Ku Klux
Klan in Southeastern North Carolina, 1950-1952."
Unpublished Master's Thesis, University of North
Carolina at Chapel Hill, 1970.

8. OHIO

457. Howson, Embrey B. "The Ku Klux Klan in Ohio After
World War I." Unpublished Master's Thesis, Ohio State
University, 1951.

9. OKLAHOMA

458. Steers, Nina A. "The Ku Klux Klan in Oklahoma in the
1920's." Unpublished Master's Thesis, Columbia
University, 1965.

10. OREGON

459. Rothwell, Charles Easton. "The Ku Klux Klan In the
State of Oregon." Unpublished Bachelor's Thesis,
Reed College, 1924.

460. Saalfield, Lawrence J. "Forces of Prejudice in
Oregon, 1920-1925." Unpublished Master's Thesis,
Catholic University of America, 1950.

461.   Toy, Eckard V., Jr. "The Ku Klux Klan in Oregon; Its Character and Program." Unpublished Master's Thesis. University of Oregon, 1959.

11.   TENNESSEE

462.   Alexander, Thomas B. "Prelude to Ku Kluxism in Tennessee." Unpublished Master's Thesis, Vanderbilt University, 1940.

463.   Kent, Ann Poindexter. "The Ku Klux Klan in Tennessee." Unpublished Master's Thesis, University of Tennessee, 1935. 134pp.

464.   McFarlin, Brenda Mack. "The Ku Klux Klan in Middle Tennessee, 1866-1869." Unpublished Master's Thesis, Middle Tennessee State University, 1971.

465.   Sherrod, Isa Lee. "The Ku Klux Movement in Tennessee." Unpublished Master's Thesis, George Peabody College, 1935.

12.   TEXAS

466.   Torrence, Lois E. "The Ku Klux Klan in Dallas, 1915-1928: An American Paradox." Unpublished Master's Thesis, Southern Methodist University, 1948.

COUNTRY

1.   CANADA

467.   Calderwood, William. "The Rise and Fall of the Ku Klux Klan in Saskatchewan." Unpublished Master's Thesis, University of Saskatchewan, 1968.

GENERAL WORKS

468.   Baker, Earlene T. "The Ku Klux Klan of the 1920's." Unpublished Master's Thesis, Memphis State, 1960.

469.   Jackson, Charles Oliver. "The Ku Klux Klan 1915-1924: A Study in Leadership." Unpublished Master's Thesis, Emory University, 1962.

470.   Johnson, Guy B. "The New Ku Klux Movement." Unpublished Master's Thesis, University of Chicago, 1922.

471.   Pack, James Edward. "The Sociology of A Social Movement: The Ku Klux Klan." Unpublished Master's Thesis, University of Tennessee, 1950. 196pp.

472.   Schuelke, H.T.   "The Nature of Vigilantism." Unpub-
        lished Master's Thesis, University of Chicago, 1943.

473.   White, Tom Murray.   "The 'Birth of A Nation':   An
        Examination of Its Sources, Content, and Historical
        Assertions About Reconstruction." Unpublished
        Master's Thesis, University of Chicago, 1952.

4
Ku Klux Klan
Materials

OFFICIAL DOCUMENTS

A SELECTED LIST

MEN OF KU KLUX KLAN

474. Ku Klux Klan. The ABC Of The Knights of The Ku Klux Klan, Chartered Under The Laws Of The State Of Georgia. Atlanta, Ga.: Knights of the Ku Klux Klan, 1917, 8pp.

475. Ku Klux Klan. America For Americans. Tucker, Ga.: Knights Of The Ku Klux Klan, n.d., 4pp.

476. Ku Klux Klan. A Message From Hon. James R. Venable, President, National Knights of the Ku Klux Klan, Concerning the KKK's Problems, Programs, and Purposes. Tucker, Ga.: National Knights of the Ku Klux Klan, n.d., 2pp.

477. Ku Klux Klan. An Introduction to The Knights of The Ku Klux Klan. Tuscaloosa, Al.: United Klans of America, 1966, 22p.

478. Ku Klux Klan. An Introduction To The Knights Of The Ku Klux Klan. Tuscaloosa, Al.: United Klans of America, n.d., 4pp.

479. Ku Klux Klan. Articles On The Klan And Elementary Klankraft. Atlanta, Ga.: Ku Klux Klan, 1924.

480. Ku Klux Klan. Big Western Kentucky KKK Rally, Henderson, Ky., Saturday, June 12, 192- and All Day Meeting KKK Sunday, July 4th, 192-. n.d., n.p.

481. Ku Klux Klan. Catalogue Of Official Robes And Banners. Atlanta, Ga.: Knights of the Ku Klux Klan, 1925, 28pp.

482. Ku Klux Klan. Certificates. Farmville, Va., 1922.

483.   Ku Klux Klan. Child Dilemma: Parent Concern for
        United Nations Educational, Scientific and Cultural
        Organization. Tuscaloosa, Al: United Klans of
        America, Inc., n.d.

484.   Ku Klux Klan. Come Now Let Us Reason Together...,
        1927. 14pp.

485.   Ku Klux Klan. Constitution and Laws of the Knights
        of the Ku Klux Klan (Incorporated). Altanta, Ga:
        Knights of the Ku Klux Klan, 1921. 96pp.

486.   Ku Klux Klan. Constitution and Laws of the Knights
        of the Ku Klux Klan (Incorporated). Atlanta, Ga:
        Knights of the Ku Klux Klan, 1921. 34pp.

487.   Ku Klux Klan. Constitution and Laws of the Knights
        of the Ku Klux Klan, Incorporated. Atlanta, Ga:
        Knights of the Ku Klux Klan. 1926. 61pp.

488.   Ku Klux Klan. Constitution and Laws of the Knights
        of the Ku Klux Klan, Incorporated. Atlanta, Ga:
        Knights of the Ku Klux Klan, 1934. 60pp.

489.   Ku Klux Klan. Constitution and Laws of the U.S.
        Klans, Knights of the Ku Klux Klan. Atlanta, Ga:
        Knights of the Ku Klux Klan, 1955. 47pp.

490.   Ku Klux Klan. Constitution and the Ritual of the
        Knights of the White Camelia. Morgantown, West
        Virginia, 1904. 32pp.

491.   Ku Klux Klan. Creed. Richmond?, 192?

492.   Ku Klux Klan. Famous Klan Speeches By William J.
        Simmons, Edward Y. Clarke, and Caleb A. Ridley.
        Atlanta, Ga: Ku Klux Klan, 1923.

493.   Ku Klux Klan. Fight Communism: You Are Eligible To
        Join the United Klans of America, Inc. Tuscaloosa,
        Al: Knights of the Ku Klux Klan, n.d. 2pp.

494.   Ku-Klux Klan. Alachua Klan No. 46. Floridians, Take
        Your Stand, Citizens of Gainesville Wake Up! Citi-
        zens of Florida, Shall We Always Be Indifferent?
        Gainesville, Fl: 1923.

495.   Ku Klux Klan. Funeral Services. Atlanta, Ga: Knights
        of the Ku Klux Klan, 1924. 5pp.

496.   Ku Klux Klan. Georgia. Klorero. Minutes. 1st - 1924?
        annual.

497.   Ku Klux Klan. Grand Realm Council of British Colum-
        bia, Vancouver Klan No. 1 Resolution...adopted...
        Friday 7th... December 1928. Vancouver, B.C.: The
        Council, 1928.

498. Ku Klux Klan. (Henry) Ford Has A Redder Idea.
      Tuscaloosa, Al: United Klans of America, n.d. 2pp.

499. Ku Klux Klan. Ideals of the Ku Klux Klan.   n.p.:
      n.d., 1915? 8pp.

500. Ku Klux Klan. Ideals of the Ku Klux Klan. Atlanta,
      Ga: Assn. of Ga. Klans..., 1925. 8pp.

501. Ku Klux Klan. Imperial Instruction. Document No. 1.
      Atlanta, Ga: 1918.

502. Ku Klux Klan. The Imperial Night Hawk. Atlanta:
      K.K.K. Publishers, 1923. 3 pamphlets.

503. Ku Klux Klan. Inspirational Addresses Delivered at
      the Second Imperial Klanvocation Held in Kansas City,
      Missouri, September 23, 24, 25, and 26, 1924. Kansas
      City?, Mo: Knights of the Ku Klux Klan Inc., 1924.
      78pp.

504. Ku Klux Klan. In the Matter of the Charges and Spe-
      cifications Against Klansman David Curtis Stephenson,
      Involving a Major Offense. Trial Before Tribunal...
      Evansville, Oh: Knights of the Ku Klux Klan, 1924.
      26pp.

505. Ku Klux Klan. K of K vs. K of C; Knights of the Klan
      Versus Knights of Columbus. n.p., 1924? 64pp.

506. Ku Klux Klan. Klan Building; An Outline of Proven
      Klan Methods For Successfully Applying the Art of
      Klankraft in Building and Operating Local Klans.
      Atlanta? 1925: 16pp.

507. Ku Klux Klan. Klan in Action; A Manual of Leader-
      ship for Officers of Local Klans. Atlanta: American
      Printing and Manufacturing Co., 1922.

508. The Ku Klux Klan in Alexandria and Rapides Parish;
      Fuqua the Ku Klux Kandidate. New Orleans: Bouan-
      Chaud Campaign Committee, 1924. 4pp.

509. The Klan Inside Out. Chicago, 1924.

510. Ku Klux Klan. Klansman's Manual, Compiled and Issued
      Under Direction and Authority of the Knights of the
      Ku Klux Klan, Incorporated. Atlanta: Buckhead, 1924.
      86pp.

511. Ku Klux Klan. Kloran. 4th ed. Atlanta: Ga: Knights
      of the Ku Klux Klan, 1916. 54pp.

512. Kloran, Knights Kamellias. Primary Order of Knight-
      hood. Property of Knights of the Ku Klux Klan...
      1925. 31pp.

513.   Ku Klux Klan. Kloran, Knights of the Ku Klux Klan;
        First Degree Character. Atlanta, Ga: Knights of the
        Ku Klux Klan, 1916. 11pp.

514.   Ku Klux Klan. The Knights of the Ku Klux Klan Were,
        Organized As A Fraternal Organization in Atlanta,
        Georgia, in 1915 and Granted their First Charter on
        July 1, 1916, The Society also Uses the Name Invisible
        Empire, Knights of the Ku Klux Klan, Inc., It is
        Commonly Known as Ku Klux Klan. n.p.n.d.

515.   Ku Klux Klan. Kloran. Atlanta, Ga: Knights of the
        Ku Klux Klan, 1916. 54pp.

516.   Ku Klux Klan. Know The United Nations: A Page
        From American History, 1945-1962. Tuscaloosa, Al:
        United Klans of America, Inc. n.d. 6pp.

517.   The K.K.K. Katechism; Pertinent Question, Pointed
        Answers. Columbus, Oh: Patriot Publishing Co., 1924.
        72pp.

518.   Ku Klux Klan. Minutes of the Imperial Kloneilium,
        Knights of the Ku Klux Klan; Meeting of May 1 and 2,
        1923, which Ratified W.J. Simmons Agreement with the
        Knights of the Ku Klux Klan, Together With Certified
        Copies of all Litigation Instituted by W.J. Simmons
        Against the Imperial Wizard and the Knights of the
        Ku Klux Klan. Atlanta, 1923. 60pp.

519.   Official Document v. 1 October 1926. Atlanta, GA:
        Office of the Grand Dragon, 1926.

520.   Ku Klux Klan. Papers Read at the Meeting of Grand
        Dragons, Knights of the Ku Klux Klan, At the First
        Annual Meeting Held at Asheville, North Carolina,
        July 1923; Together With Other Articles of Interest
        to Klansmen. Asheville, N.C.: n.p. 1923? 136pp.
        Located at the University of North Carolina at Chapel
        Hill.

521.   Ku Klux Klan. Papers Read at the Meeting of Grand
        Dragons, Knights of the Ku Klux Klan at their First
        Annual Meeting...Together with Other Articles of
        Interest to Klansmen. Atlanta, Ga: Knights of the
        Ku Klux Klan, 1923. 22pp.

522.   Ku Klux Klan. The Practice of Klanishness. Atlanta:
        Ku Klux Klan, 1918. 7pp.

523.   Ku-Klux-Klan. Prescript of the ** Order of the Ku-
        Klux-Klan. Pulaski, Tn: Pulaski Citizen Office,
        1867. 16pp.

524.   Ku-Klux Klan. Prescript of the *** Order of the Ku
        Klux Klan. New York: American Photo-Lithograph Co.,
        18-? 16pp.

525.   Proceedings of the Second Imperial Klanvocation, Held
       in Kansas City, Missouri, September 23-26, 1924.
       Atlanta, Ga: n.p., 1924.

526.   Ku Klux Klan. Realm of Indiana Marion County Klan.
       No. 3. Local Constitution. Marion: Ku Klux Klan,
       1924.

527.   Ku-Klux Klan. Revised and Amended Prescript of the
       Order of the ***. Pulaski, Tn, 1868. 24pp.

528.   Ku-Klux Klan. Revised and Amended Prescript of Ku
       Klux Klan. Morgantown, West Va., 1904. 32pp.

529.   Ku-Klux Klan. Revised and Amended Prescript of Ku-
       Klux Klan. Baton Rouge, La., 1908. 2pp.

530.   Ku Klux Klan. Secret Work of Ritual. Little Rock,
       Ark.: Parke-Harper. n.d. 4pp.

531.   Ku Klux Klan. Some Questions About the National Coun-
       cil of Churches That Need Straight Answers. Granite
       Quarry, N.C.: United Klans of America, Inc., 1966?
       4pp.

532.   Ku Klux Klan. The International Jew: The Jew in
       Character and Business, Dearborn Independent. A
       publication of Henry Ford. May 22, 1920. Reprinted
       and published by the Knights of the Ku Klux Klan.
       Atlanta, Ga: 1941. 18pp.

533.   Ku Klux Klan. The Seven Symbols of the Klan. Tucker,
       Ga: National Knights of the Ku Klux Klan, Inc., n.d.
       11pp.

534.   Ku Klux Klan. The Truth About The Book Sabotage: Ex-
       posing The Evil Plot to Destroy the United States
       Congress and Americans Who Support It. Atlanta, Ga:
       Knights of the Ku Klux Klan, 1942. 22pp.

535.   Ku Klux Klan. We, The Klan, Believe. Granite Quarry,
       N.C., n.d.

536.   Ku Klux Klan. Why You Should Become A Klansman.
       Tucker, Ga: Knights of the Ku Klux Klan, n.d. 2pp.

WOMEN OF THE KU KLUX KLAN

A SELECTED LIST

537.   Women of the Ku Klux Klan. Catalogue of Official
        Robes and Banners. Little Rock, Ark.: H.G. Pugh,
        193?. 61pp.

538.   Women of the Ku Klux Klan. Constitution and Laws of
        the Women of the Ku Klux Klan, Accepted and Adopted
        June 2nd, 1923, at Washington, D.C. Incorporated
        June 8th, 1923, at Little Rock, Ark. Little Rock:
        Ark.: Parke-Harper Publishing Co., 1924? 72pp.

539.   Women of the Ku Klux Klan. Constitution and Laws
        of the Women of the Ku Klux Klan. Adopted By First
        Imperial Klanvocation at St. Louis, Missouri on the
        Sixth Day of January, 1927. St. Louis, MO: 1927. 73pp.

540.   Women of the Ku Klux Klan. Constitution and Laws of
        the Women of the Ku Klux Klan, Adopted By First
        Imperial. Klanvocation at St. Louis, Missouri, on
        the Sixth Day of January, 1927. Little Rock, Ark.:
        H.G. Pugh & Company, 1934. 22p.

541.   Women of the Ku Klux Klan. Installation Ceremonies.
        en.p., n.d., 16pp.

542.   Ku Klux Klan. Kloran, for Ritual of the Women of the
        Ku Klux Klan. Little Rock, Arkansas: Women of the
        Ku Klux Klan 1923. 38pp.

543.   Women Of the Ku Klux Klan. Printed Forms. n.p., 192-,
        Contents. Form 2D-1. Application for Admission to
        the Second Degree.- Form 1010. P.H. Application for
        Membership. Form 113-10M BKS - 8-10-23. Official
        Order on Klabee -Form K-112-20M BKS - 8-10-23.

Klabee's Official Receipt - Form 132-P.H. - Membership Card. 8pp.

544.   Women of the Ku Klux Klan. Ritual of the Tri-K-Klub/ Women of the Ku Klux Klan. Little Rock, Ark.: Parke-Harper Publishing Co., 1925. 20pp.

545.   Women of the Ku Klux Klan. Second Degree. Obligation. First Section. en.p., n.d. 4pp.

546.   Women of the Ku Klux Klan. Women of America! The Past! The Present! The Future! Outline of Principles and Teaching, Women of the Ku Klux Klan Incorporated. Little Rock, Ark., Imperial Headquarters: Women of the Ku Klux Klan, 1923. 16pp.

BROADSIDES

A SELECTED LIST

547. Simmons, William J. Article in Reply to Charges Made
      Against the Ku Klux Klan. n.p., 192? 4pp. Broadside.

548. Ku-Klux Klan. Alachua Klan No. 116. Floridians, Take
      Your Stand. Citizens of Gainesville, Wake Up! Citi-
      zens of Florida, Shall We Always Be Indifferent?
      Gainesville, Fla., 1923. Broadside.

549. Ku Klux Klan. Certificates. Farmville, Va., n.p.
      1922. Broadside.

550. Ku Klux Klan. Big Western Kentucky KKK Rally. Hen-
      derson, Ky., Saturday, June 12, 192? and All day
      meeting K.K.K.,Sunday, July 4th. p. 192-? Broadsides.

551. Ku Klux Klan. The Ku-Klux Reign of Terror. Synopsis
      of a Portion of the Testimony Taken By the Congres-
      sional Investigating Committee. n.p., n.p. 1872.
      Broadside.

552. Ku Klux Klan. The Ku-Klux Organization - Ku-Kluxism
      and Democracy. The Ku Ku Reign of Terror. n.p. n.p.,
      1872? Broadside.

553. Ku Klux Klan. A Collection of Broadsides, Cards,
      Folders and Pamphlets Written and Published by the
      Ku Klux Klan. 24 pieces. Located in the Rare Book
      Room at Duke University, Durham, N.C.

554. Outrages [KKK] in North Carolina. n.p.: n.p. 1870.
      Broadside. Located at the University of North Caro-
      lina at Chapel Hill.

555.   <u>Ku Klux Kismet March</u>. Arkansas Press: Walter Ardrell
Riggs, 1924. Folio sheet music. Cover illustration
of hooded Klansman mounted on a hooded horse and
waving an American flag, another standing in the
background holding a burning cross. Music by Mary
Gue, arrgd., by Riggs.

POEMS

556.   Lynch, James Daniel. <u>Redpath; or The Ku Klux Tribu-
nal. A Poem</u>. Columbus, Miss.: Excelsior Printing
Establishment, 1877. 59pp.

557.   Simmons, William Joseph. <u>America's Menace; or, The
Enemy Within (an epitome) Including "America, my
America," the Most Powerfully Appealing Patriotic
Poem Ever Penned. A clarion call to patriotic action</u>.
Atlanta, Ga: Bureau of Patriotic Books, 1926. 235pp.

558.   Stroud, Malden (Mrs.). <u>Poems and Other Matter on the
Ku Klux Klan</u>. Hammond, Ind.: Printed for the Protestant Non-Klan Society, 1925. 87pp.

NOVELS

559.   Alligood, Katherine (Porter). <u>The Flaming Cross: A
Novel of the Klan in Alabama in the 1880's</u>. New York:
Exposition Press, 1956. 138pp.

560.   Braddon, Russell. <u>The Proud American Boy</u>. New York:
St. Martin's Press, 1961. 280pp. A fictional ac-
count of the Ku Klux Klan.

561.   Burnett, Hallie S. <u>This Heart, This Hunter</u>. New
York: Holt & Co., 1953. 310pp. A fictional account
of the Ku Klux Klan.

562.   Dixon, Thomas. ....<u>The Leopard's Spot; A Romance
of the White Man's Burden - 1865-1900</u>. New York:
Doubleday, Page & Co., 1902. 465pp.

563.   _____. <u>The Clansman: An Historical Romance of
the Ku Klux Klan</u>. New York: Doubleday, Page & Co.,
1905. 374pp.

564.   _____. <u>The Traitor: A Story of the Fall of the
Invisible Empire</u>. New York: Doubleday, Page & Co.,
1907. 331pp.

565.   _____. <u>The Black Hood</u>. New York: D. Appleton &
Co., 1924. 336pp.

566.   Foster, V. Ray. <u>Rebel Blood, A Novel</u>. New York:
New Exposition Press, 1954. 224pp. A fictional
account of the Ku Klux Klan activities in the South.

567.   Jerome, Thomas J. Ku Klux Klan No. 40. A Novel.
        Raleigh, North Carolina: Edwards, 1895. 259pp. A
        novel on the reconstruction South which seeks to
        justify the ruthless tactics of the Klan on the
        basis of the misguided rule of the Republicans and
        Blacks.

568.   Rubin, Victor. Tar And Feathers: An Entrancing Post-
        War Romance in Which the Ku Klux Klan, Its Principles
        and Activities Figure Prominently, Based on Fact.
        Chicago: Universal Press, 1923, 262pp.

569.   Saxon, William Andrew. Knight Vale of the K.K.K.: A
        Fiction Story of Love, Patriotism, Intrigue and Ad-
        venture. Columbus, OH.: Patriot Publishing Co.,
        1924. 160pp.

570.   Stilwell, Hart. Campus Town. Garden City, N.Y.:
        Doubleday & Co., 1950. 273pp. A fictional story
        of Ku Klux Klan activities in a Southwestern city
        in the 1920's.

571.   Swayze, George B.H. Yarb and Cretine; or, Rising
        From Bonds. Boston: The C.M. Clark Publishing Co.,
        1906. 414pp. A fictional account of the Ku Klux
        Klan.

572.   Walsh, Paul E. KKK... New York: Avon Publications,
        1956. 127pp.

573.   Who Brought Slaves To America. Denham Spring, La.:
        Empire Publishing, 1981(?)

PLAYS

574.   Americans on Guard. Worcester, Ma. Eureka Pub-
        lishers, ca. 1925. Four act play depicting a state
        governor's campaign for re-election on a platform
        endorsed by the Ku Klux Klan and his initiation into
        the organization.

575.   Reid, Mayme. The Headless Horseman. New York:
        French. 36pp. A play depicting the role of the
        Ku Klux Klan in the disfranchisement of the Negro
        in the South.

5

Government Documents

A SELECTED LIST

576. Forrest, N. B. Testimony of General N. B. Forrest Before
      the Congressional Committee of the United States Senate.
      Senate Report No. 41, Forty-Second Congress, Second
      Session, 1869. Washington, D.C.: Government Printing
      Office, 1903, pp.116-118.

577. United States Congress. House Miscellaneous Documents,
      40th Congress, 3rd Session, No. 52 (Georgia) and No. 53
      (Mississippi), (serial 1385). The Joint Committee on Re-
      construction took testimony about Klan activity in those
      states.

578. Unites States Congress. House. House Miscellaneous Docu-
      ments, 41st Congress, 1st Session, No. 12 & 13 (serial
      1402), - a contested congressional election with Repub-
      licians alleging that the Klan terrorized the opposition.
      Washington: Government Printing Office, 1871.

579. United States Congress. House. Committee on Rules. The
      Ku Klux Klan. Hearings Before The Committee On Rules,
      House of Representatives, 67th Congress, 1st Session.
      Washington: Government Printing Office, 1921, 184pp.

580. United States Congress. Senate. Select Committee to In-
      vestigate Alleged Outrages In The Southern States.
      Report on the Alleged Outrages In The Southern States,
      by the Select Committee of the Senate. March 10, 1871.
      Washington: Government Printing Office, 1871. John
      Scott, Chairman.

581. United States Congress. Senate Reports, 42nd Congress,
      1st Session, No. 1, 1871 - A Senate Investigation into
      Klan Activity.

582.   United States Congress. <u>Joint Select Committee to</u>
       <u>Inquire Into the Condition of Affairs in the Late</u>
       <u>Insurrectionary States.</u> Washington: Government
       Printing Office, 1872. Thirteen volumes containing a
       congressional investigation of conditions caused by
       the Ku Klux Klan in North Carolina, Georgia, Alabama,
       Florida, and Mississippi.

583.   United States. Congress. Senate. Joint Select
       Committee to Inquire Into the Condition of Affairs in
       the Late Insurrectionary States...<u>The Ku Klux Con-</u>
       <u>spiracy.</u> Washington: Government Printing Office,
       1872.   13v. 1484-96. 42d Cong. 2d sess. Senate rept.
       41.   This report is in 13 parts and contains besides
       the report of the committee, the views of the
       minority and the testimony taken by the committee.

584.   United States. Congress. Senate. Committee On
       Privileges and Elections. <u>Hearings Before Subcom-</u>
       <u>mittee of the Committee on Privileges and Elections</u>,
       <u>United States Senate, Sixty-Eighth Congress, First</u>
       <u>Session, Pursuant to S. Res. 97 Authorizing the</u>
       <u>Investigation of Alleged Unlawful Practices in the</u>
       <u>Election of a Senator From Texas.</u> May 8, 9, 12, 13,
       14, and 16, 1924. Pts. 1-3. Washington: Government
       Printing Office, 1924.   "Statement relative to mate-
       riality, etc., of evidence tending to support the
       allegations of the contest and protest with respect
       to the true nature of the organization known as the
       Knights of the Ku Klux Klan": Vol. 3, pp. 656-705.

585.   United States Congress. Senator from Texas. <u>Hearings</u>
       <u>Before a Subcommittee of the Committee on Privileges</u>
       <u>and Election, United States Senate, 67th Congress,</u>
       <u>1st and 2nd Session</u>. Washington: Government Printing
       Office, 1924.

586.   United States. Congress. Alleged Outrages in Louisi-
       ana. Congressional record, 67th Cong. 3d sess., v.
       63, nos. 2-3 (current file), p. 13-15; 32-7. Speeches
       in the Senate, Nov. 21, 1922, by Senators Randsdell
       and Walsh of Mass., No. 2, p. 13-15. Speeches in
       the House, Nov. 22, 1922, by Representatives Answell,
       Wilson and Sandlin, no. 3, pp. 32-7. Article from
       Washington Post by George Rothwell Brown, Nov. 19,
       1922, no. 3, pp. 32-3. Washington: Government
       Printing Office, 1924.

587.   United States Congress. House. Committee on Un-
       American Activities. <u>Activities of Ku Klux Klan Or-</u>
       <u>ganizations in the United States, Parts 1-5</u>. Wash-
       ington, D.C.:   Government Printing Office, 1966.

588.   United States Congress. House. <u>Hearings Regarding</u>
       <u>H.R. 15678, H.R. 15689, H.R. 15744, H.R. 15754, and</u>
       <u>H.R. 16099, Bills to Curb Terrorist Organizations</u>.
       Washington, D.C.:   Government Printing Office, 1966.

589.   United States Congress. House. The Present-Day Ku
        Klux Klan Movement. Washington, D.C.: Government
        Printing Office, 1967.

6
Elected Officials' Speeches

1. INDIANA

590. Pratt, Daniel Darwin. "Extension of Ku Klux Act."
Speech of Hon. Daniel D. Pratt of Indiana, delivered
in the Senate of the United States, May 17, 1872.
Washington,: F. & J. Rives & G. A. Bailey, 1872, 16pp.

2. MARYLAND

591. Butler, Benjamin Franklin. "Ku Klux Outrages In The
South. The Work Of The Democratic Party." Speech of
Hon. Benjamin F. Butler in the House of Representatives,
April 4, 1871: to which is added his reply to the
personal attacks of Mr. Ritchie and Mr. Swann of Mary-
land, in discussing the same bill. Washington: M'Gill
& Witherow, 1871, 24pp.

3. MISSISSIPPI

592. Ames, Adelbert. "Extension of The Ku Klux Act." Speech
of Hon. Adelbert Ames of Mississippi, in the Senate of
the United States, May 20, 1872. Washington: Congressional Globe Office, 1872, 8pp.

593. Barry, Henry W. "Ku Klux Democracy." Speech of Hon.
Henry W. Barry of Mississippi, delivered in the House
of Representatives, April 5, 1871. Washington: F. & J.
Rives & G. A. Bailey, 1871, 15pp.

4. NORTH CAROLINA

594. Cobb, Clinton L. "Enforcement of Fourteenth Amendment."
Speech of Honorable Clinton L. Cobb, of North

Carolina, in the House of Representatives, April 4, 1871. Washington, D.C.: Congressional Globe, n.d. 8pp.

595.   Harris, James H. Speech of Hon. James H. Harris on the Militia Bibb, Delivered in the North Carolina House of Representatives, Monday, January 17th, 1870. Raleight, N.C.: n.p. 1870. 24pp.

596.   Moore, William A. "Law and Order vs. Ku Klux Violence." Speech of Col. William A. Moore, of Chowan [County]. Delivered in the House of Representatives, January 19, 1870. n.p.: n.p., n.d. 8pp.

597.   Pool, John. "Protection of Life, etc., At the South ---Enforcement of Fourteenth Amendment." Speech of Honorable John Pool of North Carolina, Delivered in the Senate of the United States, April 5 and 12, 1871. Washington, D.C.: Rives, 1871. 32pp.

598.   Shober, Francis E. "Enforcement of Fourteenth Amendment." Speech of Honorable Francis E. Shober of North Carolina, in the House of Representative, April 1, 1871. Washington, D.C.: Congressional Globe, n.d. 4pp.

599.   Waddell, Alfred M. "Condition of the South." Speech of Honorable Alfred M. Waddell of North Carolina, in the House of Representatives, April 13, 1872. Washington, D.C.: Rives, 1872. 14pp.

5. OHIO

600.   Sherman, John. "Ku Klux Outrages." Speech of Hon. John Sherman of Ohio, Delivered in the Senate of the United States of America, March 18, 1871. Washington: F. & J. Rives & G.A. Bailey, 1871. 16pp.

601.   Stevenson, Job E. "Ku Klux Klan. Let us Protect the People in the Enjoyment of Life, Liberty, and Property, and Impartial Suffrage in Peace." Speech of Hon. Job E. Stevenson, of Ohio, Delivered in the House of Representatives, April 4, 1871. Washington: F. & J. Rives & G.A. Bailey, 1871. 36pp.

602.   _____. "Ku-Klux Conspiracy." Speech of Hon. Job E. Stevenson, of Ohio, Delivered in the House of Representatives, May 30, 1872. Washington, D.C., 1872, 8pp.

6. PENNSYLVANIA

603.   Scott, John. "Protection of Life, etc. at the South." Speech of Honorable John Scott, of Pennsylvania, Delivered in the Senate of the United States, March 22 and 23, 1871. Washington, D.C.: F. & J. Rives, 1871. 31pp.

604.   Scott, John. "Extension of Ku Klux Act." Speech Of
        Honorable John Scott, of Pennsylvania, in the Senate
        of the United States, May 17, 1872. Washington, D.C.:
        Congressional Globe, 1872. 16pp.

7
Kourier Magazine Articles

KU KLUX KLAN MATERIALS

A SELECTED LIST

STATES

1. ALABAMA

605. "A Resolution of Alabama Klansmen." The Kourier Magazine. Vol. 9, January, 1933, p. 4.

606. "Action Started By Alabama Klansmen." The Kourier Magazine. Vol. 10, November, 1934, p. 32.

607. "Evangelistic Klankraft In Alabama." The Kourier Magazine. Vol. 4, February, 1928, p. 22-23.

608. "Church Building By A Klan In Arkansas." The Kourier Magazine. Vol. 1, June, 1925, p. 14.

2. CALIFORNIA

609. An Important Message From The Knights Of The Ku Klux Klan Of California To Parents." The Kourier Magazine. Vol. 9, Feburary, 1933, p. 5-6.

610. "An Important Message From The Knights of the Ku Klux Klan Of California To Public School Authorities And Teachers." The Kourier Magazine. Vol. 9, April, 1933, p. 10-11.

611. "Blazing Cross Tells California Klan Is Riding." The Kourier Magazine. Vol. 9, January, 1933, p. 28.

612. "California Klan Defies Reds, Lines Up Against Communism." The Kourier Magazine. Vol. 9, May, 1933, p. 18-19.

613. "Crime and Kidnappings Cause California Klans To Appeal To Lawyers." The Kourier Magazine. Vol. 9, August, 1933, pp. 16-18.

614. "Fires Reveal Ku Klux Klan Revival Plan." The Kourier Magazine. Vol. 10, April, 1934, p. 28.

615. "Fiery Crosses Blaze on U.C.L.A. Campus." The Kourier Magazine. Vol. 11, May, 1935, p. 31.

616. "Fiery Cross Warns Hollywood Vice Lords." The Kourier Magazine. Vol. 10, September, 1934, p. 31.

617. "Follow California's Lead." The Kourier Magazine. Vol. 11, June, 1935, p. 20.

618. "Huge Cross Flames At San Francisco." The Kourier Magazine. Vol. 10, May, 1934, p. 28.

619. "Klan Demands Liquor Head Be Ousted." The Kourier Magazine. Vol. 10, June, 1934, p. 6.

620. "Klan Petitions School Board." The Kourier Magazine. Vol. 11, April, 1935, p. 28.

621. "The KKK Ride." The Kourier Magazine. Vol. 10, June, 1934, p. 29.

622. "Lotteries Hit In K.K.K. Probe." The Kourier Magazine. Vol. 10, September, 1934, p. 23.

623. "A Message By The Knights of The Ku Klux Klan Realm of California Addressed To The Public Employees of This Community." The Kourier Magazine. Vol. 10, 1933, pp. 20-22.

624. "A Message By The Knights of The Ku Klux Klan Realm of California Addressed To The Enforcement Officers of This Community." The Kourier Magazine. Vol. 9, October, 1933, pp. 30-32.

625. "A Message By The Knights of The Ku Klux Klan Realm of California To The Ministers of The Gospel." The Kourier Magazine. Vol. 9, June, 1933, pp. 9-11.

626. "Mixed Marriages Meanace California." The Kourier Magazine. Vol. 10, July, 1934, p. 6.

627. "Widows' And Orphans' Fund of California." The Kourier Magazine. Vol. 9, March, 1933, p. 5.

3.   COLORADO

628. "Klan In Denver Fights Jobless." The Kourier Magazine. Vol. 9, January, 1933, p. 10.

629.   "Klan Libraries." The Kourier Magazine. Vol. 3,
       February, 1927, p. 27.

4. CONNECTICUT

630.   "Address By A Connecticut Klansman." The Kourier
       Magazine. Vol. 3, November, 1927, p. 20.

631.   "Israel Putnam Klan." The Kourier Magazine. Vol. 4,
       April, 1928, pp. 31-32.

5. FLORIDA

632.   "Pinellas Klan Shows Way." The Kourier Magazine.
       Vol. 9, November, 1934, p. 37.

633.   "Klan Attacked By Florida Communists." The Kourier
       Magazine. Vol. 10, October, 1934, pp. 5-7.

634.   "Crawford Out Of Hospital." The Kourier Magazine.
       Vol. 9, January, 1933, p. 10.

635.   "The Klans Respond To Florida." The Kourier Maga-
       zine. Vol. 3, December 1926, p. 18.

6. GEORGIA

636.   "Griffin Klansmen Start Action." The Kourier Maga-
       zine. Vol. 11, June, 1935, p. 3.

637.   "Just Try And Break Us Up." The Kourier Magazine.
       Vol. 10, March, 1934, p. 16.

638.   Green, Samuel. "A Message From The Grand Dragon Of
       Georgia." The Kourier Magazine. Vol. 7, January,
       1931, p. 23.

7. ILLINOIS

639.   "Illinois Klansman Wins Kourier Contest." The
       Kourier Magazine. Vol. 11, May, 1935, p. 19.

640.   "Klan Has Eye On Morton High, School Citizen Warns."
       The Kourier Magazine. Vol. 9, April, 1933, p. 18.

641.   "Our Best Klanvocation." The Kourier Magazine.
       Vol. 4, September, 1928, pp. 56-57.

8. INDIANA

642.   "Hammond Klatter." The Kourier Magazine. Vol. 9,
       June, 1933, p. 20.

643.   "Indiana And The Klan." The Kourier Magazine. Vol.
       1, March, 1925, pp. 22-24, 31.

644. "Klan Holds 5 Day Fete Over July 4." The Kourier
Magazine. Vol. 10, August, 1934, p. 32.

645. "Ku Klux Klan Re-enters Indiana Political Arena."
The Kourier Magazine. Vol. 11, April, 1935, p. 6.

9. KANSAS

646. "A Report On The Klan In Kansas." The Kourier Magazine. Vol. 2, May, 1926, pp. 25-26.

647. "Klan Program." The Kourier Magazine. Vol, 1, March,
1925, p. 19.

648. "Kansas Grand Dragon Notes Many Changes." The Kourier
Magazine. Vol. 9, September, 1933, pp. 20-21.

10. MARYLAND

649. "Maryland Klan Stages Celebration." The Kourier
Magazine. Vol. 10, September, 1934. p. 32.

11. MICHIGAN

650. "Junior Klansmen." The Kourier Magazine. Vol. 1,
October, 1925, pp. 14-16.

12. MISSOURI

651. "Dr. Wm. M. Campbell Cancels $9,000 Debts For Poor
Patients." The Kourier Magazine. Vol. 9, April,
1933, p. 25.

652. "A Resolution Of Missouri Klansmen." The Kourier
Magazine. Vol. 9, January, 1933, p. 9.

13. NEBRASKA

653. "Speaker For Klan Is Heard By Many." The Kourier
Magazine. Vol. 10, February, 1934, p. 32.

14. NEW YORK

654. "The Klan And The Negro." The Kourier Magazine.
Vol. 1, February, 1925, p. 8.

655. "Refuse Klan Business." The Kourier Magazine. Vol.
10, May, 1934, p. 10.

656. "White Supremacy Is Gravely Menaced By Long Island
Negroes." The Kourier Magazine. Vol. 9, August,
1933, p. 19.

15. OHIO

657. "Columbusites Will Be Initiated In Ku Klux Klan." The
Kourier Magazine. Vol. 10, September, 1934, p. 32.

16. OKLAHOMA

658.   "K.K.K. Hold Rousing Meeting." The Kourier Magazine.
        Vol. 10, May, 1934, p. 15.

659.   "Oklahoma Drive Begins." The Kourier Magazine. Vol.
        10, November, 1934, p. 30.

660.   "Oklahoma Klan Rides Against Alien Radicals." The
        Kourier Magazine. Vol. 10, September, 1934, p. 31.

17. PENNSYLVANIA

661.   "Example of 'Tolerance' Of Klan's Enemies." The
        Kourier Magazine. Vol. 11, September, 1935, p. 10.

662.   "Pennsylvania Klan Backs Dr. Wirt." The Kourier
        Magazine. Vol. 10, May, 1934, p. 13.

18. SOUTH CAROLINA

663.   "The Klan And Lynching." The Kourier Magazine. Vol.
        3, January, 1927, p. 11.

664.   "Nudists Clothe When Klan Visit Rumored." The
        Kourier Magazine. Vol. 10, November, 1934, p. 29.

665.   "South Carolina: Enthusiasm In Klan At High Pitch."
        The Kourier Magazine. Vol. 9, June, 1933, pp. 27-29.

666.   "South Carolina." The Kourier Magazine. Vol. 4,
        March, 1928, p. 27.

19. TEXAS

667.   "Dallas Jury Vindicates Doctor Evans." The Kourier
        Magazine. Vol. 6, June, 1930, p. 10.

668.   "Fiery Cross Blazes Warning To Dance Halls." The
        Kourier Magazine. Vol. 10, March, 1934, p. 27.

669.   "New Note." The Kourier Magazine. Vol. 1, May, 1925,
        p. 10.

670.   "Priest Forbids Roman Catholics To Take Part In
        George Washington Celebration." The Kourier Maga-
        zine. Vol. 8, June, 1932, pp. 15-16.

671.   "Ku Klux Aid Church Work." The Kourier Magazine.
        Vol. 10, June, 1934, p. 29.

672.   "Revival of Texas Klan." The Kourier Magazine.
        Vol. 11, December, 1934, p. 35.

20. VIRGINIA

673.   "Ballston Klan No. 6 of Virginia." The Kourier Magazine. Vol. 8, May, 1932, p. 20.

674.   "Baskin Warns of Vicious Radicals." The Kourier Magazine. Vol. 10, 1934, p. 31.

21. WASHINGTON, D.C.

675.   "They Marched." The Kourier Magazine. Vol. 2, November, 1926, pp. 23-24.

22. WISCONSIN

676.   "Cloverland Klan Association No. 5." The Kourier Magazine. Vol. 9, January, 1933, p. 18.

GENERAL

677.   "Abraham Lincoln---Hiram Wesley Evans: A Character Analogy." The Kourier Magazine. Vol. 2, October, 1926, pp. 6-7.

678.   "A.C.L.U. Checks Klan Growth." The Kourier Magazine. Vol. 9, November, 1934, p. 37.

679.   "Address Delivered By Dr. H.W. Evans." The Kourier Magazine. Vol. 2, November, 1926, pp. 1-10.

680.   "Address Delivered By Mrs. Robbie Gill Comer." The Kourier Magazine. Vol. 2, November, 1926, pp. 11-22.

681.   "Address of Imperial Official." The Kourier Magazine. Vol. 1, December, 1924, pp. 22-28.

682.   "Address of the Imperial Commander - Women of the Ku Klux Klan." The Kourier Magazine. Vol. 7, August, 1931, p. 12.

683.   "Alien Invasion." The Kourier Magazine. Vol. 10, April, 1934, pp. 8-10.

684.   "Al Smith." The Kourier Magazine. Vol. 3, June, 1927, p. 12.

685.   "America Saved By Klan Strategy." The Kourier Magazine. Vol. 10, July, 1934, p. 23.

686.   "American Political Economy And The Klan." The Kourier Magazine. Vol. 8, April, 1932, pp. 14-16

687.   "Americana States Klan Plea For Immigration Restriction." The Kourier Magazine. Vol. 10, June, 1934, pp. 18-19.

688. "Another Great Victory For The Klan." The Kourier
      Magazine. Vol. 6, July, 1930, pp. 3-4.

689. "The Answer." The Kourier Magazine. Vol. 8, August,
      1932, p. 6.

690. "Appreciation of Dr. Hiram W. Evans." The Kourier
      Magazine. Vol. 2, September, 1926, p. 7.

691. "Are Klansmen Fanatical, Intolerant, Bigoted?" The
      Kourier Magazine. Vol. 4, January, 1928, p. 26.

692. "Ask Them Why?--- Tell Them To Buy." The Kourier
      Magazine. Vol. 7, January, 1931, p. 22.

693. "An Awakened Citizenship." The Kourier Magazine.
      Vol. 1, August, 1927, pp. 20-21.

694. "Be Charitable Toward Klansmen." The Kourier Maga-
      zine. Vol. 11, January, 1935, p. 17.

695. "Below The Mason and Dixon Line." The Kourier Maga-
      zine. Vol. 3, April, 1927, pp. 19-20.

696. "The Better Klan Magazine." The Kourier Magazine.
      Vol. 5, April, 1929, pp. 1-3.

697. "Buckaroo Bill Speaks On Klan." The Kourier Maga-
      zine. Vol. 8, July, 1932, pp. 11-12.

698. "Building By Lectures In Closed Meetings." The
      Kourier Magazine. Vol. 6, October, 1930, pp. 13-14.

699. "The Call Of The Klan." The Kourier Magazine. Vol.
      8, January, 1932, pp. 1-4.

700. "The Call Of The Klan." The Kourier Magazine. Vol.
      8, June, 1932, p. 12.

701. "Can The Klan Come Back?" The Kourier Magazine.
      Vol. 10, January, 1934, p. 13.

702. "Causes For Rise And Growth Of Ku Klux Klan." The
      Kourier Magazine. Vol. 3, February, 1927, pp. 16-17.

703. "Charges Nazis Seek Klan Aid." The Kourier Magazine.
      Vol. 9, November, 1933, pp. 19-20.

704. "Chief Of Klan Joins Fight On League Court." The
      Kourier Magazine. Vol. 10, May, 1934, p. 13.

705. Clark, Clifton. "A Klansman's Loyalty." The Kourier
      Magazine. Vol. 5, June, 1929, p. 6-11; September,
      1929, p. 39-43. Vol. 6, December, 1929, p. 26-29;
      Vol. 6, June, 1930, pp. 30-33.

706.   "Come Now, Let Us Reason Together." The Kourier
        Magazine. Vol. 1, March, 1925, pp. 1-5.

707.   "Constitutional Provisions Governing The Imperial
        Klanvocation." The Kourier Magazine. Vol. 12,
        October, 1936, p. 1-3.

708.   "Co-Operation Welcomed In Fight On Reds." The
        Kourier Magazine. Vol. 11, October, 1935, p. 6-8.

709.   "The Coughlin Menace: A Challenge." The Kourier
        Magazine. Vol. 10, March, 1934, pp. 13-14.

710.   "County Commissioners Deny Report Revived Klan
        Dictates Political Course." The Kourier Magazine.
        Vol. 10, February, 1934, pp. 26-27.

711.   "Country Singer Charlie Daniels Mad At Klan For Using
        His Song As Background Music For Commercials Promo-
        ting A Cross-Lighting Klan Rally." The National Ob-
        server. December 13, 1975, p. 6.

712.   "Dangers of Communism To The Church And The Klan."
        The Kourier Magazine. Vol. 9, June, 1933, pp. 18-19.

713.   Darling, Paul I. "The Klan Has Answered." The
        Kourier Magazine. Vol. 5, February, 1929, pp. 28-29.

714.   "Do We Mean It?" The Kourier Magazine. Vol. 10,
        August, 1934, p. 21-22.

715.   "Do We Need A Klan?" The Kourier Magazine. Vol. 9,
        December, 1932, p. 14.

716.   "Delusions of Security." The Kourier Magazine.
        Vol. 10, March, 1934, p. 6.

717.   "Economics, Psychology and Klankraft." The Kourier
        Magazine. Vol. 8, August, 1932, pp. 13-14.

718.   "Education Of A Klansman." The Kourier Magazine.
        Vol. 8, June, 1932, pp. 18-19.

719.   "The Empire Invisible." The Kourier Magazine. Vol.
        7, April, 1931, p. 13.

720.   "An Estimate Of Modern Klan-Kraft." The Kourier
        Magazine. Vol. 2, April, 1926, pp. 21-23.

721.   Evans, Hiram. "Alienism In The Democracy." The
        Kourier Magazine. Vol. 3, April, 1927, pp. 1-8;
        May, 1927, pp. 1-8; May, 1927, pp. 29-32; July, 1927,
        pp. 1-4; September, 1927, pp. 1-4.

722.   _____. "Causes Of Klan Growth." The Kourier
        Magazine. Vol. 6, January, 1930, p. 12-16; February,

1930, p. 12-19; April, 1930, p. 11-19; May, 1930, pp. 6-12.

723.   _____. "Communism Rampant." The Kourier Magazine. Vol. 8, September, 1932, pp. 1-3.

724.   _____. "The Destiny Of The Klan." The Kourier Magazine. Vol. 2, July, 1926, p. 1-2; August, 1926, p. 1-6; September, 1926, pp. 11-15.

725.   _____. "Hour For Action At Hand." The Kourier Magazine. Vol. 10, August, 1934, pp. 3-4.

726.   _____. "Impressions Of The Klanvocation." The Kourier Magazine. Vol. 7, August, 1931, p. 2.

727.   _____. "The Klan's Next Duty." The Kourier Magazine. Vol. 2, February, 1926, pp. 1-7.

728.   _____. "Our Crusading Army." The Kourier Magazine. Vol. 2, October, 1926, pp. 2-5.

729.   _____. "Our Half Won War." The Kourier Magazine Vol. 5, May, 1929, pp. 6-10.

730.   _____. "Sons Of America Arm For Battle." The Kourier Magazine. Vol. 11, December, 1934, pp. 1-9.

731.   _____. "Where The Klan Stands Today." The Kourier Magazine. Vol. 4, September, 1928, pp. 1-12.

732.   "Every Klansman, Regardless." The Kourier Magazine. Vol. 8, March, 1932, pp. 6-7.

733.   "An Exalted Cyclops Speaks To His Klan." The Kourier Magazine. Vol. 9, February, 1933, pp. 13-15.

734.   "Excerpts From Closing Address of Dr. Evans." The Kourier Magazine. Vol. 3, December, 1926, pp. 21-22.

735.   "Exit 'Scholarship'." The Kourier Magazine. Vol. 11, May, 1935, p. 6.

736.   "Fiery Cross First." The Kourier Magazine. Vol. 8, April, 1932, p. 19.

737.   "Fifth Biennial Imperial Klanvocation." The Kourier Magazine. Vol. 6, October, 1930, pp. 8-9.

738.   "Fifth Biennial Klanvocation." The Kourier Magazine. Vol. 6, August, 1930, p. 6.

739.   "Forethought." The Kourier Magazine. Vol. 6, August, 1930, pp. 11-15.

740.   "Forward To Victory In 1935." The Kourier Magazine.
       Vol. 11, January, 1935, pp. 1-4.

741.   "Germany Steals Klan Thunder." The Kourier Magazine.
       Vol. 10, March, 1934, p. 5.

742.   "Getting Members To Attend Klanklaves." The Kourier
       Magazine. Vol. 6, September, 1930, pp. 27-28.

743.   "A Grand Dragon's Letter." The Kourier Magazine.
       Vol. 4, December, 1927, p. 27.

744.   "A Grand Dragon's Easter Message." The Kourier Maga-
       zine. Vol. 3, April, 1927, p. 15.

745.   "Grand Dragon's Message To Georgia Klansmen." The
       Kourier Magazine. Vol. 8, February, 1932, pp. 20-21.

746.   "Grapes And Wild Grapes." The Kourier Magazine.
       Vol. 1, March, 1925, pp. 26-31.

747.   "G.W. Price." The Kourier Magazine. Vol. 10, April,
       1934, p. 30

748.   Hamlett, William A. "Be Klannish Toward Klansmen."
       The Kourier Magazine. Vol. 9, January, 1933, pp. 1-3.

749.   H.E.R. "What Is The Klan? Is It A Religion." The
       Kourier Magazine. Vol. 3, February, 1927, pp. 14-15.

750.   "Hiram Wesley Evans." The Kourier Magazine. Vol. 2,
       September, 1926, pp. 5-6.

751.   "Honorable Klannishness." The Kourier Magazine.
       Vol. 1, May, 1925, pp. 31-32.

752.   "I Challenge You." The Kourier Magazine. Vol. 10,
       July, 1934, p. 28.

753.   "Ideals and Principles Of The Ku Klux Klan." The
       Kourier Magazine. Vol. 12, October, 1936, pp. 14-19.

754.   "Illuminated Crosses." The Kourier Magazine. Vol. 3,
       December, 1926, pp. 16-17.

755.   "The Imperial Klanvocation." The Kourier Magazine.
       Vol. 8, August, 1932, pp. 15-16.

756.   "Imperial Wizard High Lights." The Kourier Magazine.
       Vol. 1, February, 1925, p. 24.

757.   "Improvements In Klan Ritualism." The Kourier Maga-
       zine. Vol. 4, September, 1928, pp. 58-65.

758.   "In Memoriam." The Kourier Magazine. Vol. 10, June,
       1934, p. 45.

759.   "Is It Worth The Effort." The Kourier Magazine.
        Vol. 7, January, 1931, p. 21.

760.   "Is Ritualism In The Klan Necessary." The Kourier
        Magazine. Vol. 8, February, 1932, pp. 18-19.

761.   "Is The Klan Enough?" The Kourier Magazine. Vol. 9,
        September, 1933, pp. 26-28.

762.   "Is The Ku Klux Klan A Blessing Or A Menace?" The
        Kourier Magazine. Vol. 1, June, 1925, p. 8.

763.   "Inspirational Address." The Kourier Magazine.
        Vol. 2, March, 1926, pp. 16-17.

764.   "A Jew Writes On The Klan." The Kourier Magazine.
        Vol. 5, January, 1929, p. 21.

765.   J.R.B. "Are You A Stranger Among Klansmen?" The
        Kourier Magazine. Vol. 3, February, 1927, pp. 6-7.

766.   "Judge Ben Lindsey Pays His Respects To The Klan."
        The Kourier Magazine. Vol. 7, April, 1931, p. 14.

767.   "Junior Klansmen." The Kourier Magazine. Vol. 1,
        March, 1925, pp. 16-18.

768.   "The Junior Klan." The Kourier Magazine. Vol. 8,
        September, 1932, p. 15.

769.   "Kansas Klansmen On Parade." The Kourier Magazine.
        Vol. 3, December, 1926, p. 19.

770.   "Klan Activities In The States." The Kourier Maga-
        zine. Vol. 2, August, 1926, pp. 6-12; October,
        1926, p. 30.

771.   "The Klan Army." The Kourier Magazine. Vol. 7,
        October, 1931, pp. 5-8.

772.   "The Klan And The Constitution." The Kourier Maga-
        zine. Vol. 8, August, 1932, pp. 5-6.

773.   "The Klan And The Eighteenth Amendment." The Kourier
        Magazine. Vol. 3, November, 1927, pp. 17-19.

774.   "The Klan And The Flag." The Kourier Magazine.
        Vol. 1, July, 1925, pp. 14-16.

775.   "A Klan Meditation." The Kourier Magazine. Vol. 3,
        February, 1927, pp. 19-21.

776.   "The Klan And The Public School." The Kourier Maga-
        zine. Vol. 1, May, 1925, pp. 25-27.

777.   "The Klan And The Reformation." The Kourier Magazine.
        Vol. 1, June, 1925, pp. 27-28.

778.   "The Klan As A Nation Builder." The Kourier Maga-
        zine. Vol. 1, March, 1925, pp. 8-11.

779.   "The Klan Creed." The Kourier Magazine. Vol. 8,
        July, 1932, p. 25.

780.   "Klan Fight In The Legislature." The Kourier Maga-
        zine. Vol. 9, June, 1933, p. 30.

781.   "The Klan In Action." The Kourier Magazine. Vol. 1,
        February, 1925, pp. 22-23.

782.   "The Klan In Action." The Kourier Magazine. Vol. 6,
        November, 1930, pp. 10-13.

783.   "The Klan In Action." The Kourier Magazine. Vol. 7,
        December, 1930, pp. 29-31; January, 1931, pp. 35-48;
        February, 1931, pp. 30-47; March, 1931, pp. 33-47;
        April, 1931, pp. 29-48; May, 1931, pp. 23-25, 28-52;
        June, 1931, pp. 31-47; July, 1931, pp. 34-56; August,
        1931, pp. 32-48; September, 1931, pp. 31-49; November,
        1931, pp. 33-50.

784.   "The Klan In Action." The Kourier Magazine. Vol. 8,
        December, 1931, pp. 31-50; January, 1932, p. 32-48;
        February, 1932, pp. 31-49; March, 1932, pp. 31-49;
        April, 1932, pp. 24-48; May, 1932, pp. 29-49; June,
        1932, pp. 31-49; July, 1932, pp. 32-48; August, 1932,
        pp. 28-41; September, 1932, pp. 31-42; October, 1932,
        pp. 33-45; November, 1932, pp. 32-42.

785.   "The Klan In Action." The Kourier Magazine. Vol. 9,
        December, 1932, pp. 32-46; January, 1933, pp. 37-48;
        February, 1933, pp. 33-48; March, 1933, pp. 29-48;
        April, 1933, pp. 35-48; May, 1933, pp. 32-48; June,
        1933, pp. 31-48; July, 1933, pp. 31-48; August, 1933,
        pp. 33-48; September, 1933, pp. 38-48; October, 1933,
        pp. 40-48; November, 1933, pp. 26-48.

786.   "The Klan In Action." The Kourier Magazine. Vol. 10,
        December, 1933, pp. 30-48; January, 1934, pp. 30-44;
        February, 1934, pp. 36-47.

787.   "Klan Joins In Seeking Probe By Grand Jury." The
        Kourier Magazine. Vol. 10, June, 1934, p. 20.

788.   "Klan Kiddies Korner." The Kourier Magazine. Vol. 3,
        February, 1927, pp. 30-31.

789.   "The Klan Krier." The Kourier Magazine. Vol. 10,
        March, 1934, pp. 33-43; April, 1934, pp. 33-45; May,
        1934, pp. 35-42, 46; June, 1934, pp. 36-44; July,
        1934, pp. 36-47; August, 1934, pp. 35-43; September,

1934, pp. 35-39; October, 1934, pp. 45-48; November, 1934, pp. 43-48.

790. "The Klan Krier." The Kourier Magazine. Vol. 11, December, 1934, pp. 41-48; January, 1935, pp. 41-48; February, 1935, pp. 41-48; March, 1935, pp. 41-48; April, 1935, pp. 40-48; May, 1935, pp. 37-48.

791. "Klan Memorial Address." The Kourier Magazine. Vol. 8, July, 1932, p. 15.

792. "Klan Mobilizes For Action." The Kourier Magazine. Vol. 10, July, 1934, pp. 1-3.

793. "Klan Pays Tribute To Departed Leader." The Kourier Magazine. Vol. 10, July, 1934, p. 14.

794. "Klan Perpetuated As Militant Crusade." The Kourier Magazine. Vol. 11, March, 1935, p. 24.

795. "The Klan Pioneers." The Kourier Magazine. Vol. 11, July, 1935, pp. 27-28.

796. "The Klan Platform." The Kourier Magazine. Vol. 8, July, 1932, p. 24.

797. The Klan Principles." The Kourier Magazine. Vol. 8, January, 1932, p. 10.

798. "The Klan Of The Reconstruction Era." The Kourier Magazine. Vol. 12, October, 1936, pp. 6-7.

799. "The Klan -- Review And Pre-view." The Kourier Magazine. Vol. 4, April, 1928, p. 27.

800. "Klan Speaker Points To Communist Move As Menace To World." The Kourier Magazine. Vol. 9, August, 1933, pp. 29-30.

801. "The Klan Speaks To The Protestant Church." The Kourier Magazine. Vol. 7, November, 1931, pp. 19-22.

802. "Klan Solves Unemployment." The Kourier Magazine. Vol. 10, March, 1934, p. 12.

803. "The Klan of Tomorrow." The Kourier Magazine. Vol. 12, October, 1936, pp. 11-13.

804. "The Klan of Yesterday." The Kourier Magazine. Vol. 12, October, 1936, pp. 8-10.

805. "Klanhaven." The Kourier Magazine. Vol. 2, November, 1926, p. 27.

806. "Klanism vs. Catholicism." The Kourier Magazine. Vol. 3, April, 1927, pp. 25-26.

807. "Klankraft In New York." The Kourier Magazine. Vol. 7, April, 1931, p. 16.

808. "Klankraft vs. Communism." The Kourier Magazine. Vol. 10, September, 1934, p. 20.

809. "Klankraft's National Crusade." The Kourier Magazine. Vol. 11, April, 1935, pp. 24-25.

810. "The Klan And The Press." The Kourier Magazine. Vol. 7, April, 1931, p. 10.

811. "Klan Conduct." The Kourier Magazine. Vol. 8, February, 1932, p. 16.

812. "The Klan And The Flag." The Kourier Magazine. Vol. 7, June, 1931, p. 4.

813. "Klan Fundamentals." The Kourier Magazine. Vol. 11, January, 1935, p. 20.

814. "The Klan Itself." The Kourier Magazine. Vol. 9, November, 1933, p. 18.

815. "The Klan Kreed." The Kourier Magazine. Vol. 7, March, 1931, p. 25.

816. "A Klan Program." The Kourier Magazine. Vol. 9, May, 1933, p. 10.

817. "The Klan: Protestantism's Ally." The Kourier Magazine. Vol. 1, August, 1925, pp. 9-13.

818. "The Klan Speaks." The Kourier Magazine. Vol. 7, August, 1931, pp. 5-6.

819. "The Klan's Mission-Americanism." The Kourier Magazine. Vol. 1, November, 1925, pp. 4-12.

820. "The Klan's Next Duty - Send Home Every Unfit Alien." The Kourier Magazine. Vol. 9, December, 1932, pp. 1-3.

821. "A Klansman's Creed." The Kourier Magazine. Vol. 7, December, 1930, p. 20.

822. "A Klansman's Loyalty." The Kourier Magazine. Vol. 11, April, 1935, p. 32.

823. "A Klansman's Oath." The Kourier Magazine. Vol. 7, December, 1930, p. 21.

824. "A Klansman's Obligation." The Kourier Magazine. Vol. 7, December, 1930, p. 19.

825. "A Klansman's Prayer." The Kourier Magazine. Vol. 7,
      March, 1931, p. 13.

826. "Klansmen--Take The Message To America..Now." The
      Kourier Magazine. Vol. 9, June, 1933, pp. 26-27.

827. "The Klarion Kall." The Kourier Magazine. Vol. 10,
      February, 1934, pp. 18-21.

828. "Klavern Konduct." The Kourier Magazine. Vol. 8,
      April, 1932, p. 8.

829. "Klavern Konduct Important." The Kourier Magazine.
      Vol. 11, January, 1935, p. 16.

830. "The Klokard - His Part In Klan Building." The Kouri-
      er Magazine. Vol. 8, March, 1932, p. 14.

831. "Klanvokation Issue." The Kourier Magazine. Vol. 12,
      October, 1936, entire issue.

832. "Klansmen, Think As Well As Act!" The Kourier Maga-
      zine.. Vol. 3, November, 1927, p. 21.

833. "Knights of The Ku Klux Klan." The Kourier Magazine.
      Vol. 11, August, 1935, pp. 26-28.

834. "The Knights Of The Ku Klux Klan Is Now 17 Years Of
      Age. The Huskiest Organization of Its Age In America
      Today." The Kourier Magazine. Vol. 9, January, 1933,
      p. 16.

835. "The Ku Klux Klan As A Nation Builder." The Kourier
      Magazine. Vol. 9, December, 1932, pp. 15-19.

836. "The Ku Klux Klan In American History." The Kourier
      Magazine. Vol. 6, July, 1930, pp. 11-12.

837. "Ku Klux Reborn." The Kourier Magazine. Vol. 10,
      December, 1933, p. 19.

838. "A Letter From Missouri's Grand Kligrapp To An Exalted
      Cyclops." The Kourier Magazine. Vol. 9, January,
      1933, pp. 17-18.

839. "A Letter To All Klansmen From The Grand Dragon of
      Texas." The Kourier Magazine. Vol. 9, February,
      1933, p. 7.

840. "Life of Klan Dragon Threatened." The Kourier Maga-
      zine. Vol. 11, March, 1935, p. 7.

841. "Looking Back." The Kourier Magazine. Vol. 10,
      March, 1934, pp. 17-18.

842. "A Message." The Kourier Magazine. Vol. 9, January,
      1933, p. 15

843.   "A Message From The Imperial Wizard." The Kourier
       Magazine. Vol. 1, February, 1925, pp. 1-2.

844.   "Message of Dr. H.W. Evans." The Kourier Magazine.
       Vol. 3, March, 1927, pp. 1-8.

845.   "The Message Of The Klan." The Kourier Magazine.
       Vol. 8, September, 1932, pp. 9-11.

846.   "A Message To The Klan." The Kourier Magazine. Vol.
       8, October, 1932, pp. 12-13.

847.   Miller, Henry C. "Klancraft Architecture." The
       Kourier Magazine. Vol. 5, June, 1929, pp. 11-12.

848.   "Militant or Military?" The Kourier Magazine. Vol.
       10, January, 1934, p. 23.

849.   "The Minister And The Klan." The Kourier Magazine.
       Vol. 2, November, 1926, pp. 25-26.

850.   "Modern Klankraft." The Kourier Magazine. Vol. 8,
       August, 1932, pp. 1-3.

851.   "A More Democratic Constitution." The Kourier Maga-
       zine. Vol. 4, September, 1928, pp. 66-70.

852.   "The Name Ku Klux Defined." The Kourier Magazine.
       Vol. 1, February, 1925, p. 7.

853.   "National Dedication Services." The Kourier Maga-
       zine. Vol, 1, January, 1925, pp. 10-11.

854.   "National Education Program." The Kourier Magazine.
       Vol. 1, December, 1924, pp. 8-9.

855.   "The Need Of The Ku Klux Klan." The Kourier Magazine.
       Vol. 2, March, 1926, pp. 26-28; April, 1926, pp. 10-
       13.

856.   "The New Klancilium." The Kourier Magazine. Vol. 7,
       January, 1931, pp. 5-8.

857.   "New Leisure Hours Should Be Used To Promote Klan-
       kraft." The Kourier Magazine. Vol. 9, September,
       1933, p. 34.

858.   "New Year's Message From The Imperial Wizard." The
       Kourier Magazine. Vol. 7, January, 1931, p. 3.

859.   "Official Document No. 875 & 876." The Kourier Maga-
       zine. Vol. 11, May, 1935, pp. 24-25.

860.   "On Guard." The Kourier Magazine. Vol. 7, February,
       1931, pp. 14-15.

861.   "One Hundred Per Cent Americanism." The Kourier
        Magazine. Vol. 8, August, 1932, p. 4.

862.   "Onward Christian Klansmen." The Kourier Magazine.
        Vol. 2, January, 1926, pp. 2-4.

863.   "The Open Door." The Kourier Magazine. Vol. 3,
        January, 1926, pp. 2-4.

864.   "An Open Letter To Knights Of The Ku Klux Klan." The
        Kourier Magazine. Vol. 3, May, 1927, pp. 12-16.

865.   "Opening Prayer." The Kourier Magazine. Vol. 8,
        February, 1932, p. 19.

866.   "Our Duty." The Kourier Magazine. Vol. 8, December,
        1931, pp. 5-6.

867.   "Our Public Schools." The Kourier Magazine. Vol. 4,
        January, 1928, pp. 12-19.

868.   "Our Public Schools: Klan's Attitude vs. Catholic
        Church's." The Kourier Magazine. Vol. 11, September,
        1934, pp. 1-3.

869.   "Over The Top." The Kourier Magazine. Vol. 10,
        February, 1934, pp. 13-16.

870.   Parvis, Pauline. "A Big Job For The Klan." The
        Kourier Magazine. Vol. 5, March, 1929, p. 32.

871.   "The Philosophy Of Successful Klankraft." The
        Kourier Magazine. Vol. 6, August, 1930, p. 10.

872.   "The Pope vs. The Klan." The Kourier Magazine.
        Vol. 5, September, 1929, p. 48.

873.   "Preamble To The Constitution of The Klan." The
        Kourier Magazine. Vol. 12, October, 1936, pp. 20-21.

874.   "Propaganda - The Menace." The Kourier Magazine.
        Vol. 8, September, 1932, pp. 5-6.

875.   "Program Launched At Klanvokation." The Kourier
        Magazine. Vol. 10, September, 1934, pp. 3-4.

876.   "Proves The Klan Charges." The Kourier Magazine.
        Vol. 1, November, 1925, pp. 21-22.

877.   "Providence And The Invisible Empire." The Kourier
        Magazine. Vol. 6, September, 1930, pp. 23-24.

878.   "The Reason For The Klan." The Kourier Magazine.
        Vol. 11, March, 1935, p. 8.

879.   "Religion And Klankraft." The Kourier Magazine.
        Vol. 8, July, 1932, p. 14.

880.   "Religion In The Klan." The Kourier Magazine, Vol.
        8, December, 1931, p. 14.

881.   "Reporter Pictures Feelings At Open Air Klan Meeting."
        The Kourier Magazine. Vol. 10, August, 1934, pp. 19-
        20.

882.   Rieseberg, Harry E. "Are There Slackers In The Ku
        Klux Klan?" The Kourier Magazine. Vol. 5, January,
        1929, p. 8.

883.   Roach, A.C. "Keeping America American." The Kourier
        Magazine. Vol. 8, August, 1932, pp. 7-8.

884.   "A Rock To Build Upon." The Kourier Magazine. Vol.
        11, February, 1935, p. 8.

885.   "Roy Frankhouser, Former Klan Leader And Leader Of
        American Nazi Party Is Government Agent." The
        Kourier Magazine. Vol. 11, August, 1935, p. 7.

886.   "Sacred Obligation Of A Klansman." The Kourier Maga-
        zine. Vol. 1, August, 1925, pp. 26-29.

887.   "Said President Coolidge,So Says The Klan." The
        Kourier Magazine. Vol. 1, April, 1925, p. 28.

888.   "Samuel Hoyt Venable - Imperial Klabee." The Kourier
        Magazine. Vol. 7, January, 1931, p. 9.

889.   "Says Klan Urged Doctor To Kill Babies." The Kourier
        Magazine. Vol. 7, May, 1931, p. 8.

890.   "Service." The Kourier Magazine. Vol. 8, April,
        1932, pp. 17-19.

891.   "They Shall Not Pass." The Kourier Magazine. Vol.
        8, July, 1932, p. 13.

892.   Shaw, H.C. "Paul's Message To Klansmen." The Kourier
        Magazine. Vol. 7, October, 1931, p. 4-5.

893..   "Sheares Of Thought Gleaned From The Mind Of Hiram
        Wesley Evans." The Kourier Magazine. Vol. 2, Sep-
        tember, 1926, pp. 8-10.

894.   "The Spirit Of The Fathers." The Kourier Magazine.
        Vol. 3, February, 1927, pp. 12-13.

895.   "Spiritual Re-Birth Of The Klan." The Kourier Maga-
        zine. Vol. 2, April, 1926, pp. 30-32.

896.   "Star Spangled Banner--Long May It Wave." The Kourier Magazine. Vol. 11, July, 1935, pp. 18-23.

897.   "Successful Operation Is The Result of Perfect Operation." The Kourier Magazine. Vol. 9, June, 1933, pp. 12-13.

898.   "Suggestions For A Klan Library." The Kourier Magazine. Vol. 4, December, 1927, pp. 15-15.

899.   "Suggestions To An Exalted Cyclops." The Kourier Magazine.

900.   "The True American." The Kourier Magazine. Vol. 2, March, 1926, pp. 8-12.

901.   "True Valuation." The Kourier Magazine. Vol. 8, December, 1931, pp. 7-8.

902.   "Turns Theater Over To Klan." The Kourier Magazine. Vol. 10, May, 1934, p. 45.

903.   "Under The Fiery Cross." The Kourier Magazine. Vol. 5, April, 1929, pp. 7-9; May, 1929, pp. 16-22; October, 1929, pp. 16-21; November, 1929, pp. 25-30; Vol. 6, January, 1930, pp. 18-21; February, 1930, pp. 19-20; April, 1930, pp. 20-21; May, 1930, pp. 17-20.

904.   "Victory Over Defeat." The Kourier Magazine. Vol. 8, September, 1932, p. 4.

905.   "Vocational Klannishness." The Kourier Magazine. Vol. 6, July, 1930, pp. 5-7.

906.   "Wanted - Klan Salesmen." The Kourier Magazine. Vol. 7, April, 19, 31, pp. 7-9.

907.   "We Are Building." The Kourier Magazine. Vol. 4, July, 1928, pp. 30-32.

908.   "We Give Thanks." The Kourier Magazine. Vol. 7, December, 1930, pp. 5-6.

909.   "What Can I Do?" The Kourier Magazine. Vol. 1, October, 1927, pp. 27-28.

910.   "What Can The Klan Do Today?" The Kourier Magazine. Vol. 9, October, 1933, pp. 35-36.

911.   "What Christmas Means To The Klansman." The Kourier Magazine. Vol. 2, December, 1925, pp. 1-2.

912.   "What Christmas Means To A Klansman." The Kourier Magazine. Vol. 8, December, 1931, pp. 1-3.

913.   "Why I Joined The Klan." The Kourier Magazine, Vol.
       2, December, 1925, pp. 12-13.

914.   "What Is The Klan?" The Kourier Magazine. Vol. 8,
       January, 1932, pp. 11-12.

915.   "What The Klan Needs." The Kourier Magazine. Vol. 3,
       May, 1927, p. 28.

916.   "Why The Klan Opposes Communism." The Kourier
       Magazine. Vol. 9, June, 1933, p. 11.

917.   "What Price Tolerance?" The Kourier Magazine.
       Vol. 3, March, 1927, pp. 27-30.

918.   "What Shall It Profit A Klansman." The Kourier
       Magazine. Vol. 7, December, 1930, p. 8.

919.   "What The Symbols of The Ku Klux Klan Mean To Me."
       The Kourier Magazine. Vol. 10, December, 1933, pp.
       16-17.

920.   "The White Man Must Solve The Race Problem." The
       Kourier Magazine. Vol. 10, August, 1934, p. 34.

921.   "White Supremacy." The Kourier Magazine. Vol. 8,
       August, 1930, pp. 2-6.

922.   "Why Attend Klan Meetings?" The Kourier Magazine.
       Vol. 8, July, 1932, p. 18.

923.   "Why I Joined The Klan." The Kourier Magazine.
       Vol. 8, July, 1932, pp. 19-20.

924.   "Why The Klan." The Kourier Magazine. Vol. 7,
       January, 1931, p. 11.

925.   "Why Klansmen Should Read The Kourier Magazine."
       The Kourier Magazine. Vol. 7, January, 1931, pp. 19-
       20.

926.   "What The Local Klan Needs Most." The Kourier Maga-
       zine. Vol. 6, May, 1930, pp. 15-16; September, 1930,
       pp. 29-30.

927.   "Why Mask The Klan If It Is One Hundred Percent
       American?" The Kourier Magazine. Vol. 1, August,
       1925, p. 32.

928.   "With The Editor." The Kourier Magazine. Vol. 1,
       September, 1925, pp. 1-3.

929.   "With The Editor." The Kourier Magazine. Vol. 3,
       March, 1927, p. 12-14; April, 1927, p. 31-32; June,
       1927, pp. 29-32.

930.   "A Word From Germany." The Kourier Magazine. Vol. 1,
        February, 1925, p. 9.

931.   "Ye Shall Know The Truth And The Truth Shall Set You
        Free." The Kourier Magazine. Vol. 6, November,
        1930, pp. 3-9.

932.   "Younger Men Must Rebuild The Klan." The Kourier
        Magazine. Vol. 10, January, 1934, pp. 1-2.

933.   "Your Klan Kard-What Does It Mean To You?" The
        Kourier Magazine. Vol. 8, March, 1932, p. 13.

EUROPE

934.   "Klan Wins Long World Court Fight." The Kourier
        Magazine. Vol. 5, April, 1929, p. 6.

POEMS, PRAYERS, AND SONGS

A SELECTED LIST

POEMS

935. "A Call To The Klan." The Kourier Magazine. Vol. 7, August, 1931, p. 7.

936. "A Klansman." The Kourier Magazine. Vol. 8, July, 1932, p. 18.

937. "Awake! Klansmen." The Kourier Magazine. Vol. 8, June, 1932, p. 16.

938. "The Degree Master." The Kourier Magazine. Vol. 8, March, 1932, p. 12.

939. "Each In His Own Tongue." The Kourier Magazine. Vol. 3, February, 1927, p. 18.

940. "Efficiency." The Kourier Magazine. Vol. 7, July, 1931, p. 23.

941. "The Fiery Cross." The Kourier Magazine. Vol. 4, April, 1928, p. 32.

942. "The Fiery Cross." The Kourier Magazine. Vol. 7, November, 1931, p. 24.

943. "The Fiery Cross." The Kourier Magazine. Vol. 8, April, 1932, p. 16.

944. "God In The Klan." The Kourier Magazine. Vol. 7, February, 1931, p. 24.

945. "God In The Klan." The Kourier Magazine. Vol. 7, August, 1931, p. 24.

946.   "I Am." The Kourier Magazine. Vol. 3, February, 1927, pp. 22-23.

947.   "Klansmen." The Kourier Magazine. Vol. 8, May, 1932, p. 16.

948.   "My Klan." The Kourier Magazine. Vol. 8, May, 1932, p. 14.

949.   "The Klansman." The Kourier Magazine. Vol. 8, January, 1932, p. 4.

950.   "Transformation." The Kourier Magazine. Vol. 3, October, 1927, p. 22.

PRAYER

951.   Blount, Asa C. "A Klansman." The Kourier Magazine. Vol. 6, September, 1930, p. 1.

SONGS

952.   "A Klan Hymn." The Kourier Magazine. Vol. 7, October, 1931, p. 25.

953.   "Onward, Klansmen." The Kourier Magazine. Vol. 8, January, 1932, p. 8.

954.   "Song Of The Klan." The Kourier Magazine. Vol. 8, May, 1932, p. 6.

8
General Works

STATES

A SELECTED LIST

1. ALABAMA

955. "Accused Alabama Klansman Dies After A Heart Attack."
New York Times. March 11, 1966, p. 18.

956. Adams, Val. "A.B.C. Charges Wallace Aide Seized Film Of
Shelton Greeting." New York Times, June 28, 1968, p. 83.

957. "Ala. Black Convicted For Shooting Klansman." Washington
Star. October 3, 1980, p. A7.

958. "Alabama D.A. Reopens Probe Of F.B.I. Informant In Ku
Klux Klan." Washington Post. August 4, 1978, p. 21A.

959. "Alabama Flogger Freed." Pittsburgh Courier. September
22, 1928, p. 8.

960. "Ala. Jury Indicts Ex-FBI Informer In '65 Civil Rights
Death Case." New Orleans Times Picayune. October 2,
1978, p. 1.

961. "Ala Rape Trial Involving Retarded Black Man Viewed."
Chicago Tribune. September 24, 1978, p. 14.

962. "Ala Troopers Patrol In Wake Of Racial Clash At KKK
Rally." Chicago Tribune. May 27, 1979, p. 3.

963. "Alabama Aide Accuses Wallace Of Contributing To Klan
Success." New York Times. October 17, 1965, p. 77.

964. "Alabama Aims At Ku Klux Klan." Pittsburgh Courier.
July 23, 1927, p. 5.

965.   "Alabama Aroused." Outlook. Vol. 147, November 2, 1927, p. 261.

966.   "Alabama Band Flogs Man, Burns His Home." New York Times. September 11, 1927, p. 17.

967.   "Alabama Couple Sue F.B.I. Citing Peril To Marriage." New York Times. April 30, 1977, p. 8.

968.   "Alabama Flogger Gets 8-Year Sentence; Convicted Of Abducting Boy From Church." New York Times. August 5, 1927, p. 1.

969.   "Alabama Floggings Charged To 18 Men." New York Times. September 17, 1927, p. 3.

970.   "Alabama Grand Jury Ending Klan Inquiry." New York Times. July 9, 1949, p. 28.

971.   "Alabama Grand Jury Opens Flogging Action." New York Times. October 11, 1927, p. 20.

972.   "Alabama Holds Second Trial In Civil Rights Case." National Observer. October 25, 1965, p. 3.

973.   "U.S. Grand Jury In Alabama Indicts 20 Ku Klux Klan Members." Los Angeles Times. April 5, 1979, p. 4.

974.   "Alabama Judge Rules Klan Must Testify." New York Times. April 18, 1927, p. 16.

975.   "Alabama Klan Aims New Laws At Press." New York Times. August 21, 1927, Sect. 2, p. 4.

976.   "Alabama Juries Rule On Civil Rights Cases." National Observer. December 6, 1965, p. 3.

977.   "Ala. Judge Sentences 8 Ku Klux Klansmen Arrested During March." San Francisco Chronicle. September 6, 1979, p. 6.

978.   "Alabama Klan Chief Orders Ban On Hoods." New York Times. June 26, 1949, p. 33.

979.   "Alabama Klan Leader Refuses To Talk About Liuzzo Slaying." New York Times. February 5, 1966, p. 14.

980.   "Alabama Klansman Guilty In Vietnamese Rights Case.: New York Times. January 16, 1980, p. 16.

981.   "Alabama Klansman Starts Prison Term." New York Times. January 5, 1966, p. 13.

982.   "Alabama Klansmen Face Murder Trial." The Charlotte Observer. September 25, 1966.

983.   "Alabama Klansmen Restore The Mask." New York
        Times. August 12, 1928, p. 12.

984.   "Alabama Kluxers Warn." Pittsburgh Courier.   June
        28, 1930, p. 1.

985.   "Alabama Law Enforcement." New York Times.   July
        12, 1927, p. 24.

986.   "Alabama Law Enforcement." New York Times.   July
        18, 1927, p. 16.

987.   "Alabama Mother Of 5 Told 'Klan Is Coming To See
        You'." Washington Post. June 20, 1949.

988.   "Alabama Orders Recall Of Guard." New York Times.
        May 30, 1961, p. 1,7.

989.   "Alabama Outlaws Wearing Of Masks." New York Times.
        June 29, 1949, p. 54.

990.   "Alabama Politics." New York Times.   December 28,
        1929, p. 9.

991.   "Alabama Prosecutor Quits Ku Klux Klan." New York
        Times.   October 20, 1927, p. 12.

992.   "Alabama Publisher Faces New Warrant." New York
        Times.   February 11, 1927, p. 44.

993.   "Alabama Slaying Is Called Planned." New York
        Times.   May 31, 1960, p. 22.

994.   "Alabama To Battle Heflin And The Klan." Pitts-
        burgh Courier.   September 6, 1930, p. 8B.

995.   "Alabama To Fight Ban On Prosecuting F.B.I. In-
        former." New York Times.   October 7, 1980, p. B15.

996.   "Alabama U.S.A." New York Times.   May 22, 1961,
        p. 30.

997.   "Alabama Watched In Crackdown." Christian Science
        Monitor. July 19, 1949, p. 15.

998.   "Alabama Widens Its Fight On Klan." New York Times.
        July 23, 1949, p. 24.

999.   "Alabama Witness Of Alleged Slaying Admits An
        Error." New York Times.   June 2, 1976, p. 17.

1,000. "Alabama Trial Set Today In 1963 Church Bombing."
        New York Times.   November 14, 1977, p. 59.

1,001. "Alabamian Who Agreed To Testify On Klan Is Killed."
        New York Times.   June 6, 1979, p. 14.

1,002.   "Alabamian Will Not Testify At Klan Trial." Pittsburgh Courier. September 10, 1927, p. 1.

1,003.   "Alabamians To Battle Heflin And The Klan." Pittsburgh Courier. September 6, 1930, p. 8.

1,004.   "Alabama's Floggers." Literary Digest. Vol. 95, October 29, 1927, pp. 11-12.

1,005.   "A License To Murder." Ebony. Vol. 21, December, 1965, pp. 148-149.

1,006.   "Alleged Klansman Slain In Alabama." New York Times. September 13, 1959, p. 23.

1,007.   Anderson, Jack. "Klan Rallies In Alabama." Washington Post. August 26, 1979, p. 7D.

1,008.   "Anti-Klan Bill Wins." Christian Science Monitor. June 28, 1949, p. 3.

1,009.   "Asks Governor Graves To End Alabama Klan." New York Times. October 28, 1927, p. 19.

1,010.   "Assails Graves On Klan." New York Times. November 9, 1927, p. 22.

1,011.   "Attorney Pleads With Jury: Set Retarded Black Man Free." New York Recorder. November 22, 1980, p. 6.

1,012.   Ayres, B. Drummond, Jr. "Alabamian Guilty In '63 Church Blast That Killed 4 Girls." New York Times. November 19, 1977, pp. 1,8.

1,013.   _____. "Case Goes To Jury In Birmingham In '63 Church Bombing Fatal To 4." New York Times. November 18, 1977, p. 18.

1,014.   Barrett, George. "Montgomery: Testing Ground." New York Times Magazine. December 16, 1956, Sect. 6, pp. 8-9, 98-50.

1,015.   "Bars Freedom Rides." New York Times. June 3, 1961, p. 18.

1,016.   Beirman, Irving. "Alabama Rips Off The Hood." Christian Science Monitor. Magazine Section, July 2, 1949, p. 3.

1,017.   "Bias Leader Arrested." New York Times. January 24, 1957, p. 30.

1,018.   Bigart, Homer. "Shotguns Bar Negro Worshiper From Church." Washington Post. September 22, 1955, p. 59.

1,019.   "Bill To Outlaw KKK Paramilitary Training By Ala.
          Rep." Jet. Vol. 59, October 23, 1980, p. 5.

1,020.   "Biracial Jury Frees Kluxer." The Greensboro
          (N.C.) Daily News. September 28, 1966.

1,021.   "Biracial Jury Frees 2d Klansman In Death Of
          Mrs. Viola Liuzzo." The Winston-Salem (N.C.)
          Journal. September 28, 1966.

1,022.   "Biracial Jury Gets Klan Murder Case." The Char-
          lotte (N.C.) Observer. September 28, 1966.

1,023.   "Birmingham Is Boiling." Afro-American. September
          14, 1963, pp. 1, 5.

1,024.   "Black Activists And Ku Klux Klansmen Stage Peace-
          ful March In Ala." Los Angeles Times. June 10,
          1979, p. 1.

1,025.   "Black Denied Shift Of Trial In Shooting Of a Klans-
          man." New York Times. February 27, 1980, p. 12.

1,026.   "Black Held In Klansman Shooting." New York Times.
          May 29, 1979, p. 16.

1,027.   "Black Man Arrested In Shooting of KKK Member
          During Ala. Clash." Chicago Tribune. May 29,
          1979, p. 3.

1,028.   "Blacks And The Klan Clash Again In Selma, After
          Decade of Peace." New York Times. April 15, 1979,
          p. 16.

1,029.   "Blacks March In Decatur, Ala., Ignoring Taunts
          Of KKK Members." Chicago Tribune. June 10, 1979,
          p. 2.

1,030.   "Black Protest March And Klan Counter March In
          Decatur, Ala., Eyed." Los Angeles Times. June 5,
          1979, p. 1.

1,031.   "Blacks Seek $1 Million In Suit Against Klan."
          Washington Post. November 16, 1980, p. A8.

1,032.   "Bombing Suspect Pleads Not Guilty." New York
          Times. October 29, 1977, p. 71.

1,033.   "Bombs Laid To KKK." Christian Science Monitor.
          February 11, 1957, p. 14.

1,034.   Bonventre, Peter. "KKK Tries To Ride Again."
          Newsweek. Vol. 93, June 18, 1979, p. 31.

1,035.   "Boycott." New York Times. March 30, 1965, p. 46.

1,036.   "Brochure Backs Wallace." New York Times. May 22, 1970, p. 46.

1,037.   Brooks, Thomas, Jr. "Ku Klux Klansman Who Is Accused Of Fatal Church Bombing Free On Bond." Atlanta Daily World. October 9, 1977, p. 1.

1,038.   Brown, Warren. "Ex-Klan Informer Hits Birmingham Police." Washington Post. July 30, 1978. p. A2.

1,039.   _____. "FBI Informer In Ku Klux Klan." Washington Post. October, 1, 1978, p. 1C.

1,040.   _____. "Top FBI Klansman Describes How He Battered Bus Riders." Washington Post. July 19, 1978, p. A2.

1,041.   Brownell, Blaine A. "Birmingham, Alabama: New South City In The 1920's." Journal of Southern History. Vol. 38, February, 1972, pp. 21-48.

1,042.   Bryant, Pat. "Cross Burning Preceded Lynching Of Mobile Youth." Cleveland Call And Post. April 18, 1981, p. 1,2.

1,043.   Calvin, Floyd J. "Moten Courageously Defied Alabama Klan." Pittsburgh Courier. March 10, 1928, p. 3.

1,044.   "Camera Smashed By Klan, Is Charge." New York Times. September, 25, 1949, p. 81.

1,045.   "Car On Loan Burned." New York Times. May 23, 1961, p. 26.

1,046.   "Carter And The KKK." New Republic. Vol. 136, February 4, 1957, p. 6.

1,047.   "Carter Re-Election Campaign." New York Times. August 28, 1980, p. B8.

1,048.   "Charges Against 4 Dropped." New York Times. June 10, 1979, p. 26.

1,049.   "Charges In Floggings." New York Times. May 24, 1961, p. 22.

1,050.   "Charter To Negro Group." New York Times. 19, November, 1946, p. 6.

1,051.   "Chief To Produce Records." Christian Science Monitor. July 27, 1949, p. 16.

1,052.   "Civil Rights Case In Haynesville, Alabama, Discussed." National Observer. May 10, 1965, p. 2.

1,053.   Coleman,Louis. "The Klan Revives." Nation. Vol.
          139, July 4, 1934, p. 20.

1,054.   "Continues Flogging Trials." New York Times.
          November 25, 1927, p. 23.

1,055.   "Controversy Over FBI's Ku Klux Klan Informer In
          Alabama Viewed." Washington Post. July 12, 1978,
          p. 2A.

1,056.   "Coors Sues Rights Group It Says Linked It To Klan."
          New York Times. December, 23, 1981, p. A14.

1,057.   "Court Condemns Klan." New York Times. October 29,
          1926, p. 48.

1,058.   "Cross Burnings Lead To Arrests." New York Times.
          March 28, 1960, pp. 25.

1,059.   "Cross Burning Warns Reds." New York Times.
          July 16, 1950, p. 61.

1,060.   Daniell, F. Raymond. "New York Attacked In Scotts-
          boro Trial." New York Times. April 8, 1933, p. 30.

1,061.   "Decatur Mayor Urges Town To Boycott Race Marches."
          New York Times. June 8, 1979, p. A14.

1,062.   "Defeat Of Heflin Is Urged By Alabama Women's Lea-
          gue." New York Times. April 27, 1929, p. 1.

1,063.   "Defers New Action In Scottsboro Case." New York
          Times. November 8, 1932, p. 13.

1,064.   "Defiant Governor: John Malcolm Patterson." New
          York Times. May 22, 1961, p. 26.

1,065.   "Demonstrations By Blacks And Ku Klux Klansmen In
          Alabama Viewed." San Francisco Chronicle. June 18,
          1979, p. 2A.

1,066.   "Demonstrators Confront Klansmen In Mobile, Ala-
          bama." New Orleans Times Picayne. September 25,
          1977, p. 14.

1,067.   "De Priest Gets Telegram From Klan." Pittsburgh
          Courier. July 5, 1930, p. 2.

1,068.   "Deputized Klansmen Aid Sheriff in Ala. Manhunt
          (of a Black man)." Pittsburgh Courier, October 15,
          1949, p. 20.

1,069.   De Selding, Peter B. "When Prejudice Changes Its
          Address." New York Times. November 26, 1979,
          p. A21.

1,070.   "Dozens Questioned In Alabama." The New York Times.
          March 27, 1960, pp. 74.

1,071.   "Dr. King Is Shifted To Safer Jail Cell." New York
          Times. November 2, 1967, p. 34.

1,072.   "Dr. King Is Speaker Near Rally By Klan." New York
          Times. December 31, 1967, p. 32.

1,073.   "Dynamite Blast Wrecks Carport Under House of
          Alabama Negro." New York Times. December 1, 1964,
          p. 44.

1,074.   "8 Whites Freed On Bond In Alabama Racial Unrest."
          New York Times. July 8, 1979, p. 18.

1,075.   Emerson, Gloria. "Dr. King To Lead Liuzzo Pro-
          tests." New York Times. October 24, 1965, p. 1,
          78.

1,076.   "Ex-FBI Dir. Hoover Blocked Trial of KKK In Ala.
          Church Bombing." Chicago Tribune. February 18,
          1980, p. 11.

1,077.   "Ex-FBI Informer Indicted In 1965 Murder of Civil
          Rights Worker." New Orleans Times Picayune.
          September 21, 1978, p. 6.

1,078.   "Ex-Informant Criticizes FBI." Washington Post.
          December 2, 1978, p. A3.

1,079.   "Ex-Klansman Convicted of Shooting At Negroes."
          Washington Post. May 26, 1963.

1,080.   "Ex-Klansman Indicted In '63 Bombing That Killed
          4." New York Times. September 27, 1977, p. 20.

1,081   "Ex-Klansman Out On A Technicality." New York
          Times. April 15, 1976, p. 39.

1,082.   "Ex-Mayor Of Birmingham To Aid Klansman's Trial."
          New York Times. September 21, 1966, p. 32.

1,083.   "Family of Slain Rights Worker Seeks $2 Million
          From F.B.I." New York Times. December 29, 1977,
          p. B6.

1,084.   "FBI Informant Reacts." Washington Post. December
          17, 1980, p. A10.

1,085.   "F.B.I. Spy Denies Admitting To Killing Of Viola
          Liuzzo." New York Times. July 18, 1980, p. 6.

1,086.   "FBI's Top Informer In Ku Klux Klan In The 1960's
          Interviewed." Washington Post. July 19, 1978,
          p. 2A.

1,087.   "Fed. Grand Jury Indicts KKK Member In Ala. Over
          NAACP Incidents." Chicago Tribune. April 5, 1979,
          Sect. 3, p. 15.

1,088.   Feidelson, Charles N. "Alabama's Super Government."
          Nation. Vol. 125, September 28, 1927, pp. 311-312.

1,089.   "5 Suits Against Time, Inc., Dismissed By Federal
          Judge." New York Times. February 10, 1966, p. 29.

1,090.   Fleming, Walter L. "The Ku-Klux Testimony Relating
          To Alabama." Gulf States Historical Magazine.
          Vol. 2, November, 1903, pp. 155-160.

1,091.   "Floggers Are Fined In Alabama Court." The New
          York Times. August 2, 1927, p. 10.

1,092.   "Flogging Inquiries Increase In Alabama." The New
          York Times. July 18, 1927, p. 32.

1,093.   "Flogging Jury Called." New York Times. August
          27, 1927, p. 15.

1,094.   "Flowers Says U.S. Refused To Aid Him In Klan In-
          quiry." New York Times. April 19, 1966, p. 20.

1,095.   Foley, Albert S. "KKK In Mobile, Ala." America.
          Vol. 96, December 8, 1956, pp. 298-299.

1,096.   "Former FBI Agent Says His Killing Of Man Covered
          Up In Alabama." Houston Post. July 31, 1978,
          p. 25A.

1,097.   "Former Ku Klux Klan Informer For The FBI Inter-
          viewed." Washington Post. July 30, 1978, p. 2A.

1,098.   "14 Arrested In Klan Cleanup." Christian Science
          Monitor. July 12, 1949, p. 16.

1,099.   "4th Klansman Guilty." New York Times. February
          21, 1958, p. 10.

1,100.   Franklin, Ben A. "4 Alabama Klansmen Charged; 3
          Released on $50,000 Bond." New York Times. March
          27, 1965, p. 10.

1,101.   _____. "Klan Chief Calls 2 Rights Deaths Part
          of Red Plot." New York Times. March 28, 1965,
          pp. 1,58.

1,102.   "Gary Rowe." New York Times. October 8, 1978,
          p. 42.

1,103.   "Gary Thomas Rowe, Jr." New York Times. November
          6, 1978, p. 53.

1,104.   Gordon, Gregory. "Planning 'Race War,' KKK Trains Its Troops At Camp In Alabama." New York Daily World. November 25, 1980, pp. 2,11.

1,105.   "Government By Law Or 'Clan'?" Washington Evening Star. August 20, 1915.

1,106.   "Government Or The Ku Klux Klan." Pittsburgh Courier. August 4, 1923, p. 8.

1,107.   "Governor Acts To Crack Down On Klan." Christian Science Monitor. August 17, 1957, p. 3.

1,108.   "Governor Graves Is Alarmed." Pittsburgh Courier. July 23, 1927, editorial page.

1,109.   Graham, Fred P. "Ex-Klan Lawyer Center Of Dispute." New York Times. March 1, 1969, p. 16.

1,110.   _____. "President Is Cool To Klan Inquiry By Alabama's Attorney General." New York Times. July 4, 1965, p. 25.

1,111.   _____. "3 Alabama Klansmen Indicted In The Slaying of Mrs. Liuzzo." New York Times. April 23, 1965, p. 15.

1,112.   "Grand Jury Assails Klan In Alabama." New York Times. August 24, 1927, p. 15.

1,113.   Graves, John Temple, 2nd. "Blow To Klan Seen In Heflin's Defeat." New York Times. January 9, 1938, Sect. 4, p. 7.

1,114.   Greenhaw, Wayne. "Remembering Bobby Shelton and The Ku Klux Klan." New York Times. July 8, 1978, p. 19.

1,115.   Greene, Johnny. "Ku Klux Klan In Alabama." Los Angeles Times. August 19, 1979, Sect. 5, p. 3.

1,116.   "Group Of KKK Marchers Peacefully Disarmed In Alabama." Los Angeles Times. August 12, 1979, p. 1.

1,117.   "Guerrilla Warfare Unit Of Ku Klux Klan In Training At Base In Alabama." San Francisco Chronicle. September 30, 1980, p. 4.

1,118.   "Guilty In Mutilation." New York Times. November 8, 1957, p. 20.

1,119.   "Gunshot Interrupts Klan Rally." New York Times. June 25, 1979, p. 12.

1,120.   Halberstam, David. "Meriwether Strove For Accord
          Behind Scenes In Montgomery." New York Times.
          May 24, 1961, p. 24.

1,121.   "Harlem Letter Warns Birmingham Officials." New
          York Times. July 3, 1930, p. 6.

1,122.   Harmetz, Aljean. "Informer Is Subject Of TV Movie."
          New York Times. July 14, 1978, p. 6.

1,123.   Harrigan, Susan. "A Seedbed Of Racial Conflict."
          Wall Street Journal. September 10, 1979, p. 22.

1,124.   Harris, Art. "17 Years Later, Marchers Retrace
          The Bloody Route Of History." Washington Post.
          February 18, 1982, p. A2.

1,125.   "Haynesville Verdict." New York Times. October 24,
          1965, Sect. 4, pp. 1,2.

1,126.   "Head Jailed For Refusing Records." Christian
          Science Monitor. August 3, 1949, p. 10.

1,127.   "Head Resigns In Flogging Protest." Christian
          Science Monitor. July 21, 1949, p. 3.

1,128.   Herbers, John. "Klan Undercover Agent Studied
          Racial Strife For Alabama Committee." New York
          Times. February 9, 1966, p. 27.

1,129.   _____. "Union Violence Laid To Alabama Klan."
          New York Times. February 8, 1966, p. 22.

1,130.   "High-Standing Flogger." New York Times. July
          28, 1927, p. 18.

1,131.   "Hines To Seek Advice On Tuskegee Dispute." New
          York Times. July 6, 1923, p. 3.

1,132.   "Hold Everything." Time. Vol. 54, July 25, 1949,
          p. 12.

1,133.   "Hoover Hid KKK's Role In Alabama Church Bombing."
          Jet. Vol. 57, March 13, 1980, p. 7.

1,134.   "House To Study Alabama Floggings." Christian
          Science Monitor. June 22, 1949, p. 7.

1,135.   "How Klan Castrated Negro (in Alabama in 1957)."
          Muhammad Speaks. January 1963, pp. 3-5.

1,136.   "Huntsville, Ala. Jaycees Pay KKK To Stay Away
          From Fair." New Orleans Times Picayune.
          September 28, 1975, p. 5.

1,137.   "Indict 36 Klansmen In Alabama County." New York Times. October 16, 1972, p. 5.

1,138.   "Industries Urged To Shun Alabama." New York Times. April 3, 1965, p. 14.

1,139.   "Informant: Attacks Ordered." Washington Post. November 30, 1980, p. A15.

1,140.   "Injunction Cites Rival Klansmen." New York Times. May 22, 1961, p. 27.

1,141.   "Injunction In Alabama." New York Times. August 7, 1957, p. 7.

1,142.   "It Sure Was Pretty." Time. Vol. 54, November 7, 1949, p. 24.

1,143.   "Jailed For Killing Night Attacker." New York Times. June 15, 1925, p. 6.

1,144.   Jenkins, Ray. "Alabama Slaying Laid To Klansmen." New York Times. February 27, 1976, p. 13.

1,145.   _____. "Defense Questions Photo Identification In Bomb Trial." New York Times. November 16, 1977, p. 18.

1,146.   _____. "Witness In Church-Bombing Trial Links Dynamite To The Defendant." New York Times. November 17, 1977, p. 18.

1,147.   "Judge Blocks Rights Slaying Case." New York Times. June 14, 1980, p. 7.

1,148.   "Judge Condemns Violence." Christian Science Monitor. February 12, 1957, p. 6.

1,149.   "Jury Chosen In Slaying Of Girl In Church Blast." New York Times. November 15, 1977, p. 19.

1,150.   "Jury With Negroes Acquits Klansman In Liuzzo Slaying." New York Times. September 28, 1966, pp. 1,24.

1,151.   Kahn, Joseph P. "Southern Justice." New York Times. March 10, 1979, p. 19.

1,152.   "Kasper At Klan Rally." New York Times. October 7, 1956, p. 44.

1,153.   "Katzenbach Vows To Aid Klan Study." New York Times. July 7, 1965, p. 16.

1,154.   "Killed By Kluxers." Newsweek. Vol. 35, March 13, 1950, p. 22.

1,155.   King, Wayne. "Alabama Official Expects To Find 1963 Killers Of Four Black Girls." New York Times. March 10, 1976, p. 14C.

1,156.   _____. "'Give Police A Chance,' Rally Leader Urges Klansmen." New York Times. May 28, 1979, p. 8.

1,157.   _____. "Klan And Blacks March Through Tense Decatur." New York Times. June 10, 1979, p. 26.

1,158.   _____. "Klansmen Begin A White-Rights March In Alabama." New York Times. August 10, 1979, p. 9.

1,159.   _____. "Newly Resurgent Klan In Alabama Is Closely Watched By U.S. Agents." New York Times. May 15, 1979, p. 14.

1,160.   _____. "164 Klan Marchers In Alabama Arrested Over Permit." New York Times. August 13, 1979, p. 14.

1,161.   _____. "Racism Rebounds In Part Of South." New York Times. July 5, 1979, pp. 1,12.

1,162.   _____. "2 Klansmen And A Black Woman Are Shot In A Street Clash In Alabama." New York Times. May 27, 1979, p. 26.

1,163.   "KKK Crusades In Selma, As Blacks Shout Insults." Jet. Vol. 56, May 3, 1979, p. 5.

1,164.   "KKK Group Cited For Lack Of Parade Permit At Montgomery Limits." Chicago Tribune. August 13, 1979, p. 6.

1,165.   "KKK In Alabama." New York Times. October 3, 1978, p. 57.

1,166.   "KKK In Alabama." New York Times. October 4, 1978, p. 78.

1,167.   "KKK In Alabama." New York Times. October 14, 1978, p. 63.

1,168.   "KKK Invades The University Of Alabama." The Daily Worker. February 8, 1956, p. 5.

1,169.   "KKK Is Reported Turning Out." New York Times. September 1, 1948, p. 13.

1,170.   "Klan Leases Property Near Black Muslims In Alabama." National Observer. February 9, 1970, p. 13.

1,171.   "KKK And Blacks Stage Marches In Alabama And Mississippi." New Orleans Times Picayune. June 10, 1979, p. 2.

1,172.   "KKK And SCLC Hold Marches In Decatur, Alabama."
         Washington Post. June 10, 1979, p. 3A.

1,173.   "KKK Arms For Rally In Decatur, Ala." New Orleans
         Times Picayune. May 28, 1979, p. 3.

1,174.   "KKK Clash With SCLC During Decatur, Ala. March
         Leaves 4 Injured." New Orleans Times Picayune.
         May 27, 1979, p. 3.

1,175.   "KKK Continues Trek Retracing Martin Luther King
         Jr.'s March." New Orleans Times Picayune. August
         11, 1979, p. 2.

1,176.   "KKK Group Hits Rival KKK Group's March On Mont-
         gomery." New Orleans Times Picayune. August 14,
         1979, p. 2.

1,177.   "KKK Marches In Decatur, Ala. To Protest Weapons
         Ban." New Orleans Times Picayune. February 25,
         1979, p. 5B.

1,178.   "KKK Marchers Jeered As They Begin March To Mont-
         gomery, Ala." New Orleans Times Picayune. August
         10, 1979, p. 2.

1,179.   "KKK Members Protest Shooting Of 2 Members During
         Ala. Rally." Chicago Tribune. May 28, 1979,
         Sect. 4, p. 3.

1,180.   "KKK Protests Cambodian Refugees Coming To Birming-
         ham, Alabama." Atlanta Daily World. September 1,
         1981, p. 1.

1,181.   "KKK Threatens Negro Veterans." People's Voice.
         May 3, 1947, p. 8.

1,182.   "KKK Threats To Florence Officials." New York
         Times. February 21, 1923, p. 9.

1,183.   "The KKK Tries To Rise Again." Newsweek. Vol. 93,
         June 18, 1979, p. 31.

1,184.   "Klan Active In Mobile." New York Times. Sep-
         tember 19, 1956, p. 20.

1,185.   "Klan Activities Described At A Hearing In Alabama."
         New York Times. April 21, 1980, p. 14.

1,186.   "Klan And Blacks Clash." New York Times. Septem-
         ber 25, 1977, p. 37.

1,187.   "Klan And Blacks Create Tensions At Carter Cam-
         paign Opening In Ala." Los Angeles Times. Sep-
         tember 2, 1980, p. 7.

1,188.   "Klan And Foes." New York Times. March 12, 1978,
          p. 26.

1,189.   "Klan Attack On Negroes Arouse Town." Christian
          Science Monitor. August 15, 1957, p. 4.

1,190.   "Klan Beats Newsman." New York Times. March 24,
          1957, p. 62.

1,191.   "Klan 'Bums' Blamed In Beating of Woman." New
          York Times. June 13, 1949, p. 13.

1,192.   "Klan Book Disappears From Booth At Show." The
          New York Times. May 16, 1925, p. 22.

1,193.   "Klan Boosting Public Image, Says Wizard." The
          Knoxville Journal. September 28, 1977.

1,194.   "Klan Charges Persecution." New York Times. March
          2, 1969, p. 16.

1,195,   "Klan Chief To Try To Produce Names." Christian
          Science Monitor. July 30, 1949, p. 12.

1,196.   "Klan Drops Secretiveness At Alabama Fair Display."
          New York Times. October 9, 1964, p. 64.

1,197.   "Klan-Elected; Becomes Foe Of Nightriders." Pitts-
          burgh Courier. October 22, 1972, p. 1.

1,198.   "Klan Fast Losing Out In Alabama." Pittsburgh
          Courier. June 4, 1927, p. B7.

1,199.   "Klan Gives Negro, 107, Radio." New York Times.
          December 23, 1948, p. 40.

1,200.   "Klan Governor Roused By Flogging Of Girl." New
          York Times. July 11, 1927, p. 9.

1,201.   "Klan Group Planning For National Action." New
          York Times. December 19, 1949, p. 44.

1,202.   "Klan Holds Alabama Rally." New York Times. Au-
          gust 26, 1956, p. 16.

1,203.   "Klan In Alabama Rallies To Heflin." New York
          Times. December 28, 1929, p. 9.

1,204.   "Klan Lawyer Killed In Traffic Crash." New York
          Times. August 21, 1965, p. 9.

1,205.   "Klan Leader Admits Attack On Minister." New York
          Times. December 21, 1978, p. 20.

1,206.   "Klan Leader Arrested." Birmingham Times. May 21-
          23, 1981, p. 1.

1,207.   "Klan Leader Criticizes U.S. Report And Asserts, 'We Violate No Law'." _New York Times_. November 25, 1980, p. A12.

1,208.   "Klan Leader Held In Shooting." _New York Times_. January 25, 1957, p. 16.

1,209.   "Klan Leader Sues To Keep F.B.I. From Destroying Political Files." _New York Times_. July 12, 1977, p. 26.

1,210.   "Klan Leader To Resign." _New York Times_. November 4, 1965, p. 35.

1,211.   "Klan Libel Bill Killed By Strategy." _New York Times_. August 26, 1927, p. 17.

1,212.   "Klan Loses." _Pittsburgh Courier_. December 31, 1927, p. 1.

1,213.   "Klan March Is Halted Outside Montgomery And Guns Are Seized." _New York Times_. August 12, 1979, p. 31.

1,214.   "Klan Members Hold 'Leadership' Session." _Washington Post_. November 30, 1980, p. A4.

1,215.   "Klan Officials Deny Sending DePriest Message." _Pittsburgh Courier_. July 5, 1930, p. B8.

1,216.   "Klan Opposes Vorter Society." _Chicago Defender_. November 30, 1946, p. 4.

1,217.   "Klan Parades In Selma, Ala." _Pittsburgh Courier_. September 6, 1958, p. B1.

1,218.   "Klan Plans March." _Washington Star_. September 1, 1980, p. A5.

1,219.   "Klan Raids In Birmingham." _New York Times_. January 5, 1926, p. 15.

1,220.   "Klan Rally In Selma." _New York Times_. April 16, 1979, p. D13.

1,221.   "Klan-Robed Man Shot By Blacks Says His 'Initiation' Was A Ruse." _New York Times_. May 6, 1979, p. 58.

1,222.   "Klan Rule." _Crisis_. Vol. 35, January, 1928, pp. 12-13.

1,223.   "Klan Sends Warning." _Pittsburgh Courier_. July 12, 1930, p. 2.

1,224.   "Klan Threatens Tuskegee." _Pittsburgh Courier_. July 14, 1923, pp. 1,14.

1,225.   "Klan To Challenge Law Barring Alabama March."
         Washington Star. August 28, 1980, p. A5.

1,226.   "Klan Trial Postponed Till Today." Winston-Salem
         Journal. September 27, 1966.

1,227.   "Klan Warns League Here." New York Times. Febru-
         ary 24, 1948, p. 13.

1,228.   "Klan Will Discard Its Masks On Feb. 22, Alabama
         Hears." New York Times. January 22, 1928, p. 1.

1,229.   "Klansman, Eaton, Dies In Alabama." New Bern Sun
         Journal. March 10, 1966.

1,230.   Klansman Backs Survival Camps That Teach Warfare
         To Children." New York Times. December 1, 1980,
         p. B12.

1,231.   "Klansman Begins Term Today." New York Times.
         January 4, 1966, p. 7.

1,232.   "Klansman Draws Another Term." The Greensboro
         Daily News. February 26, 1966.

1,233.   "Klansman Found Guilty of Killing." New York
         Times. March 10, 1974, p. 26.

1,234.   "Klansman Free In Murder Case of Rights Man."
         The New Bern Sun Journal. September 28, 1966.

1,235.   "Klansman Freed In Liuzzo Slaying." The Durham
         Morning Herald. September 28, 1966.

1,236.   "Klansman Gets 180 Days." New York Times. April
         11, 1925, p. 9.

1,237.   "Klansman Jailed For Mutilation Case." New York
         Times. November 1, 1957, p. 14.

1,238.   "Klansman In Liuzzo Case Gets 30 Days For Fighting."
         New York Times. October 21, 1966, p. 25.

1,239.   "Klansman Scores Johnson." New York Times. March
         28, 1965, p. 58.

1,240.   "Klansman To Get New Trial In Killing Of Black
         Minister." New York Times. April 8, 1974, p. 30.

1,241.   "Klansman To Go On Trial For Slaying." Pittsburgh
         Courier. August 6, 1927, pp. 1,4.

1,242.   "The Klansman Who Wore Many Hoods." New York
         Times. July 16, 1978, Sect. 4, p. 1.

1,243.   "Klansman's Killer Freed In Alabama." New York
         Times. June 1, 1960, p. 33.

1,244. "Klansmen Apologize." _New York Times_. March 25, 1957, p. 13.

1,245. "Klansmen Are Taunted At A Birmingham March." _New York Times_. July 29, 1979, p. 16.

1,246. "Klansmen Charged With Beating Two Ala. Ministers." _Jet_. Vol. 57, February 7, 1980, p. 8.

1,247. "Klansmen From 15 States Attend Funeral For Murphy." _New York Times_. August 23, 1965, p. 18.

1,248. "Klansmen Preparing To Parade Unmasked In Alabama." _New York Times_. August 22, 1949, p. 11.

1,249. "Klansmen Seized In Alabama Are Accused Of A 1957 Killing." _New York Times_. February 22, 1976, p. 48.

1,250. "Klansmen's Trial Ends In Alabama Floggings." _New York Times_. December 1, 1927, p. 56.

1,251. "Ku Klux Klansmen Begin White Power March Through Alabama." _San Francisco Chronicle_. August 10, 1979, p. 5.

1,252. "Ku Klux Klan Continues March To Montgomery, Alabama." _Washington Post_. August 11, 1979, p. 9A.

1,253. "A Ku Klux - G.O.P. - Heflin Alliance." _New York Times_. August 28, 1930, p. 18.

1,254. "KKK In Alabama." _Charlotte (N.C.) Observer_. July 6, 1923.

1,255. "Ku Klux Klan Informer Indicted In 1965 Slaying." _Washington Post_. September 21, 1978, p. 1A.

1,256. "Ku Klux Initiate 500 Klansmen." _New York Times_. January 28, 1921, p. 6.

1,257. "Ku Klux Klan Demonstration In Decatur, Alabama, Viewed." _San Francisco Chronicle_. May 28, 1979, p. 8.

1,258. "KKK In Tuskegee." _Mobile (Ala.) Register_. July 5, 1923.

1,259. "KKK In Tuskegee." _Savannah Tribune_. July 12, 1923.

1,260. "KKK In Tuskegee." _Norfolk Journal and Guide_. July 14, 1923.

1,261. "KKK In Tuskegee." _Pittsburgh Courier_. August 4, 1923.

1,262.   "Ku Klux Klan Holds National Leadership Conference
         In Birmingham, Ala." Houston Post. November 30,
         1980, p. 8D.

1,263.   "Ku Klux Klan March In Alabama." Christian Science
         Monitor. August 14, 1979, p. 24.

1,264.   "Ku Klux Klan March In Alabama Ends." San Francisco
         Chronicle. August 11, 1980, p. 26.

1,265.   "Klansmen March In Alabama To Protest Bombing In-
         dictment." New Orleans Times Picayune. October 9,
         1977, p. 8.

1,266.   "Ku Klux Klan March In Mobile, Ala." Washington
         Post. September 25, 1981, p. 6A.

1,267.   "Ku Klux Klan Marches In Selma, Alabama." Wash-
         ington Post. August 10, 1979, p. 6A.

1,268.   "Ku Klux Klan March In Selma, Alabama, Viewed."
         Los Angeles Times. August 10, 1979, p. 11.

1,269.   "Ku Klux Klan March Near Selma, Alabama." Christian
         Science Monitor. August 10, 1979, p. 2.

1,270.   "Ku Klux Klan On White Power March Through Alabama."
         Houston Post. August 11, 1979, p. 12A.

1,271.   "Ku Klux Klansman Arrested In Alabama During White
         Power March." San Francisco Chronicle. August 13,
         1979, p. 5.

1,272.   "Ku Klux Klansmen In Alabama Indicted In Shootings."
         New York Times. April 5, 1979, p. 19.

1,273.   "Ku Klux Klansmen Indicted In Alabama." Christian
         Science Monitor. April 6, 1979, p. 2.

1,274.   "Ku Klux Klansmen's White Rights March In Alabama
         Viewed." San Francisco Chronicle. August 11,
         1979, p. 3.

1,275.   Kunstel, Marcia. "In Selma, A Bridge Links Eras."
         New York Times. August 25, 1979, p. 17.

1,276.   "A Law Enforcer." New York Times. December 5,
         1927, p. 22.

1,277.   Lawrence, W.H. "200 More U.S. Marshals Being Sent
         To Alabama; F.B.I. Jails 4 In Bus Fire." New
         York Times. May 23, 1961, pp. 1,26.

1,278.   "Lawsuit By Rights Group Seeks Bar To Klansmen In-
         timidating Blacks." New York Times. November 5,
         1980, p. A12.

1,279.   "Lawyer Cites Lie Tests In Rights Worker's Death."
New York Times. February 3, 1979, p. 3.

1,280.   "Leader Resigns Over Teen Marriage." Christian
Science Monitor. June 12, 1957, p. 10.

1,281.   "Legislation Strikes At Cowardice." Christian
Science Monitor. July 2, 1949, p. M3.

1,282.   Lewis, Anthony. "Capital Opposes Ban On Bus
Rides." New York Times. June 3, 1961, p. 18.

1,283.   _____. "400 U.S. Marshals Sent To Alabama As
Montgomery Bus Riots Hurt 20; President Bids State
Keep Order." New York Times. May 21, 1961, pp. 1,
78.

1,284.   Loftus, Joseph A. "Marshals Alert For Race Crises."
New York Times. May 23, 1961, p. 26.

1,285.   _____. "U.S. Puts Length Of Deputies' Stay Up
To Alabamans." New York Times. May 24, 1961, pp.
1, 24.

1,286.   "Looking Backward At KKK At University Of Alabama
Campus." The Daily Worker. February 9, 1956, p. 5.

1,287.   Lowther, William. "Donning Robes, Fanning Flames."
MacLeans. Vol. 92, August 27, 1979, p. 26.

1,288.   Lytle, Stewart and Chris Conway. "Ku Klux Klan,
With A New Face, Makes Comeback; FBI Not Impressed."
Knoxville News-Sentinel. July 24, 1978.

1,289.   "Man Of 61 Is Flogged." New York Times. August 10,
1927, p. 11.

1,290.   "March By Ku Klux Klansmen." San Francisco Chronicle. August 14, 1979, p. 38.

1,291.   "March Of Time." New York Times. August 14, 1979,
p. 16.

1,292.   Marro, Anthony. "Informer Is Backed On Witness
Dispute." New York Times. July 19, 1978, p. 7.

1,293.   _____. "Justice Department Investigating Report Linking Informer To Violent Crime." New York
Times. July 13, 1978, pp. 1, 13.

1,294.   "Mask And Muzzle." New York Times. August 27,
1927, p. 12.

1,295.   "Mask Ban Splits Klan In Alabama." New York Times.
June 27, 1949, p. 38.

1,296.   Matthews, Ralph. "Afro Unearths Secret Ku Klux
          Document In Alabama Encouraging Lynchings." Afro-
          American. February 17, 1934.

1,297.   McClory, Robert. "Alabama Bishop Sees Klan Revival."
          National Catholic Reporter. Vol. 15, June 29, 1979,
          p. 7.

1,298.   Middlebrooks, Acton E. "Alabama Votes To Unmask
          Klan." Christian Century. Vol. 66, July 20, 1949,
          p. 871.

1,299.   Miller, Judy and Mark Miller. "Conviction Of A Ku
          Klux Killer." Sepia. Vol. 29, October, 1980,
          pp. 22-26.

1,300.   "Miners Say Ku Klux Should Be Wiped Out." Chicago
          Defender. April 16, 1921, p. 2.

1,301.   "Mistrial Declared In Klan Beating Case." New York
          Times. December 13, 1949, p. 39.

1,302.   Montgomery, Paul L. "Wallace Pledge." New York
          Times. March 27, 1965, pp. 1, 10.

1,303.   "Montgomery, Ala., Police Confront KKK Marchers And
          Seize Arms." Chicago Tribune. August 12, 1979,
          p. 14.

1,304.   "Montgomery Bars Klan Masks." New York Times.
          July 22, 1923, p. 16.

1,305.   "Montgomery Defeats Klansman For Mayor." New York
          Times. May 17, 1927, p. 32.

1,306.   "Montgomery Under Martial Law; Troops Called After
          New Riot; Marshals And Police Fight Mob." New
          York Times. May 22, 1961, pp. 1, 28.

1,307.   "Moral Lashes For Alabama Floggers." Literary
          Digest. Vol. 95, December 17, 1927, p. 32.

1,308.   "More Racial Unrest In Birmingham." New York Times.
          July 7, 1979, p. 6.

1,309.   "Moton - The Champion Blunderer." New York Amster-
          dam News. August 15, 1923, p. 12.

1,310.   "Moton May Be Given Hot Reception By Irate Negroes."
          New York Amsterdam News. August 15, 1923, p. 3.

1,311.   "Negro Juror At Klansman Trial Certain." Charlotte
          Observer. October 27, 1966.

1,312.   "A Negro Minister." New York Times. August 16,
          1957, p. 10.

1,313.   "Negroes - Darrow vs. Klan." _Time_. Vol. 9, March
          21, 1927, p. 12.

1,314.   "Negroes Dominate Jury List In Alabama Slaying
          Trials." _Winston-Salem Journal_. September 25,
          1966.

1,315.   "Negroes In Birmingham Protest On Registration."
          New York Times. January 6, 1966, p. 11.

1,316.   "New Flogging Case Barred In Alabama." _New York
          Times_. July 14, 1927, p. 25.

1,317.   "New Furor Over An Old Informant: G.T. Rowe, Jr.,
          FBI Informer On Ku Klux Klan Activities." _Time_.
          Vol. 112, July 24, 1978, p. 17.

1,318.   "New Wave of Trouble In Decatur, Ala., Between KKK
          And Blacks Eyed." _Chicago Tribune_. August 19,
          1979, Sect. 2, p. 12.

1,319.   "Night-riding In Alabama." _Commonweal_. Vol. 50,
          July 8, 1949, p. 309.

1,320.   "9 Ku Klux Klansmen Convicted In Alabama Racial
          Violence Case." _Los Angeles Times_. June 15, 1979,
          p. 15.

1,321.   "9 Of 12 Klansmen Are Guilty On Charges Of Terror-
          ism." _New York Times_. June 15, 1979, p. A12.

1,322.   "1963 Bombing Inquiry Reopened." _New York Times_.
          February 22, 1980, p. D15.

1,323.   "Not Political Move, Says Evans." _New York Times_.
          December 28, 1929, p. 9.

1,324.   "Not The Hospital - But Our Boys." _Pittsburgh
          Courier_. July 28, 1923, p. 14.

1,325.   "107 Year Old Former Slave Received A Ku Klux Klan
          Gift." _N.Y. Herald Tribune_. December 23, 1948.

1,326.   "1,000 At Klan Meeting." _New York Times_. November
          25, 1956, p. 79.

1,327.   "1,000 Robed Klansmen Parade In Tuskegee In Protest
          On Negro Hospital Personnel." _New York Times_.
          July 4, 1923, p. 1.

1,328.   "1,200 At Klan Meeting." _New York Times_. September
          9, 1956, p. 83.

1,329.   "Parade Fizzles." _Christian Science Monitor_.
          August 22, 1949, p. 14.

1,330.   "Pass Anti-Flogging Bill." New York Times. August
          31, 1927, p. 18.

1,331.   "Pastor Welcomes Klan." New York Times. October
          23, 1956, p. 36.

1,332.   "Plan To Indict Klan Reported In Alabama." Wash -
          ington Post. July 23, 1949.

1,333.   "Plead Guilty In Flogging." New York Times.
          August 9, 1927, p. 14.

1,334.   "Police Arrest KKK Marchers On Montgomery, Alabama.
          New Orleans Times Picayune. August 13, 1979, p. 1.

1,335.   "Police Arrest 198 In Ku Klux Klan For Illegal
          Parade In Alabama." Houston Post. August 13,
          1979, p. 8B.

1,336.   "Police Block KKK March On Montgomery And Confis-
          cate Weapons." New Orleans Times Picayune.
          August 12, 1979, p. 3.

1,337.   "Police Break Up Ku Klux Klan March To Montgomery,
          Alabama." Washington Post. August 13, 1979, p.
          2A.

1,338.   "Police Prevent Ku Klux Klansmen From Entering
          Montgomery, Ala." Washington Post. August 12,
          1979, p. 12A.

1,339.   Popham, John N.   "Test In High Court Is Sought By
          Klan." New York Times. July 18, 1949, pp. 1,10.

1,340.   "Protest Erupts Into Violence." Christian Science
          Monitor. September 16, 1977, p. 2.

1,341.   "Racial Unrest In Decatur, Alabama." Washington
          Post. September 17, 1978, p. 15A.

1,342.   "Radio Station Smeared." New York Times. May 30,
          1958, p. 41.

1,343.   Raines, Howell. "Alabama Requests Informer's Re-
          turn." New York Times. December 22, 1978, p. 11.

1,344.   _____. "F.B.I. Cover-Up Seen In 60's Klan
          Attacks." New York Times. February 17, 1980,
          pp. 1, 16.

1,345.   _____. "F.B.I. Informant In Klan Asserts He
          Shot And Killed A Black In '63." New York Times.
          July 11, 1978, pp. 1A, B7.

1,346.   _____. "Federal Report Says Hoover Barred Trial
          For Klansmen In '63 Bombing." New York Times.
          February 18, 1980, p. 12.

1,347.   . "Informer For F.B.I. Suspect In Bombing."
New York Times. July 9, 1978, pp. 1,20.

1,348.   . "Inquiries Link Informer For F.B.I. To
Major Klan Terrorism In '60's." New York Times.
July 17, 1978, pp. 1, 12.

1,349.   . "KKK In Alabama." New York Times.
September 20, 1978, p. 8.

1,350.   . "Police Given Data On Boast By Rowe."
New York Times. July 14, 1978, p. 1, 6.

1,351. "Rash of Racial Violence To Be Investigated By
F.B.I." New York Times. May 7, 1979, p. 12. .

1,352. Rawls, Wendell, Jr. "Klan Group In Alabama Training
For 'Race War'." New York Times. September 28,
1980, p. 26.

1,353. "Reagon Criticism Fails To Alienate Klansman."
New York Times. September 3, 1980, p. B15.

1,354. "Rearmament Of KKK In Wake Of Decatur, Ala., Incident Discussed." Chicago Tribune. June 3, 1979,
Sect. 3, p. 12.

1,355. Reed, Roy, "Dr. King To Step Up Drive For Alabama
Civil Rights." New York Times. March 28, 1965,
pp. 1,58.

1,356.   . "High Alabama Aid Lays Death To Klan,
Assails Police Head." New York Times. August 22,
1965, pp. 1,28.

1,357.   . "Klan Trial Jury Retires For Night."
New York Times. December 3, 1965, p. 35.

1,358.   . "Klansman Freed In Liuzzo Killing."
New York Times. October 23, 1965, pp. 1,21.

1,359.   . "Liuzzo Prosecutor Asks Juror Purge."
New York Times. October 20, 1965, pp. 1,29.

1,360.   . "2d Liuzzo Trial Will Open Today." New
York Times. October 18, 1965, p. 24.

1,361.   . "White Supremacist Jurors Approved In
Liuzzo Trial." New York Times. October 21, 1965,
pp. 1,28.

1,362.   . "Witness To Slaying Cites Harassment On
Road Earlier." New York Times. March 27, 1965,
pp. 1, 10.

1,363.   "Registration Check Reveals Half Of Kluxers Can't
         Vote In Ala." _Pittsburgh Courier_. October 1,
         1949, p. 11.

1,364.   Reid, T. R.   "FBI Embroiled In Controversy Over
         Klan Informer In Alabama." _Washington Post_. July
         12, 1978, p. A2.

1,365.   _____.   "Justice Dept. Vows Swift Probe Of FBI
         Informant's Role." _Washington Post_. July 13, 1978,
         p. A10.

1,366.   "Rights Aide Silent On Police-Klan Link." _New
         York Times_. May 23, 1961, p. 26.

1,367.   "Robed Alabama Mob Lashes Husband; Third Victim Of
         Hooded Gang In Week." _New York Times_. June 16,
         1949, p. 58.

1,368.   "Robert Creel." _New York Times_. August 1, 1965,
         p. 57.

1,369.   Roberts, Gene.   "A Negro Student Slain In Alabama."
         New York Times. January 5, 1966, pp. 1, 12.

1,370.   _____.   "Tuskegee Finds Slaying Witness." _New
         York Times_. January 6, 1966, p. 11.

1,371.   _____.   "U.S. Role Upheld In Selma Voting."
         New York Times. May 18, 1966, p. 24.

1,372.   Rogers, William W.   "Boyd Incident: Black Belt
         Violence During Reconstruction." _Civil War History_.
         Vol. 21, December, 1975, pp. 302-329.

1,373.   "R.R. Moton Wires K.K.K." _New York Amsterdam News_.
         August 8, 1923, p. 1.

1,374.   Rugaber, Walter.   "Carmichael, Out Of Jail, Leads
         A March In Alabama." _New York Times_. June 14,
         1967, p. 31.

1,375.   "The 'Sacred Bond'." _New York Times_. December 2,
         1927, p. 22.

1,376.   Salisbury, Harrison E.   "Race Issue Shakes Alabama
         Structure."   _New York Times_. April 13, 1960,
         pp. 1, 33.

1,377.   "Say Race Men Wore K.K.K." _Chicago Defender_.
         July 22, 1922, p. 13.

1,378.   "Says Alabama Klan Is Not In Politics." _New York
         Times_. December 29, 1929, Sect. 2, p. 1.

1,379.   "Says Mayor And Police Are Of Klan." Pittsburgh
          Courier. August 13, 1937, p. 1.

1,380.   "Says Moton Admitted Telegram." New York Amsterdam
          News. August 29, 1923, p. 1.

1,381.   Schieffelin, William J. "Most Unforgettable
          Character I've Met: R.R. Moton." Readers Digest.
          Vol. 57, November, 1950, pp. 25-28.

1,382.   _____. "Most Unforgettable Character I've Ever
          Met." The Negro Digest. Vol. 9, February, 1951,
          pp. 66-68.

1,383.   "Seek New Trial." Atlanta Daily World. March 5,
          1978, pp. 1,4.

1,384.   "Seeks Klan Delegation." New York Times. August
          10, 1927, p. 14.

1,385.   "Seize Klan Records In Alabama Inquiry." New York
          Times. October 15, 1927, p. 2.

1,386.   "Senator Of The Klan." Pittsburgh Courier. June
          9, 1928, editorial page.

1,387.   "Send The Klan A Message." New York Times. June
          8, 1979, p. A30.

1,388.   "Sentenced As Kidnapper." New York Times. August
          7, 1927, Sect. 2, p. 1.

1,389.   "A Settling Of Accounts." New York Times. Novem-
          ber 20, 1977, Sect. 4, p. 3.

1,390.   "7 Held In Alabama For Cross-Burning." New York
          Times. September 28, 1958, p. 11.

1,391.   "The Sheets, The Sheets!" Pittsburgh Courier.
          August 4, 1923, p. 8.

1,392.   "Shelton, Klan Leader, Goes To Prison For Con-
          tempt." New York Times. February 15, 1969, p. 13.

1,393.   Shepari, Scott. "KKK In Alabama." New York Times.
          September 19, 1978. p.6.

1,394.   Shepherd, William G. "The Whip Hand." Collier's.
          Vol. 81, January 7, 1928, pp. 8-9, 44-45.

1,395.   _____. "The Whip Wins." Collier's. Vol. 81,
          January 14, 1928, pp. 10-11, 30,32.

1,396.   "Shots In The Shadows." Newsweek. Vol. 49,
          February 4, 1957, p. 26.

1,397.   Sitton, Claude. "Activity Of Klan Rises In Alabama."
          New York Times. September 27, 1959, p. 59.

1,398.   _____. "Alabamans Act To Bar Violence At Uni-
          versity." New York Times. November 24, 1962,
          p. 10.

1,399.   _____. "U.S. Court Enjoins Freedom Riders In
          Alabama Trips." New York Times. June 3, 1961,
          pp. 1,18.

1,400.   _____. "Wallace Curbed In School Fight." New
          York Times. February 4, 1964, p. 22.

1,401.   Sloan, John Z. "The Ku Klux Klan And The Alabama
          Election of 1872." Alabama Review. Vol. 17,
          April, 1965, pp. 113-124.

1,402.   "Small Klan Group Marches." New York Times.
          December 1, 1980. p. B12.

1,403.   "Smith Hanged In Effigy." New York Times. July 8,
          1928, p. 2.

1,404.   Snell, William R. "Fiery Crosses In The Roaring
          Twenties: Activities Of The Revised Klan In Ala-
          bama, 1915-1930." Alabama Review. Vol. 23,
          October, 1970, pp. 256-276.

1,405.   "The South Learns Something." Pittsburgh Courier.
          October 29, 1927, Editorial page.

1,406.   "Squibbs." Pittsburgh Courier. July 21, 1923, p.
          8.

1,407.   "The State." New York Times. October 14, 1952,
          p. 35.

1,408.   Stephens, Harold W. "Mask And Lash In Crenshaw."
          North American Review. Vol. 225, April, 1928, pp.
          435-442.

1,409.   Stern, Laurence. "Klan Sex Lives Called Target."
          Washington Post. December 3, 1978, p. A4.

1,410.   Stuart, Reginald. "Kin Of Klan Victim Seek More
          Answers." New York Times. July 12, 1978, p. 11.

1,411.   "Subpoena The Klan." America. Vol. 96, February
          9, 1957, p. 520.

1,412.   "Suspect And 4 Seized." New York Times. September
          29, 1977, p. 18.

1,413.   "Take A Stand Against The Klan." Arizona Informant.
          March 11, 1981, p. 1.

1,414.   Tate, Franklin. "SCLC And KKK Debate." Birmingham
          (Ala.) Times. May 7-9, 1981, pp. 1,8.

1,415.   "Terror Inquiry To Resume." New York Times.
          July 27, 1949, p. 48.

1,416.   "Testimony Begins In Alabama Trial Of Black Man
          Who Shot Klansman." New York Times. September 30,
          1980, p. 16.

1,417.   "Third Klansman Is Arrested In Alabama March
          Violence." New York Times. May 30, 1979, p. 10.

1,418.   Thomas, Rex. "FBI Testimony Expected Today In
          Murder Case." New York Times. May 30, 1979, p. 10.

1,419:   _____. "Klansman Goes On Trial Today In Murder
          Case." The New York Bern (N.C.) Sun Journal.
          September 26, 1966.

1,420.   "Thomas Rowe's Involvement With Ku Klux Klan."
          National Observer. April 26, 1965, p. 2.

1,421.   Thompson, Jerry. "Alabama Doctor's Home Klan Re-
          cruiting Station." The Tennessean. December 9,
          1980.

1,422.   Thornton, J. Mills, III. "Alabama Politics, J.
          Thomas Heflin, And The Expulsion Movement of
          1929." Alabama Review. Vol. 21, April, 1968,
          pp. 83-112.

1,423.   "Threat Bars Parade." New York Times. December 18,
          1959, p. 18.

1,424.   "Threatens Subpoenas." New York Times. April 23,
          1965, p. 15.

1,425.   "3 Alabama Whites Seized In Blast At Negro Church."
          New York Times. December 14, 1964, p. 43.

1,426.   "Three Face Trial In Flogging Charge." Christian
          Science Monitor. November 1, 1949, p. 11.

1,427.   "3 Klansmen Gain Probation For Guilty Pleas In
          Violence." New York Times. June 23, 1979, p. 6.

1,428.   "3 Klansmen Held In Negro Torture." New York Times.
          September 8, 1957, p. 66.

1,429.   "3 KKK Members Win Probation In Ala." New Orleans
          Times, Picayune. June 24, 1979, p. 36.

1,430.   "3 Named As Klan Members Plead Not Guilty In
          Murder." New York Times. March 16, 1976, p. 18.

1,431.   "3 Whites Indicted In '57 Black Death." New York
         Times. March 6, 1976, p. 51.

1,432.   "Trial Starts For 2 In Racial Bombing." New York
         Times. May 28, 1957, p. 51.

1,433.   "To Try Alabama Floggers." New York Times. July
         10, 1927, p. 7.

1,434.   "To Try 34 Alabamans As Floggers." New York Times.
         November 21, 1927, p. 3.

1,435.   "Top Klan Official Quits In Alabama." New York
         Times. July 22, 1949, p. 38.

1,436.   "Transcript Of Johnson's Statement On The Arrests
         In Alabama." New York Times. March 27, 1965,
         p. 11.

1,437.   "Trial By Jury." Newsweek. Vol. 66, November 1,
         1965, p. 36.

1,438.   Trillin, Calvin. "U.S. Journal: Luverne, Ala:
         G.T. Miller's Plan." New Yorker. Vol. 46, August
         29, 1970, pp. 53-58.

1,439.   "Trio Jailed For Attacking Women." New York Times.
         July 27, 1927, p. 48.

1,440.   "The Tuskegee Case." Pittsburgh Courier. August
         4, 1923, p. 8.

1,441.   "Tuskegee Veteran's Hospital." Opportunity. Vol.
         2, January, 1924, p. 31.

1,442.   "20 Members Of Ku Klux Klan Indicated In Alabama."
         Washington Post. April 5, 1979, p. 2A.

1,443.   "Twice Flogged, Then Shot." New York Times.
         October 27, 1927, p. 1.

1,444.   "Two Crosses Burned." New York Times. January 24,
         1957, p. 30.

1,445.   "Two Held For Grand Jury." New York Times. May
         30, 1961, p. 7.

1,446.   "200 Ku Klux Klan Members Arrested Outside Mont-
         gomery, Alabama." Los Angeles Times. August 13,
         1979, p. 1.

1,447.   "Un-American Klan." Economist. Vol. 215, April
         3, 1965, pp. 48, 50.

1,448.   "Underwood Backs Fight Against Klan." New York
         Times. August 22, 1927, p. 22.

1,449.   "U.S. Asked To Ban Book In Alabama." New York
         Times. February 8, 1970, p. 27.

1,450.   "U.S. Atty. Brooks Drops Conspiracy Case Against
         4 Klansmen In Ala." New Orleans Times Picayune.
         June 9, 1979, p. 15.

1,451.   "U.S. Fails To Enjoin Birmingham Police." New York
         Times. June 1, 1961, pp. 1,23.

1,452.   "U.S. Judge Blocks Alabama From Prosecuting Infor-
         mer." New York Times. October 3, 1980, p. A12.

1,453.   "U.S. Justice Dept. Vows Probe Into FBI Agent's
         Role In KKK Case." Washington Post. July 13,
         1978, p. 10A.

1,454.   "U.S. Lawyers Link Klan To Violence." New York
         Times. May 31, 1961, p. 24.

1,455.   "Violence In Alabama." New York Times. June 12,
         1967, p. 88.

1,456.   "W.J. Simmons." New York Times. November 7, 1923,
         p. 15.

1,457.   "Wallace Is Urged To Check On Klan." New York
         Times. April 23, 1965, p. 15.

1,458.   "Want Roster Of Alabama Klan." Pittsburgh Courier.
         July 23, 1927, p. 1.

1,459.   Weisman, Steven R. "President Denounces The Klan."
         New York Times. September 2, 1980, pp. A1, B8.

1,460.   "What They Said Last Week." Pittsburgh Courier.
         July 21, 1923, p. 8.

1,461.   Wicker, Tom. "The Perennial Klan." New York Times.
         March 20, 1979, p. 19.

1,462.   _____. "New Life For The Klan." New York Times.
         March 18, 1979, Sect. 4, p. 21.

1,463.   "Wilkins Suggests Alabama Secede." New York Times.
         May 21, 1961, p. 77.

1,464.   Williams, Dennis A. "The Informant." Newsweek.
         Vol. 92, July 24, 1978, p. 41.

1,465.   "With Malice Afore Thought." Time. Vol. 55,
         March 13, 1950, p. 24.

1,466.   Wolf, Rebecca. "Hate Incidents Rising In Mont-
         gomery." Washington Post. January 21, 1982,
         p. Md. 6.

1,467.   Wooten, James T. "Black Muslims Would Sell Farm
          To Klan." New York Times. March 17, 1970, p. 32.

1,468.   "Worker Reporter In Kleagle's Ala. Office As He
          Phone - Talks." Daily Worker. February 12, 1956,
          p. 5.

1,469.   "Would End Klan Parades." New York Times. May
          26, 1922, p. 30.

2. ARIZONA

1,470.   Abbey, Sue W. "The Ku Klux Klan In Arizona, 1921-
          1925." Journal of Arizona History. Vol. 14,
          Spring, 1973, pp. 10-30.

1,471.   "Ariz. Meads To Probe Klan Label As 'Equal Oppor-
          tunity Employer'." Los Angeles Times. June 2,
          1980, Sect. 3, p. 11.

1,472.   "Arizona To Probe Decision To List Klan Equal
          Opportunity Employer." San Francisco Chronicle.
          June 2, 1980, p. 1.

1,473.   "Arizona To Probe Listing Of KKK As Equal Oppor-
          tunity Employer." Chicago Tribune. June 2, 1980,
          p. 15.

1,474.   "Brand 'K' On Breast Of Man." Chicago Defender.
          April 1, 1922, p. 1.

1,475.   "KKK" 'Equal Opportunity Employer'." Washington
          Post. June 2, 1980, p. A2.

1,476.   "KKK Offers Jobs To All In Sheet-Sewing Drive."
          Jet. Vol. 58, June 19, 1980, p. 5.

1,477.   "Klan Candidate Loses In Arizona." New York Times.
          September 11, 1924, p. 3.

1,478.   "A Needed Discrimination." New York Times.
          June 4, 1980, p. B20.

1,479.   "Posted In Arkansas." Washington Daily News.
          May 20, 1959, p. 2.

1,480.   "Two Indictments." New York Times. June 20, 1922,
          p. 21.

3. ARKANSAS

1,481.   Alexander, Charles C. "Defeat, Decline, Disintegra-
          tion: The Ku Klux Klan In Arkansas, 1924 and After."
          Arkansas Historical Quarterly. Vol. 22, Winter,
          1963, pp. 310-331.

1,482. _____. "White Robes In Politics: The Ku Klux Klan In Arkansas, 1922-1924." _Arkansas Historical Quarterly_. Vol. 22, Fall, 1963, pp. 195-214.

1,483. _____. "White Robed Reformers: The Ku Klux Klan Come To Arkansas, 1921-1922." _Arkansas Historical Quarterly_. Vol. 22, Spring, 1963, pp. 8-23.

1,484. "Ambushers Plead Guilty." _New York Times_. November 22, 1922, p. 9.

1,485. "Arkansas To Bar Klansmen From Jury." _New York Amsterdam News_. December 13, 1922, p. 3.

1,486. "Arson Attempt Fails." _New York Times_. June 10, 1959, p. 74.

1,487. "Black Man And The Ku Klux Klan Letter." _San Francisco Chronicle_. June 11, 1979, p. 42.

1,488. "Black Man Plans Barbeque For Ku Klux Klan Rally In Arkansas." _San Francisco Chronicle_. June 2, 1979, p. 5.

1,489. "Dislikes Ku Klux Klan." _New York Times_. September 6, 1958, p. 6.

1,490. "Imperial Wizard Suing Klan Head For $100,000." _Pittsburgh Courier_. June 9, 1923, p. 2.

1,491. "Klan Ambushed, 1 Killed." _New York Times_. November 17, 1922, p. 4.

1,492. "Klan Candidate Second In Arkansas." _New York Times_. August 13, 1924, p. 1.

1,493. "Klan Leader Is Arrested." _New York Times_. June 10, 1979, p. 26.

1,494. "Klan Leader Says F.B.I. Financed Some Factions." _New York Times_. June 19, 1979, p. 18.

1,495. "Klan Loses In Arkansas." _New York Times_. August 14, 1924, p. 2.

1,496. "Ku Klux Klan Murders, Flogs In Southwest." _Chicago Defender_. December 24, 1921, p. 2.

1,497. "Masked Vigilanters Kill 1 In Arkansas." _New York Times_. November 30, 1922, p. 14.

1,498. "McRae First In Arkansas." _New York Times_. August 9, 1922, p. 6.

1,499. "Mechanic Is Guilty In Death of Negro." _New York Times_. February 27, 1966, p. 44.

1,500.   Reed, Roy. "Widespread Racial Violence Persists In
         Eastern Arkansas Farming Area." New York Times.
         October 10, 1971, p. 55.

1,501.   Sitton, Claude. "Farbus To Resist Any Interferring
         By Federal Force." New York Times. September 3,
         1958, pp. 1,23.

1,502.   _____. "Little Rock Asks Peace At Schools."
         New York Times. August 11, 1959, pp. 1,16.

1,503.   "Sues Klan Emperor For $100,00." New York Times.
         May 25, 1923, p. 6.

1,504.   "Suspect In Murder Called A Klansman." New York
         Times. February 26, 1966, p. 22.

1,505.   "10,000 In Klan Parade At Little Rock, Ark."
         New York Times. July 5, 1924, p. 6.

1,506.   "Will Break Ground For $125,000 Hospital To Be
         Erected By Klansmen At El Dorado, Arkansas."
         Imperial Night-Hawk. June 27, 1923, p. 8.

4. CALIFORNIA

1,507.   "ACLU And KKK At Camp Pendleton." Los Angeles
         Times. December 30, 1976, Sect. 2, p. 4.

1,508.   "ACLU Files Suit Against Marine Corps On Behalf
         Of KKK." New Orleans Times Picayune. February
         10, 1977, p. 2.

1,509.   "ACLU Represents Both Sides In Marine Corp - Ku
         Klux Klan Case." Los Angeles Times. December 24,
         1976, Sect. 2, p. 1.

1,510.   "ACLU Role In Ku Klux Klan Suit Against Marine
         Corps. Discussed." Washington Post. January 29,
         1977, p. 4A.

1,511.   "ACLU Role In Camp Pendleton KKK Issue." Los
         Angeles Times. January 13, 1977, Sect. 2, p. 4.

1,512.   "ACLU Sues Marine Corps In Behalf of Ku Klux Klan."
         Los Angeles Times. February 10, 1977, p. 18.

1,513.   "ACLU Sues Pentagon In Behalf of Klansmen." New
         York Times. February 11, 1979, p. 14.

1,514.   "ACLU To File Suit In Behalf Of Camp Pendleton Ku
         Klux Klan." Los Angeles Times. December 10,
         1976, p. 10.

1,515.   "ADL Praises California Law On Extremist Groups
         Training Camps." Atlanta Daily World. November
         3, 1981. p. 3.

1,516.   "AFL In California Hits Reds In Films." New York
          Times. June 19, 1946, p. 18.

1,517.   "Allegations Of Ku Klux Klan Unit On Marine Base
          Discussed." Chicago Tribune. January 30, 1977,
          p. 20.

1,518.   "American First Gives Calif. Kluxer $500." People's
          Voice. May 4, 1946, p. 11.

1,519.   "American Legion In California Calls KKK Un-Ameri-
          can." San Francisco Examiner. May 4, 1922, p. 17.

1,520.   "An Inside Look At Cal. KKK's Preparations For
          Imperial Wizard." San Francisco Chronicle.
          February 9, 1981, p. 1.

1,521.   "Anaheim Ousts Klan Trustee." New York Times.
          February 4, 1925, p. 2.

1,522.   "Anti-KKK Bill Topic Of Debate." Watts (Calif.)
          Star Review. June 5, 1981, p. 1.

1,523.   "Anti-Klan Group Wrecks Frisco Theater Showing 1915
          Birth Of A Nation." Variety. Vol. 299, June 18,
          1980, p. 1.

1,524.   "Anti-Klan Protest Leads To Melee." New York
          Times. July 31, 1978, p. 10.

1,525.   "Anti-Ku Klux Klan Melee In Oxnard, California
          Eyed." Houston Post. August 1, 1978, p. 2A.

1,526.   "Anti-Nazi, Anti-Klan Bill Okayed By Cal. Senate."
          Los Angeles Times. July 10, 1981, Sect. 2, p. 6.

1,527.   "Atty. Leonard Weinglass To Serve In Camp Pendleton
          KKK Case." Los Angeles Times. January 13, 1977,
          p. 25.

1,528.   "Authorities Don't Plan To Interfere With KKK
          Border Patrol." Los Angeles Times. October 20,
          1977, p. 3.

1,529.   "Backs LaFollette To 'Save' Capitalism." New York
          Times. October 25, 1924, p. 10.

1,530.   "Being Stupid Held A Right As Judge Rules For Klan."
          Durham Morning Herald. September 29, 1966.

1,531.   "Bell Orders Ku Klux Klan To Disband Border Patrol."
          New York Times. October 28, 1977, p. 10.

1,532.   "Bill Outlawing Violence." Criminal Justice Issues.
          Vol. 6, June, 1981, p. 10.

1,533.   "Black Lawyers In Calif. Urge Outlawing Of KKK."
         Jet. Vol. 59, November 13, 1980, p. 8.

1,534.   "Black Marine Admits Attack On Whites At Camp
         Pendleton." Los Angeles Times. December 30, 1976,
         p. 3.

1,535.   "Black Marine Is Fined In Barracks Attack." New
         York Times. September 16, 1977, p. 16.

1,536.   "Black Marine Sentenced For Attack At Camp Pendle-
         ton." Los Angeles Times. January 14, 1977, p. 21.

1,537.   "Black Marine Sentenced For Camp Pendleton Attack."
         Los Angeles Times. June 23, 1977, p. 18.

1,538.   "Black Marines Battle Ku Klux Klan At Camp Pendle-
         ton Base." Black Scholar. Vol. 8, April, 1977,
         pp. 46-49.

1,539.   "Brown Still Around." Washington Star. November
         2, 1980, p. A2.

1,540.   Browning, Frank. "Ku Klux Klan Pushes To Recruit
         More Youths As Terrorism Escalates." (Howard
         University) Hilltop. November 20, 1981, pp. 2,8.

1,541.   "Cal. Assembly Candidate Welcomes KKK Endorsement."
         Los Angeles Times. May 24, 1976, p. 2.

1,542.   "Cal. Assembly Com. Okays Diluted Version Of Klan-
         Nazi Bill." Los Angeles Times. August 18, 1981,
         p. 21.

1,543.   "Cal. Atty. Gen. Deukmejian Pushes For Law To
         Banish KKK." San Francisco Chronicle. January
         30, 1981, p. 6.

1,544.   "Cal. Atty. Gen. Warns Of Ku Klux Klan Growth In
         The State." San Francisco Chronicle. September
         30, 1980, p. 1.

1,545.   "Cal. Cities Refusal To Issue Permits May Halt Klan
         Protest." Los Angeles Times. November 7, 1979,
         Sect. 2, p. 8.

1,546.   "Cal. Dem. Party Disavows Klansman's Candidacy
         For Congress." Los Angeles Times. June 22, 1980,
         p. 3.

1,547.   "Cal. Dem. Party Disavows Nomination Of Ku Klux
         Klan Leader." San Francisco Chronicle. June 23,
         1980, p. 9.

1,548.   "Cal. Dems. Won't Support Klansman Who Won Con-
         gressional Primary." Houston Post. June 5, 1980,
         p. 8A.

1,549.   "Cal. Democrats Begin Conv. With Denial Of KKK
Member." San Francisco Chronicle. January 17,
1981, p. 8.

1,550.   "Cal. Democratic Leaders Endorse GOP Candidate
Over Klansman." Los Angeles Times. June 6, 1980,
Sect. 2, p. 2.

1,551.   "Cal. Gov. Brown Forms Task Force To Counteract
Ku Klux Klan." San Francisco Chronicle. June 24,
1980, p. 10.

1,552.   "Calif. Legis. To Outlaw Bad Ideas - Letters."
Los Angeles Times. February 9, 1981, Sect. 2, p. 8.

1,553.   "Cal. Sen. Watson Defends Bill Aimed At Ku Klux
Klan." Los Angeles Times. January 30, 1981, p. 3.

1,554.   "Cal. Sen. Watson's Letter On U.S. Freedom -
Letters." Los Angeles Times. March 3, 1981,
Sect. 2, p. 4.

1,555.   "Cal. Senate Com. Actions On Banning Racist Orgs."
Los Angeles Times. May 1, 1981, Sect. 2, p. 10

1,556.   "Cal. Senate Com. Clears Anti-Ku Klux Klan Bill."
Los Angeles Times. June 4, 1981, p. 3.

1,557.   "Cal. Officials Probe Ku Klux Klan Detective
Agency." Washington Post. December 14, 1979,
p. 46A.

1,558.   "Cal. Senate Com. Okays Bill Outlawing Klan And
Other Racist Groups." Los Angeles Times. April
30, 1981, p. 3.

1,559.   "Cal. Senate Okays Bill Designed To Block KKK And
Nazi Protests." Los Angeles Times. July 9, 1981,
p. 3.

1,560.   "Calif. Senate Oks Bill To Reduce KKK Violence."
Jet. Vol. 60, August 6, 1981, p. 8.

1,561.   "Cal. Sen. Watson Writes Letter On Feb. 4th Editorial On Freedom." Los Angeles Times. February
22, 1981, Sect. 5, p. 4.

1,562.   "California Gets KKK." Greensboro Daily News.
September 30, 1966, p. 1.

1,563.   "California KKK Charter Revoked." New York Times.
May 22, 1946, p. 23.

1,564.   "California Klan Planning Directory Of Businesses."
New York Times. September 21, 1977, p. 16.

1,565.   "California Klansman Runs For Congress." National Catholic Reporter. Vol. 16, July 4, 1980, pp. 6-7.

1,566.   "California Klux Shake-Up." New York Times. May 25, 1922, p. 10.

1,567.   "Camp Pendleton Black Marines Case." Washington Post. December 9, 1976.

1,568.   "Camp Pendleton Comdr. Says Some KKK Members Transferred." Los Angeles Times. November 30, 1976, p. 3.

1,569.   "Camp Pendleton KKK Leader Transferred To East Coast Air Base." Los Angeles Times. December 4, 1976, Sect. 2, p. 1.

1,570.   "Catholic Diocese Of San Diego Urges Resistance To Ku Klux Klan." Los Angeles Times. October 3, 1980, Sect. 2, p. 8.

1,571.   "Chavez Suggests The Possibility Of Nationwide Lettuce Boycott." New York Times. February 11, 1979, p. 58.

1,572.   "Civil Rights Activist Jesse Jackson Eyes Camp Pendleton Case." Los Angeles Times. December 9, 1976, p. 25.

1,573.   "Civilian Atty. Clashes With Presiding Officer In Marine KKK Case." Los Angeles Times. January 1, 1977, p. 16.

1,574.   "Claim That Marine Klansmen Remain At Pendleton Disputed." Los Angeles Times. November 25, 1977, p. 34.

1,575.   "The Clansman Strikes Rocks In Sacramento." Chicago Defender. May 13, 1922, p. 1.

1,576.   "Coast AFL Orders Communist Inquiry." New York Times. June 22, 1946, p. 9.

1,577.   "College Board Approves Anti-KKK Resolution." Los Angeles Herald-Dispatch. May 1, 1981, p. 1.

1,578.   "Community Leaders Blast KKK Recruitment Booth In S.B. Central City Mall." Precinct (San Bernadino) Reporter. September 17, 1981, p. 3.

1,579.   "Conditions Causing Racial Friction Ordered Curbed." Christian Science Monitor. December 17, 1976, p. 2.

1,580.   "Constable Killed In Ku Klux Raid." New York Times. April 26, 1972, p. 4.

1,581.   "Defendants In Camp Pendleton KKK Case File For Venue Change." Los Angeles Times. January 27, 1977, p. 2.

1,582.   "Dem. Party Challenges KKK Member Metzger's Right To Com. Seat." Los Angeles Times. January 17, 1981, p. 23.

1,583.   "Democratic Party Views Cal. Victories By Dymally And Metzger." Los Angeles Times. June 5, 1980, p. 3.

1,584.   "Democrats Disavow Nominee From Klan." New York Times. June 6, 1980, p. 17.

1,585.   "Demonstrators Assemble Outside Showing Of Movie For KKK In Cal." Washington Post. July 31, 1978, p. 15A.

1,586.   "Demonstrators Battle Oxnard, Cal. Police At KKK Meeting." Chicago Tribune. July 31, 1978, p. 3.

1,587.   "Demonstrators Disrupt Ku Klux Klan Meeting In Castro Valley." San Francisco Chronicle. August 20, 1979, p. 1.

1,588.   "Demonstrators And Klansmen Clash Outside Marine Hearing." Washington Post. December 7, 1976.

1,589.   "Demonstrators On Coast Clash With Klan Members." New York Times. August 21, 1979, p. 15.

1,590.   "Denounces Ku Klux Klan." New York Times. May 21, 1922, p. 12.

1,591.   "Developments Concerning Camp Pendleton And Ku Klux Klan Viewed." Los Angeles Times. December 2, 1976, p. 3.

1,592.   "Dispute Erupts Within San Diego Chapter Of ACLU Over KKK." New Orleans Times Picayune. January 30, 1977, p. 2.

1,593.   Dumas, Carol. "KKK Rally Flops." Sacramento Observer. April 2-8, 1981, p. F1.

1,594.   "Eight Black Marines In KKK Case Seek Release." Los Angeles Times. February 17, 1977, p. 24.

1,595.   "Eight Black Marines In KKK Case Win Release." Los Angeles Times. February 20, 1977, p. 15.

1,596.   Emmons, Steve. "Anaheim Regime: Once It Was The Klan." Los Angeles Times. September 6, 1970, p. G8.

1,597. "Firearms Found In Car Of Camp Pendleton KKK Leader."
        Los Angeles Times. December 5, 1976, Sect. 2, p. 6.

1,598. "Fiery Cross Burns Again." New York Times. July
        15, 1946, p. 25.

1,599. "Fontana, Cal. School Board Allows KKK To Use
        School For Rally." Los Angeles Sentinel. Novem-
        ber 5, 1981, p. 4A.

1,600. "Fontana Police Separate Groups During Protest
        Against KKK." Los Angeles Times. August 10, 1980,
        p. 20.

1,601. "Former Members Liken Black Panthers To The Klan."
        New York Times. April 9, 1969, p. 44.

1,602. "43rd Congressional Dst. Candidate Tom Metzger."
        Los Angeles Times. June 15, 1980, Sect. 5, p. 4.

1,603. "43rd Dst. Residents Tell Reasons For Giving
        Klansman Victory." Los Angeles Times. June 15,
        1980, p. 1; June 16, 1980, p. 3.

1,604. "43 Klansmen Indicted For California Raid;
        Accused Of Kidnapping And Intent To Murder." New
        York Times. June 8, 1922, p. 1.

1,605. "14 Camp Pendleton Marines May Face Attempted
        Murder Charges." Los Angeles Times. December 8,
        1976, Sect. 2, p. 1.

1,606. "14 Robed KKK Members Hold Rally Across From Cal.
        Capitol Bldg." San Francisco Chronicle. April 2,
        1981, p. 3.

1,607. Good, Neil. "Cal. Politics Allowing Klansmen To
        Win." Los Angeles Times. September 10, 1980,
        Sect. 2, p. 5.

1,608. "GOP Rep. Burgener's Campaign Against Klansman
        Metzger Viewed." Los Angeles Times. November 3,
        1980, Sect. 2, p. 1.

1,609. "The Grand Dragon Runs For Congress." Present
        Tense. Vol. 8, Summer, 1981, pp. 25-30.

1,610. Holles, Everett R. "Marines In Klan Openly Abused
        Blacks At Pendleton, Panel Hears." New York Times.
        January 9, 1977, p. 34.

1,611. Holles, Everett R. "Suit Defending Klan Causing
        Dissension In Coast A.C.L.U." New York Times.
        February 20, 1977, p. 20.

1,612. "Increasing KKK Activities In California." San
        Francisco Chronicle. March 2, 1981, p. 40.

1,613. "Intelligence Probe Of KKK Unit At Camp Pendleton Under Way." Los Angeles Times. December 12, 1976, p. 83.

1,614. "Intruders Not Welcome." New York Times. October 21, 1977, p. 18.

1,615. "Investigation Of KKK Incident At Camp Pendleton Continues." Los Angeles Times. November 29, 1976, p. 3.

1,616. "The Invisible Empire In Los Angeles." San Francisco Chronicle. March 7, 1922, p. 1.

1,617. "KKK Activity In California Discussed." Bilalian News. November 6, 1981, p. 11.

1,618. "The KKK Candidate For Congress." Newsweek. Vol. 95, June 16, 1980, p. 27.

1,619. "KKK Candidate Metzger's Meeting With Neo-Nazi Fugitive Discussed." San Francisco Chronicle. October 23, 1980, p. 1.

1,620. "KKK Congressional Candidate Pelted With Cans In San Diego." Los Angeles Times. July 15, 1980, Sect. 2, p. 6.

1,621. "KKK Cross Burning In Ceres, Cal." San Francisco Chronicle. February 24, 1981, p. 36.

1,622. "KKK Cross Burning Stirs Up Ceres, Cal." San Francisco Chronicle. February 23, 1981, p. 1.

1,623. "KKK Leader Metzger Surprised To Learn He Is Not NAACP Member." San Francisco Chronicle. February 19, 1981, p. 3.

1,624. "KKK Leader Tom Metzger - Letters." Los Angeles Times. April 23, 1978, Sect. 6, p. 4.

1,625. "KKK Member Losing U.S. Congressional Race In San Diego City." San Francisco Chronicle. November 5, 1980, p. 3.

1,626. "KKK Member Ousted As Cal. Dem. Delegate, N. Pelosi Named Chmn." San Francisco Chronicle. January 18, 1981, Sect. B, p. 1.

1,627. "KKK Official Metzger's Bid For Cal. Congressional Seat Viewed." Los Angeles Times. May 29, 1980, p. 3.

1,628. "KKK Recruitment Rally In San Jose Ended By Protesters." San Francisco Chronicle. April 12, 1981, p. 4.

1,629,   "KKK, South Africa Get Official Greenlight." Pre-
          cinct (San Bernardino) Reporter. September 17,
          1981, p. 1.

1,630.   "KKK's Use Of Goon Tactics On Calif. Bar." Houston
          Post. December 12, 1977, p. 2C.

1,631.   "Klan." Washington Post. October 4, 1980, p. A4.

1,632.   "Klan Candidate." Washington Star. October 29,
          1980, p. A8.

1,633.   "Klan Charge Was Blow To Sen. McAdoo." N.Y.
          Amsterdam News. September 10, 1938, Sect. 2, p. 2.

1,634.   "Klan 'Border Watch' Ignites Stormy Debate."
          Christian Science Monitor. November 1, 1977, p. 26.

1,635.   "Klan Film-Showing Provokes Tension." Washington
          Post. July 31, 1978, p. A15.

1,636.   "Klan Gobbles Up Los Angeles Cops One By One."
          Chicago Defender. April 22, 1922, p. 1.

1,637.   "Klan Held Active In Marine Base." New York Times.
          November 28, 1976, p. 12.

1,638.   "Klan Leader Is Expected To Be Democratic Nominee."
          New York Times. June 3, 1980, p. B10.

1,639.   "Klan Leader Loses." Washington Star. November 5,
          1980, p. A8.

1,640.   "Klan Leader Says Blacks Attacked Wrong Marines."
          New York Times. November 29, 1976, p. 18.

1,641.   "Klan Leader Says Blacks Attacked Wrong Marines In
          California." Houston Post. November 29, 1976,
          p. 12A.

1,642.   "Klan Member Running In Cal.'s 43rd Congressional
          District Noted." San Francisco Chronicle. June 1,
          1980, p. 18A.

1,643.   "Klan Member Wins Calif. Primary In Most Populous
          District In U.S." Washington Star. June 5, 1980,
          pp. A5.

1,644.   "Klan Opponent Hooted." New York Times. August 23,
          1922, p. 32.

1,645.   "Klan Pickets Attacked." New York Times. December
          7, 1976, p. 22.

1,646.   "Klan Symbol Fired At Home Of Family Battling Re-
          strictions." Los Angeles Sentinel. May 16, 1946.

1,647.   "Klan Temple Is Destroyed By Explosion." _Pittsburgh Courier_. December 4, 1926, p. 8.

1,648.   "Klan To Clean City Of Vice." _Chicago Defender_. May 13, 1922, p. 16.

1,649.   "Klan Vows Revenge After Fight." _New York Times_. March 17, 1980, p. B11.

1,650.   "The Klandidate." _Nation_. Vol. 231, July 5, 1980, p. 4-5.

1,651.   "Klansman Candidate Calls For End To Affirmative Action Programs." _San Francisco Chronicle_. May 5, 1980, p. 9.

1,652.   " 'Klansman' Disappears Again." _New York Times_. April 24, 1965, p. 19.

1,653.   "Klansman Gets Life Prison Term In Death Of Member, An Informer." _New York Times_. June 17, 1979, p. 10.

1,654.   "Klansman, Hoping For 2d Surprise, Wages Lonely Campaign On Coast." _New York Times_. August 31, 1980, p. 42.

1,655.   "Klansmen Interviewed On Ku Klux Klan Members On Cal. Marine Base." _Washington Post_. December 3, 1976, p. 1.

1,656.   "Klansman Joins NAACP." _New York Recorder_. February 21, 1981, p. 12.

1,657.   "Klansman Metzger Discusses Loss To U.S. Rep. Burgener." _Los Angeles Times_. November 6, 1980, Sect. 2, p. 1.

1,658.   "Klansman Running For Congress Finds Support In Rural California." _Washington Star_. June 9, 1980, p. A3.

1,659.   "Klansman Running For Congressional Seat - Gratsmith Cartoon." _San Francisco Chronicle_. June 13, 1980, p. 50.

1,660.   "Klansman Running For Congress Ousted By San Diego Democrats." _New York Times_. October 29, 1980, p. A22.

1,661.   "Klansman Tom Metzger Names Fellow Member To Cal. Dem. Post." _Los Angeles Times_. June 8, 1980, Sect. 2, p. 5.

1,662.   "Klansman Tom Metzger's Political Message To The People Viewed." _San Francisco Chronicle_. June 16, 1980, p. 8.

1,663.   "Klansman Tom Metzger Reports On Campaign Gifts In
          House Race." Los Angeles Times. October 27, 1980,
          Sect. 2, p. 4.

1,664.   "Klansman Wins Calif. Congressional Primary." Jet.
          Vol. 58, June 26, 1980, p. 5.

1,665.   "Klansman's Victory In Congressional Race In Cal.
          Confirmed." San Francisco Chronicle. June 18,
          1980, p. 44.

1,666.   "Klansman's Victory For U.S. House Bid-Interland:
          Cartoon." Los Angeles Times. June 19, 1980,
          Sect. 2, p. 7.

1,667.   "Klansmen Stoned In San Jose." New York Times.
          April 12, 1981, p. 36.

1,668.   "Klux Write Death Notes To Pastor." Chicago
          Defender. May 27, 1922, p. 3.

1,669.   "Kluxers Are Busy Again In California." Pittsburgh
          Courier. February 5, 1927, p. 3.

1,670.   "Ku Klux Klan Accused Of Trying To Exploit Oxnard
          Slayings." Los Angeles Times. July 22, 1978,
          Sect. 2, p. 1.

1,671.   "Ku Klux Klan Activity In California." Chicago
          Defender. November 3, 1979, p. 6.

1,672.   "Ku Klux Klan At Camp Pendleton - Letter." Los
          Angeles Times. February 8, 1977, Sect. 2, p. 4.

1,673.   "Ku Klux Klan Comes To California." San Francisco
          Examiner. January 2, 1921, p. 70.

1,674.   "Ku Klux Klan Endorses Candidate In California."
          Washington Post. May 25, 1976, p. 1.

1,675.   "Ku Klux Klan Gets Approval For Oceanside, Cal.
          Rally." Los Angeles Times. September 1, 1979,
          Sect. 2, p. 1.

1,676.   "Ku Klux Klan Holds Rally In San Luis Obispo." San
          Francisco Chronicle. November 18, 1979, p. 10A.

1,677.   "Ku Klux Klan In Bakersfield (California)." Bakers-
          field Daily Californian. October 10, 1921, p. 1.

1,678.   "Ku Klux Klan In Bakersfield (California)."
          Bakersfield Daily Californian. February 21, 1922,
          p. 1; March 4, 1922, p. 1.

1,679.   "Ku Klux Klan In Bakersfield (California)."
          Bakersfield Daily Californian. January 15, 1923,
          p. 1.

1,680.   "Ku Klux Klan In Bakersfield (California)."
          San Francisco Examiner. February 22, 1922, p. 13.

1,681.   "Ku Klux Klan In Berkeley (California)." San
          Francisco Examiner. April 3, 1923, p. 1.

1,682.   "Ku Klux Klan In California," San Francisco
          Examiner. May 25, 1922, p. 1.

1,683.   "Ku Klux Klan In California." Interpreter Of
          Americanism. July 17, 1922, p. 1.

1,684.   "Ku Klux Klan In California." Los Angeles Times.
          October 8, 1946, p. 9.

1,685.   "KKK Incident At Camp Pendleton." Los Angeles
          Times. December 5, 1976, Sect. 8, p. 19.

1,686.   "Ku Klux Klan In Fresno (California)." Bakersfield
          Daily Californian. May 5, 1922, p. 1.

1,687.   "Ku Klux Klan In Fresno (California)." Los Angeles
          Times. June 6, 1922, p. 1.

1,688.   "Ku Klux Klan In Fresno (California)." San
          Francisco Chronicle. April 29, 1922, p. 2.

1,689.   "Ku Klux Klan In Fresno (California)." San
          Francisco Examiner. May 2, 1922, p. 8; May 3, 1922,
          p. 1.

1,690.   "Ku Klux Klan In Hanford (California)." Los Angeles
          Times. April 30, 1922, p. 1.

1,691.   "Ku Klux Klan In Kern County (California)." Bakers-
          field Daily Californian. July 27, 1922, p. 1.

1,692.   "The Ku Klux Klan In Kern County (California)."
          Midway Driller. March 10, 1922, p. 1.

1,693.   "Ku Klux Klan In Kern County (California)."
          San Francisco Chronicle. March 5, 1922, p. 10.

1,694.   "Ku Klux Klan In King County (California)." Los
          Angeles Times. May 7, 1922, p. 2.

1,695.   "Ku Klux Klan In Los Angeles." Los Angeles Times.
          July 19, 1921, p. 17.

1,696.   "Ku Klux Klan In Maryville (California)." San
          Francisco Chronicle. March 10, 1922, p. 7.

1,697.   "Ku Klux Klan In Modesto (California)." Bakersfield
          Daily Californian. May 2, 1922, p. 2.

1,698.   "Ku Klux Klan In Modesto (California)." San
          Francisco Chronicle. November 18, 1923, p. 53.

1,699.   "Ku Klux Klan In Monterey - Santa Cruz (California)."
          San Francisco Examiner. December 22, 1923, p. 5.

1,700.   "Ku Klux Klan In Northern California." San
          Francisco Chronicle. October 5, 1922, p. 1.

1,701.   "Ku Klux Klan In Oakland (California)." San
          Francisco Chronicle. March 12, 1922, p. 48.

1,702.   "Ku Klux Klan In Palo Alto (California)." San
          Francisco Chronicle. December 11, 1923, p. 1.

1,703.   "Ku Klux Klan In Red Bluff (California)." San
          Francisco Examiner. May 17, 1922, p. 2.

1,704.   "Ku Klux Klan In Richmond (California)." Richmond
          Daily Independent. June 24, 1924, p. 9.

1,705.   "Ku Klux Klan In Richmond (California)." Richmond
          Daily Independent. September 6, 1924, p. 1.

1,706.   "Ku Klux Klan In Roseville (California)." Sacra-
          mento Bee. April 18, 1923, p. 9.

1,707.   "Ku Klux Klan In Roseville (California)." Sacra-
          mento Bee. August 26, 1923, p. 1.

1,708.   "Ku Klux Klan In Roseville (California)." San
          Francisco Examiner. February 16, 1923, p. 8.

1,709.   "Ku Klux Klan In Sacramento (California)."
          Sacramento Bee. April 10, 1922, p. 1.

1,710.   "Ku Klux Klan In Sacramento (California)." Sacra-
          mento Bee. May 4, 1922, p. 1.

1,711.   "Ku Klux Klan In Sacramento (California)." San
          Francisco Chronicle. July 28, 1921, p. 17.

1,712.   "Ku Klux Klan In Sacramento (California)." San
          Francisco Examiner. May 6, 1921, pp. 2,14.

1,713.   "Ku Klux Klan In San Francisco." San Francisco
          Chronicle. March 9, 1922, p. 24.

1,714.   "Ku Klux Klan In San Francisco." San Francisco
          Examiner. April 28, 1922, p. 28.

1,715.   "Ku Klux Klan In San Francisco." San Francisco
          Examiner. May 14, 1922, p. 1.

1,716.   "Ku Klux Klan In San Joaquin Valley (California)."
          San Francisco Examiner. July 7, 1921, p. 7.

1,717.   "Ku Klux Klan In San Jose (California)." San Francisco Chronicle. March 15, 1922, p. 18.

1,718.   "Ku Klux Klan In San Jose (California)." San Francisco Examiner. September 23, 1921, p. 6.

1,719.   "Ku Klux Klan In San Mateo (California)." San Francisco Chronicle. March 27, 1922, p. 5.

1,720.   "Ku Klux Klan In Santa Cruz (California)." San Francisco Chronicle. June 6, 1924, p. 1.

1,721.   "Ku Klux Klan In Stockton (California)." San Francisco Chronicle. September 20, 1921, p. 6.

1,722.   "Ku Klux Klan In Stockton (California)." San Francisco Chronicle. October 19, 1922, p. 1.

1,723.   "Ku Klux Klan Member Addresses Paramount City Council." Los Angeles Times. March 4, 1981, Sect. 2, p. 3.

1,724.   "Ku Klux Klan Members At Camp Pendleton." Los Angeles Times. December 7, 1976, Sect. 2, p. 7.

1,725.   "Ku Klux Klan Members Clash With Oceanside Hecklers At Rally." San Francisco Chronicle. March 17, 1980, p. 6.

1,726.   "Ku Klux Klan Near Oakland (California)." San Francisco Chronicle. March 4, 1922, p. 2.

1,727.   "Ku Klux Klan Plans Border Patrol To Help Fight Illegal Alien Problem." New York Times. October 18, 1977, p. 80.

1,728.   "Ku Klux Klan Plan To Use Oceanside, Cal. Park Causes Dispute." Los Angeles Times. August 16, 1979, Sect. 2, p. 1.

1,729.   "Ku Klux Klan Rally In Oceanside Ends Following Clash With Crowd." Los Angeles Times. March 16, 1980, p. 3.

1,730.   "KKK Showing Of Movie,"Birth Of Nation,"Causes Demonstration." New Orleans Times Picayune. July 31, 1978, p. 5.

1,731.   "Ku Klux Klan Signs Found In The 'Angel City'." Pittsburgh Courier. May 22, 1937, p. 24

1,732.   "Ku Klux Klan Sues Paper." New York Times. August 4, 1921, p. 15.

1,733.   "Ku Klux Klan Threats Close Bar In Lakeside, California." New Orleans Times Picayune. December 4, 1977, p. 8.

1,734.   "Ku Klux Klansman Tom Metzger's Bid For Congres-
          sional Seat Viewed." Los Angeles Times. April
          24, 1980, Sect. 2, p. 1.

1,735.   Kotkin, Joel. "Calif. Klansman Nominated For
          Congress As Democrat." Washington Post. June 8,
          1980, p. A4.

1,736.   "JDL Protests ACLU Defense Of Klan Activities At
          Camp Pendleton." Los Angeles Times. December 15,
          1976, p. 35.

1,737.   "Judge Grants Acquittal Of Black Marine In Camp
          Pendleton Case." Los Angeles Times. February 1,
          1977, p. 20.

1,738.   "Latin Groups Call On Fed. And State Officials To
          Halt Klan Patrols." Los Angeles Times. October
          21, 1977, p. 3.

1,739.   "Leader Of Camp Pendleton KKK Struck Outside Ct.
          Hearing Site." Los Angeles Times. December 7,
          1976, Sect. 2, p. 3.

1,740.   "Leftists Storm KKK Show In Oxnard, Calif."
          Christian Science Monitor. August 1, 1978, p. 2.

1,741.   Lindsey, Robert. "Klan Candidate Exploits A
          Vein Of Fear." New York Times. June 8, 1980,
          p. 24.

1,742.   _____. "Marines Transfer Leader Of Klan To
          Ease Tension At Camp Pendleton." New York Times.
          December 4, 1976, p. 10.

1,743.   _____. "Uneasy Peace Seen In Marine Camp After
          Attack On Whites By Blacks." New York Times.
          December 2, 1976, p. 18.

1,744.   "Local Members Of The KKK In Sacramento." Sacra-
          mento Bee. May 5, 1922, p. 1.

1,745.   "Los Angeles Citizens Put Klansmen To Rout."
          Chicago Defender. May 27, 1922, p. 2.

1,746.   "Los Angeles Is Pacific Coast Headquarters Of
          Ku Klux Klan." San Francisco Examiner. September
          21, 1921, p. 1.

1,747.   "Marine Accused Of Assault On Whites Faces Trial."
          New York Times. December 24, 1976, p. 8.

1,748.   "Marine Base Chief Expresses KKK Retaliation
          Views." Houston Post. December 17, 1976, p. 4A.

1,749.   "Marine Base KKK Chief Transferred Against Will."
          New Orleans Times Picayune. December 4, 1976,
          p. 21.

1,750.   "Marine Command At Camp Pendleton Transfer Ku Klux
          Klan Members." Washington Post. November 30,
          1976, p. 1.

1,751.   "Marine Commander Says KKK Movement At Pendleton
          'Miniscule'." Los Angeles Times. December 17,
          1976.

1,752.   "Marine Corps Probes Ku Klux Klan Activity On
          California Base." Washington Post. November 29,
          1976, p. 1.

1,753.   "Marine KKK Case - Orange Cty. ACLU Letter." Los
          Angeles Times. January 16, 1977, Sect. 5, p. 4.

1,754.   "Marine Spokesman Says 14 Black Marines Going
          Through Pretrial." Los Angeles Times. December
          18, 1976, Sect. 2, p. 12.

1,755.   "Marine Tells Of Hearing Threats To Harm Blacks."
          New York Times. December 29, 1976, p. 10.

1,756.   "Marines To Try 9 Blacks Accused In Camp Pendleton
          Attack." Los Angeles Times. July 14, 1977, Sect.
          2, p. 8.

1,757.   "Marines Chief Cautions Against Racial Friction."
          New York Times. December 17, 1976, p. 18.

1,758.   "Marin City, H.S. Football Team Members Suspended
          For Racial Incident." San Francisco Chronicle.
          November 7, 1980, p. 3.

1,759.   "The Marines Need To Be Told." New York Times.
          January 14, 1977, p. 22.

1,760.   "Mary Bacon." New York Times. July 5, 1975, p. 7.

1,761.   "Mary Bacon." New York Times. July 18, 1975,
          p. 25.

1,762.   "M'Adoo Accused Of Tie With Klan." New York
          Times. August 24, 1938, p. 9.

1,763.   Melching, Richard. "The Activities Of The Ku
          Klux Klan In Anaheim, California, 1923-1925."
          Southern California Quarterly. Vol. 56, Summer,
          1974, pp. 175-196.

1,764.   "Melee Erupts At California Klan Rally." New York
          Times. March 16, 1980, p. 26.

1,765.   "Merced Oks Klan March." California Advocate.
          May 22, 1981, p. 1.

1,766.   "Military Judge Stops Court- Martial Of Blacks."
          New York Times. March 18, 1977, p. 12.

1,767.   "Mob Attacks S.F. Theater Showing Film." Los
          Angeles Times. June 15, 1980, Sect. 5, p. 4.

1,768.   "NAACP Ousts Klansman." California (Fresno)
          Advocate. February 20, 1981, p. 1.

1,769.   "National Minority Advisory Council And California
          KKK." Baltimore Afro-American. December 22, 1979,
          p. 5.

1,770.   "Negro Gets 'KKK' Threat." New York Times. Decem-
          ber 14, 1946, p. 9.

1,771.   "Negroes Start Petition." New York Times. Sep-
          tember 15, 1946, p. 2.

1,772.   "New York Woman Returns $500 To KKK U.S. House
          Candidate Metzger." Los Angeles Times. August 15,
          1980, Sect. 2, p. 12.

1,773.   "1981 Cal. Democratic Convention Viewed." San
          Francisco Chronicle. January 19, 1981, p. 10.

1,774.   "No Ku Klux Wanted." Chicago Defender. September
          3, 1921, p. 16.

1,775.   "Nomination Of Klansman Metzger For U.S. House
          Post." Los Angeles Times. June 28, 1980, Sect.
          2, p. 4.

1,776.   "Oceanside Bans KKK From Using Community Center
          For Rally." Los Angeles Times. August 18, 1979,
          Sect. 2, p. 1.

1,777.   "Oceanside Mayor Holds Press Conf. On Police Speed
          To Klan Rally." Los Angeles Times. March 18,
          1980, Sect. 2, p. 2.

1,778.   "Official Ballot Counting Widens Klansman Metzger's
          Victory." Los Angeles Times. June 19, 1980, p. 3.

1,779.   "On Defending The Ku Klux Klan." New York Times.
          April 18, 1977, p. 30.

1,780.   "1 Of 9 Black Marines Pleads Guilty In Attack On
          Whites In California." New York Times. August
          25, 1977, p. 12.

1,781.   "One Person Arrested Near Calif. Klan Rally."
          Washington Post. February 23, 1981, p. A13.

1,782.   "Out Of The Cave." _Time_. Vol. 47. June 3, 1946,
          p. 25.

1,783.   Parker, Paula. "The Ku Klux Congressman." _Black
          Enterprise_. Vol. 11, October, 1980, p. 24-25.

1,784.   "Party Seeks Ouster Of Klan Leader." _Washington
          Star_. October 26, 1980, p. A4.

1,785.   "A Patriotic Idea." _Scoop U.S.A_. (Philadelphia).
          November 14, 1980, p. 1.

1,786.   "Pictorial On KKK Cross Burning In Ceres, Cal."
          San Francisco Chronicle. February 23, 1981, p. 3.

1,787.   "Political Donation To KKK Congressional Candidate
          Backfires." _Los Angeles Times_. July 30, 1980,
          Sect. 2, p. 1.

1,788.   "Private Investigator Linked To Ku Klux Klan In
          Calif." _San Francisco Chronicle_. December 14,
          1979, p. 4.

1,789.   "Probe Into KKK Group At Camp Pendleton Viewed."
          Houston Post. November 10, 1977, p. 24A

1,790.   "Proposed Calif. Bill To Halt New Ideas - Conrad
          Cartoon." _Los Angeles Times_. February 6, 1981,
          Sect. 2, p. 7.

1,791.   "Proposed State Law To Ban Bad Ideas In Califor-
          nia." _Los Angeles Times_. February 4, 1981,
          Sect. 2, p. 4.

1,792.   "Protesters Jeer Ex-Klan Leader Duke During Cal.
          State U. Speech." _Los Angeles Times_. November
          12, 1980, Sect. 2, p. 1.

1,793.   "Put Ku Klux Holy Terror Behind Bars." _Chicago
          Defender_. July 22, 1922, p. 1.

1,794.   "Race Issue - A Dilemma At Pendleton." _Christian
          Science Monitor_. December 13, 1976, p. 7.

1,795.   "Report Card: KKK Makes The Grade." _New West_.
          Vol. 6, January 1981, p. 7.

1,796.   "Rules Against Klansmen." _New York Times_.
          August 22, 1922, p. 18.

1,797.   "_San Bernardino Sun_ Bans Ads From Ku Klux Klan."
          Los Angeles Times. August 19, 1980, Sect. 4, p. 5.

1,798.   "San Diego Bishop Not To Give Votes To Klansman."
          New York Times. October 5, 1980, p. 24.

1,799.   "San Diego Bishop Urges Defeat Of Klansman."
            National Catholic Reporter. Vol. 16, October 17,
            1980, pp. 3-4.

1,799a.   "San Diego Cty. Dem. Com. Expels Klansman Metzger
            From Local Party." Los Angeles Times. October
            20, 1978, Sect. 2, p. 2.

1,799b.   "San Diego Laymen Assail KKK Congressional Candi-
            ate Metzger." Los Angeles Times. July 16, 1980,
            Sect. 2, p. 3.

1,799c.   "San Diego Urban League Links Camp Pendleton
            Racial Attack To KKK." Los Angeles Times.
            November 28, 1976, p. 3.

1,799d.   "San Francisco Public Officials Members Of KKK."
            San Francisco Examiner. May 17, 1922, p. 2.

1,799e.   "San Diego KKK And Pendleton Appointment To CRC."
            Michigan Chronicle. December 12, 1981, p. 6A.

1,799f.   "San Jose Mayor Hayes Supports 3rd Rally In Issue
            Over KKK." San Francisco Chronicle. April 9,
            1981, p. 2.

1,799g.   "San Jose Protestors Thwart KKK Rally." Jet.
            Vol. 60, May 7, 1981, p. 5.

1,799h.   "Say Cross Burnings By Klan Should Have Attention
            Of Dies." Pittsburgh Courier. March 2, 1940,
            p. 5.

1,799i.   "16 Camp Pendleton Marines Listed As Klansmen."
            New Orleans Times Picayune. December 3, 1976,
            p. 2.

1,799j.   "Sims Hits Curley And Klan." New York Times.
            March 31, 1923, p. 2.

1,799k.   "60 Torch-Carrying Men Found Easy To Unmask."
            New York Times. January 21, 1966, p. 27.

1,799l.   "State Employees Can Not Be Members Of The KKK
            And Work For California." Sacramento Bee. May
            12, 1922, p. 1.

1,799m.   "10,000 Turn Out To See Klan Rally On The Coast."
            New York Times. September 19, 1966, p. 30.

1,799n.   "10th Black Marine To Face Trial In Klan Case."
            Los Angeles Times. April 21, 1977, Sect. 2, p. 3.

1,799o.   "3 AWOL Marine KKK Members Surrender To Authori-
            ties." Los Angeles Times. January 5, 1977, p. 3.

1,799p.   "Three Marines Fail To Appear To Testify At Corps.
Hearing." New York Times. January 4, 1977, p. 36.

1,799q.   "3 Marines Fail To Appear At Camp Pendleton Hearing." Los Angeles Times. January 4, 1977, p. 3.

1,799r.   "To Arrest Ku Klux Raiders." New York Times.
April 27, 1922, p. 19.

1,799s.   "Tom Metzger, California Ku Klux Klan Leader, Interviewed." Los Angeles Sentinel. November 8, 1979,
p. 4A.

1,799t.   "Tom Metzger As Candidate For San Diego City Suprs."
Los Angeles Times. March 10, 1978, Sect. 2, p. 6.

1,800.   "Tom Metzger, Candidate In Cal's. 43rd Congressional
District, Viewed." Chicago Tribune. October 5,
1980, Sect. 3, p. 1.

1,801.   "Tom Metzger, KKK Leader In California, Interviewed." Los Angeles Times. April 16, 1978,
Sect. 2, p. 1.

1,802.   "Top Black Law Enforcement Officials Meet In
Inglewood." Los Angeles Times. June 23, 1980,
p. 3.

1,803.   "Tracking Down The Metzger Vote In San Siego Cty.
Viewed." San Francisco Chronicle. June 16, 1980,
p. 8.

1,804.   "Trial For Black Marine." Christian Science Monitor. December 27, 1976, p. 27.

1,805.   "Turn Light On Plot Of Klan Cops." Chicago
Defender. April 29, 1922, p. 1.

1,806.   "2 Alleged Klansmen Ordered Back To Camp Pendleton
In KKK Case." Los Angeles Times. December 15,
1976, p. 28.

1,807.   "2 Black Marines Sentenced For 1976 Camp Pendleton
Attack." Los Angeles Times. October 22, 1977,
Sect. 2, p. 5.

1,808.   "2 Held In Alleged Attempt To Kill Klan Candidate
Metzger." San Francisco Chronicle. September 18,
1980, p. 53.

1,809.   "2 More General Court Martials Ordered For Camp
Pendleton Marines." Los Angeles Times. February
15, 1977, p. 2.

1,810.   "2 Suspected Ku Klux Klan Members To Testify In
Marines Defense." New Orleans Times Picayune.
December 15, 1976, Sect. 2, p. 2.

1,811.   "U.S. Congressional Candidate Metzger Faces Dem. Party Ouster." Los Angeles Times. October 24, 1980, p. 14.

1,812.   "U.S. Is Out As Defendant In Marines-Klan Lawsuit." New York Times. February 25, 1978, p. 6.

1,813.   "U.S. Military Appeal Ct. Halts Trial Of Black Marines." Los Angeles Times. March 10, 1977, p. 3.

1,814.   "U.S. Rep. Burgener's Campaign Against Klansman Metzger Discussed." Los Angeles Times. September 22, 1980, p. 1.

1,815.   "U.S. Sen. Cranston Opposes Klansman Metzger's Bid For Congress." Los Angeles Times. June 7, 1980, Sect. 2, p. 1.

1,816.   "U.S. Sen. Endorses Klansman's Foe In U.S. Congressional Race." San Francisco Chronicle. June 7, 1980, p. 7.

1,817.   "U.S. Marines Transfer Camp Pendleton Ku Klux Klan Chief." Washington Post. December 4, 1976, p. 1.

1,818.   "U.S. Rep. Burke Says She Has No Objections To Klan On Bases." Los Angeles Times. December 16, 1976, p. 3.

1,819.   Wheeldin, Don and Charles Glenn. "KKK Cross Burned At Home Of Negro Candidate In L.A." Daily Worker. June 3, 1952, p. 8.

1,820.   "William S. Coburn." New York Times. June 20, 1922, p. 21.

1,821.   Williams, Dennis A. and William J. Cook. "Mistaken Identity; Causing Racial Harassment At Camp Pendleton Marine Base." Newsweek. Vol. 88, December 13, 1976, pp. 35, 37.

5.   COLORADO

1,822.   "Activity Of Ku Klux Klan In Colo. Viewed." Denver Post. November 18, 1979, p. 37.

1,823.   "Calls On Klan To Explain." New York Times. February 26, 1922, Sect. 8, p. 22.

1,824.   Casey, Lee. "When The Klan Controlled Colorado." Rocky Mountain News. June 17, 18, 19, 1946.

1,825.   "Colo. District Court To Hear Klan Official Case." Denver Post. December 29, 1979, p. 11.

1,826.   "Colo. Ku Klux Klan Head Files Suit Seeking Assault Prosecutor." Denver Post. November 1, 1979, p. 53.

1,827.   "Colo. Ku Klux Klan Leader Denied Court Appointed Atty. In Case." Denver Post. November 9, 1979, p. 24.

1,828.   "Colorado Klan Candidates Win." New York Times. September 12, 1924, p. 2.

1,829.   "Colorado Klan Men In Lead." New York Times. September 11, 1924, p. 3.

1,830.   "Colorado Law Has Teeth To Gnaw Ku Klux." Chicago Defender. April 8, 1922, p. 2.

1,831.   "Communist Workers Party In Denver Reacts To N.C. KKK Shootings." Denver Post. November 7, 1979, p. 57.

1,832.   "Cross Is Burned Near Nightclub That Backed Fund For Black Boy." New York Times. April 1, 1979, p. 36.

1,833.   Davis, James H. "Colorado Under The Klan." Colorado Magazine. Vol. 42, Spring, 1965, pp. 93-108.

1,834.   "Denver Area Radio Show Host Claims Threat By Klansman." Denver Post. November 7, 1979, p. 56.

1,835.   "Denver Man Flees From Klan; Law To Aid Him." Chicago Defender. March 18, 1922, p. 2.

1,836.   "Dragon Gets Time To Plead." New York Times. January 11, 1925, p. 5.

1,837.   "Dragon Of Ku Klux Arrested In Denver." New York Times. January 10, 1925, p. 13.

1,838.   "Form Anti-Klan Body In Colorado." New York Times. May 13, 1925, p. 2.

1,839.   Goldberg, Robert A. "Beneath The Hood And Robe: A Socioeconomic Analysis Of Ku Klux Klan Membership In Denver, Colorado, 1921-1925." Western Historical Quarterly. Vol. 11, April, 1980, pp. 181-198.

1,840.   Hamil, Harold. "When The Klan Visited Sterling High." Denver Post Empire Magazine. October 27, 1974, pp. 49, 51.

1,841.   "Increasing Activity Of Ultra Rightist Groups In Colo. Viewed." Denver Post. November 18, 1979, p. 37.

1,842.   Keith, Adam. "K.K.K. ... Klose Kall In Kolorado."
         Denver. Vol. 1, August, 1965, pp. 24-27.

1,843.   "Klan In Colorado Prison." _New York Times_.
         November 29, 1929, p. 17.

1,844.   "Klan Opposed In Colorado." _New York Times_. March
         17, 1922, p. 20.

1,845.   "Klan Officials Rush By Plane To Denver To Halt
         Wholesale Colorado Secession." _New York Times_.
         July 19, 1925, p. 1.

1,846.   "Klan Provokes Assaults On Children, Judge Ben
         Lindsey Says, Scoring It." _New York Amsterdam
         News_. July 15, 1925, p. 16.

1,847.   "Klan Puts Coolidge Ahead In Colorado." _New York
         Times_. October 2, 1924, p. 4.

1,848.   "Klan Sweeps Colorado." _New York Times_. November
         6, 1924, p. 3.

1,849.   "Klan Wins In Denver Vote." _New York Times_.
         May 21, 1925, p. 16.

1,850.   "Klansman Free On Plea." _New York Times_. August
         9, 1925, p. 2.

1,851.   "Ku Klux Klan Grand Wizard David Duke Is Inter-
         viewed On KWBZ." _Denver Post_. January 9, 1979,
         p. 13.

1,852.   "Ku Klux Klan Grand Wizard Interview At KWBZ."
         Denver Post. January 8, 1979, p. 3.

1,853.   "Ku Klux Klan March Against Colo. Zionist Founda-
         tion - Letter." _Denver Post_. July 9, 1979, p. 19.

1,854.   "Ku Klux Klan Members Picket Colo. Zionist Federa-
         tion In Denver." _Denver Post_. July 2, 1975, p. 2.

1,855.   "Ku Klux Klan Pickets Ralph Abernathy Speech In
         Colorado." _Denver Post_. March 30, 1979, p. 3.

1,856.   "Ku Klux Meeting In Denver Prevented." _New York
         Amsterdam News_. July 25, 1923, p. 3.

1,857.   "Ku Klux Threat To Negro Messenger For Gov. Shoup."
         New York Times. March 14, 1922, p. 1.

1,858.   Lindsey, Ben B. "The Beast In A New Form." _New
         Republic_. Vol. 41, December 24, 1924, p. 121.

1,859.   _____. "My Fight With The Ku Klux Klan."
         Survey Graphic. Vol. 54, June 1, 1925, pp. 271-274.

1,860.   Marriner, Gerald L. "Klan Politics In Colorado."
          Journal of the West. Vol. 15, January, 1976,
          pp. 76-101.

1,861.   Mazzulla, Fred and Jo Mazzulla. "A Klan Album."
          Colorado Magazine. Vol. 42, Spring, 1965, pp.
          109-113.

1,862.   "Minute Men To Form A Nation-Wide Order." New
          York Times. August 17, 1925, p. 16.

1,863.   "Not Dead But Sleeping." Chicago Defender.
          March 11, 1922, p. 12.

1,864.   "Protest Held In Denver Against Ku Klux Klan Role
          In N.C. Murders." Denver Post. November 12,
          1979, p. 3.

1,865.   "Refuses Ku Klux Klan Incorporation In Colorado."
          New York Times. March 19, 1922, p. 1.

1,866.   "Resigns From The Klan." New York Times. July
          23, 1925, p. 10.

1,867.   Speers, L.C. "Colorado Hurries Downfall Of Klan."
          New York Times. September 26, 1926, Sect. 9,
          pp. 3,12.

1,868.   Taylor, Ralph C. "Klan Controlled Colorado Poli-
          tics In 1920's." Pueblo Chieftain. March 12,
          1961.

1,869.   "Wheeler Attacks Senator Phillips." New York
          Times. September 30, 1924, p. 9.

1,870.   "Youth Accuses Ku Klux." New York Times. January
          8, 1925, p. 12.

1,871.   Zylstra, Don. "When The Ku Klux Klan Ran Denver."
          Denver Post Roundup. January 5, 1958, pp. 5,7.

6.   CONNECTICUT

1,872.   "Aborted Rally At Meriden, Conn." Washington Post.
          July 12, 1981. p. A10.

1,873.   "Another Klan Rally Held But Audience Is Smaller."
          Washington Post. September 15, 1980, p. A14.

1,874.   "Arms Guard Heflin." New York Times. June 10,
          1929, p. 27.

1,875.   "As The 'Imperial Wizard' Talked." New York Times.
          September 21, 1980, Sect. 23, p. 3.

1,876.   "Beginning To See The Light." New York Times.
          January 6, 1926, p. 26.

1,877.   "Blacks, Hispanics Beset Klansmen." Washington
          Post. March 22, 1981, p. A7.

1,878.   "Bloodied Klansman." Washington Star. March 22,
          1981, p. A1.

1,879.   "Citizen Defies Klan." Pittsburgh Courier.
          January 26, 1929, p. 4.

1,880.   "Clash Marks Klan Rally In Connecticut Town."
          Washington Post. September 14, 1980, p. A15.

1,881.   "Connecticut Journal." New York Times. September
          27, 1981, Sect. 23, p. 3.

1,882.   "Connecticut Klan Will Enter Politics." New York
          Times. August 19, 1923, p. 2.

1,883.   "Connecticut Outlaws KKK Training Camps." Atlanta
          (Ga.) Voice.   June 13, 1981, p. 2.

1,884.   "Connecticut Ticket Will Be Anti-Klan." New York
          Times. September 16, 1924, p. 2.

1,885.   "Crowd Breaks Up Klan Rally." New York Times.
          July 12, 1981, p. 24.

1,886.   Devries, Hilary. "Connecticut Klan Rally Erupts
          In Violence." Christian Science Monitor. March
          23, 1981, p. 2.

1,887.   "8 Injured And 9 Arrested At Rally Of K.K.K. In
          Rural Connecticut." New York Times. September 14,
          1980, p. 46.

1,888.   "Four Seized At A "Calm" Klan Rally (in Conn.)."
          Newark, (N.J.) Sunday Star-Ledger. March 21, 1982,
          p. 8.

1,889.   "Its Records Stolen, Ku Klux Klan Alleges: Asks
          Court To Stop Publication In Magazine."   New
          York Times. July 21, 1923, p. 1.

1,890.   Jones, J.R. "Memories Of Danbury." Katallagate.
          Vol. 3-4, Winter/Spring, 1972, pp. 26-27.

1,891.   "K.K.K. On Highway Puzzles Greenwich." New York
          Times. September 28, 1925, p. 34.

1,892.   "KKK Painted On Norwalk Home." New York Times.
          April 23, 1964, p. 31.

1,893.   "Klan And Anti-Klan Demonstrators Clash In Meriden,
          Connecticut." Bilalian News. July 31, 1981, p. 7.

1,894. "Klan Cited As Menace To Nation." Pittsburgh
Courier. January 9, 1926, p. 1.

1,895. "Klan Cross Fires Woods." New York Times. May 13,
1925, p. 15.

1,896. "Klan Demands Probe Of Clash In Connecticut."
Washington Star. March 23, 1981, p. A2.

1,897. "Klan Disrupts A Fair." New York Times. June 25,
1923, p. 15.

1,898. "Klan Foes Rally In Connecticut." Washington
Star. September 14, 1980, p. A7.

1,899. "Klan Holds Rally After Imperial Wizard Is Arrested." New York Times. September 15, 1980, p. B9.

1,900. "Klan Inquiry Halts Police Drill Order." New York
Times. December 26, 1922, p. 3.

1,901. "Klan Leader Arrested At Connecticut Rally."
Jet. Vol. 59, October 2, 1980, p. 7.

1,902. "Klan Bans Parade In Election Campaign; Denies
Organized Crusade Against Smith." New York Times.
August 3, 1928, p. 4.

1,903. "Klan Rally Attacked By Community." Scoop, U.S.A.
(Phila.). March 27, 1981, p. 1.

1,904. "Klan Stages 2nd Conn. Rally; 'Wizard' Faces Gun
Charge." Washington Star. September 15, 1980,
p. A2.

1,905. "Klan Stirs Up Stamford." New York Times. July
15, 1924, p. 19.

1,906. "Klan Suits Dismissed." Washington Post. November 4, 1981, p. A8.

1,907. "Klan To Seek Federal Probe Of Connecticut Rally
Violence." Washington Post. March 23, 1981,
p. B4.

1,908. "Klan 'Wrecking Crew' Aimed At Politicians."
New York Times. January 8, 1923, p. 4.

1,909. "Klansmen Bloodied By Angry Crowd In Meriden,
Conn." Washington Star. March 22, 1981, p. A7.

1,910. "Klansmen Decorate Hale Statue." New York Times.
June 7, 1928, p. 17.

1,911. "Klansmen Get 'Rocky' Reception In Conn." Jet.
Vol. 60, April 9, 1981, p. 13.

1,912.   "Klansmen Hide Behind Police As Counterrally Erupts In Conn." Los Angeles Times.   March 22, 1981, p. 4.

1,913.   "Klansmen Make Quiet Appearance." New York Times. July 13, 1981, p. B2.

1,914.   "Klan's Rally Routed By Barrage Of Rocks On Street In Meriden." New York Times. July 12, 1981, p. 25.

1,915.   "Ku Klux In Connecticut." New York Times. September 4, 1921, p. 11.

1,916.   "KKK Rally Turns Into Bloody Confrontation In Meriden, Conn." New Orleans Times Picayune. March 22, 1981, p. 5.

1,917.   "Louisiana Based KKK Group Arrested Following Rallies In Conn." Chicago Tribune. September 15, 1980, p. 6.

1,918.   Madden, Richard L. "Connecticut Troopers Get A New Chief." New York Times. May 16, 1981, p. 26.

1,919.   _____. "Donald Long: Man In The Middle Of Dispute." New York Times. April 5, 1981, Sect. 23, p. 1,15.

1,920.   _____. "Klan Rally Inquiry Faults Connecticut's State Police." New York Times. May 7, 1981, p. B2.

1,921.   "Mrs. Waldron Freed Of Charge By Klan." New York Times. December 6, 1924, p. 11.

1,922.   "Must Get Permits For Fiery Cross." New York Times. August 9, 1924, p. 2.

1,923.   "Mutiny In The Invisible Empire." Independent. Vol. 116, January 16, 1926, pp. 58-59.

1,924.   "Name Bingham In Connecticut." New York Times. September 11, 1924, p. 6.

1,925.   "New Haven Klansmen Disband Their Unit." New York Times. January 5, 1926, p. 13.

1,926.   "Petty Officers Accused Of Aiding Klan Before Naval Board At New London." New York Times. October 11, 1924, p. 17.

1,927.   "Police Mutiny Due To Klan Activity." New York Times. December 25, 1922, p. 1.

1,928.   "7 Are Injured By Rocks As Connecticut Rally By Klan Is Broken Up." New York Times. March 22, 1981, p. 38.

1,929.   "6,000 Klansmen Celebrate." New York Times.
          August 12, 1928, Sect. 2, p. 22.

1,930.   "Stamford Policeman Is Sentinel For Klan." New
          York Times. September 15, 1924, p. 23.

1,931.   "300 Protest K.K.K. In Danbury March." New York
          Times. October 22, 1979, p. B2.

1,932.   "Troopers Assail Inaction On Klan." New York Times.
          March 24, 1981, p. B2.

1,933.   "Violence Erupts At KKK Rally In Connecticut."
          Atlanta Daily World. July 14, 1981, p. 1.

1,934.   "The Visible Empire In Connecticut." New York
          Times. March 29, 1981, Sect. 4, p. F5.

1,935.   Tomasson, Robert E. "School Program To Counter The
          Klan." New York Times. July 19, 1981, Sect. 23,
          p. 1,15.

1,936.   Wald, Matthew L. "Meriden Resents Image Caused
          By Klan Clashes." New York Times. July 18, 1981,
          p. 26.

1,937.   _____. "Town Abuzz At Prospect Of Klan Rally."
          New York Times. August 31, 1980, Sect. 23, p. 3.

7.   DELAWARE

1,938.   "Delaware Klan Aide Held On Two Weapons Charges."
          New York Times. November 8, 1965, p. 24.

1,939.   "Delaware Klan In Political Fight." New York Times.
          April 10, 1966, p. 60.

1,940.   "Delaware KKK Leader Sentenced In Gun Sale Case."
          New Orleans Times Picayune. October 22, 1981, p.
          19.

1,941.   "Delaware N.A.A.C.P. Opposes Klux Meet." New York
          Amsterdam News. August 15, 1923, p. 7.

1,942.   "Five Shot In Riot At Klan Initiation." New York
          Times. September 1, 1923, p. 5.

1,943.   "Klan Aide's Plan To Resign Told." New York Times.
          November 14, 1965, p. 75.

1,944.   "Klan Draws 2,000 In Delaware Rally." New York
          Times. August 1, 1965, p. 57.

1,945.   "Klan Fight In Delaware." New York Times. Sep-
          tember 10, 1924, p. 2.

1,946.   "Klan Is Blamed For Night Raid On Center At Delaware U. Campus." New York Times. December 15,
1970, p. 37.

1,947.   "Klan Sets Delaware Rally." New York Times.
July 28, 1965, p. 40.

1,948.   "Klansmen Held On Weapon's Charge." New Bern
(N.C.) Sun-Journal. March 14, 1966, p. 1.

8. FLORIDA

1,949.   "Action By Florida Governor." New York Times.
August 17, 1957, p. 7.

1,950.   "Argument Is Begun In Florida Floggings." New
York Times. May 22, 1936, p. 16.

1,951.   Armbrister, Trevor. "Portrait Of An Extremist."
Saturday Evening Post. Vol. 237, August 22-29,
1964, pp. 80-83.

1,952.   "'Associate' Of Klan Accused In Bombing." New York
Times. March 5, 1964, p. 27.

1,953.   "Attacks State Case In Flogging Case." New York
Times. May 14, 1936, p. 52.

1,954.   "Bias Report Cites Bombing In Florida." New York
Times. December 30, 1951, p. 16.

1,955.   Bigart, Homer. "St. Augustine Aides Say They
Cannot Keep Peace." New York Times. June 27,
1964, pp. 1, 10.

1,956.   _____. "St. Augustine Awaits Steps To Ease
Race Strife." New York Times. July 3, 1964, p. 8.

1,957.   "Black Ballots." Time. Vol. 33, May 15, 1939,
p. 19.

1,958.   "Black Leader Blames Unrest On President." Washington Post. February 10, 1982, p. A4.

1,959.   "Bombing Reward Raised." New York Times. January
10, 1952, p. 60.

1,960.   "Boy Scouts Warn Of Parade Boycott." New York
Times. May 30, 1976, p. 20.

1,961.   "Break Away From Klan." New York Times. November 4, 1928, p. 23.

1,962.   "Brutal Outrages Reported." Christian Science
Monitor. March 26, 1953, p. 19.

1,963.   Carter, Elmer A. "The Ku Klux Klan Marches Again."
          Opportunity. Vol. 17, June, 1939, p. 163.

1,964.   "Celery Men Warned To Leave Florida." New York
          Times. May 13, 1925, p. 23.

1,965.   Chalmers, David. "The Ku Klux Klan In The Sunshine
          State: The 1920's." Florida Historical Quarterly.
          Vol. 43, 1964, pp. 209-215.

1,966.   "CIO Charges Klan Threatened Negro." New York
          Times. August 7, 1946, p. 12.

1,967.   "Collins Target In Florida." New York Times.
          March 27, 1960, p. 74.

1,968.   "A Correction." New York Times. April 3, 1936, p. 33.

1,969.   "Courage In Florida." Norfolk Journal And Guide.
          May 13, 1939, p. 8.

1,970.   "Cross Is Thrust Through Door." New York Times.
          November 13, 1965, p. 34.

1,971.   "Crosses Blaze In Miami." New York Times. May 2,
          1939, p. 28.

1,972.   "Defense In Tampa Helps Speed Trial." New York
          Times. October 11, 1937, p. 38.

1,973.   "Denies Klan Will Unmask." New York Times.
          February 7, 1928, p. 20.

1,974.   "Deputy In Florida Assailed By Judge." New York
          Times. August 19, 1964, p. 26.

1,975.   "Doctor Testifies As Flogging Victim." New York
          Times. April 21, 1936, p. 3.

1,976.   Doherty, Herbert J. Jr. "Florida And The Presi-
          dential Election Of 1928." Florida Historical
          Quarterly. Vol. 26, October, 1947, pp. 174-186.

1,977.   "Fail To Bar Negro Chorus." New York Times.
          October 19, 1938, p. 14.

1,978.   "Film Picketed In Florida." New York Times.
          August 17, 1957, p. 7.

1,979.   "Fire Damages Home Of Suspect In Blast." New York
          Times. April 26, 1964, p. 78.

1,980.   "First Flogging Case Shifted From Tampa." New
          York Times. April 1, 1936, p. 4.

1,981.   "5 Are Convicted In Flogging Case." New York Times.
          May 24, 1936, pp. 1, 21.

1,982.   "5 Klansmen's Trial Hears Home Bomber." New York
         Times. July 4, 1964, p. 4.

1,983.   "5 More Held In Bombing Of Florida Negro's Home."
         New York Times.   March 13, 1964, p. 20.

1,984.   "5 Whites Accused In St. Augustine." New York
         Times. July 25, 1964, p. 9.

1,985.   "Fla. KKK Will Arm For Protection." Baltimore Afro-
         American. July 16, 1977, p. 7.

1,986.   "Flees Florida Town After Being Beaten, Tarred,
         Feathered." Pittsburgh Courier. January 20, 1923,
         p. 1.

1,987.   Fleming, G. James. "Miamian Who Flouted Klan Wins
         Admiration Of NAACP Delegates." Norfolk Journal
         And Guide. July 8, 1939, Sect. 2, p. 11.

1,988.   "Flogged Men Testify." New York Times. October
         9, 1937, p. 9.

1,989.   "Floggers Get Four Years." New York Times. August
         8, 1936, p. 28.

1,990.   "Flogging Trial Halts For New Jury Panel." New
         York Times. March 31, 1936, p. 46.

1,991.   "Flogging Witness Tells Of Seizure." New York
         Times. April 19, 1936, p. 27.

1,992.   "Florida Anti-Klan Act Signed." New York Times.
         May 9, 1951, p. 57.

1,993.   "Florida Ban On Masks Gains." New York Times.
         April 17, 1951, p. 22.

1,994.   "Florida Boy Scouts Cancel March With Ku Klux
         Klan." New Orleans Times Picayune. June 1, 1976,
         p. 12.

1,995.   "Florida City Denies Permit For Ku Klux Klan
         Parade." New York Times. March 20, 1977, p. 26.

1,996.   "Florida City Ousts High Leader Of Klan." New
         York Times. December 4, 1960, p. 80.

1,997.   "Florida Curbs Klan." New York Times. March 14,
         1958, p. 17.

1,998.   "Florida Governor Warns Ku Kluxers." Pittsburgh
         Courier. March 22, 1958, p. 2.

1,999.   "Florida House Votes Mask Ban." New York Times.
         April 25, 1951, p. 23.

2,000.   "Florida Is Being Lobbied For Anti-Klan Legislation."
          SCLC Magazine. Vol. 10, March/April, 1981, p. 51.

2,001.   "Florida Klan Forms 'Confederate Army'." New York
          Times. July 16, 1952, p. 15.

2,002.   "Florida Klan Head Indicted For Libel." New York
          Times. February 13, 1952, p. 24.

2,003.   "Florida Klan In Open." New York Times. October
          13, 1953, p. 18.

2,004.   "Florida Klan To Give $1,000 To Black." New York
          Times. June 6, 1976, p. 26.

2,005.   "Florida Klansmen Plan To Ride On Election Eve."
          New York Times. October 28, 1939, p. 20.

2,006.   "Florida Overturns Curb On Klan." New York Times.
          December 19, 1939. p. D19.

2,007.   "Florida Panels Approve Unmasking Klan Bills."
          Jet. Vol. 60, May 21, 1981, p. 19.

2,008.   "Florida Senate Votes Mask Ban." New York Times.
          May 1, 1951, p. 31.

2,009.   "Florida Stands By Black." New York Times. Sep-
          tember 19, 1937, p. 39.

2,010.   "Florida Town Grants Man Parade Sought For 3 Years."
          New York Times. July 10, 1978, p. 14.

2,011.   "4 Give Up To U.S. Marshal In Miami On Perjury
          Charges In Terrorism." New York Times. December
          1, 1952, p. 1.

2,012.   "4 Inquirers Comb Florida Bombing." New York
          Times. December 28, 1951, p. 13.

2,013.   "4 Negroes Beaten At St. Augustine." New York
          Times. July 18, 1964, p. 6.

2,014.   "G.A. Davis." New York Times. August 21, 1923,
          p. 5.

2,015.   "Gov. Cone Defends Florida Violence." New York
          Times. October 22, 1937, p. 25.

2,016.   "Gives New Evidence In Tampa Lashings." New York
          Times. October 10, 1937, p. 25.

2,017.   Goodwyn, Larry. "Anarchy In St. Augustine."
          Harper's Magazine. Vol. 230, January, 1965,
          pp. 74-81.

2,018.   Herbers, John. "Florida Sheriff Called Klan Ally."
          New York Times. June 4, 1964, p. 18.

2,019.   _____. "Klan Is An Issue In St. Augustine."
          New York Times. June 7, 1964, p. 48.

2,020.   _____. "Police-Klan Ties Hinted In Florida."
          New York Times. June 3, 1969, p. 19.

2,021.   _____. "300 At Klan Meeting Applaud Slurs On
          Negroes." New York Times. May 4, 1964, p. 25.

2,022.   _____. "200 Whites March At St. Augustine."
          New York Times. June 13, 1964, p. 21.

2,023.   "Homeless Shun Relief Gift Of Ku Klux Klan."
          Chicago Defender. May 13, 1922, p. 3.

2,024.   "Identify Accused In Flogging Trial." New York
          Times. October 12, 1937, p. 52.

2,025.   "Implicate Sergeant In Tampa Flogging." New York
          Times. May 5, 1936, p. 46.

2,026.   "Indicted For Flogging." New York Times. Decem-
          ber 25, 1935, p. 14.

2,027.   Ingalls, Robert. "1935: The Murder Of Joseph
          Shoemaker." Southern Exposure. Vol. 8, Summer,
          1980, pp. 64-68.

2,028.   "Integration Hit By Florida Klan." New York Times.
          July 22, 1956, p. 32.

2,029.   "Jury Picked To Try Tampa Policemen." New York
          Times. October 8, 1937, p. 48.

2,030.   "Justice Department Investigates Klan Outrage In
          Miami." Iowa Bystander. June 15, 1939.

2,031.   "Kasper Cites Jews In Florida Speech." New York
          Times. March 3, 1957, p. 68.

2,032.   King, Wayne. "Racial Incidents In Pensacola
          Prompt Attempts By Klan To Get New Members." New
          York Times. March 18, 1975, p. 74.

2,033.   "K.K.K. Denies Incidents." New York Times. July
          16, 1951, p. 21.

2,034.   "K.K.K. Parades In Florida." New York Times.
          June 30, 1957, p. 48.

2,035.   "KKK To Reward Black Police Agent." Washington
          Evening Star. June 6, 1976.

2,036.   "Klan Blamed For 30 Wooden Crosses Set Ablaze Over
         Florida." New Orleans Times Picayune. May 15,
         1972, p. 18.

2,037.   "Klan Buster Enters Senate Race In Florida." Daily
         Worker. August 19, 1950, p. 15.

2,038.   "Klan Challenges Busing." New York Times. Sep-
         tember 9, 1977, p. 18.

2,039.   "Klan Chief Is Resigning." New York Times. Decem-
         ber 30, 1960, p. 5.

2,040.   "Klan Chief Recruiting Army Against Negroes."
         Daily Worker. July 17, 1952, p. 3.

2,041.   "Klan-Clad Invaders Wreck A Night Club." New York
         Times. November 17, 1937, p. 2.

2,042.   "Klan Denies Any Part In Flogging Murder; Replies
         To Rumors Eve Of Florida Trial." New York Times.
         October 4, 1937, p. 3.

2,043.   "Klan Denies Involvement." New York Times.
         December 30, 1951, p. 16.

2,044.   "Klan Ex-Head In Florida Race." New York Times.
         May 30, 1954, p. 19.

2,045.   "Klan For Negroes?" Newsweek. Vol. 42, October
         26, 1953, p. 43.

2,046.   "Klan Fought In Florida." New York Times. January
         29, 1949, p. 7.

2,047.   "Klan Group Disavowed." New York Times. July 22,
         1956, p. 32.

2,048.   "The Klan In Florida." New Republic. Vol. 91,
         June 9, 1937, p. 118.

2,049.   "Klan Linked To String Of Burning Crosses In Flori-
         da." Los Angeles Times. March 26, 1972, p. 9A.

2,050.   "Klan Marches Again In Florida." New York Times.
         September 1, 1938, p. 46.

2,051.   "Klan Nemesis In Florida Speaks For Association."
         New York Amsterdam News. June 10, 1939, p. 2.

2,052.   "Klan Orders 2 Pastors Out Of Fla. Town." Chicago
         Defender. March 16, 1940, p.

2,053.   "Klan Pushes Petition." New York Times. September
         29, 1954, p. 29.

2,054.   "Klan Scores Supreme Court." New York Times. August 5, 1956, p. 43.

2,055.   "Klan Trial Opens In Florida." New York Times. July 1, 1964, p. 22.

2,056.   "Klan Watches Florida Hotels, Seeking Mrs. Rip Rhinelander." New York Times. December 15, 1925, p. 1.

2,057.   "Klansman Freed In Bombing Trial." New York Times. July 6, 1964, p. 19.

2,058.   "Klansman Acquitted In Beatings." New York Times. September 21, 1980, p. 46.

2,059.   "Klansmen Blasts NAACP At Rally." Pittsburgh Courier. September 6, 1958, p. 21.

2,060.   "Klansmen In Alabama Defy A Ban On Firearms." New York Times. February 25, 1979, p. 33.

2,061.   "Klansmen Jeered." New York Times. February 20, 1977, p. 26.

2,062.   "Ku Klux Klansmen March Through Pensacola, Fla." New Orleans Times Picayune. May 25, 1975, p. 20.

2,063.   "KKK Members March In Davie, Fla., Capping Fight To Demonstrate." New Orleans Times Picayune. July 9, 1978, p. 2.

2,064.   "Klansmen Parade In Harding Tribute." New York Times. August 8, 1923, p. 2.

2,065.   "Ku Klux Klan." New York Star. November 3, 1948.

2,066.   "Ku Klux Klan Declining." Bilalian News. February 27, 1976, p. 18.

2,067.   "The KKK Burned Crosses In Florida After Wallace Won The Presidential Primary." National Observer. April 8, 1972, p. 6.

2,068.   "Ku Klux Klan Fights St. Augustine Integration." Sepia. Vol. 13, September 1964, pp. 16-18.

2,069.   "KKK Recruits Members In Lake Wales, Fla." New Orleans Times Picayune. February 21, 1975, Sect. 2, p. 3.

2,070.   "Ku Klux Klan Recruits Children." Florida (Jacksonville) Star. December 6-12, 1980, p. 2.

2,071.   McMillan, George. "The Klan Scourges Old St. Augustine." Life. Vol. 56, June 26, 1964, p. 21.

2,072.   "Mechanic Given 7 Years In Negro Home Bombing."
          New York Times. April 18, 1964, p. 16.

2,073.   "Miami Negroes Vote, Defying Klan Threat." New
          York Times. May 3, 1939, p. 7.

2,074.   "Miami Night Life Loses 'Hot Spots'." New York
          Times. November 22, 1937, p. 2.

2,075.   "More Eloquent Than Words." New York Amsterdam
          News. May 13, 1939, p. 1.

2,076.   "Mutilation Laid To Florida Klan." New York Times.
          April 11, 1936, p. 32.

2,077.   "N.A.A.C.P. Inquiry Set." New York Times. August
          22, 1956, p. 27.

2,078.   "Negro Aid Group Will Lose Funds." New York Times.
          September 15, 1956, p. 6.

2,079.   "Negroes Defy Klan By Voting." New York Times.
          September 15, 1938, p. 20.

2,080.   "New Delay Ordered In The Flogging Trial." New
          York Times. May 1, 1936, p. 8.

2,081.   "New Klan Rally Slated." New York Times. July 24,
          1956, p. 8.

2,082.   "Official Once In The Klan." New York Times.
          March 16, 1949, p. 30.

2,083.   "Ousts 6 In Flogging Case." New York Times. May
          2, 1936, p. 8.

2,084.   Peck, Ralph L. "Lawlessness In Florida, 1868-1871."
          Florida Historical Quarterly. Vol. 40, October,
          1961, pp. 164-185.

2,085.   Perlmutter, Nathan. "Bombing In Miami's Anti-
          Semitism And The Segregationists." Commentary.
          Vol. 25, June 1958, p. 498-503.

2,086.   "Police Chief's Club Called Klan Front." New York
          Times. February 24, 1966, p. 18.

2,087.   "Posse Kills Negro, Florida Fugitive." New York
          Times. July 27, 1949, p. 48.

2,088.   "Prosecution Rests In Florida Flogging." New York
          Times. May 13, 1936, p. 9.

2,089.   "Racial Clash In Florida." New York Times. July
          19, 1966, p. 18.

2,090.   "Rector Flogged." Pittsburgh Courier. January 20, 1923, p. 1.

2,091.   "Reds Ask Support In Attack On Klan." New York Times. March 29, 1936, p. 12.

2,092.   "Refuses To Testify In Florida Flogging." New York Times. May 12, 1936, p. 5.

2,093.   "Reign Of Terror Charged." New York Times. March 3, 1953, p. 9.

2,094.   "Rights Aides Freed On Bond In Florida Contempt Case." New York Times. February 10, 1968, p. 31.

2,095.   "Sam Coleman." New York Times. June 12, 1976, p. 11.

2,096.   "Says Flogging Victim Was Held By Police." New York Times. May 6, 1936, p. 12.

2,097.   "Says Tampa's Chief Shielded Floggers." New York Times. May 7, 1936, p. 32.

2,098.   "Shake-up In Tampa Police." New York Times. February 20, 1936, p. 5.

2,099.   Sherrill, Robert. "The New Klan (Tallahassee, Fla.)." New York Post. July 27, 1964, p. 27.

2,100.   "Shoemaker's Brother Heard." New York Times. October 12, 1937, p. 52.

2,101.   Shuler, Rev. A.C. "Address Delivered By The Emperor To Knights of The KKK, at Monticello (Fla.)." Southern Gospel. September-October, 1949, pp. 1-3.

2,102.   Sims, Harris G. "Emboldened Ku Klux Klan Again Is Active In Florida." New York Times. November 21, 1937, Sect. 4, p. 7.

2,103.   Sitton, Claude. "Strain Showing In St. Augustine." New York Times. May 31, 1964, p. 50.

2,104.   "Six Are Acquitted In Flogging Death." New York Times. October 15, 1937, p. 16.

2,105.   "6 Men Are Indicted In Florida Terror." New York Times. June 4, 1953, p. 26.

2,106.   "State Rests Case In Florida Flogging." New York Times. October 13, 1937, p. 44.

2,107.   "Students' Strike Leads To Breaking Up Of Southern College." Pittsburgh Courier. November 3, 1923, p. 15.

2,108.   "Suicide In Flogging Case." New York Times. January 25, 1936, p. 32.

2,109.   "Taken From Jail By Kidnappers." New York Times. August 20, 1923, p. 2.

2,110.   "Ten-Hour Arguments End." New York Times. May 15, 1936, p. 52.

2,111.   "10 Men Face Trial In Fatal Flogging." New York Times. March 21, 1936, p. 3.

2,112.   "Terrorism In Florida." New York Times. December 28, 1951, p. 20.

2,113.   "Testimony Ended In Flogging Trial." New York Times. May 19, 1936, p. 2.

2,114.   "Thomas Assails Tampa Flogging." New York Times. December 12, 1936, p. 8.

2,115.   "Trammell Has Big Lead." New York Times. June 8, 1922, p. 21.

2,116.   "Threat For Evelyn Nesbit." New York Times. December 15, 1924, p. 14.

2,117.   "3 Testify In Bombings." New York Times. October 14, 1952, p. 47,

2,118.   Treaster, Joseph B. "Tide Of Refugees Swells As Vessel With 500 Docks." New York Times. May 12, 1980, p. B7.

2,119.   "Two Are Acquitted In Flogging Trial." New York Times. May 17, 1936, p. 7.

2,120.   "Two Top Officials Of New Klan Group Arrested In Florida." New York Times. October 30, 1965, p. 12.

2,121.   "Voting In Florida Primary Takes On New Life After KKK Threats." Norfolk Journal and Guide. May 13, 1939, p. 1.

2,122.   White, Walter F. "Election By Terror In Florida." New Republic. Vol. 25, January 12, 1921, pp. 195-197.

2,123.   "Who's Afraid Of The KKK?" Afro-American. May 13, 1939.

2,124.   "Witness Refuses To Testify In Bombing Of Negro Home." New York Times. November 24, 1964, p. 26.

2,125.   "W.L. Davis, Imperial Wizard Of The Ku Klux Klan
          Inciting A Gathering." Illustrated London News.
          Vol. 238, January 21, 1961, p. 94.

2,126.   Wood, Junius B. "Communism Denied At Flogging
          Trial." New York Times. April 23, 1936, p. 14.

2,127.   _____. "Failed To Present Flogging Evidence."
          New York Times. April 29, 1936, p. 29.

2,128.   _____. "Flogging Trials Ordered To Go On."
          New York Times. March 26, 1936, p. 48.

2,129.   _____. "Flogging Victims Are Put On Trial?"
          New York Times. May 8, 1936, p. 9.

2,130.   _____. "Groups In Florida Defend Floggings."
          New York Times. May 11, 1936, p. 20.

2,131.   _____. "Jury Picking Lags In Flogging Trial."
          New York Times. March 28, 1936, p. 10.

2,132.   _____. "Lawyers In Clash At Flogging Trial."
          New York Times. April 30, 1936, p. 20.

2,133.   _____. "Patriotism Made Issue In Flogging."
          New York Times. March 27, 1936, p. 7.

2,134.   _____. "Police Identified In Tampa 'Red'
          Raid." New York Times. April 28, 1936, p. 44.

2,135.   _____. "Red Attack Delays In Flogging Trial."
          New York Times. March 25, 1936, p. 11.

2,136.   _____. "Rules For Defense In Flogging Trial."
          New York Times. April 24, 1936, p. 22.

2,137.   _____. "Wide Plot Alleged In Fatal Flogging."
          New York Times. March 22, 1936, p. 42.

2,138.   "Shelton Statement." New York Times. August 1,
          1965, p. 57.

9. GEORGIA

2,139.   "Abducted By Robed Band." New York Times.
          February 5, 1939, p. 37.

2,140.   "Accuse Klan Of Contempt." New York Times. July
          26, 1922, p. 2.

2,141.   "Acquit Macon Klansman." New York Times.
          September 16, 1923, p. 23.

2,142.   "Again, The Klan." Time. Vol. 47, May 20, 1946,
          p. 20.

2,143.   "Aid Is Offered To Driver." New York Times.
          July 5, 1977, p. 12.

2,144.   "Aid To Schools And Anti-Klan Bill Defeated In
          Georgia." New York Times. February 19, 1950,
          Sect. 4, p. 6.

2,145.   "Albany, Ga. Has First KKK Parade In 20 Years."
          Pittsburgh Courier. January 11, 1949, p. 2.

2,146.   "Anti-Klan Bias Charged." New York Times.
          October 23, 1951, p. 27.

2,147.   Arnall, Ellis. "My Battle Against The Klan."
          Coronet. Vol. 20, October, 1946, pp. 3-8.

2,148.   "Arnall Checks Klan Here." New York Times.
          August 8, 1966, p. 23.

2,149.   "Arnall Moves To Dissolve Klan." Christian Century.
          Vol. 63, July 3, 1946, p. 829.

2,150.   "Arnall Speaks For All Of Us." New York Times.
          June 1, 1946, p. 12.

2,151.   "Asks Ku Klux Receiver." New York Times. November
          11, 1922, p. 17.

2,152.   "Atlanta, Klan's Capital, Bans Wearing Of Masks."
          New York Times. May 3, 1949, p. 19.

2,153.   "Atlanta NAACP Demands End To KKK Terror."
          Atlanta (Ga.) Voice. July 4, 1981, p. 2.

2,154.   "Atlanta's Course Surprising." New York Times.
          September 21, 1921, p. 14.

2,155.   "Atlanta's School Plea." New York Times. March
          24, 1960, p. 25.

2,156.   "Attacks Gov. Walker." New York Times. September
          4, 1924, p. 5.

2,157.   "Auto Smashes Into Crowd At KKK Rally In Plains,
          Ga." Los Angeles Times. July 3, 1977, p. 1.

2,158.   "Background Details Of Man Who Disrupted Klan
          Rally Emerge." Los Angeles Times. July 8, 1977,
          p. 9.

2,159.   "Baptists Can Invite Klansmen To Church." New York
          Times. July 30, 1947, p. 23.

2,160.   Benet, William R. "Fan Mail." Saturday Review Of
          Literature. Vol. 32, January 1, 1949, p. 32-33.

2,161.   Bennett, Carl D. "Methodists Not Alone In Georgia."
         Christian Century. Vol. 66, January 26, 1949, pp.
         114-115.

2,162.   "Big Influx Of Klansmen." New York Times. April
         5, 1923, p. 21.

2,163.   "Biracial Unit Bars Plan To Sell Farm." New York
         Times. March 2, 1957, p. 19.

2,164.   "Blacks, KKK In Ga. Confrontation." Washington
         Post. February 21, 1982, p. 10A.

2,165.   "Black Students In Atlanta Attempt Debate With KKK."
         Jet. Vol. 60, March 26, 1981, p. 26.

2,166.   "Black Veterans Plan Training To Fight KKK." Jet.
         Vol. 54, November 13, 1980, p. 5.

2,167.   "Black Writer Beaten At Klan Meeting." Washington
         Evening Star. September 1, 1975, p. 1.

2,168.   "Blackmail Charges Hurled In Klan Probe." Pitts-
         burgh Courier. April 14, 1923, p. 1.

2,169.   "Blacks Hold Protest March In Town In Central
         Georgia." New York Times. April 27, 1980, p. 26.

2,170.   "Black Students In Atlanta Attempt Debate With
         KKK." Jet. Vol. 60, March 26, 1981, p. 26.

2,171.   "Bomb Rips A House In Atlanta Tension." New York
         Times. November 1, 1946, p. 2.

2,172.   "Book Tells Of Stern Maddox Order On Marchers."
         New York Times. July 6, 1968, p. 19.

2,173.   "Borglum And The Klan." New York Amsterdam News.
         March 11, 1925, p. 16.

2,174.   Boyd, Thomas. "Defying The Klan." Forum. Vol.
         76, July, 1926, pp. 48-56.

2,175.   "Brands Macon Floggers." New York Times. Sep-
         tember 8, 1923, p. 15.

2,176.   "Bright To Quit Macon." New York Times. April 8,
         1923, p. 14.

2,177.   "Broken Monopoly." Time Vol. 55, March 20, 1950,
         p. 20.

2,178.   "Bullies Bare KKK Plot In Georgia." Afro-American.
         February 1, 1947, p. 1,2.

2,179.   "The Burning Of A Cross." New York Times.
         September 6, 1976, p. 23.

2,180.   "Burnings In Georgia." New York Times. March 27, 1960, p. 74.

2,181.   "Busbee Clears Extradition Of Ex-F.B.I. Informer." New York Times. February 8, 1979, p. 16.

2,182.   "Button Down Bed Sheets." Newsweek. Vol. 62, August 26, 1963, pp. 32-33.

2,183.   "Car Crashes Rally Of KKK In Plains, Ga." Houston Post. July 3, 1977, p. 7.

2,184.   "Car Plows Into Ku Klux Klan Rally In Plains, Georgia." Los Angeles Times. July 3, 1977, p. 1.

2,185.   "Caucasian Community Being Planned By Klan." Washington Evening Star. March 23, 1964.

2,186.   "Charges Klan Swung Georgia To M'Adoo." New York Times. March 21, 1924, p. 3.

2,187.   "Chief In Atlanta Jeered By Racists." New York Times. September 6, 1961, p. 23.

2,188.   "Church Backs Ex-Chaplain Of Klan." New York Times. June 14, 1923, p. 21.

2,189.   "Churchwomen Act To Unmask Klan. Christian Science Monitor. January 19, 1951, p. 14.

2,190.   "Civil Rights Group Confronts Klan." Washington Post. March 23, 1964.

2,191.   "Civil Rights Jury Out A Day." New York Times. December 16, 1949, p. 25.

2,192.   "Clarke Quits Klan." Chicago Defender. October 14, 1921, p. 3.

2,193.   "Clarke Quits Klan, And Mrs. Tyler Too." New York Times. September 25, 1921, p. 14.

2,194.   "Clarke Resignation Stirs Ku Klux Klan." New York Times. September 26, 1921, p. 5.

2,195.   "Colescott 'At A Loss'." New York Times. February 1, 1942, p. 35.

2,196.   "Columbians Sued On Charter Recall." New York Times. November 6, 1946, p. 24.

2,197.   "Columbus Blacks Reported Anxious About KKK Patrols." Atlanta Daily World. March 2, 1978, pp. 1, 4.

2,198.   "Columbus, Ga., Blacks Uneasy About KKK Patrols."
          Atlanta Daily World. March 2, 1978, p. 1.

2,199.   "Commission Rule Ordered For Klan." New York
          Times. April 8, 1923, p. 22.

2,200.   "Condemns Night Riding." New York Times. December
          16, 1922, p. 8.

2,201.   "Confession Read In Penn's Slaying." New York
          Times. September 3, 1964, p. 18.

2,202.   "Convicted In Flogging." New York Times. April
          26, 1940, p. 17.

2,203.   "Conviction Of Attacker Of KKK Rally." Christian
          Science Monitor. October 27, 1977, p. 2.

2,204.   "Criticizes The Associated Press." New York Times.
          January 12, 1923, p. 10.

2,205.   "Crosses Of Fire." Newsweek. Vol. 27, April 8,
          1946, pp. 21-22.

2,206.   "A Curious Phase Of Klanism." New York Times.
          February 9, 1926, p. 24.

2,207.   Davis, Elmer. "Georgia Beats Klan Plank." New
          York Times. June 29, 1924, pp. 1, 2.

2,208.   Davis, Peter. "18 In Hospital After Klan Rally
          Crash." Washington Post. July 4, 1977, p. A2.

2,209.   "Defies Klan Ban On Smith." New York Times.
          May 28, 1928, p. 3.

2,210.   "Defies Ku Klux In Race For Mayor Of Atlanta."
          New York Times. August 7, 1922, p. 17.

2,211.   DePoris, Gene. "Slump Will Aid KKK, Georgia Offi-
          cial Warns." PM. August 13, 1946.

2,212.   "Divisible Invisible Empire." Newsweek. Vol. 32,
          July 19, 1948, p. 20.

2,213.   "Dog Eat Dog." Pittsburgh Courier. November 10,
          1923, p. 16.

2,214.   Douglas, Francis P. "Big KKK Expansion Seen If
          Talmadge Becomes Governor." Washington Evening
          Star. June 14, 1946.

2,215.   "Dragon Of Klan Asserts He Is On Talmadge Staff."
          New York Times. June 29, 1949, p. 54.

2,216.   "Driven From Georgia Town." New York Amsterdam
           News. March 7, 1923, p. 1.

2,217.   "Driver At Klan Rally Where 29 Were Hurt Is Bound
           Over To Jury." New York Times. August 11, 1977,
           p. B8.

2,218.   "Driver Faces 19 Assault Charges In Klan Incident."
           New York Times. July 4, 1977, p. 5.

2,219.   "Driver Pleads In Jail Break." New York Times.
           January 15, 1978, p. 23.

2,220.   "Driver Says He Tried To Disrupt Klan Rally."
           New York Times. September 6, 1977, p. 24.

2,221.   "Drops Coach In Klan Row." New York Times.
           February 21, 1948, p. 15.

2,222.   Du Bois, W.E.B. "Savings Of Black Georgia."
           Outlook. Vol. 69, September 14, 1901, pp. 128-130.

2,223.   "Dunce Caps On Parade." New York Times. November
           28, 1960, p. 30.

2,224.   "Edicts Of The Imperial Palace." New York Times.
           July 8, 1924, p. 18.

2,225.   "18 In Hospital After Plains, Ga. Klan Rally Crash."
           Washington Post. July 4, 1977, p. 2A.

2,226.   "Election Eve In Georgia." New Republic. Vol. 119,
           September 6, 1948, p. 10.

2,227.   "11 Year Old Boy Slays Klansman." Chicago Defender.
           December 17, 1921, p. 1.

2,228.   "Emperor Samuel II Elected." Christian Science
           Monitor. August 29, 1949, p. 14.

2,229.   "Emperor Simmons Gains Control Of Klan By Court
           Action Which Ties Up All Funds. New York Times.
           April 4, 1923, p. 1.

2,230.   "Erwin A Klan Fighter." New York Times. June 30,
           1924, p. 6.

2,231.   Evans, Rowland and Robert Novak. "The Lesser
           Georgia Evil." Durham Morning Herald. October
           22, 1966.

2,232.   "Evans, Head Of Ku Klux Klan, Is A Guest As
           Atlanta Catholics Dedicate Cathedral." New York
           Times. January 19, 1939, p. 21.

2,233.   "Even Georgia Is On Klan's Trail." New York
            Amsterdam News. September 12, 1923, p. 7.

2,234.   "Ex-Marine Disrupts Klan Rally In Plains, Ga."
            New York Amsterdam News. July 9, 1977, p. C2.

2,235.   "FBI And Georgia Probing Klan." People's Voice.
            March 27, 1948, p. 4.

2,236.   "FBI Hunts Klansman In Shooting." Charlotte (N.C.)
            Observer. May 7, 1966.

2,237.   "FBI Joins In Klansman Manhunt." Greensboro (N.C.)
            Daily News. May 7, 1966.

2,238.   "FBI Probe Asked Of Klan Revival." People's
            Voice. February 28, 1948, p. 2.

2,239.   "FBI To Begin Inquiry In Rural Georgia Threats."
            New York Times. July 27, 1981, p. A8.

2,240.   "Fears Klan Will Kill Him." New York Times.
            March 3, 1923, p. 9.

2,241.   "Federal Aid Given In Fight On Klan." New York
            Times. August 21, 1923, p. 5.

2,242.   "Federal Aide Threatened." New York Times.
            August 30, 1949, p. 28.

2,243.   "Federal Case Rests In Georgia Flogging." New
            York Times. December 2, 1949, p. 27.

2,244.   "Fed. Judge In Ga. Refuses To Cite KKK In Protest
            Against Aliens." New Orleans Times Picayune.
            July 23, 1981, p. 3.

2,245.   "Federal Jury Told Klansman Clubbed Negro With
            Pistol." New York Times. July 6, 1966, p. 16.

2,246.   "Female Ku Kluxers Parade Atlanta Streets."
            California Eagle. December 16, 1922, p. 4,
            Section 2.

2,247.   "Financial Aid Offered Man Charged In Assault At
            KKK Meeting In Ga." Houston Post. July 5, 1977,
            p. 14A.

2,248.   "Fire At Mrs. Tyler, Threaten Simmons." New York
            Times. October 12, 1921, p. 5.

2,249.   "5 Jailed On Bus Route." New York Times. May 26,
            1961, p. 18.

2,250.   "Flogger Gets Jail Term." New York Times. May 18,
            1940, p. 34.

2,251.   "Flogger Of Woman Convicted By Jury." New York Times. July 10, 1927, p. 7.

2,252.   "Floggers Arrested In Macon Crusade; Residents Arming." New York Times. August 20, 1923, p. 1.

2,253.   "Floggers Lose Appeal." New York Times. December 2, 1941, p. 11.

2,254.   "Flogging Jury Finds 3 Deputies In Klan." New York Times. March 14, 1940, p. 12.

2,255.   "Flogging Victim Says Sheriff Ignored Plea." New York Times. November 30, 1949, p. 56.

2,256.   "Ford Gets Backing Of Klansmen." Chicago Defender. June 3, 1922, p. 1.

2,257.   "Forrest Tells Aims Of Ku Klux College." New York Times. September 12, 1921, p. 15.

2,258.   "4 Flogged In Georgia." New York Times. July 28, 1950, p. 11.

2,259.   "4 In Racial Slaying Face Georgia Trial." New York Times. August 15, 1964, p. 9.

2,260.   "The Four Klansmen." Newsweek. Vol. 64, August 17, 1964, pp. 29-30.

2,261.   "Fox, Atlanta Klan Slayer, Gets Life Term; Victim's Widow Wanted Severer Penalty." New York Times. December 22, 1923, p. 1.

2,262.   Franklin, Ben A. "Klan Jury Shown Arms Of Accused." New York Times. June 30, 1966, p. 23.

2,263.   _____. "2 Of 6 Klansmen Convicted Of Plot To Harm Negroes." New York Times. July 9, 1966, p. 1.

2,264.   _____. "Witness Links 2 To Penn Slaying." New York Times. July 1, 1966, p. 19.

2,265.   "Freed Klansmen To Fight New Penn Case Charges." New York Times. September 6, 1964, p. 34.

2,266.   Furniss, Jim. "Evidence To Outlaw Klan Declared Ready." Atlanta Constitution. June 9, 1946.

2,267.   "Future Of 'Empire' Hangs In Doubt." Christian Science Monitor. August 19, 1949, p. 12.

2,268.   "Ga. Klan Protests Flag Desecration." Greensboro (N.C.) Daily News. April 4, 1966.

2,269.   "Ga. Klansman Wounds Wife In Hospital. Greensboro (N.C.) Daily News. May 6, 1966.

2,270.   "Ga. Sen. Bond Protests Ex-KKK Leader's Upcoming College Speech." New Orleans Times Picayune. February 26, 1981, p. 19.

2,271.   "Georgia Klan Again Suspect (in Cross Burning)," Pittsburgh Courier. October 8, 1949, p. 20.

2,272.   "General Klan Session Opens In Atlanta." New York Times. November 29, 1922, p. 23.

2,273.   "Georgia Acts To Dissolve Ku Klux Klan." PM. June 21, 1948.

2,274.   "Georgia Also On Trial." New York Times. December 30, 1926, p. 18.

2,275.   "Georgia Approves Bill Outlawing Klan Camps." Jet. Vol. 60, April 30, 1981, p. 28.

2,276.   "Georgia Bans Klan." People's Voice. June 1, 1946, p. 9.

2,277.   "Georgia Baptist Head Says Klansmen Are OK In Church." PM. July 30, 1947.

2,278.   "Georgia Bars Plan To Kill Klan Bill." New York Times. January 19, 1949, p. 22.

2,279.   "Georgia Bill Outlaws Klan Hood." New York Times. February 8, 1939, p. 44.

2,280.   "Georgia Candidates Shunning The Klan." New York Times. September 8, 1924, p. 3.

2,281.   "Georgia Christianity OK's K.K.K." California Eagle. June 30, 1923, p. 1.

2,282.   "Georgia Christianity OK's Ku Klux." Pittsburgh Courier. June 23, 1923, p. 4.

2,283.   "Georgia Civil-Rights Trial Fnded With Jury In 48-Hour Deadlock." New York Times. December 18, 1949, pp. 1,58.

2,284.   "Georgia Considers Bills Outlawing Klan Camps." Jet. Vol. 60, March 26, 1981, p. 38.

2,285.   "Georgia Debates Klan Issue." New York Times. December 1, 1946, Sec. 4, p. 9.

2,286.   "Georgia Ex-Klansman Backs Negro Charges." New York Times. December 1, 1949, p. 37.

2,287.   "Georgia Flogger Gets Year On Chain Gang." New York Times. July 17, 1927, Sect. 2, p. 3.

2,288. "Georgia Floggings Are Investigated." New York Times. March 12, 1940, p. 11.

2,289. "Georgian Found Guilty In Assault At KKK Rally." Houston Post. October 26, 1977, p. 2A.

2,290. "Georgia Girl Appears With KKK." Washington Post. December 12, 1948.

2,291. "Georgia Governor Acts On Macon Cases." New York Times. August 19, 1923, p. 2.

2,292. "Georgia Hood Ban Voted." New York Times. January 16, 1951, p. 32.

2,293. "Georgia House Committee Bans Dog Fighting But Not KKK Camps." Atlanta Daily World. December 18, 1981, p. 1.

2,294. "Georgia Jails Third Klansman." New York Times. May 25, 1940, p. 6.

2,295. "Georgia Judge Hits Race Intolerance." New York Times. June 5, 1926, p. 14.

2,296. "Georgia Kills A Bill To Unmask The Klan." New York Times. January 21, 1949, p. 5.

2,297. "Georgia Klan Case Is Hailed In South." New York Times. March 19, 1950, Sect. 4, p. 10.

2,298. "Georgia Klan Chief Ex-Policeman Chief." New York Times. August 28, 1949, p. 61.

2,299. "Georgia Klan Chief Gets Customs Office." New York Times. August 23, 1925, p. 24.

2,300. "Georgia Klan Chief Quits To Help Build 'A United America'." New York Times. April 29, 1968, p. 29.

2,301. "Georgia Klan Girds For Segregation March July 20." Norfolk Journal and Guide. July 20, 1963, p. 15.

2,302. "Georgia Klan Hits Whip." Pittsburgh Courier. November 5, 1927, p. 1.

2,303. "Georgia Klan Parades." New York Times. February 26, 1956, p. 87.

2,304. "Georgia Klan To Admit 100 While 'Peculiar Cross' Burns." Washington Post. July 23, 1948.

2,305. "Georgia Klan Vote Threat Fails." New York Times. March 11, 1948, p. 40.

2,306. "Georgia Klansmen Burn Fiery Cross." New York Times. October 21, 1945, p. 33.

2,307.   "Georgia Klan Vote Threat Fails." New York Times.
          March 11, 1948, p. 40.

2,308.   "Georgia Klansmen Burn Fiery Cross." New York
          Times. October 21, 1945, p. 33.

2,309.   "Georgia Law Urged To End Subversion." New York
          Times. August 20, 1946, p. 15.

2,310.   "Georgia Mayor Unmasks Three Klansmen And Says He
          May Be Their Judge And Jury." New York Times.
          May 23, 1949, p. 25.

2,311.   "Georgia Ministers Call KKK Cross Sacrilegious."
          Pittsburgh Courier. January 1, 1949, p. 3.

2,312.   "Georgia Moves To Prosecute 4 As Slayers Of Negro
          Educator." New York Times. August 8, 1964, p. 7.

2,313.   "Georgia Newspaper Picketed By Klan." New York
          Times. December 11, 1960, p. 57.

2,314.   "Georgia Opens War On Masked Mobs." New York
          Times. December 29, 1926, p. 2.

2,315.   "Georgia Orders Action To Revoke Charter Of Klan."
          New York Times. May 31, 1946, p. 1.

2,316.   "Georgia Police Sent To Balk Klan Rally." New
          York Times. March 24, 1948, p. 26.

2,317.   "Georgia Republican Row." New York Times. January
          22, 1921, p. 4.

2,318.   "Georgia Says Klan Sought Band Help." New York
          Times. November 10, 1946, p. 23.

2,319.   "Georgia Senator And Group Charge U.S. Agency With
          Harassment." Los Angeles Times. June 24, 1980,
          p. 13.

2,320.   "Georgia Senator Called A Klansman." New York
          Times. August 25, 1924, p. 2.

2,321.   "Georgia Sniper Kills A Negro Educator." New York
          Times. July 12, 1964, pp. 1,52.

2,322.   "Georgia To Check Report Of A Klan Training Camp."
          New York Times. October 31, 1980, p. A14.

2,323.   "Georgia Weighs Revocation Of All Charters For
          Klan." New York Times. October 20, 1965, p. 29.

2,324.   "Georgian, 30, Convicted Of Assault At Klan Rally."
          New York Times. October 26, 1977, p. 18.

2,325.   "Georgians Urge Feds To Collect From Klan." *Chicago Defender*. September 28, 1946, p. 7.

2,326.   "Georgia's Governor Dares Mob Action." *New York Times*. March 6, 1948, p. 11.

2,327.   "Georgia's Mask Ban Is Law." *New York Times*. January 31, 1951, p. 27.

2,328.   "Goldwater Is Supported By Georgia Klan Leader." *New York Times*. July 26, 1964, p. 38.

2,329.   "Gov. Dorsey, Ga. Denounces Ku Klux Klan Orator As Liar." *New York Age*. April 2, 1921, pp. 1,2.

2,330.   "Government Questioning." *New York Times*. December 13, 1949, p. 39.

2,331.   "Green, Klan Chief, Dies At His Home." *New York Times*. August 19, 1949, p. 1.

2,332.   "Griffin, Ga. C-Of-C Distressed By KKK Float In Yule Parade." *Houston Post*. December 13, 1980, p. 13C.

2,333.   "Group Including 2 Blacks Assaulted At Klan Meeting." *New York Times*. August 31, 1975, p. 39.

2,334.   "Guilt Is Upheld In Ku Klux Case." *New York Times*. May 27, 1951, p. 55.

2,335.   "Halts Klan Injunction." *New York Times*. September 19, 1923, p. 5.

2,336.   "Hardwick Declares Klan Rules Georgia." *New York Times*. July 7, 1924, p. 3.

2,337.   Hatcher, George. "Georgia Court Action Aimed At Legal Basis Of The Klan." *New York Times*. June 23, 1946, Sec. 4, p. 7.

2,338.   _____. "Klan On March In Georgia." *New York Times*. March 28, 1948, Sect. 4, p. 7.

2,339.   _____. "Klan Openly Backs Talmadge In Georgia Campaign." *New York Times*. August 15, 1948, Sect. 4, p. 6.

2,340.   _____. "Public Activities Of Gerogia's K.K.K. Are Increasing." *New York Times*. August 10, 1947, Sect. 4, p. 8.

2,341.   _____. "Rivival Of Klan Is Linked To Negro Voting, Labor Drive." *New York Times*. May 19, 1946, Sect. 4, p. 6.

2,342.   "Head Of Klan Orders Members Unmasked." New York
          Times. August 9, 1949, p. 27.

2,343.   "Held For Flogging Woman." New York Times. June
          14, 1927, p. 29.

2,344.   "Held In Georgia Lashing." New York Times.
          March 6, 1950, p. 13.

2,345.   Herbers, John. "F.A.A. Rented Space In Klan
          Building." New York Times. November 4, 1965,
          p. 35.

2,346.   _____. "Klan Aide Urged 'Acts Of Violence'."
          New York Times. November 3, 1965, p. 21.

2,347.   "Highlights Of SCLC-IFCO Conference On Ku Klux
          Klan." Atlanta Daily World. December 16, 1979,
          p. 1.

2,348.   Hinton, Harold B. "Klan Head Denies National
          Status." New York Times. June 19, 1946, p. 22.

2,349.   "Hooded Hoodlums." Atlanta Constitution. June 6,
          1946.

2,350.   "Hoods Down." Newsweek. Vol. 35, April 17, 1950,
          p. 67.

2,351.   Howard, James T. "Rankin Committee Postively
          Won't Quiz Georgia KKK." PM. May 28, 1946.

2,352.   Huie, William B. "Murder: The Klan On Trial;
          L. Penn Case." Saturday Evening Post. Vol. 238,
          June 19, 1965, pp. 86-89.

2,353   "Humphrey Backs Proposal For An Investigation Of
          Klan." New York Times. February 14, 1965, p. 49.

2,354.   "'Imperial Edict' On Mask Wearing." Christian
          Science Monitor. August 8, 1949, p. 14.

2,355.   "Indicts Klan Editor For Atlanta Killing." New
          York Times. November 7, 1923, p. 15.

2,356.   "Is Talmadge Policy 'Hands Off' Ga. KKK?" Pitts-
          burgh Courier. May 7, 1949, p. 11.

2,357.   "J.B. Stoner Suspended As Lawyer." New York
          Times. November 9, 1980, p. 54.

2,358.   "Jailed In Negro Beatings." New York Times.
          March 18, 1950, p. 30.

2,359.   "Joseph Lowry Speaks As SCLC-IFCO Anti-Klan Con-
          ference Ends." Atlanta Daily World. December 18,
          1979, p. 1.

2,360.   "Judge Asks Revoke Charter." Christian Science Monitor. October 19, 1965, p. 2.

2,361.   "Judge Dismisses Extradition Suit By Rowe, Ex-Informer For The FBI." New York Times. June 6, 1980, p. 16.

2,362.   "Jury For Klan Trial Selected." New York Times. October 21, 1977, p. D13.

2,363.   "Jury Picked To Try Two In Penn Slaying." New York Times. September 1, 1964, p. 20.

2,364.   "Jury Weighs Car Crash At Klan Rally In Plains." New York Times. October 25, 1977, p. 18.

2,365.   "The Justice Department." New York Times. November 4, 1978, p. 36.

2,366.   Kennedy, Stetson. "Evidence Offered To McGrath For Retrial Of Georgia Floggers." Daily Compass. December 19, 1949, p. 3.

2,367.   _____. "How Many Of Georgia's 200,000 Negroes Will Defy KKK?" New York Star. September 7, 1948.

2,368.   _____. "The Ku Klux Klan Is Riding Again." Daily Compass. December 5, 1949, p. 3.

2,369.   _____. "Klan Sure Of Acquittal In Flogging, Plan To March (in Georgia)." Daily Compass. December 12, 1949, p. 3.

2,370.   _____. "Inside Georgia's Klan." Salute. December, 1946, pp. 20-23.

2,371.   _____. "Kluxer Claims 1500 'Watchdogs' Against 'Invasion'." PM. March 24, 1947, p. 4.

2,372.   _____. "PM Writer Defies KKK Vow To 'Get' Him." PM. August 4, 1947.

2,373.   King, Wayne. "Carter's Church To Admit Blacks And Keep Minister." New York Times. November 15, 1976, pp. 1,24.

2,374.   _____. "Maddox Forced Into Runoff For Georgia Governor." New York Times. August 14, 1974, p. 14.

2,375.   "KKK And NAACP Compete For Spotlight During Ga. Marches." New Orleans Times Picayune. August 20, 1979, p. 4.

2,376.   "KKK And NAACP Hold Marches In Columbus, Ga." New Orleans Times Picayune. August 19, 1979, p. 2.

2,377. "KKK Bid To Hold Meeting At Spaulding Cty., Georgia, School Eyed." Atlanta Daily World. December 29, 1981, p. 1.

2,378. "K.K.K. Fails To Get U.S. Protection For Its Rally." Atlanta Daily World. July 10, 1977, p. 2.

2,379. "KKK Leader Believed Target During Rally in Ga." New Orleans Times Picayune. July 4, 1977, p. 1.

2,380. "KKK Meeting At Georgia School Building." Atlanta Daily World. December 29, 1981, p. 6.

2,381. "KKK Move To Close Integrated Farm." Christian Science Monitor. February 25, 1957, p. 14.

2,382. "The KKK Plays To Slim Crowd." People's Voice. February 14, 1948, p. 21.

2,383. "KKK Rally Staged In Plains, Ga." Baltimore Afro-American. July 9, 1977, p. 8.

2,384. "KKK Rides Again: Hits Daily For 'Unfair' News." Norfolk Journal And Guide. December 2, 1929, p. 4.

2,385. "KKK Threatens Capital Residents." Pittsburgh Courier. December 14, 1929, p. 2.

2,386. "KKK Urged To Remain Peaceful In Columbus, Ga., By Police Chief." Atlanta Daily World. February 26, 1978, p. 1.

2,387. "KKK Warned To Remain Peaceful In Columbus." Atlanta Daily World. February 26, 1978, p. 1.

2,388. "Klan Admits 700 In Cross-Lit Rites." New York Times. July 24, 1948, p. 28.

2,389. "Klan And Negroes March In Atlanta." New York Times. November 27, 1960, pp. 1, 66.

2,390. "A Klan Appointment." New York Times. October 17, 1925, p. 14.

2,391. "Klan Arson Plan Is Told To House." New York Times. November 5, 1965, p. 24.

2,392. "Klan Asks Ban On Reds." New York Times. March 3, 1940, p. 9.

2,393. "Klan Asks End Of Suit." New York Times. July 4, 1946, p. 21.

2,394. "Klan At Soldier's Burial." New York Times. September 26, 1951, p. 33.

2,395. "Klan Bans Masks From Its Regalia." New York Times. April 18, 1940, p. 48.

2,396. "Klan Blamed For Exodus From South." Pittsburgh Courier. August 11, 1923, p. 3.

2,397. "Klan Boom Looms In Georgia: Plenty Of Rope." Pittsburgh Courier. January 25, 1947, pp. 1, 4.

2,398. "Klan Breach Widens." Pittsburgh Courier. September 22, 1923, p. 2.

2,399. "Klan Bund Backer Sets Georgia Move." New York Times. September 8, 1946, p. 17.

2,400. "Klan Burning Crosses Again In Georgia." Washington Post. October 21, 1945.

2,401. "Klan Burns A Cross Before Georgia Vote." New York Times. March 3, 1948, p. 3.

2,402. "Klan Burns Cross In Georgia Town." New York Times. February 4, 1948, p. 6.

2,403. "Klan Candidate Wins." New York Times. September 21, 1922, p. 2.

2,404. "Klan Control Fight Splits Three Ways." New York Times. April 7, 1923, p. 15.

2,405. "Klan Demonstrates At Banquet For Comr. In Augusta, Ga." Atlanta Daily World. August 23, 1977, p. 3.

2,406. "Klan Dragon Denies Any Plot On Arnall." New York Times. June 23, 1946, p. 42.

2,407. "Klan Editor Kills Simmon's Counsel In Atlanta Office." New York Times. November 6, 1923, pp. 1-5.

2,408. "The Klan Embarrasses Georgia's Governor." People's Voice. March 20, 1948, p. 19.

2,409. "Klan Enforces White Primary (in Georgia)." People's Voice. April 24, 1948, p. 8.

2,410. "Klan Favors Equal Chance For Negro, Green Declares." Washington Evening Star. December 11, 1948.

2,411. "Klan Flogging Trial Frees 2 Of Accused." New York Times. December 3, 1949, p. 28.

2,412. "Klan Founder Asks Restraining Order." Pittsburgh Courier. April 7, 1923, p. 1.

2,413. "Klan Funds Tied Up By An Injunction." New York Times. June 1, 1923, p. 14.

2,414. "Klan Harassment Unites Blacks And Whites." SCLC Magazine. Vol. 10, October/November, 1981, pp. 54-55.

2,415. "Klan Head Accepts Catholic Invitation." New York Times. January 17, 1939, p. 11.

2,416. "Klan Heads Differ At Whipping Trial." New York Times. November 24, 1949, p. 22.

2,417. "Klan Here Accused Of Ties With Bund." New York Times. August 13, 1946, p. 1.

2,418. "Klan Is Accused Of A Revolt Plot." New York Times. June 21, 1946, p. 46.

2,419. "Klan Issue Grows In Georgia Poll." New York Times. June 1, 1946, p. 14.

2,420. "Klan Issues Warning On 2 Wallace Talks." New York Times. November 19, 1947, p. 23.

2,421. "Klan Kidnap Raid Reported." New York Times. July 27, 1949, p. 48.

2,422. "Klan Killing Stirs Wrath Of Atlanta." New York Times. March 17, 1940, Sect. 4, p. 10.

2,423. "Klan Losing Power In Its Birthplace." New York Times. November 18, 1923, Sect. 2, p. 1.

2.424. "Klan Meeting Disrupter Denied Visitors After Escape Attempt." Atlanta Daily World. January 8, 1978, p. 2.

2,425. "Klan Money Used To Clean Up 'Black Belt'." Pittsburgh Courier. November 10, 1923, p. 4.

2,426. "Klan Officials Deny Morality Charges." New York Times. September 20, 1921, p. 19.

2,427. "Klan Organizer Gets 12 Months." New York Times. July 4, 1935, p. 3.

2,428. "Klan Parades In Atlanta Negro Section; Onlooker Takes Hood And Wears It." Black Dispatch. November 20, 1937.

2,429. "Klan Pickets Banquet For Commissioner." Atlanta Daily World. August 23, 1977, p. 3.

2,430. "Klan Raider Is Killed." New York Times. March 11, 1926, p. 24.

2,431.   "Klan Rally Rammer Denied All Visitors During Escape Probe." _Atlanta Daily World_. January 8, 1978, p. 2.

2,432.   "Klan Reborn On Stone Mountain." _Christian Century_. Vol. 63, June 5, 1946, p. 726.

2,433.   "Klan Rebuffed." _Washington Post_. January 23, 1982, p. A10.

2,434.   "Klan Rebuffed On Koinonia Farm Suggestion." _Christian Science Monitor_. March 2, 1957, p. 15.

2,435.   "Klan Receiver Refused." _New York Times_. February 21, 1923, p. 19.

2,436.   "Klan Sells Atlanta Block." _New York Times_. February 16, 1928, p. 37.

2,437.   "Klan Shows Are Outlawed." _Pittsburgh Courier_. February 18, 1939, p. 23.

2,438.   "Klan Supports Clarke." _New York Times_. October 7, 1922, p. 20.

2,439.   "Klan Surrenders Georgia Charter." _New York Times_. June 14, 1947, p. 30.

2,440.   "Klan Suspends 4 Arrested In Slaying Of Educator." _New York Times_. August 9, 1964, p. 66.

2,441.   "Klan Takes Over Supper." _New York Times_. May 21, 1950, p. 45.

2,442.   "Klan Terrorists Linked To Killing." _New York Times_. June 8, 1946, p. 38.

2,443.   "Klan To Don Masks Again." _New York Times_. November 13, 1922, p. 16.

2,444.   "Klan Tyrant Out." _Chicago Defender_. January 21, 1922, p. 2.

2,445.   "Klan Wants Segregation - 'Or Else'." _Washington Post_. November 18, 1947.

2,446.   "Klan Warns Coach To Get Out Of Town." _New York Times_. February 5, 1948, p. 17.

2,447.   "Klan Wars On C.I.O. In Georgia Areas." _New York Times_. December 11, 1938.

2,448.   "Klan Welcomes Investigation." _New York Times_. March 26, 1950, p. 77.

2,449.   "Klan Wins Delay On Georgia's Suit." New York
Times. November 30, 1946., p. 32.

2,450.   "Klan Wizard Shorn Of Full Authority." New York
Times. May 8, 1923, p. 17.

2,451.   "Klansman Accused Of Shooting Wife." Charlotte
Observer. May 6, 1966.

2,452.   "Klansman Assails Clarke." New York Times. June
26, 1922, p. 4.

2,453.   "Klansman Helps Negro On Project." New York Times.
January 28, 1968, p. 59.

2,454.   "Klansman Helps Negroes." Washington Post. March
27, 1965.

2,455.   "Klansman Is Held In Kidnapping Of Georgia Sheriff
In Drug Inquiry." New York Times. October 8,
1980, p. A16.

2,456.   "Klansman Protest." New York Times. September 17,
1961, p. 66.

2,457.   "Klansman Sentenced In Shooting." Charlotte
Observer. August 14, 1966.

2,458.   "Klansman To Speak At Atlanta University Center."
Atlanta (Ga.) Voice. March 14, 1981, p. 10.

2,459.   "Klansmen Are Given 10 Years." Charlotte Observer.
July 10, 1966, p. 4A.

2,460.   "Klansmen Freed In Negro's Death." New York Times.
September 5, 1964, pp. 1, 9.

2,461.   "Klansmen Given Maximum Term For Rights Violation."
Durham Morning Herald. July 10, 1966, p. 8A.

2,462.   "Klansmen Given Terms In Slaying." Greensboro
Daily News. July 10, 1966.

2,463.   "Klansmen In Georgia More To 'Cut' Davis; Allege
Negro Equality Talk, Which He Denies." New York
Times. October 29, 1924, p. 1.

2,464.   "Klansmen Kidnap Bright And Mrs. Pace, Beat Man
Senseless." New York Times. April 5, 1923, p. 1.

2,465.   "Klansmen Kluxed By The Klus: Just Ku Kluxin'
Around." The Messenger. Vol. 5, December, 1923,
p. 920.

2,466.   "Klansmen Scold Paper." New York Times. November 27, 1939, p. 7.

2,467.   "Klansmen Sentenced In Georgia." Winston-Salem
          Journal. July 10, 1966.

2,468.   "Konstitutional Rites." Newsweek. Vol. 66,
          November 8, 1965, p. 34.

2,469.   "Ku Klux Acts Today On Clarke Resignation." New
          York Times. September 27, 1921, p. 32.

2,470.   "Ku Klux Head Made Leader Of College." Chicago
          Defender. August 27, 1921, p. 3.

2,471.   "Ku Klux Klan." Nation. Vol. 162, June 8, 1946,
          p. 678.

2,472.   "Ku Klux Klan Boasts 25,000 Georgia Members."
          Chicago Defender. December 8, 1945.

2,473.   "KKK March In Macon, Ga. Reported To Be Peaceful."
          Atlanta Daily World. December 4, 1979, p. 8.

2,474.   "Ku Klux Klan Insurgents Gain Ground On Simmons."
          Chicago Defender. January 14, 1922, p. 1.

2,475.   "Ku Klux Klan Leaders Well Fitted To Correct
          Morals Of Communities." The Messenger. Vol. 3,
          October, 1921, pp. 261-262.

2,476.   "Ku Klux Klan Meets." New York Times. May 9,
          1922, p.33.

2,477.   "Ku Klux Klan Plans School." New York Times.
          January 8, 1960, p. 8.

2,478.   "Ku Klux Klan To Attend Wrightsville, Ga., Blacks
          March." Houston Post. April 12, 1980, p. 18A.

2,479.   "The Ku Klux Klan Tries A Comeback." Life. Vol.
          20, May 27, 1946, pp. 42-44.

2,480.   "Ku Klux Officials Escape Indictment." New York
          Times. September 24, 1921, p. 16.

2,481.   "Ku Klux Present Head Of Order $25,000 Home."
          Chicago Defender. May 14, 1921, p. 1.

2,482.   "Ku Klux Seek Money For 'Kultur' College."
          Chicago Defender. January 21, 1922, p. 1.

2,483.   "Ku Klux To Build 'Hall Of Invisibles'." New
          York Times. September 19, 1921, p. 17.

2,484.   "Ku Klux To Discard Its Masks In Public." New
          York Times. July 23, 1922, p. 1.

2,485.   "Ku Klux Unmasking Denied." New York Times.
          July 25, 1922, p. 27.

2,486.   "Ku Klux Warn White Editor To Halt Attack."
          Chicago Defender. May 7, 1921, p. 1.

2,487.   "Ku Klux Warns Members." New York Times. August
          9, 1922, p. 6.

2,488.   "Labor In Georgia Asks Klan Inquiry." New York
          Times. May 11, 1946, p. 40.

2,489.   "Labor Wants Probe Of Klan." People's Voice.
          May 18, 1946, p. 3.

2,490.   "Law Hits Terrorism." Christian Science Monitor.
          February 10, 1951, p. 14.

2,491.   "Law Sought To Ban Masked Klan Parade." New York
          Times. December 9, 1948, p. 41.

2,492.   "Leader Of KKK On Personal Staff Of Governor
          Talmadge." Afro-American. July 9, 1949, p. 1.

2,493.   LeFlore, John. "Hooded Group In Georgia Revival."
          Chicago Defender. October 27, 1945.

2,494.   "Legislature Bans Masks In Georgia." New York
          Times. January 20, 1951, p. 19.

2,495.   "Macon, Ga. Prepares For KKK March Through The
          City." Atlanta Daily World. November 30, 1979,
          p. 1.

2,496.   "Macon Klan Organizer Arrested." New York Times.
          September 11, 1923, p. 19.

2,497.   "Maddox Called Aid To Klan." Durham Morning
          Herald. November 30, 1966.

2,498.   "Maddox Names Ex-Law Partner Of Klan Leader As
          Party Official." New York Times. October 15,
          1966, p. 14.

2,499.   "Maddox Turns Aside Klan 'Endorsement'." New York
          Times. August 12, 1974, p. 49.

2,500.   "Man Claims Memory Loss Before Car Hits KKK Rally
          Stage." Houston Post. October 23, 1977, p. 3A.

2,501.   "Man Who Drove Into Rally Of Klan Is Recaptured."
          New York Times. December 28, 1977, p. 14.

2,502.   "Mayor James Peterson." New York Times. July 9,
          1949, p. 28.

2,503.   McLean, Phillip J. "Klan Reborn On Stone Moun-
           tain." _Christian Century_. Vol. 63, June 5, 1946,
           p. 726.

2,504.   _____. "Southern Liberals Oppose Klan."
           Christian Century. Vol. 63, June 5, 1946, p. 726.

2,505.   McWilliams, Carey. "The Klan: Post War Model."
           Nation. Vol. 163, December 14, 1946, pp. 691-692.

2,506.   "Mechanic Pleads Innocent In Klan Rally Assault."
           New York Times. October 18, 1977, p. 16.

2,507.   "Minister Denounces Klan." _New York Times_.
           July 18, 1949, p. 10.

2,508.   "Ministers Denounce Georgia Klan." _Christian
           Century_. Vol. 66, January 5, 1949, p. 6.

2,509.   "Miss KKK." _Newsweek_. Vol. 32, December 20,
           1948, p. 22.

2,510.   "Miss Lillian Says Sight Impaired During Accident
           At KKK Rally." _Houston Post_. October 22, 1977,
           p. 8A.

2,511.   "Mistrial In Bombing Case." _New York Times_.
           January 26, 1952, p. 30.

2,512.   "Moderates Concerned." _Christian Science Monitor_.
           April 6, 1967, p. 1.

2,513.   "A More Civilized Curriculum." _New York Times_.
           June 10, 1946, p. 20.

2,514.   Moseley, Clement Charlton. "Latent Klanism in
           Georgia, 1890-1915." _Georgia Historical Quarterly_.
           Vol. 56, 1972, pp. 115-135.

2,515.   _____. "The Political Influence Of The Ku Klux
           Klan In Georgia, 1915-1925." _Georgia Historical
           Quarterly_. Vol. 57, Summer, 1973, pp. 235-255.

2,516.   "Moton's 'Good-Will' Tour." _New York Amsterdam
           News_. December 13, 1922.

2,517.   "Mountain's Owners Bar Klan And Foes." _New York
           Times_. June 17, 1946, p. 23.

2,518.   "Move To Clean Up 'Hooded Ruffians'." _New York
           Times_. February 14, 1927, p. 10.

2,519.   "Mrs. Pace's Story Of Outrage." _New York Times_.
           April 5, 1923, p. 1, 8.

2,520. "Mrs. Tyler Resigns Klan Post As Aid To Imperial Kleague." New York Times. January 5, 1922, p. 1.

2,521. Mugleston, William F. "Julian Harris, The Georgia Press, And The Ku Klux Klan." Georgia Historical Quarterly. Vol. 59, Fall, 1975, pp. 284-295.

2,522. "NAACP Members May Attend KKK Meeting In Georgia School." Atlanta Daily World. December 31, 1981, p. 1.

2,523. "Negro And Klansman Join In Atlanta Plan." New York Times. January 24, 1968, p. 55.

2,524. "Negro Voters Defy Klan." New York Times. March 23, 1948, p. 28.

2,525. "Negro Whippings In Georgia Raise Issue Of Action By Federal Court On Civil Rights." New York Times. November 22, 1949, p. 18.

2,526. "Negroes Advised To Demand Rights." New York Times. July 5, 1962, p. 14.

2,527. "Negroes Harassed, Klan Trial Is Told." New York Times. July 7, 1966, p. 22.

2,528. "Negro Teams Barred." New York Times. November 30, 1956, p. 16.

2,529. "Negro's Murder Laid To 2 In Klan." New York Times. July 8, 1966, p. 16.

2,530. "Negroes Shun Polls After Klan Threats." People's Voice. March 6, 1948, p. 2.

2,531. "Night Riding Ga. Flogger Is Sentenced." Chicago Defender. May 4, 1940.

2,532. "Nightmare On Pine Mountain." Time. Vol. 51, March 22, 1948, pp. 24-25.

2,533. "1940: 'The Police Just Laughed'." Southern Exposure. Vol. 8, Summer, 1980, p. 69.

2,534. "No Negroes Vote After Klan Threat." New York Times. March 4, 1948, p. 15.

2,535. "Old Ku Klux Klan Headquarters Still Stands In Atlanta." Atlanta Daily World. June 1, 1978, p. 1.

2,536. "100 Ku Klux Klansmen March Through Cartersville, Georgia." Atlanta Daily World. November 27, 1979, p. 1.

2,537. "100 March In Georgia." New York Times. November 25, 1979, p. 44.

2,538.   "$190,000 Bond Set For Man Who Used Car To Break Up KKK Rally." Atlanta Daily World. July 5, 1977, p. 1.

2,539.   "170 Ask Receiver For Ku Klux Klan." New York Times. December 29, 1921, p. 9.

2,540.   "Orders Klan Into Court." New York Times. September 16, 1923, p. 23.

2,541.   "Organizer Of Klan At Flogging Trial." New York Times. September 12, 1923, p. 21.

2,542.   Ottley, Roy. "I Met The Grand Dragon." Nation. Vol. 169, July 2, 1949, pp. 10-11.

2,543.   " 'Outsider' Issue Stirs Albany, Ga." New York Times. August 13, 1962, pp. 1, 13.

2,544.   "Pace Kidnappers Elude Police Hunt." New York Times. April 6, 1923, p. 1.

2,545.   "Parading Klansmen Fired On In Georgia." New York Times. August 8, 1949, p. 30.

2,546.   Pearson, Drew. "Herman Talmadge Splits Klan." Washington Post. January 28, 1948.

2,547.   "Pearson Links Klan To Talmadge Plans." New York Times. July 22, 1946, p. 23.

2,548.   "Pearson's Charges Denied By Talmadge." New York Times. July 23, 1946, p. 27.

2,549.   "Penn Murder Trial Hears 2 Witnesses." New York Times. September 2, 1964, p. 27.

2,550.   "Plains, Georgia, Alters Parade Ordinance After Klan Rally." New Orleans Times Picayune. July 11, 1977, p. 14.

2,551.   "Plains, Ga. Mayor Expects KKK Rallies." Atlanta Daily World. July 14, 1977, p. 2.

2,552.   "Playing With Fire." Time. Vol. 53, January 3, 1949, p. 42.

2,553   "Police Records." New York Times. March 3, 1923, p. 9.

2,554.   Popham, John N. "Dual Racial Stand Voted In Georgia." New York Times. February 18, 1951, p. 48.

2,555.   " 'Powerless' To Stop KKK Rallies: Mayor." Atlanta Daily World. July 14, 1977, p. 2.

2,556. "President Lauds Mayor Of Georgia Town Who Unmasked Three Members Of Klan." New York Times. June 7, 1949, p. 29.

2,557. "Pressure Charged In Georgia Flogging." New York Times. November 29, 1949, p. 16.

2,558. Pretshold, Karl. "Georgia's Arnall Opens All-Out Battle Against Klan." PM. May 31, 1946.

2,559. "Probe Of Slayings Is Aim Of Marchers." Richmond Times-Dispatch. February 21, 1982, p. A2.

2,560. "Proposes To Sue Klan To Account For Fund. New York Times. May 20, 1928, p. 22.

2,561. "Prospective Jurors Queried In Private In Negro's Slaying." New York Times. June 28, 1966, p. 25.

2,562. "Protectors Of Womanhood." Time. Vol. 51, February 16, 1948, p. 26.

2,563. "Protest And Counter Protest." New York Times. July 5, 1962, p. 14.

2,564. Racine, Philip N. "The Ku Klux Klan, Anti-Catholicism, And Atlanta's Board Of Education, 1916-1927." Georgia Historical Quarterly. Vol. 57, Spring, 1973, pp. 63-75.

2,565. "Ready To Call Troops In Georgia." New York Times. August 21, 1923, p. 5.

2,566. Reed, Roy. "Victim Of Attack Is Held In Georgia." New York Times. October 14, 1965, p. 40.

2,567. Rimer, Sara and Tom Sherwood. "Ex-Klansman Ordered To Pay Victims." Washington Post. April 28, 1982, p. C6.

2,568. "Rogge Scrutinizes Georgia Floggings." New York Times. March 21, 1940, p. 13.

2,569. Rovere, Richard H. "The Klan Rides Again." Nation. Vol. 150, April 6, 1940, pp. 445-446.

2,570. "Sanders Studies Revocation Of Georgia's Klan Charters." New York Times. October 19, 1965, p. 28.

2,571. "Santa Claus Foils Mask Ban." New York Times. February 19, 1939, p. 36.

2,572. "Say Gunmen Harass Klan." New York Times. October 13, 1921, p. 9.

2,573.   "Says Klan Met In Capitol." New York Times. September 18, 1923, p. 5.

2,574.   "School Board In Georgia Backed On Klan Meeting." New York Times. December 26, 1981, p. 12.

2,575.   Schulz, William E. "Speeding Car Cuts A Swath Through Plains Klan Rally." Washington Post. July 3, 1977, p. A3.

2,576.   "SCLC And IFCO Sponsor Anti-KKK Conference In Atlanta." Atlanta Daily World. December 13, 1979, p. 1.

2,577.   "Seizes Klan Chaplain As Intoxicated In Car." New York Times. October 18, 1923, p. 23.

2,578.   "Serve More Warrants For Macon Floggings." New York Times. September 9, 1923, p. 18.

2,579.   Shankman, Arnold. "Julian Harris And The Ku Klux Klan." Mississippi Quarterly. Vol. 28, Spring, 1975, pp. 147-169.

2,580.   "Sheet, Sugar Sack and Cross." Time. Vol. 51, March 15, 1948, p. 29.

2,581.   "Sheriff Indicted In Flogging Incident." Christian Science Monitor. May 11, 1949, p. 6.

2,582.   "Sheriff Is Convicted In Georgia Flogging." New York Times. March 10, 1950, p. 17.

2,583.   "Sheriff Says Klan Took Two Prisioners." New York Times. December 10, 1949, p. 28.

2,584.   Shipp, Bill. "Initiation Night At The Klan Hall." Twin City Sentinel. February 24, 1965.

2,585.   "Shots At Klansmen Free Georgia Negro." New York Times. March 5, 1950, p. 77.

2,586.   "Simmons Charges Klan Fund Diverted." New York Times. April 6, 1923, p. 19.

2,587.   "Simmons, Ex-Wizard Of Klan, Plans 'Caucasian Crusade' For Whites." Pittsburgh Courier. August 2, 1930, p. 3.

2,588.   Sitton, Claude. "Georgia Students Riot On Campus; Two Negroes Out." New York Times. January 12, 1961, pp. 1, 20.

2,589.   _____. "Georgia U. Moves To Guard Negroes." New York Times. January 16, 1961, p. 15.

2,590.   _____. "Klansmen Stage Albany, Ga. Rally."
                New York Times. September 4, 1962, p. 26

2,591.   _____. "Negroes And Klan Picket In Atlanta."
                New York Times. February 2, 1964, p. 64.

2,592.   _____. "Negroes And Klansmen Clash In Atlanta
                As U.N. Group Visits City." New York Times.
                January 26, 1964, pp. 1, 34.

2,593.   _____. "Negroes Resume Atlanta Sit-Ins After
                Sidewalk Clash With Klan." New York Times.
                January 20, 1964, p. 15.

2,594.   _____. "Negroes To Step Up Pressure In Atlanta."
                New York Times. January 19, 1964, pp. 1, 43.

2,595.   _____. "Race Issue Stirs Georgia Primary."
                New York Times. September 3, 1962, p. 13.

2,596.   _____. "Troopers Upheld On Klan's Rally."
                New York Times. July 10, 1962, p. 24.

2,597.   _____. "U.S. Judge Weighs Georgia U. Action."
                New York Times. January 13, 1961, pp. 1, 32.

2,598.   "6 Georgia Klansmen Due For Trial Jan. 11." New
                York Times. December 1, 1964, p. 44.

2,599.   "6 Klansmen Face Charges In Harassment Of Negroes."
                New York Times. November 30, 1964, p. 50.

2,600.   "Sixty Years Of Night Terrorism Exposed." Chicago
                Defender. October 8, 1921, p. 2.

2,601.   "Smug KKK Count On White Jury In Penn Killing."
                Muhammad Speaks. July 8, 1960, p. 6.

2,602.   "Social Equality In Georgia." Pittsburgh Courier.
                July 2, 1927, Editorial page.

2,603.   "Steals Ku Klux Klan Cloth, Say." Pittsburgh
                Courier. May 12, 1928, p. 5.

2,604.   "A South Georgia Mayor." New York Times. June 13,
                1949, p. 13.

2,605.   "Sues Klan For $100,000." New York Times. October
                11, 1921, p. 4.

2,606.   "Summary Of KKK Activity In N.J., Texas And
                Carterville, Ga." Bilalian News. December 14,
                1979, p. 4.

2,607.   "Surrenders In Klan Case." New York Times.
                December 24, 1923, p. 5.

2,608.   Swim, Allan L. "Hate Peddlers." _Washington Daily News_. December 10, 1945.

2,609.   "Talmadge Frees Three Floggers." _New York Times_. December 9, 1942, p. 17.

2,610.   Taylor, Charles S. "Old Headquarters Of KKK Still Stands On Roswell Rd." _Atlanta Daily World_. June 1, 1978, pp. 1, 4.

2,611.   "Tells Of Murder And Kidnapping." _New York Times_. August 21, 1923, p. 5.

2,612.   "$10,000 Is Offered For Lynchers; Georgia Police Inquiry Thwarted." _New York Times_. July 28, 1946, pp. 1, 12.

2,613.   "Terrorists Arrests Now 10 In Georgia." _New York Times_. March 31, 1940, p. 5.

2,614.   "Their Method That Of The Klan." _New York Times_. April 7, 1923, p. 12.

2,615.   "Then School Bells Rang." _Newsweek_. Vol. 60, September 17, 1962, pp. 31-32, 34.

2,616.   "Stiffer Blows Needed To Control." _Christian Science Monitor_. August 10, 1949, p. 7.

2,617.   "Sumpter City Sheriff Says Car Aimed At Klan Chief In Ga. Incident." _Houston Post_. July 4, 1977, p. 1C.

2,618.   "They Had A City For Victim." _New York Times_. April 7, 1923, p. 12.

2,619.   "This Judge Knows It As It Is." _New York Times_. June 7, 1926, p. 18.

2,620.   "Thompson Pushes Georgia Klan Case." _New York Times_. March 21, 1947, p. 4.

2,621.   "3 Hooded Men Win First Test In Court." _New York Times_. June 14, 1949, p. 26.

2,622.   "300 Women In Masks Parade In Atlanta." _New York Times_. November 23, 1922, p. 23.

2,623.   "3 Klansmen Fined." _New York Times_. May 30, 1961, p. 7.

2,624.   "3 Linked To Floggings." _New York Times_. March 23, 1940, p. 3.

2,625.   "3 Newsmen Say Klan Held, Drugged Them." _New York Times_. March 14, 1948, p. 76.

2,626.   "3,500 At Klan Rally." New York Times. September
         30, 1956, p. 52.

2,627.   "Time Blocks Prosecution Of Ga. KKK." Chicago
         Defender. November 16, 1946, p. 3.

2,628.   "To Try Klan Slayer Dec. 12." New York Times.
         November 11, 1923, p. 18.

2,629.   "Topics Of The Times." New York Times. September
         12, 1946, p. 6.

2,630.   "Triumph Over Tolerance." Pittsburgh Courier.
         January 28, 1939, p. 10.

2,631.   "Truck Driver Who Hit Ku Klux Klan Crowd Arraigned
         In Sumpter Ct." Los Angeles Times. July 4, 1977,
         p. 1.

2,632.   "Two Atlanta Ku Klux Officials Resign." New York
         Times. September 22, 1921, p. 3.

2,633.   "2 Georgia KKK Units Set Up Rival Group." New
         York Times. June 30, 1948, p. 21.

2,634.   "2 Klansmen Convicted, 4 Freed In Penn Case."
         Washington Post. July 9, 1966.

2,635.   "Two Klansmen Deny Guilt In Penn Case." New York
         Times. September 4, 1964, p. 11.

2,636.   "Two Macon Victims Tell Of Floggings." New York
         Times. September 13, 1923, p. 23.

2,637.   "Two More Floggings." New York Times. August 19,
         1923, p. 2.

2,638.   "2 Students Indicted." New York Times. January
         20, 1961, p. 19.

2,639.   "2 Tried For Penn's Murder Released On $25,000
         Bonds." New York Times. September 9, 1964, p. 20.

2,640.   "War Is Again Raging Within Ku Klux Klan."
         Pittsburgh Courier. June 30, 1923, p. 8.

2,641.   "Warrants Issued For Klan Officials." New York
         Times. April 5, 1923, p. 21.

2,642.   Wesberry, James P. "K.K.K. Holds Cross-Burning
         Near Atlanta." Christian Century. Vol. 74,
         January 9, 1957, p. 54.

2,643.   "White Driver Rams Klan Rally In Plains, Injuring
         30." New York Times. July 3, 1977, pp. 1, 10.

2,644.   "White Man Drives Car Into Ku Klux Klan Rally."
          Chicago Tribune. July 3, 1977, p. 2.

2,645.   "White Protest Meeting Held." New York Times.
          July 5, 1962, p. 14.

2,646.   "Willacoochee, Ga., Mayor Seeks FBI Aid To Stop
          Racial Violence." Atlanta Daily World. July 28,
          1981, p. 1.

2,647.   "With Klan's Help, Incident On School Bus Disrupts
          Two Lives." Augusta (Ga.) News-Review. June 20,
          1981, pp. 1, 7.

2,648.   "Woman In Klan Case Held In Tennessee." New York
          Times. December 16, 1923, p. 18.

2,649.   "Women Terrorists Reported." New York Times.
          March 31, 1940, p. 5.

2,650.   "Youth Drives Car Through Ku Klux Klan Rally In
          Plains, Georgia." Washington Post. July 3, 1977,
          p. 3A.

10. HAWAII

2,651.   "Hawaii Bars Klan Movies, Demand Pastor Quit
          Pulpit." Chicago Defender. September 16, 1922,
          p. 1.

2,652.   "Ku Klux Klan In Hawaii." New York Times.
          October 19, 1922, p. 44.

11. IDAHO

2,653.   "Condemn Klan In Idaho." New York Times. August
          28, 1924, p. 3.

2,654.   "Council Tells Police To 'Shoot To Kill' In War
          Against K.K.K." Pittsburgh Courier. September 29,
          1923, p. 8.

2,655.   "The Klan's Man In Idaho A Card-Carrying Negro."
          New York Times. February 25, 1965, p. 18.

2,656.   "Negro Who Joined Klan Reported Missing In Idaho."
          New York Times. April 22, 1965, p. 14.

2,657.   "Police Told To Kill Hooded Raiders." New York
          Times. September 19, 1923, p. 5.

12. ILLINOIS

2,658.   "Agnew Deplores 'Scruffy' Youths." New York Times.
          May 12, 1971, p. 26.

2,659.   "Arrests Herrin Klansmen." New York Times.
          October 21, 1924, p. 6.

2,660.   "Assail Barring Of Klan On Juries." New York Times.
          January 9, 1923, p. 3.

2,661.   "Assails Dawes On Klan." New York Times. September
          1, 1924, p. 3.

2,662.   "Aurora, Illinois Blacks Protest Ku Klux Klan Acti-
          vities." Chicago Tribune. March 12, 1975, p. 4.

2,663.   "Aurora, Illinois City Council Condemns KKK
          Activities." Chicago Tribune. March 19, 1975,
          Sect. 3, p. 18.

2,664.   "Beavers To Start Battle Against Ku Klux Sunday."
          Chicago Defender. October 15, 1921, pp. 5-6.

2,665.   "Big Rockford Crowd Hears Davis Urge 'Common
          Honesty'." New York Times. September 6, 1924,
          pp. 1, 3.

2,666.   "Blames Klan For Fire." New York Times.   October
          19, 1924, pp. 26-27.

2,667.   " 'Bloody Williamson'." New York Times.   January
          27, 1925, p. 12.

2,668.   "Bomb Threat At Hotel." New York Times.   January
          29, 1923, p. 17.

2,669.   "Branded With 'K.K.K.'." New York Times.   August
          12, 1924, pp. 21-22.

2,670.   "Called Klansman; Sues." New York Times.   February
          3, 1923, p. 14.

2,671.   "Calls Wrigley Klansman." New York Times.
          February 8, 1923, p. 16.

2,672.   Chenery, William L. "Herrin - The 'Sore Spot' Of
          The Nation." New York Times. September 14, 1924,
          Sect. 9, pp. 1, 12.

2,673.   "Chi Kluxers Plan To Double Cross Oscar De Priest."
          Pittsburgh Courier. September 8, 1928, p. 8.

2,674.   "Chicago Bars Ku Klux." New York Times. September
          20, 1921, p. 19.

2,675.   "Chicago Daily Papers To Refuse Ku Klux Ad."
          Chicago Defender. April 9, 1921, p. 1.

2,676.   "Chicago Judge Bars Klansmen As His Jurors."
          Chicago Defender. September 23, 1922, pp. 2-3.

2,677.   "Chicago Ku Klux Admit 4,650 In Night Spectacle Near
          City." New York Times. August 21, 1922, p. 1.

2,678.   "Chicago Millionaire To Sue Ku Klux Klan." Cali-
         fornia Eagle. February 17, 1923, pp. 1-2.

2,679.   "Chicago Opens War On Ku Klux Klan." New York
         Times. November 12, 1922, Sect. 2, p. 1.

2,680.   "Church Recants In Denunciation Of Ku Kluxers."
         Chicago Defender. October 14, 1922, pp. 2-3.

2,681.   "City Council Of Chicago Scores Ku Klux Klan."
         Chicago Defender. September 24, 1921, pp. 3-4.

2,682.   "Colored Representative Applies For Membership!"
         Pittsburgh Courier. June 16, 1923, p. 10.

2,683.   "Comeback Of Ku Klux Klan In Illinois Discussed."
         Chicago Tribune. March 16, 1975, p. 1.

2,684.   "Con Admits To KKK Killings." Pittsburgh Courier.
         June 13, 1981, p. 1.

2,685.   "County Klans Gather For Fight." New York Times.
         February 10, 1924, p. 16.

2,686.   "Court Enjoins Publication Of Ku Klux Klan Member-
         ship." New York Times. May 13, 1923, Sect. 2,
         p. 1.

2,687.   "Cross Burns At Negro's New Home." Charlotte
         Observer. March 14, 1966, p. 1.

2,688.   "Dennis Kucinich And The Ku Klux Klan." Chicago
         Defender. October 20, 1979, p. 9A.

2,689.   "Disputes Herrin Picture." New York Times.
         August 26, 1924, p. 10.

2,690.   "Dodges Putting Blame For Herrin Shooting." New
         York Times. May 26, 1924, p. 17.

2,691.   "Dr. Black Is Freed In Herrin Murder." New York
         Times. September 7, 1924, p. 20.

2,692.   "Editor Abbott's Comment On Ku Klux Klan Order."
         Chicago Defender. August 27, 1921, pp. 3-4.

2,693.   "Equal Rights League Opens War On Klan." Chicago
         Defender. September 3, 1921, pp. 8-9.

2,694.   "Eyewitness Tells Of Herrin Battle." New York
         Times. January 27, 1925, p. 5.

2,695.   "Faces Klan Foes At Herrin Meeting." New York
         Times. February 3, 1925, p. 19.

2,696.   "Federal Arrests Stir Chicago's Ire." New York
          Times. April 3, 1928, pp. 1, 2.

2,697.   "Fight KKK Revival In Illinois. New York Age.
          April 8, 1939, pp. 1-2.

2,698.   "500 Klansmen Renew Williamson Raids." New York
          Times. January 21, 1929, p. 2.

2,699.   "Following A Bad Precedent." New York Times.
          September 17, 1921, p. 12.

2,700.   "For Chicago Klan Inquiry." California Eagle.
          December 23, 1922, p. 6, Sect. 2.

2,701.   "For Chicago Klan Inquiry." New York Times.
          December 5, 1922, p. 3.

2,702.   "4 Slain In Herrin; Glenn Young Victim." New York
          Times. January 25, 1925, p. 1.

2,703.   "George T. Kersey Loses: Influence Of The Ku Klux
          Klan Shown In The State Legislature." Broad Ax.
          May 9, 1925, p. 2.

2,704.   "Guard Called For Cicero Tomorrow." New York
          Times. September 3, 1966, p. 48.

2,705.   "Gun Play And Sudden Death In Herrin." Literary
          Digest. February 21, 1925, pp. 34, 36, 38, 40.

2,706.   "Herrin Grand Jury Acts." New York Times. February
          13, 1925, p. 25.

2,707.   "Herrin Klan Arrests Judge, Alleging Fraudulent
          Voting." New York Times. April 16, 1924, p. 25.

2,708.   "Herrin Klansmen Convicted Of Assault In Feb. 8
          Rioting." New York Times. August 29, 1924, p. 1.

2,709.   "Herrin Officer Kills To Save Comrade." New York
          Times. February 2, 1925, pp. 1, 2.

2,710.   "Herrin On A Carouse Defies Klan And 'Drys'."
          New York Times. December 26, 1923, p. 25.

2,711.   "Herrin Peace Plan Ratified By Klan." New York
          Times. February 8, 1925, p. 7.

2,712.   "Herrin Preachers Would Oust Sheriff." New York
          Times. September 3, 1924, p. 21.

2,713.   "Herrin Sheriff And Aids Arrested." New York
          Times. September 2, 1924, p. 21.

2,714.   "Herrin Sheriff Will Leave County As Means Of Peace." New York Times. February 6, 1925, p. 1.

2,715.   "Herrin Widow Tells How Klansmen Slew Husband In Battle." New York Times. September 4, 1924, pp. 1, 4.

2,716.   "Herrin Witnesses Testify Secretly." New York Times. April 18, 1926, p. 19.

2,717.   "Hides Five Days In Woods To Escape Klan's Hot Tar." Chicago Defender. September 24, 1921, pp. 3-4.

2,718.   "Hold 3 In Klan Shooting." New York Times. June 27, 1924, p. 19.

2,719.   "Hooded Klansmen Burn De Priest In Effigy In Chicago." Pittsburgh Courier. August 23, 1930, p. 1.

2,720.   "Illinois Anti-Klan Bill Is Law." New York Times. June 28, 1923, p. 2.

2,721.   "Illinois Bars Mock Klan." New York Times. August 16, 1947, p. 6.

2,722.   "Illinois House Gets Anti-Klan Bill." New York Times. January 17, 1923, p. 8.

2,723.   "Illinois Rep. Henry Wants KKK Amendment Added To Bill On Gangs." Chicago Defender. July 16, 1981, p. 2.

2,724.   "Ill. Legis. Comm. Issues Report On State's Ku Klux Klan Chapter." Los Angeles Times. October 29, 1976, p. 5.

2,725.   "Ill. Legislative Comm. Report On Ku Klux Klan Viewed." New Orleans Times Picayune. May 15, 1975, Sect. 4, p. 2.

2,726.   "Ill. Legis. Investigating Comm. Views Status Of KKK In Illinois." Chicago Tribune. November 4, 1979, Sect. 2, p. 9.

2,727.   "Jackson Gives Local Ku Klux Solar Plexus." Chicago Defender. June 3, 1922, pp. 4-5.

2,728.   Janson, Donald. "Cicero Issues Permit For March Today." New York Times. September 4, 1966, p. 54.

2,729.   _____. "Dr. King And 500 Jeered In 5 Mile Chicago March." New York Times. August 22, 1966, pp. 1, 3.

2,730.   _____. "Sheriff Asks Dr. King To Call Off
          Cicero March." New York Times. August 23, 1966,
          p. 35.

2,731.   "Kahane Calls Violence Necessary." New York Times.
          July 5, 1977, p. 12.

2,732.   "Kidnapped Police Chief Returns." New York Times.
          February 11, 1924, p. 2.

2,733.   "KKK; Festering Sore In Chicago." Sepia. Vol. 17,
          June, 1963, pp. 60-65.

2,734.   "KKK In Chicago." Broad Ax. August 26, 1922, p. 1.

2,735.   "KKK Reportedly Urges Black Family Out Of Aurora,
          Ill." Chicago Tribune. August 18, 1975, Sect. 2,
          p. 7.

2,736.   "Klan Aids Dry Raiders." New York Times. February
          4, 1924, p. 23.

2,737.   "Klan Bans Parade Until After Election." New York
          Times. July 20, 1928, p. 5.

2,738.   "Klan Donation Is Declined By A Colored Congrega-
          tion." New York Times. September 17, 1924, p. 1.

2,739.   "Klan Hearings Planned. New York Times. January
          11, 1968, p. 29.

2,740.   "Klan In Election Fight." New York Times. April
          3, 1923, p. 25.

2,741.   "The Klan In Illinois." New York Times. October
          25, 1924, p. 14.

2,742.   "Klan Law And Order." New York Times. September
          1, 1924, p. 12.

2,743.   "Klan Leaders Indicted For Extortion." New York
          Times. April 26, 1924, p. 3.

2,744.   "Klan Papers's Plant Wrecked By Bomb." New York
          Times. April 7, 1923, p. 15.

2,745.   "Klan To Make Fight On Chicago Fireman." New York
          Times. January 28, 1923, Sect. 1, Part 2, p. 5.

2,746.   "Klan Warned In Illinois." New York Times.
          October 31, 1965, p. 35.

2,747.   "Klan Warns Marion Officials." New York Times.
          August 21, 1923, p. 5.

2,748.   "Klan Warns Resorts." New York Times. July 12, 1925, Sect. 2, p. 2.

2,749.   "Klansman Reported Senate Group Aide." New York Times. July 12, 1930, p. 4.

2,750.   "Klansmen Admit Attacking Doctor." New York Times. June 16, 1922, p. 17.

2,751.   "Klansmen Aid Raides, By Drys At Herrin." New York Times. December 25, 1923, p. 3.

2,752.   "Klansmen In Chicago's Pay." New York Times. November 30, 1922, p. 21.

2,753.   "Klansmen In Chicago To Be Exposed." Chicago Defender. September 10, 1922, pp. 2-3.

2,754.   "Klansmen Light A Fiery Cross." New York Times. September 1, 1924, p. 3.

2,755.   "Klansmen Take Office In Marion, Ill." New York Times. December 2, 1924, p. 27.

2,756.   "Klansmen Take Police Officer." New York Times. February 10, 1924, p. 16.

2,757.   "Ku Klux Invade Chicago." Chicago Defender. August 20, 1921, pp. 1, 3.

2,758.   "Ku Klux Klan Condemned By Illinois House." Chicago Defender. June 25, 1921, pp. 8-9.

2,759.   "Ku Klux Klan Organization A Bad Influence." Christian Century. Vol. 38, September 8, 1921, p. 4.

2,760.   "Leaders In War Exiled From Herrin." New York Times. September 6, 1924, p. 13.

2,761.   "Lure Of Jack O'Lantern." Chicago Defender. August 27, 1921, pp. 16-17.

2,762.   "Martial Law Asked By Herrin Sheriff." New York Times. February 1, 1925, p. 1.

2,763.   "Meddlers Get No Help." New York Times. January 30, 1925, p. 16.

2,764.   "Members Of Race 'Pass' And Join The Ku Kluxers." Chicago Defender. August 26, 1922, pp. 3-4

2,765.   "Miners Strike Against Klan." New York Times. February 10, 1924, p. 16.

2,766.   "Nation-Wide War On Ku Klux Klan Is Launched Here."
          Chicago Defender. August 19, 1922, pp. 3-4.

2,767.   "Negro's Klan Bill Beaten." New York Times.
          June 12, 1925, p. 6.

2,768.   "Negro's Klan Membership Is Revoked By The Wizard."
          New York Times. February 26, 1965, p. 14.

2,769.   "New Rift Seen At Herrin." New York Times.
          February 4, 1925, p. 14.

2,770.   "Nine Klansmen Under Arrest." New York Times.
          September 1, 1924, p. 3.

2,771.   "Offices Of 'Dawn' K.K.K. Organ. Bombed." New
          York Amsterdam News. April 11, 1923, pp. 3-4.

2,772.   "Orders Klan Out Of Herrin." New York Times.
          January 11, 1924, p. 9

2,773.   "Organizing To Fight The Ku Klux Klan." New York
          Times. September 16, 1921, p. 12.

2,774.   Oulahan, Richard V. "Gunmen's Sway At Polls Feared
          In Chicago Today; 8,000 Guards For Primary." New
          York Times. April 10, 1928, pp. 1, 2.

2,775.   _____. "Negro Newspaper Opposes Hoover." New
          York Times. October 20, 1928, p. 4.

2,776.   "Parker Says Nation Must Unmask Klan." New York
          Times. February 27, 1923, p. 21.

2,777.   "Pastor Eulogizes Young For 'Clean-Up'." New York
          Times. January 30, 1925, p. 19.

2,778.   "Put Military Rule In Force At Herrin." New York
          Times. February 11, 1924, p. 1.

2,779.   "Raps Klan In Urbana." New York Amsterdam News.
          April 15, 1939, p. 17.

2,780.   "The Reformation Of Herrin." Literary Digest.
          Vol. 86, August 1, 1925, pp. 28-29.

2,781.   Reinitz, Bertrand. "Stranger Than Fiction." New
          York Times. February 1, 1925, Sect. 8, p. 2.

2,782.   "Religious Issue Up In Chicago Election." New
          York Times. April 3, 1923, p. 25.

2,783.   "Reputed Klan Head Held." New York Times. May 2,
          1967, p. 2.

2,784.   "Resolutions Seek Ban On Klux Jurors." Chicago
          Defender. October 14, 1922, p. 2.

2,785.   "Results Of Chicago Inquiry." New York Times.
          October 5, 1921, p. 18.

2,786.   "Rev. Brown Assails Ku Klux Before Big Crowd."
          Chicago Defender. June 3, 1922, p. 9.

2,787.   "Robed Speaker Arrested." Durham Morning Herald.
          August 22, 1966, p. 1.

2,788.   "Says Klansmen Go Armed." New York Times.
          February 28, 1923, p. 19.

2,789.   "Seventh Herrin Victim Dies." New York Times.
          September 30, 1924, p. 9.

2,790.   Sexton, George. "I Attended Secret Meeting Of
          Chicago Ku Klux Klan Outfit." Daily Worker.
          December 27, 1949, p. 5.

2,791.   "Scene Of Bloody Strife." New York Times. August
          31, 1924, p. 2.

2,792.   "Secret Klan Inquiry By Chicago Aldermen." New
          York Times. December 9, 1922, p. 4.

2,793.   "Shoot Down Two As Young's Foes." New York Times.
          May 25, 1924, p. 16.

2,794.   "Signs Illinois Anti Ku Klux Klan Bill." Pittsburgh
          Courier. July 14, 1923, p. 2.

2,795.   "6 Chicago Policemen Charged With Klan Activity."
          New York Times. December 29, 1967, p. 20.

2,796.   "Six Killed At Polls In Herrin Klan Riot." New
          York Times. April 14, 1926, pp. 1, 3.

2,797.   "Six Killed In New Klan Clash At Herrin; Sheriff
          And Men Besieged In Hospital; State Rushes Troops
          To Rioting Town." New York Times. August 31, 1924,
          pp. 1, 2.

2,798.   "Soldiers Go To Marion, Ill., As Klan Trouble Is
          Feared." New York Times. November 6, 1924, p. 21.

2,799.   "Soldiers On Guard Keep Herrin Quiet." New York
          Times. April 15, 1926, p. 2.

2,800.   "Some Lay Shooting To The Sheriff." New York Times.
          September 4, 1924, p. 4.

2,801.   "State Troops Patrol Streets." New York Times.
          August 31, 1924, p. 2.

2,802.   "Store In Herrin Bombed." New York Times. April
          11, 1925, p. 5.

2,803.   "Sues Anti-Klan Organ." New York Times. March 16,
         1923, p. 3.

2,804.   "10,000 At Burial Of Young By Klan." New York
         Times. January 30, 1925, p. 19.

2,805.   "They're Safer Without Their Sheriff. New York
         Times. February 7, 1925, p. 5.

2,806.   "Thirty-Two Warrants Issued." New York Times.
         September 2, 1924, p. 21.

2,807.   "Thomas Shot:First Witnesses Testify." New York
         Times. January 28, 1925, p. 9.

2,808.   "Thomas Wounded In Previous Battle." New York
         Times. January 25, 1925, p. 30.

2,809.   Tibbs, W.H. "The Ku Klux Klan In Chicago." The
         Messenger. Vol. 2, December, 1919, pp. 27-28.

2,810.   "To Aid Chicago Klansmen." New York Times.
         January 25, 1923, p. 19.

2,811.   "To Censor Anti-Klan Paper." New York Times.
         February 16, 1923, p. 8.

2,812.   "To Contest Legal Right Of Ku Klux Klansmen."
         Chicago Defender. August 27, 1921, p. 4.

2,813.   "To Try Herrin Policemen." New York Times.
         February 11, 1925, p. 28.

2,814.   "Troops Called Out In Herrin Dry War." New York
         Times. January 9, 1924, p. 1.

2,815.   "Troop Commander Finds Sheriff Barracaded In The
         Herrin Hospital After The Fight." New York Times.
         August 31, 1924, p. 1.

2,816.   "Troops Awe Herrin At Klan Burials." New York
         Times. April 17, 1926, p. 5.

2,817.   "Troops Guard Herrin." New York Times. November 5,
         1924, p. 2.

2,818.   "Troops Hold Herrin After Slaying Of 4, Including
         Young." New York Times. January 26, 1925, p. 1.

2,819.   "Troops Hold Herrin While Klan,Its Foes And Wets
         Make War." New York Times. February 10, 1924,
         pp. 1, 16.

2,820.   "Troops Keep Peace After Herrin Fight." New York
         Times. September 1, 1924, pp. 1, 3.

2,821.   "Troops Sent To Herrin." New York Times.   January
          25, 1925, p. 30.

2,822.   "Twelve Are Indicted For Herrin Murders; Sheriff,
          Judge And State's Attorney Named." New York Times.
          October 5, 1924, p. 1.

2,823.   "20 Witnesses Fail To Fix Herrin Blame." New York
          Times. January 29, 1925, p. 13.

2,824.   "2 Policemen Tied To Klan." New York Times.
          January 3, 1968, p. 28.

2,825.   "Two Shot At Herrin; Troops Called Out." New York
          Times. February 9, 1924, p. 1.

2,826.   "Victorious But Undefended." New York Times.
          June 15, 1925, p. 14.

2,827.   "Wears Ku Klux Garb To Grave." Chicago Defender.
          May 20, 1922, p. 13.

2,828.   Wieck, Agnes.   "Ku Kluxing In The Miners' Country."
          New Republic.   Vol. 38, March 26, 1924, pp. 122-
          124.

2,829.   "Williamson Asked For 'Clean-Up'." New York
          Times. December 25, 1923, p. 3.

2,830.   "Wounds Delay Klan Raider's Trial." New York Times.
          August 20, 1924, p. 17.

2,831.   "Young, Herrin Klan Leader, And Wife Shot And
          Wounded By Gunmen In Auto Ambush." New York Times.
          May 24, 1924, p. 1.

2,832.   "Young Known As 'Man-Killer'." New York Times.
          January 25, 1925, pp. 1, 34.

13.   INDIANA

2,833.   "Again Hunt Trial Of Klan In Indiana." New York
          Times. July 7, 1927, p. 7.

2,834.   "Alma Mater, K.K.K." New Republic.   Vol. 36,
          September 5, 1923, pp. 35-36.

2,835.   "Anti-Klan Editor's Appeal Is Dismissed By Supreme
          Court For Delay Of Records." New York Times.
          January 4, 1927, p. 3.

2,836.   "Asks Indiana Klan Ouster." New York Times.
          January 5, 1928, p. 7.

2,837.   "The Assembled Klansmen." New York Times.
          May 14, 1924, p. 2.

2,838.   "At It Again." New York Times. October 17, 1926, Sect. 2, p. 8.

2,839.   "Attorney Files Writ To See Stephenson." New York Times. August 23, 1927, p. 7.

2,840.   "A Ban Against Union Coal Miners." New York Times. October 5, 1921, p. 18.

2,841.   "Bares Klan Terror In Indiana Reign." New York Times. February 21, 1928, p. 15.

2,842.   "Bars Klan And Rival Parades On 4th." New York Times. June 27, 1923, p. 21.

2,843.   "Booze Opens War To Kill Klan Heads." Chicago Defender. September 16, 1922, p. 3.

2,844.   Betten, Neil. "Nativism And The Klan In Town And City: Valparaiso And Gary, Indiana." Studies In History And Society. Vol. 4, Spring 1973, pp. 3-16.

2,845.   Buckner, George W., Jr. "Probe A Rebirth Of Hoosier Klan." Christian Century. Vol. 63, November 27, 1946, p. 1446.

2,846.   Budenz, Louis Francis. "There's Mud On Indiana's White Robes." Nation. Vol. 125, July 27, 1927, pp. 81-82.

2,847.   "Call Klan Un-American." New York Times. January 27, 1923, p. 15.

2,848.   "Campaign Funds Plot Laid To Mayor Duvall." New York Times. May 18, 1927, p. 2.

2,849.   "Church Snubs Klan Gift." Chicago Defender. October 14, 1922, p. 1.

2,850.   "Clear Troops Of Klan Activity." New York Times. January 25, 1923, p. 17.

2,851.   "Covering Its Tracks." New York Times. October 28, 1926, p. 24.

2,852.   "Cross Burned In Anderson, Indiana, Where NAACP Director To Speak." Baltimore Afro American. December 5, 1981, p. 3.

2,853.   Crosson, David. "What's The Risk? Controversial Exhibits Challenge The Romantic Past." History News. Vol. 36, April, 1981, pp. 17-19.

2,854.   "D.C. Stephenson Called Insane In Report Of Psychiatrist On Former Head Of Ku Klux." New York Times. August 10, 1945, p. 17.

2,855.   "Demands Ku Klux Secrets." New York Times. January 17, 1928, p. 17.

2,856.   "Demands Vote Recount; Gets K.K.K. Threat." Chicago Defender. May 27, 1922, p. 1.

2,857.   "Democrats To Fight For Indiana's Vote." New York Times. September 11, 1924, p. 3.

2,858.   "A Dictatorship Of Adolescents." Pittsburgh Courier. October 8, 1927, Editorial page.

2,859.   "Drift Toward Davis Noted In Indiana." New York Times. October 19, 1924, Sect. 2, pp. 1, 2.

2,860.   "Drops Clarke Liquor Case." New York Times. April 30, 1924, Sect. 2, p. 2.

2,861.   Duffus, R.L. "A Political Volcano Seethes In Indiana." New York Times. October 2, 1927, Sect. 9, p. 1.

2,862.   "Duvall Admits Aid To Backers In Klan." New York Times. September 20, 1927, p. 31.

2,863.   "Duvall Case Goes To The Jury Today." New York Times. September 22, 1927, p. 31.

2,864.   "Duvall Took Cash To 'Protect' Public." New York Times. September 21, 1927, p. 31.

2,865.   "Dying Empire In Indiana." New York Times. October 12, 1926, p. 26.

2,866.   "Evans In Indiana To Tell His Side." New York Times. November 9, 1923, p. 4.

2,867.   "Ex-Chief Of Klan Free." New York Times. December 23, 1956, p. 32.

2,868.   "Ex-Dragon To Surrender." New York Times. April 20, 1925, p. 4.

2,869.   "Fight For Freedom Of The Press." Literary Digest. Vol. 90, August 14, 1926, pp. 9-10.

2,870.   "Firm On Ousting Indiana Klan." New York Times. February 23, 1928, p. 2.

2,871.   "Five Indiana Klansmen Held In Possession Of Dynamite." New York Times. August 22, 1969, p. 17.

2,872.   "5 Men Are Seized In Indiana For 'Hate' Activity For The Klan." New York Times. August 1, 1965, p. 57.

2,873. "Four Attacks Fail On Editor's Home. New York
        Times. November 26, 1926, p. 2.

2,874. Frost, Stanley. "The Klan Shows Its Hand In
        Indiana." Outlook. Vol. 137, June 4, 1924,
        pp. 187-190.

2,875. Gardner, Virginia. "Klansmen Crusade For Dewey."
        New Masses. Vol. 53, October 31, 1944.

2,876. "Gary Citizens Raise Money For Fight." Pittsburgh
        Courier. October 22, 1927, p. 2.

2,877. "Gary's Young Kluxers." Pittsburgh Courier.
        October 15, 1927, Editorial page.

2,878. Gordon, Elaine A. "Local Group Organizes Against
        Racist Attacks." Gary (Ind.) Crusader. November
        29, 1980, pp. 1, 2.

2,879. "Hand Of Klan In Strike." Pittsburgh Courier.
        October 8, 1927, pp. 1, 5.

2,880. Harrison, Morton. "Gentlemen From Indiana."
        Atlantic. Vol. 141, May, 1928, pp. 676-686.

2,881. "Has No Klan Connections, Senator Ralston Declares."
        New York Times. June 29, 1924, p. 13.

2,882. "He Can't Believe Them Bad." New York Times.
        October 30, 1923, p. 18.

2,883. "His Harder Task Remains." New York Times.
        April 2, 1923, p. 16.

2,884. "Hits Indiana Dry League." New York Times.
        July 22, 1927, p. 3.

2,885. "Hold Klansmen Who Had Dynamite." New York Times.
        December 28, 1922, p. 7.

2,886. "Indiana." New York Times. October 22, 1924.
        p. 20.

2,887. "Indiana Acts On Klan." New York Times. November
        11, 1946, p. 29.

2,888. "Indiana And The Klan." New York Times. June 7,
        1924, p. 12.

2,889. "Indiana Begins To Boil." New York Times. May 14,
        1924, p. 18.

2,890. "Indiana Delegation Solid For Ralston." New York
        Times. June 6, 1924, pp. 1, 3.

2,891.   "Indiana Democrats Assail Power Of Klan." New York Times. January 8, 1926, p. 6.

2,892.   "Indiana Dragon Sues High Klan Officer." New York Times. May 14, 1924, p. 2.

2,893.   "Indiana Editor Accuses Mayor Of Klan Bargain." New York Herald Tribune. October 7, 1926, p. 12.

2,894.   "Indiana Faces Klan Issue." New York Times. May 13, 1924, p. 3.

2,895.   "Indiana For Coolidge By Big Vote." New York Times. May 7, 1924, p. 1.

2,896.   "Indiana Governor Is Silent On Klan." New York Times. August 12, 1927, p. 5.

2,897.   "Indiana Has 85,000 In Klan." New York Times. July 6, 1923, p. 2.

2,898.   "Indiana Klan Chief Advises Members To Get Shotguns." New York Times. August 25, 1974, p. 59.

2,899.   "Indiana Klan Sued On Book." New York Times. May 20, 1927, p. 12.

2,900.   "Indiana Ku Klux Klan Group Attends Gov. Wallace Rally." Chicago Tribune. April 26, 1972, Sect. 3, p. 18.

2,901.   "Indiana Police Battle Anti-KKK Demonstrators In Kokomo." Chicago Tribune. April 27, 1980, p. 8.

2,902.   "Indiana Police Stop Confrontation." New York Times. April 28, 1980, p. 16.

2,903.   "Indiana Politician Quits Ku Klux Klan." New York Times. March 31, 1923, p. 8.

2,904.   "Indiana Politics." New York Times. November 8, 1929, p. 24.

2,905.   "Indiana Swayed Entirely By Klan." New York Times. November 7, 1923, p. 15.

2,906.   "Indianapolis To Get New Morning Paper." New York Times. February 21, 1924, p. 2.

2,907.   "Jackson Runs Behind Ticket." New York Times. November 6, 1924, p. 3.

2,908.   Janson, Donald. "Klan's Influence In Indiana Denied." New York Times. August 22, 1965, p. 51.

2,909.   "A Jovial Cyclops." New York Times. October 22, 1926, p. 20.

2,910.   "Judge Bans Klan Session." New York Times.
November 6, 1965, p. 60.

2,911.   "Judge Bars Ku Klux Klan From Holding Indiana
Rally." New York Times. August 11, 1967, p. 34.

2,912.   "KKK." Indiana House Of Representatives Journal.
74th Session, 1925, p. 751.

2,913.   "KKK." Indiana Senate Journal. 74th Session,
1925, pp. 132, 792.

2,914.   "KKK Plans Anti-Amnesty March On Camp Atterbury,
Ind." New Orleans Times Picayune. October 11,
1974, p. 17.

2,915.   "Klan A 'Swindle', Ex-Official Says." New York
Times. March 7, 1928, p. 9.

2,916.   "The Klan 'Backs' A College." Literary Digest.
Vol. 78, September 15, 1923, pp. 43-46.

2,917.   "Klan Buys University." New York Amsterdam News.
August 22, 1923, pp. 7-8.

2,918.   "Klan Dominates In Indiana Fight." New York Times.
October 16, 1924, p. 10.

2,919.   "Klan Editor To Quit National Democrat." New York
Times. July 12, 1925, p. 5.

2,920.   "Klan Enemy Gets Appeal." New York Times. July
20, 1926, p. 3.

2,921.   "Klan Figure Free In A 1925 Murder." New York
Times. December 22, 1956, p. 10.

2,922.   "Klan Gets University." New York Times. August
16, 1923, p. 17.

2,923.   "Klan Ghost Bobs Up Again In Indiana; Republican
Leader Quits As Committee-Man." New York Times.
June 14, 1944, pp. 34-35.

2,924.   "Klan Is Victor In Indiana." New York Times.
May 8, 1924, pp. 1, 4.

2,925.   "Klan Pastor Asks Heaven To Stem Us." Chicago
Defender. July 1, 1922, pp. 1, 2.

2,926.   "A Klan Senator From Indiana." Literary Digest.
Vol. 87, November 14, 1925, pp. 16-17.

2,927.   "A Klan Shock In Indiana." Literary Digest.
Vol. 81, May 24, 1924, p. 14.

2,928.   "Klan Sues To Hold Rallies." New York Times.
          May 20, 1966, p. 36.

2,929.   "Klan To Take Owls, Says Convict Head." New York
          Times. December 30, 1922, pp. 26-27.

2,930.   "A Klan University." New York Times. July 28,
          1923, p. 6.

2,931.   "Klan Will Open Its University To All." New York
          Times. August 17, 1923, p. 16.

2,932.   "Klan Willing To Take University." New York Times.
          July 27, 1923, p. 15.

2,933.   "Klansmen Cross Indiana." New York Times. October
          16, 1967, p. 49.

2,934.   "Ku Klux Klan In Indiana Won't Wear Klan-Made
          Robes." National Observer. August 9, 1975, p. 5.

2,935.   "Ku Klux Klan Members In Indiana Called Klans-
          persons Says Chicago Sun-Times Editorial."
          National Observer. March 29, 1975, p. 13.

2,936.   "Ku Klux Klan Seeks Recruits In Indiana Town."
          Chicago Tribune. May 5, 1975, Sect. 2, p. 30.

2,937.   "Ku Klux Leader Denied New Trial." Pittsburgh
          Courier. February 4, 1939, p. 4.

2,938.   "Ku Klux Murderer Gets Sentence Cut." New York
          Times. March 5, 1950, pp. 77-78.

2,939.   "Ku Klux Won't Buy Valparaiso School." New York
          Times. September 6, 1923, p. 19.

2,940.   "Lyons And The Klan." New York Times. April 7,
          1923, p. 12.

2,941.   "Machine Gun Squads Patrol Gary, Ind., As Students
          Seek To End School Strike." New York Times.
          September 29, 1927, p. 1.

2,942.   Markey, Morris. "Why Did Indiana Free The Klan
          Killer?" Coronet. October, 1950, pp. 94-100.

2,943.   Martin, John B. "Beauty And The Beast; The
          Downfall of D.C. Stephenson, Grand Dragon Of The
          Indiana K.K.K." Harper's Magazine. Vol. 189,
          September, 1944, pp. 319-329.

2,944.   "Masquerade Of Innocents." New York Times.
          November 7, 1926, Sect. 2, p. 8.

2,945.   Mellett, Lowell. "Klan And Church." Atlantic
          Monthly. Vol. 132, November, 1923, pp. 586-592.

2,946. Merritt, Dixon. "Klan And Anti-Klan In Indiana." _Outlook_. Vol. 144, December 8, 1926, pp. 465-469.

2,947. Moore, Samuel T. "Consequences Of The Klan." _Independent_. Vol. 113, December 20, 1924, pp. 534-536.

2,948. _____. "How The Kleagles Collected The Cash." _Independent_. Vol. 113, December 13, 1924, pp. 517-519.

2,949. _____. "A Klan Kingdom Collapses." _Independent_. Vol. 113, December 6, 1924, pp. 473-475.

2,950. "Morgan City, Ind. Ku Klux Klan Meeting Discussed." _Chicago Tribune_. July 19, 1975, Sect. N1, p. 4.

2,951. Moscow, Warren. "Indiana Republicans Drop Wills In Favor Of Jenner For Senate." _New York Times_. June 14, 1946, pp. 15-16.

2,952. "N.A.A.C.P. President Denies Membership In Gary's Black Klan." _Pittsburgh Courier_. November 26, 1927, p. 2.

2,953. "Name Klan Vice President." _New York Times_. January 26, 1926, p. 12.

2,954. "Negroes Form A New Klan Body." _New York Times_. February 11, 1925, p. 14.

2,955. "New Klan Has 'Nightgown'." _New York Times_. January 23, 1926, p. 17.

2,956. "Ninety-two Indiana Klans Will Receive Charters At Kokomo On Fourth Of July." _Imperial Night-Hawk_. June 27, 1923, p. 5.

2,957. "No Clean Sheets For The Klan. _New York Times_. April 29, 1980, p. 22.

2,958. "No Room For KKK, Racist Pranks at Purdue Pres." _Jet_. Vol. 59, October 9, 1980, p. 30.

2,959. " 'No School' - Ku Klux." _Messenger_. Vol. 5, October, 1923, pp. 831-832.

2,960. "Offer To Save University." _New York Times_. September 22, 1923, p. 4.

2,961. "Official Halts Sale of Anti-Klan Weekly." _New York Times_. July 26, 1926, p. 15.

2,962. "100,000 Klansmen Go To Fort Wayne." _New York Times_. November 10, 1923, p. 15.

2,963.   "One Paper Dared To Criticize." _New York Times_.
          November 8, 1923, p. 18.

2,964.   "Only 5,000 Of Klan Invade Fort Wayne." _New York
          Times_. November 11, 1923, p. 18.

2,965.   Oulahan, Richard V. "Dry Forces Control Indiana
          Situation." _New York Times_. October 24, 1928, p.
          8.

2,966.   "President's Step Splits Indiana." _New York Times_.
          August 10, 1927, p. 8.

2,967.   "Ready To Take University." _New York Times_.
          August 18, 1923, p. 4.

2,968.   "Recovering From Evil Rule." _New York Times_.
          January 9, 1926, p. 16.

2,969.   "Rise Of The Ku Klux Klan In Indiana Reported."
          New Orleans Times Picayune. December 10, 1972,
          p. 28.

2,970.   "School Accepts KKK Book For Students, Limits Use."
          Jet. Vol. 58, July 31, 1980, p. 54.

2,971.   "Seeks Indiana Data In Pennsylvania." _New York
          Times_. July 29, 1927, p. 2.

2,972.   "Sees K.K.K. Slipping." _Pittsburgh Courier_.
          August 27, 1927, p. 4.

2,973.   Shepherd, William G. "Indiana's Mystery Man."
          Collier's. Vol. 79, January 8, 1927, pp. 8-9,
          47-49.

2,974.   "Silence Is Not Heroic." _New York Times_.
          November 3, 1923, p. 12.

2,975.   "The Spirit Of Indiana." _Pittsburgh Courier_.
          October 8, 1927, editorial page.

2,976.   "A Startling Charge." _Pittsburgh Courier_.
          November 12, 1927, Editorial page.

2,977.   "Stephenson Extradition Signed." _New York Times_.
          November 18, 1950, p. 9.

2,978.   "Stephenson Says Klan Lynched And Burned." _New
          York Times_. April 2, 1928, p. 9.

2,979.   "Taggart Summons Democrats To Fight." _New York
          Times_. January 10, 1926, Sect. 2, p. 1.

2,980.   Taylor, Alva W. "What The Klan Did In Indiana."
          New Republic. Vol. 52, November 16, 1927, pp. 330-
          332.

2,981.   Thornbrough, Emma L. "Segregation In Indiana
          During The Klan Era Of The 1920's." Mississippi
          Valley Historical Review. Vol. 47, March, 1961,
          pp. 594-618.

2,982.   "3 Policemen Hurt In Kokomo Clash." New York
          Times. September 15, 1969, p. 51.

2,983.   "Unmasking In Indiana." New York Times. July 13,
          1927, p. 22.

2,984.   "Victory In Gary." Crisis. Vol. 35, January,
          1928, pp. 13, 30.

2,985.   "Watson Promises To Back Klan Man." New York
          Times. May 22, 1924, p. 19.

2,986.   "Will Seek New Trial For D.C. Stephenson." New
          York Times. January 7, 1928, p. 4.

2,987.   Wilson, William E. "Long, Hot Summer In Indiana;
          1924." American Heritage. Vol. 16, August,
          1965, pp. 56-64.

2,988.   "The World Aids Editor." New York Times. August
          2, 1926, p. 17.

                    14. IOWA

2,989.   "Ia. Legion Goes After Klan." The (Iowa)
          Bystander. January 20, 1923, p. 1.

2,990.   "Iowa Klansmen Attacked." New York Times.
          July 25, 1926, Sect. 2, p. 2.

2,991.   "Iowa Town Riot Over Klan." New York Times.
          July 25, 1926, p. 3.

2,992.   Jones, Joseph. "Knights Of The Ku Klux Klan On
          The Rise In Iowa." Iowa Bystander. November 27,
          1980, pp. 1, 12.

2,993.   "KKK Put On College Doors." New York Times.
          November 3, 1957, p. 63.

2,994.   "Klan Candidate Beaten In Iowa." New York Times.
          March 10, 1926, p. 4.

2,995.   "Klan Must Pay City Taxes In Iowa." New York
          Times. January 6, 1928, p. 9.

2,996.   "Legion Endorses Anti-Klan Bill." New York
          Times. January 16, 1923, p. 13.

2,997.   "Mrs. Cook Is Buried With Ku Klux Rites." New
          York Times. September 11, 1925, p. 5.

2,998.   "Shots Mark Klan Session." New York Times.
          July 27, 1927, p. 6.

2,999.   "United States Senator Steck." New York Times.
          October 30, 1926, p. 3.

3,000.   "University Trustees Vanish In Des Moines."
          New York Times. June 2, 1929, p. 20.

                    15. KANSAS

3,001.   "Allen Hits Klan And Bigots." New York Times.
          November 1, 1922, p. 21.

3,002.   "Allen Out To Drive Klan From Kansas." New York
          Times. October 30, 1922, p. 1.

3,003.   "Arrest In Klan Ouster." New York Times. March
          3, 1923, p. 3.

3,004.   "Asserts Kansas Klan Rises To Fight Smith." New
          York Times. February 9, 1928, p. 8.

3,005.   "Bans Klan Parade." Chicago Defender. July 22,
          1922, p. 3.

3,006.   "Confirmation From A Strange Source." American
          Federationist. Vol. 29, December, 1922, pp. 905-
          906.

3,007.   "Denies Kansas Klan A New Hearing." New York
          Times. February 15, 1925, p. 16.

3,008.   "Family Defies KKK Efforts To Chase It Out Of
          Town." Afro American. November 5, 1949, p. 3.

3,009.   "Fears Klan Revival If Smith Is Named." New
          York Times. January 29, 1928, p. 2.

3,010.   "A Governing Governor." New York Times. October
          31, 1922, p. 14.

3,011   Griffith, Charles B. and Donald W. Stewart. "Has
          A Court Of Equity Power To Enjoin Parading By The
          Ku Klux Klan In Mask?" Central Law Journal.
          Vol. 96, November 20, 1923, pp. 384-393.

3,012.   "Hit Klan In Kansas." New York Times. August 28,
          1924, p. 3.

3,013.   Jones, Lila L. "The Ku Klux Klan In Eastern
          Kansas During The 1920's." Emporia State Research
          Studies. Vol. 23, Winter, 1975, pp. 5-41.

3,014.   "Kansas And The Ku Klux." California Eagle.
          August 17, 1923, p. 10.

3,015.   "Kansas Dime 'Moral' Finally Explained." New
          York Times. December 17, 1926, p. 42.

3,016.   "Kansas High Court Outlaws The Klan." New York
          Times. January 11, 1925, p. 16.

3,017.   "Kansas House Bars Klan." New York Times. March
          6, 1925, p. 24.

3,018.   "Kansas Klan Asks Ouster Rehearing." New York
          Times. February 1, 1925, p. 24..

3,019.   "Kansas Klan Defies White By Burning A Fiery
          Cross." New York Times. September 24, 1924, p. 1.

3,020.   "Kansas Klan Must Answer." New York Times.
          January 21, 1923, p. 20.

3,021.   "Kansas Mayor Labels Klan A Crime-Breeder."
          Chicago Defender. May 20, 1922, pp. 3-4.

3,022.   "Kansas Mayor Lashed After Assailing Klan."
          New York Times. October 17, 1922, p. 2.

3,023.   "Kansas Parades Enjoined In Kansas." New York
          Times. December 20, 1925, p. 3.

3,024.   "Kansas Refuses A Charter To Klan." New York
          Times. July 2, 1925, p. 21.

3,025.   "Kansas Refuses To Charter Ku Klux." New York
          Amsterdam News. July 8, 1925, p. 10.

3,026.   "The Klan In Kansas." New York Times. August 30,
          1924, p. 8.

3,027.   "Klan May Yet Win White's Forgiveness." New York
          Times. April 25, 1925, p. 17.

3,028.   "Klan Organizer Jailed In Kansas." New York Times.
          March 2, 1923, p. 6.

3,029.   "Klansmen Send Taffy To Race Hospital; Note."
          Chicago Defender. June 17, 1922, p. 2.

3,030.   "Letter Signed K.K.K. Warns Capper's Paper." New
          York Times. July 27, 1921, p. 15.

3,031.   McCormick, Anne O'Hare. "Editor White Tilts At
          The Kansas Klan." New York Times. October 5,
          1924, Sect. 9, p. 11

3,032.   "Mr. White Challenges The Klan." Outlook. Vol.
          138, October 1, 1924, p. 154.

3,033.   "Ouster Suit Against The Ku Klux Klan." New York
          Times. November 11, 1922, p. 17.

3,034.   "A Perturbed Kansas Spirit." New York Times.
          September 4, 1924, p. 18.

3,035.   "Says Kansas Klan Ousted Democrats." New York
          Times. November 4, 1924, p. 2.

3,036.   "Simplicity Of The Kansas K.K.K." New York Times.
          September 6, 1926, p. 14.

3,037.   "Slow Primaries In Kansas." New York Times.
          August 1, 1926, p. 28.

3,038.   Sloan, Charles W., Jr. "Kansas Battles The Invi-
          sible Empire: The Legal Ouster Of The KKK From
          Kansas, 1922-1927." Kansas Historical Quarterly.
          Vol. 57, Autumn, 1974, pp. 393-409.

3,039.   "Suit Filed To Oust Klan From Kansas." New York
          Times. November 22, 1922, p. 23.

3,040.   "Their Victory Really Was A Defeat." New York
          Times. November 19, 1924, p. 20.

3,041.   "Tries To Push Klan Case." New York Times.
          December 28, 1922, p. 7.

3,042.   "W.A. White To Run As Foe Of The Klan." New York
          Times. September 21, 1924, pp. 1, 25.

3,043.   "Wants Klan Named In Kansas Convention." New York
          Times. August 26, 1924, p. 2.

3,044.   "White Assails Klan In Topeka Stronghold." New
          York Times. September,29, 1924, p. 2.

3,045.   "White Declares Fight On Klan Will Be Won." New
          York Times. November 6, 1924, p. 3.

3,046.   "White Starts Fight On Kansas Klan." New York
          Times. September 11, 1924, p. 4.

3,047.   "White Would Oust Klan In Kansas." New York Times.
          October 10, 1924, p. 3.

3,048.   "Why Kansas Bans The Klan." Literary Digest.
          Vol. 75, November 11, 1922, pp. 13-14.

3,049.   "William Allen White's War On The Klan." Literary
          Digest. Vol. 83, October 11, 1924, pp. 16-17.

16.   KENTUCKY

3,050.   "Asks Receivership For Kentucky Klan." New York
          Times. April 8, 1925, p. 23.

3,051.   "Bars Ku Klux From Juries." New York Times. June 2, 1924, p. 2.

3,052.   "Court Blocks Klan Rally." New York Times. August 12, 1967, p. 15.

3,053.   "Emmett Andrew Carr." New York Times. October 2, 1952, p. 16.

3,054.   "Forbid Ku Klux Meeting." New York Times. September 16, 1921, p. 12.

3,055.   "Kentucky Picks Duvall." New York Times. November 4, 1925, p. 4.

3,056.   "Judge Sets Klan Meet On Courthouse Lawn." New York Amsterdam News. September 12, 1923, p. 1.

3,057.   "Jury To Investigate Klan." New York Times. September 28, 1921, p. 4.

3,058.   "Klan Chief Sues Editor For $100,000." New York Times. June 11, 1924, p. 16.

3,059.   "Klan Is Outlawed In Kentucky." Christian Century. Vol. 63, September 25, 1946, pp. 114-116.

3,060.   "Klan Killed In Kentucky." Chicago Defender. September 21, 1946, p. 7.

3,061.   "Klan Lined Up Against Smith." Pittsburgh Courier. September 1, 1928, p. 4.

3,062.   "Klan Loses Fight In Louisville, Ky." Pittsburgh Courier. September 1, 1928, p. 9.

3,063.   "Klan March In Kentucky." New York Times. August 16, 1976, p. 34.

3,064.   "Klan Sued In Kentucky." New York Times. September 21, 1925, p. 10.

3,065.   "Klan Unwanted." New York Times. May 4, 1967, p. 30.

3,066.   "Ku Klux Drops Fight Against Louisville Ban." New York Times. September 18, 1921, p. 21.

3,067.   "Mayor Of Louisville Fights Ku Klux Klan." New York Times. August 23, 1921, p. 10.

3,068.   Robinson, Douglas. "Dr. King Presses Louisville Fight." New York Times. May 4, 1967, p. 30.

3,069.   "Runs Amuck With Gun After Ku Klux Meeting." Chicago Defender. September 23, 1922, pp. 1-2.

3,070.   Stevens, William K.   "Guard Called Out In Louisville Riot." New York Times. September 7, 1975, pp. 1, 45.

3,071.   "Suit To End Klan Filed By Kentucky." New York Times. July 23, 1946, p. 14.

3,072.   "2 In KKK Arrested For Fire-Bombing." Washington Star. June 24, 1981, p. A7.

3,073.   "260 In Klan March In Kentucky Town." New York Times. July 4, 1976, p. 39.

3,074.   "Will Leads In Louisville." New York Times. November 4, 1925, p. 4.

3,075.   "Woman Fined For Using Profanity To Police, Klan." Cincinnati (Ohio) Herald. June 20, 1981, pp. 1, 10.

17. LOUISIANA

3,076.   "ACLU Assists Ku Klux Klan In Getting School Gym For Rally." New Orleans Times Picayune. November 17, 1975, p. 8.

3,077.   "Accused Klansmen Flee Louisiana." New York Times. April 15, Sect. 1, Part 2, p. 4.

3,078.   "Alibi For Skipwood Is Offered By Klan." New York Times. January 16, 1923, p. 13.

3,079.   "Alleged Klansmen Indicted In 1965 New Orleans Fires." New York Times. June 22, 1966, p. 32.

3,080.   "Americans Who Need Explanation." New York Times. January 10, 1923, p. 22.

3,081.   "Andrews And Daniel Tell How Mob Flogged; Recognized No One." Washington Post. January 7, 1923, p. 6.

3,082.   "Another Form Of The Same Thing." New York Times. November 7, 1923, p. 16.

3,083.   "Anti-Klan Candidate Wins In Louisiana." California Eagle. April 14, 1923, p. 6.

3,084.   "Armed Force Protects Negroes In Rights March Through Louisiana." New York Times. August 19, 1967, pp. 1, 12.

3,085.   "Arrest Dr. M'Koin, Reputed Klan Head, As Mer Rouge Slayer." New York Times. December 27, 1922, p. 1.

3,086.   "Attorney General Coco." New York Times. January 4, 1923, p. 21.

3,087.   "Bars Two Judges As Klansmen From Louisiana Appeal Court." New York Times. March 15, 1923, p. 1.

3,088.   "Bastrop Grand Jury Fails To Indict Klan Murderers." New York Amsterdam News. March 21, 1973, p. 2.

3,089.   "Bastrop's Celebrated Case." New York Times. January 6, 1923, p. 12.

3,090.   Benjamin, Philip. "Core Is Planning Louisiana Drive." New York Times. April 12, 1965, p. 49.

3,091.   Bentley, Max. "Let's Brush Them Aside; How One Man Preached The Gospel Of Fairness To All." Collier's. Vol. 74, November 22, 1924, pp. 21, 47.

3,092.   "Blacks Plan To Confront Klan At New Orleans March." New York Times. November 26, 1978, p. 27.

3,093.   "Brother Says Teegerstrom Is Safe." New York Times. January 3, 1923, p. 19.

3,094.   Brown, George Rothwell. "Ku Klux Klan Rules Louisiana, Governor Asserts; To Ask President To Act; State Officers Powerless." Washington Post. November 19, 1922, p1.

3,095.   "Calls On Klansmen To Resign." New York Times. January 14, 1923, p. 23.

3,096.   "Captain J.K. Skipwith." New York Times. January 27, 1923, p. 15.

3,097.   Chalk, David. "Klanswomen, In The New South The Ku Klux Klan Is Very Much A Family Affair." New Dawn. Vol. 1, September, 1976, pp. 37-41.

3,098.   "Charges Dropped Against 2 Suspects In Destrehan, La. Case." New Orleans Times Picayune. November 2, 1974, p. 26.

3,099.   "Citizens Of This Section." New York Times. January 2, 1923, p. 17.

3,100.   "Civil Rights Injunctions - Louisiana." Race Relations Labor Review. Vol. 10, Winter, 1965, pp. 1449-1467.

3,101.   "Clean Bill Of Health." New York Times. August 1, 1965, p. 57.

3,102.   Cline, Leonard L. "In Darkest Louisiana." Nation. Vol. 116, March 14, 1923, pp. 292-293.

3,103.   "Coco Accuses Skipwith." New York Times. April 14, 1923, p. 21.

3,104.   "Coco To Identify Mer Rouge Slayers." New York Times. January 18, 1923, p. 9.

3,105.   "Condemns Mob Murders." New York Times. January 9, 1923, p. 5.

3,106.   "Controversy Over Handshake At Rapides Parish School Hearing Eyed." New Orleans Times Picayune. January 18, 1981, p. 8.

3,107.   Corrigan, Richard. "Louisiana Klan Chief Testifies He Burned Data." Washington Post. January 5, 1966.

3,108.   "Ct. Bars Shreveport, La., Ku Klux Klan Auditorium Meeting." New Orleans Times Picayune. August 1, 1973, p. 7.

3,109.   "Court Upholds Convictions Of 2 In Mrs. Liuzzo's Death." New York Times. April 28, 1967, p. 30.

3,110.   Crider, Bill. "KKK In Louisiana." New York Times. August 26, 1978, p. 109.

3,111.   "David Duke Fails To Get Restraining Order For Liberty Monument." New Orleans Times Picayune. February 6, 1981, p. 17.

3,112.   "Dealing With The Klan." New York Times. November 21, 1922, pp. 18-19.

3,113.   "Demonstration." New York Times. September 3, 1962, p. 13.

3,114.   "Denounces Klan As Hearing Ends." New York Times. January 26, 1923, p. 19.

3,115.   "Deplorable But Not Peculiar." New York Times. March 17, 1923, p. 12.

3,116.   Dillon, Merton L. "Captain Jason W. James, Anti-Frontier Democrat." New Mexico Historical Review. Vol. 31, April, 1956, pp. 89-101.

3,117.   Du Bois, W.E.B. "The Shape Of Fear." North American Review. Vol. 223, June, 1926, pp. 291-304.

3,118.   "Eight More Arrests Expected This Week In Mer Rouge Crime." New York Times. January 8, 1923, pp. 1, 4.

3,119.   "Ex-Klansman Links Mer Rouge Murders With Ku Klux
          Band." New York Times. January 10, 1923, pp. 1, 5.

3,120.   "Ex-Klansman Tells Of Flogging Youth." New York
          Times. January 12, 1966, pp. 1, 19.

3,121.   "Ex-Klansman Tells Of Louisiana Violence." Wash-
          ington Evening Star. January 11, 1966.

3,122.   "Ex-Sheriff On Trial In Bastrop Klan Case." New
          York Times. November 7, 1923, p. 15.

3,123.   "Expect Naming Of 2 In Mer Rouge Crime." New York
          Times. January 15, 1923, p. 15.

3,124.   "Expect 30 Arrests In Klan Case Soon." New York
          Times. January 22, 1923, p. 17.

3,125.   "Explosion Reveals Wire-Bound Bodies Of Supposed
          Ku Klux Victims In Lake; Louisiana Governor Sends
          More Troops." New York Times. December 23, 1922,
          pp. 1-2.

3,126.   "FBI In New Orleans Set Up Group To Discredit Klan
          In 1960's." New Orleans Times Picayune. November
          30, 1977, p. 1.

3,127.   "Fines 4 Of Klan In Bastrop." New York Times.
          November 9, 1923, p. 4.

3,128.   "First Arrest Made in Supposed Klan Mer Rouge
          Murders." New York Times. December 24, 1922, p. 1.

3,129.   "Five Farmers Murdered." Chicago Defender. July
          16, 1921, pp. 1-2.

3,130.   Fleming, Walter L. "A Ku Klux Document."
          Mississippi Valley Historical Review. Vol. 1,
          March, 1915, pp. 575-578.

3,131.   "For Them Murder Is Justified." New York Times.
          December 26, 1922, p. 12.

3,132.   "Forty Arrests Expected." New York Times.
          January 30, 1923, p. 21.

3,133.   "Four Found Guilty In Morehouse Trial." New York
          Times. November 6, 1923, p. 5.

3,134.   "Funds Queried In KKK Plot." Pittsburgh (Pa.)
          Courier. July 11, 1981, p. 1.

3,135.   "Fuqua Now In The Lead." New York Times. January
          19, 1924, p. 4.

3,136.   "Gets Klan Warning." Pittsburgh Courier. January
          20, 1923, p. 1.

3,137. "Girl Names M'Koin In Ku Klux Case." New York
        Times. January 9, 1923, p. 5.

3,138. "Gov. Earl Long." New York Times. February 13,
        1952, p. 24.

3,139. "Governor Parker." New York Times. January 3,
        1923, p. 19.

3,140. "Gov. Parker Admits Mission On Ku Klux, But Denies
        He Will Ask For Drastic Action." New York Times.
        November 20, 1922, p. 1.

3,141. "Governor Parker Started Inquiry." New York Times.
        March 16, 1923, p. 3.

3,142. "Governor Will Not Ask For Federal Troops." New
        York Times. November 20, 1922, p. 1.

3,143. "Government Men Get Pistols Back." Washington
        Post. January 7, 1923, p. 6.

3,144. "Gov't. Must Stop Kluxers, New Orleans National
        Maritime Union (NMU) Declares." Daily Worker.
        July 29, 1946, p. 5.

3,145. "Guns Guard Search For Victims Of Mob." New York
        Times. December 22, 1922, p. 2.

3,146. "Head Of KKK Splinter Group In New Orleans Enters
        Plea In Dynamite Case." New Orleans Times
        Picayune. October 21, 1981, p. 6.

3,147. "Held For Ku Klux Slaying." New York Times.
        March 14, 1922, p. 3.

3,148. Herbers, John. "Hearing On Klan Shifts Emphasis."
        New York Times. January 5, 1966, p. 13.

3,149. _____. "Klan Haunts Louisiana City That Can-
        celed Hay's Rights Talk." New York Times. January
        9, 1965, p. 13.

3,150. _____. "Klan Is Said To Retain Its Control Of
        Bogalusa Despite Court Order." New York Times.
        January 6, 1966, p. 11.

3,151. "HEW Hits Snag On Klan Plea To Use La. School."
        New Orleans Times Picayune. November 28, 1976,
        p. 32.

3,152. "HEW To Rule On Ku Klux Klan Request To Use La.
        School Auditorium." Washington Post. November
        28, 1976.

3,153. "Holds Martial Law Over Heads Of Klan." New York
        Times. January 25, 1923, p. 21.

3,154.   "Hooded Men Escape Indictment By Jury In Mer Rouge
          Case." New York Times. March 16, 1923, pp. 1, 3.

3,155.   "Hooded Murderers Of Mer Rouge Men Known To Agents."
          New York Times. December 25, 1922, p. 63.

3,156.   "Hundred Saw Two Men Kidnapped." New York Times.
          December 23, 1922, p. 2.

3,157.   "Hunt Teegestrom Near New Orleans." New York Times.
          January 28, 1923, Sect. 1, Part 2, p. 5.

3,158.   "Hylan Praises Parker For Fight On Klan." New
          York Times. December 24, 1922, p. 2.

3,159.   "If Ever A Devil..." Time. Vol. 86, November 5,
          1965, pp. 109-110.

3,160.   "Inciting Crowd Testimony Is Refuted By Klansman."
          New Orleans Times Picayune. May 26, 1977, p. 16.

3,161.   "Initiating A Negro Into The Ku Klux Klan."
          Messenger. Vol. 5, January, 1923, pp. 562-563.

3,162.   "Inquiry By F.B.I. Asked." New York Times.
          January 20, 1964, p. 15.

3,163.   "Invisible Power Of Ku Klux Is Said To Rule
          Louisiana In Washington Paper's Story Of Appeal
          To Harding." New York Times. November 20, 1922,
          p. 2.

3,164.   "IRS Releases Records On 99 Political And Activist
          Groups." New Orleans Times Picayune. November 18,
          1974, p. 1.

3,165.   "Jeff Burnett." New York Times. January 9, 1923,
          p. 5.

3,166.   "Jeff. Detective Testifies At Ku Klux Klan Trial."
          New Orleans Times Picayune. May 24, 1977, p. 8.

3,167.   "Jeff. School Bd. To Ban KKK If Racial Tension
          Become Excessive." New Orleans Times Picayune.
          May 10, 1979, p. 16.

3,168.   "Jeff. School System Okays KKK Use Of School For
          Meeting." New Orleans Times Picayune. May 9,
          1979, p. 2.

3,169.   "Join 'Invisible Empire'." New York Times.
          January 7, 1923, p. 20.

3,170.   "Judge Warns Klan, Orders Gun Hunt, At Murder
          Hearing." New York Times. January 6, 1923, pp. 1,
          7.

3,171.   "Kidnap A Witness Against Man Held As Ku Klux Slayer." New York Times. January 1, 1923, pp. 1, 7.

3,172.   King, Wayne. "Klan Radio Ads Seek Public Support." New York Times. November 24, 1975, p. 33.

3,173.   "KKK Activity On LSU Campus Reported." New Orleans Times Picayune. April 24, 1974, Sect. 3, p. 2.

3,174.   "KKK Chief D. Duke Addresses La. Taxpayer's Assn. Meeting." New Orleans Times Picayune. August 25, 1974, p. 26.

3,175.   "KKK Concludes Convention With Nominations For U.S. Pres." New Orleans Times Picayune. September 3, 1974, p. 5.

3,176.   "Ku Klux Klan Demonstrators Arrested In Shreveport, La." New Orleans Times Picayune. August 12, 1973, p. 16.

3,177.   "Ku Klux Klan Elects 19 Year Old Grand Dragon, D. Johnson." New Orleans Times Picayune. July 10, 1974, p. 2.

3,178.   "KKK In Louisiana." New York Times. August 27, 1978, p. 10.

3,179.   "KKK Leader Arrives In Destrehan, La. As Violence Subsides." New Orleans Times Picayune. October 10, 1974, p. 1.

3,180.   "KKK Leader Duke And Aide Warner To Face Trial In Gretna." New Orleans Times Picayune. August 21, 1979, p. 12.

3,181.   "KKK Leader Duke Gets Suspended Sentence For Metairie Incident." New Orleans Times Picayune. November 29, 1979, p. 3.

3,182.   "KKK Leader Duke Guilty Of Riot Charge In Jeff. Parish." New Orleans Times Picayune. August 24, 1979, p. 1.

3,183.   "KKK Leader Duke Views Rally Plans At Metairie School." New Orleans Times Picayune. May 11, 1979, p. 4.

3,184.   "KKK Leader To Meet To Nominate 1976 Pres. Candidate." New Orleans Times Picayune. December 14, 1974, Sect. 3, p. 4.

3,185.   "KKK Loses Ruling In School Use Suit." New Orleans Times Picayune. April 21, 1976, p. 16.

3,186.   "KKK March In N.O." Chicago Tribune. December 3,
          1978, Sect. 2, p. 6.

3,187.   "KKK Meeting In La - Letters." New Orleans Times
          Picayune. May 13, 1976, p. 20.

3,188.   "KKK Newspaper Ad - Letter." New Orleans Times
          Picayune. August 31, 1974, p. 18.

3,189.   "KKK Plans To Patrol Streets If Police Strike
          During Carnival." New Orleans Times Picayune.
          February 15, 1979, p. 5.

3,190.   "Ku Klux Klan Pickets New Orleans Airport Sheraton
          Hotel." New Orleans Times Picayune. September 7,
          1975, p. 16.

3,191.   "KKK Protest At Morial's Inauguration - Letter."
          New Orleans Times Picayune. April 30, 1978, p. 40.

3,192.   "KKK Protesters Gather Outside Jeff. Courthouse."
          New Orleans Times Picayune. September 3, 1979,
          p. 16.

3,193.   "KKK Rally At Metairie School Viewed." New Orleans
          Times Picayune. May 12, 1979, p. 18.

3,194.   "KKK Rally In New Orleans - Letters." New Orleans
          Times Picayune. December 7, 1978, p. 18.

3,195.   "Ku Klux Klan Refused Use Of School For Rally."
          New Orleans Times Picayune. November 20, 1975,
          p. 11.

3,196.   "KKK Rep. Protests Alexandria, La. Police Order On
          Flags." Chicago Defender. October 3, 1979, p. 5.

3,197.   "KKK, Rightists Stir Tense Town." Charlotte
          Observer. April 3, 1966, p. 1.

3,198.   "KKK Threatens To Picket In Louisiana Busing Feud."
          San Francisco Chronicle. January 8, 1981, p. 30.

3,199.   "Klan Burns Cross To Open Quarters In Louisiana
          Busing Feud." New York Times. April 17, 1976,
          p. 12.

3,200.   "Klan Candidates Lose In Louisiana Contest." New
          York Times. March 28, 1923, p. 31.

3,201.   "Klan Convictions In Killings Upheld." New York
          Times. July 18, 1969, p. 31.

3,202.   "Klan Does Not Choose Its Victims." Chicago
          Defender. January 28, 1922, p. 8.

3,203.   "Klan Faced With Murder Charge." New York Amsterdam
          News. December 27, 1922, pp. 1-2.

3,204.   "Klan Gets Involved In School Bias Case. Washington
          Star. January 11, 1981, p. A6.

3,205.   " 'Klan Hall' Trap Injures Two Boys." New York
          Times. October 9, 1967, p. 20.

3,206.   "Klan Head Assails Mer Rouge Hearing." New York
          Times. January 27, 1923, p. 15.

3,207.   "Klan Hearing Turns To Missing Witness." New York
          Times. January 23, 1923, p. 23.

3,208.   "The Klan In Louisiana." New York Times. September
          4, 1962, p. 32.

3,209.   "Klan In Louisiana Burning Crosses." New York
          Times. September 3, 1962, p. 13.

3,210.   "The Klan In Morehouse." New York Times. January
          11, 1923, p. 20.

3,211.   "Klan Jury To Hear Mer Rouge Evidence." New York
          Times. March 6, 1923, p. 24.

3,212.   "Klan Leader Fined For Inciting Riot In La."
          Jet. Vol. 57, January 3, 1980, p. 8.

3,213.   "Klan May Disban In La." Afro-American. December
          22, 1956, p. 6.

3,214.   "Klan Opponents Win In Louisiana Fight." Pittsburgh
          Courier. April 7, 1923, p. 14.

3,215.   "Klan Raid Victim, Dragged From Home, Says Skipwith
          Led." New York Times. January 14, 1923, pp. 1, 23.

3,216.   "Klan Kash & Karry: 'No Comment'." Southern
          Exposure. Vol. 8, Summer, 1980, pp. 54-55.

3,217.   "Klan Leader Arrested In Scuffle." New York Times.
          September 14, 1976, p. 36.

3,218.   "Klan Leader Plans Action." New York Times.
          December 30, 1922, p. 26.

3,219.   "Klan Plans To Raise Fund For Defense of Beckwith."
          New York Times. October 12, 1973, p. 13.

3,220.   "Klan Shows Hand In Louisiana Politics." Pittsburgh
          Courier. October 15, 1927, p. 1.

3,221.   "Klan Stronghold Gets Jewish Sheriff." New York
          Times. February 26, 1924, p. 11.

3,222. "Klan Sues For $200,000." New York Times. August 11, 1974, p. 39.

3,223. "Klan Threatens A Mayor." New York Times. December 2, 1922, p. 2.

3,224. "Klan Threats Block Speech In Louisiana On Racial Problems." New York Times. January 6, 1965, p. 28.

3,225. "Klan To Expel Legislators." New York Times. June 15, 1924, Sect. 2, p. 3.

3,226. "Klan To Wage Bitter Political Battle." New York Times. January 28, 1923, Sect. 1, Part 2, p. 5.

3,227. "Klan Usurped Law In Reign Of Terror, Mayor Testifies." New York Times. January 12, 1923, pp. 1, 10.

3,228. "Klan Views Avowed By Confederates." New York Times. April 13, 1923, p. 20.

3,229. "Klan Wizard Injured During New Orleans Lee Birthday Celebration." Washington Post. January 20, 1972, p. 2A.

3,230. "Klansman Calls Inciting Riot Charge 'Big Joke'." New Orleans Times Picayune. May 27, 1977, p. 6.

3,231. "Klansman Hurt In March." New York Times. January 20, 1972, p. 55.

3,232. "Klansman Named As Kidnapper Of 2 Mer Rouge Victims." New York Times. January 19, 1923, pp. 1, 8.

3,233. "Klansmen Arrested In La. For Unlawful Demonstration." New Orleans Times Picayune. August 13, 1973, p. 5.

3,234. "Klansmen Meted 6 Months In Jefferson Jail." New Orleans Times Picayune. April 17, 1976, p. 1.

3,235. "Klansmen Parade To New Lodge In Bogalusa, La." New Orleans Times Picayune. April 17, 1976, p. 1.

3,236. "Klansman Witness Denies He's Slayer." New York Times. January 17, 1923, p. 8.

3,237. "Klansmen Renew Mer Rouge Terror." New York Times. November 27, 1922, p. 2.

3,238. "Klansmen Turn On McKoin." New York Times. December 30, 1922, p. 26.

3,239. "Knights Of KKK Realm Of La. Sues E. Baton Rouge School Board." New Orleans Times Picayune. April 30, 1977, p. 4.

3,240.   "Knights Of The Ku Klux Klan Hold Rally In Walker, La." New Orleans Times Picayune. April 6, 1975, p. 40.

3,241.   "Ku Klux And Crime." New Republic. Vol. 33, January 17, 1923, pp. 189-190.

3,242.   "Ku Klux Effort To Rule Courts Of State Hinted." Pittsburgh Courier. April 14, 1923, p. 13.

3,243.   "Ku Klux Furnished Evidence To Convict." Pittsburgh Courier. June 23, 1923, p. 1.

3,244.   "Ku Klux Justice." New York Amsterdam News. March 21, 1923, p. 2.

3,245.   "Ku Klux Klan Appeals School Bus Ruling." New Orleans Times Picayune. November 22, 1975, p. 5.

3,246.   "Ku Klux Klan Drives Negroes From Homes." New York Amsterdam News. December 13, 1922, pp. 2-3.

3,247.   "The Ku Klux Klan In Louisiana." New York Times. December 24, 1922, p. 12.

3,248.   "Ku Klux Klan Leader Disrupts Louisiana Statue Ceremony." Houston Post. July 31, 1976, p. 16F.

3,249.   "The Ku Klux Mischief." New York Times. November 23, 1922, p. 20.

3,250.   "Ku Klux Klan Parade In N.O. French Quarter Described." Chicago Tribune. November 27, 1978, p. 3.

3,251.   "Ku Klux Klan Parades In Ville Platte, Louisiana." New Orleans Times Picayune. April 30, 1972, p. 2.

3,252.   "Ku Klux Klan Picketing Of Adult Book Store - Letter." New Orleans Times Picayune. August 24, 1973, p. 10.

3,253.   "Ku Klux Klan Publicity Proclaims Its Rebirth." Southern School News. Vol. 7, March, 1961, p. 9.

3,254.   "Ku Klux Klan Weekend Recruitment Program In La. Viewed." New Orleans Times Picayune. September 1, 1974, Sect. 3, p. 2.

3,255.   "Ku Klux Klan Rally At St. Bernard Civic Auditorium Viewed." New Orleans Times Picayune. June 22, 1975, p. 2.

3,256.   "Ku Klux Question Makes House Flurry." New York Times. November 23, 1922, p. 3.

3,257.   "Labor Chief's Home Damaged By Bomb." New York
          Times. July 20, 1967, p. 25.

3,258.   "Leader Reports Students Are Recruited For Klan."
          New York Times. January 27, 1978, p. 10.

3,259.   "Long Tells Klan Head To Stay Out Of State." New
          York Times. August 18, 1934, p. 5.

3,260.   "La. ACLU Exec. Director On Klan Rights." New
          Orleans Times Picayune. June 23, 1977, p. 20.

3,261.   "Louisiana Governor Comes To Washington To See
          What Can Be Done With The Ku Klux Klan; Mentions
          Disappearance Of Several Men." New York Times.
          November 20, 1922, pp. 1, 2.

3,262.   "Louisiana Governor Won't Name Any Klansman For
          Office." New York Times. February 18, 1923, p. 1.

3,263.   "Louisiana Guardsmen Refuse To Drill Under Klan
          Captain." New York Times. March 30, 1923, p. 19.

3,264.   "Louisiana Klan Goes On Trial Today." New York
          Times. January 5, 1923, p. 17.

3,265.   "Louisiana March Nears Its Climax." New York
          Times. August 20, 1967, p. 40.

3,266.   "Louisiana Primary Close On Klan Issue." New York
          Times. January 18, 1924, p. 19.

3,267.   "Louisiana Primary Puts Klan In Fight." New York
          Times. January 15, 1924, p. 11.

3,268.   "La. Ct. Denies Request To Increase Bond For Ku
          Klux Klan Head." New Orleans Times Picayune.
          April 19, 1978, p. 12.

3,269.   "La. Dst. Judge Wicker Postpones Trial Of KKK Head
          David Duke." New Orleans Times Picayune. July 6,
          1979, p. 15.

3,270.   "La. Gov. Issues Statement On KKK Offer To Quell
          Violence." New Orleans Times Picayune. October 9,
          1974, p. 1.

3,271.   "La. Judge Orders KKK Leader Not To Leave Again."
          New Orleans Times Picayune. April 13, 1978, p. 13.

3,272.   "La. Klansmen Chiefs Plan Dem. Delegate Selection
          Suit." New Orleans Times Picayune. May 22, 1972,
          p. 5.

3,273.   "La. KKK Involved As Boston Anti-Bus Protest Halts
          Traffic." New Orleans Times Picayune. December 13,
          1975, p. 14.

3,274.   "La. Ku Klux Klan Leader Expands Activities."
          Washington Post. August 17, 1979, p. 4A.

3,275.   "La. KKK Visits La. House Hearing On Anti-Discrimi-
          nation." New Orleans Times Picayune. June 6, 1974,
          Sect. 4, p. 23.

3,276.   "La. Supreme Ct. Reverses Conviction Of 2 Klansmen
          On Riot Charges." New Orleans Times Picayune.
          September 6, 1978, p. 10.

3,277.   "La. Rep. Alexander May Unite Blacks Against
          Possible KKK Forces." New Orleans Times Picayune.
          February 17, 1979, p. 6.

3,278.   "Lester Maddox Repudiates Ku Klux Klan Endorsement."
          New Orleans Times Picayune. August 13, 1974, p. 15.

3,279.   "Louisiana Student Interviewed On Busing Feud."
          San Francisco Chronicle. January 8, 1981, p. 30.

3,280.   "Louisiana To Fight The Klan Without Federal Aid
          Now." New York Times. November 21, 1922, pp. 1, 4.

3,281.   "Louisiana Troops Are Sent To Guard Hearings On
          Kidnapping Of 5 Citizens By Hooded Men." New York
          Times. December 20, 1922, p. 1.

3,282.   "La. Senate Com. Approves Bill On Open Public
          Meetings. New Orleans Times Picayune. July 30,
          1976, p. 6.

3,283.   "Louisianians Send Indignant Denials." New York
          Times. November 21, 1922, p. 4.

3,284.   "Louisiana Voters Go To Polls Today." New York
          Times. August 13, 1966, p. 9.

3,285.   "Machine Gunners Protect State's Attorneys Sent
          By Governor For Mer Rouge Inquiry." New York Times.
          December 23, 1922, p. 1.

3,286.   "Martial Law Order Ready In Louisiana." New York
          Times. January 4, 1922, p. 21.

3,287.   "The Mask, Not The Murder." Pittsburgh Courier.
          January 20, 1963.

3,288.   "Masked Klansmen Routed From Church." Pittsburgh
          Courier. September 1, 1923, pp. 3-4.

3,289.   "McKoin Fights Extradition." New York Times.
          December 28, 1922, p. 7.

3,290.   "McKoin Returns Voluntarily." New York Times.
          January 4, 1923, p. 21.

3,291.   "Medical Report Tells How Bones Of Two Mob Victims Were Broken." Washington Post. January 7, 1923, p. 6.

3,292.   "Men, Convicted On Evidence Of Klan, Reprieved." Pittsburgh Courier. October 27, 1923, p. 15.

3,293.   "The Menace Of Mer Rouge." New York World. January 8, 1923, p. 1.

3,294.   "Mer Rouge Mayor Gets Death Threat." New York Times. January 31, 1923, p. 15.

3,295.   "Mer Rouge Murders Unpunished." Literary Digest. Vol. 76, March 31, 1923, pp. 10-11.

3,296.   "Mer Rouge 'Victims' Are Alive, Doctor Says." New York Times. February 14, 1923, p. 3.

3,297.   "Mer Rouge Witness Gone A Second Time." New York Times. January 2, 1923, p. 17.

3,298.   "Missing Witness Back To Klansmen." New York Times. January 30, 1923, p. 21.

3,299.   "More Federal Agents Summoned." New York Times. December 31, 1922, p. 18.

3,300.   "Morehouse Klansmen Surrender To Sheriff." New York Times. April 20, 1923, p. 8.

3,301.   "Murders Laid To Ku Klux Klan." New York Times. December 30, 1922, p. 26.

3,302.   "Murders Of Mer Rouge." Literary Digest. Vol. 76, January 13, 1923, pp. 10-12.

3,303.   "National Klan Leader Fined For Inciting To Riot In South." New York Times. November 30, 1979, p. A20.

3,304.   "New Charges To Be Made." New York Times. January 1, 1923, p. 7.

3,305.   "New Orleans Black Events Rescheduled To Avoid KKK Parade." New Orleans Times Picayune. November 22, 1978, p. 5.

3,306.   "New Orleans Churches Federation Asks Dock Bd. To Cancel KKK Mtg." New Orleans Times Picayune. May 13, 1976, p. 10.

3,307.   "New Orleans Council Actions Summarized." New Orleans Times Picayune. April 11, 1975, p. 2.

3,308.   "New Orleans Dock Bd. Seeks Cancellation Of KKK Lease." New Orleans Times Picayune. May 8, 1976, p. 20.

3,309.   "New Orleans Issues KKK Parade Permit For Same Day As Black Festivities." *New Orleans Times Picayune*. November 18, 1978, p. 1.

3,310.   "New Orleans Klan Rallies Early, Missing Irate Blacks." *New York Times*. November 27, 1978, p. 16.

3,311.   "New Orleans Mayor Discusses Right Of KKK To Stage Parade In This City." *New Orleans Times Picayune*. November 23, 1978, p. 13.

3,312.   "New Orleans Mayor's Handling Of KKK Request For March." *New Orleans Times Picayune*. December 8, 1978, p. 14.

3,313.   "New Orleans Police Avert Confrontation As KKK And Blacks Rally Downtown." *New Orleans Times Picayune*. November 27, 1978, p. 4.

3,314.   "New Orleans Police Chief Parsons Explains How He Handled KKK-Black Marchers." *New Orleans Times Picayune*. December 3, 1978, p. 1.

3,315.   "Night Riders Out; 2 Kidnappers Named." *New York Times*. January 20, 1923, pp. 1, 6.

3,316.   "100 Armed Deputies To Guard Klan Trial." *New York Times*. November 5, 1923, p. 19.

3,317.   "OEO Investigates KKK." *Christian Science Monitor*. March 19, 1969, p. 2.

3,318.   "Paper Denies Charges." *New York Times*. January 7, 1966, p. 9.

3,319.   "Parker, A Fighting Governor; Ku Klux Has Met Its Match." *New York Times*. December 31, 1922, Sect. 8, p. 3.

3,320.   "Parker May Declare Martial Law." *New York Times*. January 3, 1923, p. 19.

3,321.   "Parker To Join Conference." *New York Times*. December 28, 1922, p. 7.

3,322.   "Parker Writes On Klan." *New York Times*. December 28, 1922, p. 7.

3,323.   " 'Pelican Klub' Wars On Cohen." *Pittsburgh Courier*. October 29, 1927, p. 3.

3,324.   "Perjury Inquiry Started." *New York Times*. December 31, 1922, p. 18.

3,325.   "Physicians Offer To Aid McKoin." *New York Times*. December 28, 1922, p. 7.

3,326.   "Placed Under Arrest." New York Times. January
         30, 1923, p. 21.

3,327.   Powledge, Fred. "Armed Negroes Make Jonesboro
         An Unusual Town." New York Times. February 21,
         1965, p. 52.

3,328.   "Predict Indicting In Mer Rouge Crime." New York
         Times. December 30, 1922, p. 26.

3,329.   "Prisoner Held For Mer Rouge Murders Denies He's
         In Klan." New York Times. December 26, 1922,
         pp. 1, 3.

3,330.   "Prompt Action." New York Times. January 31, 1923,
         p. 15.

3,331.   "Quit Morehouse Parish." New York Times. March
         11, 1923, p. 18.

3,332.   "Racism Is Issue In Clash Over New Orleans Monu-
         ment." New York Times. January 18, 1981, p. 20.

3,333.   Reed, Rex. " 'Like They Could Eat Your Heart Out'."
         New York Times. August 21, 1966, Sect. 2, p. 9.

3,334.   Reed, Roy. "How Beckwith Was Cleared In Bombing
         Case." New York Times. January 21, 1974, p. 10.

3,335.   "Removal Of A Marker Linked To Klan Urged." New
         York Times. September 12, 1976, p. 43.

3,336.   "Report On Mutilated Bodies." New York Times.
         October 31, 1923, p. 19.

3,337.   "Rescheduling Creole Feast Due To KKK Parade."
         New Orleans Times Picayune. November 25, 1978,
         p. 14.

3,338.   "Reversal In Klan Case Asked." New York Times.
         January 20, 1967, p. 21.

3,339.   Rugaber, Walter. "Negroes Wind Up Louisiana
         March." New York Times. August 21, 1967, p. 27.

3,340.   "Say U.S. Attorney Tried To Save Klan In Federal
         Inquiry." New York Times. December 28, 1922,
         pp. 1, 3.

3,341.   "Says Case Is Perfect In Mer Rouge Crime." New
         York Times. December 31, 1922, p. 18.

3,342.   "Says Hylan Financed Inquiry At Mer Rouge." New
         York Times. February 6, 1923, p. 4.

3,343. "Says Klan Checked Mer Rouge Inquiry." New York Times. October 31, 1923, p. 19.

3,344. "Says Klan Not In Politics." New York Times. November 21, 1922, p. 4.

3,345. "Says Klansmen Led Kidnapers." New York Times. December 28, 1922, p. 7.

3,346. "Says Louisiana Is Calm." New York Times. November 20, 1922, p. 2.

3,347. "Says Skipwith Gave Phone Stop Order." New York Times. January 24, 1923, p. 21.

3,348. "Says Skipwith's Son Guarded Victims On Murder Truck." New York Times. January 21, 1923, pp. 1, 20.

3,349. "SCLC Opens Annual Convention In New Orleans, Assault On Black Life Discussed." New Orleans Times Picayune. August 12, 1981, p. 20.

3,350. "Secret Service Men Still Track Klan." New York Times. January 29, 1923, p. 17.

3,351. "Seek Evidence Against McKoin." New York Times. December 31, 1922, p. 18.

3,352. "Senator Long." New York Times. August 18, 1934, p. 5.

3,353. "Sentences Passed In Invasion Plot." New York Times. July 2, 1981, p. A15.

3,354. "Shreveport Official Hits Dismissal Of Ku Klux Klan Charges." New Orleans Times Picayune. August 15, 1973, p. 9.

3,355. "Site In New Orleans Chosen For Rally Of The Ku Klux Klan - Letter." New Orleans Times Picayune. December 14, 1978, p. 18.

3,356. "Southern Exposure." Newsweek. Vol. 72, November 25, 1968, pp. 111-112.

3,357. "State's Evidence On Mer Rouge Crime." New York Times. January 28, 1923, Sect. 1, Part 2, p. 5.

3,358. "Their Hoods Do Serve Them Well." New York Times. December 21, 1922, p. 14.

3,359. "Their One Plea Is Empty." New York Times. January 12, 1923, p. 14.

3,360. "Think Klan Victims Crushed By Tractor." New York Times. March 9, 1923, p. 17.

3,361.   "Think Parker Knew Secret Of Lake La Fourche When
He Opened War On Klan." _Washington Post_. January
7, 1923, p. 7.

3,362.   "Thirty Klansmen Face Indictment In Mer Rouge Case."
New York World. January 19, 1923.

3,363.   "This Seems Too Much For Belief." _New York Times_.
January 8, 1923, p. 16.

3,364.   "Times Receives Denials." _New York Times_.
November 21, 1922, p. 4.

3,365.   "To Arrest 20 Of Klan In Louisiana Cases." _New
York Times_. April 17, 1923, p. 14.

3,366.   "To Select Bastrop Jury." _New York Times_. February
13, 1923, p. 14.

3,367.   "To Study Klan Case Panel." _New York Times_.
February 16, 1923, p. 8.

3,368.   "To Tell Of Louisiana Klan." _New York Times_.
October 27, 1923, p. 5.

3,369.   "Torture Devices Used On Victims Of Mer Rouge Mob."
New York Times. January 7, 1923, pp. 1, 20.

3,370.   "Troops Seek Bodies In Louisiana Lakes." _New York
Times_. December 21, 1922, p. 6.

3,371.   "Trial Of KKK Leader David Duke Viewed." _New
Orleans Times Picayune_. August 22, 1979, p. 13.

3,372.   "Trial Of KKK Leader Duke In Gretna Continues."
New Orleans Times Picayune. August 23, 1979, p. 14.

3,373.   "250 Masked Men Act In Louisiana Shooting." _New
York Times_. November 28, 1922, p. 23.

3,374.   "2 Guilty In Plot To Oust Dominican Government."
Washington Post. June 21, 1981, p. A9.

3,375.   "2 KKK Leaders Guilty Of Inciting To Riot." _New
Orleans Times Picayune_. May 28, 1977, p. 1.

3,376.   "2 KKK Members Arrested In Connection With Ky.
Bombing Case." _New Orleans Times Picayune_.
June 24, 1981, p. 17.

3,377.   "2 KKK Members Arrested In Metairie Held Under Bond
In Bomb Case." _New Orleans Times Picayune_. June
25, 1981, Sect. 5, p. 3.

3,378.   "2 Klansmen Appeal Convictions In Jefferson Parish
Incidents." _New Orleans Times Picayune_. March 3,
1978, Sect. 3, p. 4.

3,379.   "2 Klansmen Convicted In Plot To Overthrow Dominican Regime." Washington Star. June 21, 1981, p. D16.

3,380.   "2 On Baton Rouge School Board Receive 'KKK' Visits At Home." New York Times. February 25, 1961, p. 6.

3,381.   "2 Protests Reported At Liberty Monument In New Orleans." New Orleans Times Picayune. January 25, 1981, p. 3.

3,382.   "TV Newsman In South Beaten." New York Times. April 20, 1964, p. 59.

3,383.   "United Klans Of America Holds Rally In Covington, La." New Orleans Times Picayune. July 25, 1976, p. 38.

3,384.   "United Klans Of America Rally Held At St. Bernard Auditorium." New Orleans Times Picayune. August 14, 1977, p. 16.

3,385.   "Urges McKoin To Return." New York Times. December 30, 1922, p. 26.

3,386.   "U.S. Appeals Ct. Hears Arguments On KKK Use Of School." New Orleans Times Picayune. May 11, 1978, Sect. 6, p. 12.

3,387.   "U.S. Court Begins Contempt Charges In La. School Integration Case." Los Angeles Times. January 8, 1981, p. 20.

3,388.   "U.S. Court Issues Injunction Against La. School's Anti-KKK Policy." Houston Post. August 24, 1978, p. 6A.

3,389.   "U.S. Ct. Rules Baton Rouge School Board Must Pay Costs In KKK Case." New Orleans Times Picayune. February 24, 1981, Sect. 2, p. 4.

3,390.   "U.S. Ct. Rules On E. Baton Rouge School's Barring Of KKK." New Orleans Times Picayune. August 26, 1978, p. 15.

3,391.   "U.S. Ct. Rules On Ku Klux Klan Use Of Baton Rouge School." New Orleans Times Picayune. January 23, 1979, p. 4.

3,392.   "U.S. Judges Enjoin Klan In Bogalusa." New York Times. December 2, 1965, pp. 1, 36.

3,393.   "U.S. Opposed Klan's Use Of School For A Meeting." New York Times. December 23, 1976, p. 12.

3,394.   "W.J. Bryant Against Klan." New York Times. August 30, 1924, p. 4.

3,395.   Walsh, Robert K.   "Bogalusa School Aide Takes 5th At
           Klan Probe." Washington Evening Star. January 6,
           1966, p. 1.

3,396.   _____. "Former Klansman Tells Of Burnings,
           Whippings." Washington Evening Star. January 11,
           1966, p. 1.

3,397.   "Warrants Out For Klan In Morehouse." New York
           Times. April 19, 1923, p. 21.

3,398.   "WBOX And The KKK. Newsweek. Vol. 66, August 16,
           1965, pp. 75-76.

3,399.   "White Men Bar Attack Planned By Klansmen."
           Chicago Defender. September 30, 1922, p. 3.

3,400.   "Whites In Louisiana Town Take Control Of Poverty
           Board From Negroes." New York Times. March 16,
           1969, p. 68.

3,401.   "Who The Bogalusa (La.) Klansmen Are." Militant.
           December 13, 1965.

3,402.   "Wholesale Alibis To Be Klan's Plea; Klux Witnesses
           Build Skipwith's." New York World. January 16,
           1973, p. 1.

3,403.   "Witness Identifies Gray As One Of Klan Kidnapping
           Band On Night Of Murder." New York World. January
           18, 1923,

3,404.   "Witness Was Told Mer Rouge Victims 'Knew Too
           Much'." New York Times. January 13, 1923, p. 1.

3,405.   "Witnesses Identify 7 More Klansmen Of Kidnapping
           Band." New York Times. January 11, 1923, pp. 1, 6.

3,406.   Wrench, Evelyn. "English-Speaking World."
           Spectator. Vol. 130, March 24, 1923, pp. 506-507.

3,407.   "You Can Say Positively." New York Times. January
           2, 1923, p. 17.

18. MAINE

3,408.   "Charges Brewster Boasts Klan Votes." New York
           Times. June 14, 1928, p. 10.

3,409.   Collins, Frederick L.   "Way Down East With The
           Ku Klux Klan." Collier's. Vol. 72, December 15,
           1923, pp. 12, 29.

3,410.   "Complimenting The Maine Voters." New York Times.
           September 5, 1924, p. 16.

3,411.   "Dawes Attacks Ku Klux In Maine." New York Times.
          August 24, 1924, pp. 1, 2.

3,412.   "Democrats Predict Victory In Maine." New York
          Times. September 7, 1924, pp. 1, 26.

3,413.   "Dirigo Ku Klux." New York Times. September 12,
          1923, p. 18.

3,414.   "How Klan Figures In Maine Election." New York
          Times. August 31, 1924, Sect. 2, p. 2.

3,415.   "Klan Company Is Sued." New York Times. May 13,
          1924, p. 2.

3,416.   "Klan Issue In Maine Derided By Willis." New York
          Times. August 28, 1924, p. 3.

3,417.   "Klan Makes Issue In Maine Politics." New York
          Times. September 10, 1923, p. 19.

3,418.   "Klansmen Help Elect Two Maine Mayors." New York
          Times. March 4, 1924, p. 4.

3,419.   "Lacking Prime Qualifications." New York Times.
          September 7, 1924, Sect. 2, p. 4.

3,420.   "Maine And The Klan." New York Times. September
          10, 1924, p. 20.

3,421.   "Maine Democrats Organize Women." New York Times.
          September 5, 1924, p. 3.

3,422.   "Maine Democrats Show Republicans Raised Klan
          Issue." New York Times. September 3, 1924,
          pp. 1, 2.

3,423.   "Maine Know-Nothingism." New York Times. July
          22, 1924, p. 14.

3,424.   "The Maine Primaries." New York Times. June 20,
          1928, p. 24.

3,425.   "Maine Republicans Fear Radical Vote." New York
          Times. September 4, 1924, p. 3.

3,426.   "The Maine Rumpus." New York Times. November 27,
          1926, p. 16.

3,427.   "Portland City Council." New York Times. March
          19, 1929, p. 12.

3,428.   "The Pride Of Aroostook." New York Times.
          November 23, 1926, p. 28.

3,429.   "Psychiatric Test Is Ordered For Klan
Suspect." _Washington Post_. July 30, 1981, p. B6.

3,430.   "Republicans Worry Over Split In Maine." _New York
Times_. July 21, 1924, p. 3.

3,431.   "Thinks Democrats May Carry Maine." _New York Times_.
September 5, 1924, p. 3.

3,432.   "Thrift, Kamelia, Thrift!" _New York Times_. October
2, 1923, p. 6.

3,433.   "Warns Klan In Maine." _New York Times_. November
2, 1922, p. 10.

3,434.   Weiss, John K. "How Brewster Deserted A Republican
To Back Klan-Supported Democrat." _PM_. August 13,
1947, pp. 3-4.

3,435.   _____. "Support Of KKK Helped Brewster Climb
His Political Ladder." _PM_. August 12, 1947, pp.
3-4.

19. MARYLAND

3,436.   "ACLU Attacks Anti-KKK Zoning Rule." _Washington
Star_. July 10, 1981, p. B1.

3,437.   "Annapolis, Md. Plaque Marking Roots Landmark
Removed By KKK." _New Orleans Times Picayune_.
September 24, 1981, Sect. 4, p. 12.

3,438.   "Annapolis Unveils New Kunta Kinte Memorial
Plaque." _Washington Post_. November 23, 1981, p.
B2.

3,439.   "Anti-Klan Month In County." _Prince George's
(Md.) Journal_. May 29, 1981, p. A2.

3,440.   "An Anti-Lynching Senator." _New York Times_.
August 12, 1923, Sect. 2, p. 4.

3,441.   "Archbishop Rouses Klan." _New York Times_.
November 30, 1922, p. 21.

3,442.   "Arrest Of 10 In Md. And Del. Thwarts Plan To
Bomb NAACP Offices." _New Orleans Times Picayune_.
May 23, 1981, p. 3.

3,443.   "Baltimore Allows More Core Pickets." _New York
Times_. May 17, 1966, p. 34.

3,444.   "Baltimore Bookman Fights Against KKK Terrorism;
New Era Bookshop." _Publisher's Weekly_. Vol. 191,
March 27, 1967, pp. 35-36.

3,445.   "Baptist Bids Church Fight Segregation." New York
          Times. November 18, 1964, p. 41.

3,446.   Bigart, Homer. "Friend Of Rap Brown Dies With
          2d Man In Auto Blast." New York Times. March 11,
          1970, pp. 1, 34.

3,447.   Brown, Chip. "Klan's Einsteins Slice At Life's
          Complexities." Washington Post. July 3, 1980, Md. 1.

3,448.   _____. "Klansmen Outnumbered By Newsmen At
          Md. Rally." Washington Post. June 30, 1980, p.
          A7.

3,449.   Chase, Anne. "The Klansman." Prince Georges
          (Md.) Journal. July 25, 1980, pp. A1, A7.

3,450.   "Crosses Burned At Harford." Washington Star.
          January 29, 1981, p. B1.

3,451.   "Cross Burning In Maryland Counties Discussed."
          Washington Post. April 20, 1977, p. 1C.

3,452.   "Deny M'Koin Is Klan Member." New York Times.
          December 31, 1922, p. 18.

3,453.   "Disapproves 'Red Knights'." New York Times.
          September 9, 1923, Sect. 1, Part 2, p. 8.

3,454.   "Eastern Shore Officials Split On Response To
          KKK Rally." Washington Post. November 5, 1981,
          p. B4.

3,455.   "8 Held For Conspiracy To Bomb N.A.A.C.P. Center."
          New York Times. May 22, 1981, p. A14.

3,456.   "8 Held In Alleged Plot To Bomb NAACP Site."
          Washington Star. May 22, 1981, p. B1.

3,457.   "Feds Crack KKK Conspiracy To Bomb NAACP In Md."
          Augusta (Ga.) News-Review. June 13, 1981, p. 1.

3,458.   "Fed. Judge Sentences Md. KKK Leader In Bombing
          Of NAACP Hdqrs." New Orleans Times Picayune.
          September 25, 1981, p. 8.

3,459.   "Fire Engine Guards Church As The Klan Dedicates
          It." New York Times. August 25, 1924, p. 1.

3,460.   "Five Suspects Linked To Cross Burning." Washington
          Star. June 1, 1981, p. A5.

3,461.   Gettlin, Bob. "Few Interested In Its Message,
          The Klan Found." Washington Star. June 30, 1980,
          pp. D1, D3.

3,462.   _____ . "20 Klansmen Hold Peaceful Rally At Rural Frederick County Site." Washington Star. June 29, 1980, p. A6.

3,463.   "Hate-Mongers." Washington Post. July 14, 1981, p. A12.

3,464.   "Hecklers At Baltimore Rally Interrupt Kennedy Speech." New York Times. May 7, 1980, p. B7.

3,465.   "Hughes Calls For Battle Against 'Hate-Mongers'." Washington Post. July 3, 1981, p. B6.

3,466.   "Kinte's Plaque Stolen." Washington Post. September 24, 1981, p. B5.

3,467.   "KKK Gets Frederick Permit." Washington Star. June 12, 1980, p. D1.

3,468.   "KKK Leader Gets 15 Years." Prince Georges (Md.) Journal. September 25, 1981, p. A4.

3,469.   "KKK 'Plot' To Bomb NAACP Chapter Foiled." Jet. Vol. 60, June 11, 1981, p. 8.

3,470.   "KKK Said To Recruit In Md. Schools." Washington Star. February 5, 1981, p. B1.

3,471.   "KKK Steals 'Roots' Plaque." Prince George's (Md.) Journal. September 24, 1981, p. B8.

3,472.   "Klan Assails LaFollette." New York Times. August 18, 1924, p. 4.

3,473.   "Klan Burns Crosses In Maryland Town." New York Times. November 8, 1965, p. 21.

3,474.   "Klan Card Causes Trouble." Pittsburgh Courier. February 16, 1929, p. 2C.

3,475.   "Klan Credited In Theft Of Kunta Kinte Memorial." Jet. Vol. 61, October 15, 1981, p. 7.

3,476.   "Klan Ghosts Guard Coffin In Maryland." Chicago Defender. January 21, 1922, p. 1, Part 2.

3,477.   "Klan Leader Charged In Plot Goes Before Judge Today." Washington Star. May 29, 1981, p. B3.

3,478.   "Klan Leader Claims Group Is Arming For 'Race War'." Washington Star. May 24, 1981, p. F5.

3,479.   "Klan Members Strike Deal In Cross-Burning Charges." Washington Star. July 25, 1981, p. B2.

3,480.   "Klan NAACP To Hold Rallies." _Washington Star_.
          April 3, 1981, p. B1.

3,481.   "Klan Plans 2nd Frederick Rally." _Washington Star_.
          October 2, 1980, p. B1.

3,482.   "Klan Postpones March." _New York Times_. June 14,
          1966, p. 20.

3,483.   "Klan Protest Draws More Than Klan Rally On
          Eastern Shore." _Washington Post_. November 9,
          1981, p. B22.

3,484.   "Klan Rallies Again In Frederick County."
          Washington Star. October 20, 1980, p. B1.

3,485.   "Klan Rally Draws 2,000 In Maryland." _New York
          Times_. November 7, 1965, p. 74.

3,486.   "Klan Stages A Cross-Burning In Frederick, NAACP
          Has Rally." _Washington Post_. April 6, 1981,
          p. B20.

3,487.   "Klan Wizard Pleads Innocent." _Washington Star_.
          June 27, 1981, p. B1.

3,488.   "Klan Wizard Resigns." _New York Times_. March
          28, 1967, p. 36.

3,489.   "Klansman Is Questioned In Alleged Death Threat."
          Washington Star. June 19, 1981, p. B4.

3,490.   "KKK Leader Found Guilty." _Washington Post_.
          August 29, 1981, p. A14.

3,491.   "KKK Members Distribute Literature In Cambridge,
          Maryland." _Baltimore Afro-American_. October 31,
          1981, p. 3.

3,492.   "Ku Klux Klan Rally In Gamber, Md. Eyed."
          Washington Post. May 26, 1975, p. 1C.

3,493.   "Klansmen Rare At Shore Rally." _Prince Georges
          (Md.) Journal_. November 9, 1981, p. A10.

3,494.   "A Ku Klux Klan Speaker." _New York Times_.
          July 18, 1966, p. 17.

3,495.   "Kunta Kinte Plaque." _Atlanta Daily World_.
          September 27, 1981, p. 4.

3,496.   "Kunta Kinte Plaque Dedicated In Annapolis And
          Then Stolen." _Bilalian News_. October 9, 1981, p. 4.

3,497.   "Kunta Kinte Plaque Stolen In Maryland; KKK Calling
          Card Left." _Atlanta Daily World_. September 25,
          1981, p. 1.

3,498.   Lowy, Joan. "Racial Vandalism Probed At Black
          Baptist Church." _Washington Star_. September 10,
          1980, pp. B1, B4.

3,499.   "Make Cross Burning A Felony: Baltimore Group."
          Jet. Vol. 58, March 20, 1980, p. 7.

3,500.   "Maryland Dragon Quits." _New York Times_. June 30,
          1926, p. 6.

3,501.   "Md. Klan Chief Indicted In Plot Against NAACP."
          Washington Star. June 17, 1981, p. C2.

3,502.   "Maryland Student Held In Alleged Klan Plot."
          Knoxville Journal. March 3, 1977.

3,503.   "Maryland Teachers Assn. Denounce KKK Activity."
          Jet. Vol. 59, February 26, 1981, p. 15.

3,504.   "Maryland Teachers Combat The Klan." _Prince
          George's (Md.) Journal_. March 26, 1982, p.A10.

3,505.   "Md. Teen-Ager Is Sentenced In Cross-Burning
          Incident." _Washington Post_. March 19, 1982,
          p. B8.

3,506.   "Maryland Town Forbids Ku Klux Klan Meeting."
          Pittsburgh Courier. June 23, 1923, p. 12.

3,507.   McKinney, Gwen. "Klan Bomb Targeted For NAACP
          Defused." _Philadelphia Tribune_. May 26, 1981,
          pp. 1, 11.

3,508.   "McKoin Back In Baltimore." _New York Times_.
          February 16, 1923, p. 8.

3,509.   "McKoin May Drop His Fight." _New York Times_.
          January 2, 1923, p. 17.

3,510.   "M'Keldin Blocks Bookshop Ouster." _New York Times_.
          March 27, 1967, p. 23.

3,511.   "M'Koin on Request Leaves Johns Hopkins." _New
          York Times_. February 7, 1923, p. 19.

3,512.   "More Klan Arrests In Md." _Washington Star_.
          June 2, 1981, p. B1.

3,513.   Morris, Gregg. "Five Montgomery Teen-Agers Are
          Charged in Cross Burning." _Washington Star_.
          June 19, 1981, pp. C1, C3.

3,514.   Muscatine, Alison, and Ronald D. White. "Cross-
          Burning." Washington Post. September 25, 1981,
          pp. B1, B10.

3,515.   "Negro Paper Quits Hoover." New York Times.
          October 26, 1928, p. 11.

3,516.   "Ordinance To Ban Klan Rallies Opposed By Maryland
          ACLU." Washington Post. July 10, 1981, p. C4.

3,517.   "Pr. George's City Exec. Kelly Supports Cross
          Burning Penalty." Washington Post. May 4, 1977,
          p. 1B.

3,518.   "Pr. Geo. Cty. Exec. Lawrence Hogan's Inaugural
          Remarks." Washington Post. December 6, 1978,
          p. 22A.

3,519.   "Prison For Masked Band." New York Times.
          December 27, 1922, p. 2.

3,520.   "Reagan Is Asked To Speak Against Racial Violence."
          Washington Star. November 30, 1980, p. D3.

3,521.   "Refuses Armory For Klan." New York Times.
          December 23, 1922, p. 2.

3,522.   Richards, Bill. "Black Couple Given Harsh
          Welcome." Washington Post. September 2, 1975,
          p. 1.

3,523.   "Ritchie Refuses To Give Up M'Koin." New York
          Times. January 3, 1923, p. 19.

3,524.   "Ritchie Says Davis Will Win Maryland." New York
          Times. September 12, 1924, p. 2.

3,525.   "Rocks Are Thrown As Klan And CORE Picket At
          Tavern In Baltimore." New York Times. May 31,
          1966, p. 28.

3,526.   Saperstein, Saundra and Neil Henry. "11-Month
          Undercover Probe Led To Md. Klan Arrests."
          Washington Post. May 24, 1981, pp. D1, D5.

3,527.   Sims, Patsy. "Ku Klux Klan In Maryland."
          Washington Post. January 22, 1978, p. 10.

3,528.   "Soldiers Wear Ku Klux Sheets." Chicago Defender.
          August 26, 1922, p. 13.

3,529.   "10 Alleged KKK Members Arrested By Fed. Agents
          In Maryland." San Francisco Chronicle.
          May 23, 1981, p. 4.

3,530.   "Tiff Mars Klan Rally." Washington Star. July
          27, 1981, p. B1.

3,531.   "To Hear McKoin Wednesday." New York Times.
          February 1, 1923, p. 7.

3,532.   "A Tractor Must Be Ready." New York Times.
          August 26, 1924, p. 10.

3,533.   "3 Charged In Cross Burning." Washington Post.
          December 17, 1981, p. C12.

3,534.   "200 Take K.K.K. Oath Before 1,000 Klansmen."
          Washington Evening Star. June 28, 1922, p. 1.

3,535.   "Try To Burn Ku Klux Home." New York Times.
          February 10, 1923, p. 8.

3,536.   "Two In Klan Robes Disrupt Fundamentalist Service."
          Washington Post. February 2, 1982, p. B5.

3,537.   "2 Md. Klansmen Get Jail For Cross Burning."
          Washington Post. January 7, 1982, p. C3.

3,538.   Weil, Martin. "Alleged Klan Plot Cited In Arrest
          Of 8." Washington Post. May 22, 1981, p. B8.

3,539.   White, Ronald. R. "Exposing Hate In Reason's
          Light." Washington Post. October 1, 1981, p.
          Md. 1.

3,540.   _____. "Police See Increase In Harassment."
          Washington Post. July 3, 1981, pp. B1, B6.

3,541.   Zilg, Jerry. "Militant Youth, Labor Confront KKK
          Rally." Worker's World. Vol. 13, June 25, 1971,
          p. 2.

20. MASSACHUSETTS

3,542.   "Alleged Rioters Held." New York Times. August
          4, 1925, p. 5.

3,543.   "Bay State Bars Brewster." New York Times.
          October 26, 1924, p. 6.

3,544.   "Besiege 150 Klansmen." New York Times. April 1,
          1925, p. 23.

3,545.   "Bishop Repudiates Klan." New York Times. April
          5, 1923, p. 21.

3,546.   "Blacks Bused From Boston Withdrew From School."
          New York Times. July 21, 1978, p. 10.

3,547.   "Boston Demonstration Against Knights Of KKK Acti-
          vities Eyed." Chicago Defender. December 10,
          1979, p. 5.

3,548. "Bottle Misses Heflin But Cuts Policeman." New York Times. March 19, 1929, p. 12.

3,549. "Busing Protests Spread To East Boston." New York Times. September 21, 1974, p. 60.

3,550. "Calls Prof. Ward A Red." New York Times. November 2, 1937, p. 13.

3,551. "Can Harvard Students Be Klansmen?" New York Times. October 24, 1923, p. 18.

3,552. "Charge Klan Guards Impersonate Police." New York Times. September 6, 1926, p. 30.

3,553. "Condemns Ku Klux Klan." New York Times. January 16, 1923, p. 13.

3,554. "Demonstrators Attack Ku Klux Klan Members In Boston." Washington Post. October 16, 1978, p. 5A.

3,555. "Fiery Cross Near New Monastery." New York Times. November 1, 1925, Sect. 2, p. 1.

3,556. "Fiery Crosses Blaze Up In Massachusetts Towns." New York Times. October 2, 1937, p. 2.

3,557. "Fifty Hurt In Two Bay State Klan Battles; In One 500 Foes Clash With 200 Knights." New York Times. July 30, 1924, p. 1.

3,558. "Fights Klan In Boston." New York Times. September 19, 1921, p. 17.

3,559. "Finds 13 Guilty In Klan Riot." New York Times. August 19, 1924, p. 36.

3,560. "Five Shot Near Klan Field." New York Times. August 11, 1925, p. 12.

3,561. "Groton Church Lightless." New York Times. July 9, 1926, p. 33.

3,562. "Harvard In Grip Of The Ku Klux Klan." California Eagle. January 27, 1923, p. 1.

3,563. "Harvard Warned Of Coming Klan Drive And Assault On Discrimination Bar." New York Times. October 23, 1923, p. 1.

3,564. "Harvard's Klan Scare Considered A Joke." New York Times. November 22, 1922, p. 23.

3,565. "Heflin Not So Hot In Brockton." Pittsburgh Courier. March 30, 1929, p. 3.

3,566. "Held For Klan Riots." New York Times. June 21, 1925, p. 15.

3,567. "Hundreds In Klan Riot." New York Times. September 19, 1925, p. 9.

3,568. Kifner, John. "South Boston, A 'Town' Of Irishmen, Feels As If It's A Persecuted Belfast." New York Times. September 23, 1974, p. 40.

3,569. "KKK Unit Plans To Help Boston White Resistance Organize." New Orleans Times Picayune. September 18, 1974, p. 12.

3,570. "Klan Clash Prisoners Are Jailed And Fined." New York Times. August 1, 1924, p. 13.

3,571. "Klan Propaganda Seen." New York Times. November 25, 1923, p. 22.

3,572. "Klan Threatens Six Children Of Mayor." New York Times. January 29, 1923, p. 17.

3,573. "Klan Warning At Harvard." New York Times. November 21, 1922, p. 4.

3,574. "Ku Klux At Work." Chicago Defender. July 8, 1922, p. 13.

3,575. "Ku Klux Stirs Worcester." New York Times. September 24, 1923, p. 3.

3,576. "Leave Klan Robe For Him." New York Times. January 17, 1923, p. 9.

3,577. "Links Klan With Others." New York Times. February 8, 1923, p. 16.

3,578. "Mason Condemns Ku Klux." New York Times. June 17, 1922, p. 26.

3,579. "Massachusetts House Condemns Klan." New York Times. January 17, 1923, p. 8.

3,580. "Mayors Warn Ku Klux." New York Times. October 7, 1922, p. 15.

3,581. "Mob Of 800 In Worcester Beats Klansmen And Wrecks Cars After Order's Big Meeting." New York Times. October 19, 1924, p. 1.

3,582. "More Arrests Made In Klan Rioting." New York Times. August 2, 1924, p. 10.

3,583. "Mr. Heflin Dodges A Bottle." Pittsburgh Courier. May 4, 1929, Editorial page.

3,584. "Mud Hurled At Heflin By Bay State Crowd." New York Times. March 18, 1929, p. 8.

3,585. "Negroes Protest Klan At Harvard." New York Times. October 24, 1923, p. 12.

3,586. "1,000 In Bay State Engage In Klan Row." New York Times. August 13, 1925, p. 21.

3,587. "Police Sergeant Was The Target." New York Times. April 25, 1929, p. 6.

3,588. "Prison Guards Fired For Using KKK Masks In Massachusetts Prison." Baltimore Afro-American. June 17, 1978, p. 8.

3,589. "Quits Klan Because of Cowardly Policy." New York Amsterdam News. December 6, 1922, p. 1.

3,590. "Says Ford Men Aid Nazi Efforts Here." New York Times. October 17, 1937, p. 17.

3,591. "Scores Are Hurt In Bay State Klan Riots; Three Arrested After Siege In Farmhouse." New York Times. August 3, 1925, p. 1.

3,592. "Senate By 70 To 14 Votes Heflin Down." New York Times. May 2, 1929, p. 1.

3,593. "16 Klansmen Held For Bay State Riot." New York Times. August 12, 1925, p. 23.

3,594. Stone, Elizabeth. "KKK Scum In Boston: 'Real Issue In Niggers'." Militant. Vol. 38, October 18, 1974, p. 4.

3,595. "Talk Of Klan Recruiting." Christian Science Monitor. August 28, 1970, p. 6.

3,596. "There She Is, But Where Is She At?" New York Times. August 14, 1925, p. 12.

3,597. "300 Klansmen Stoned In Massachusetts." New York Times. May 4, 1925, p. 14.

3,598. "Three Shot In Attack On Klansmen By Crowd After Initiation Ceremonies Near Haverhill." New York Times. July 31, 1924, p. 1.

3,599. "Thwart Klan Or Close Harvard." New York Amsterdam News. November 7, 1923, p. 7.

3,600. "To Investigate Klan Riot." New York Times. October 20, 1924, p. 18.

3,601.   "Two Held In Klan Disorders." New York Times.
        June 12, 1925, p. 6.

3,602.   "Two Klan Foes Beaten." New York Times. May 20,
        1925, p. 10.

3,603.   "Upholds Klan Meetings." New York Times. October
        22, 1923, p. 25.

3,604.   "Young Socialists Oppose The Klan." New York Times.
        January 2, 1923, p. 17.

3,605.   Wilson, Steve. "KKK In Boston." New York Times.
        October 16, 1978, p. 30.

21. MICHIGAN

3,606.   "ACLU Sues FBI In 1965 Death Of Civil Rights Worker,
        Viola Liuzzo." Chicago Tribune. July 6, 1979,
        p. 6.

3,607.   "Anti-Klan Bill Backed In Michigan." New York Times.
        April 25, 1923, p. 23.

3,608.   "Anti-Klan Hecklers Scuffle With Police." New
        York Times. June 27, 1980, p. 14.

3,609.   "Anti-Ku Klux Klan Rally Held In Downtown Detroit."
        Chicago Defender. November 19, 1979, p. 19.

3,610.   "Army Patrols End Detroit Riotings:Death Toll At
        29." New York Times. June 23, 1943, pp. 1, 12.

3,611.   Beichman, Arnold. "Klan Backing Jeffries For Re-
        Election, Rival Charges." PM. November 1, 1943,p.6.

3,612.   "Bombings Admitted By Dying Klansmen." New York
        Times. March 2, 1974, p. 11.

3,613.   "Branded Minister Tells Of Horrors As Senses
        Return." New York Times. July 14, 1924, pp. 1, 5.

3,614.   "Branded Pastor Able To Return To Home." New York
        Times. July 15, 1924, p. 19.

3,615.   Catledge, Turner. "Asks 'Give And Take' For
        Detroit Peace." New York Times. June 30, 1943,
        p. 42.

3,616.   "Communists Shown At Work In Klan." New York Times.
        September 27, 1922, p. 11.

3,617.   "Couzens Nominated By Large Majority." New York
        Times. September 11, 1924, pp. 1, 3.

3,618.   "Declares Organization Doomed." New York Times.
          May 31, 1936, p. 10.

3,619.   "Detroit Bars Klan Parade." New York Times.
          October 13, 1921, p. 9.

3,620.   "Detroit Council Hearing On KKK." Michigan
          Chronicle. August 29, 1981, p. A3.

3,621.   "Detroit KKK Mobs Attack." Daily Worker.
          September 18, 1955, p. 16.

3,622.   "Detroit Police Put Out Klan Cross." New York
          Times. December 26, 1923, p. 25.

3,623.   "Detroit Prohibits Ku Klux Film." New York Times.
          September 18, 1921, p. 21.

3,624.   "Detroit Will Vote On The Klan Today." New York
          Times. November 3, 1925, p. 8.

3,625.   Dispute Over Alleged KKK Incident At Ford Plant
          Eyed." Michigan Chronicle. October 20, 1979, p.
          1A.

3,626.   "Disruption In Detroit." Charlotte (N.C.) Observer.
          June 27, 1980, p. A1.

3,627.   "Dying Klansman 'Confesses' To Bombing." Black
          Panther. Vol. 10, March 16, 1974, p. 5.

3,628.   Everett, Arthur W. "Michigan Klan Is Quiescent,
          But Grand Jury Investigates." Washington Evening
          Star. August 22, 1946, p. 4.

3,629.   "Find Missing Pastor In Delirium, Branded On Back
          With K.K.K." New York Times. July 13, 1924, pp.
          1, 2.

3,630.   "Five Are Indicted In Pontiac Bombing." New York
          Times. October 21, 1971, p. 19.

3,631.   "5 Ku Klux Klansmen Found Guilty Of Pontiac, Mich.
          Bombing." Washington Post. May 22, 1973, p. 5C.

3,632.   "Four With Klan Ties Sentenced For Attacks."
          Washington Post. January 14, 1981, p. A5.

3,633.   "G.O.P. Leaders Are Embarrassed By A Racist
          Nominee In Michigan." New York Times. August 31,
          1980, p. 43.

3,634.   Harsch, Ernie. "Klansmen Arrested In Michigan
          Bombing." Militant. Vol. 35, September 24, 1971,
          p. 14.

3,635.   Howard, G.D.   "Ku Klux Klan Head Opens Campaign
         Offices." Pittsburgh Courier. September 17, 1927,
         p. 12.

3,636.   "Judge Refuses To Dismiss Federal Tort Claim."
         Criminal Justice Issues. Vol. 6, June, 1981,
         pp. 8-9.

3,637.   "Kelly Acts To Ease Detroit Riot Curb." New York
         Times. June 24, 1943, pp. 1, 12.

3,638.   "K.K.K. Blamed For Barring Race Voters." Pittsburgh
         Courier. November 19, 1921, p. 1.

3,639.   "KKK In Detroit." New York Times. October 27,
         1978, p. 34.

3,640.   "KKK Wants To Parade In Detroit; 'Let'em March,'
         Councilman Says." Jet. Vol. 58, June 26, 1980,
         p. 53.

3,641.   "Klan Elects Flint Mayor." New York Times. July
         17, 1924, p. 17.

3,642.   "Klan Gets A Daily Paper." New York Times. April
         17, 1924, p. 20.

3,643.   "Klan Is Routed In Detroit." New York Times.
         November 5, 1925, p. 8.

3,644.   "Klan Must Toe Mark In Mich." New York Amsterdam
         News. September 5, 1923, p. 2.

3,645.   "Klan Offers Reward For K.K.K. Branders." New York
         Times. July 20, 1924, p. 26.

3,646.   "Klan Plea Bargain Deal Too Lenient?" Michigan
         Chronicle. December 6, 1980, p. 1.

3,647.   "Klan Plot To Bomb Pontiac, Mich. School Buses
         Outlined." Washington Post. April 13, 1973, p. 6A.

3,648.   "Klan Vows To Fight Rally Restrictions." Washington
         Star. August 2, 1980, p. A5.

3,649.   "Klansmen Free On Bond, Jury To Probe Blast."
         Washington Post. September 11, 1971, p. 4A.

3,650.   Lissner, Will. "New Flogging Laid To Black Legion;
         Five Are Arrested." New York Times. May 27, 1936,
         pp. 1, 9.

3,651.   _____. "Says Leader Urged Black Band To Kill."
         New York Times. May 3, 1936, p. 10.

3,652. "Many Deaths Laid To 'Black Legion'; Klan Link Charged." New York Times. May 24, 1936, p. 1.

3,653. Michael, Charles R. "Vote In Maryland War On All Fronts." New York Times. November 2, 1938, p. 7.

3,654. "Mich. ACLU Unit To Sue FBI In 1965 Murder Of Civil Rights Worker." Chicago Tribune. July 5, 1979, p. 11.

3,655. "Michigan Inquiry Sought." New York Times. January 18, 1923, p. 9.

3,656. "Michigan Mask Law Aimed At Klan." New York Times. August 31, 1923, p. 10.

3,657. Peterson, Iver. "Cover-Up Inquiry Is Cited In Suit By Kin Of A Slain Rights Marcher." New York Times. February 22, 1980, p. D15.

3,658. "Pontiac Bombing Charged To Klan. New York Times. September 10, 1971, pp. 1, 16.

3,659. "Protest Ban On 'Burning Cross'." New York Times. November 4, 1947, p. 31.

3,660. "Protest Over Klan-Nazi Request In Detroit Viewed." San Francisco Chronicle. June 27, 1980, p. 36.

3,661. Salpukas, Agis. "Wider Plot Laid To Pontiac Klan." New York Times. September 11, 1971, p. 54.

3,662. Serrin, William. "F.B.I. Facing A Suit In '65 Rights Killing." New York Times. July 5, 1979, p. A11.

3,663. "6 Klansmen Arrested In Pontiac Bombings." Washington Post. September 10, 1971, p. 1A.

3,664. "Smith Winning In Detroit." New York Times. November 4, 1925, p. 4.

3,665. Stevens, William K. "5 Ex-Klansmen Convicted In School Bus Bomb Plot." New York Times. May 22, 1973, p. 21.

3,666. Stewart, Agnes. "Activist Pastor Kluxer's Target." Michigan Chronicle. March 7, 1981, pp. 1, 4.

3,667. _____. "Move To Curb Anti-Black Terrorism." Michigan Chronicle. April 4, 1981, pp. 1, 4.

3,668. "Strong Klan Vote Seen In Michigan." New York Times. September 12, 1924, p. 3.

3,669.   "Students Applaud Anderson." New York Times.
          September 3, 1980, p. B12.

3,670.   "Tear Bombs Scatter Detroit Mob Of 5,000 Which
          Masses Before Anti-Klan Meeting." New York Times.
          October 22, 1924, p. 1.

3,671.   Tremblay, William C. "Reporter Joins KKK, Finds
          Tames Yes Man." Editor & Publisher. Vol. 100,
          May 20, 1967, p. 15.

3,672.   "U.A.W. Says Klan Fomented Strike." New York Times.
          June 7, 1943, p. 18.

3,673.   "U.S. Drops Charges In Pontiac Bombing." New York
          Times. October 23, 1974, p. 30.

3,674.   Woodford, Frank B. "Detroit Uncertain Over Riot's
          Cause." New York Times. June 27, 1943, Sect. 2,
          p. 12.

3,675.   Wooten, James T. "Rally In Michigan Town Is A
          Study In Confusion When Wallace Doesn't Appear."
          New York Times. May 9, 1972, p. 24.

                    22. MINNESOTA

3,676.   "Ask Klan To Dissolve Minneapolis Branch." New
          York Times. May 28, 1923, p. 2.

3,677.   Harris, Abraham I. "The Klan On Trial." New
          Republic. Vol. 35, June 13, 1923, pp. 67-69.

3,678.   "Klan Loses Another Mayor." Pittsburgh Courier.
          June 23, 1923, p. 10.

3,679.   "Ku Klux Propose Mob Rule To Get Man Convicted."
          Chicago Defender. April 23, 1921, p. 13.

3,680.   Linder, John. "Minn. Students Picket Speech By
          Klansman." Militant. Vol. 38, October 25, 1974,
          p. 23.

                    23. MISSISSIPPI

3,681.   "ACLU Fails In Bid To Let KKK Participate In Miss.
          Parade." Los Angeles Times. April 4, 1972, p. 12.

3,682.   "ACLU To Aid KKK Gain A Place In Jackson, Miss.
          Parade." Los Angeles Times. April 2, 1972, p. 2A.

3,683.   "Alabamian Is Guilty In Bombing Attempt." New York
          Times. November 28, 1968, p. 24.

3,684.   "Abduction Of Klan Official Reported In Mississippi."
          New York Times. December 22, 1967, p. 21

3,685.   "All-White Jury Acquits 3 In Klan." New York Times. May 11, 1969, p. 80.

3,686.   "Alleged Klansman Is Freed In Slaying Of Negro." New York Times. December 10, 1967, p. 44.

3,687.   Anderson, Jack. "Miss. Paper Editor's Battle With Ku Klux Klan." Washington Post. May 26, 1981, p. 11B.

3,688.   "Argument Set In Jackson." New York Times. December 1, 1964, p. 44.

3,689.   "Beckwith, Accused Murderer, Is Silent On Klan Activity." New York Times. January 13, 1966, p. 13.

3,690.   Bigart, Homer. "Sheriff And Deputy Arrested On Return From 'Whiskey Raid'." New York Times. December 5, 1964, pp. 1, 18.

3,691.   _____. "Wide Klan Plot Is Hinted In One Of 3 Rights Killings." New York Times. November 29, 1964, pp. 1, 41.

3,692.   "Bilbo Boasts Of KKK Membership." New York Amsterdam News. August 17, 1946, p. 6.

3,693.   "Bilbo KKK Avowal Stumps Mississippi." New York Times. August 14, 1946, p. 14.

3,694.   "Biracial Woodcutters Union Battles KKK In Mississippi." Chicago Defender. December 8, 1979, p. 4.

3,695.   "Blacks And Ku Klux Klansmen March In Tupelo, Mississippi." Washington Post. June 11, 1978, p. 6A.

3,696.   "Black And White Union Woodcutters Battle KKK In Mississippi." Baltimore Afro-American. December 22, 1979, p. 3.

3,697.   "Blacks Protest Klan In Mississippi." Baltimore Afro-American. June 17, 1978, p. 7.

3,698.   "Black Protest And Ku Klux Klan Reaction In Tupelo, Miss. Viewed." Chicago Tribune. August 8, 1978, p. 1.

3,699.   "Blast In Mississippi Damages Parsonage." New York Times. November 16, 1967, p. 40.

3,700.   "Boast On Bombs Is Laid To Mississippi Klansman." New York Times. February 4, 1966, p. 16.

3,701.   "Bombing Arsenal Found In M'Comb." New York Times.
          October 6, 1964, p. 24.

3,702.   "Bombing Charges Dropped In Case Of 2 Linked To
          Klan." New York Times. August 10, 1968, p. 11.

3,703.   "Bowers Free On Bond Set At $25,000." The Meridian
          Star. April 1, 1966.

3,704.   Buckley, Thomas. "Core Says F.B.I. Has 'Witness'."
          New York Times. December 6, 1964, p. 44.

3,705.   "Buckley Is Convicted On Kidnapping Count." The
          Jackson Clarion-Ledger. February 8, 1968.

3,706.   "Bush Doubts Reagan Harm From Remarks On The Klan."
          New York Times. September 4, 1980, p. B11.

3,707.   "Case Dismissed." New York Times. December 11,
          1964, p. 38.

3,708.   Chalmers, David. "The Ku Klux Klan In Politics
          In The 1920's." Mississippi Quarterly. Vol. 18,
          Fall, 1965, pp. 234-247.

3,709.   "Charges Against Reporter In Mississippi Are
          Dropped." New York Times. November 29, 1978,
          p. 18.

3,710.   "Charges Dismissed In Rights Slaying." New York
          Times. January 28, 1966, p. 38.

3,711.   "Civil Rightists And Ku Klux March In Tupelo,
          Mississippi." New Orleans Times Picayune. June
          11, 1978, p. 46.

3,712.   "Conviction In Negro's Death Upheld By Mississippi
          Court." New York Times. November 25, 1969, p. 33.

3,713.   "Cross-Burning In Miss. Reported." Atlanta Daily
          World. October 13, 1977, p. 1.

3,714.   "Cross Burning Is Reported By Negro Woman." The
          Meridian Star. March 10, 1967, p. 1.

3,715.   Cunningham, Morris and Robert Gordon. "Klan
          Leader Escapes As FBI Charges 13 In Hattiesburg
          Death." The Memphis (Tenn.) Commercial Appeal.
          March 29, 1966, p. 1.

3,716.   Dearman, Stanley. "KLAN-LOCAL: Meridian Minister
          Subpoenaed To Appear Before House Committee." The
          Meridian Star. November 6, 1965, p. 1.

3,717.   "Defense Motions In Dahmer Case Denied By Cox."
          The Meridian Star. June 16, 1967, p. 1.

3,718.   Donald, David. H.   "The Scalawag In Mississippi Re-
          construction." Journal of Southern History. Vol.
          10, November, 1944, pp. 447-460.

3,719.   Dunbar, Anthony. "Conspiracy On Conspiracy."
          Katallagete. Vol. 3, Winter, 1971, pp. 33-38.

3,720.   Edmonson, Ben G. "Pat Harrison And Mississippi In
          The Presidential Elections Of 1924 and 1928."
          Journal Of Mississippi History. Vol. 33, November,
          1971, pp. 333-350.

3,721.   "11 KKK Members Jailed In Mississippi." Washington
          Star. November 10, 1980, p. A6.

3,722.   "11 Klansmen Are Arrested For Distributing Litera-
          ture." New York Times. November 10, 1980, p. A16.

3,723.   "11 Men Nabbed At Hattiesburg In Dahmer Case."
          The Meridian Star. January 25, 1968, p. 1.

3,724.   "Evers Says Klan Regroups But Negroes Will Meet
          It." New York Times. October 12, 1967, p. 39.

3,725.   "Ex-Klan Leader Arrested On Negro Murder Charge."
          New York Times. November 19, 1968, p. 93.

3,726.   "Ex-Leader Of Klan Accused Of Murder." New York
          Times. January 23, 1969, p. 21.

3,727.   "Eyewitness Is Reported." New York Times. Decem-
          ber 6, 1964, p. 43.

3,728.   "Face 'Rights' Charges." Christian Science
          Monitor. March 3, 1967, p. 2.

3,729.   "Facts Needed In Mississippi." New York Times.
          August 15, 1964, p. 20.

3,730.   "FBI Arrests 13 Klansmen In Slaying." New Bern
          (N.C.) Sun-Journal. March 29, 1966, p. 1.

3,731.   "F.B.I. Declines Comment." New York Times.
          December 6, 1964, p. 44.

3,732.   "F.B.I. Made Arrests Under Criminal Code." New
          York Times. December 5, 1964, p. 18.

3,733.   "FBI Probes Activity In Tupelo." Christian
          Science Monitor. June 26, 1978, pp. 2-3.

3,734.   "F.B.I. Special Agent Who Smashed Klan Resuming
          Old Post." New York Times. December 26, 1972,
          p. 17.

3,735.   "FBI Still Hunts Klan Wizard." Charlotte (N.C.)
Observer. March 29, 1966, p. 1.

3,736.   "Federal Jury May Probe Dahmer Case." The Meridian
Star. June 2, 1966, p. 1.

3,737.   "15 In Klan Indicted In A Negro Slaying." New
York Times. June 24, 1966, p. 1.

3,738.   "15 Klansmen Deny Guilt In Slaying Of Negro
Merchant." New York Times. August 2, 1966, p. 12.

3,739.   "Firebomb Trial To Open." New York Times. April
28, 1969, p. 29.

3,740.   "Fire Ruins Market Of Natchez Mayor." New York
Times. January 1, 1966, p. 21.

3,741.   Franklin, Ben A. "Subpoena Calls Evers From His
District On Last Day Of Mississippi Campaign."
New York Times. March 11, 1968, p. 35.

3,742.   Gordon, Robert. "FBI Charges 14 In Hattiesburg;
Neshoba Trials Get Court OK, 13 Already Arrested
In CR Leader's Death." The Meridian Star. March
28, 1966, p. 1.

3,743.   Graham, Fred P. "Supreme Court Rejects Appeal Of
Klansmen In Rights Slayings." New York Times.
February 28, 1970, p. 19.

3,744.   "Grenada Visit Of King May Bring Klan There."
New Bern (N.C.) Sun-Journal. September 20, 1966,
p. 1.

3,745.   Halberstam, David. "Hostility Meets Rights Workers." New York Times. July 3, 1964, p. 8.

3,746.   Hearn, Philip D. "KKK, Blacks March Peacefully
In Miss." Atlanta Daily World. June 13, 1978,
pp. 1, 6.

3,747.   Herbers, John. "Dr. King Seeks Marshals To Help
Negroes To Vote." New York Times. July 23, 1964,
p. 15.

3,748.   _____. "F.B.I. Arrests 21 In Mississippi In
Murder Of 3 Rights Workers; Law Officers And
Pastor Held." New York Times. December 5, 1964,
pp. 1, 18.

3,749.   _____. "Gains In Mississippi." New York Times.
October 6, 1964, p. 24.

3,750.   _____. "Klansmen Rally Around Beckwith."
New York Times. April 12, 1964, p. 42.

3,751. _____. "Leaders In Mississippi Klan Linked To Violence In McComb." New York Times. January 19, 1966, p. 24.

3,752. _____. "M'Comb Bombings Laid To 3 Whites." New York Times. October 2, 1964, p. 27.

3,753. _____. "Mississippians Raise Funds For 21 Held In Killings." New York Times. December 7, 1964, p. 38.

3,754. _____. "Mississippi Bars Rights Trial Now." New York Times. December 6, 1964, pp. 1, 43.

3,755. _____. "Mississippi Klan Feared A Civil Rights 'Invasion'." New York Times. January 17, 1966, p. 23.

3,756. _____. "Mrs. Johnson Held Target Of Klan Plot." New York Times. January 14, 1966, pp. 1, 35.

3,757. _____. "Negroes Anxious On Rights Trial." New York Times. December 9, 1964, p. 43.

3,758. _____. "Tension Persists In M'Comb, Miss." New York Times. September 27, 1964, p. 41.

3,759. _____. "U.S. Aide Frees 19 In Rights Deaths; Bars F.B.I.'s Data." New York Times. December 11, 1964, pp. 1, 34.

3,760. _____. "U.S. Drops Charge Against 20th Man In Rights Slayings." New York Times. December 12, 1964, pp. 1, 19.

3,761. _____. "White Man Linked To Slain Negroes." New York Times. January 15, 1966, pp. 1, 28.

3,762. "How 'Al' Smith Fared In Mississippi." Nation. Vol. 125, September 14, 1927, pp. 244-245.

3,763. Hunter, Marjorie. "Dulles Requests More F.B.I. Agents For Mississippi." New York Times. June 27, 1964, pp. 1, 10.

3,764. "Imperial Wizard Abolishes Mississippi Branch Of Klan." New York Times. November 1, 1966, p. 17.

3,765. "In Fayette, The Whites Blinked In Disbelief." New York Times. September 14, 1969, Sect. 4, p. 5.

3,766. "Jackson Bombing Puzzles Officials: More Of Same Feared." The Meridian Star. November 20, 1967, p. 1.

3,767.   "Jackson Report Says 'Informer' Was Witness:
          Neshoba Case Aired By Federal Panel." The Meridian
          Star. February 22, 1967, p. 1.

3,768.   " 'Jesus No'!" Newsweek. Vol. 64, December 21,
          1964, pp. 21-22.

3,769.   Johnson, Thomas A. "Below Tupelo's Calm, A Residue
          Of Tension." New York Times. January 30, 1979,
          p. 10.

3,770.   "Judge Declares Mistrial." Christian Science
          Monitor. January 28, 1969, p. 14.

3,771.   "Jury Clears A Klan Leader Of Sub Machine Gun
          Charge." New York Times. January 19, 1968, p. 45.

3,772.   "Jury Clears Klansman In Mississippi Bombing."
          New York Times. August 9, 1968, p. 17.

3,773.   Keeter, Terry. "Arraignment Slated April 12 In
          Neshoba CR Slaying Case: At Federal Building Here."
          The Meridian Star. March 22, 1967, p. 1.

3,774.   _____. "Explosion Rips Negro's Home At Laurel:
          Cox's Warning Not Recalled By Blast." The Meridian
          Star. November 15, 1967, p. 1.

3,775.   _____. "New Indictments In Dahmer Case: 16
          Now Charged With Conspiracy In Firebomb Slaying."
          The Meridian Star. March 27, 1968, p. 1.

3,776.   _____. "State Action Seen In Dahmer Slaying:
          Consideration By Grand Jury Seems Certain, Murder
          Indictments Could Result." The Meridian Star.
          November 9, 1967, p. 1.

3,777.   "Killing Shocks Mississippians." New York Times.
          January 12, 1966, p. 19.

3,778.   King, Wayne. "Black Protest Is Monitored By Klan As
          A Mississippi Boycott Continues." New York Times.
          July 9, 1978, p. 26.

3,779.   "KKK And Blacks March Peacefully In Mississippi."
          Atlanta Daily World. June 13, 1978, p. 1.

3,780.   "KKK Forces Miss. Congressional Candidate To
          Resign Over Nazi Tif." New Orleans Times Picayune.
          May 16, 1981, p. 4.

3,781.   "KKK Heckles Civil Rights Demonstrators In Magee,
          Miss." New Orleans Times Picayune. July 22, 1979,
          p. 10.

3,782.   "KKK In Mississippi." New York Times. August 29,
         1978, p. 45.

3,783.   "KKK In Mississippi." New York Times. September
         2, 1978, p. 97.

3,784.   "KKK In Mississippi." Vicksburg (Miss.) Weekly
         Republican. June 23, 1868, p. 1.

3,785.   "KKK In Mississippi." Vicksburg (Miss.) Weekly
         Republican. November 1, 1868, p. 1.

3,786.   "KKKomical?" Jet. Vol. 59, October 23, 1980, p. 5.

3,787.   "KKK Protests Black Rally In Mississippi." Houston
         Post. October 6, 1978, p. 25C.

3,788.   "KKKer Details Firebomb Killing." Washington Afro-
         American. March 19, 1968, p. 1.

3,789.   "Klan And 3 Men Fined $1-Million In Slaying Of
         Negro In Mississippi." New York Times. November
         14, 1968, p. 1.

3,790.   "Klan Gets Equal Time." New York Times. November
         3, 1965, p. 21.

3,791.   "Klan In Mississippi Opens Fight On Smith." New
         York Times. September 30, 1927, p. 16.

3,792.   "Klan Kolum." The Lexington (Miss.) Advertiser.
         November 16, 1923, p. 1.

3,793.   "Klan Leader Goes On Trial." New York Times.
         May 15, 1968, p. 32.

3,794.   "Klan Leader In Mississippi Posts Bond On Gun
         Charge." New York Times. December 23, 1967, p. 48.

3,795.   "Klan Leader, Object Of Hunt, To Surrender." The
         Greensboro (N.C.) Daily News. March 31, 1966, p. 1.

3,796.   "Klan Moves Into Mississippi." New York Times.
         March 26, 1950, p. 49.

3,797.   "Klan Order Cited In Rights Slaying." New York
         Times. February 2, 1966, p. 18.

3,798.   "Klan Raids Net Cache Of Arms." The Durham (N.C.)
         Morning Herald. March 30, 1966, p. 13A.

3,799.   "Klan Rally In Jackson." Washington Post. October
         5, 1980, p. A12.

3,800.   "Klan Rally In Jackson, Miss., Attracts About 500
         Persons." New York Times. October 5, 1980, p. 28.

3,801.   "Klan Warns Firemen To Leave Jobs." Chicago
          Defender. September 3, 1921, p. 1.

3,802.   "Klan Wizard Gives Self Up To Law." New Bern (N.C.)
          Sun-Journal. March 31, 1966, p. 1.

3,803.   " 'Klans' Last Stand." Christian Science Monitor.
          December 15, 1967, p. 1.

3,804.   "Klansman Arrested After Evers Threat." New York
          Times. September 10, 1969, p. 1.

3,805.   "Klansman Guilty In Bomb Slaying." New York Times.
          July 20, 1968, p. 25.

3,806.   "Klansman Is Freed On $25,000 Bond." New Bern
          (N.C.) Sun-Journal. April 1, 1966, p. 1.

3,807.   "Klansmen Face Federal Court In Mississippi." New
          Bern (N.C.) Sun-Journal. March 28, 1966, p. 1.

3,808.   "Ku Klux Klan." The Aberdeen (Miss.) Weekly.
          August 13, 1926, p. 1; September 3, 1926, p. 4;
          October 8, 1926, p. 1; October 29, 1926, p. 1;
          February 24, 1928, p. 1.

3,809.   "Ku Klux Klan." The Baptist (Miss.) Record.
          October 21, 1921, p. 13; November 10, 1921, p. 7;
          December 21, 1922, p. 14; February 21, 1922, p.
          11; June 21, 1923, p. 8.

3,810.   "Ku Klux Klan." The Hattiesburg (Miss.) American.
          October 30, 1920, p. 1; February 8, 1921, p. 8;
          February 10, 1921, p. 1; September 2, 1921, pp. 1,
          5; September 3, 1921, p. 1; September 19, 1921, p.
          5; April 6, 1922, p. 8.

3,811.   "Ku Klux Klan." Laurel (Miss.) Leader. May 12,
          1926; October 30, 1926.

3,812.   "KKK And White Militants In Mississippi." National
          Observer. May 25, 1964, p. 8.

3,813.   "Ku Klux Klan Holds Rallies In Mississippi."
          National Observer. August 2, 1965, p. 6.

3,814.   "Ku Klux Klansmen Lose Bid To Join In Mississippi
          Parade." Washington Post. April 4, 1972, p. 2A.

3,815.   "Ku Klux Klans Of The Reconstruction Period In
          Missouri." Missouri Historical Review. Vol. 37,
          July, 1943, pp. 441-450.

3,816.   "Ku Klux Klan's White Knights." Newsweek. Vol. 64,
          December 21, 1964, pp. 22-24.

3,817.   "Lawyer Claims 'New Evidence' In Klan Case. The
          Meridian Star. April 4, 1966, p. 1.

3,818.   Loftus, Joseph A. "Poverty Hearing Set In
          Mississippi." New York Times. April 10, 1967, p.
          13.

3,819.   "Malice Toward Some." Newsweek. Vol. 67, April
          11, 1966, pp. 39-40.

3,820.   "March News Aide Says He's Klan Spy." New York
          Times. June 23, 1966, p. 25.

3,821.   "Marchers Accuse Police Of Pushing." New York Times.
          January 16, 1966, p. 62.

3,822.   Marx, Andrew and Tom Tuthill. "1978: Mississippi
          Organizes." Southern Exposure. Vol. 8, Summer,
          1980, pp. 73-76.

3,823.   "Mayor Evers Claims Bust Of KKK Cross-Burning
          Ceremony." Atlanta Daily World. October 13, 1977,
          p. 1.

3,824.   "Mayor On TV Raps Klan." Christian Science Monitor.
          October 20, 1965, p. 3.

3,825.   McNeilly, J.S. "Enforcement Act Of 1871 And Ku
          Klux Klan In Mississippi." Mississippi Historical
          Society Publications. 1906, pp. 107-171.

3,826.   "Meridian Pastor Issued Subpoena." The Jackson
          Clarion-Ledger. November 7, 1965.

3,827.   "Meredith Will Head March In Returning To Missis-
          sippi." New York Times. May 12, 1966, p. 21.

3,828.   Minor, Bill. "A Black Paper And Night Riders In
          A Pickup Truck." Washington Post. January 25,
          1982, p. A9.

3,829.   "Mississippi Blacks Report Klan Activity Is Rising."
          New York Times. November 8, 1977, p. 16.

3,830.   "Mississippi Bomber Loses Court Appeal." New York
          Times. June 2, 1970, p. 16.

3,831.   "Mississippi Death Laid To Klansmen." New York
          Times. April 7, 1967, p. 22.

3,832.   "Mississippi Is Urged To Stay Calm Today As Kennedy
          Visits." New York Times. March 18, 1966, p. 78.

3,833.   "Mississippi Klansman Guilty In Negro Slaying."
          Washington Evening Star. March 16, 1968, p. 1.

3.834.   "Mississippi Klansmen Arrested." The Winston
          Salem (N.C.) Journal. March 29, 1966, p. 1.

3,835.   "Miss. Members Protest Stance Of ACLU On K.K.K."
          Baltimore Afro-American. October 1, 1977, p. 3.

3,836.   "The Mississippi Murders: 21 Arrests." Newsweek.
          Vol. 64, December 14, 1964, pp. 21-22.

3,837.   "Mississippi Rabbi Sees Rise In Bias. New York
          Times. September 20, 1967, p. 34.

3,838.   "Mississippi Union Defies Klan In Ad." New York
          Times. November 20, 1964, p. 19.

3,839.   "Mississippi White Is Held In Shooting At Negro
          Home." New York Times. September 4, 1964, p. 13.

3,840.   "Mississippians Start Drive On Ku Klux Klan."
          Chicago Defender. April 8, 1922, pp. 3-4.

3,841.   "Mistrial Declared In A Bombing Case." New York
          Times. August 1, 1968, p. 38.

3,842.   Moore, Roy Kingsley. "G-Man With A Smile." New
          York Times. December 5, 1964, p. 19.

3,843.   "More Klansmen Called." New York Times. January
          7, 1966, p. 9.

3,844.   "More Trials In Dahmer Killing Due This Term?"
          The Meridian Star. May 8, 1968, p. 1.

3,845.   "Murder Convictions Stands." New York Times.
          April 22, 1970, p. 64.

3,846.   "Natchez Negroes Protest Mistrial In Racial Slaying."
          New York Times. April 12, 1967, p. 51.

3,847.   Neier, Aryeh. "Mississippi Relives Its '60s."
          Nation. Vol. 227, September 23, 1978, pp. 265-267.

3,848.   Nelson, Jack. "FBI Holds Klansman As Memphis Bank
          Robber: Called Top 'Hit' Man For White Knights;
          His Car Used In Meridian Bomb Case." Los Angeles
          Times. July 13, 1968, p. 1.

3,849.   . "Terror In Mississippi." New South.
          Vol. 23, Fall, 1968, pp. 41-57.

3,850.   "Nightriders Kill Mississippi Negro." New York
          Times. January 11, 1966, p. 10.

3,851.   "19 Named In New Indictments In 3 Mississippi
          Rights Killings." New York Times. March 1, 1967,
          pp. 1, 28.

3,852.   "Nobody Turn Me 'Round; Anti-Klan Demonstrations In Natchez, Miss." _Time_. Vol. 86, October 15, 1965, pp. 31-32.

3,853.   "Officers Told Klan's Leader Is Dangerous." _New Bern (N.C.) Sun-Journal_. March 29, 1966, p. 1.

3,854.   "1,000 Queried By Bureau." _New York Times_. December 6, 1964, p. 44.

3,855.   "Pastor Charges Bombing To Jackson's 'Decent And Responsible People'." _Meridian Star_. November 21, 1967, p. 1.

3,856.   Pearce, John. "Five Bombings Recall Terror Of 1964." _Meridian Star_. November 26, 1967, p. 1.

3,857.   Peterson, John. "The Klan Is Trying To Decide Which Way To Go." _National Observer_. June 2, 1969, p. 1.

3,858.   "Policeman Reports Murder Plot." _Christian Science Monitor_. October 14, 1967, p. 14.

3,859.   "The Police Say Klan Vows War On Law." _New York Times_. July 4, 1968, p. 16.

3,860.   "Put On Defensive." _Christian Science Monitor_. January 30, 1969, p. 1.

3,861.   "Rabbi Links Blast To A Slaying Plot." _New York Times_. November 23, 1967, p. 50.

3,862.   Raines, Howell. "Klan Patrols Tupelo As 400 Blacks March." _New York Times_. May 7, 1978, p. 26.

3,863.   Raspberry, William. "Black Boycott Of Okolona, Miss., Merchants." _Chicago Tribune_. August 21, 1979, Sect. 2, p. 3.

3,864.   " 'Rebel Flag' Rally Called Against RFK." _Greensboro (N.C.) Daily News_. March 15, 1966, p. 1.

3,865.   "Recent Civil Strife Sparks Revival Of KKK In Tupelo, Miss." _Los Angeles Times_. July 9, 1978, p. 8.

3,866.   Reed, Roy. "Mississippi Whites Join Blacks To Listen To Evers At Labor Rally." _New York Times_. September 24, 1971, p. 47.

3,867.   _____. "Philadelphia, Miss., Easing Memories Of Violence." _New York Times_. March 4, 1971, pp. 1, 19.

3,868.   _____ . "Release Of Klansman, Jailed For Killing Black Leader, Is Decried In Mississippi." New York Times. December 24, 1972, p. 17.

3,869.   _____ . "13 Mississippi Klansmen Seized In Negro's Death." New York Times. March 29, 1966, pp. 1, 24.

3,870.   _____ . "3 Mississippi Whites Held In Alleged Plot To Assassinate Evers." New York Times. September 11, 1969, p. 19.

3,871.   "Reporter's Case In KKK Rally Transferred To Miss. Justice Court." New Orleans Times Picayune. June 15, 1978, p. 18.

3,872.   "Restaurants Desegregated Quietly In McComb, Miss." New York Times. November 19, 1964, pp. 1, 25.

3,873.   "Rich Planter Leads Mississippi Klansmen." Chicago Defender. August 6, 1921, pp. 2-3.

3,874.   "Rights Unit Wins A Hearing On Suit." New York Times. December 23, 1964, p. 23.

3,875.   "Rights Workers Were Warned They Faced Possible Beatings." New York Times. December 5, 1964, p. 19

3,876.   Roberts, Gene. "Marchers Upset By Negro Apathy." New York Times. June 14, 1966, p. 19.

3,877.   _____ . "A Southern City Fights The Klan." New York Times. October 22, 1965, p. 32.

3,878.   Rugaber, Walter. "All-White Jury Picked As Trial Of 18 In Slaying Of 3 Rights Workers Begins In Mississippi." New York Times. October 10, 1967, p. 21.

3,879.   _____ . "Defense Calls 2 Negroes As Character Witnesses For Mississippi Klan Chief." New York Times. October 17, 1967, p. C31.

3,880.   _____ . "Informer Links Klan To Rights Slayings." New York Times. October 12, 1967, p. 1.

3,881.   _____ . ""The Klan: The Knights Are A Bit Bedraggled." New York Times. January 7, 1968, Sect. 4, p. 6.

3,882.   _____ . "2 Rights Killings Face Court Again." New York Times. February 21, 1967, p. 26.

3,883.   _____ . "2,000 In March Decry Natchez Killing." New York Times. March 1, 1967, p. 28.

3,884.   _____ . "Witness Tells Of Role In Slaying Of Rights Workers." New York Times. October 13, 1967, pp. 1, 43.

3,885.   "Sam Borders On Trial For Murder." Christian Science Monitor. January 24, 1969, p. 3.

3,886.   "Sam Bowers Subpoenaed In KKK Probe." Meridian Miss. Star. October 27, 1965, p. 1.

3,887.   Sartor, William. "Greenville, Miss.: Klan vs. The Liberals." New York Herald Tribune. August 22, 1960, p. 1.

3,888.   Schardt, Arlie. "A Mississippi Mayor Fights The Klan." Reporter. Vol. 34, January 27, 1966, pp. 39-40.

3,889.   "S.D. Redmond Target Of Ku Klux Klan Threat." Chicago Defender. November 12, 1921, pp. 1-2.

3,890.   " 'Sensational' Cases May Be Re-Opened: Neshoba, Hattiesburg Civil Rights Cases Face Federal Grand Jury Investigation?" Meridian Star. February 19, 1962, p. 1.

3,891.   Sitton, Claude. "Chaney Was Given A Brutal Beating." New York Times. August 8, 1964, p. 7.

3,892.   _____ . "Mississippi Town Fears New Strife." New York Times. June 7, 1964, p. 54.

3,893.   "16 Whites Indicted In Mississippi Death." New York Times. March 28, 1968, p. 29.

3,894.   "Sketches Of Mississippi Suspects." New York Times. December 5, 1964, p. 18.

3,895.   "Still No Report By The Grand Jury; Dahmer Killing Case Now Being Aired." Meridian Star. February 24, 1967, p. 1.

3,896.   "Supreme Court Rejects Appeals Of Seven Klan Members Convicted Of Conspiracy In Triple Slaying In Mississippi In 1964." National Observer. March 2, 1970, p. 3.

3,897.   "Suspect Says He Saw Companions Slay Negro." Washington Evening Star. June 18, 1966, p. 1.

3,898.   "Suspected Bomber In Mississippi Shot." New York Times. July 1, 1968, p. 1.

3,899.   "10 Are Indicted In Mississippi For Racial Bombing Last Year." New York Times. April 11, 1968, p. 34.

3,900.   "10 Indicted In A Rights Slaying Plead Not Guilty
         In Mississippi." New York Times. January 26,
         1968, p. 17.

3,901.   "Tension Between Klansmen And Blacks In Tupelo,
         Grows." New Orleans Times Picayune. May 8, 1978,
         p. 3.

3,902.   "Terrorism Today." Christianity Today. Vol. 22,
         September 22, 1978, pp. 12-16.

3,903.   "Terrorist Bomb Rips Front Of Rabbi's Home."
         Santa Fe New Mexican. November 22, 1967, p. 1.

3,904.   "13 Klansmen Held For Grand Jury In Death Of Negro
         Civil Rights Leader In Mississippi." New York
         Times. April 13, 1966, p. 27.

3.905.   "13 Klansmen Seized In Firebomb Death Of Negro
         Rights Leader." Washington Post. March 29, 1966,
         p. 1.

3,906.   "13 Of KKK Held In Negro's Death." Durham (N.C.)
         Morning Herald. March 29, 1966, pp. 6B-7B.

3,907.   "3 Men Held In Mississippi On Charge Of Killing
         Negro." New York Times. July 8, 1966, p. 13.

3,908.   "Three Mississippi Klansmen Held On Charge of
         Kidnapping." New York Times. November 11, 1967,
         p. 20.

3,909.   "3 Whites Arrested In Death Of Negro Outside Of
         Natchez." New York Times. June 15, 1966, p. 27.

3,910.   "To Testify In 'Rights' Case." Christian Science
         Monitor. October 13, 1967, p. 2.

3,911.   "Trap For A Terrorist." Newsweek. Vol. 72, July
         15, 1968, p. 31A.

3,912.   "Trial Begins." New York Times. April 29, 1969,
         p. 34.

3,913.   "Trial Set For Oct. 9 In '64 Rights Deaths." New
         York Times. September 2, 1967, p. 13.

3,914.   "Tupelo Ban On Protests Declared Unconstitutional."
         New York Times. May 24, 1978, p. 16.

3,915.   "Tupelo Miss. Braces For Ku Klux Klan-Demonstrators'
         Clash." New Orleans Times Picayune. May 6, 1978,
         p. 12.

3,916.   "12th Dahmer Case Suspect Arrested." Jackson
         Clarion-Ledger. January 26, 1968.

3,917.   "12 Deny Conspiracy In Mississippi Death." New York Times. April 18, 1967, p. 34.

3,918.   "12 Surrender On Conspiracy." Christian Science Monitor. March 2, 1967, p. 2.

3,919.   "2 Agents Of F.B.I. Shot At; 7 Seized At Cross Burning." New York Times. January 5, 1966, p. 12.

3,920.   "Two Indicted In Mississippi In Attack On Jewish Leader." New York Times. November 15, 1968, p. 34.

3,921.   "Two Men Arrested In Mississippi Cross Burning." New Orleans Times Picayune. August 23, 1977, p. 10.

3,922.   "Trial Of Ex-Klansmen Ends In Mistrial For Fourth Time." New York Times. July 27, 1969, p. 55.

3,923.   "U.S. Intervention Asked." New York Times. January 11, 1966, p. 10.

3,924.   "U.S. Official Seized In Fight Arising From Klan Rally." New York Times. June 11, 1978, p. 26.

3,925.   "U.S. Re-indicts 12 In '66 Negro Killing." New York Times. March 2, 1967, p. 1.

3,926.   "U.S. Reported Investigating Police And Klan In Tupelo." New York Times. June 25, 1978, p. 26.

3,927.   "Venue Charge Unlikely." New York Times. December 5, 1964, p. 18.

3,928.   "The Violence Trap." Nation. Vol. 210, March 9, 1970, pp. 261-262.

3,929.   "White Churches Unite To Help After Bombing." Meridian Star. November 20, 1967, p. 1.

3,930.   "White Floggers Out On Bond." Pittsburgh Courier. May 10, 1930, p. 3.

3,931.   Whitehead, Don. "Murder In Mississippi; Condensation Of Attack On Terror." Reader's Digest. Vol. 97, September, 1970, pp. 191-196, 198-202, 208-210, 213-228.

3,932.   Wilson, Walter. "Meridian Massacre Of 1871." The Crisis. Vol. 81, February, 1974, pp. 49-52.

3,933.   "Women At Sanderson Farms Continue Strike." Off Our Backs. Vol. 10, June, 1980, p. 2.

3,934.   Wooten, James T. "Inquiry On F.B.I. In Klan Death Urged." New York Times. Arpil 8, 1970, p. 28.

3,935.   . "Klan Head Called Planner Of Slaying."
New York Times.   January 24, 1969, p. 95.

3,936.   . "Klansman's Trial Ends In Hung Jury."
New York Times.   January 26, 1969, p. 49.

24. MISSOURI

3,937.   "Count On Reed's Help." New York Times.   October
26, 1924, p. 14.

3,938.   "Davis Seems Likely To Carry Missouri." New York
Times.   October 21, 1924, p. 3.

3,939.   "Demonstrators Break Up Klan Rally (in Hannibal,
Missouri). The (Newark, N.J.) Sunday Star-Ledger.
April 25, 1982, Section One, p. 20.

3,940.   "Denounces Ku Klux." New York Times.   September
21, 1921, p. 19.

3,941.   "Detestable Help Is Refused." New York Times.
November 13, 1922, p. 14.

3,942.   "Evans Seeks Kansas City Building." New York Times.
November 9, 1923, p. 4.

3,943.   "Evidence Of KKK Activity In Missouri." St. Louis
Argus.   December 3, 1981, Sect. 2, p. 4.

3,944.   "Fears Klan Influence, Asks For All Race Jury."
Pittsburgh Courier.   October 20, 1923, pp. 2-3.

3,945.   "Goldman Defends Truman." New York Times.
October 29, 1944, p. 38.

3,946.   "Klan Accusation Traced." New York Times.
October 27, 1944, p. 14.

3,947.   "Klan In Missouri Election." New York Times.
April 3, 1924, p. 3.

3,948.   "Klan Is Opposed By G.O.P. In St. Louis."
Pittsburgh Courier.   September 15, 1923, p. 13.

3,949.   "Klan Offers To Fight Crime." New York Times.
March 19, 1976, p. 25.

3,950.   "Klan Protesters Driven Back." Washington Post.
April 25, 1982, p. A6.

3,951.   "Klan Representative Urges Muslim To Go To Africa."
New York Times.   November 14, 1977, p. 20.

3,952.   "Klansmen Stir Funeral Party By Queer Rites."
Chicago Defender.   October 7, 1922, pp. 3-4.

3,953.   Kneeland, Douglass E. "Hooting Crowd Disperses
Nazis Attempting To March In South St. Louis."
New York Times. March 12, 1978, p. 26.

3,954.   "Ku Klux Klan Visited Colored Churches In Kansas
City, Mo." Broad Ax. August 26, 1922, p. 1.

3,955.   "Missouri Democrats Sent Uninstructed." New York
Times. April 17, 1924, p. 3.

3,956.   "Missouri Klan Attacks Reed." New York Times.
October 12, 1922, p. 11.

3,957.   "Opens Doors On Klansmen." New York Times. July
13, 1924, p. 3.

3,958.   "Preacher Resigns From Klan." New York Times.
October 13, 1921, p. 9.

3,959.   "Primary 'Lessons'." New York Times. August 6,
1926, p. 14.

3,960.   "Reed Of Missouri Speaks For Davis." New York
Times. October 29, 1924, p. 9.

3,961.   "Reed Praises Davis." New York Times. August 24,
1924, p. 6.

3,962.   "Refuse Ku Klux Gift." New York Times. November
11, 1922, p. 22.

3,963.   "Reports Klan Service At Capitol." New York Times.
February 15, 1924, p. 10.

3,964.   "Rob Church Safe; Leave K.K.K. Note." Pittsburgh
Courier. April 2, 1927, p. 1.

3,965.   "Simmons Slinks From Ga. To St. Louis, Klan Wilts."
Chicago Defender. October 1, 1921, pp. 1-2.

3,966.   "Sims Denounces Klan." New York Times. February
27, 1923, p. 21.

3,967.   Smith, Terence. "Carter Assails Reagan Remark
About The Klan As An Insult To The South." New
York Times. September 3, 1980, p. B8.

3,968.   " 'White Man's World' Really Doesn't Exist."
Charlotte (N.C.) Observer. August 8, 1966, p. 1.

3,969.   "Wrecks Klan Store In Kansas City." New York Times.
October 25, 1923, p. 3.

25.   MONTANA

3,970.   "Montana Democrats Reply." New York Times.
September 12, 1924, p. 3.

3,971.   "Montana Troubles All Party Leaders." New York Times. October 11, 1924, p. 2.

3,972.   "Sheriff Warns Ku Klux Leader To Leave Town." Chicago Defender. August 27, 1924, p. 3.

3,973.   Yerxa, Fendall W. "Johnson Hits Extremism." New York Times. October 13, 1964, pp. 1, 35.

26. NEBRASKA

3,974.   "Omaha Fights Klan." Pittsburgh Courier. May 17, 1930, p. B9.

3,975.   Paul, Justus F. "The Ku Klux Klan In The 1936 Nebraska Election." North Dakota Quarterly. Vol. 39, No. 4, Autumn 1971, pp. 64-70.

27. NEVADA

3,976.   "KKK's Message Has No Listeners." Las Vegas Review Journal. April 13, 1981, p. 10A.

28. NEW HAMPSHIRE

3,977.   Bodden, Bonny. "KKK In New Hampshire." New York Times. October 15, 1978, p. 46.

3,978.   "Branded Man Disappears." New York Times. July 14, 1924, p. 5.

3,979.   "F.B.I. Inquiry Sought." New York Times. October 26, 1960, p. 26.

3,980.   "KKK In New Hampshire." New York Times. October 12, 1978, p. 40.

3,981.   "Protestors Meet KKK Pro-Nuclear Rally At Seabrook, N.H. Plant." Houston Post. October 15, 1978, p. 17A.

3,982.   "10,000 Klansmen Meet." New York Times. June 2, 1924, p. 2.

3,983.   "2 KKK Members And Motorcycle Gang Laud N.H. A-Plant Construction." New Orleans Times Picayune. October 15, 1978, p. 3.

29. NEW JERSEY

3,984.   "Affidavit Backs Ashbury Charges." New York Times. April 9, 1924, p. 23.

3,985.   "Against Klan In Politics." New York Times. November 4, 1923, Sect. 2, p. 1.

3,986.   "All But One Endorsed By Klan Win." New York Times.
          May 29, 1924, p. 2.

3,987.   "Anti-Klan Crowd Smashes Windows." New York Times.
          June 7, 1923, p. 21.

3,988.   "Anti-Klan Speaker Rescued By Police." New York
          Times. June 18, 1925, p. 11.

3,989.   "Appellate Division Upholds Cross-Burning Con-
          viction." New York Times. January 3, 1974, p.
          75.

3,990.   "Armed Men Guard Services At Church." New York
          Times. May 7, 1923, p. 15.

3,991.   "Arrest Of 22 Klan Members At Jersey Home Foils
          Group's Plans For Rally." New York Times.
          November 25, 1974, p. 44.

3,992.   "Asbury Park Mayor Accused In Pulpits." New York
          Times. April 7, 1924, p. 7.

3,993.   "Asks Golden Rule In Foreign Affairs." New York
          Times. March 25, 1926, p. 12.

3,994.   "Atlantic City Acts To Curb Klansmen." New York
          Times. November 23, 1923, p. 19.

3,995.   "Atlantic City Elks' Lodge Votes To Expel Members
          Of Ku Klux Klan From The Order." New York Times.
          October 19, 1923, p. 1.

3,996.   "Atlantic City Man Warned By Ku Klux." New York
          Times. January 12, 1923, p. 10.

3,997.   "Atlantic City Voters Defeat Klan In Bitter Fight:
          Ku Klux Candidate For Mayor Supported By Nutter
          And Lightfoot Get Only 4 Few Colored Ballots."
          Afro-American. May 23, 1924, pp. 1, 2.

3,998.   "Awaits Klan With Gun." New York Times. August
          4, 1927, p. 21.

3,999.   "Bar Catholic Books From High School." New York
          Times. March 21, 1923, p. 6.

4,000.   "Bar Klan From Parade." New York Times. December
          9, 1923, p. 10.

4,001.   "Barnegat, N.J. Police Prepare For KKK Demonstra-
          tion." New Orleans Times Picayune. August 11,
          1979, p. 2.

4,002.   "Big Klan Meeting Tonight." New York Times. May
          10, 1923, p. 8.

4,003.   "Bill To Bar Cross-Burning Attacked By Liberties
          Union." New York Times. May 7, 1967, p. 53.

4,004.   "Black Lawyer Ousted In N.J. Klan Case." Washington
          Post. March 27, 1971, p. 6A.

4,005.   Blom, Arnold. "Jersey Police Suspect Revival
          Of KKK Activity." PM. August 24, 1945, p. 1.

4,006.   "Bombs And Crosses Set Off Near Ball." New York
          Times. October 12, 1924, p. 8.

4,007.   "Bound Brook Mob Raids Klan Meeting." New York
          Times. May 2, 1923, pp. 1, 3.

4,008.   "Bundsmen Linked To Defense Plants." New York
          Times. October 3, 1940, pp. 1, 14.

4,009.   "Burn Fiery Cross At Citizen's Home." New York
          Times. August 5, 1926, p. 33.

4,010.   Butterfield, Fox. "Teachers Reach Pact In Newark."
          New York Times. April 3, 1971, p. 33.

4,011.   "Calls Ku Klux Cowards." New York Times. April 6,
          1925, p. 3.

4,012.   "Camp Cross Burning Laid To Jersey Klan." New
          York Times. August 15, 1948, p. 19.

4,013.   "Ceremonies, In New Jersey." New York Times. May
          31, 1926, p. 17.

4,014.   "Church Floor Falls; Many Klansmen Hurt." New
          York Times. August 18, 1924, p. 15.

4,015.   "Citizens To Fight Klan." New York Times. November
          19, 1923, p. 17.

4,016.   "Civil Rights Units Scored On Tactics." New York
          Times. May 20, 1966, p. 21.

4,017.   Clarity, James F. "Atlantic City Fears Rise In
          Klan Activity." New York Times. June 20, 1978,
          p. B2.

4,018.   "Clergyman Prefers Ku Klux To K. Of C." New York
          Times. May 22, 1922, p. 15.

4,019.   "Congregation Hears Plan For Junior Klan." New
          York Times. April 20, 1925, p. 4.

4,020.   "Cripple Says Klan Fired Home, Beat Him." New York
          Times. September 18, 1926, p. 6.

4,021.   "Cross Burned In Jersey As Black Makes Speech."
          New York Times. October 2, 1937, p. 2.

4,022.   "Cross-Burning Stirs Jerseyans." New York Times.
          April 9, 1967, p. 56.

4,023.   "Davis Is Assailed At Klan Gathering." New York
          Times. August 31, 1924, p. 3.

4,024.   "Defies Klan, Stays In Town." New York Times.
          January 19, 1927, p. 8.

4,025.   "Denies Anti-Klan Meeting." New York Times.
          May 6, 1923, p. 4.

4,026.   "Denies He Is In Klan." New York Times. December
          16, 1922, p. 8.

4,027.   "Denies Split Over Klan." New York Times. March
          25, 1925, p. 13.

4,028.   "Diploma Refused To Student In Klan." New York
          Times. November 13, 1979, p. B2.

4,029.   "Disabled Princeton Veteran Vows To Continue
          Battle Against Klan." Raleigh News & Observer.
          July 6, 1969, p. 3.

4,030.   "Ex-Chaplain Arms To Repel Klansmen." New York
          Times. February 1, 1925, p. 18.

4,031.   "Ex-Klansmen Sentenced In Jersey." New York Times.
          April 12, 1981, p. 40.

4,032.   "Faced By Klan Problem." New York Times. February
          24, 1924, p. 18.

4,033.   "Fiery Cross In Yard Protests Wedding." New York
          Times. November 7, 1925, p. 7.

4,034.   "Fiery Cross On Mountain." New York Times. July
          5, 1922, p. 20.

4,035.   "Finds Office In Red And 'KKK' On Door." New York
          Times. June 15, 1923, p. 21.

4,036.   "Fire Three Klan Crosses." New York Times.
          December 26, 1923, p. 25.

4,037.   "First Klan Funeral Is Held In Jersey." New York
          Times. November 28, 1923, p. 19.

4,038.   "15,000 Klansmen Gather." New York Times.
          May 24, 1925, p. 3.

4,039.   "Fire Cross And Bombs As Klansmen Meet." New York
          Times. April 4, 1924, p. 3.

4,040.   "500 Rout Speaker At Klan Meeting." New York Times.
          June 5, 1923, p. 4.

4,041.   "5,000 At Klan Initiation." New York Times.
          September 20, 1925, p. 20.

4,042.   "5,000 At Klan Klavern." New York Times. August
          1, 1926, p. 2.

4,043.   "Flag In Fireworks Set Ablaze By Klan." New York
          Times. July 14, 1924, p. 5.

4,044.   "40 Klansmen Invade Church In Newark." New York
          Times. March 13, 1923, p. 10.

4,045.   "40,000 Klansmen To Rally In Jersey." New York
          Times. July 3, 1924, p. 6.

4,046.   Gardner, Sandra. "Grand Dragon Says He's A 'Family
          Man'." New York Times. September 13, 1981, Sect.
          11, p. 16.

4,047.   _____. "Schools Seeking To Counter Ku Klux
          Klan." New York Times. September 13, 1981,
          Sect. 11, pp. 1, 17.

4,048.   "Girl Found In Woods, Ill." New York Times.
          October 12, 1925, p. 8.

4,049.   Goldberg, David M. "Is The Klan On The Rise In
          Jersey?" New York Post. March 30, 1971, p. 58.

4,050.   "Head Of New Jersey Klan Quits Without Explanation."
          New York Times. June 23, 1966, p. 44.

4,051.   "Hibernians To Fight Klan." New York Times.
          August 6, 1922, p. 22.

4,052.   "Hooded Klansmen At A Funeral." New York Times.
          February 16, 1925, p. 22.

4,053.   "House Panel To Get Jersey Klan Report." New York
          Times. October 21, 1965, p. 27.

4,054.   Janson, Donald. "Atlantic City Judge Orders Ban
          On Ku Klux Klan." New York Times. July 15, 1978,
          p. 47.

4,055.   _____. "Is Klan Role In The State Waning?"
          New York Times. August 26, 1979, Sect. 11, p. 1.

4,056.   _____. "Plan For Klan Rally In Vineland Stirs
          Counter-Plan For A 'Brotherhood Vigil'." New York
          Times. November 18, 1979. Sect. 11, pp. 12-13.

4,057.   "Jersey Asks A Ban On Big Klan Rally." New York
           Times. May 19, 1966, p. 40.

4,058.   "Jersey D.A. Moves To Kill Klan Roots." New York
           Amsterdam News. October 26, 1946, p. 8.

4,059.   "Jersey Democrats To Name The Klan." New York
           Times. October 1, 1924, p. 10.

4,060.   "Jersey Klan Member Jailed 6 Months In Cross
           Burning." New York Times. January 14, 1973, p. 58.

4,061.   "Jersey Klan Head Sued By Ziegler Kin." New York
           Times. March 13, 1926, p. 10.

4,062.   "Jersey Klan Fights Smith." New York Times.
           September 9, 1928, p. 2.

4,063.   "Jersey Klan Fights German In Schools." New York
           Times. November 25, 1922, p. 3.

4,064.   "Jersey Klan Endorses Republican Nominees." New
           York Times. November 3, 1924, p. 2.

4,065.   "Jersey Klans Women In Outdoor Initiation." New
           York Times. August 19, 1923, p. 2.

4,066.   "Jersey Klansmen Rally." New York Times. July 20,
           1924, p. 26.

4,067.   "Jersey Klansmen To Remove Hoods." New York Times.
           November 19, 1923, p. 17.

4,068.   "Jersey Kleagle Is Dead." New York Times. August
           6, 1924, p. 13.

4,069.   "Jersey Ku Klux Hold Rites At Man's Grave." New
           York Times. May 26, 1922, p. 20.

4,070.   "Jersey Ku Klux Klan Seeks State Charter; Files
           Membership Rules And Purposes." New York Times.
           October 3, 1923, p. 1.

4,071.   "Jersey Methodists Ask Taylor Recall." New York
           Times. April 16, 1940, p. 21.

4,072.   "Jersey Pastor Quits Klan." New York Times.
           October 13, 1927, p. 18.

4,073.   "Jersey Platform Split On Two Issues." New York
           Times. October 8, 1924, p. 4.

4,074.   "Jersey Platforms Differ." New York Times.
           October 3, 1924, p. 4.

4,075.   "Jersey Winds Up Bitter Campaigns." New York Times.
           May 10, 1927, p. 22.

4,076.   Johnston, Richard J.H.   "Jersey A.C.L.U. To Join
          Defense Of 3 Accused Of Cross-Burning."   New York
          Times.   March 7, 1971, p. 31.

4,077.   "Kan The Klan His Slogan."   New York Times.   April
          16, 1925, p. 7.

4,078.   King, Jan.   "The Bedsheets Are Flapping Again."
          New York Times.   December 30, 1957, Sect. 11, p. 16.

4,079.   "K.K.K. Flowers Removed."   New York Times.   August
          24, 1924, p. 5.

4,080.   "KKK Holds National Meeting In The State."   New
          Brunswick (N.J.) Daily Home News.   July 9, 1924,
          p. 1.

4,081.   "KKK And Nazis' Held In N.J. As Ga. And Texas KKK
          Activists Act."   New Orleans Times Picayune.
          November 25, 1979, p. 19.

4,082.   "KKK And Nazi Party Members Arrested Before New
          Jersey KKK Rally."   Chicago Defender.   November
          26, 1979, p. 5.

4.083.   "K.K.K. Threatens Judge."   New York Times.
          February 10, 1923, p. 8.

4,084.   "K. Of P. Defies Klan Order Not To Parade."
          Pittsburgh Courier.   September 29, 1923, p. 2.

4,085.   "Klan Active At Cape May."   New York Times.
          February 22, 1924, p. 16.

4,086.   "Klan Aids Negro Church."   New York Times.   June
          17, 1924, p. 33.

4,087.   "Klan Appeals To Citizens."   New York Times.
          August 3, 1924, p. 14.

4,088.   "Klan At Church Service."   New York Times.   May
          28, 1923, p. 2.

4,089.   "Klan Baptizes Twin Girls."   New York Times.
          August 18, 1924, p. 15.

4,090.   "Klan Cancels Rally As Troopers Gather."   New York
          Times.   May 21, 1966, p. 15.

4,091.   "Klan Celebrates Mother's Day."   Christian Century.
          Vol. 42, May 21, 1925, pp. 677-681.

4,092.   "Klan Charter Attacked."   New York Times.   October
          11, 1923, p. 22.

4,093.   "Klan Chief To Speak In Jersey City." New York
Times. April 17, 1927, p. 12.

4,094.   "Klan Cross In Jersey City." New York Times.
August 17, 1923, p. 2.

4,095.   "Klan Cross Is Destroyed." New York Times. July
15, 1923, Sect. 2, p. 1.

4,096.   "Klan Crosses Burn At Hammonton." New York Times.
July 27, 1925, p. 19.

4,097.   "Klan Crosses Go Begging." New York Times. August
3, 1946, p. 28.

4,098.   "Klan Defender Very Ill." New York Times.
April 19, 1925, p. 24.

4,099.   "Klan Disclaims Warnings." New York Times.
June 16, 1924, p. 9.

4,100.   "Klan Dragon Calls Smith Unfit." New York Times.
September 9, 1928, p. 4.

4,101.   "Klan Fights German Study." New York Times.
August 26, 1922, p. 20.

4,102.   "Klan Foes Write To Silzer." New York Times.
September 2, 1923, p. 4.

4,103.   "Klan Gives Rector $100." New York Times. March
6, 1923, p. 24.

4,104.   "Klan Has 'Americanism' Rally At Bund Camp; Members
Of Both Orders Mingle In Jersey." New York Times.
August 19, 1940, p. 1.

4,105.   "Klan Has Summer Resort." New York Times. June
20, 1926, Sect. 2, p. 17.

4,106.   "Klan Head Assails Smith." New York Times. April
18, 1927, p. 3.

4,107.   "Klan Holds Down Service In Jersey." New York Times.
April 17, 1933, p. 3.

4,108.   "Klan Holds Parade In Jersey." New York Times.
February 12, 1940, p. 34.

4,109.   "Klan In Dawn Service." New York Times. April 22,
1935, p. 9.

4,110.   "Klan In New Jersey Launches Campaign Against Gov.
Smith." New York Times. May 6, 1928, p. 21.

4,111.   "Klan Initiates 400 In A Jersey Field." New York
Times. July 2, 1924, p. 14.

4,112.   "Klan Initiates 652." New York Times. July 24, 1923, p. 23.

4,113.   "Klan Is Defended In Two Churches." New York Times. June 18, 1923, p. 7.

4,114.   "Klan Is Forbidden To March In Atlantic City." Pittsburgh Courier. November 24, 1923, p. 10.

4,115.   "Klan Keeps Watch On Politics Here." New York Times. September 15, 1937, p. 1.

4,116.   "Klan Leader And 5 Held In Jersey Cross-Burning." New York Times. May 15, 1966, p. 73.

4,117.   "Klan Leader Held In Jersey." New York Times. December 17, 1941, p. 19.

4,118.   "Klan Loses Jersey Suit." New York Times. September 21, 1929, p. 9.

4,119.   "Klan March In Jersey." New York Times. November 20, 1978, Sect. 2, p. 2.

4,120.   "Klan Members Build Hall." New York Times. August 2, 1925, p. 3.

4,121.   "Klan Not Named In Jersey." New York Times. October 2, 1924, p. 3.

4,122.   "Klan Parade Shifts." New York Times. July 6, 1926, p. 8.

4,123.   "Klan Parades With Electric Cross." New York Times. August 9, 1924, p. 2.

4,124.   "Klan Plans Parade At Belmar, N.J." New York Times. June 20, 1926, Sect. 2, p. 2.

4,125.   "Klan Plans Radio Station." New York Times. February 26, 1925, p. 15.

4,126.   "Klan Posters Trap Pastor." New York Times. October 4, 1928, p. 2.

4,127.   "Klan Rally Vents Anti-Smith Feeling." New York Times. July 5, 1980, p. 6.

4,128.   "Klan Refuses To March Unmasked." New York Times. June 19, 1926, p. 25.

4,129.   "Klan Removes Welcome Sign At Princeton." Raleigh (N.C.) News & Observer. July 6, 1969, p. 3.

4,130.   "Klan Seeks Jersey Members." New York Times. November 28, 1965, p. 36.

4,132.   "Klan Seeks To Get Land." New York Times. January 29, 1928, p. 8.

4,133.   "Klan Threat To Parade Even If Blood Is Shed Brings Ban On Hooded Order In Atlantic City." New York Times. November 16, 1923, p. 1.

4,134.   "Klan Threatens Boy With Rope And Knife." New York Times. May 10, 1923, pp. 1, 8.

4,135.   "Klan Threatens Congress Candidate." New York Times. September 19, 1924, p. 5.

4,136.   "Klan Threatens To Parade." New York Times. July 5, 1926, p. 13.

4,137.   "Klan To Build A Home." New York Times. July 16, 1924, p. 6.

4,138.   "Klan To Hold More Jersey Klaverns." New York Times. May 4, 1923, p. 6.

4,139.   "Klan Tries To Recruit Policemen In Newark." Washington Post. January 8, 1966, p. 1.

4,140.   "Klan Votes On Strike." New York Times. October 22, 1924, p. 9.

4,141.   "Klan Warns Three Towns." New York Times. January 31, 1924, p. 30.

4,142.   "Klan Will Hold Daylight Meeting." New York Times. June 2, 1923, p. 13.

4,143.   "Klan's Flag Returned By Women." Pittsburgh Courier. December 4, 1926, p. 4.

4,144.   "Klansman Out On Bail." New York Times. July 28, 1925, p. 28.

4,145.   "Klansman Unmasks To Speak In Church." New York Times. June 4, 1923, p. 3.

4,146.   "Klansman's Attack Stirs Methodists." New York Times. March 28, 1926, p. 19.

4,147.   "Klansmen Aroused By Dickson Murder." New York Times. September 29, 1923, p. 9.

4,148.   "Klansmen Cheered In March To Church." New York Times. May 21, 1923, p. 15.

4,149.   "Klansmen Honor American Mothers." New York Times. May 11, 1925, p. 19.

4,150.   "Klansmen In Negro Church." New York Times.
          June 15, 1925, p. 6.

4,151.   "Klansmen Initiate 75 More In Newark." New York
          Amsterdam News. December 20, 1922, p. 1.

4,152.   "Klansmen Initiate 75 More In Newark." New York
          Times. December 13, 1922, p. 5.

4,153.   "Klansmen Invited To Negro Church." New York
          Amsterdam News. June 17, 1925, pp. 1-2.

4,154.   "Klansmen Protest 'Invasion Of Mobs'." New York
          Times. June 17, 1923, p. 3.

4,155.   "Klansmen Visit Church." New York Times. September
          8, 1924, p. 15.

4,156.   "Kleagle Talks In Dark." New York Times.
          September 29, 1923, p. 9.

4,157.   "Knocks Off Hoods, Beats 3 Klansmen." New York
          Times. June 25, 1923, p. 15.

4,158.   "Ku Klux Aids Children." New York Times. Decem-
          ber 28, 1922, p. 7.

4,159.   "Ku Klux Cheered On March." New York Amsterdam
          News. May 23, 1923, p. 3.

4,160.   "Ku Klux Klan Membership Campaign." Christian
          Science Monitor. January 15, 1966, p. 3.

4,161.   "Ku Klux Klan Takes $25 Gift To Church." New York
          Times. May 16, 1922, p. 14.

4,162.   "Ku Klux Klan Warning Drives Worshipers Away."
          Chicago Defender. October 8, 1921, p. 2.

4,163.   "Ku Klux Klansmen Invade A Church." New York
          Times. October 23, 1922, p. 1.

4,164.   "Ku Klux Now Has 50 Klans In Jersey." New York
          Times. August 30, 1921, p. 19.

4,165.   "Ku Klux Protest Honor To Late Dean." New York
          Times. June 22, 1922, p. 36.

4,166.   "Ku Klux Rankles Jersey; Fiery Crosses On Mount."
          Chicago Defender. April 22, 1922, pp. 1-2.

4,167.   "Ku Klux Revolt Starts In Jersey." New York Times.
          December 22, 1923, p. 13.

4,168.   "Ku Klux Signals Flash On Patterson." New York
          Times. April 16, 1922, p. 20.

4,169.   "Ku Kluxers Visit Churches." New York Times.
          December 25, 1922, p. 3.

4,170.   "Lays Separation To Klan." New York Times. March
          27, 1927, p. 19.

4,171.   "Letters Start Body Hunt." New York Times. April
          19, 1923, p. 21.

4,172.   "Lightfoot Gets Ku Klux Warning." New York Amster-
          dam News. December 13, 1922, p. 1.

4,173.   "Mayor Hague Won't Let Klan Parade; Tells Grand
          Klokard He Fears Rioting." New York Times. June
          17, 1926, p. 25.

4,174.   "Methodist Bishop Defends The Negro." New York
          Times. March 4, 1926, p. 11.

4,175.   Mintz, David A and Paul Stagg." A Call For A New
          Commitment." New York Times. January 13, 1980,
          Sect. 11, p. 26.

4,176.   "Mixed Crowd Break Up Ku Klux Meeting." Pittsburgh
          Courier. June 16, 1923, pp. 3-4.

4,177.   "The Mob Spirit At Perth Amboy." New York Times.
          September 1, 1923, p. 10.

4,178.   "Negroes And Klansmen March In Church Parade." New
          York Times. September 27, 1925, p. 1.

4,179.   "New Clue In Hall Murder." New York Times.
          September 16, 1924, p. 10.

4,180.   "New Jersey Folks Arm When Told Of Ku Klux Klan."
          Chicago Defender. August 27, 1921, p. 9.

4,181.   "New Jersey Boy Klansman Stirs Dispute Over Klan
          Rally." Los Angeles Times. October 5, 1979,
          Sect. 1A, p. 10.

4,182.   "N.J. High School Refuses To Give Diploma To Ku
          Klux Klan Youth." Houston Post. November 13,
          1979, p. 14A.

4,183.   "N.J. Klan Pledges Tar And Feathers." Washington
          Post. March 17, 1971, p. 3A.

4,184.   "New Jersey Klans Campaign For Schools." The
          Kourier Magazine. Vol. 9, September, 1933, p. 37.

4,185.   "New Jersey Pastor Gets 'K.K.K.' Threat." New
          York Times. April 19, 1923, p. 21.

4,186.   "New Jersey Plans Move To Abolish Klan By Making
          Its State Charter Inoperative." New York Times.
          July 31, 1946, p. 48.

4,187.   "N.J. Klan Threat Stirs Bootleggers." New York
          Times. January 15, 1924, p. 23.

4,188.   "Now Heresy Invades The Klan." New York Times.
          December 24, 1923, p. 10.

4,189.   "Officer Dims Klan Cross." New York Times.
          August 29, 1925, p. 13.

4,190.   "150 Initiated Into Klan." New York Times.
          June 30, 1924, p. 4.

4,191.   "$100,000 Club For Klan." New York Times.
          August 23, 1924, p. 3.

4,192.   "Pastor Calls Klan A Church Hope." New York Times
          August 9, 1926, p. 18.

4,193.   "Pastor Gets 2 Warrants." New York Times. August
          7, 1927, Sect. 2, p. 9.

4,194.   "Pastor Wants A Pistol." New York Times. June
          27, 1925, p. 14.

4,195.   "Pastor's Critics Give Bail." New York Times.
          August 10, 1927, p. 23.

4,196.   "Paterson, Defying Klan, Honors Dean." New York
          Times. June 23, 1922, p. 36.

4,197.   "Paterson Mayor To Drop Employees Linked To Klan."
          New York Times. December 2, 1965, p. 36.

4,198.   "Perth Amboy Mob In Anti-Klan Riot; Scores Are
          Beaten." New York Times. August 31, 1923, pp. 1,
          10.

4,199.   "Perth Amboy Shaky After Rout Of Klan." New York
          Times. September 1, 1923, p. 4.

4,200.   "Police Seize Klan Wreath." New York Times.
          February 23, 1923, p. 15.

4,201.   "Policemen Seize 17 Before J.D.L. Holds Hightstown
          Protest." New York Times. April 5, 1971, p. 66.

4,202.   Porter, Russell B. "Hague Holds Reds Lack Civil
          Rights; Defends His Ban." New York Times. June
          17, 1938, p. 1.

4,203.   "Preacher Asks Klan Riot Inquiry." New York
          Times. July 15, 1928, p. 5.

4,204.   "Preacher Rebuked By Grand Dragon." The Kourier
Magazine. Vol. 10, May, 1934., p. 22.

4,205.   "Press Finds Klan Is Quiet In Jersey." New York
Times. February 16, 1923, p. 8.

4,206.   "Promise To Unmask Ku Klux In Jersey." New York
Times. April 11, 1923, p. 24.

4,207.   "Proskauer Scores New Deal Policies." New York
Times. November 3, 1940, p. 59.

4,208.   "Protests Against Ban On Ku Klux Parade." New
York Times. June 20, 1926, p. 8.

4,209.   "Race Clash Feared If Klansmen March." New York
Times. August 18, 1924, p. 15.

4,210.   "Recruiting By Klan Pressed In Newark In Residence
Areas." New York Times. January 8, 1966, p. 23.

4,211.   "Report Klan Losing Strength In Jersey." New York
Times. April 5, 1924, p. 17.

4,212.   "Robed Riders Lead Public Klan Parade." New York
Times. June 3, 1923, Sect. 1, Part 2, p. 8.

4,213.   "Says Elks Will Fight Klan." New York Times.
October 23, 1923, p. 30.

4,214.   "Says Klan Menaces Him." New York Times. August
1, 1924, p. 13.

4,215.   "Says Klan Will Win Nomination." New York Times.
September 24, 1924, pp. 22.

4,216.   "Senate Recalls Jersey Bridge Act." New York Times.
February 17, 1925, p. 12.

4,217.   "Senator Leap Makes Address To Children At K.K.K.
Supper At Salem, N.J." The Kourier Magazine.
Vol. 9, May, 1933, p. 12.

4,218.   "7 Held After Klan Meets." New York Times.
August 24, 1923, p. 2.

4,219.   Shear, Jeffrey. " 'I Ranted And Raved'." New
York Times. January 20, 1981, Sect. 11, p. 15.

4,220.   _____. "Klansman, 18, Fights For A Diploma."
New York Times. January 20, 1980, Sect. 11, p. 1.

4,221.   "Silzer Hits Ku Klux Klan." New York Times.
January 25, 1923, p. 21.

4,222.   "Silzer To Ignore Klan." New York Times. June 19,
1923, p. 23.

4,223.   "Smith Man Elected At Heflin Meeting." New York
Times. June 25, 1928, p. 21.

4,224.   "Start Reformed Plan." New York Times. January
11, 1924, p. 9.

4,225.   Sullivan, Ronald. "Jersey Klan Plans Cross-Burning
Rally On May 23." New York Times. April 13, 1966,
p. 26.

4,226.   _____. "Newark's White Citizen Patrol, Opposed
By Governor, Sees Itself As Antidote To Fear And
Riots." New York Times. June 24, 1968, p. 23.

4,227.   "Sullivan Denies Klan Backing." New York Times.
November 2, 1925, p. 3.

4,228.   "Sunday Films Fought In Plainfield By Klan." New
York Times. August 15, 1926, p. 15.

4,229.   "Tear Down Fiery Cross." New York Times. July 19,
1923, p. 8.

4,230.   "Telling Of Graft, Official Quits Klan." New
York Times. October 6, 1923, p. 4.

4,231.   "Tells Of Klan Fight Over Hoboken Leader." New
York Times. February 15, 1923, p. 21.

4,232.   "10,000 Masked Men Hold A Klan Parade." New York
Times. September 2, 1924, p. 12.

4,233.   "Their Ideals Plainly Illustrated." New York Times.
May 11, 1923, p. 16.

4,234.   "They Never Deserve Any Praise." New York Times.
July 17, 1923, p. 18.

4,235.   "Thirteen Crosses Burned In Jersey." New York Times.
November 26, 1923, p. 14.

4,236.   "Thousands Of Klan Leave Jersey Camp." New York
Times. July 6, 1924, p. 6.

4,237.   "Threatening Letters Sent By Ku Klux Klan." New
York Times. June 15, 1924, p. 17.

4,238.   "Three-Day Klan Fete At Sesquicentennial." New
York Times. June 18, 1926, p. 23.

4,239.   "Three Fined As Klansmen." New York Times.
September 8, 1926, p. 12.

4.240.   "Toward Newark School Peace." New York Times.
          April 3, 1971, p. 28.

4,241.   "Trenton To Fight Ku Klux." New York Times.
          August 17, 1921, p. 11.

4,242.   "A Tribute To Major Washburn." New York Times.
          September 23, 1924, p. 22.

4,243.   "12,000 Klansmen Hold A Parade In Jersey." New
          York Times. August 16, 1925, p. 25.

4,244.   "25,000 Catholics Parade." New York Times.
          October 13, 1924, p. 17.

4,245.   "Two Cleared Of Rape Charges." New York Times.
          March 1, 1980, p. 24.

4,246.   "2 Klan Chiefs Subpoenaed To Testify To Jersey
          Jury." New York Times. December 3, 1965, p. 30.

4,247.   Waggoner, Walter H. "Cross-Burning Conviction Of
          2 Is Reversed By Appeals Court." New York Times.
          June 22, 1974, p. 62.

4,248.   Waldron, Martin. "New Jersey Journal." New York
          Times. January 20, 1980, Sect. 11, p. 3.

4,249.   "Will Try Pastor's Critics." New York Times.
          August 8, 1927, p. 17.

4,250.   Willcox, Isobel. "Hackensack Is Recalled As
          Hostile Racist Town." New York Times. July 15,
          1973, p. 82.

4,251.   "Wizard To Fly To Klan." New York Times. July 4,
          1926, p. 8.

4,252.   "Woman Gets Fire Threat." New York Times. June
          24, 1923, p. 10.

4,253.   "Women's Klan Incorporated." New York Times.
          December 1, 1923, p. 20.

4,254.   "Would Legalize Bingo." New York Times. September
          14, 1946, p. 10.

4,255.   "Would Oust Klan Officers." New York Times.
          September 21, 1921, p. 19.

4,256.   "Wouldn't Join The Klan." New York Times. May
          25, 1925, p. 20.

4,257.   "Ziegler Is Returning To Face Klan Charges." New
          York Times. July 23, 1925, p. 20.

4,258.   "Ziegler Rearrested As Embezzler." New York Times.
           December 22, 1925, p. 35.

30. NEW MEXICO

4,259.   "Fall Is Big Issue In New Mexico Race." New York
           Times. October 28, 1924, p. 3.

4.260.   "Judge In New Mexico Defies Sender Of Ku Klux
           Threats." New York Times. July 12, 1923, p. 1.

4,261.   "New Mexico Democrats Hit Klan." New York Times.
           September 18, 1924, p. 3.

31. NEW YORK

4,262.   "Abducted Druggist Is Found In Hotel." New York
           Times. August 28, 1924, p. 19.

4,263.   "Accuse Yonkers Police." New York Times. October
           29, 1923, p. 6.

4,264.   "Action Of Young Kluxers Scored." Pittsburgh
           Courier. June 5, 1937, p. 1, 4.

4,265.   "Al Smith 'Sits On' Kluxers." Pittsburgh Courier.
           January 7, 1928, p. 1.

4,266.   "Aldermen Pledge Aid In War On Klan." New York
           Times. November 29, 1922, p. 1.

4,267.   "All Action On The Klan Left To Prosecutors."
           New York Times. November 29, 1928, p. 24.

4,268.   "Alleged Klansmen Held On 2 Charges." New York
           Times. February 3, 1923, p. 14.

4,269.   "Anderson Talks Of Ku Klux Klan." New York Times.
           September 9, 1923, Sect. 2, p. 1.

4,270.   "Anti-Klan Law Put Up To Prosecutors." New York
           Times. November 23, 1981, p. 45.

4,271.   "Anti-Klan Law Repeal Sought In Assembly." New
           York Times. February 1, 1924, p. 19.

4,272.   "Anti-Klan Rally Held In Amityville, New York."
           New York Amsterdam News. July 25, 1981, p. 3.

4,273.   "Anti Ku Klux Meeting Draws A Large Crowd."
           Chicago Defender. October 15, 1921, p. 9.

4,274.   "Appeals In Klan Case Decided." New York Times.
           April 7, 1928, p. 15.

4,275.   "Appomattox Republican Club To Discuss Ku Klux Klan." New York Amsterdam News. December 13, 1922, p. 4.

4,276.   "Argue Klan Law Validity." New York Times. November 25, 1925, p. 2.

4,277.   "Arrest In Row Over Klan." New York Times. May 19, 1924, p. 4.

4,278.   "Ascribe To Klan Attack On Smith." New York Times. March 1, 1923, p. 19.

4,279.   "Ashurst Discusses Nation's Problems." New York Times. March 15, 1926, p. 7.

4,280.   "Asks Klan, Reds Be Outlawed." New York Times. July 16, 1949, p. 14.

4,281.   "Asks Miller To Stop Klan." New York Times. November 15, 1922, p. 23.

4,282.   "Assemblyman Says He Was In Klan In '27." New York Times. February 9, 1952, p. 8.

4,283.   "Attention Mustn't Be Diverted." New York Times. February 27, 1923, p. 18.

4,284.   "Ban On Parade Of Klan." New York Times. July 12, 1927, p. 24.

4,285.   "Band In Klan Regalia Attacks Gypsy Camp." New York Times. June 27, 1926, p. 19.

4,286.   "Bankhead Resorts To Fish." New York Times. September 17, 1937, p. 12.

4,287.   "Banton Denies He's A Ku Klux." New York Times. September 9, 1921, p. 10

4,288.   "Bar Klan From Parade." New York Times. May 14, 1930, p. 56.

4,289.   "Bar Ku Klux Here, Mayor Tells Police." New York Times. January 12, 1921, p. 4.

4,290.   Berry, Abner W. "Bi-Partisan Klan Here Gunning For Benjamin J. Davis." Daily Worker. December 13, 1948, p. 1.

4,291.   _____. "Has The KKK Infiltrated Into Yonkers City Hall?" Daily Worker. April 10, 1952, p. 3.

4,292.   "Bids Klan Not To Parade." New York Times. May 28, 1928, p. 14.

4,293.   Bigart, Homer. "City Aide Accused As A Klan Leader."
          New York Times. October 22, 1965, p. 31.

4,294.   _____. "Coroner Affirms Burros's Suicide." New
          York Times. November 2, 1965, p. 20.

4,295.   _____. "Jewish-Born Klansman Apparent Suicide."
          New York Times. November 1, 1965, pp. 1, 52.

4,296.   "Bill Against Klan Hits Dry League." New York
          Times. February 23, 1923, p. 4.

4,297.   "Binghamton Klan In Street Battle." New York Times.
          August 28, 1923, p. 19.

4,298.   "Binghamton Sees Only 1,540 Of Klan." New York
          Times. July 5, 1924, p. 6.

4,299.   "Blazing Cross Appears." New York Times. February
          3, 1924, Sect. 1, Part 2, p. 6.

4,300.   "Bloomfield Church Splits Over Klan Aid." New York
          Times. March 24, 1925, p. 2.

4,301.   "Bonus Bonds Win Leader's Support." New York
          Times. January 25, 1923, p. 21.

4,302.   "Bootlegger Gang Kills A Policeman." New York Times.
          May 17, 1924, p. 1.

4,303.   Borders, William. "Buckley Predicts Edge On
          Liberals." New York Times. October 25, 1965, pp.
          1, 29.

4,304.   "Boys Get 'K.K.K.' Warning." New York Times.
          August 13, 1922, p. 28.

4,305.   "Brooklyn Has A Mystery." New York Times. January
          27, 1923, p. 12.

4,306.   "Building Defenses Against The Haters." New York
          Times. December 30, 1923, Sect. 21, p. 12.

4,307.   "Burn Cross On Church Lot." New York Times. May
          11, 1924, p. 17.

4,308.   "Butler And Siegel Assail Ku Klux." New York
          Times. November 20, 1922, p. 2.

4,309.   "Call Mass Meeting For Fight On Klan." New York
          Times. January 19, 1923, p. 8.

4,310.   "Called Klan Victim." New York Times. September
          2, 1924, p. 21.

4,311.   "Called Ku Klux Body." New York Times. December 15, 1924, p. 3.

4,312.   "Calls For Repudiation." New York Times. December 25, 1922, p. 3.

4,313.   "Calvary Church Expels Ku Klux Lecturer, Who Boasted Dr. Straton Was Afraid To Act." New York Times. December 29, 1922, p. 1.

4,314.   "Calvary Meeting Avoids Ku Klux." New York Times. November 30, 1922, p. 21.

4,315.   "Calvary Not A Klan Nest, Says Straton." New York Times. November 20, 1922, p. 2.

4,316.   Calvin, Floyd J. " 'Angostura Bitters' Denies Ku Klux Klan." Messenger. Vol. 5, February, 1923, pp. 591-592.

4,317.   "Candidate Charges 'Ku Klux' Threat." New York Times. October 2, 1922, p. 10.

4,318.   "Candidate Not A Klan." New York Times. November 8, 1927, p. 6.

4,319.   "Catholic Weekly Calls Klan A Curse." New York Times. December 1, 1922, p. 11.

4,320.   "Ceiling Of 'Heaven' Falls On Disciples." New York Times. March 8, 1937, p. 21.

4,321.   "Celebration Of Lincoln's Birthday." The Freeman. Vol. 6, February 28, 1923, pp. 579-581.

4,322.   "Chambers Of Black Judge Defaced During Break-In." New York Times. January 18, 1981, p. 27.

4,323.   "Charlotte Mills Asks Governor's Aid." New York Times. September 28, 1922, p. 1.

4,234.   "Civil War Veteran Routs 12 Ku Kluxers." New York Times. May 31, 1924, p. 2.

4,325.   "Clergyman Held As Smith Libeler." New York Times. June 27, 1924, p. 21.

4,326.   "Clergyman Better Keep Out." New York Times. May 22, 1924, p. 16.

4,327.   "Close Fight On Klan." New York Times. November 7, 1923, p. 3.

4,328.   "Cohalan Sees Plot To Steal Primary." New York Times. September 1, 1925, p. 3.

4,329.   "Col. Felder To Lead Fight On Klan Here." New York
         Times. December 20, 1922, p. 11.

4,330.   Coley, Lem. "Bigotry On L.I. Then And Now." New
         York Times. December 2, 1979, Sect. 21, p. 26.

4,331.   "Columbus Orator Attacks The Klan." New York Times.
         October 13, 1924, p. 17.

4,332.   "Cortland Kleagle Is Arrested." New York Times.
         April 12, 1924, p. 10.

4,333.   "Couldn't Find Klan Klave." New York Times.
         February 4, 1923, Sect. 1, Part 2, p. 4.

4,334.   "Court Shifts Trial Because Of Ku Klux." New York
         Times. July 9, 1924, p. 8.

4,335.   "Court Warns Klan Out Of Brooklyn." New York Times.
         January 27, 1923, p. 15.

4,336.   "Crews Warns Voters Against Pressure." New York
         Times. September 20, 1938, p. 5.

4,337.   "Cross Burned At Store." New York Times. September
         16, 1928, p. 18.

4,338.   "Cross-Burners 'Stupid'." New York Times.
         September 28, 1949, p. 29.

4,339.   "Cross Is Fired Near Scene Of Klan Attack On Smith."
         New York Times. December 21, 1923, p. 19.

4,340.   "Crowds Tear Ku Klux Flowers From Grave." Pitts-
         burgh Courier. June 9, 1923, p. 4.

4,341.   "Davis, Smith, Dawes And Roosevelt Open Intensive
         Drive Here." New York Times. October 26, 1924,
         pp. 1, 14.

4,342.   "Dead Klan Spy Accused." New York Times. September
         5, 1924, p. 7.

4,343.   "Death Threat Sent To Columbia Negro." New York
         Times. April 5, 1924, p. 6.

4,344.   "Declines To Oust Negro." New York Times. April
         8, 1924, p. 14.

4,345.   "Detectives Watch Meeting For Klan." New York
         Times. March 6, 1923, p. 24.

4,346.   "Defends Klan, Sees Hylan As A Hamam." New York
         Times. December 2, 1922, p. 14.

4,347.   "Defiance Is Soon Abandoned." New York Times.
          June 4, 1923, p. 14.

4,348.   "Demand Ku Klux Klan To Make Public Report."
          Chicago Defender. April 2, 1921, p. 8.

4,349.   "Demands Tioga Klan Roll." New York Times.
          September 12, 1924, p. 2.

4,350.   "Denial May Be Confession." New York Times.
          November 22, 1922, p. 20.

4,351.   "Denies Fixing Blame In Klan Row." New York Times.
          August 2, 1927, p. 12.

4,352.   "Denounces Klan In Sermon." New York Times. March
          18, 1923, Sect. 1, Part 2, p. 8.

4,353.   "Destroy Burning Cross On Palisades." New York
          Times. May 9, 1927, p. 27.

4,354.   "Dewey Blasts Bilbo; Outlaws Klan." New York
          Amsterdam News. October 19, 1946, p. 4.

4,355.   "Dewey Pledges Fight On Ku Klux As Long As He Is
          Governor." Washington Evening Star. August 19,
          1946, p. 1.

4,356.   "A Donation." New York Times. May 10, 1923, p. 8.

4,357.   "Doubts Stoning By Klan." New York Times. September
          2, 1924, p. 12.

4,358.   "Dr. Chas. H. Roberts Defeated." Messenger.
          Vol. 6, December, 1924, pp. 374,388.

4,359.   "Drug Package Sent To State Senator." New York
          Times. March 28, 1923, p. 1.

4,360.   "Druggist, Threatened By Alleged Klansmen, Torn From
          Wife On Street And Kidnapped." New York Times.
          August 27, 1924, p. 1.

4,361.   "Dynamite Under Fiery Cross Imperils Lives Of
          Firemen Called To Put Out Flames." New York Times.
          March 19, 1924, p. 1.

4,362.   "Effort To Bar N.Y. Klan Rally Fail." Baltimore
          Afro-American. July 23, 1977, p. 7.

4,363.   Egan, Leo. "State Gains Hailed." New York Times.
          November 3, 1946, pp. 1, 2.

4,364.   "Elements That Are Discordant." New York Times.
          June 1, 1927, p. 26.

4,365.   "Enright Warns Ku Klux." New York Times. September
          18, 1921, p. 21.

4,366.   "Evans Attacks Smith At Big Klan Rally." New York
          Times. July 10, 1927, p. 20.

4,367.   "Explain Ku Klux Incident." New York Times. June
          8, 1924, p. 23.

4,368.   "Explains Klan Invitation." New York Times.
          May 25, 1923, p. 19.

4,369.   "Father Criticizes Boy Murder Inquiry." New York
          Times. December 11, 1923, p. 23.

4,370.   "Fear Klan's Hand In Trial." New York Times.
          September 29, 1927, p. 31.

4,371.   "Fears Klan Interference." New York Times. January
          20, 1923, p. 6.

4,372.   "Few Mourn Dead Klan Leader, Who Is Recalled As A
          'Loner'." New York Times. November 1, 1965, p. 53.

4,373.   "Fiery Cross At Speedway." New York Times. July
          7, 1924, p. 4.

4,374.   "Fiery Cross Brings Columbia Negro Aid." New York
          Times. April 4, 1924, p. 7.

4,375.   "Fiery Cross Found After Party In L.I." New York
          Times. July 6, 1966, p. 15.

4,376.   "Fiery Cross Greets Negro." New York Times.
          July 18, 1926, Sect. 2, p. 1.

4,377.   "Fiery Cross Near K. Of C." New York Times.
          August 25, 1924, p. 2.

4,378.   "Fiery Cross On The Hudson." New York Times.
          March 3, 1923, p. 14.

4,379.   "Fiery Klan Crosses Light Long Island." New York
          Times. October 14, 1923, p. 14.

4,380.   " 'Fiery Cross' Is Barred." New York Times.
          August 30, 1936, Sect. 2, p. 6.

4,381.   "15 Klansmen Assist Dry Chief In Drive." New York
          Times. May 19, 1924, p. 4.

4,382.   "Finds Fiery Cross In Yard." New York Times.
          March 27, 1923, p. 14.

4,383.   "Fired From Welfare Job." Christian Science
          Monitor. November 26, 1965, p. 5.

4,384.   "Fist Fights Mark Klan Celebration." New York Times.
          August 21, 1927, p. 24.

4,385.   "500 Klansmen Defy 1,000 Police In Song." New York
          Times. May 31, 1928, p. 14.

4,386.   "Five New York Radio Outlets." New York Times.
          October 1, 1937, p. 11.

4,387.   "5,000 At Funeral Of Slain Klansman Join War On
          Liquor." New York Times. May 21, 1924, p. 1.

4,388.   "Flag For Klan Pole." New York Times. December
          15, 1924, p. 19.

4,389.   "Flagpole Splits Town." New York Times. November
          9, 1924, p. 20.

4,390.   "Flaming Cross In Park Near Negro Cabaret Believed
          To Be First Ku Klux Sign In City." New York Times.
          July 12, 1923, p. 1.

4,391.   "Flaming Crosses Show Klan At Port Jervis." New
          York Times. April 23, 1923, p. 16.

4,392.   "Fliers Drop Klan Tracts." New York Times. Decem-
          ber 17, 1923, p. 2.

4,393.   "Foes Of Klan Win Fight In Buffalo." New York
          Times. September 17, 1924, p. 10.

4,394.   "4 Admit Cross Burning." New York Times. September
          14, 1949, p. 31.

4,395.   "Fortieth Enright Rumor." New York Times. January
          10, 1923, p. 7.

4,396.   "Four Arrested For Fiery Crosses." New York Times.
          August 28, 1926, p. 25.

4,397.   "400 In Ithaca College Protest." New York Times.
          November 13, 1979, p. B6.

4,398.   "Frat Man In Klan Reported 'Missing'." New York
          Times. December 11, 1921, p. 9.

4,399.   "Free Alleged Klansmen." New York Times. February
          22, 1923, p. 30.

4,400.   Fremont-Smith, Eliot. "A Disaster Of A Life."
          New York Times. October 9, 1967, p. 45.

4,401.   "Garvey Case Brings Ku Klux Giant Here." New York
          Times. February 8, 1923, p. 16.

4,402.   "Garvey Denounced At Negro Meeting." New York
          Times. August 7, 1922, p. 7.

4,403.   "Gets Her Trial Moved On Plea Against Klan." New
          York Times. February 17, 1925, p. 10.

4,404.   "Goldstein Moves To Outlaw Klan." New York Times.
          April 30, 1946, p. 23.

4,405.   Goldstein, Tom. "Appeals Court Backs Prison Guard
          Who Refused To Reply On K.K.K." New York Times.
          April 4, 1979, p. B1.

4,406.   Gordon, Albert J. "CIO Shipbuilders Bar Communists."
          New York Times. September 27, 1946, p. 2.

4,407.   "Gov. Smith Says Machold Is A Liar; Derides
          Roosevelt." New York Times. October 29, 1924, p. 1.

4,408.   "Governor Declines Klan's Invitation." New York
          Times. July 3, 1928, p. 2.

4,409.   "Grand Jury Blames Police In Klan Row." New York
          Times. July 28, 1927, p. 21.

4,410.   "Guard For World Building." New York Times.
          September 9, 1921, p. 2.

4,411.   "Guns And Munitions Seized Here; Klan Or Irish
          Suspected." New York Times. February 25, 1923, pp.
          1, 5.

4,412.   "Hangs Klan Warning On Katonah Hall." New York
          Times. September 3, 1923, p. 8.

4,413.   "Harvey Aide Called In Queens Inquiry." New York
          Times. March 23, 1929, p. 21.

4,414.   "Harvey On Stand At Trial Of Paino." New York
          Times. April 17, 1929, p. 29.

4,415.   "Harvey Rejected Bribe Of $200,000." New York
          Times. February 8, 1929, p. 1.

4,416.   "Hazing Case Brings Inquiry By Walker Into All
          Hospitals." New York Times. June 22, 1927, pp. 1,
          10.

4,417.   "Hazing In Hospital Upheld By Alumni." New York
          Times. June 25, 1927, p. 4.

4,418.   "Hearst Denounces Smith In His Reply." New York
          Times. September 4, 1925, p. 18.

4,419.   "Hecklers Break Up Ku Klux Meeting; Klan's First
          Appearance In Long Island." New York Times.
          November 7, 1922, p. 19.

4,420.   "Heflin Gets Data On Klan Parade Row." New York
          Times. January 7, 1928, p. 29.

4,421.   "Heflin Hints He Might Support Gov. Smith." New
          York Times. July 31, 1928, p. 6.

4,422.   "Heflin Scores Smith In Albany Suburb." New York
          Times. June 18, 1928, pp. 1, 12.

4,423.   "Heflin To Talk In Queens." New York Times. June
          21, 1928, p. 4.

4,424.   "Heflin To Talk To Freeport Klan." New York Times.
          July 28, 1928, p. 2.

4,425.   "Heflin's 'Reward' Goes To Klan Paper." New York
          Times. July 6, 1928, p. 23.

4,426.   "Held As Klan Plotters." New York Times. September
          30, 1923, p. 10.

4,427.   Hentoff, Nat. "A Man Lost." New York Times Book
          Review. October 1, 1967, Sect. 7, p. 18.

4,428.   "High Court Upholds Buffalo Klan Arrest." New
          York Times. May 23, 1925, p. 25.

4,429.   "High Court Upholds New York Klan Law." New York
          Times. November 20, 1928, p. 1.

4,430.   "Hirshfield Accuses Color Of Klanism." New York
          Times. September 14, 1923, p. 21.

4,431.   "His Scheme Worked Far Too Well." New York Times.
          December 19, 1922, p. 18.

4,432.   "Hold First Klan Funeral." New York Times.
          September 4, 1924, p. 4.

4,433.   "How They Escaped Publicity." New York Times.
          July 21, 1923, p. 8.

4,434.   "Hunt Ku Klux Here." New York Times. January 13,
          1921, p. 4.

4,435.   "Hylan Plans To Quit Public Life At End Of Term
          As Mayor." New York Times. November 27, 1922, p.
          1.

4,436.   "Identified As Kidnapper." New York Times.
          August 31, 1924, p. 11.

4,437.   "Imperial Wizard Has Conference With Mr. Garvey."
          Chicago Defender. July 8, 1922, pp. 2-3.

4,438.   "In The Long, Hot And Tragic Summer Of 1964."
          New York Times. October 25, 1973, p. 34.

4,439.   "Investigates Klan Charge." New York Times.
          July 19, 1927, p. 8.

4,440.   "It's Not Over Yet! KKK - 22 Caliber Connection?"
          Buffalo (N.Y.) Challenger. November 6, 1980, pp. 1,
          8.

4,441.   "Jamaica Klan Case Again Delayed." New York Times.
          August 24, 1927, p. 1.

4,442.   "Jamaica Klan Hall Sold." New York Times. March
          4, 1928, Sect. 2, p. 4.

4,443.   "Jewish GI's Fight Klan." New York Times. June 10,
          1946, p. 3.

4,444.   Johnson, Laurie. "Anti-Defamation League Says
          Rockaway's Klan Plans Cross-Burnings. New York
          Times. April 21, 1977, p. B4.

4,445.   "Joke Book Author Gets Klux Warning." New York
          Amsterdam News. August 8, 1923, p. 1.

4,446.   "Judge Enjoins Klan As A Corporation." New York
          Times. July 26, 1923, p. 1.

4,447.   "Judge Rebukes Klansmen." New York Times. March
          10, 1926, p. 20.

4,448.   "Judge Scores The Klan." New York Times. March
          18, 1926, p. 25.

4,449.   "Judge Tiernan On Klan." New York Times. March
          30, 1925, p. 17.

4,450.   "K Of C Hear Klan Denounced." New York Times.
          March 30, 1925, p. 20.

4,451.   Kaplan, Morris. "Rightist Is Linked To A TNT
          Plot Here." New York Times. August 12, 1969, p. 26.

4,452.   Kaufman, Michael T. "Upstate Prison Teacher
          Defends His Klan Role." New York Times. December
          23, 1974, p. 24.

4,453.   "Kids Admit Faking KKK Terror On L.I." New York
          Amsterdam News. August 10, 1946, p. 2.

4,454.   Kihss, Peter. "Liberties Group Back Klan In
          Dispute With Lefkowitz." New York Times. April
          26, 1977, p. 64.

4,455.   _____. "Police Say The Klan In Far Rockaway
          Has No Impact." New York Times. April 25, 1977,
          p. 57.

4,456.   "Kills Himself; Asked Klan Funeral." New York Times.
          March 22, 1924, p. 13.

4,457.   "K.K.K. Again Burns Cross In Yonkers." New York
          Amsterdam News. July 15, 1939, pp. 2-3.

4,458.   "KKK Attacks Muslim's Home In Copiague (New York)."
          New York Amsterdam News. July 11, 1981, p. 3.

4,459.   "KKK Fraud Uncovered In New York." People's Voice.
          May 4, 1946, p. 4.

4,460.   "K.K.K. Cross Burns At Mattituck." New York Times.
          August 7, 1939, p. 2.

4,461.   "Klan Aboard In Buffalo." New York Times. March
          24, 1924, p. 3.

4,462.   "Klan Accepts Veto On Jamaica Parade." New York
          Times. May 21, 1928, p. 23.

4,463.   "Klan Admits Secret Change In Papers." New York
          Times. July 29, 1923, p. 2.

4,464.   "Klan Aids Grange Fund." New York Times. February
          24, 1924, p. 15.

4,465.   "Klan Aids Hospital Fund." New York Times.
          March 28, 1923, p. 2.

4,466.   "The Klan And New York State." Pittsburgh Courier.
          April 21, 1923, p. 14.

4,467.   "Klan Asks New York To Police Its March. New York
          Times. July 2, 1966, p. 13.

4,468.   "Klan Asks Smith Inquiry." New York Times.
          December 24, 1927, p. 7.

4,469.   "Klan Asks To Parade Memorial Day." Pittsburgh
          Courier. May 24, 1930, p. 4.

4,470.   "Klan At Queens Funeral." New York Times. October
          7, 1927, p. 29.

4,471.   "Klan Backs Candidate." New York Times. September
          12, 1925, p. 5.

4,472.   "Klan Burial At Patchogue." New York Times.
          May 1, 1924, p. 10.

4,473.   "Klan Burns Cross On Columbia Campus." The
          Messenger. Vol. 6, May, 1924, pp. 137-138.

4,474.   "Klan Burns Cross On Harvey's Lawn." New York
          Times. June 11, 1930, p. 29.

4,475.   "Klan Carries Gold To Pastor In Church." New York Times. November 21, 1922, p. 4.

4,476.   "Klan Celebrates On Merrick Road." New York Times. July 5, 1927, p. 4.

4,477.   "Klan Challenges Walker." New York Times. November 10, 1927, p. 3.

4,478.   "Klan Chief Places Blame." New York Times. November 2, 1965, p. 20.

4,479.   "Klan Clubhouse Fired At Port Washington." New York Times. October 10, 1928, p. 17.

4,480.   "Klan Converts Told To Fight Tammany." New York Times. October 8, 1923, p. 2.

4,481.   "Klan Cross Disturbs Jacobstein's Audience." New York Times. August 5, 1928, p. 17.

4,482.   "Klan Cross Is Set Up." New York Times. May 31, 1936, p. 10.

4,483.   "Klan 'Cross' Protests Mixing In Cabarets." Pittsburgh Courier. August 4, 1923, pp. 2-3.

4,484.   "Klan Cross Stirs Yonkers." New York Times. March 16, 1923, p. 3.

4,485.   "Klan Cross Torn Down." New York Times. October 15, 1923, p. 1.

4,486.   "Klan Dedicates Children's Home. New York Times. July 11, 1926, p. 7.

4,487.   "Klan Defended By Rector." New York Times. November 27, 1922, p. 2.

4,488.   "The Klan Defies A State." Literary Digest. Vol. 77, June 9, 1923, pp. 12-13.

4,489.   "Klan Demonstration At Hempstead." New York Times. August 23, 1924, p. 3.

4,490.   "Klan Denies Intimidation." New York Times. March 19, 1923, p. 11.

4,491.   "Klan Drive On Here; Hylan Tells Police To Rout Them Out." New York Times. November 24, 1922, pp. 1, 4.

4,492.   "Klan Dying Up-State." New York Times. October 10, 1926, p. 27.

4,493.   "Klan Enjoined By New York Justice." Pittsburgh Courier. August 4, 1923, pp. 1-2.

4,494.   "Klan Fails To File Its Membership List." New York
           Times. June 23, 1923, p. 13.

4,495.   "Klan Fails To Stop Barrett's Wedding." New York
           Times. April 26, 1926, p. 1.

4,496.   "Klan Frightens Negroes." New York Times. July 12,
           1923, p. 29.

4,497.   "Klan Gets A Place In Jamaica Parade." New York
           Times. May 24, 1927, p. 14.

4,498.   "Klan Gives Church Donation Of $25." Pittsburgh
           Courier. December 15, 1923, pp. 1-2.

4,499.   "Klan In Freeport Election." New York Times.
           March 16, 1925, p. 11.

4,500.   "The Klan In This State." New York Times. October
           9, 1923, p. 20.

4,501.   "Klan Initiates 100." New York Times. August 28,
           1924, p. 3.

4,502.   "Klan Initiates 300." New York Times. October 22,
           1923, p. 21.

4,503.   "Klan Initiates 200." New York Times. July 3,
           1923, p. 8.

4,504.   "Klan Injunction Signed." New York Times. August
           20, 1923, p. 2.

4,505.   "Klan Inquiry Pressed." New York Times. January
           24, 1929, p. 12.

4,506.   "Klan Is Formed In Middleton." New York Times.
           January 11, 1923, p. 6.

4,507.   "Klan Is Outlawed In New York State." New York
           Times. July 30, 1946, p. 25.

4,508.   "Klan Is Suffolk Issue." New York Times.
           November 1, 1925, Sect. 2, p. 2.

4,509.   "Klan Issue Brings Out Binghamton Voters." New
           York Times. October 19, 1925, p. 25.

4,510.   "Klan Issue Raised At Murder Trial." New York
           Times. October 22, 1924, p. 9.

4,511.   "Klan Issue Up Again In Suffolk Politics." New
           York Times. September 17, 1925, p. 3.

4,512.   "Klan Jams Meeting In New Public School." New
           York Times. December 3, 1930, p. 27.

4,513.   "Klan Kleagle Guilty Of Having Blackjack." New
          York Times. February 1, 1923, p. 3.

4,514.   "Klan Klonvocation Lights Huge Crosses." New York
          Times. September 27, 1926, p. 7.

4,515.   "Klan Leader Debates Racial Bias With Ralph
          Abernathy At Campus." New York Times. October 5,
          1979, p. 26.

4,516.   "Klan Leader Here To Fight Platform." New York
          Times. June 22, 1924, p. 3.

4,517.   "Klan Lecturer Aroused." New York Times. February
          7, 1923, p. 19.

4,518.   "Klan Letters Sent To Grand Jurors." New York Times.
          December 12, 1922, p. 3.

4,519.   "Klan Lights Cross At Quiet Meeting." New York
          Times. September 8, 1936, p. 29.

4,520.   "Klan Loses In Nassau." New York Times. March 22,
          1926, p. 21.

4,521.   "Klan Made Outlaw Organization In N.Y." New York
          Amsterdam News. August 22, 1923, p. 1-2.

4,522.   "Klan Meeting At Huntington." New York Times.
          November 19, 1923, p. 17.

4,523.   "Klan Meets At Freeport." New York Times. Septem-
          ber 3, 1933, Sect. 2, p. 4.

4,524.   "Klan Meets At Peekskill." New York Times.
          September 4, 1928, p. 14.

4,525.   "Klan Members Get Delay." New York Times. June
          8, 1927, p. 27.

4,526.   "Klan Met In High School." New York Times. April
          10, 1925, p. 3.

4,527.   "Klan Offers $1,000 In Race Attack Case." New York
          Times. December 13, 1921, p. 15.

4,528.   "Klan Offers Trophy Cup." New York Times. August
          28, 1923, p. 19.

4,529.   "Klan On Long Island." New York Times. October
          28, 1923, Sect. 2, p. 1.

4,530.   "Klan Ordered To Attend Hoover Meet." Pittsburgh
          Courier. November 3, 1928, p. 78.

4,531.   "Klan 150,000 Strong." New York Amsterdam News.
          January 3, 1923, pp. 10-11.

4,532.   "Klan Organ Opens War On Wadsworth." _New York Times_.
          September 26, 1926, p. 2.

4,533.   "Klan Parade A Mile Long." _New York Times_. November
          8, 1923, p. 3.

4,534.   "Klan Parade Ends In General Fight." _New York Times_.
          November 9, 1928, p. 3.

4,535.   "Klan Parades In Riverhead." _New York Times_.
          August 22, 1926, p. 4.

4,536.   "Klan Pastor Defies Mayor And Police." _New York
          Times_. November 28, 1922, p. 23.

4,537.   "Klan Pays Mortgage Of The African Methodist
          Episcopal Church." _Broad Ax_. January 24, 1925,
          p. 1.

4,538.   "Klan Pays Negro Church Debt." _New York Times_.
          November 29, 1924, p. 15.

4,539.   "Klan Permanently Outlawed In N.Y." _New York
          Amsterdam News_. October 17, 1923, p. 7.

4,540.   "Klan Pillow At Monument." _New York Times_. June
          1, 1926, p. 2.

4,541.   "Klan Plans Block Party." _New York Times_. May
          22, 1924, p. 19.

4,542.   "Klan Plans Jamaica Lodge." _New York Times_. July
          8, 1928, p. 13.

4,543.   "Klan Plans State Temple." _New York Times_. April
          20, 1925, p. 18.

4,544.   "Klan Plans To Enter State Campaign, Seeking To
          Name Members In Primaries." _New York Times_.
          June 22, 1925, p. 3.

4,545.   "Klan 'Posts' Syracuse." _New York Times_. July
          27, 1924, p. 2.

4,546.   "Klan Prize Is Awarded." _New York Times_. September
          4, 1923, p. 19.

4,547.   "Klan Protests Ignored." _New York Times_. May 23,
          1928, p. 25.

4,548.   "Klan Protests In Queens." _New York Times_. June
          30, 1927, p. 56.

4,549.   "Klan Quits Binghamton." _New York Times_. July
          7, 1924, p. 17.

4,550.   "Klan Rally Leader Arrested." Washington Post.
          January 15, 1981, p. A13.

4,551.   "Klan Rebuked In Will." New York Times. October
          10, 1928, p. 16.

4,552.   "Klan Renews Fight On The Walker Law." New York
          Times. March 25, 1925, p. 9.

4,553.   "Klan Republicans Capture Suffolk." New York Times.
          April 13, 1924, p. 5.

4,554.   "Klan Row In Parade Goes To Grand Jury." New York
          Times. July 13, 1927, p. 14.

4,555.   "Klan Said To Make No Progress Here." New York
          Times. November 2, 1965, p. 20.

4,556.   "Klan Scores Tammany Hall." New York Times.
          September 5, 1933, p. 19.

4,557.   "Klan Seeks To March In Mount Kisco." New York
          Times. May 9, 1930, p. 5.

4,558.   "Klan Session Open After Hasty Move." New York
          Times. September 6, 1936, p. 12.

4,559.   "Klan Slips Through Loophole In Law." New York
          Times. January 14, 1926, pp. 1, 6.

4,560.   "Klan 'Suspension' 'Amuses' Harvey." New York
          Times. June 9, 1929, p. 24.

4,561.   "Klan Threatens Nominee." New York Times. October
          27, 1923, p. 5.

4,562.   "Klan To Boycott New York City." California Eagle.
          December 23, 1922, p. 4, Section 2.

4,563.   "Klan To Celebrate In Vacant Lot." New York Times.
          July 3, 1927, p. 8.

4,564.   "Klan To Meet In Batavia." New York Times.
          August 22, 1924, p. 3.

4,565.   "Klan To Meet Where Smith Speaks." New York Times.
          August 5, 1924, p. 21.

4,566.   "Klan To Obey Injunction." New York Times. August
          17, 1923, p. 2.

4,567.   "Klan To Stage Rally." New York Times. May 21,
          1925, p. 16.

4,568.   "Klan Un-Masonic; Declares Leaders." Pittsburgh
          Courier. May 17, 1924, p. 3.

4,569.   "Klan Urges Pastors To War On Catholics." New York
           Times. July 1, 1923, p. 14.

4,570.   "Klan Visits Church To Keep Out Negroes." New York
           Times. October 14, 1929, p. 25.

4,571.   "Klan Would Scare Colored Postman From Long Island
           Home." Broad Ax. August 21, 1926, p. 2.

4,572.   " 'Klan' Wreath Draws Crowd To Hale Statue." New
           York Times. June 7, 1927, p. 29.

4,573.   "Klanism Means Just That." New York Times. Decem-
           ber 1, 1923, p. 12.

4,574.   "Klans Get Time Extension." New York Times. June
           2, 1923, p. 13.

4,575.   "Klan's Hand Seen In Veteran's Bureau." New York
           Times. October 10, 1924, pp. 1, 10.

4,576.   "Klan's Nemesis Honored." New York Times. May
           30, 1947, p. 22.

4,577.   "Klan's Orators Soon To Defy Hylan Here." New York
           Times. December 3, 1922, Sect. 1, Part 2, p. 5.

4,578.   "Klan's Pistols Only Wood, Police Discover; Worn
           With Uniforms To Cow Foes At Rallies." New York
           Times. July 6, 1928, p. 23.

4,579.   "The Klansman And His Prisoners." New York Times.
           April 13, 1979, p. 26.

4,580.   "Klansman Attacks Smith." New York Times. Decem-
           ber 17, 1923, p. 14.

4,581.   "Klansman-Teacher Is Ousted By State From Prison
           Post." New York Times. December 24, 1974, p. 42.

4,582.   "Klansmen Are Barred From State Of N.Y." Pittsburgh
           Courier. October 20, 1923, p. 2.

4,583.   "Klansmen Burn Cross At Rally Amid Protests In
           Hamilton, N.Y." New York Times. July 10, 1977,
           p. 42.

4,584.   "Klansmen Contradict Mayor's Statement." New York
           Times. December 23, 1927, p. 12.

4,585.   "Klansmen Get Brick Shower." Pittsburgh Courier.
           November 17, 1928, p. 12.

4,586.   "Klansmen In Hoods At Bier Of Policeman." Pitts-
           burgh Courier. August 2, 1930, p. B9.

4,587.   "Klansmen March To Negro Church Service, Profess
          Friendship And Give $200 In Gold." New York Times.
          November 10, 1924, p. 1.

4,588.   "Klansmen On Screen Cheered By N.Y. Audience."
          California Eagle. December 23, 1922, p. 4, Sect. 2.

4,589.   "Klansmen On Screen Cheered By Audience!" New
          York Amsterdam News. December 13, 1922, pp. 1, 3.

4,590.   "Klansmen Parade On Merrick Road." New York Times.
          July 12, 1925, p. 4.

4,591.   "Klansmen Routed By Suffolk Vote." New York Times.
          March 22, 1926, p. 21.

4,592.   "Klansmen Serve On Affirmative Action Panel At
          N.Y. Prison." Houston Post. October 17, 1981, p.
          10A.

4,593.   "Klansmen To Honor Slain Policeman." New York
          Times. May 19, 1924, p. 4.

4,594.   "Klansmen Visit Church." New York Times. September
          17, 1923, p. 18.

4,595.   "Kleagle Of New York State Klan In Court." New
          York Amsterdam News. August 1, 1923, pp. 1-2.

4,596.   "Kleagle Sues For $15,000." New York Times. May
          23, 1923, p. 7.

4,597.   "Klokard Haywood Here To Aid Ku Klux." New York
          Times. February 5, 1923, p. 4.

4,598.   "Kluxers Raid Kiddie's Camp." Pittsburgh Courier.
          August 30, 1930, p. B2.

4,599.   "Knights Of Columbus Shake Faith In Klan." New
          York Times. April 16, 1923, p. 18.

4,600.   Knowles, Clayton. "Crusade On Klan Pledged By
          Mead." New York Times. October 25, 1946, p. 1.

4,601.   _____. "Mead Calls Dewey Lax On 'Bilboism'."
          New York Times. October 28, 1946, p. 10.

4,602.   _____. "Mead Charges Foe Fails To Curb Klan,
          'Smears' Liberals." New York Times. November 2,
          1946, p. 1.

4,603.   "Ku Klux And Legion Fight At Monument To 9 Heroes
          Of War." New York Times. November 30, 1923, pp. 1,
          3.

4,604.   "Ku Klux Bill Tightened." New York Times. April
          18, 1923, p. 26.

4,605.   "Ku Klux Denounced By Masonic Leader; Police Fight
          Starts." New York Times. November 25, 1922, pp.
          1, 4.

4,606.   "Ku Klux Donates To Fund." New York Times. August
          13, 1922, Sect. 2, p. 4.

4,607.   "Ku Klux Evangelist Opens Fight To Stay With
          Baptist Church." New York Times. November 26,
          1922, pp. 1, 20.

4,608.   "Ku Klux 'Empress' Comes Here To Shop." New York
          Times. September 11, 1921, p. 22.

4,609.   "Ku Klux Getting Active; Hold Meetings In New York,"
          Chicago Defender. December 24, 1921, p. 9.

4,610.   "Ku Klux Klan Alarmed." New York Times. January
          25, 1921, p. 10.

4,611.   "Ku Klux Klan Asks To Be Incorporated." New York
          Times. June 2, 1923, p. 13.

4,612.   "Ku Klux Klan Denounced." New York Times. June 3,
          1924, p. 10.

4,613.   "Ku Klux Klan Gives $25 To Negro Church Toward New
          Building; Extends Best Wishes." New York Times.
          December 9, 1923, p. 1.

4,614.   "Ku Klux Klan Openly Defies New Law; Holds Big
          Meetings All Over State; Hundreds Join; Governor
          Denounced." New York Times. May 28, 1923, pp. 1, 2.

4,615.   "Ku Klux Klan Rally In New York." Washington Post.
          July 5, 1975, p. 4A.

4,616.   "Ku Klux Klan Reported Active In Queens Area."
          Christian Science Monitor. April 22, 1977, p. 2.

4,617.   "Ku Klux Klan Threatens St. Albans Families."
          PM. August 1, 1946, p. 1.

4,618.   "Ku Klux Lecturer Under Fire 3 Hours." New York
          Times. December 9, 1922, pp. 1, 4.

4,619.   "Ku Klux Session At Port Jervis." New York Times.
          August 3, 1922, p. 3.

4,620.   Lacey, D. "KKK-Type Harassment In NYC Mayoral Cam-
          paign." New York Amsterdam News. September 5, 1981,
          p. 1.

4,621.   "La Guardia Defies Agents He Accuses." New York
          Times. March 17, 1927, p. 14.

4,622.   "Law Group Here Asks City And U.S. To Curb Vigilan-
          tes." New York Times. February 10, 1966, p. 30.

4,623.   "Law For Others, Not For The Ku Klux Klan!" Outlook.
          Vol. 134, June 9, 1923, pp. 109-110.

4,624.   "Law Makers At Capital Flay Ku Klux Order." Chicago
          Defender. October 22, 1921, pp. 8-9.

4,625.   "Leaps Out Of Hospital Window." New York Times.
          April 19, 1923, p. 21.

4,626.   "Lefkowitz Loses Move Against Klan." New York Times.
          January 15, 1976, p. 37.

4,627.   "Lefkowitz Orders Inquiry." New York Times.
          November 10, 1965, p. 7.

4,628.   "Legally Outlawed." New York Amsterdam News.
          October 17, 1923, p. 12.

4,629.   "Legislature Kills Dry Enforcement Act After Long
          Fight On Last Day Of Session, Smith Will Sign Repeal,
          His Friends Say." New York Times. May 5, 1923,
          pp. 1, 2.

4,630.   "A Letter From The Ku Klux Klan." New York
          Amsterdam News. August 8, 1923, pp. 7-8.

4,631.   "Letter Threatens Life Of Justice Tompkins." New
          York Times. July 28, 1923, p. 5.

4,632.   "Lockport Officers Battle 600 Of Klan." New York
          Times. October 20, 1923, p. 17.

4,633.   "Long Island Getting Its Reward." New York Times.
          June 10, 1923, p. 10.

4,634.   "Long Island Sees Biggest Klan Crowd." New York
          Times. June 22, 1923, pp. 1, 10.

4,635.   "Loyless To Be Editor Of Tolerance." New York
          Times. March 10, 1923, p. 14.

4,636.   "Magistrates With Dale On Klan Fiat." New York
          Times. January 28, 1923, Sect. 1, Part 2, p. 5.

4,637.   "Mahoney Charges Campaign Frauds." New York Times.
          September 16, 1937, p. 2.

4,638.   "Man Arrested Here In Nazi-Like Garb." New York
          Times. April 2, 1972, p. 72.

4,639.   "Man Found Slashed With K.K.K. On Chest." New
          York Times. November 2, 1928, p. 16.

4,640. "Many Groups To Celebrate." New York Times. July 1, 1927, p. 13.

4,641. "Many Klan Letters Given Out In Buffalo." New York Times. September 21, 1924, p. 25.

4,642. "Masked Klansmen In Brooklyn Pulpit Defies Police Ban." New York Times. December 11, 1922, pp. 1, 4.

4,643. "Masons Feel Slighted." New York Times. June 22, 1927, p. 27.

4,644. "Mayor Gets $5,000 Demand By K.K.K." New York Times. September 29, 1921, p. 19.

4,645. "Mayor Says Klan Paraded Illegally." New York Times. December 22, 1927, p. 10.

4,646. "Mayor Won't Upset Ban On Klan Parade." New York Times. May 22, 1928, p. 29.

4,647. Mazo, Earl. "Wagner Assails Miller Charges." New York Times. August 5, 1964, p. 37.

4,648. "Meeting To Discuss New Ku Klux Activity." New York Times. November 12, 1930, p. 11.

4,649. "Membership In Klan Barred To Employees Of Prisons In State." New York Times. September 4, 1975, p. 37.

4,650. "Memorial Service Marred By 'K.K.K.'." New York Times. May 31, 1924, p. 2.

4,651. "Menaced By Klan, Druggist To Move." New York Times. September 5, 1924, p. 36.

4,652. "Middleton Has A Flaming Cross." New York Times. December 26, 1923, p. 8.

4,653. "Ministers Suspect Racism After Five Churches Burned." Jet. Vol. 58, May 29, 1980, pp. 8-9.

4,654. " 'Missing' Ku Kluxer Tells Of An Attack." New York Times. December 12, 1921, p. 5.

4,655. "Moon Church Seeks U.S. Inquiry On Fire At Group's Upstate Camp." New York Times. August 10, 1980, p. 20.

4,656. "Move Announced To Bar Ku Klux Klan For Changes In Incorporation Certificate." New York Times. July 24, 1923, p. 1.

4,657. "Move To Kick Ku Klux Klan Out Of New York State." Cleveland Call And Post. May 11, 1946, p. 1.

4,658.   "Murder Charges." <u>Wall Street Journal</u>. November
          5, 1979, p. 1.

4,659.   "Murder Trial Stayed." <u>New York Times</u>. May 25,
          1925, Sect. 1, Part 2, p. 6.

4,660.   "Name Klansmen, Goldstein Asked." <u>Daily Worker</u>.
          July 31, 1946, p. 5.

4,661.   "Nassau Klan Rise Denied." <u>New York Times</u>.
          August 25, 1949, p. 25.

4.662.   "Nassau Village Elect." <u>New York Times</u>. March 17,
          1926, p. 3.

4.663.   "Negro At Columbia Defies His Critics." <u>New York
          Times</u>. April 3, 1924, p. 12.

4,664.   "Negro Here To Aid Integration Fight." <u>New York
          Times</u>. September 19, 1956, p. 20.

4,665.   "Negro Introduces Bill To Bar Klan." <u>New York
          Times</u>. February 7, 1923, p. 19.

4,666.   "Negro Questions Talesmen On Klan." <u>New York
          Times</u>. June 26, 1928, p. 42.

4,667.   "Negro Receives A Message." <u>New York Times</u>.
          December 6, 1922, p. 4.

4,668.   "Neo-Nazi Party Demotes Aide Who Hid Jewish Back-
          ground." <u>New York Times</u>. November 5, 1965, p. 26.

4,669.   "New Deal No Issue In City, Says Smith." <u>New York
          Times</u>. September 16, 1937, p. 4.

4,670.   "New York Banker Backing Reactionary Klan."
          <u>California Eagle</u>. December 23, 1922, p. 3, Sect.
          3.

4,671.   "New York Church Expels Ku Klux Klan Leader
          Haywood." <u>New York Age</u>. January 6, 1923, p. 1.

4,672.   "New York Klan Hearing Is Begun." <u>New York Amster-
          dam News</u>. August 15, 1923, p. 7.

4,673.   "New York Mayor Denounces The Ku Klux Order."
          <u>Chicago Defender</u>. September 3, 1921, pp. 9-10.

4,674.   "New York To Enforce Anti Ku Klux Klan Law."
          <u>Pittsburgh Courier</u>. June 2, 1923, p. 1.

4,675.   "New Yorkers Back Anti-Klan Plank." <u>New York
          Times</u>. June 10, 1924, pp. 1, 3.

4,676.   "New York's Anti-Klan Outburst." *Literary Digest*.
          Vol. 75, December 23, 1922, pp. 31-32.

4,677.   "New York's Only Legal KKK Unit." *Washington Post*.
          January 1, 1976.

4,678.   "N.Y. Prison Employees Warned To Quit The KKK."
          New Orleans Times Picayune. September 4, 1975, p.
          2.

4,679.   "N.Y. State To Enforce Anti-Ku Klux Klan Law."
          Pittsburgh Courier. June 21, 1923, p. 1.

4,680.   "Newcombe Won't Ask Indictment Of Harvey."
          New York Times. April 28, 1929, p. 23.

4,681.   "No Complaints Against Klan." *New York Times*.
          January 14, 1926, p. 6.

4,682.   "No Ku Klux Case Yet, Grand Jury Released." *New
          York Times*. December 30, 1922, p. 26.

4,683.   "No Record Of Any Inwood Case." *New York Times*.
          May 31, 1936, p. 10.

4,684.   North, Joseph. "Klansman Warns Of Those Peek-
          skills." *Daily Worker*. September 15, 1949, p. 1.

4,685.   "N.Y. Dissolves KKK; Two Other States Plan Suits."
          Chicago Defender. July 10, 1945, p. 1.

4,686.   "N.Y. Police Give District Attorney List Of 800
          In Klan." *California Eagle*. December 23, 1923,
          pp. 4-5, Sect. 2.

4,687.   "N.Y. Woman And Man Whipped By Klan." *New York
          Amsterdam News*. April 11, 1923, pp. 3-4.

4,688.   "Officials Elected In Westchester." *New York
          Times*. March 17, 1926, p. 3.

4,689.   "One Epidemic Comes To An End." *New York Times*.
          March 23, 1926, p. 26.

4,690.   "100,000 Klansmen Plan Parade Here." *New York
          Times*. June 24, 1923, p. 11.

4,691.   "1,000 Klansmen Assembled." *New York Times*.
          February 22, 1925, p. 14.

4,692.   "1,000 Out To See Klan Hold Funeral." *New York
          Times*. November 16, 1924, p. 19.

4,693.   "Pastor Defends Klan." *New York Times*. October
          15, 1923, p. 17.

4,694.   "Pastor, Home Bombed, Again Aids Raiders." New
          York Times. April 19, 1924, p. 4.

4,695.   "Patchgut Klan Parades." New York Times. August
          2, 1925, p. 7.

4,696.   "Peace Is Better Than War." New York Times.
          April 4, 1924, p. 18.

4,697.   Perlmutter, Emanuel. "Little Klan Influence Seen
          Here; No Early Investigation Expected." New York
          Times. November 1, 1965, p. 52.

4,698.   "Permit Klan Carnival." New York Times. August
          7, 1924, p. 16.

4.699.   Phillips, McCandlish. "State Klan Leader Hides
          Secret Of Jewish Origin." New York Times.
          October 31, 1965, pp. 1, 85.

4,700.   "Place Pickets In Theater's Door To Halt Play."
          Chicago Defender. May 14, 1921, pp. 2-3.

4,701.   "Platform Crashes At Heflin Meeting Of 10,000
          Klansmen." New York Times. June 17, 1928, pp.
          1, 21.

4,702.   "Police Ban Fascist And Klan Parades." New York
          Times. June 4, 1927, p. 19.

4,703.   "Police Give Banton List Of 800 In Klan." New
          York Times. December 6, 1922, pp. 1, 4.

4,704.   "Police Give Bodyguard To Gigli For Month." New
          York Times. January 24, 1925, p. 16.

4,705.   "Police Seize 8 Here As Ku Klux Plotters." New
          York Times. January 26, 1923, pp. 1, 12.

4,706.   "Preaches On Klan, Attacks Its Foes." New York
          Times. February 19, 1923, p. 32.

4,707.   "Prisoners 'Protectors'." New York Times. April
          25, 1979, p. 22.

4,708.   "Prosecutor Asks List Of Kings Klan Members."
          New York Times. August 3, 1946, p. 3.

4,709.   "Prosecutor Blames Klan." New York Times. July
          29, 1927, p. 3.

4,710.   "Protest Anti-Klan Bill." New York Times.
          February 7, 1923, p. 3.

4,711.   "Protest Klan Acts In Church." New York Times.
          October 16, 1923, p. 22.

4,712.   "Publicity To Them Is Fatal." New York Times.
          May 25, 1923, p. 20.

4,713.   "Queens Klan Boasts 1,200." New York Times.   March
          16, 1923, p. 3.

4,714.   "Queens Klan Seeks Parade Permit." New York Times.
          May 17, 1928, p. 22.

4,715.   "Queens Klansman Aide To Sheriff." New York Times.
          January 19, 1928, p. 14.

4,716.   "Queens Motor Bureau Aide Ousted; Accused Of In-
          corporating Klan." New York Times. May 7, 1946,
          p. 1.

4,717.   "Rabbi Flays Klan; Urges 'Fair Play'." Pittsburgh
          Courier. March 1, 1924, pp. 1-2.

4,718.   "Raps Effort To Kill Anti-Klan Law." New York
          Times. February 12, 1924, p. 28.

4,719.   "Real Estate Agent Gets Klan Letter." New York
          Amsterdam News. July 18, 1923, pp. 1, 3.

4,720.   "Receiver Of Klan Letter In Court." New York
          Amsterdam News. August 1, 1923, pp. 1-2.

4,721.   "Refuse Klan Parade Plea." New York Times.   June
          25, 1925, p. 14.

4,722.   Reinholz, Mary. "A Visit To A KKK Koffee Klatch
          In Upstate New York." New Dawn. Vol. 1, September,
          1976, p. 36.

4,723.   "Reports Threats To Kidnap Heflin." New York Times.
          June 29, 1928, p. 9.

4,724.   "Republican Sweep In Suffolk County." New York
          Times. November 4, 1925, p. 6.

4,725.   "Republicans Back Building Program." New York
          Times. February 19, 1925, p. 21.

4,726.   "Rev. Brown Assails Ku Klux Before Big Crowd."
          Chicago Defender. June 3, 1922, pp. 9-10.

4,727.   "A Right Thing Done In A Wrong Way." New York
          Times. January 18, 1923, p. 14.

4,728.   "Rights Of Corrections Guards To Be KKK Members
          Fought." New York Amsterdam News. November 26,
          1977, p. 1.

4,729.   "Rioting Mars Parade Of Geneva (N.Y.) Klan."
          New York Times. September 4, 1927, p. 17.

4,730.   "Robeson Demands Violence Inquiry." New York Times.
         August 29, 1949, pp. 19, 23.

4,731.   "Robeson Will Sing Near Melee Scene." New York
         Times. September 2, 1949, pp. 1, 10.

4,732.   "Roosevelt Nominated For Governor; Anti-Klan Plank
         Is Forced Through; Oil Issue Injected By The
         Democrats." New York Times. September 26, 1924,
         p. 1.

4,733.   "Rules Against Klan In Walker Law Case." New York
         Times. November 8, 1924, p. 3.

4,734.   "Sanctions Klan Rally." New York Times. July 3,
         1930, p. 2.

4,735.   Saxon, Wolfgang. "Prison Teacher Suspended In
         State Study Of K.K.K. New York Times. December
         22, 1974, p. 14.

4.736.   "Say Hylan Has List Of Klan Policemen." New York
         Times. March 11, 1923, p. 3.

4,737.   "Say 30 Policemen Belong To Ku Klux." New York
         Times. March 10, 1923, p. 12.

4,738.   "Says Catholics Stir Religious Fight." New York
         Times. July 16, 1925, p. 22.

4,739.   "Says Klan Altered Its Incorporation." New York
         Times. August 14, 1923, p. 36.

4,740.   "Says Tammany 'Wets' Make Klan Members." New York
         Times. October 1, 1923, p. 9.

4,741.   "Says The Klan Is Neutral." New York Times.
         August 25, 1924, p. 2.

4,742.   "Says Women Here Flock To Join Klan." New York
         Times. September 13, 1921, p. 5.

4,743.   "Seek Cross Fire Clue." New York Times. December
         26, 1922, p. 3.

4,744.   "Seeks Injunction Against Ku Klux Klan." New York
         Times. July 25, 1923, p. 7.

4,745.   "Seeks Klansman's Arrest." New York Times. August
         5, 1924, p. 36.

4,746.   "Seeks To Force Klan To Reveal Members." New York
         Times. January 17, 1923, p. 8.

4,747.   "Seized Klan Wreath Ordered Replaced." New York
         Times. May 31, 1923, pp. 1, 10.

4,748. "Senator Means Not A Klansman, He Says." New York Times. February 24, 1927, p. 16.

4,749. "Sent To Workhouse After Ku Klux Row." New York Times. November 2, 1927, p. 2.

4,750. "Service For Klan Spoiled By Bottle." New York Times. September 7, 1936, p. 19.

4,751. "72 Klansmen Flee As Police Approach." New York Times. January 30, 1923, p. 21.

4,752. "Sherman Gets Order Restraining Klan." New York Times. August 22, 1923, p. 16.

4,753. "Sherman Is Said To Plan Court Fight On Klan For Violating Walker Law And Injunction." New York Times. August 28, 1924, p. 1.

4,754. "Shots At Klansmen Stir Binghamton." New York Times. July 6, 1924, p. 12.

4,755. "Signs Bill Forcing Klansmen Into Open." New York Times. May 24, 1923, p. 3.

4,756. "Silent On Klan Decision." New York Times. November 21, 1928, p. 35.

4,757. "Six Seized Planning Raid." New York Times. July 14, 1928, p. 5.

4,758. Smith, Baxter. "The Klan Rides At Naponoch." Militant. Vol. 39, January 24, 1975, p. 11; April 4, 1975, p. 24.

4,759. "Smith Assails Klan, But Would Be Just." New York Times. December 30, 1927, pp. 1, 7.

4,760. "Smith Carries Fight On Hylan To Queens; Mayor Answers Him In A Radio Speech; Craig Says Hylan Punished Labor Bank." New York Times. August 29, 1925, pp. 1, 2.

4,761. "Smith Opens Campaign Against Hylan; Says City Needs Mayor Of More Ability; Calls 5-Cent Fare Issue A Smoke Screen." New York Times. August 28, 1925, pp. 1, 2.

4,762. "Smith Shuns Klan As An Issue Here." New York Times. September 16, 1937, p. 14.

4,763. "Smith Tells Hearst To Keep Hands Off Democracy Here." New York Times. September 3, 1925, pp. 1, 3.

4,764. "Smith's Decision Is Due Next Week." New York Times. September 5, 1924, p. 3.

4,765. "Smith's State Aides Disagree Over Klan." New York Times. June 13, 1924, p. 17.

4,766. "Socialists Plan High School Work." New York Times. February 19, 1923, p. 32.

4,767. "Staley Enjoins The Ku Klux Klan Here From Acting As Chartered Fraternal Body." New York Times. August 15, 1923, p. 1.

4,768. "Startling The Villagers." New York Times. September 5, 1923, p. 14.

4,769. "Starts Nation-Wide Fight On Klan Here." New York Times. December 8, 1922, p. 19.

4,770. "State Assailed On Klan Ruling." New York Times. September 5, 1975, p. 33.

4,771. "State Head Defends Klan." New York Times. February 2, 1925, p. 2.

4,772. "State Klan Loses Jury Trial Chance." New York Times. September 11, 1923, p. 19.

4,773. "State Official Due For Quiz On Klan." New York Times. May 1, 1946, p. 52.

4,774. "State Officials Await Next Move By Klan." New York Times. August 16, 1923, p. 5.

4,775. "State Officials Fear New Anti-Klan Law May Fail To Force Publicity Of Membership." New York Times. June 9, 1923, p. 1.

4,776. "State Republicans Divided On The Klan." New York Times. September 24, 1924, p. 2.

4,777. "State To Intervene In Rothenberg Case." New York Times. December 12, 1923, p. 17.

4,778. "State Will Not Prosecute Ku Klux Klan; Attorney General Finds Walker Law Less Careful." New York Times. July 12, 1923, p. 1.

4,779. "Strife Splits Klan Of Ulster County." New York Times. January 2, 1926, p. 15.

4,780. "Such Men Really Should Go." New York Times. March 12, 1923, p. 14.

4,781. "Talley Invites Klan Here." New York Times. November 27, 1922, p. 2.

4,782. "Tammany Turns To Judicial Slate." New York Times. September 22, 1927, p. 9.

4,783.   "Tells Of Seizing Oath Of State Klan." New York
          Times. January 23, 1929, p. 3.

4,784.   "Tells Secret Rites Of Klan To Police." New York
          Times. February 2, 1923, p. 17.

4,785.   "10,000 At Klan Gathering." New York Times.
          September 2, 1930, p. 21.

4,786.   "10,000 Klansmen Burn Cross At Oceanside." New
          York Times. July 26, 1925, Sect. 2, p. 16.

4,787.   "Terrorism Charged To Liquor Runners." New York
          Times. May 30, 1924, p. 17.

4,788.   "A Terrible Blow At The Klan." New York Times.
          January 14, 1926, p. 24.

4,789.   "Text Of Governor Dewey's Campaign Address At
          Cooper Union Rally." New York Times. November 3,
          1946, p. 3.

4,790.   "Text Of Gov. Smith's Brooklyn Speech Supporting
          Senator Walker For Mayor." New York Times.
          August 28, 1925, pp. 1, 2.

4,791.   "Text Of The Oath Taken By 200 New Members Of The
          Ku Klux Klan Sworn In Near Buffalo." New York
          Times. May 28, 1923, p. 1.

4,792.   "There Are Klansmen In New York." New York Times.
          October 4, 1921, p. 14.

4,793.   "They Announce They Will Be Lawbreakers." New
          York Times. May 29, 1923, p. 14.

4,794.   "They Did Not Know Their Trade." New York Times.
          July 13, 1923, p. 14.

4,795.   "They Had No Law To Enforce." New York Times.
          December 13, 1922, p. 20.

4,796.   "3 Flaming Crosses Fired By The Ku Klux To
          Frighten Negroes In Long Island Towns." New York
          Times. February 13, 1923, p. 1.

4,797.   "3,500 Withdraw From Klan." New York Times.
          September 25, 1925, p. 21.

4,798.   "30,000 See Klan Parade." New York Times.
          September 21, 1924, p. 25.

4,799.   "Thomas Scores Roosevelt." New York Times.
          September 26, 1924, p. 7.

4,800.   "Thos. Dixon Repudiates Klan." New York Amsterdam
          News. January 24, 1923, pp. 1, 2.

4,801.   "Threatened By Klan." New York Times. August 20,
          1924, p. 20.

4,802.   "3 L.I. Youths Admit Forming Own 'Klan'." New York
          Times. January 30, 1957, p. 14.

4,803.   "3,000 At Klan Gathering." New York Times.
          May 22, 1925, p. 4.

4,804.   "3,000 At Klan Rally But Hear No Heflin." New
          York Times. July 5, 1928, p. 21.

4,805.   "To Bring Criminal Action Against Buffalo Klan
          Heads." New York Times. September 9, 1924, p. 1.

4,806.   "To Enforce Ku Klux Law In Suffolk." New York
          Times. May 29, 1923, p. 19.

4,807.   "To Name Klansmen Here." New York Times. January
          21, 1923, p. 20.

4,808   "To Oust Klansmen From City Payroll." New York
          Times. December 10, 1922, p. 7.

4,809.   "Told Not To Rent To Negroes By K.K.K." New York
          Times. July 13, 1923, p. 16.

4,810.   "Tolerance, Anti-Klan Organ, Appears Today." New
          York Times. January 13, 1923, p. 6.

4,811.   "Town Board Ousts Nyack Police Chief." New York
          Times. July 22, 1925, p. 4.

4,812.   "20,000 At Jubilee Of Klan Near ISLIP." New York
          Times. September 24, 1923, p. 4.

4,813.   "Two Boys, 13, Held In Klan 'Warnings'." New York
          Times. August 2, 1946, p. 21.

4,814.   "Two Freed In Ku Klux Klan Row." New York Times.
          October 6, 1923, p. 6.

4,815.   "Two Grand Juries To Sift Activities Of Ku Klux
          Here." New York Times. December 5, 1922, pp. 1,
          3.

4,816.   "2 Guilty In Klan Parade." New York Times.
          October 26, 1927, p. 2.

4,817.   "Two Held In Ku Klux Case." New York Times.
          August 27, 1922, p. 15.

4,818.   "Two Klansmen Held For Trial As Rioters." New
          York Times. October 25, 1923, p. 3.

4,819.   "Two Klansmen Killed In Quarrel In Buffalo." New
York Times. September 1, 1924, p. 3.

4,820.   "2 KKK-Related Incidents Reported In Copiague, New
York." New York Amsterdam News. July 11, 1981,
p. 3.

4,821.   "Two Paraders To Be Tried." New York Times. June
17, 1927, p. 26.

4,822.   "Two Things That Go Together." New York Times.
June 23, 1923, p. 10.

4,823.   "An Unappreciated Decoration." New York Times.
May 30, 1940, p. 16.

4,824.   "Unmasking Rites Here." New York Times. February
23, 1928, p. 2.

4,825.   "Unnamed Talks For Klan." New York Times. January
19, 1923, p. 8.

4,826.   "Upholds State Law, Ends Klan Secrecy." New York
Times. January 13, 1926, pp. 1, 13.

4,827.   "Upstate Klansmen Split." New York Times.
September 18, 1925, p. 28.

4,828.   "Urges Complaint By Klan." New York Times. June
4, 1927, p. 19.

4,829.   "Urges Klan To Lower Its Racial Barriers."
Pittsburgh Courier. July 14, 1923, p. 2.

4,830.   "USO Employs Klan Suspect, Fund Secretary Fired
By N.Y. State." Chicago Defender. November 9, 1946,
p. 2.

4,831.   "Vandals Strike In Nyack." New York Times. June
22, 1966, p. 35.

4,832.   "Vanguard Of Klan Enters Binghamton." New York
Times. July 4, 1924, p. 14.

4,833.   "Vassar Protesters Ask Rules Against Racist Acts."
New York Times. March 6, 1977, p. 53.

4,834.   "Wagner Denounces Klan." New York Times. September
14, 1937, p. 19.

4,835.   "Walker Insists Law On Klan Be Enforced." New
York Times. January 15, 1926, p. 4.

4,836.   "Walker Law Test Up In Supreme Court." New York
Times. October 5, 1926, p. 5.

4,837. "Walton Will Speak Here Soon On Klan." New York
        Times. August 28, 1924, p. 3.

4,838. "Want Smith To Run On Anti-Klan Plank." New York
        Times. July 25, 1924, pp. 1, 3.

4,839. "Wants No Queens Riot On Memorial Day." New York
        Times. May 9, 1928, p. 18.

4,840. "Wants Parade Allowed." New York Times. July 7,
        1927, p. 24.

4,841. "Warren Denies Klan Petition To Parade In Queens
        July 4." New York Times. June 18, 1927, p. 19.

4,842. "Warren Lifts Ban But Paraders Balk." New York
        Times. May 29, 1928, p. 27.

4,843. "Warren Refuses Permit For Parade." New York Times.
        May 20, 1928, p. 2.

4,844. "Warren Testifies In Klan Investigation." New York
        Times. July 21, 1927, p. 14.

4,845. "Westchester Klan Revives, Backs Nazis." New York
        Times. September 9, 1934, p. 5.

4,846. "Winchester Klan To Face Prosecution." New York
        Times. November 30, 1928, p. 20.

4,847. "Westchester Pastor Quits After Klan Row." New York
        Times. October 9, 1932, p. 19.

4,848. Wicker, Tom. "Catch-22 Behind Bars." New York
        Times. May 22, 1979, p. A19.

4,849. "Will Ask Annulment Of Klan's Charters." New
        York Times. September 20, 1923, p. 3.

4,850. "Will Move To Arrest Buffalo Klansmen." New York
        Times. September 18, 1924, p. 5.

4,851. "Will Permit Klan To Hold Meetings." New York
        Times. January 31, 1923, p. 15.

4,852. "Would Arm Against Klan." New York Times. January
        12, 1923, p. 10.

4,853. "Would Investigate Klan In This State." New York
        Times. January 16, 1924, p. 5.

4,854. "Wreath From Klan Is Again Removed." New York
        Times. June 1, 1923, p. 14.

4,855. "Writs For Klansmen." New York Times. July 27,
        1923, p. 12.

4,856.   Yaffe, Richard A. "N.Y. Outlaws Klan; 1100 Names
           To FBI." PM. July 30, 1946,

4,857.   "Yonkers Klan Cyclops Questioned By Police." New
           York Times. January 28, 1923, Sect. 1, Part 2, p. 5.

4,858.   "Yonkers Raiders Held." New York Times. July 15,
           1928, p. 4.

4,859.   Young, James C. "Torch Of The Ku Klux Burns Close
           To New York." New York Times. June 8, 1924,
           Sect. 8, p. 4.

4,860.   "Young Men Call Fiery Cross A Joke." New York
           Times. January 4, 1923, p. 13.

32. NORTH CAROLINA

4,861.   "Accused Of Taking Klan's Funds." New York Times.
           September 17, 1922, p. 17.

4,862.   "Achievement For Lawfulness." Christian Science
           Monitor. June 19, 1952, p. E4.

4,863.   "ACLU Criticizes Ban Of Maxton Klan Rally."
           Greensboro (N.C.) Daily News. March 21, 1966, p. 1.

4,864.   "ACLU Defense Of Nazi Party And KKK - Letters."
           Washington Post. January 14, 1981, p. 14A.

4,865.   "ACLU Says Klan Case Acts Ended." Greensboro
           (N.C.) Daily News. March 30, 1966, p. 1.

4,866.   "Acoustics Expert Traces Shot In Greensboro Case."
           New York Times. September 26, 1980, p. A12.

4,867.   "Acquittals In Greensboro, N.C. Slayings -
           Oliphant Cartoon." San Francisco Chronicle.
           November 24, 1980, p. 52.

4,868.   "Acquittals in N.C. Slayings." San Francisco
           Chronicle. November 19, 1980, p. 66.

4,869.   "Acquittals Of Klansmen And Nazis Protested In
           Greensboro, N.C." San Francisco Chronicle.
           November 21, 1980, p. 32.

4,870.   "Acquitted Klansman Exchanges Shots With Unknown
           Assailant." Forest City (N.C.) Daily Courier.
           November 20, 1980, p. 3.

4,871.   "Acquitted Klansman Exchanges Shots With An
           Unknown Gunman." New York Times. November 20,
           1980, p. A27.

4,872.   "Acquitted Klansman Is Target Of Shots." Washington
           Star. November 20, 1980, p. A3.

4,873.   " 'Active' Klan Membership In N.C. Viewed As
          'Dwindling'." Durham (N.C.) Morning Herald.
          December 24, 1969, p. B5.

4,874.   "Active Klan Units Buy Boss Cadillac." Raleigh
          (N.C.) News And Observer. October 12, 1965, p. 1.

4,875.   Adams, Hoover. "Attempt To Corrupt Juror Charged
          To N.C. Klan Trio." Raleigh (N.C.) News And
          Observer. June 22, 1966, p. 1.

4,876.   "Add: KKK Business In North Carolina." Greensboro
          (N.C.) Daily News. November 3, 1966, p. 1.

4,877.   Ader, Paul. "Capt. John Lea Tells Of Death In
          Court House." Durham (N.C.) Herald Sun. April
          21, 1941, p. 1.

4,878.   _____. "Caswell Night Riders... Lea Family
          Played Large Part Ku Klux Klan Affairs."
          Greensboro (N.C.) Daily News. April 20, 1941, p. 1.

4,879.   "After Klan Boycott, Business Normal." Charlotte
          (N.C.) Observer. November 15, 1966.

4,880.   "After Seven Days Deliberation Klansmen Cleared
          Of Murder Charges." (Fort Pierce, Fla.) Chronicle.
          November 20, 1980, pp. 1, 8.

4,881.   "Agent Says 6 Nazis Planned 'Week Of Terror'."
          New York Times. September 16, 1981, p A16.

4,882.   "Agitators Are Threat Feared In Klan Rally."
          New Bern (N.C.) Sun-Journal. August 13, 1966, p. 1.

4,883.   "All Equal Before The Law." Greensboro (N.C.)
          Daily News. November 22, 1966, p. 1.

4,884.   "All Quiet After Funeral March." New York Times.
          November 13, 1979, p. A18.

4,885.   "All Klan Data Given-Bruton." Greensboro (N.C.)
          Daily News. July 20, 1966, p. 1.

4,886.   "All-White Jury Acquits KKKs And Nazis." Norfolk
          (Va.) Journal & Guide. November 19, 1980, pp. 1,
          3.

4,887.   "All-White Jury Acquits KKK Members And 2 Nazis
          Of Murder In N.C." Los Angeles Times. November
          18, 1980, p. 1.

4,888.   "All-White Jury Frees Klansmen." California
          Advocate. November 21, 1980, pp. 1, 2.

4,889.   "All-White Jury Selected In Trial Of 6 Nazis In
Carolina Bomb Plot." New York Times. July 14,
1981, p. A23.

4,890.   "All-White Jury To Sit In KKK Trial In N.C." Jet.
Vol. 58, August 21, 1980, p. 28.

4,891.   "Alleged Klan Weapons Shown At Murder Trial."
Washington Star. August 7, 1980, p. A5.

4,892.   "Alleged Klansmen's Trial In Robeson Postponed By
Court." Durham (N.C.) Morning Herald. May 13,
1952, Sect. 2, p. 4.

4,893.   "Amendment Deadlocks Cross Bill." Raleigh (N.C.)
News & Observer. May 17, 1967, p. 3.

4,894.   "Analysis Of Shootings At Anti-Klan March In
Greensboro, N.C." Baltimore Afro-American.
November 17, 1979, p. 3.

4,895.   "Anderson Denies Data On N.C. Klan Withheld."
Durham (N.C.) Morning Herald. July 21, 1966, p. 1.

4,896.   Andrews, Simmons. "City Council Here Adopts
Ordinance Outlawing Masks." Raleigh (N.C.) News
And Observer. January 4, 1950, p. 1.

4,897.   "Anniversary Service Marks Deaths At Anti-Klan
Rally." New York Times. November 3, 1980, p. A20.

4,898.   "Another Attempt Is Aimed At Smashing KKK In State."
Durham (N.C.) Morning Herald. March 5, 1952, p. 1.

4,899.   "Another Columbus KKK Night Rider Granted Parole."
Durham (N.C.) Morning Herald. June 11, 1953, p. 5.

4,900.   "Another Klan Group Gets North Carolina Charter."
Raleigh (N.C.) News & Observer. July 30, 1965, p. 1.

4,901.   "Anson County Klan 'Defeats' Negro Sunday School
Class." Charlotte (N.C.) Observer. February 27,
1966, p. 1.

4,902.   "The Answer To Terror Was Death." Greensboro
(N.C.) Daily News. May 24, 1970, p. 1.

4,903.   "Anti-KKK Fight Shapes Up." Raleigh News &
Observer. August 17, 1955, p. 1.

4,904.   "Anti Klan Committees Organize." Black Scholar.
Vol. 11, November/December, 1979, pp. 81-82.

4,905.   "Anti-Klan Demonstrators March In Greesnboro, N.C."
New York Times. February 3, 1980, p. 22.

4,906.   "Anti-Klan Groups To March In N.C." Washington
          Post. November 11, 1979, p. 7A.

4,907.   "Anti-Klan, Nazi Action Urged." Washington Post.
          November 19, 1980, p. A8.

4,908.   "Anti-Klan Rally In N.C. Viewed." San Francisco
          Chronicle. November 11, 1979, p. 10.

4,909.   "Anti-Ku Klux Klan Demonstration In Greensboro,
          N.C. Viewed." Los Angeles Times. February 3,
          1980, p. 6.

4,910.   "Anti-Ku Klux Klan March In Greensboro, N.C.
          Noted." San Francisco Chronicle. February 3,
          1980, p. A2.

4,911.   "Apparently Moore Is Not Seeking Showdown." Daily
          Reflector. July 4, 1966, p. 1.

4,912.   "Appeals Of 7 Klansmen Argued In Federal Court."
          Durham (N.C.) Morning Herald. October 7, 1952,
          p. B4.

4,913.   "Appel Says Staff Got Most Data." Raleigh (N.C.)
          News & Observer. October 26, 1965, p. 1.

4,914.   Arisman, J. Michael. "Gathering Of The Klan."
          Commonweal. Vol. 82, June 11, 1965, pp. 373-374.

4,915.   "Arraignment Off In Klan Case." New York Times.
          June 6, 1980, p. 17.

4,916.   "Arson Probed In Church Used By Klan." The
          Independent. March 1, 1979, p. 1.

4,917.   "As Probers Produce Records, Reluctant Klan Dragon
          Mum." Daily Reflector. October 21, 1965, p. 1.

4,918.   "Assault Costs Klanswoman." Charlotte (N.C.)
          Observer. August 27, 1966, p. 1.

4,919.   "Assassination Of Carpetbagger In Courthouse At
          Yanceyville Occurred 100 Years Ago Today."
          The Danville (Va.) Bee. May 21, 1970, p. 1.

4,920.   "The Association Of Carolina Klans." Whitesville
          (N.C.) News Reporter. February 16, 1952, p. 1.

4,921.   "At Klan Fair Booth." Durham (N.C.) Morning
          Herald. October 15, 1966, p. 1.

4,922.   "Attend KKK Rally." Winston Salem (N.C.) Journal.
          October 6, 1966, p. 1.

4,923.   "Attorney Claims His Phone 'Bugged'." Raleigh
          (N.C.) News & Observer. July 19, 1969, p. 3.

4,924.   "Author Hits Klan Probe As Mistake." Raleigh (N.C.)
          News and Observer. October 21, 1965, p. 1.

4,925.   Babington, Charles. "Police At Scene Not Told Klan
          Was Approaching." Greensboro Daily News. November
          4, 1979, p. Al.

4,926.   "Back To Little Big Horn." Winston-Salem (N.C.)
          Journal. March 11, 1966, p. 1.

4,927.   "Bad Medicine For The Klan; Robeson County, N.C."
          Life. Vol. 44, January 27, 1958, pp. 26-28.

4,928..   "Baptist Group Hits Resurgence Of KKK." Raleigh
          News And Observer. October 29, 1965, p. 1.

4,929..   Barbash, Fred and Art Harris. "Klansmen, Nazis
          Found Not Guilty." Washington Post. November 18,
          1980, pp. Al, All.

4,930.   Barbour, Charles. "Court Blocks Robeson Klan
          Rally March 27." Durham Morning Herald. March
          18, 1966, p. 1.

4,931.   Barker, Karlyn. "3 Widows Of The Greensboro
          Marches Rage Against The Decision." Washington
          Post. November 19, 1980, p. A2.

4,932.   Barrington, Charles. "35 Arrested Carrying Guns."
          Greensboro Daily News. November 12, 1979, p. 1.

4,933.   Batten, James K. "All Southern Cast Closes Curtain
          On Klan Probe." Charlotte Observer. February 27,
          1966, p. 3B

4,934.   _____. "Once-Robust Klan Is Clearly Ailing."
          Charlotte Observer. February 27, 1966, p. 1.

4,935.   _____. "Seven Klan Chiefs Plead Not Guilty."
          Charlotte Observer. March 12, 1966, p. 1.

4,936.   "Begins Youth Drive Over State." Raleigh (N.C.)
          News & Observer. January 24, 1968, p. 3.

4,937.   "Behavior Of Klan's Guards Denounced By Gov.
          Moore." Winston-Salem Journal. August 4, 1966,
          p. 1.

4,938.   "Believes KKK Is 'Fair Game'." Daily Reflector.
          February 16, 1965, p. 1.

4,939.   Berry, Steve. "Jury Ponders Fate Of Klansmen,
          Nazis In Deaths Of 5 Communists." Washington
          Post. November 10, 1980, p. A21.

4,940.   Betts, Jack. "FBI Worker To Divide N.C. Klans?"
          Greensboro Daily News. December 6, 1975, p. 1.

4,941.   "Big Gains Scored By Carolina Klan." New York
          Times. September 6, 1964, p. 34.

4,942.   "Big Sign Causes Strife: Smithfield." Raleigh
          (N.C.) News & Observer. May 22, 1967, p. 24.

4,943.   "Birchers Are In, Klan Out." Raleigh (N.C.)
          News & Observer. September 23, 1967, p. 22.

4,944.   "Black Americans' New Fears." World Press Review.
          Vol. 28, August, 1981, pp. 21-23.

4,945.   "Black Leader Calls For Nazis, Klansmen Retrial."
          Jet. Vol. 59, December 4, 1980, p. 15.

4,946.   "Black Protestor Slain While Protecting Children
          At N.C. Anti-Klan Rally." Jet. Vol. 57, November
          2, 1979, pp. 6-7.

4,947.   "Blacks Criticize Carolina Verdict On 6 Klansmen."
          New York Times. November 19, 1980, p. A24.

4,948.   "Blacks Plan Klan Protest In Wilmington." Raleigh
          News & Observer. July 2, 1971, p. 9.

4,949.   "Blacks Shocked At Verdict Against Klansmen And
          Nazis." Miami (Fla.) Times. November 20, 1980,
          p. 1.

4,950.   "Blurred Emotions." Washington Star. November 21,
          1980, p. A12.

4,951.   "Bombs, Threats Kill Anson 'Freedom Of Choice'."
          Raleigh News & Observer. September 18, 1966, p. 1.

4,952.   "Bond Cut In Klan Chief Case." Winston-Salem
          (N.C.) Journal. March 16, 1966, p. 1.

4,953.   "Booth (KKK) Back At Johnston Fair." Raleigh
          (N.C.) News & Observer. October 5, 1967, p. 6.

4,954.   "Booth (KKK) Removed From Johnston County Fair."
          Raleigh (N.C.) News & Observer. October 4, 1967,
          p. 3.

4,955.   Boyd, Blanche McCrary. "Ambush: An Inquiry Into
          The Holy War In Greensboro." The Village Voice.
          Vol. 25, May 26, 1980.

4,956.   Brawley, James. "Klan Fighters Ambushed At
          Shober Bridge." The Salisbury (N.C.) Evening Post.
          March 8, 1970, p. 1.

4,957.   Braxton, Lee. "They Spoke Out For Decency."
          Rotarian. Vol. 83, September, 1953, pp. 29, 55-56.

4,958.   "Broughton: Klan Help Unsolicited." Raleigh News
          & Observer. April 24, 1968, p. 5.

4,959.   "Bruton Denies Klan Reports Under Cover." Raleigh
          News & Observer. July 20, 1966, p. 1.

4,960.   "Bruton Says All KKK Data Handed Group." Durham
          Morning Herald. July 20, 1966, p. 1.

4,961.   Bryant, Pat. "Justice vs. The Movement."
          Southern Exposure. Vol. 8, Summer, 1980, pp. 79-87.

4,962.   "Buck Passed And Lost." Raleigh News & Observer.
          December 13, 1967, p. 4.

4,963.   "A Burning Problem." New York Times. October 31,
          1957, p. 9.

4,964.   Burton, W.C. "Ex-Member Of Klan Gets $100 Fine."
          Greensboro (N.C.) Daily News. March 19, 1966, p. 1.

4,965.   _____. "The Klan Killed Him In The County
          Courthouse." Greensboro (N.C.) Daily News. May
          24, 1970, p. 1.

4,966.   "A Busy Weekend." Greensboro Daily News. August
          2, 1966, p. 1.

4,967.   "Cameraman Testifies." Washington Post. August
          23, 1980, p. C1.

4,968.   Campbell, Kenneth. "Many Who Watched Marchers Just
          Curious, Not Sympathetic." Greensboro Daily News.
          November 12, 1979.

4,969.   "Candidate Is Silent On Klan Question." Charlotte
          Observer. April 30, 1966.

4,970.   "Candidates Affiliated With Klan Don't Fare Well
          In Primary." Raleigh News & Observer. May 30,
          1966, p. 1.

4,971.   "Card-Carrying Klansman Faces Shooting Case."
          New Bern (N.C.) Sun Journal. July 9, 1966,

4,972.   "Carolina Governor Asks Drinking Law And Curbs On
          Klan." New York Times. February 10, 1967, p. 18.

4,973.   "Carolina Governor Seeks Meeting." New York Times.
          November 25, 1980, p. A12.

4,974.   "Carolina Klan Aide Shot Dead At Home." New York
          Times. December 13, 1965, p. 48.

4,975.   "Carolina Klan Chief Accused Of Perjury In Divorce
          Trial." New York Times. January 13, 1966, p. 13.

4,976.   "Carolina Klan Exhibit Called A White Version Of
          'Roots'." New York Times. February 24, 1979, p. 8.

4,977.   "Carolina Klan Yields In A Sign Feud." New York
          Times. July 6, 1969, p. 35.

4,978.   "Carolina Revokes Charter Of KKK." Afro-American.
          July 2, 1949, p. 3.

4,979.   Carr, Jim. "Carnival-Like Atmosphere Pervades Ku
          Klux Klan Meet." Durham (N.C.) Morning Herald.
          October 3, 1966, p. 1.

4,980.   _____. "Guards For Klan Rally Eject 5 Duke
          Students." Durham (N.C.) Morning Herald. October
          3, 1966, p. 1.

4,981.   Carr, Sonny and Baldwin Renner. "Klansmen Hold
          Rally Under Police Guard." Raleigh News &
          Observer. November 7, 1966, p. 1.

4,982.   Carroll, Ginny. Communists, Klan Familiar Bitter
          Enemies." Raleigh News And Observer. November
          11, 1979, p. 1.

4,983.   Carter, Sanders. "Two Klansmen Convicted For
          'Conspiracy'." New (N.C.) Bern Sun Journal. July
          9, 1966.

4,984.   "Cases Against 4 Alleged Klansmen Are Dismissed."
          Durham (N.C.) Morning Herald. March 9, 1952, p. 1.

4,985.   "Cases Against Four Men." New York Times.
          March 9, 1952, p. 19.

4,986.   Cassels, Felicia M. "Not Guilty Verdict For Klans-
          men Draws Protest." Carolina (Durham) Times.
          November 22, 1980, p. 1, 6.

4,987.   "Catfish Cole Might Change Complexion of N.C. Klan."
          Raleigh News & Observer. March 30, 1967, p. 1.

4,988.   " 'Catfish' Cole Quits Klan Job." Charlotte (N.C.)
          Observer. July 12, 1966, p. 1.

4,989.   "Catfish Will Stick With Ku Klux Klan." Raleigh
          News & Observer. March 15, 1958, p. 1.

4,990.   "The Cautious Approach Can Hurt." Durham (N.C.)
          Morning Herald. August 5, 1966, p. 1.

4,991.   "Chaplain: Klan's Aim Is To Block Out Reds."
          Raleigh News & Observer. July 17, 1965, p. 1.

4,992.   "Chaplain Of N.C. Klan." New York Times. September 22, 1966, p. 54.

4,993.   Chapman, G.C. "Cold Night, Harassment For Kluxers." Daily Reflector. January 19, 1966, p. 1.

4,994.   _____. "2 Pitt Kluxers Arrested Sunday Demonstrating." Daily Reflector. March 5, 1966, p. 1.

4,995.   "Charges Dropped Against 16 In KKK In Greensboro, N.C. Shootings." Houston Post. November 27, 1980, p. 12A.

4,996.   "Charlotte Chief Pledges To Fight Klan." Raleigh News & Observer. December 10, 1949, p. 1.

4,997.   "Chief Klan Investigator Quits In North Carolina." New York Times. June 25, 1966, p. 16.

4,998.   "Chief Of Police Waives Hearing On 'Challenge'." Daily Reflector. March 29, 1966.

4,999.   "Chiefs Deny Ouster: Shelton Jones." Raleigh News & Observer. June 9, 1967, p. 1.

5,000.   "Churchmen To Serve Klan Dinner." Raleigh News & Observer. September 23, 1965.

5,001.   "Cities Brace For Verdict In Klan Case." Charlotte (N.C.) Observer. November 12, 1980, p. B1.

5,002.   "Cities Must Carry Load, Says Britt." Raleigh News & Observer. October 23, 1966.

5,003.   "City Manager Supports Lawson." Daily Reflector. March 30, 1966.

5,004.   "Civic Club To Hear Klan Chief And Foe." Greensboro Daily News. November 4, 1966, p. B9.

5,005.   "Civil Rights Leaders Call For Fed. Probe Of N.C. Rally Murders." Houston Post. November 5, 1979, p. A25.

5,006.   "Civil Rights Leaders Seek U.S. Action In N.C.-KKK- Nazi Case." Chicago Tribune. November 19, 1980, p. 2.

5,007.   "Civil Rights Leaders Urge U.S. Action In N.C. Slayings." San Francisco Chronicle. November 19, 1980, p. 2.

5,008.   "Claims Challenge." Daily Reflector. March 28, 1966.

5,009.   Clark, Robin. "A City Of Fear, Anger And Appre-
hension." Charlotte (N.C.) Observer. November 19,
1980, p. 10A.

5,010.   "Class Struggle Said Cause For Shooting In Anti-
KKK Rally." New Orleans Times Picayune. November
5, 1979, p. 13.

5,011.   Clay, Charles. "Seawell, Moore Collide Over
Status Of Klan." Fayetteville Observer. June
10, 1966.

5,012.   Clay, Russell. "Hodges Ties Goldwaterism To Klan
Rise." Raleigh News & Observer. October 31, 1965.

5,013.   _____. "Injunction Bars Klan From Robeson
Rally." Raleigh News & Observer. March 18, 1966.

5,014.   _____. "Klan Prober Quits, Cites Secrecy In
SBI." Raliegh News & Observer. July 26, 1966.

5,015.   _____. "Moore Puts Klan Strength At 618."
Raleigh News & Observer. October 29, 1965.

5,016.   _____. "No Action Against Klan." Raleigh
News & Observer. June 7, 1966.

5,017.   _____. "No Case Exists For Taking Klan Charter."
Raleigh News & Observer. July 1, 1966.

5,018.   _____. "Seawell Blasts Klan." Raleigh News &
Observer. January 22, 1966.

5,019.   _____. "Seawell Building 'Case' For Eure."
Raleigh News & Observer. May 5, 1966.

5,020.   _____. "State Decides No Case Exists For Taking
Klan Charter." Raleigh News & Observer. July, 1, 1966.

5,021.   _____. "State Not Deciding Yet On Klan
Legality." Raleigh News & Observer. June 11, 1966.

5,022.   _____. "State Plans Injunction Against Klan."
Raleigh News & Observer. March 17, 1966.

5,023.   _____. "Tar Heels Reject State's Label of No.
I For Klan." Raleigh News & Observer. October
24, 1965.

5,024.   _____. "Terry Hurls A Warning At The Klan."
Raleigh News & Observer. June 23, 1964.

5,025.   Clay, William. "The Greensboro Decision: A
National Tragedy." Florida (Jacksonville) Star.
December 6-12, 1980, p. 2.

5,026.   "Cleric Group Brands Klan As Un-American." Raleigh
          News & Observer. May 12, 1965.

5,027.   "Closing Arguments Begin In Trial Of 6 Klansmen
          Accused In 5 Deaths." New York Times. October
          28, 1980, p. A20.

5,028.   Clotfelter, Jim. "KKK Asks Trading Stamps To
          Get Plane For Leaders." Durham Morning Herald.
          July 23, 1965.

5,029.   _____. "Over Klan Name, Technical Tangle."
          Durham Morning Herald. June 27, 1965.

5,030.   Cohen, Richard. "Justice In The Streets: A Victory
          For Lunacy." Washington Post. November 27, 1980,
          p. B1, B9.

5,031.   Cole, Willard G. "Hamilton Gets Four Years In
          Ku Klux Klan Conspiracy." Raleigh News & Observer.
          July 31, 1952.

5,032.   _____. "Klan Trials Move Near End." Raleigh
          News & Observer. July 26, 1952.

5,033.   _____. "Klan Trio Freed; Sentences Today."
          Raleigh News & Observer. July 29, 1952.

5,034.   _____. "Man Hears Guilty Verdict In Columbus
          Flogging Case." Raleigh News & Observer. July 25,
          1952.

5,035.   _____. "Members Of Klan Empire Will Hear
          Sentence Today." Raleigh News & Observer. July
          30, 1952.

5,036.   "Cole Fights Return To N.C. On Inciting - Riot
          Charges." Asheville (N.C.) Citizen. January 23,
          1958.

5,037.   Coleman, Milton. "Thousands In Greensboro Con-
          demn Klan." Washington Post. February 3, 1980,
          p. A5.

5,038.   "Columbus Flogging Trials May Be Ended Tomorrow."
          Durham Morning Herald. July 27, 1952, Sect. 3,
          p. 11.

5,039.   "Columbus Jury Indicts Accused Ex-Klansmen On
          Charges Of Flogging." Durham Morning Herald.
          April 2, 1952, p. 1.

5,040.   "Columbus Jury Indicts Hamilton; 50 More Facing
          Flogging Arrests." Raleigh News & Observer.
          June 20, 1952.

5,041.   "Columbus Klan Trial Jury Recesses Without Action."
          Durham Morning Herald. April 1, 1952, p. 1.

5,042.   "Columbus Klan Trials Put Off Until Monday."
          Durham Morning Herald. April 30, 1952, p. 1.

5,043.   "Comment On Klan 'Evasive'." Virginian Pilot.
          July 23, 1966.

5,044.   "Committee Says KKK Needs Money." New Bern Sun-
          Journal. April 2, 1966.

5,045.   "Communist Cited At N.C. Klan Trial." Washington
          Post. August 30, 1980, p. A25.

5,046.   "Communist Workers Party Buries 5 Members In
          Greensboro, N.C." Los Angeles Times. November 12,
          1979, p. 1.

5,047.   "Communist Workers Party On Death In Greensboro,
          N.C. - Letter." Baltimore Afro-American.
          November 24, 1979, p. 4.

5,048.   "Communist Workers Party View On Ct. Verdict."
          Chicago Tribune. November 21, 1980, p. 1.

5,049.   "Communists And Anti-Klan Protestors March Through
          N.C. Town." Washington Post. November 12, 1979,
          p. 26A.

5,050.   "Communists And Police Clash Outside N.C. Trial."
          Christian Science Monitor. June 17, 1980, p. 2.

5,051.   "Communists Hold Memorial For 5 Killed In Gunfight
          In N.C." Houston Post. November 3, 1980, p. 24A.

5,052.   "Confederate Knights Formed By Dorsett." Durham
          Morning Herald. August 23, 1967.

5,053.   Connor, R.D.W. "Ku Klux Klan And Its Operations
          In North Carolina." North Carolina University
          Magazine. Vol. 30, April, 1900, pp. 224-234.

5,054.   _____. "The Ku Klux Klan And Its Operations In
          North Carolina. North Carolina University Maga-
          zine. New Series, Vol. 17, 1960, pp. 224-234.

5,055.   "Continuing Probe Of Crash In Guilford County."
          Raleigh News & Observer. July 30, 1967, p. 13.

5,056.   "Convictions Of KKK Members Upheld." Durham
          (N.C.) Morning Herald. October 4, 1952, p. 3.

5,057.   Cooper, David. "Governor Denies SBI Withheld
          Information About Ku Klux Klan." Winston-Salem
          Journal. July 27, 1966.

5,058.   _____. "Klan Plans Upset Robeson." Winston-
          Salem Journal. March 15, 1966.

5,059.   _____. "Leaflets Linked To Klan." Winston-
          Salem Journal. November 8, 1966.

5,060.   _____. "N.C.'s Attempt To Block Rally Unique
          In History Of Klan." Winston-Salem Journal.
          March 18, 1966.

5,061.   _____. "Opinion Of Officials Differs On Klan
          Files." Winston-Salem Journal. July 20, 1966.

5,062.   _____. "Ruckus History Of Klan Files And SBI
          Is Study In Confusion." Winston-Salem Journal.
          July 29, 1966.

5,063.   _____. "Seawell Says Klan Rally Site Unwise."
          Winston-Salem Journal. March 10, 1966.

5,064.   _____. "State May Ban Fair Booth Of Klan,
          Others." Winston-Salem Journal. October 26, 1966.

5,065.   _____. "The State Moves Against The Klan's
          Rally In Robeson." Winston-Salem Journal.
          March 18, 1966.

5,066.   _____. "State To Ask Court To Halt Klan Rally."
          Winston-Salem Journal. March 17, 1966.

5,067.   _____. "Students Taunt Klansmen In Parade At
          Durham." Winston-Salem Journal. April 25, 1965,
          p. 1.

5,068.   "Copying Father." New York Times. April 21, 1980,
          p. 14.

5,069.   " 'Cornfield' Image Of Klan Said Gone." Durham
          Morning Herald. January 20, 1970.

5,070.   "A Correction." New York Times. January 21, 1952,
          p. 10.

5,071.   "Costly Practice." Raleigh News & Observer. March
          27, 1966.

5,072.   "Court Bars A Klan Rally." New York Times. March
          18, 1966, p. 22.

5,073.   "Court Finds Klanswoman Guilty." Greensboro Daily
          News. August 27, 1966.

5,074. "Court Order Blocks Klan Maxton Rally." New Bern Sun. March 18, 1966.

5,075. "Court Order Delays A Klan Rally In Robeson." Daily Reflector. March 18, 1966.

5,076. "Court Ruling Due Tomorrow On KKK Cases." Durham Morning Herald. May 4, 1952, p. 1.

5,077. "Court Says Klan Has Right To Stage Rally In Robeson." Greensboro Daily News. April 19, 1966.

5,078. "Court To Hear Final Pleas In Klan Trial." Washington Star. October 26, 1980, p. A8.

5,079. Covington, Howard. "N.C. Klans Break Ties With Parent." Charlotte Observer. September 9, 1969.

5,080. Cowan, Allen and Lee Weisbecker. "3 Haunting Gunshots In Greensboro." Charlotte (N.C.) Observer. November 19, 1980, pp. A1, A9.

5,081. "Crackdown On Klan State's Biggest Story During '52." Durham (N.C.) Morning Herald. December 31, 1952, p. 1.

5,082. "Cracking Down On Klan." Christian Science Monitor. January 13, 1966, p. 1.

5,083. Craven, Charles. "Jury Convicts Cole In Lumberton Trial." Raleigh News & Observer. March 14, 1958.

5,084. _____. "Klansmen Face Johnston Trial." Raleigh News & Observer. June 23, 1966.

5,085. _____. "Memories Of Klan Rout Hangs Over Peaceful Robeson Field." Raleigh News & Observer. March 20, 1966.

5,086. _____. "Rift Growing In N.C. Klan." Raleigh News & Observer. April 25, 1967.

5,087. _____. "Robeson County Indiana Uprising Against The KKK." South Atlantic Quarterly. Vol. 57, Fall, 1958, pp. 433-442.

5,088. _____. "Seawell: Color Is Not A Factor." Raleigh News & Observer. March 27, 1966.

5,089. _____. "3 Admit Cross-Burning In Wake." Raleigh News & Observer. February 22, 1952.

5,090. _____. "Vanceboro Store Visit Recalled." Raleigh News & Observer. January 30, 1965.

5,091.   "Criminal Justice And The Klan." Miami Times.
          November 20, 1980, p. 4.

5,092.   "Cripple Tells How Klan Bounced Him." Charlotte
          Observer. July 13, 1966.

5,093.   "Crippled Man Not To Press Klan Charges." New
          Bern Sun Journal. July 13, 1966.

5,094.   "Cross Burned At Editor's Home." Daily Reflector.
          April 12, 1965.

5,095.   "Cross Burned In Pembroke Area." Daily Reflector.
          March 17, 1966.

5,096.   "Cross-Burning Action 'Interests' Governor."
          Raleigh News & Observer. December 9, 1966.

5,097.   "Cross-Burning, Arson Attempt." Daily Reflector.
          October 13, 1966.

5,098.   "Cross Fires Reported." Raleigh News & Observer.
          May 29, 1964.

5,099.   "Cross Is Burned In Minister's Yard." Charlotte
          Observer. April 19, 1966.

5,100.   "Cross Is Burned In Moore, Robeson Case Said
          Prank." Durham Morning Herald. March 11, 1952,
          p. 1.

5,101.   "Crossburners Ordered To Begin Jail Terms."
          Raleigh News & Observer. September 23, 1967,
          p. 22.

5,102.   "Crosses Are Burned In Eastern N.C." Daily
          Reflector. May 29, 1964.

5,103.   "Crosses Burned Last Night In Simpson Area."
          Daily Reflector. April 13, 1966.

5,104.   "Crowds Jeer In Raleigh As Negroes Meet." New
          Bern Sun Journal. August 15, 1966.

5,105.   "Cumberland County Invaded By Night Riders; Tenant
          Family Abandon Home." Durham Morning Herald.
          February 21, 1952, Sect. 1, p. 1.

5,106.   Cunningham, Dwight F. "Residents Pleading Keep
          Radicals Out." Greensboro Daily News. November
          7, 1979.

5.107.   "Curb On Klan Pickets Sought." Durham Morning
          Herald. March 24, 1966.

5,108.   "Curbing The Klan." Winston-Salem Journal.
          August 13, 1966.

5,109.   "Curious Eye Klan In March." Raleigh News &
          Observer. April 25, 1965.

5,110.   "CWP Renews Claim That Government Planned Killings."
          Charlotte (N.C.) Observer. November 18, 1980, p.
          3A.

5,111.   "Cyclops Of Klan Is Jailed Again." Raleigh News
          & Observer. December 15, 1965.

5,112.   "Dan Calls Klan 'Sorry' Outfit." Raleigh News &
          Observer. October 26, 1966.

5,113.   Daniels, Lee A. "Party Behind Anti-Klan Protest
          Sees Government Role In Deaths." New York Times.
          November 5, 1979, p. B13.

5,114.   "A Dare That Ignited A Slaughter." Time. Vol.
          115, June 30, 1980, p. 25.

5,115.   "Death Of Suspected Kluxer May Be Suicide." Daily
          Reflector. December 13, 1965.

5,116.   "Deaths At Anti-Klan Rally In Greensboro, N.C."
          Bilalian News. November 23, 1979, p. 2.

5,117.   "Deaths At Anti-KKK Rally In Greensboro, N.C.."
          New York Amsterdam News. November 10, 1979, p. 16.

5,118.   "Deaths During Anti-Klan March In Greensboro, N.C."
          Baltimore Afro-American. November 17, 1979, p. 4.

5,119.   "Delegates To N.C. NAACP Convention Hit 'Black
          Power'." Durham Morning Herald. October 17,
          1966.

5,120.   "Democrats Make Best Of Touchy Situation." Greens-
          boro Daily News. October 1, 1966.

5,121.   "Demonstration At Anti-KKK Marchers N.C. Funerals."
          New York Amsterdam News. November 17, 1979, p.1.

5,122.   "Demonstrators Scuffle With Police At Klan Nazi
          Trial In N.C." San Francisco Chronicle. June 17,
          1980, p. 5.

5,123.   "Developments In Aftermath Of Greensboro, N.C.
          Rally Deaths." Atlanta Daily World. November 18,
          1979, p. 1.

5,124.   "Developments Move Swiftly As State Acts To Begin
          Flogging Trial Today." Durham Morning Herald.
          May 6, 1952, p. 1.

5.125.   "Did Klan Boss Break North Carolina Law." Raleigh
          News & Observer. October 21, 1965.

5,126.   "The Director's Corner...From Salisbury To Greens-
          boro: A Tale Of Two Cities." IFCO News. (In-
          terreligious Foundation For Community Organization).
          Vol. 7, April, 1980, p. 2.

5,127.   "Dismissal In Klan Case Weighed." New York Times.
          February 10, 1980, p. 30

5,128.   "Disputes Built Up To Confrontation." Charlotte
          (N.C.) Observer. November 18, 1980, p. 6A.

5,129.   "Dissension Riddles Klan In Carolina." Raleigh News
          & Observer. September 18, 1969, p. 1.

5,130.   "Doing A Grand Job." Raleigh News & Observer.
          July 26, 1952.

5,131.   "Don't Link NAACP, Ku Klux Klan." Charlotte
          Observer. November 30, 1966.

5,132.   "Dorsett Sees Split In Klan." Raleigh News &
          Observer. April 2, 1967.

5,133.   Doster, Joe. "Democrats Attack Leaflets On Race."
          Charlotte Observer. November 8, 1966.

5,134.   "Dr. King And Klan Both To Appear In Raleigh
          Saturday." Durham Morning Herald. July 27, 1966.

5,135.   "Dragon Afraid He'll Lose Driving Rights." Raleigh
          News & Observer. November 24, 1965.

5,136.   "Dragon: Hard-Core Klan Tops Genuine Democracy."
          Raleigh News & Observer. September 23, 1966.

5,137.   "Dragon Jones Goes To Jail." Raleigh News & Ob-
          server. March 25, 1969, p. 1.

5,138.   "Dragon Loses License." Raleigh News & Observer.
          December 8, 1965.

5,139.   "Dragon Says Klan Had No Role In Boycott Of Store."
          Durham Morning Herald. November 1, 1966.

5,140.   "Dragons Get 1 Year Sentences." Raleigh News &
          Observer. March 15, 1969, p. 1.

5,141.   "Drama Of 1870: 'Chicken' Stephens Executed By
          Klan." Greensboro Daily News. May 24, 1970.

5,142.   "Duel Challenge Charge Faces Greenville Chief."
          Greensboro Daily News. March 30, 1966.

5,143.   "Duel Offer Is Charged." Greensboro Daily News.
          March 29, 1966.

5,144. "Dueling Trial Is Ended In Non-Suit." New Bern Sun-Journal. April 16, 1966.

5,145. "Duke Students Join Klansman In Protest." Raleigh News & Observer. April 24, 1968, p. 28.

5,146. "Duke Students Seek Relief From Abuse At Klan Rally." Winston Salem Journal. October 4, 1966.

5,147. Dunn, Mamie. " 'Fighting For White Rights'." Durham Morning Herald. December 29, 1974.

5,148. _____. "A Gathering Of The Klan." Durham Morning Herald. December 29, 1974.

5,149. _____. "The Klan: A History of Fear And Prejudice." Durham Morning Herald. December 29, 1974.

5,150. "Dunn Ministers In Klan Protest." Raleigh News & Observer. May 21, 1965.

5,151. Dunnigan, Alice A. "Nothing New About Klan-Indian Clashes." Pittsburgh Courier. March 1, 1958, p. 7.

5,152. "Durham KKK Offers Reward In Bombing." Raleigh News & Observer. June 24, 1970, p. 9.

5,153. "Edenton Termed By Klan Leader As 'Klansville'." Durham Morning Herald. March 12, 1966.

5,154. "Eight Indicted On Riot Charges In Violence At Anti-Klan Rally." Washington Star. May 3, 1980, p. A4.

5,155. "Eight Klansmen Acquitted In Intimidation Trial." Raleigh News & Observer. January 20, 1968, p. 1.

5,156. "8 More Indicted In Carolina In Deaths At Anti-Klan Rally." New York Times. May 3, 1980, p. 8.

5,157. "Eight More Indicted In Greensboro." Washington Post. May 3, 1980, p. B7.

5,158. "11 Ex-Klansmen Arrested In Another Major Blow At Night Riders In N.C.; 15 Arrested In Robeson, Klan Membership Cited." Durham Morning Herald. February 28, 1952, p. 1.

5,159. "Eleven More Arrested In Carolina Terrorism." New York Times. February 28, 1952, p. 28.

5,160. Ellis, C.P. and Studs Terkel. " 'Why I Quit The Klan'." Southern Exposure. Vol. 8, Summer, 1980, pp. 95-100.

5,161.   "Elm City Action Of Klan Scored By Presbyterians."
          Durham Morning Herald. June 26, 1964, Sect. D, p. 6.

5,162.   "Elm City Board Blasts Klan." Durham Morning Herald.
          June 24, 1964, p. 12.

5.163.   "ENC Klan Rally Ends In Shootout." Asheville
          Citizen-Times. July 6, 1969.

5,164.   "End Of The Klan." Raleigh News & Observer. May
          12, 1952.

5,165.   Erwin, Kate. "Baptists May Flay Klansmen."
          Raleigh News & Observer. November 16, 1965.

5,166.   _____. "Coach: No Civil Rights In Football."
          Raleigh News & Observer. September 18, 1966.

5,167.   _____. "Tar Heel Baptist Resolution Blasts
          Klan." Raleigh News & Observer. November 17,
          1965.

5,168.   "Eure Disputes Case Of Klan." Greensboro Daily
          News. September 27, 1966.

5,169.   Evans, Rowland and Robert Novak. "A Test For 'Black
          Power'." Greensboro Daily News. August 8, 1966.

5,170.   "Events Leading To Killings At The Anti-KKK Rally
          In N.C. Eyed." San Francisco Chronicle. November
          5, 1979, p. 1.

5,171.   "Evidence Deceptive - Moore." Raleigh News &
          Observer. October 22, 1965.

5,172.   "Evidence In 3 More Klan Cases Heard In Columbus
          Court." Durham Morning Herald. July 26, 1952,
          p. 7.

5,173.   Ewing, Cortez A.M. "Two Reconstruction Impeach-
          ments." North Carolina Historical Review. Vol.
          15, July 1938, pp. 204-230.

5,174.   "Ex-Deputy Cites Klan Activities." Raleigh News
          & Observer. October 2, 1968, p. 3.

5,175.   "Ex-Exalted Cyclops Tells Of Threats By Klan Group."
          Raleigh News & Observer. August 13, 1966.

5,176.   "Ex-KKK Man Gets Threats." Raleigh News &
          Observer. October 14, 1965.

5,177.   "Ex-Klansman Candidate In Jail." Charlotte
          Observer. May 7, 1966.

5,178.   "Ex-Wizard Disowns Klan; Urges It Be Disbanded."
          New York Times. October 23, 1953, p. 16.

5,179. "Explosions Shake New Bern Peace." _Daily Reflector_.
        January 25, 1965.

5,180. "Extra Officers On Duty In Terror-Ridden Surry."
        Durham (N.C.) Morning Herald. March 4, 1952, p. 1.

5,181. "Extra Police Duty Slated In Wilmington." _Raleigh
        News & Observer_. July 3, 1971, p. 17.

5,182. "Fair Bluff Man Is Under $5,000 Bond On Flogging
        Count." _Durham Morning Herald_. April 11, 1952,
        p. 2.

5,183. Fairlie, Henry. "An Englishman Goes To A Klan
        Meeting." _N.Y. Times Magazine_. May 23, 1965, pp.
        26-27, 83-85.

5,184. Falk, Lawrence. "Klan Linen Gets Public Airing."
        Raleigh News & Observer. June 18, 1967.

5,185. "The Fallout From Greensboro." _New York Times_.
        November 20, 1980, p. A34.

5,186. "Fast Dragon May Lose License For 60 Days."
        Raleigh News & Observer. November 27, 1965.

5,187. "FBI Accuses 13 Of Flogging." _Christian Science
        Monitor_. November 17, 1953, p. 12.

5,188. "FBI Action Curbs KKK." _Christian Science Monitor_.
        February 25, 1952, p. 7.

5,189. "FBI Agent Tells Of Klan's Terror." _Raleigh News
        & Observer_. January 17, 1968, p. 3.

5,190. "FBI Agent Brands Purported KKK Letter Here A
        Fake." _Durham Morning Herald_. March 4, 1952,
        Sect. 2, p. 1.

5,191. "FBI Arrests 10 Ex-Tarheel Klansmen On Charge Of
        Kidnapping, Flogging." _Durham Morning Herald_.
        February 17, 1952, Sect. 1, p. 1.

5,192. "FBI Ordered To Probe Klan Shooting Of Blacks
        After Acquittal." _San Francisco Chronicle_. July
        24, 1980, p. 5.

5,193. "FBI Sees Tapes Of Anti-Klan Rally." _Christian
        Science Monitor_. November 5, 1979, p. 2.

5,194. "FBI Team Dispatched To Probe Shootout." _Raleigh
        News & Observer_. November 6, 1979.

5,195. "Fed. Action Sought Against 6 In KKK Acquittal
        Of Murders In N.C." _Houston Post_. November 19,
        1980, p. 1B.

5,196.   "Fed. Judge Declares Mistrial In Alleged Nazi Bomb
          Plot In N.C." New Orleans Times Picayune. July
          19, 1981, p. 32.

5,197.   "Federal Charges Possible." Forest City (N.C.)
          Daily Courier. November 18, 1980, p. 7.

5,198.   "Federal Court Names KKK Jurors." Raleigh News &
          Observer. May 2, 1952.

5,199.   "Federal Trial Of 11 Accused Klansmen Will Open
          Tomorrow." Durham Morning Herald. May 11, 1952,
          p. 1.

5,200.   "Feud Between KKK And Communist Workers Party In
          N.C." Chicago Defender. November 10, 1979, p. 5.

5,201.   "Fiery Cross Burned At High Point." Raleigh News
          & Observer. March 20, 1947.

5,202.   "5th Flogging In Columbus Reported; Fear Is Riding
          The Night." Durham Morning Herald. January 17,
          1952, p. 1.

5,203.   "A Fifth Person Died." Wall Street Journal.
          November 6, 1979, p. 1.

5,204.   "5th Person Dies From Shooting At N.C. Anti-Klan
          Rally." Washington Post. November 6, 1979,
          p. 8A.

5,205.   "5th Victim Of Klan Dies Of Wounds From Weekend
          Shooting In N.C." San Francisco Chronicle.
          November 6, 1979, p. 3.

5,206.   "15th Man Is Held In Rally Deaths; 4 Other Suspects
          On Bond." New York Times. November 16, 1979, p.
          A9.

5,207.   "50 More May Be Cited In Nightriding Terrorism."
          Durham Morning Herald. June 20, 1952, p. 1.

5,208.   "Final Arguments." New York Times. November 1,
          1980, p. 12.

5,209.   "Final Arguments Tomorrow In Klansmen's Murder
          Trial." New York Times. October 27, 1980, p. A16.

5,210.   "Final Klan Trial Arguments Start; Carolina City
          Is Bracing For Verdict." New York Times. November
          4, 1980, p. A16.

5,211.   "Final Witness In Klan Probe To Be Stoner."
          Greensboro Daily News. February 23, 1966.

5,212.   "Finish The Job!" <u>Raleigh News & Observer</u>. May 14, 1952.

5,213.   "5 In Klan Charged In Dynamite Plot." <u>New York Times</u>. February 22, 1958, p. 32.

5,214.   "5 Killed And 9 Wounded At Anti-KKK Rally In Greensboro, N.C." <u>Atlanta Daily World</u>. November 6, 1979, p. 1.

5,215.   "Five Klansmen Given Cross-Burning Terms." <u>Raleigh News & Observer</u>. July 1, 1967, p. 1.

5,216.   "Five Klansmen Jailed For School Bomb Plot." <u>Raleigh News & Observer</u>. February 17, 1958.

5,217.   "Five Receive Terms In Klan Hut Burning." <u>Raleigh News & Observer</u>. October 23, 1968, p. 3.

5,218.   "Five Waive Hearing In Klan Hall Fire." <u>Raleigh News & Observer</u>. April 20, 1968, p. 3.

5,219.   "Flogging Arrests Rise." <u>New York Times</u>. April 24, 1952, p. 13.

5,220.   "A Flogging For The Klan." <u>Time</u>. Vol. 60, August 11, 1952, p. 21.

5,221.   "Flogging Hearing Delayed." <u>New York Times</u>. February 26, 1952, p. 14.

5,222.   "Flogging Jury Selected." <u>New York Times</u>. May 8, 1952, p. 28.

5,223.   "Flogging Victim Says He Was Beaten Until Numb; Ex-Members Blame Klan." <u>Durham Morning Herald</u>. May 9, 1952, p. 1.

5,224.   "Following Of K.K.K. In State Has Dropped To 2,817, Audit Shows." <u>Greensboro Daily News</u>. May 16, 1926.

5,225.   "Formal Arraignment Slated Today For Former Klansmen." <u>Durham Morning Herald</u>. April 3, 1952, p. 1.

5,226.   "Former Chief Sues, Charging Conspiracy." <u>Raleigh News & Observer</u>. June 29, 1970, p. 3.

5,227.   "Former Klan Attorney Joins Morgan's Staff." <u>Raleigh News & Observer</u>. November 8, 1969, p. 24.

5,228.   "Former Klan Leader Paroled." <u>New York Times</u>. February 23, 1954, p. 47.

5,229.   "Former Klansman Begins Sentence." <u>Durham Morning Herald</u>. May 7, 1966.

5,230.   "Former Klansman's Funeral." Raleigh News &
          Observer. September 13, 1967, p. 1.

5,231.   "Former N.C. Statesman Would Be Silenced Today."
          Daily Reflector. October 2, 1964.

5,232.   "Former Potentate Of Klan Paroled." Durham Morning
          Herald. February 23, 1954, p. 1.

5,233.   "Forsyth County, N.C. Opens Door To KKK Despite
          Threat Of Violence." Library Journal. Vol. 106,
          June 1, 1981, p. 1156.

5,234.   "4 Anti-Klan Demonstrators Killed In Greensboro,
          N.C." Baltimore Afro-American. November 10, 1979,
          p. 1.

5,235.   "Four Bullet Holes Found In Home Of Klansman's
          Father." Durham Morning Herald. March 21, 1966.

5,236.   "4 Deaths At Anti-Klan Rally Laid To One Defendant."
          New York Times. November 6, 1980, p. A16.

5,237.   "4 Deny Part In Flogging Of Johnson." Durham
          Morning Herald. May 10, 1952, p. 1.

5,238.   "Four Die In Greensboro Shootout When Anti-Klan
          Rally Disrupted." Raleigh News & Observer.
          November 4, 1979, pp. 1, 16.

5,239.   "Four Die In Shootings At Anti- Ku Klux Klan Rally
          In N.C." San Francisco Chronicle. November 4,
          1979, p. 1A.

5,240.   "4 Ex-Klansmen Testify Against 7 Others Faced
          With Kidnapping Counts." Durham Morning Herald.
          May 13, 1952, p. 1.

5,241.   "4 Killed At Anti-Ku Klux Klan Rally In N.C."
          Washington Post. November 4, 1979, p. 5A.

5,242.   "4 Killed At N.C. Communist Party Anti-Ku Klux
          Klan Rally." Houston Post. November 4, 1979, p. 1A.

5,243.   "4 Killed During Greensboro Rally." Charlotte
          Observer. November 4, 1979, pp. 1, 7.

5,244.   "4 Klansmen, 2 Nazi's Freed In N.C. Slayings."
          Louisiana (New Orleans) Weekly. November 22, 1980,
          pp. 1, 5.

5,245.   "4 Men In Klan Robes Walk Out Of Integrated Caro-
          lina Service." New York Times. November 28, 1964,
          p. 34

5,246.   "Four People Slain At Anti-Ku Klux Klan Rally In
         North Carolina." Los Angeles Times. November 4,
         1979, p. 1.

5,247.   "4 Slain, 10 Hurt In Gun Battle At Anti-Klan March."
         New York Daily News. November 4, 1979.

5,248.   "4 Youths Nabbed, Accused Of Crossburning In Ire-
         dell." Durham Morning Herald. March 14, 1952,
         Sect. 2, p. 7.

5,249.   "14 Accused Of Killings At Greensboro, N.C. Anti-
         Klan Rally." Chicago Defender. November 6,
         1979, p. 2.

5,250.   "14 Alleged Former Klansmen Seized On Charges Of
         Kidnapping, Flogging: Bitter Woman Tells How KKK
         Beat Her Brother." Durham Morning Herald.
         November 17, 1953, p. 1.

5,251.   "14 Alleged KKK Members Held On Flogging Charge."
         Durham (N.C.) Morning Herald. January 20, 1953,
         p. 1.

5,252.   "14 To Be Arraigned Today In Deaths At Anti-Klan
         Rally." New York Times. January 18, 1980, p. 10.

5,253.   "4th Greensboro Juror." Charlotte (N.C.) Observer.
         June 28, 1980, p. 2C.

5,254.   "Franklinton Bus Object Of Special Precautions."
         Durham Morning Herald. December 3, 1966.

5,255.   "Free Access In Forsyth County." Wilson Library
         Bulletin. Vol. 53, June, 1979, p. 683.

5,256.   Friscia, Alberta. "Killers Set Free: Drive Con-
         tinues To Ban Klan, Nazis." New York Daily World.
         November 19, 1980, pp. 3, 10.

5,257.   "From Ambush." Daily Reflector. November 7, 1966.

5,258.   "Fund Use Eyed In Klan Probe." Raleigh News &
         Observer. October 20, 1965.

5,259.   "Funeral Held For 4 Victims In Greensboro Rally
         Slaying." New Orleans Times Picayune. November
         12, 1979, p. 13.

5,260.   "A Funeral Procession." Wall Street Journal.
         November 2, 1979, p. 1.

5,261.   "Funny Faces For Ku Klux Klan Members." New Bern
         Sun-Journal. April 4, 1966.

5,262.   "Gardner Calls On Backer To Disclaim Line To Klan;
Disavow Klan Link, Stickley Tells Foe." Raleigh
News & Observer. April 25, 1968, p. 27.

5,263.   Gatewood, William B., Jr. "Politics And Piety In
North Carolina: The Fundamentalist Crusade At High
Tide, 1925-1927." North Carolina Historical Review.
Vol. 42, July, 1965, p. 275-290.

5,264.   "George Dorsett Organizes Splinter Groups."
Raleigh News & Observer. August 23, 1967, p. 3.

5,265.   "Getting Results." Raleigh News & Observer. March
3, 1952.

5,266.   " 'Go To Georgia' Eure Tells Ousted Kluxers."
Raleigh News & Observer. June 3, 1967, p.22.

5,267.   "Godwin Says Klan On Rise." Winston Salem Journal.
November 24, 1966.

5,268.   "Good Neighbor Chairman's Remarks Backfire In
Hyde." Raleigh News & Observer. November 20,
1968, p. 6.

5,269.   "Good Preparation For Klan Rally." Charlotte
Observer. August 16, 1966.

5,270.   "GOP Backs Klan Victors In Rowan." Charlotte
Observer. November 15, 1966.

5,271.   "Governor Calls For Probe Of Strong-Armed Kluxers."
Raleigh News & Observer. August 4, 1966.

5,272.   "Governor Denounces Actions Of Security Guards In
Klan." Durham Morning Herald. August 4, 1966.

5,273.   "Governor Lends No New Word On Klan Rally Probe."
Durham Morning Herald. August 9, 1966.

5,274.   "Governor Moore And The Klan Rally." Greensboro
Daily News. August 4, 1966.

5,275.   "Governor Orders Guardsmen To Stand By For Klan
Rally." Durham Morning Herald. August 13, 1966.

5,276.   "Governor Says Klan Now Has 6,000 Members."
Greensboro Daily News. September 22, 1966.

5,277.   "Governor Says Task Force To Eye All Law Violators."
Raleigh News & Observer. January 7, 1966.

5,278.   "Grand Dragon Claims News, TV Members." Raleigh
News & Observer. August 16, 1966.

5,279.   "Grand Dragon Defends Right Of Klansmen To Pull
         Jury Duty." Raleigh News & Observer. November 23,
         1966, p. 12.

5,280.   "Grand Dragon Denies Klan Membership Is On Decline."
         Greensboro Daily News. January 4, 1967.

5,281.   " 'Grand Dragon' Is Bound Over On Perjury Charge."
         Daily Reflector. March 16, 1966.

5,282.   "Grand Dragon Is Sworn In As A Special Deputy In
         Rowan." Raleigh News & Observer. September 28,
         1968, p. 1.

5,283.   "Grand Dragon Perjury Case Is Continued." Greens-
         boro Daily News. February 26, 1966.

5,284.   "Grand Dragon Plans To Incorporate Klan." Raleigh
         News & Observer. June 21, 1965.

5,285.   "Grand Dragon Rents Hall; Officers Ready." Greens-
         boro Daily News. August 12, 1966.

5,286.   "Grand Dragon Robert Jones: Special Deputy Role
         Lost." Raleigh News & Observer. October 1, 1968,
         p. 1.

5,287.   "Grand Dragon Says Boycott Not By Klan." Daily
         Reflector. October 28, 1966.

5,288.   "Grand Dragon Says Klan Still Growing." Raleigh
         News & Observer. November 17, 1964.

5,289.   "Grand Dragon Says Vote Shows Klan Is Wanted."
         Daily Reflector. June 30, 1964.

5,290.   "Grand Dragon Sees Smear Try." Daily Reflector.
         February 2, 1965.

5,291.   "Grand Jury Indicts 14 Ku Klux Klansmen In N.C.
         Rally Killings." San Francisco Chronicle.
         December 14, 1979, p. 40.

5,292.   "Grand Jury Refuses To Indict Klansmen For Killing
         Of Black Man." Black Panther. Vol. 6, May 15,
         1971, p. 5.

5,293.   "Grand Jury To Air Counts Against Alleged Klansmen."
         Durham Morning Herald. March 14, 1952, p. 1.

5,294.   Grant, Jim. "Insurrection In Wilmington."
         Southern Patriot. Vol. 29, March 1971, p. 2.

5,295.   _____. "Rebellion In Oxford." Southern Patriot.
         Vol. 28, June, 1970, p. 1.

5,296.   Gray, Farnum. "Judge Bans Klansmen From Forsyth
          Jury." Winston-Salem (N.C.) Journal. November 22,
          1966, p. 1.

5,297.   "Greatest State." Raleigh (N.C.) News & Observer.
          August 1, 1966, p. 1.

5,298.   "Greensboro Asks Review Of Police Role At Klan
          Rally." New York Times. November 21, 1979, p. A16.

5,299.   "Greensboro Damage Suit." Washington Post.
          January 1, 1981, p. A2.

5,300.   "Greensboro Demonstration Is Planned By Nazi
          Leader." New York Times. February 5, 1980, p. 16.

5,301.   "Greensboro Joins Suit Against Dorsett, Pals."
          Raleigh (N.C.) News & Observer. September 9, 1967,
          p. 2.

5,302.   "Greensboro, N.C. Murder Verdict Reheats KKK Emo-
          tions." Christian Science Monitor. November 19,
          1980, p. 1.

5,303.   "Greensboro, N.C. Probe Of Police And Shootings."
          Christian Science Monitor. November 27, 1979, p. 2.

5,304.   "Greensboro Reports Backs Police Work At Fatal
          Rally." New York Times. November 27, 1979, p. A18.

5,305.   "Greensboro Riot Trial." Washington Post. June 16,
          1980, p. A12.

5,306.   "Greensboro, N.C. Seeks Renewed Racial Progress
          After Klan Trial." Christian Science Monitor.
          November 24, 1980, p. 6.

5,307.   "Greensboro To Be Studied As Klan Site." Durham
          (N.C.) Sun. January 3, 1950, p. 1.

5,308.   "Greensboro Trial: Bigotry Or Justice?" U.S. News
          And World Report. Vol. 89, December 1, 1980, p. 14.

5,309.   "Greensboro Trail Dropped." Washington Post.
          November 27, 1980, p. A2.

5,310.   "Greensboro's Violence." Greensboro (N.C.) Daily
          News. November 11, 1979, p. 1.

5,311.   "Grocer Claiming Klan Boycott Says Business Better."
          Durham (N.C.) Morning Herald. October 31, 1966.

5,312.   "Grocer Says Klan Denies Store Boycott." Winston-
          Salem (N.C.) Journal. October 29, 1966, p. 1.

5,313.   Gruson, Lindsey. "After Violence, Community
          Leaders Ask For Calm." Greensboro (N.C.) Daily
          News. November 4, 1979, p. A4.

5,314.   _____. "Police Suspect WVO Fired First Shot."
          Greensboro (N.C.) Daily News. November 11, 1979,
          p. 1.

5,315.   Gruson, Lindsey and Charles Babington. "Slain
          Man 'Was Firing' Gun At Klan Group, Witness Says."
          Greensboro (N.C.) Daily News. November 10, 1979,
          p. 1.

5,316.   "Guilford Candidate A Klan Member." Charlotte
          (N.C.) Observer. May 5, 1966.

5,317.   "Guilford Restraining Dorsett, 12 Others."
          Raleigh (N.C.) News & Observer. September 23,
          1967, p. 3.

5,318.   "Gunfire In Greensboro." America. Vol. 141, Novem-
          ber 17, 1979, pp. 292-310.

5,319.   "Gunfire In N.C. Killing 5 Communist Marchers
          Remembered." Los Angeles Times. April 27, 1980,
          p. 1.

5,320.   "Guns Barred In Wilmington, N.C., After Sniping And
          Racial Unrest." New York Times. October 6, 1971,
          p. 22.

5,321.   Hackney, Brent and Steve Berry. "CWP Members
          Refusing To Cooperate With Agents." Greensboro
          Daily News. November 7, 1979, p. 1.

5,322.   "Halifat Sheriff Thinks Klan Activities Are
          'Exaggerated'." Raleigh (N.C.) News & Observer.
          December 8, 1964.

5,323.   "Hamilton Pleads Guilty." Christian Science
          Monitor. July 22, 1952, p. 1.

5,324.   "Hamilton Pleads Innocent As Whiteville Trial
          Begins." Durham (N.C.) Morning Herald. July
          22, 1952, p. 1.

5,325.   "Hamilton, 65 Alleged Klan Members To Go On Trial
          In Whiteville Today." Durham Morning Herald.
          July 21, 1952, p. 1.

5,326.   "Hamilton's Trial Scheduled Today." Raleigh News
          & Observer. July 21, 1952.

5,327.   "Hand-Washing Law." Raleigh News & Observer.
          July 2, 1966.

5,328.   Hardee, Roy. "Ex-Klansman Tells Of Plot To Harm
Vanceboro Mayor." Raleigh (N.C.) News & Observer.
January 25, 1966.

5,329.   _____. "Greenville Chief Freed In Klan Case."
Raleigh News & Observer. April 6, 1966.

5,330.   _____. "Klan Dragon Instructed Klansmen On
Voting In First District Race." Raleigh News &
Observer. February 8, 1966, p. 1.

5,331.   _____. "Klan Revolt Is Reflected In Eastern
N.C. Ranks." Raleigh News & Observer. April 13,
1967, p. 1.

5,332.   _____. "Klan's Move In Plymouth Is Described."
Raleigh (N.C.) News & Observer. January 26, 1966,
p. 1.

5,333.   _____. "Pitt Ex-Klansman Testifies Today."
Raleigh News & Observer. January 28, 1966.

5,334.   _____. "Rural, Urban Feud Causes Pitt Klan
Rift." Raleigh News & Observer. January 27, 1966.

5,335.   Harris, Art. " 'Agonizing' Verdict In Greensboro."
Washington Post. November 21, 1980, p. A2.

5,336.   _____. "The Hardscrabble Heroes Of Hate."
Washington Post. November 19, 1980, pp. A1, A2.

5,337.   _____. "Klan Trial Opens To A Cry Of 'Sham'."
Washington Post. August 5, 1980, p. A12.

5,338.   Harris, Bernice Kelly. "Writer Rides All Unaware
In Ku Klux Klan Parade." The Southern Pines (N.C.)
Pilot. March 1, 1972, p. 1.

5,339.   Hart, Reese. "Bruton Staff Member Quits, Claims
Klan Facts Withheld." Durham (N.C.) Morning
Herald. July 26, 1966, p. 1.

5,340.   _____. "Klan Jeers Negroes Attending KKK
Rally." Charlotte (N.C.) Observer. August 15,
1966.

5,341.   _____. "Klansmen Jeer Negroes At Raleigh
Rally." Winston-Salem (N.C.) Journal. August 15,
1966, p. 1.

5,342.   _____. "O'Quinn Leaves Atty. Gen." Virginian
Pilot. July 26, 1966, p. 1.

5,343.   _____. "Seawell: Enforcement Will Stop Klan."
Raleigh News & Observer. June 20, 1966,

5,344.   Hatch, Richard W. "Negroes Integrate Rally To Dismay OK Klansmen." Greensboro (N.C.) Daily News. August 15, 1966.

5,345.   _____. "Governor Denies SBI Withholds Klan Facts." Greensboro Daily News. July 27, 1966.

5,346.   _____. "Moore Supports SBI In Hassle." Charlotte (N.C.) Observer. July 27, 1966, p. 1.

5,347.   _____. "Tar Heel Klansmen Estimated At 6,000." Raleigh (N.C.) News And Observer. September 22, 1966, p. 1.

5,348.   "Hate Propaganda Distributed Here." Raleigh News & Observer. July 1, 1965, p. 1.

5,349.   "Heap Bad Kluxers Armed With Gun. Indian Angry, Paleface Run." Ebony. Vol. 13, April, 1958, pp. 25-26, 28.

5,350.   "Hearing For Jones Is Tuesday." Winston-Salem Journal. March 13, 1966, p. 1.

5,351.   "Hearing For KKK Chief Postponed Indefinitely." Durham Morning Herald. June 11, 1952, p. 2.

5,352.   "Hearing On 1957 Klan Murder In Alabama Continues." New Orleans Times Picayune. February 27, 1976, p. 1.

5,353.   "Hearing Set." Raleigh News & Observer. August 27, 1971, p. 3.

5,354.   "Hearings Of Alleged KKK Night Riders Postponed." Durham Morning Herald. February 26, 1952, p. 1.

5,355.   "Helms Seems To Need A Rabbit's Foot." Raleigh New & Observer. July 26, 1972, p. 4.

5,356.   Henderson, Bruce. "Day For Friends, Giving Thanks." Charlotte (N.C.) Observer. November 19, 1980, pp. A1, A10.

5,357.   Henderson, Tom. "Mrs. Graves Sewed White Hoods." Greensboro Daily News. December 17, 1939, p. 1.

5,358.   Hennessee, W.E. "The Klan In Carolina." The State. November 9, 1940, pp. 5, 6, 16.

5,359.   Herbers, John. "Ex-Member Calls Klan 'The Lowest'." New York Times. January 29, 1966, p. 9.

5,360.   _____. "Gun Dealer Tells Of Sales To Klansmen." New York Times. October 26, 1965, p. 27.

5,361.   . "Hearings Believed Damaging To Klan."
Winston-Salem Journal. February, 21, 1966.

5,362.   . "Klan's National Chaplain Invokes the 5th
Amendment At House Inquiry." New York Times.
October 28, 1965, p. 29.

5,363.   . "Sheriff Says He And 6 Deputies Joined
Klan To Keep An Eye On It." New York Times.
October 27, 1965, pp. 1, 28.

5,364.   "Here Are Officials In Klan Action." Winston-
Salem Journal. March 16, 1966, p. 1.

5,365.   Herzog, Frederick. "Was Justice Done In Greensboro?
Christian Century. Vol. 97, December 17, 1980, pp.
1236-1237.

5,366.   "High Court Reverses 'Cycle Case'." Raleigh News
& Observer. December 14, 1967, p. 8.

5,367.   "Hodges: Congressional Hearings Put Ku Klux Klan
At 'Lower Ebb'." Raleigh News & Observer. November 6, 1965, p. 1.

5,368.   "Hodges Warns Klansmen Not To Breach N.C. Laws."
Asheville (N.C.) Citizen. January 31, 1958, p. 1.

5,369.   "Hold Hearing Today On Barring Of Klan." Daily
Reflector. March 31, 1966.

5,370.   Holder, Laurie. "SBI Probes Cross-Burning At
Governor's Mansion." Raleigh News & Observer.
August 15, 1964.

5,371.   . "Solons Claim No Kin With Tar Heel Klan."
Raleigh News & Observer. November 7, 1965, p. 1.

5,372.   Hollar, Keith. "The Klan: Statewide Grand Dragon
Seeks Legitimacy Through Non-Violence." Chapel
Hill (N.C.) Newspaper. March 4, 1979, pp. 1C, 5C.

5,373.   "House Group Says State Klan Active." Raleigh
News & Observer. December 12, 1967, p. 1.

5,374.   Howe, Claudia. "Klansman Who Quit Says Threats
Made." Charlotte Observer. August 12, 1966, p. 1.

5,375.   Howe, Elizabeth M. "A Ku Klux Uniform." Buffalo
Historical Society Publications. Vol. 25, 1921,
pp. 9-41.

5,376.   Huff, John. "Ellis Gives Visitors A View Of
Klan." Durham Morning Herald. February 4, 1973.

5,377.   "Humphrey Back In State For Talk Saturday." New
          Bern (N.C.) Sun-Journal. April 14, 1966, p. 1.

5,378.   "Humphrey Talk Picketed." New York Times. April
          25, 1965, p. 42.

5,379.   " 'Hunting' Klans Not Legitimate." Raleigh News
          & Observer. October 21, 1965, p. 1.

5,380.   "Hyde Negroes March Despite Visit Of Klan Grand
          Dragon." Raleigh News & Observer. November 19,
          1968, p. 1.

5,381.   "I Withheld No KKK Data - Anderson." Charlotte
          Observer. July 21, 1966.

5,382.   "Image Of Klansville, U.S.A." Durham Morning
          Herald. October 24, 1966.

5,383.   "Imperial Wizard Hamilton Returns To Whiteville In
          Different Role." Durham Morning Herald. May 27,
          1952, p. 1.

5,384.   "Imperial Wizard Sentenced." Christian Science
          Monitor. July 30, 1952, p. 1.

5,385.   "Imperial Wizard Shelton Discusses Klan Changes."
          Durham (N.C.) Morning Herald. December 29, 1974.

5,386.   "In Greensboro, Its Rhythmn vs. Anti-KKK Rally."
          Pittsburgh Courier. February 9, 1980, p. 2.

5,387.   "Indian Trio On Robeson Grand Jury." Raleigh News
          & Observer. January 21, 1958, p. 1.

5,388.   "Indians Back At Peace And The Klan At Bay." Life.
          Vol. 44, February 3, 1958, p. 36.

5,389.   "Indians May Go To Klan Rally." Greensboro Daily
          News. March 17, 1966.

5,390.   "Indians Rout The Klan." Commonweal. Vol. 67,
          January 31, 1958, p. 446.

5,391.   "Indians Shun Peace Confab With The Klan." New
          Bern Sun-Journal. March 22, 1966.

5,392.   "Indict KKK Supporters In Greensboro Bomb Plot."
          New York Recorder. March 7, 1981, p. 6.

5,393.   "Indicted Klansman Declared A Fugitive." New York
          Times. January 22, 1958, p. 17.

5,394.   "Indictment Faces Tarheel Klansmen On Perjury
          Charge." Durham Morning Herald. March 16, 1966
          p. 1.

5,395.   "Indictments For Alleged Klansmen." New Bern Sun-
           Journal. March 3, 1966, p. 1.

5,396.   "Informer Fears For Life." Raleigh (N.C.) News &
           Observer. January 22, 1968, p. 22.

5,397.   "Informer Says Mayor Assisted (China Grove)."
           Raleigh (N.C.) News & Observer. January 11, 1968,
           p. 1.

5,398.   "Injunction Should Be Permanent." Daily Reflector.
           March 19, 1966, p. 1.

5,399.   "Inner Workings Of Klan Related In Robeson Trial."
           Durham (N.C.) Morning Herald. March 28, 1952, p. 1.

5,400.   Inman, Tom. "Change Has Eroded The Ku Klux Klan."
           Raleigh News & Observer. May 21, 1965, p. 1.

5,401.   _____. "Preyer Denounces Klan, Warns It's
           Worming Deep Into Politics." Raleigh News &
           Observer. June 24, 1964, p. 1.

5,402.   _____. "Roadside Show Of The Ku Klux Klan."
           Raleigh News & Observer. August 5, 1964, p. 1.

5,403.   "Inquiries Made Into N.C. Klan." Raleigh News &
           Observer. October 11, 1946.

5,404.   " 'Interest' In K.K.K. Mostly Against It."
           Greensboro Daily News. December 30, 1949.

5,405.   " 'Invisible Empire'." Raleigh News & Observer.
           February 22, 1952.

5,406.   "Is US 70 Billboard Only Sign Of Smithfield 'Klan
           Country'?" Raleigh (N.C.) News & Observer.
           August 17, 1970, p. 3.

5,407.   Jablow, Paul. "Klan Fights Communism, Jones Says."
           Charlotte Observer. November 2, 1966, p. 1.

5,408.   "Jail Term Confirmed." New York Times. May 26,
           1959, p. 20.

5,409.   "Jail Term, $1,000 Fine Await Jones." Raleigh
           (N.C.) News & Observer. January 15, 1969, p. 1.

5,410.   "Jailer Says Man Admitted Shootings At Anti-Klan
           Rally." New York Times. August 29, 1980, p. A12.

5,411.   "Jailing Of KKK Members In Greensboro, N.C."
           Chicago Defender. November 10, 1979, p. 10B.

5,412.   "James Cole and George Dorsett To Visit Sec. Of
           State Thad Eure." Raleigh (N.C.) News & Observer.
           May 31, 1967, p. 22.

5,413.   "James Earl Ray's Attorney Hired To Defend Klansmen
          In Hyde Trial." Raleigh (N.C.) News & Observer.
          July 16, 1969, p. 3.

5,414.   "James Waller, Communist Workers Party Member Slain
          By KKK." Chicago Tribune. November 7, 1979, Sect.
          2, p. 3.

5,415.   Jarvis, Mrs. T.J. "The Conditions That Led To The
          Ku Klux Klan." The North Carolina Booklet. Vol. 1,
          #12, April 10, 1902, pp. 3-24.

5,416.   _____. "The Ku-Klux Klans." North Carolina
          Booklet. Vol. 2, May 10, 1902, pp. 3-26.

5,417.   Jeffers, Trellie L. "N.C. Central Students Hold
          Vigil Against Klan Verdict." Carolina (Durham)
          Times. November 29, 1980, p. 1.

5,418.   Jeffreys, Grady. "Crackdown Ordered On Acts Of
          Violence." Raleigh (N.C.) News & Observer.
          January 3, 1966, p. 1.

5,419.   _____. "Klan May Face Major Legal Action."
          Raleigh (N.C.) News & Observer. May 1, 1966.

5,420.   _____. "Klan Stages Capital City Street Walk."
          Raleigh News & Observer. June 27, 1965, p. 1.

5,421.   _____. "Klan Stages Raleigh Walk, County Rally."
          Raleigh News & Observer. June 27, 1965.

5,422.   _____. "Seawell To Battle Klan." Raleigh News
          & Observer. January 3, 1966.

5,423.   Jenkins, Ray. "Again, The Klan: Old Sheets, New
          Victims." Reporter. Vol. 6, March 4, 1952, pp. 29-
          31.

5,424.   _____. "Again The Klan: Old Sheets, New
          Victims." Whitesville (N.C.) News Reporter.
          March 4, 1952, pp. 29-32.

5,425.   _____. "Court Drops Ban On KKK Meeting."
          Charlotte Observer. April 19, 1966.

5,426.   _____. "Decision To Invade Robeson Indicates
          Klan's Desperate." Charlotte (N.C.) Observer.
          March 13, 1966, p. 1.

5,427.   _____. "Despite Its Ominous Klan, N.C. Still
          Wears A Crown." Charlotte Observer. August 7,
          1966, p. 1.

5,428.   _____. "Feeling Of Relief Meets Klan Arrests."
          Raleigh (N.C.) News & Observer. February 18,
          1952, p. 1.

5,429.   . "Hamilton Sentence Due Monday." _Raleigh News & Observer_. July 24, 1952, p. 1.

5,430.   . "Judge Says Klan Can't Meet, Cites Possibility Of 'Murders'." _Charlotte Observer_. March 18, 1966, p. 1.

5,431.   . "KKK, Indians May Clash At Maxton." _Charlotte Observer_. March 16, 1966, p. 1.

5,432.   . "Klan-Spawned Violence Grips County." _Raleigh News & Observer_. January 16, 1952, p. 1.

5,433.   . "Lumbees Back Out On Klan Meet - 'Nothing To Negotiate'." _Charlotte Observer_. March 22 1966, p. 1.

5,434.   . "Moore Assails Klan's Conduct." _Charlotte Observer_. August 4, 1966, p. 1.

5,435.   . "Moore: N.C. Won't Tolerate Violence." _Charlotte Observer_. March 11, 1966, p. 1.

5,436.   . "SBI Bottled Up Evidence On The Klan, Seawell Says." _Charlotte Observer_. July 19, 1966.

5,437.   . "SBI Won't Discuss Klan Data." _Charlotte Observer_. July 20, 1966.

5,438.   . "Thomas L. Hamilton Posts $10,000 Bond, Waives Extradition." _Raleigh News & Observer_. May 25, 1952.

5,439.   . "Thomas L. Hamilton, Ruler Of Ku Klux Klan, Delays Arrest By Absence From South Carolina Home; Charged With Conspiracy To Kidnap And Conspiracy To Assault In Columbus Flogging Cases." _Raleigh News & Observer_. May 24, 1952.

5,440.   . "Three Plead Guilty In Klan Case." _Raleigh News & Observer_. July 22, 1952.

5,441. "Jews Allowed On Jury In Bombing Plot Trial." _New York Times_. November 7, 1981, p. 7.

5,442. Johnsey, Arthur. "Eure Questions Rights Of King's Group To Operate In N.C." _Greensboro Daily News_. September 29, 1966, p. A4.

5,443.   . "Eure Will Receive Information That May Revoke Klan Certificate." _Greensboro Daily News_. May 5, 1966, p. 1.

5,444.   . "Klan, Birchers There, Too." _Greensboro Daily News_. October 12, 1966, p. 1.

5,445.   _____. "Klan Postpones Rally; Injunction Is
          Issued." Greensboro (N.C.) Daily News. March 18,
          1966.

5,446.   _____. "Klan To Stay At State Fair." Greensboro
          Daily News. October 1, 1966.

5,447.   _____. "Moore Uses Strong Words To Condemn
          Klan 'Bullying'." Greensboro (N.C.) Daily News.
          August 4, 1966, p. 1.

5,448.   _____. "Raleigh Officials Accused By Klan."
          Greensboro Daily News. August 15, 1966.

5,449.   _____. "Rivalry Cited As Cause Of Shakeup."
          Greensboro Daily News. December 19, 1965.

5,450.   Johnson, James Weldon. "What Do They Require?"
          New York Age. December 30, 1922, p. 1.

5,451.   Jolley, Roger. "Cripple Removed By Ku Klux Iden-
          tified As Duke Student." Durham Morning Herald.
          July 13, 1966, p. 1.

5,452.   Jones, Phyllis and Martha Nathan. "Update On
          Greensboro: Fighting For Our Civil Liberties." CRJ
          Reporter. Summer, 1981, pp. 22-24.

5,453.   "Jones Bound Over In Perjury Case. Charlotte
          Observer. March 16, 1966.

5,454.   "Jones Denies Klan Boycotting Store." Charlotte
          Observer. October 29, 1966.

5,455.   "Jones Raps Judge For Slighting Klan." Charlotte
          Observer. November 23, 1966.

5,456.   "Jones Rushes To Defense Of Klansman Jury Service."
          Greensboro (N.C.) Daily News. November 23, 1966.

5,457.   "Jones Says Klan Didn't Boycott Store." Charlotte
          Observer. November 1, 1966.

5,458.   "Jones Says Klan Includes Members From News Media."
          Durham Morning Herald. August 16, 1966.

5,459.   "Jones Says Klan Will Meet In Robeson Despite
          Pleas." Greensboro Daily News. March 17, 1966,
          p. 1.

5,460.   "Jones Says Meet Set With Indians." Durham Morning
          Herald. March 18, 1966.

5,461.   "Jones Says Shelton To Talk To Lumbees." Winston-Salem Journal. March 18, 1966.

5,462.   "Jones Taken To Prison." Raleigh (N.C.) News & Observer. March 27, 1969, p. 42.

5,463.   "Jones Wearies Of Klan Traveling." Winston-Salem Journal. November 8, 1966.

5,464.   "Judge Asks Klan To Skip Jury Duty." New York Times. November 22, 1966, p. 26.

5,465.   "Judge Declares Jury No Place For Klansmen." Greensboro Daily News. November 22, 1966.

5,466.   "Judge Declares Mistrial In Case Against Nazis." New York Times. July 19, 1981, p. 2.

5,467.   "Judge Gwyn Doesn't Want Klan On Juries." Raleigh News & Observer. November 22, 1966.

5,468.   "Judge Gwyn's Wish." Winston-Salem Journal. November 23, 1966.

5,469.   "Judge Hints Error In Sentencing Of 5." New York Times. June 15, 1969, p. 51.

5,470.   "Judge May Dismiss Appeal By Klansman." Greensboro Daily News. March 3, 1966.

5,471.   "Judge Orders Acquittal In Klan Shooting." Raleigh News & Observer. November 10, 1971, p. 23.

5,472.   "Judge Postpones Decision On Permanent KKK Ban." Charlotte Observer. April 1, 1966, p. 1.

5,473.   "Judge To Decide On Klan Rally April 18." Winston-Salem Journal. April 1, 1966, p. 1.

5,474.   "Judge To Rule On Klan's Injunction." New Bern Sun-Journal. April 18, 1966.

5,475.   "Judge Upholds Klansman." New York Times. December 3, 1971, p. 20.

5,476.   "Jurors Took 12 Major Votes Before Reaching Decision." Forest City (N.C.) Daily Courier. November 18, 1980, p. 7.

5,477.   "Jurors Weigh Klan Murder Case." New York Times. November 8, 1980, p. 7.

5,478.   "Jury Acquits Klansmen And Nazis Of Charges In N.C. Rally Slayings." San Francisco Chronicle. November 10, 1980, p. 1.

5,479.   "Jury Acquits Nazis, Klansmen In Killing." Forest
          City (N.C.) Daily Courier. November 18, 1980,
          pp. 1, 7.

5,480.   "Jury Begins Deliberations In Long Klan Murder
          Trial." Washington Star. November 8, 1980, p. A4.

5,481.   "Jury Begins Deliberation In Trial Of Nazis And
          KKK In N.C." Chicago Tribune. November 10, 1980,
          Sect. 5, p. 8.

5,482.   "Jury Finally Selected To Hear Flogging Case."
          Durham (N.C.) Morning Herald. May 8, 1952, p. 1.

5,483.   "Jury Hears Charges On Flogging In South." New
          York Times. April 1, 1952, p. 25.

5,484.   "Jury In Carolina Acquits 8 Klansmen Of Conspiracy."
          New York Times. January 20, 1968, p. 16.

5,485.   "Jury In Carolina Frees Klansmen In Five Slayings."
          New York Times. November 18, 1980, pp. 1, 20.

5,486.   "Jury Watches Film Of Violence." Washington Star.
          November 11, 1980, p. A8.

5,487.   "Just A Peaceful Rally?" Winston-Salem Journal.
          August 5, 1966, p. 1.

5,488.   "Justice Dept. To Eye Prosecution Of 6 In KKK
          For Murders In N.C." Houston Post. November 20,
          1980, p. 26A.

5,489.   Justice, John. "Kluxers Gather To Burn Cross."
          Daily Reflector. October 18, 1965.

5,490.   "Katzenback Is Summoned To Senate On Anti-Klan,
          Anti-Crime Bills." Charlotte Observer. March 20,
          1966.

5,491.   Kaufman, Naomi. "Most Of Greensboro Ignored
          Rally." Durham Morning Herald. February 4, 1980.

5,492.   _____. "3,500 March In Greensboro Against
          Klan." Raleigh News & Observer. February 3, 1980,
          pp. 1, 23.

5,493.   Kennedy, Paul D. "10 Of Klan Seized By F.B.I. In
          Carolina In Flogging Case." New York Times.
          February 17, 1952, pp. 1, 12.

5,494.   " 'Kick-em'out' Drew In Klan Konstitution."
          Raleigh (N.C.) News & Observer. June 10, 1967,
          p. 1.

5,495.   "Kidnap-Flogging Trial Of Alleged Nightriders Opens."
         Durham Morning Herald. December 2, 1954, p. 1.

5,496.   King, Adrian. "FBI Nabs Them All In Craven."
         Raleigh News & Observer. January 30, 1965.

5,497.   _____. " 'Pertinent' Data Revealed - Moore."
         Raleigh News & Observer. July 31, 1966, p. 1.

5,498.   King, Wayne. "14 Denied Bond In Slayings Of Foes
         Of Klan At Rally." New York Times. November 6,
         1979, p. A16.

5,499.   _____. "Jury Selection Challenged By Joan
         Little's Lawyers." New York Times. July 15,
         1975, p. 20.

5,500.   _____. "Klan Fights Leftists And Nazis At
         Its Exhibit." New York Times. February 27, 1979,
         p. 12.

5,501.   _____. "Six Klansmen And Nazis Going On Trial
         In Killings." New York Times. August 4, 1980,
         p. A8.

5,502.   _____. "Vengeance For Raid Seen As Motive For
         4 Killings At Anti-Klan March." New York Times.
         November 5, 1979, pp. A1, B12.

5,503.   "King And KKK Had N.C. Patrol Watch." New Bern
         Sun-Journal. August 4, 1966.

5,504.   "King, KKK In Raleigh Sunday." Charlotte Observer.
         July 29, 1966.

5,505.   "King, Klan Routine." Greensboro (N.C.) Daily
         News. July 28, 1966, p. 1.

5,506.   "KKK Activity In Columbus County, N.C." The
         Whitesville (N.C.) News Reporter. February 4,
         1952, p. 1.

5,507.   "KKK Air Settled At Jury Verdict." Raleigh News &
         Observer. May 12, 1952.

5,508.   "KKK - And NBC - Spotlight Winston-Salem Library."
         American Libraries, Vol. 10, April, 1979, p. 164.

5,509.   "KKK Carpenter Will Work On N.C. Chain Gang."
         Pittsburgh Courier. October 18, 1958, p. B2.

5,510.   "KKK Charges Against 25 Face Columbus Jury Today."
         Durham Morning Herald. June 18, 1952, p. 1.

5,511.   "KKK Chief Posts $10,000 Bond After Being Arrested
         In S.C." Durham Morning Herald. May 25, 1952, p. 1.

5,512.   "KKK Crossburning Reactivates Tarheel Klavern In
          Robeson." Durham Morning Herald. October 20,
          1956, Sect. A, p. 1.

5,513.   "KKK Dragon: I'll Work To Defeat Moore." Raleigh
          News & Observer. August 3, 1964.

5,514.   "KKK Guard, 17, Convicted, Fined." Winston-Salem
          Journal. August 24, 1966, p. 1.

5,515.   "KKK Head Backs Helms." Raleigh News & Observer.
          July 24, 1972, p. 5.

5,516.   "KKK Horns In On Wilkes Rape Case." New Bern (N.C.)
          Sun-Journal. August 15, 1966.

5,517.   "KKK In N.C." Raleigh News & Observer. February
          3, 1980.

5,518.   "KKK In North Carolina." The Tabor City (N.C.)
          Tribune. July 25, 1950, p. 1; July 26, 1950,
          p. 1; November 1, 1950, p. 1; November 15, 1950,
          p. 1; April 18, 1951, p. 4.

5,519.   "KKK In North Carolina." The Whitesville (N.C.)
          News Reporter. September 11, 1950, p. 4;
          November 26, 1950, p. 1; January 22, 1951, p. 1.;
          July 31, 1951, p. 4; December 11, 1951, p. 1;
          January 28, 1952, p. 1; February 16, 1952, p. 1.

5,520.   "KKK Karpetbaggers." The Carteret County News-
          Times. October 15, 1965.

5,521.   "KKK Leaders Blast Public Officials." Fayetteville
          (N.C.) Observer. May 15, 1966.

5,522.   "KKK Library Exhibit Causes Melee In N.C." Library
          Journal. Vol. 104, April 1, 1979, p. 776.

5,523.   "KKK Literature In Paper Tubes Probed." Goldsboro
          (N.C.) News Argus. May 26, 1966.

5,524.   "KKK Loses Suit Against Station." Raleigh News &
          Observer. June 2, 1972, p. 34.

5,525.   "KKK Member Acquitted In N.C. Murders Shot By
          Unknown Person." Houston Post. November 20,
          1980, p. 27A.

5,526.   "K.K.K. Of Washington, N.C. In Reconstruction Days."
          Raleigh News & Observer. October 22, 1922.

5,527.   "KKK Plans Rally." Greensboro (N.C.) Daily News.
          August 5, 1966.

5,528.   "KKK Probe Protested By Ardent Foe." Daily Reflector. February 16, 1965.

5,529.   "KKK Robeson Plan 'Lunatic' - Seawell." Charlotte Observer. March 17, 1966.

5,530.   "KKK Sign Tells Just One Story." Raleigh News & Observer. June 23, 1968, Sect. 3, p. 5.

5,531.   "KKK Slaying At Communist Rally In N.C." Chicago Tribune. November 11, 1979, Sect. 3, p. 1.

5,532.   "KKK Still Plans Rally Despite Plea." Winston-Salem (N.C.) Journal. March 17, 1966, p. 1.

5,533.   "KKK To Rally Near Durham." Charlotte Observer. September 23, 1966.

5,534.   "KKK Uniting 'Entire' U.S." Raleigh News & Observer. August 21, 1965, p. 1.

5,535.   "KKK Unwanted For Jury Duty In Gwyn's Court." Durham (N.C.) Morning Herald. November 22, 1966, p. 1.

5,536.   "KKK Vote Not Sought-Moore." Durham Morning Herald. June 23, 1964, p. 3.

5,537.   "KKK Will Revisit Maxton For Rally." Greensboro Daily News. March 10, 1966, p. A4.

5,538.   "The Klan." Greensboro (N.C.) Daily News. August 23, 1966, p. 1.

5,539.   "Klan Accepts Raleigh Conditions For Rally." Durham Morning Herald. August 11, 1966.

5,540.   "Klan Acquittals Seen As An Emergency Sign." Michigan Chronicle. November 29, 1980, p. 2.

5,541.   "Klan Activity Is Observed In Newton." Winston-Salem Journal. November 14, 1976, p. 1.

5,542.   "Klan Adds Papers To Its Long List Of 'Subversives'." Durham Morning Herald. August 22, 1966.

5,543.   "Klan Advertises At Carolina Fair." New York Times. October 16, 1966.

5,544.   "Klan Again Tries For Incorporation In N.C." Daily Reflector. June 23, 1965.

5,545.   "Klan Aide Pleads Guilty." New York Times. May 5, 1959, p. 17.

5,546.   "Klan Aide Avoids Jail." New York Times. September
          3, 1952, p. 26.

5,547.   "Klan Analysis." Durham (N.C.) Morning Herald.
          August 11, 1966.

5,548.   "Klan And Patriotism." Raleigh News & Observer.
          December 4, 1966.

5,549.   "Klan As Symbol." Greensboro (N.C.) Daily News.
          May 6, 1966.

5,550.   "Klan Asks Defeat Of Bond Issue." Raleigh News
          & Observer. August 9, 1966.

5,551.   "Klan Assassins Set Free." New York Daily World.
          November 19, 1980, pp. 1, 8.

5,552.   "Klan Attraction At State Fair." Durham Morning
          Herald. October 12, 1966.

5,553.   "Klan Backs Violence." Raleigh News & Observer.
          October 22, 1965.

5,554.   "Klan Balks At Hiring Off-Duty Cops." Charlotte
          Observer. August 10, 1966.

5,555.   "Klan, Barred From Arena, Files Suit In North
          Carolina." New York Times. April 20, 1967, p. 52.

5,556.   "Klan Booth At Fair." Durham Morning Herald.
          October 22, 1966.

5,557.   "Klan Booth At State Fair Is Ordered To Curb Noise."
          Daily Reflector. October 14, 1966, p. 1.

5,558.   "Klan Booth Peace Attributed To SBI." Charlotte
          Observer. October 18, 1966.

5,559.   "Klan Bosses Will Speak At Rally Near Elizabeth
          City." Raleigh News & Observer. April 13, 1967,
          p. 36.

5,560.   "Klan Bound By N.C. Law: Attorney General Rules."
          Twin City Sentinel. June 18, 1965, p. 1.

5,561.   "Klan Boycott Helps Store." New Bern Sun-Journal.
          October 31, 1966, p. 1.

5,562.   " 'Klan-Boycotted' Store Buzzes With Business
          After Publicity." Charlotte Observer. October 31,
          1966, p. 1.

5,563.   "Klan Buries Suicide Victim." New York Times.
          December 15, 1965, p. 50.

5,564.   " 'Klan Buster' Dies After Long Illness." The
Virginian Pilot. July 13, 1966.

5,565.   "Klan Can Be Restrained." Charlotte (N.C.)
Observer. July 23, 1966, p. 1.

5,566.   "Klan Can Mobilize, Leader Says." Winston-Salem
Journal. March 30, 1966, p. 1.

5,567.   "Klan Campaigns May Be Illegal." Goldsboro News
Argus. May 27, 1966, p. 1.

5,568.   "Klan Candidates Don't Fare Well In Primary."
Raleigh News & Observer. May 30, 1966.

5,569.   "Klan Case Arraignment Set." New York Times.
December 18, 1979, p. 13.

5,570.   "Klan Case In Robeson Court Today." Greensboro
Daily News. March 31, 1966, p. 1.

5,571.   "Klan Case To Test Old N.C. Law." Raleigh News
& Observer. March 26, 1952.

5,572.   "Klan Charter In State Under Fire." New Bern Sun-
Journal. May 5, 1966.

5,573.   "Klan Chartered To Do Business." Raleigh News &
Observer. July 8, 1965.

5,574.   "Klan Chief Criticizes Gwyn's Jury Views." Winston-
Salem Journal. November 23, 1966.

5,575.   "Klan Chief Draws 4 Years In Beating." New York
Times. July 31, 1952, p. 42.

5,576.   "Klan Chief Invokes Duel Law." Charlotte Observer.
March 20, 1966, p. 1.

5,577.   "Klan Chief Is Deputy Sheriff." New York Times.
September 28, 1968, p. 31.

5,578.   "Klan Chief Pleads Guilty In Flogging." New York
Times. July 23, 1952, p. 31.

5,579.   "Klan Chief Posts $5,000 Bond For Rally In Raleigh."
Durham Morning Herald. August 12, 1966.

5,580.   "Klan Chief Says He's Still No. 1." Raleigh (N.C.)
News & Observer. April 2, 1967.

5,581.   "Klan Chief Says Hiring Police Likely." Winston-
Salem Journal. August 10, 1966.

5,582.   "Klan Chief To Speak To Club." Raleigh News &
Observer. November 4, 1966.

5,583. "Klan Chief Tom Hamilton Admits He Had Part In Flogging Negro Woman." Durham Morning Herald. July 23, 1952, p. 1.

5,584. "Klan Chief's Rights Violated, Judge Says." Raleigh News & Observer. December 3, 1971, p. 31.

5,585. "Klan Chief's Trial In Flogging Starts." New York Times. July 22, 1952, p. 33.

5,586. "Klan Chief Uncertain About Rally." Winston-Salem Journal. April 19, 1966.

5,587. "Klan Chief Deny Ouster." Raleigh (N.C.) News & Observer. June 9, 1967, p. 1.

5,588. "Klan Chief's Rights Violated, Judge Says." Raleigh News & Observer. December 3, 1971.

5,589. "Klan Chief's Wife Defends Candidacy." Winston-Salem Journal. April 19, 1966.

5,590. "Klan Claims Law On Cussing Vague." Raleigh News & Observer. August 27, 1966.

5,591. "Klan Claims Major Gain In Members." Raleigh News & Observer. September 22, 1966.

5,592. "Klan Contributes Nothing." Raleigh News & Observer. September 21, 1965.

5,593. "Klan Convictions Upheld." New York Times. October 14, 1952, p. 35.

5,594. "Klan Cyclops Files For Sheriff's Race In Guilford County." Durham Morning Herald. March 3, 1966.

5,595. "Klan Cyclops In Sheriff's Race." New Bern Sun-Journal. March 3, 1966.

5,596. "Klan Demonstrates Its Meaning." Durham Morning Herald. August 2, 1966.

5,597. "Klan Dragon Claims He Is Weary." Raleigh News & Observer. November 8, 1966.

5,598. "Klan Dragon Denies Rowan Political Aims." Raleigh News & Observer. November 16, 1966.

5,599. "Klan Dragon Dodges Ban." Raleigh News & Observer. October 28, 1965.

5,600. "Klan Dragon Holds March In Monroe." Raleigh News & Observer. February 15, 1972.

5,601. "Klan Dragon Jones Goes To Jail." Raleigh News & Observer. March 25, 1969.

5,602. "Klan Dragon Sounds Off Against Road Bond Issue." Raleigh News & Observer. October 30, 1965.

5,603. "Klan Ejects Student, Moore Asks Probe." The Virginian-Pilot. July 13, 1966.

5,604. "Klan Evicts 5 Students From Rally." Winston-Salem Journal. October 3, 1966.

5,605. "Klan Expects Victory In Presidential Vote." Raleigh News & Observer. August 23, 1965.

5,606. "Klan Expose Cited In Hillman Awards." New York Times. June 11, 1953, p. 18.

5,607. "Klan Extremists Blamed By Moore." Raleigh News & Observer. September 3, 1965.

5,608. "Klan Fighter Seawell Is Interviewed." Greensboro Daily News. July 18, 1966.

5,609. "Klan Fighter Takes On New Foe." Raleigh News & Observer. May 11, 1964.

5,610. "Klan Film Pickets In South Dispersed." New York Times. September 2, 1957, p. 26.

5,611. "Klan Flogging Case Nears Jury In South." New York Times. May 10, 1952, p. 16.

5,612. "Klan Foe Arrests 32d." New York Times. March 1, 1952, p. 17.

5,613. "Klan Gives Bond As Police Prepare." Charlotte Observer. August 12, 1966.

5,614. "Klan Gives State Another Black Eye." Raleigh News & Observer. October 23, 1966.

5,615. "Klan Group Miffed Over Guidelines." Greensboro Daily News. May 8, 1966.

5,616. "Klan Growth Worries Mecklenburg Official." Raleigh News & Observer. November 6, 1965.

5,617. "Klan Guards Give Governor Cause For Greater Concern." Charlotte Observer. August 5, 1966, p. 1.

5,618. "Klan Has More Than 6,000 Members - Jones." Charlotte Observer. September 23, 1966, p. 1.

5,619. "Klan Head Declines Invite To CR Panel. Durham Morning Herald. March 30, 1966.

5,620. "Klan Head's Case Slated For Hearing." Greensboro Daily News. March 12, 1966, p. 1.

5,621.   "Klan Hearing Is Wilkinson's Topic At Duke."
          Winston-Salem Journal. February 26, 1966, p. 1.

5,622.   "Klan Hits Boycotters In Durham." Raleigh (N.C.)
          News & Observer. November 30, 1965.

5,623.   "Klan Holds Another Rally." Asheville (N.C.)
          Citizen. August 30, 1951, p. 1.

5,624.   "Klan Holds March In Wilkes Areas." Durham (N.C.)
          Morning Herald. August 14, 1966, p. 1.

5,625.   "The Klan In Better Days." Durham (N.C.) Morning
          Herald. December 29, 1974.

5,626.   "Klan Indian Violence Is Feared In Rural North
          Carolina Area." New York Times. January 17, 1958,
          p. 10.

5,627.   "Klan Is In Trouble: An Interstate Abduction Sets
          FBI On Floggers." Life. March 31, 1952, pp. 44-
          46, 49.

5,628.   "Klan In State." Durham (N.C.) Morning Herald.
          December 12, 1949, p. 1.

5,629.   "Klan Increases Its Membership." New Bern Sun-
          Journal. September 22, 1966.

5,630.   "Klan Infiltrated By FBI Agents." Daily Reflector.
          December 2, 1964, p. 1.

5,631.   "Klan Informer Fears For Life." Raleigh (N.C.)
          News & Observer. January 22, 1968.

5,632.   "Klan Injunction Is Unwise." Charlotte Observer.
          March 25, 1966.

5,633.   "Klan Is Blasted In New Hanover." Raleigh News &
          Observer. November 8, 1965, p. 1.

5,634.   "Klan Is Claiming Fewer Crimes Than Baptists, CIO
          And GOP." Raleigh News & Observer. November 10,
          1965, p. 1.

5,635.   "Klan Is Given Right To Meet In Indian Area."
          New Bern (N.C.) Sun-Journal. April 19, 1966.

5,636.   "Klan Is Over Publicized, Says Moore." Daily
          Reflector. January 6, 1966, p. 1.

5,637.   "Klan Jury Told Of 2 Bragging On Shootings." New
          York Times. October 1, 1980, p. A16.

5,638.   "Klan Konduct Rues Governor." Greensboro Daily
          News. July 14, 1966, p. 1.

5,639.   "Klan Kludd Says Hennis Bid Mistake." _Winston Salem Journal_. March 5, 1966, p. 1.

5,640.   "Klan Lawyer Matt Murphy Speaks To Sanford Rally." _Raleigh News & Observer_. May 17, 1965.

5,641.   "Klan Leader Appears On Panel In Church." _Raleigh News & Observer_. November 13, 1965, p. 1.

5,642.   "Klan Leader Blames Group For Bombing." _Raleigh (N.C.) News & Observer_. October 21, 1971, p. 57.

5,643.   "Klan Leader Death Plot Again Linked." _Greensboro Daily News_. February 22, 1966, p. 1.

5,644.   "Klan Leader Is Charged With Perjury." _Daily Reflector_. January 12, 1966.

5,645.   "Klan Leader Quits To Run For Sheriff." _Winston-Salem Journal_. March 8, 1966.

5,646.   "Klan Leader Surrenders To Begin Year In Prison." _New York Times_. March 25, 1969, p. 16.

5,647.   "Klan Leadership Secrecy Defended By N.C. Dragon." _Raleigh News & Observer_. May 25, 1965.

5,648.   "Klan Leaflets Attack Moore And Seawell." _Raleigh News & Observer_. May 18, 1966.

5,649.   "Klan Making Little Progress In South. _Raleigh News & Observer_. April 7, 1958.

5,650.   "Klan March Meets Black Harassment." _Raleigh News & Observer_. January 30, 1972, p. 5.

5,651.   "Klan Marches In Burlington." _Greensboro Daily News_. March 13, 1966.

5,652.   "Klan Marriage Another Step In Sudden N.C. Re-surgence." _Raleigh News & Observer_. May 25, 1965.

5,653.   "Klan May Need To Keep Order." _New Bern (N.C.) Sun-Journal_. August 9, 1966.

5,654.   "Klan Meeting Is Postponed Due To Snow." _The Ashville (N.C.) Citizen_. February 16, 1958, p. 1.

5,655.   "Klan Member Visits Good Neighbor Meet." _Raleigh News & Observer_. January 22, 1966.

5,656.   "Klan Must Employ Policemen To Hold Auditorium Rally." _Durham Morning Herald_. August 9, 1966, p. 1.

5,657.   "Klan, NAACP Stage Marches In Wadesboro." _Raleigh News & Observer_. June 19, 1967, p. 7.

5,658.   "Klan Nazis Go Free In Greensboro." Bay State
(Mass.) Banner. November 27, 1980, pp. 1, 21.

5,659.   "Klan, Nazi Leaders Exult Over Acquittals In
Slayings." Charlotte (N.C.) Observer. November 18,
1980, p. 3A.

5,660.   "Klan-Nazi Trial Told Of Boasting." Washington
Post. October 1, 1980, p. A5.

5,661.   "Klan, Negroes Clash Before King Speech." Greensboro Daily News. August 1, 1966.

5,662.   "Klan, Negroes Face-To-Face." Daily Reflector.
August 23, 1965.

5,663.   "Klan, Negroes Meet; Noise Is Only Result."
Durham Morning Herald. August 7, 1966.

5,664.   "Klan Opens Offices Near Granite Quarry." Charlotte
(N.C.) Observer. March 10, 1966, p. 1.

5,665.   "Klan Opponents Urge March In Washington On
Inauguration Day." New York Times. December 7,
1980, p. 29.

5,666.   "Klan Parades In Raleigh." New York Times. July
11, 1966, p. 19.

5,667.   "Klan Pickets Mount Airy Barber Shop." Winston-
Salem Journal. March 24, 1966.

5,668.   "Klan Planning For Rally In Robeson Again."
New Bern Sun-Journal. March 10, 1966, p. 1.

5,669.   "Klan Plans A Walk As Humphrey Visits." Raleigh
News & Observer. April 17, 1965, p. 1.

5,670.   "Klan Plans March Rally In Robeson." Charlotte
Observer. March 10, 1966, p. 1.

5,671.   "Klan Plans Matching Protests." Winston-Salem
Journal. July 11, 1966, p. 1.

5,672.   "Klan Plans N.C. Rally." Charlotte (N.C.)
Observer. August 5, 1966, p. 1.

5,673.   "Klan Plans Oct. 2 Rally In Durham." Raleigh News
& Observer. September 22, 1966.

5,674.   "Klan Plans Program Of Education." Raleigh (N.C.)
News & Observer. June 29, 1970, p. 1.

5,675.   "Klan Plans Rally Near Burgaw." Raleigh News &
Observer. June 24, 1964, p. 1.

5,676.   "Klan Plans State Rally At Raleigh." Durham (N.C.)
          Morning Herald. August 5, 1966.

5,677.   "Klan Plans Trial Of Tar Heel Trio." Raleigh
          (N.C.) News & Observer. April 6, 1967.

5,678.   "Klan Posts Bond For Capital Rally." Winston-Salem
          Journal. August 12, 1966.

5,679.   "Klan Prosecutor Won't Press Charges." Washington
          Star. November 27, 1980, p. A4.

5,680.   "Klan Protests In N.C., White Foes Rally In Ind."
          Jet. Vol. 58, May 15, 1980, p. 5.

5,681.   "Klan Race-Mixing Mixed With Drink." Raleigh (N.C.)
          News & Observer. October 22, 1965.

5,682.   "Klan Rallies Decision Has Been Delayed." New
          Bern Sun-Journal. April 1, 1966.

5,683.   "Klan Rallies Take Troopers Off Highways." Raleigh
          News & Observer. November 18, 1966.

5,684.   "Klan Rally." Durham Morning Herald. August 12,
          1966.

5,685.   "Klan Rally." Winston-Salem (N.C.) Journal.
          August 5, 1966.

5,686.   "Klan Rally Arrests, Charges." Charlotte (N.C.)
          Observer. August 15, 1966, p. 1.

5,687.   "Klan Rally Attracts 300 Outside Elizabeth City."
          Winston-Salem (N.C.) Journal. March 13, 1966, p. 1.

5,688.   "Klan Rally Ban Hit By ACLU Director." Durham
          Morning Herald. March 30, 1966.

5,689.   "Klan Rally Cost N.C. $7,000 For Patrolmen."
          Greensboro Daily News. August 18, 1966, p. 1.

5,690.   "Klan Rally Decision Is Due." Durham (N.C.)
          Morning Herald. April 17, 1966, p. 1.

5,691.   "Klan Rally Hearing Set Today." Winston-Salem
          Journal. March 31, 1966, p. 1.

5,692.   "Klan Rally Held Here Last Night." Daily Reflector.
          September 15, 1966.

5,693.   "Klan Rally Hits Patrol For $7,000." Durham
          Morning Herald. August 19, 1966, p. 1.

5,694.   "Klan Rally In Raleigh." Durham (N.C.) Morning
          Herald. August 5, 1966.

5,695.   "Klan Rally Incident Investigation Called." Durham
          Morning Herald. July 12, 1966.

5,696.   "Klan Rally Is Put Off." New York Times. January
          26, 1958, p. 72.

5,697.   "Klan Rally Lacked Police." Charlotte (N.C.)
          Observer. August 6, 1966, p. 1.

5,698.   "Klan-Rally Ruling Expected Monday." Charlotte
          Observer. April 17, 1966, p. 1.

5,699.   "Klan Rally Scheduled." Winston-Salem Journal.
          March 3, 1966, p. 1.

5,700.   "Klan Rally Will Alert N.C. Guard." Winston-
          Salem Journal. August 13, 1966, p. 1.

5,701.   "Klan Raps LBJ, Noted Author." Raleigh News &
          Observer. April 12, 1965.

5,702.   "Klan-Related Charges Pursued." Durham Morning
          Herald. October 4, 1966, p. 4.

5,703.   "Klan Rents Booth At Fair." New York Times.
          September 29, 1966, p. 39.

5,704.   "Klan Rents Booth Space At NC Fair." Raleigh News
          & Observer. September 28, 1966.

5,705.   "Klan Resurgence Predicted." Durham Morning Herald.
          March 9, 1966.

5,706.   "Klan Revived By Rights Crisis." Raleigh News &
          Observer. March 27, 1965.

5,707.   "Klan Revolt Reflected In Eastern NC Ranks."
          Raleigh News & Observer. April 13, 1967, p. 15.

5,708.   "Klan Revolt Threatens Over Jones' Leadership."
          Raleigh News & Observer. April 4, 1967, p. 1.

5,709.   "Klan Schedules Rally Saturday In Pender County."
          Durham (N.C.) Morning Herald. June 24, 1964,
          Sect. A, p. 12.

5,710.   "Klan Sentences Delayed." New York Times. July
          30, 1952, p. 14.

5,711.   "Klan Set To Move Into Wilmington, Leaders
          Announce." Durham (N.C.) Morning Herald. January
          6, 1950, p. 1.

5,712.   "Klan Setback." Christian Science Monitor.
          September 16, 1952, p. E4.

5,713.   "Klan Should Have 'Equal Rights'." Charlotte (N.C.) Observer. July 28, 1966.

5,714.   "Klan Signs Probed For Law Violation." Raleigh (N.C.) News & Observer. May 18, 1966.

5,715.   "Klan Slapped On Wrist." Cincinnati (Ohio) Herald. November 29, 1980, pp. 1, 11.

5,716.   "Klan Slapped On Wrist By Greensboro Jury." Gary (Ind.) Crusader. November 29, 1980, pp. 1, 2.

5,717.   "Klan Slapped On Wrist By Greensboro Jury - Cobb." Carolina (Durham) Times. November 29, 1980, p. 1.

5,718.   "Klan Spokesman In Harnett Backs Campaign Of 'Truth'." Durham (N.C.) Morning Herald. August 4, 1966.

5,719.   "Klan Spreading." Raleigh (N.C.) News & Observer. February 21, 1952.

5,720.   "Klan Stages March, N.C. Capital Rally." Durham (N.C.) Morning Herald. July 11, 1966.

5,721.   "Klan States Quiet Burlington Parade." Durham (N.C.) Morning Herald. March 13, 1966.

5,722.   "Klan Stages Rally In Morganton." Raleigh (N.C.) News & Observer. April 5, 1965.

5,723.   "Klan Starts Boycott Of Grocery." Winston-Salem (N.C.) Journal. October 27, 1966.

5,724.   "Klan Still Planning Area Meeting Today." Raleigh News & Observer. January 25, 1964.

5,725.   "Klan Threatens Raleigh Minister. Raleigh (N.C.) News & Observer. September 30, 1964.

5,726.   "Klan To Bar News Media From Rallies." Raleigh (N.C.) News & Observer. August 10, 1964.

5,727.   "Klan To Meet At Indian 'Ambush' Town." Durham (N.C.) Morning Herald. March 10, 1966.

5,728.   "Klan To Open Chapel Hill Drive 'In About 2 Weeks'." Durham (N.C.) Morning Herald. January 7, 1950.

5,729.   "Klan To Operate Booth At Fair." Durham (N.C.) Morning Herald. September 28, 1966.

5,730.   "Klan To Rent Raleigh Hall For A Rally." New Bern Sun-Journal. August 11, 1966.

5,731.   "Klan To Seek Members Among Lumbee Indians."
Asheville (N.C.) Citizen. March 21, 1966.

5,732.   "Klan Told To Seek Authority." Raleigh (N.C.)
News & Observer. June 19, 1965.

5,733.   "Klan Trial Defendant Denies Saying He Got 'His
Share'." New York Times. October 2, 1980, p. A18.

5,734.   "Klan Trial Defense Attorney Assails News Media
'Silence'." New York Times. October 29, 1980,
p. A16.

5,735.   "Klan Trial Deliberations Continue." Charlotte
(N.C.) Observer. November 14, 1980, p. 20C.

5,736.   "Klan Trial Jurors See A News Film Showing Shootings
And Arrests." New York Times. August 13, 1980,
p. A20.

5,737.   "Klan Trial Jurors See More Videotape." New York
Times. August 23, 1980, p. 9.

5,738.   "Klan Trial Nears End." New York Times. July
29, 1952, p. 16.

5,739.   "Klan Trial Testimony Ends; Closing Arguments Are
Set." New York Times. October 22, 1980, p. A18.

5,740.   "Klan Trial Winding Up." Washington Star. November
1, 1980, p. A5.

5,741.   "Klan Tries To Halt Negroes' Protest." New York
Times. February 6, 1960, p. 20.

5,742.   "Klan Trio Get Terms For School Blast Try."
Raleigh (N.C.) News & Observer. March 21, 1958.

5,743.   "Klan Unshaken Only Puzzled." Daily Reflector.
January 26, 1965.

5,744.   "Klan Upheld On Right To Hold Robeson Rally."
Durham (N.C.) Morning Herald. April 19, 1966.

5,745.   "Klan Uses Sidewalk In Smithfield March." Raleigh
(N.C.) News & Observer. September 26, 1965, p.
6.

5,746.   "Klan Verdict Polarizes Voters In Carolina City."
New York Times. November 3, 1981, p. B12.

5,747.   "Klan Visits Church For Sermon, Barbecue." Raleigh
(N.C.) News & Observer. September 27, 1965.

5,748.   "Klan Visits Wilson Integrated Service." Raleigh
(N.C.) News & Observer. November 29, 1964.

5,749.   "Klan Warned To Stay Out Of Charlotte By Police."
Afro-American. October 1, 1949, p. 20.

5,750.   "Klan Will Be Flushed Out." Raleigh (N.C.) News
& Observer. January 4, 1965.

5,751.   "Klan Will Be Topic Of Panel Discussion At UNC
Tomorrow." Chapel Hill (N.C.) Weekly. March 12, 1966

5,752.   "Klan Wizard And 23 Indicted In Carolina." New
York Times. June 20, 1952, p. 33.

5,753.   "Klan Won't Be Able To Meet In Armory." Raleigh
(N.C.) News & Observer. January 24, 1964.

5,754.   "Klan Won't Hear Black's Speech." Raleigh News &
Observer. August 13, 1971, p. 11.

5,755.   "Klandidates Faired Common." Goldsboro News-
Argus. May 30, 1966, p. 3.

5,756.   "Klan's Bid To Incorporate Is Foiled By Technical
Error." Raleigh (N.C.) News & Observer. June 23,
1965.

5,757.   "Klan's Jones To Get Hearing." Winston-Salem (N.C.)
Journal. March 15, 1966.

5,758.   "Klan's Lawyer 'Disciplined'." Raleigh (N.C.) News
& Observer. November 2, 1965.

5,759.   "Klan's Right To Hold Rally Is Defended." Winston-
Salem (N.C.) Journal. March 25, 1966.

5,760.   "Klan's Sign Is Back Up." Raleigh News & Observer.
October 12, 1972, p. 5.

5,761.   "Klan's Take In N.C. In 66 Was $125,000." Raleigh
(N.C.) News & Observer. April 11, 1967.

5,762.   "Klansman Acquitted At Concord." Raleigh (N.C.)
News & Observer. March 15, 1968, p. 14.

5,763.   "Klansman Acquitted In Rowan." Raleigh (N.C.)
News & Observer. January 16, 1968, p. 1.

5,764.   "Klansman At Trial Says Informer Led Way To
Rally." New York Times. October 8, 1980, p. A20.

5,765.   "Klansman Bailed Out By His Pals." Raleigh (N.C.)
News & Observer. November 20, 1965.

5,766.   "Klansman Charges Policeman." Raleigh News &
Observer. March 20, 1970, p. 3.

5,767. "Klansman Cole." Asheville (N.C.) Citizen.
        January 25, 1958.

5,768. "Klansman Convicted." New York Times. March 14,
        1958, p. 1.

5,769. "Klansman Convicted Of Kidnapping." Christian
        Science Monitor. May 13, 1952, p. 1.

5,770. "Klansman Donald Laughter Surrenders." Raleigh
        (N.C.) News & Observer. September 27, 1967, p. 3.

5,771. "Klansman Faces Charges?" Raleigh (N.C.) News &
        Observer. January 7, 1968, p. 4.

5,772. "Klansman Firing Upheld." Raleigh News & Observer.
        September 10, 1971, p. 3.

5,773. "Klansman Gives Views On Election." New Bern Sun-
        Journal. November 15, 1966.

5,774. "Klansman Has Larger Crowd For Speaking." New
        Bern Sun-Journal. September 9, 1966.

5,775. "Klansman Is Freed." Raleigh News & Observer.
        May 21, 1968, p. 15.

5,776. "Klansman, Others Held In New Bern Bombing."
        Twin City Sentinel. January 29, 1965, p. 1.

5,777. "Klansman Pleads Guilty In 2d Trial." Winston-
        Salem Journal. August 24, 1966.

5,778. "Klansman Posts Bond." New York Times. May 27,
        1952, p. 56.

5,779. "Klansman Rejects Carolina Jury Bid." New York
        Times. November 23, 1966, p. 26.

5,780. "Klansman Turns Self In." Greensboro Daily News.
        November 12, 1979.

5,781. "Klansman Quits, Says He Receives Threats."
        Winston-Salem Journal. August 13, 1966.

5,782. "Klansman To Face Trial On Tuesday." Raleigh News
        & Observer. June 12, 1966.

5,783. "Klansman: Warned On Corruption." Raleigh News &
        Observer. August 19, 1973, p. 6.

5,784. "Klansman, Wife Un-Clan." Charlotte (N.C.)
        Observer. March 3, 1966.

5,785. "Klansman Who Quit Tells Of Threats." New York
        Times. October 24, 1965, p. 79.

5,786.   "Klansman's Concern Bombed." New York Times.
           August 20, 1968, p. 38.

5,787.   "Klansman's Home Bombed." New York Times. August
           5, 1968, p. 39.

5,788.   "Klansman's Role Of Deputy Causes Dispute In
           Carolina." New York Times. September 30, 1968,
           p. 29.

5,789.   "Klansman's Story Denied By Faircloth." Raleigh
           (N.C.) News & Observer. April 23, 1970, p. 32.

5,790.   "Klansman's View On Hired Guards." New Bern (N.C.)
           Sun-Journal. August 10, 1966, p. 1.

5,791.   "Klansman, Out Of Jail, Runs For Sheriff." Winston-
           Salem (N.C.) Journal. March 4, 1966, pp. 11-12.

5,792.   "Klansmen Accused Of Threat." Greensboro (N.C.)
           Daily News. August 13, 1966, p. 1.

5,793.   "Klansmen At Hopewell Jeer Negro Protesters."
           Winston-Salem (N.C.) Journal. August 7, 1966.

5,794.   "Klansmen Bring In Negro." New York Times.
           June 7, 1922, p. 2.

5,795.   "Klansmen Celebrate Freedom." Forest City (N.C.)
           Daily Courier. November 19, 1980, p. 4A.

5,796.   "Klansmen Charges Dropped." Raleigh News (N.C.) &
           Observer. May 3, 1969, p. 1.

5,797.   "Klansmen Chase Young Negroes." Winston-Salem
           (N.C.) Journal. August 1, 1966.

5,798.   "Klansmen Employ Chalmers To Study Judge's Actions."
           Raleigh News & Observer. November 20, 1965.

5,799.   "Klansmen Injured By Unknown Sniper." New Bern
           (N.C.) Sun-Journal. November 7, 1966, p. 1.

5,800.   "Klansmen March In Wilkes County." Winston-Salem
           (N.C.) Journal. August 14, 1966.

5,801.   "Klansmen May Face Assault Warrants." Durham (N.C.)
           Morning Herald. August 9, 1966.

5,802.   "Klansmen May Sue Neighbors: Greensboro." Raleigh
           (N.C.) News & Observer. August 23, 1967, p. 3.

5,803.   "Klansmen, Nazis Not Guilty In Rally Slayings."
           Washington Star. November 18, 1980, pp. A1, A6.

5,804.   "Klansmen Offer Aid To Sheriff In Dynamiting."
         New Bern Sun-Journal. April 11, 1966.

5,805.   "Klansmen Seek Some Assembly Posts In N.C." New
         Bern Sun-Journal. August 16, 1966.

5,806.   "Klansmen State Ride At Benson." Raleigh News &
         Observer. April 10, 1968, p. 16.

5,807.   "Klansmen To Get Hearing In Court Of Appeals
         Today." Durham Morning Herald. October 6, 1952,
         p. 3.

5,808.   "Klansmen's Capture Described At Trial." Washington
         Star. August 6, 1980, p. A2.

5,809.   "Klavern Head Plans Action On Grounds Of Discrimi-
         nation." Durham Morning Herald. January 20, 1958.

5,810.   "Klobbered In Karolina." Newsweek. Vol. 40,
         August 11, 1952, p. 24.

5,811.   "Kluxers Circulate Leaflets In Concord, N.C."
         Pittsburgh Courier. July 2, 1949, p. 11.

5,812.   "The Knights Of The Ku Klux Klan Is Watching You."
         Raleigh News & Observer. October 4, 1964.

5,813.   "Knockout Blow Seen Dealt." Christian Science
         Monitor. August 4, 1952, p. 11.

5,814.   Kroll, Eric. "A Documentary Photographer Takes
         A Ride With The Klan." American Photographer.
         Vol. 4, April, 1980, pp. 28-30.

5,815.   "Ku Klux Klan Dealt A Heavy Blow In Columbus."
         Raleigh News & Observer. May 15, 1952.

5,816.   "Ku Klux Klan Exhibit In North Carolina Discussed."
         San Francisco Chronicle. February 24, 1979, p. 5.

5,817.   "Ku Klux Klan Fires On Communist Rally In Greensboro,
         N.C." Chicago Tribune. November 4, 1979, p. 1.

5,818.   "Ku Klux Klan Head Starts Prison Term." New York
         Times. October 2, 1952, p. 16.

5,819.   "Ku Klux Klan Historic Exhibit In North Carolina
         Picketed." New Orleans Times Picayune. February
         27, 1979, p. 3.

5,820.   "Ku Klux Klan Holds Harnett Public Meeting."
         Raleigh News & Observer. November 4, 1964.

5,821.   "Ku Klux Klan Holds Parade At Burlington." Winston-
         Salem Journal. March 13, 1966.

5,822.   "Ku Klux Klan Initiates 700 As 1,500 Watch N.C. Ritual." Winston-Salem Journal. October 13, 1966, pp. 1, 12.

5,823.   "Ku Klux Klan Jury Watches Videotape Of Witness Under Hypnosis." San Francisco Chronicle. August 20, 1980, p. 5.

5,824.   "Ku Klux Klan Kandidates In Most Kounties In N.C." Greensboro News-Argus. May 26, 1966.

5,825.   "Ku Klux Klan Plans Rally In Raleigh." Asheville Citizen. July 2, 1968.

5,826.   "Ku Klux Klan Seeks New Image." Durham Morning Herald. July 25, 1965.

5,827.   " 'Law, Order' Group Reviews Events On N.C. Racial Front." Durham Morning Herald. March 23, 1966.

5,828.   "Lawmen Called To Investigate KKK 'Beatings'." Raleigh News & Observer. November 24, 1965, p. 1.

5,829.   "Lawn Cross Burning Reported In Craven." Raleigh News & Observer. July 18, 1965.

5,830.   "A Lay Sermon On The Klan." Asheville Citizen-Times. March 2, 1952.

5,831.   "Leader Of Hertford Klan Fined For Negro Assault." Raleigh News & Observer. April 5, 1967, p. 3.

5,832.   "Leader Of Klan Banishes North Carolina Chaplain." New York Times. April 5, 1967, p. 95.

5,833.   "Leaders Arrive For Convention." Raleigh News & Observer. June 27, 1970, p. 8.

5,834.   "Legal Action Against Klan Not Sighted On State Level." Raleigh News & Observer. December 12, 1967, p. 1.

5,835.   "Legal Curbs Explored On Picketing By Klan." Raleigh News & Observer. March 24, 1966.

5,836.   "Legion Balks At Klan March: Elizabeth City." Raleigh News & Observer. May 26, 1967, p. 5.

5,837.   Lemann, Nicholas. "Klansmen Vs. Communists." Washington Post. June 22, 1980, pp. A1, A17.

5,838.   "Let Klan Meet, ACLU Proposes." Durham Morning Herald. March 25, 1966.

5,839.   "Letter Is Hoax; No KKK Here, Cops Say." Durham Morning Herald. March 1, 1952, p. 1.

5,840.   Lewis, Anthony. "Free Speech And Provocation Can
          Be Hard To Separate." New York Times. November
          11, 1979, Sect. 4, p. 5.

5,841.   Lewis, Jim. "Klan Intimidation Charged." Raleigh
          News & Observer. November 23, 1966.

5,842.   _____. "Klan Strength Sinks Low In N.C."
          Raleigh News & Observer. December 24, 1969.

5,843.   Lewis, Susan. "Klan Chiefs May Be Held In Con-
          tempt." Raleigh News & Observer. November 9,
          1965.

5,844.   "Liberties Union Backs Klan Stand." New Bern Sun-
          Journal. March 25, 1966.

5,845.   "List Of Unsolved Columbus County Floggings Mounts."
          Durham Morning Herald. January 12, 1952, Sect. 1,
          p. 8.

5,846.   "A Litany Of 'Not Guilty'." Time. Vol. 116,
          December 1, 1980, pp. 25-26.

5,847.   Little, Loye. " 'Subversives' Are Targets At
          Forsyth Rally Of Klan." Winston-Salem Journal.
          August 22, 1966.

5,848.   "Lo The Poor Indian!" Chapel Hill Weekly. January
          28, 1958.

5,849.   "Local Clergy Condemn Klan In Statement." Daily
          Reflector. September 25, 1964.

5,850.   Lougee, George. "Klan Leader Declares Here LBJ
          Group's Best Recruiter." Durham Morning Herald.
          April 25, 1965.

5,851.   "Louisburg Events Orderly; Franklin Threat Probed."
          Raleigh News & Observer. December 8, 1964.

5,852.   Lowther, William. "An Agent Under The Sheets."
          Mac Leans. Vol. 93, August 4, 1980, p. 26.

5,853.   "Lumbee Indians On The Warpath." Asheville Citizen.
          January 21, 1958.

5,854.   "Lumbee Klan 'War' Reporters Turn Chicken - For
          2nd Time." Charlotte Observer. March 11, 1966.

5,855.   "Lumbees Boycott Meet With Klan At Fayetteville."
          Durham Morning Herald. March 22, 1966.

5,856.   Lynch, Bob. "Jaypee Linked To Klan." Raleigh
          News & Observer. October 29, 1965.

5,857.   MacRae, Ronnie. "Break-Away Klansmen Put Torch
To UKA Members Cards." Concord Tribune. September
13, 1969, pp. 1-2

5,858.   Maddry, Lawrence. "Kluxers Stump In Orange." Chapel
Hill Weekly. June 25, 1965.

5,859.   "Man Held In Wounding Of Two At Klan Rally."
Durham Morning Herald. November 9, 1966.

5,860.   "Man Who Threatened Self In Letter Given Freedom."
Durham Morning Herald. March 7, 1952, p. 8.

5,861.   "Many Regret Smithfield Sentences." Raleigh News
& Observer. April 13, 1969, p. 1.

5,862.   March, William. "Greensboro Rallies Blast Klan,
Recall Civil Rights Anniversary." National
Catholic Reporter. Vol. 16, February 15, 1980,
pp. 4-5.

5,863.   "Marchers Join Procession Of Activists Killed In
Anti-Klan Rally." San Francisco Chronicle.
November 12, 1979, p. 4.

5,864.   "Marchers Protest Greensboro Verdict." New York
Times. November 21, 1980, p. A16.

5,865.   Martin, Wilbur. "Testimony In Klan Hearing
Studied." New Bern Sun-Journal. February 25,
1966.

5,866.   "The Mask And The Coattail." Raleigh News &
Observer. January 20, 1958.

5,867.   "Masked White Men Assault Aged Woman." Pittsburgh
Courier. June 9, 1923, pp. 3-4.

5,868.   Masland, Tom. "Klan, Communists: Explosive Mix."
Philadelphia Inquirer. November 8, 1979.

5,869.   "Maxton Rally Plans Unchanged; Klan Cites Protection Rights." Raleigh News & Observer. January
18, 1958.

5,870.   McConville, Edward. "Portrait Of A Klansman: The
Prophetic Voice Of C.P. Ellis." Nation. Vol.
217, October 15, 1973, pp. 361-366.

5,871.   McCrary, Elissa. "CWP Dismisses Trial As Part Of
Cover-Up." Forest City Daily Courier. November
18, 1980, p. 7.

5,872.   _____. "Jury Gets Nazi/Klan Case." Forest
City Courier. November 7, 1980, p. 4.

5,873.   . "Klan/Nazi Trial Jury Setting New Record For Deliberation." *Forest City Daily Courier*. November 14, 1980, p. 3.

5,874.   McDaniel, J. Gaskill. "Historic New Bern Keeps Pride." *Raleigh News & Observer*. January 30, 1965, p. 1.

5,875.   McIver, Stuart. "The Murder Of A Scalawag." *American History Illustrated*. Vol. 8, April, 1973, pp. 12-18.

5,876.   McKnight, David. "With Pop And Prayer, Klan Meets." *Durham Morning Herald*. June 20, 1970.

5,877.   McLamb, Kinnon. "Action Urged Against Klan." *Raleigh News & Observer*. July 29, 1966.

5,878.   "Media Martyrdom: The Greensboro Shootout." *Harpers*. Vol. 260, March, 1980, pp. 95-99.

5,879.   "Melee Erupts In Hall As Klan Trial Starts." *Washington Post*. June 17, 1980, p. A6.

5,880.   "Membership In Klan Is Offered To Indians." *New York Times*. March 22, 1966, p. 43.

5,881.   "Memorial Auditorium Not Available To Klan." *Raleigh News & Observer*. July 28, 1966.

5,882.   Miller, Hannah. "Plan: "Who's Who' In KKK." *Charlotte Observer*. February 16, 1965.

5,883.   "Minister Believes Hate Led To Burning Of Tree." *Daily Reflector*. September 9, 1965.

5,884.   "Minister Claims Search At Klan Meeting." *Greensboro Daily News*. September 30, 1964.

5,885.   "Minister Told Of Threats By KKK At HUAC Hearing." *Daily Reflector*. October 25, 1965.

5,886.   "Ministerial Association Blasts Klan." *Raleigh News & Observer*. November 17, 1965.

5,887.   "Ministers Ask Klan To Stop Pitt Rallies." *Daily Reflector*. April 6, 1965.

5,888.   "Ministers Denounce Klansmen." *Raleigh News & Observer*. December 25, 1965.

5,889.   Mitchell, Jerry. "Justice Dept., N.C. Prosecutors To Meet." *Washington Afro-American*. November 22, 1980, pp. 1, 2.

5,890.   _____. "Klansmen And Nazis Acquitted In
        Slayings." Bilalian News. December 5, 1980, p. 9.

5,891.   _____. "Nazi-Klansmen Set Free." New York
        Recorder. November 22, 1980, p. 2.

5,892.   _____. "Rev. Lowery Condemns Klan Acquittals."
        New York Recorder. November 22, 1980, p. 7.

5,893.   "Moody Says No Basis For Outlawing Klan." Raleigh
        News & Observer. September 1, 1965.

5,894.   "Moore Attacks Klan's Sunday Rally Actions." New
        Bern Sun-Journal. August 3, 1966.

5,895.   "Moore Commends Warning To Klan." Durham Morning
        Herald. March 17, 1966.

5,896.   "Moore Committee Seeks Unmask Klan Membership."
        Daily Reflector. January 3, 1966.

5,897.   "Moore Condemns Lawlessness Of Klan Or Negro
        Militants." Winston-Salem Journal. July 24, 1966.

5,898.   "Moore Declares 'Absolutely' No Data On Klan
        Withheld." Durham Morning Herald. July 27, 1966.

5,899.   "Moore Denies Easing Stand Against Klan."
        Fayetteville Observer. June 10, 1966.

5,900.   "Moore Denies SBI Withheld Information." New Bern
        Sun-Journal. July 27, 1966.

5,901.   "Moore Doubts Klan So Active." Daily Reflector.
        October 25, 1965.

5,902.   "Moore Draws Fire On Remark Over NAACP And KKK."
        Durham Morning Herald. October 29, 1966.

5,903.   "Moore Gives No New Word On Klan Probe." Winston-
        Salem Journal. August 9, 1966.

5,904.   "Moore Hits Klan Growth In State." Raleigh News
        & Observer. June 20, 1965.

5,905.   "Moore Hits Lawlessness Of Negroes And White."
        Raleigh News & Observer. July 24, 1966, p. 4.

5,906.   "Moore In Blast At Ku Klux Klan." Durham Morning
        Herald. October 26, 1966, p. 12A.

5,907.   "Moore Insists No Klan Facts Were Withheld." New
        Bern Sun-Journal. July 29, 1966.

5,908.   "Moore Labels Klan Sorry Organization." Charlotte
        Observer. October 26, 1966.

5,909.   "Moore: No Action Against Klan." Raleigh News &
          Observer. June 7, 1966.

5,910.   "Moore Praises Anti-Klan Stand." Raleigh News &
          Observer. November 19, 1965.

5,911.   "Moore Says Group Is Not Anti-Klan." Charlotte
          Observer. August 4, 1966.

5,912.   "Moore Says Seawell Has His Best Wishes." Winston-
          Salem Journal. August 4, 1966.

5,913.   "Moore Tells Troops To Stand By At Rally."
          Charlotte Observer. August 13, 1966.

5,914.   "Moore's Future Steps Conjecture." Daily Reflector.
          June 15, 1966.

5,915.   "Moore's Win Seen 'Victory For Klan' By Grand
          Dragon." Durham Morning Herald. June 30, 1964,
          Sect. B, p. 10.

5,916.   "More Arrests Being Made In Columbus KKK Lashings."
          Durham Morning Herald. June 25, 1952, p. 1.

5,917.   "More Arrests Made After Murder Of Anti-Klan
          Marchers In N.C." Houston Post. November 5, 1979,
          p. A5.

5,918.   "More Jurors Sought." Charlotte Observer. June
          27, 1980, p. B2.

5,919.   "Motion Filed To Speed Jones' Perjury Trial."
          Charlotte Observer. May 5, 1966.

5,920.   "Moving In On 'Security Guards'." Greensboro
          Daily News. August 13, 1966.

5,921.   "Mrs. Jones' Filing Upsets Rowan Chief." Charlotte
          Observer. April 16, 1966.

5,922.   "Murder Trial Of 6 KKK Members Begins In North
          Carolina." Houston Post. June 17, 1980, p. 3A.

5,923.   "Murray's Job Motion Denied." Raleigh News &
          Observer. August 7, 1971, p. 3.

5,924.   "NAACP Chief Urges AFL-CIO To Renew Its Opposition
          To The KKK." San Francisco Chronicle. November 17,
          1979, p. 8.

5,925.   "NAACP: Don't Lump Us With Klan." Charlotte
          Observer. October 29, 1966.

5,926.   "NAACP President Asks Negroes To Boycott Fair."
          Winston-Salem Journal. September 30, 1966.

5,927.   "NAACP Seeks U.S. Probe of 1979 Deaths In Greensboro, N.C." Norfolk Journal & Guide. July 1, 1981, p. 1.

5,928.   Nadler, Mark. "Ku Klux Klan Country: Group's Membership Increases In Gaston, Lincoln, Catawba." Charlotte Observer. November 18, 1979, pp. 1, 6.

5,929.   "A National Disgrace Puts City In Spotlight." Chicago Tribune. November 11, 1979.

5,930.   "National Guard Brought Into Greensboro Following Deaths There." Norfolk Journal & Guide. November 16, 1979, p. 1A.

5,931.   "National Guard To Back Police At Klan Meeting." Greensboro Daily News. August 13, 1966.

5,932.   "The Natives Are Restless." Time. Vol. 71, January 27, 1958, pp. 20-21.

5,933.   "Nazi Bombing Case In N.C. Ends In Mistrial." Washington Star. July 19, 1981, p. A7.

5,934.   "Nazi Hand Seen In N.C. Klan's Reign Of Terror." Norfolk Journal & Guide. October 7, 1939, p. 5.

5,935.   "Nazi Head Sees 'White' Revolution." Forest City Daily Courier. November 18, 1980, p. 7.

5,936.   "Nazi-Klan Trial To Begin In Greensboro, N.C." San Francisco Chronicle. August 4, 1980, p. 7.

5,937.   "Nazi Motorcade Canceled, But 'Hitlerfest' Is Planned." New York Times. April 10, 1980, p. 22.

5,938.   "Nazis And Ku Klux Klansmen Set Fire To Cross At Rally In N.C." San Francisco Chronicle. April 20, 1980, p. 17A.

5,939.   "N.C. And Greensboro Officials Discuss Deaths At Anti-KKK Rally." Chicago Defender. November 5, 1979, p. 5.

5,940.   "NC Chief Jones' Release Set." Raleigh News & Observer. December 17, 1969, p. 15.

5,941.   "N.C. Counsel Quits, Charges Klan Data Is Being Withheld." Charlotte Observer. July 26, 1966.

5,942.   "N.C. Grand Dragon Banished From Klan." Raleigh News & Observer. October 10, 1975.

5,943.   "N.C. Guard Put On Alert." Washington Post. January 31, 1980, p. A22.

5,944.   "NC Klan Is Called Hate Group." Raleigh News &
          Observer. August 4, 1967, p. 3.

5,945.   "N.C. Klan Leader: The News Is Faulty." Raleigh
          News & Observer. May 23, 1965.

5,946.   "N.C. Klan 'Winning' Members." Greensboro Daily
          News. April 2, 1966, p. A7.

5,947.   "NC Klan Wizard Begins Year Term." Raleigh News
          & Observer. February 15, 1969, p. 3.

5,948.   "N.C. Klansmen And Nazis Found Not Guilty In Death
          Of 5 Communists." Houston Post. November 18, 1980,
          p. 1A.

5,949.   "N.C. Klansman Resigning; Puts 'God And Country'
          Before KKK." Raleigh News & Observer. October 22,
          1965.

5,950.   "N.C. Kluxers Warn Negro In Letter." Pittsburgh
          Courier. January 7, 1928, p. 1.

5,951.   "N.C. Mum On Security For Klan." Winston-Salem
          Journal. March 11, 1966.

5,952.   "N.C. Murder Trial In Deaths Of 5 Communists."
          Chicago Tribune. August 20, 1980, p. 1.

5,953.   "N.C. Negro Woman Reports Mob Of White Men Beat
          Her." Asheville Citizen. January 23, 1951.

5,954.   "N.C. Police Confirm Giving Man Permit Copy Of
          Anti-Klan Rally." San Francisco Chronicle.
          November 8, 1979, p. 44.

5,955.   "N.C. Police Probe Of Shootings In Anti-Klan Rally
          Viewed." San Francisco Chronicle. November 27,
          1979, p. 7.

5,956.   "N.C. Prosecutors Drop All Charges In Anti-Klan
          Deaths." Los Angeles Times. November 27, 1980,
          p. 5.

5,957.   "N.C. Prosecutors Drop Remaining Charges In KKK/
          Nazi Trial." Chicago Tribune. November 27, 1980,
          Sect. 4, p. 2.

5,958.   "N.C. Protesters In 3 Cities Hit Acquittal Of KKK-
          Nazi Killers." New York Daily World. November
          22, 1980, pp. 3, 10.

5,959.   "North Carolina Senate Bars Paramilitary Training
          Camps." New York Times. July 12, 1981, p. 33.

5,960.   "N.C. Sheriff Tells Of Joining Klan In Effort To
          Get Information." Raleigh News & Observer.
          October 26, 1965.

5,961.   "N.C. State Club To Invite Communist, Klan Speakers."
          Charlotte Observer. April 1, 1966.

5,962.   "N.C. State Fair Attendance Down." Durham Morning
          Herald. December 6, 1966.

5,963.   "N.C. Trial On Murder Of Communist Workers Party
          Members Begins." Los Angeles Times. June 17,
          1980, p. 12.

5,964.   "N.C. Won't Tolerate Illegal Actions, Sanford Warns
          Klan." Durham Morning Herald. June 23, 1964,
          Sect. A, p. 1.

5,965.   "N. Carolina Puts A Ban On Hoods." Pittsburgh
          Courier. March 5, 1927, p. 8.

5,966.   "Negro Held As Sniper At Klan." New York Times.
          November 8, 1966, p. 27.

5,967.   "Negro Leaders Oppose Klan's State Fair Booth."
          Durham Morning Herald. October 1, 1966, p. 22A.

5,968.   "Negro Shot After Klan Rally; FBI Investigates."
          Charlotte Observer. April 3, 1966.

5,969.   "Negroes Ask Removal Of KKK Signs." Raleigh News &
          Observer. November 2, 1966.

5,970.   "Negroes Deplore Growth Of KKK." Greensboro
          Daily News. August 21, 1966.

5,971.   "Negroes In Raleigh Invade Klan Rally Attended By
          5,000." New York Times. August 15, 1966, p. 17.

5,972.   "Negroes Seek Policemen In Hertford Row." New
          Bern Sun-Journal. March 14, 1966.

5,973.   "Neighbors Of Klansmen Express Surprise Over
          Violence." New York Times. November 11, 1979,
          p. 30.

5,974.   "New Klan Group Gets NC Charter." Raleigh News &
          Observer. September 16, 1967, p. 24.

5,975.   "New Klavern Linked With Cross-Burnings." Raleigh
          News & Observer. June 26, 1965.

5,976.   "New Teeth For The Grand Wizard." Raleigh News &
          Observer. January 24, 1958.

5,977.   "News Coverage Of Klan Booth." Durham Morning Herald. October 23, 1966.

5,978.   "Newsmen Belong To Klan - Jones." Greensboro Daily News. August 16, 1966.

5,979.   "Newsmen Ejected By Greenshirts; Film Is Removed." Greenville Daily Reflector. September 28, 1964.

5,980.   Newton, David. "Klan, Nazis Knew Details Of Rally." Greensboro Daily News. November 7, 1979.

5,981.   Nicholas, Wayne. "Bullet Hits Car Driven By Acquitted Klansmen." Charlotte Observer. November 21, 1980, p. C1.

5,982.   "Nine Alleged Ex-Klansmen Convicted Of Flogging Pair; Terms Suspended." Durham Morning Herald. December 4, 1954, p. 1.

5,983.   "19 Convicted In Carolinas Klan Kidnap-Flogging Case." Durham Morning Herald. May 19, 1953, Sect. 1, p. 1.

5,984.   "19 Men Face Trial Tomorrow In Klan Flogging Case Before Federal Court." Durham Morning Herald. May 17, 1953, p. 6.

5,985.   "No Clues Found In Shooting Attack On Ku Klux Klansman In N.C." Houston Post. November 21, 1980, p. 2A.

5,986.   "No Jurors Accepted." Charlotte Observer. June 25, 1980, p. C2.

5,987.   " 'No Klan Data Withheld'." Virginian Pilot. July 27, 1966.

5,988.   "No Lip From The Klan." Raleigh News & Observer. September 30, 1951.

5,989.   "No Place For 'Security Guards'." Greensboro Daily News. August 9, 1966.

5,990.   Nordan, Dave. "Louisburg Parade Draws KKK Threats." Raleigh News & Observer. December 6, 1964.

5,991.   Nordheimer, Jon. "Anti-Negro Group Vexing Police In Wilmington, N.C." New York Times. October 7, 1971, p. 25.

5,992.   _____. "Dissension Riddles Klan In Carolina." Raleigh News & Observer. September 18, 1969.

5,993.   _____. "Klan In Trouble In North Carolina." New York Times. September 17, 1969, p. 17.

5,994.   "North Carolina Accepts Klan." New York Times.
          July 8, 1965, p. 4.

5,995.   "North Carolina Bars Laws Hostile To Klan." New
          York Times. March 2, 1923, p. 6.

5,996.   "North Carolina Fair To Bar All Politics." New
          York Times. October 30, 1966, p. 13.

5,997.   "North Carolina Fights The Klan." New York Times.
          January 3, 1966, p. 24.

5,998.   "North Carolina Guardsmen On Alert In Anti-Klan
          Rally." New York Times. January 31, 1980, p. 14.

5,999.   "North Carolina: Indian Raid." Newsweek. Vol. 51,
          January 27, 1958, p. 27.

6,000.   "North Carolina Justice." New York Times. November
          30, 1980, Sect. 4, p. 16.

6,001.   "North Carolina Klan Splits With Dr. Evans."
          New York Times. February 23, 1927, p. 18.

6,002.   "North Carolina Labeled Most Active For Klan."
          Raleigh News & Observer. October 20, 1965.

6,003.   "North Carolina Opens Active War On Klan."
          Washington Evening Star. January 3, 1966.

6,004.   "North Carolina Prison Frees Klan Ex-Wizard."
          New York Times. February 5, 1954, p. 12.

6,005.   "The North Carolina Verdict." Washington Post.
          November 20, 1980, p. A18.

6,006.   "North Carolina Won't Prosecute 16 In Slayings At
          Anti-Klan Rally." New York Times. November 27,
          1980, p. A22.

6,007.   "North Carolina's Klan." Carolina Israelite."
          May-June 1966.

6,008.   "Not Active In Klan, Says Sheriff-Elect." Winston-
          Salem Journal. November 12, 1966.

6,009.   " 'Not Guilty' - Jury Didn't Vindicate Klan."
          Charlotte Observer. November 19, 1980, p. 16A.

6,010.   "Not Private." Raleigh News & Observer. August
          20, 1951.

6,011.   "Nothing Withheld - Moore." Raleigh News & Observer.
          July 27, 1966.

6,012.   "Observations." <u>Charlotte Observer</u>. August 5,
          1966.

6,013.   "Offending KKK Signs Removed From Highways."
          <u>Greensboro Daily News</u>. November 3, 1966.

6,014.   "Offers To Give Up Party Booth." <u>Daily Reflector</u>.
          October 28, 1966.

6,015.   "Official Doffs Robes To Run For Sheriff."
          <u>Christian Science Monitor</u>. March 10, 1966, p. 16.

6,016.   "Official Reports First Shot At Rally Came From
          Klan." <u>New York Times</u>. March 26, 1980, p. 19.

6,017.   "An Official View Of The Klan Rally." <u>Greensboro
          Daily News</u>. August 12, 1966.

6,018.   "Officials At Greensboro Discuss Federal Charges
          Against Klan." <u>Washington Star</u>. November 22,
          1980, p. A7.

6,019.   "Officials Set To Prevent KKK Violence." <u>New Bern
          Sun-Journal</u>. March 17, 1966.

6,020.   "Officials Suggest Outlawing Klan." <u>Asheville
          Citizen</u>. February 28, 1952.

6,021.   "Officials To Halt Klan's Picketing." <u>Winston-
          Salem Journal</u>. March 24, 1966.

6,022.   "Old English Law Used In Trial Of Kluxers."
          <u>Raleigh News & Observer</u>. February 28, 1967.

6,023.   "Old KKK House Will Be Park's Community Center."
          <u>Raleigh News & Observer</u>. December 26, 1972, p. 44.

6,024.   "Old South." <u>Newsweek</u>. Vol. 94, November 12,
          1979, p. 50.

6,025.   "On Misery Hill." <u>Southern Pines Pilot</u>. March 7,
          1952.

6,026.   "One Of Acquitted Klansmen Is Fired At In Night
          Attack." <u>Washington Post</u>. November 21, 1980, p.
          2.

6,027.   "One Simple Question." <u>Raleigh News & Observer</u>.
          March 29, 1952.

6,028.   "1,000 Will Guard Funeral Of 5 Killed At Anti-Klan
          March." <u>New York Times</u>. November 9, 1979, p. A16.

6,029.   "The Only Klan Headline Would Be Welcomed." <u>Durham
          Morning Herald</u>. February 20, 1958.

6,030.   "Only The Facade Peaceful." Durham Morning Herald.
          October 11, 1966.

6,031.   "Opposes Klan Exhibit." Durham Morning Herald.
          October 12, 1966.

6,032.   Osolin, Charles. "SBI Says Culler Is Klan Member."
          Winston-Salem Journal. May 5, 1966.

6,033.   "Other Editors Saying Klan Gets Message." Daily
          Reflector. March 22, 1966.

6,034.   "Ousted KKK Head Starts Court Fight." Raleigh
          News & Observer. July 18, 1971, p. 14.

6,035.   "Ousted Klan Leader Seeks State Action." Raleigh
          News & Observer. May 24, 1967.

6,036.   "Ousted Leader Dorsett Seeks State Action." Raleigh
          News & Observer. May 24, 1967, p. 26.

6,037.   "Outcome Of KKK-Nazi Trial In North Carolina -
          Letters." Chicago Tribune. December 3, 1980,
          Sect. 6, p. 2.

6,038.   "Outlawing The Klan May Give It Boost." Raleigh
          News & Observer. May 5, 1966.

6,039.   "Outrage At Klan Acquittal." Sacramento Observer.
          November 20-26, 1980, pp. A1, A8.

6,040.   Page, Robert C. "Moore Gives Klan Post-Fair
          Blast." Durham Morning Herald. October 30, 1966.

6,041.   _____. "Semantics Blur KKK File Facts."
          Durham Morning Herald. July 31, 1966.

6,042.   "A Painful Message From Greensboro." New York
          Times. November 25, 1980, p. A18.

6,043.   "Panel Of Jurors Drawn For Trial Of KKK Cases."
          Durham Morning Herald. May 2, 1952, p. 1.

6,044.   Parke, Richard H. "10 Ex-Klansmen Guilty In
          Flogging As U.S. Invokes Lindbergh Law." New
          York Times. May 14, 1952, p. 1.

6,045.   _____. "U.S. Puts 11 Klan On Trial In South."
          New York Times. May 13, 1952, p. 18.

6,046.   Parker, Barry. "Klan: Biggest Donor To State's
          ACLU." Raleigh News & Observer. February 15,
          1972.

6,047.   Parker, Roy Jr. "Chalmers Counsel For Klan Dragon."
          Raleigh News & Observer. October 20, 1965.

6,049.   Parker, Roy Jr. "Computer Spews Out KKK Radio
          Letters." Raleigh News & Observer. November 4,
          1965.

6,050.   _____. "Hearing Shows More Klan Activity."
          Raleigh News & Observer. October 26, 1965.

6,051.   _____. "Klan Back." Raleigh News & Observer.
          October 22, 1965.

6,052.   _____. "Klan's Kludd Raps Non-Prayer Probe."
          Raleigh News & Observer. October 28, 1965.

6,053.   _____. "Klansman Of Wayne Resigns." Raleigh
          News & Observer. October 22, 1965.

6,054.   _____. "Klansmen Face Contempt Move." Raleigh
          News & Observer. January 7, 1966.

6,055.   _____. "Lennon Votes 'No' In KKK Contempt."
          Raleigh News & Observer. February 3, 1966.

6,056.   _____. "Records Reveal Activity." Raleigh
          News & Observer. October 27, 1965.

6,057.   _____. "Rise In Klan Fever Awaited. Greensboro
          Daily News. March 13, 1966.

6,058.   _____. "Tar Heel Congressmen Size Up Klan
          Strength." Raleigh News & Observer. October 24,
          1965.

6,059.   "Party Suing Officials." New York Times. November
          4, 1980, p. A16.

6,060.   Paysour, Conrad. "Historian: Klan Ineffective
          From Reconstruction To Present." Greensboro Daily
          News. January 20, 1980.

6,061.   Paysour, LaFleur and Allen Cowan. "U.S. Ready To
          Review Testimony In Klan-Nazi Trial." Charlotte
          Observer. November 19, 1980, p. 10A.

6,062.   Peek, V. Lonnie, Jr. "Greensboro's A Sign Of The
          Trial." Michigan Chronicle. December 6, 1980,
          p. 3.

6,063.   "The People's Forum." Raleigh News & Observer.
          October 16, 1966.

6,064.   "Persecuting Klan." Charlotte Observer. March
          20, 1966.

6,065.   "Permanent Block For Klan Rally Hearing Opens
          Today." Durham Morning Herald. March 31, 1966,
          p. 3A.

6,066.   Phillips, Wayne. "Indian Raid Knits A Carolina
          Town." New York Times. January 26, 1958, p. 72.

6,067.   _____. "Klansman Fined For Maxton Role." New
          York Times. January 23, 1958, p. 13.

6,068.   Pinsky, Mark I. "Greensboro Knows Grim Struggles,
          Not Fatal Ones." New York Times. January 13,
          1980, Sect. 4, p. 5.

6,069.   _____. "Greensboro Massacre." Progressive.
          Vol. 44, January, 1980, pp. 11-12.

6,070.   "Pittsburgh Communist Workers Party Eyes N.C. KKK
          Rally Deaths." Pittsburgh Courier. November 10,
          1979, p. 1.

6,071.   "Plans Rallies In Johnston." Raleigh News &
          Observer. September 26, 1968, p. 8.

6,072.   Plott, Monte. "Hypnosis May Be Factor In Nazi
          Trial." Forest City Daily Courier. August 15,
          1980, p. 4.

6,073.   _____. "The Klan: Communists, Not Blacks Now
          Target." Greensboro Record. November 8, 1979.

6,074.   _____. "KKK Plans Push In N.C." Durham Morning
          Herald. March 11, 1979, p. 1.

6,075.   Poindexter, Jesse. "Sheriff-Elect Won't Say If
          He's A Klan Member." Winston-Salem Journal.
          November 10, 1966.

6,076.   _____. "Wilkes Klan Story Held Incomplete."
          Winston-Salem Journal. August 18, 1966.

6,077.   "Police Call For Full Forces At Raleigh Klan
          Today." Greensboro Daily News. August 14, 1966.

6,078.   "Police Chief Charged With Whipping Woman." New
          York Times. April 26, 1923, p. 8.

6,079.   "Police Chief, Klan Leader Plan Meeting." Raleigh
          News & Observer. August 6, 1971, p. 26.

6,080.   "Police Chief Rejects Klan Auxiliary Offer."
          Raleigh News & Observer. August 7, 1971, p. 3.

6,081.   "Police Chief To Answer Charge Today." Daily
          Reflector. March 30, 1966.

6,082.   "Police Moonlighting At Klan Rally Scored."
          Durham Morning Herald. August 10, 1966.

6,083. "Police Plan Secret On Maxton Klan Rally." Durham Morning Herald. March 11, 1966.

6,084. "Police Presence Keeps Greensboro March Quiet." Christian Science Monitor. November 13, 1979, p. 2.

6,085. "Police Say Klan Given Parade Permit Copy Before N.C. Murders." Houston Post. November 8, 1979, p. 8B.

6,086. "Police Should Use Measures To Restrain Klan's Guards." Charlotte Observer. August 2, 1966.

6,087. "Police Spy Cites Klan Blast Plot." Raleigh News & Observer. March 19, 1958.

6,088. "Police To Surround Site Of Klan Rally." Durham Morning Herald. August 14, 1966.

6,089. "Policeman Tells Of Sighting Klansmen Near Shooting." New York Times. August 7, 1980, p. A14.

6,090. "Powell Will Assist Prosecution Of Klan Leader In Columbus." Durham Morning Herald. June 14, 1952, p. 2.

6,091. Preslar, Lloyd. "Klan Leaders Post Bond On Charges." Winston-Salem Journal. March 12, 1966.

6,092. _____. "Klan's Biggest Gains Scored In This State, House Committee Says: 113 Units Reported In North Carolina." Winston-Salem Journal. October 20, 1965, pp. 1, 8.

6,093. _____. "Report Says Communists, Klan Similar." Winston-Salem Journal. September 11, 1966.

6,094. Press, Robert M. "Greensboro Killings Mask Black Gains." Christian Science Monitor. November 7, 1979, p. 4.

6,095. _____. "N.C. Shootings Expose Web Of Extremist Groups." Christian Science Monitor. November 6, 1979, p. 4.

6,096. _____. "Verdict Reheats KKK Emotions." Christian Science Monitor. November 19, 1980, p. 1.

6,097. Pressley, Patsy V. "Anti-Klan March Draws 7,000 To N.C." The Hilltop (Howard University). February, 1980, pp. 1, 7.

6,098   "Pressured Hookerton Grocery Is Closing." Raleigh News & Observer. July 29, 1967, p. 1.

6,100.   "Pretrial Hearings Are Set In North Carolina Slay-
          ings." New York Times. November 15, 1979, p. A24.

6,101.   "Preyer Warns Of Ku Klux Involvement In North
          Carolina's Political Scene." Durham Morning
          Herald. June 24, 1964, Sect. A, p. 12.

6,102.   "Price Of Pussyfooting." Raleigh News & Observer.
          July 12, 1966.

6,103.   "Prison For Masked Man." New York Times. January
          11, 1923, p. 6.

6,104.   "Probation Ordered In Klan Case." Raleigh News
          & Observer. May 23, 1968, p. 21.

6,105.   "Probe Indicates Ku Klux Klan And Nazis Involved
          In N.C. Killings." Washington Post. November 5,
          1979, p. 9A.

6,106.   "Probe Of Klan Ordered." Raleigh News & Observer.
          July 12, 1966.

6,107.   "Probes Say Dragon Jones Made A Large Profit From
          Widow's Fund." Raleigh News & Observer. October
          22, 1965.

6,108.   "Proper Ending." Raleigh News & Observer. July
          31, 1952.

6,109.   "Prosecution Rests Case In Murder Trial Of Klans-
          men." New York Times. September 18, 1980, p. A20.

6,110.   "Prosecution Rests In Klan Murder Trial." Washing-
          ton Star. November 7, 1980, p. A2.

6,111.   "Prosecutor In Klan-Protest Killings Terms 12
          Suspects Equally Guilty." New York Times.
          November 7, 1979, p. A23.

6,112.   "Protest Pro-KKK Verdict." Michigan Chronicle.
          November 29, 1980, pp. 1, 4.

6,113.   "Public Opinion And The Revivified Klan." Durham
          Morning Herald. January 27, 1958.

6,114.   Rabon, Roy. "Klan Group Believed One Of Strongest."
          Raleigh News & Observer. May 23, 1965.

6,115.   _____. "Klan To March Here Before King's Talk."
          Raleigh News & Observer. July 27, 1966.

6,116.   _____. "Klan Wants To Smoke Peace Pipe."
          Raleigh News & Observer. March 18, 1966.

6,117.   Rabon, Roy. "Klanswoman Fined $50 For Assault."
          Greensboro Daily News. August 27, 1966.

6,118.   _____. "Police Keep Order At Klan Rally."
          Raleigh News & Observer. August 15, 1966.

6,119.   _____. "Wake Klan Group Believed One Of
          Strongest." Raleigh News & Observer. May 23, 1965.

6,120.   "Radio Okay Denied Pitt Klansman." Raleigh News &
          Observer. September 27, 1968, p. 17.

6,121.   "Raid By 500 Indians Balks North Carolina Klan
          Rally." New York Times. January 19, 1958, pp. 1,
          41.

6,122.   "Rain Cools Tempers In Scuffle With Klan." Raleigh
          News & Observer. August 22, 1965.

6,123.   Raines, Howell. "500 March In A Procession For
          Five Slain Communists." New York Times. November
          12, 1979, p. A18.

6,124.   "Raleigh Alert On Klan Rally." New York Times.
          August 13, 1966, p. 8.

6,125.   "Raleigh Police Handled Klan And King Meetings
          Well." Winston-Salem Journal. August 12, 1966.

6,126.   "Rallies Cost State $5,541." Greensboro Daily
          News. August 4, 1966.

6,127.   "Rally, Dinner Slated In Wilmington." Raleigh
          News & Observer. June 29, 1971, p. 3.

6,128.   "Rally Draws 250 Spectators." Raleigh New &
          Observer. July 5, 1971, p. 32.

6,129.   "Rally Marks Split From United Klan." Raleigh
          News & Observer. September 16, 1969, p. 3.

6,130.   "Rally To Protect Slayings At Greensboro Is Put
          Off." New York Times. November 17, 1979, p. A10.

6,131.   "Ranks Growing, Klan Fires Out." Durham Morning
          Herald. September 25, 1966.

6,132.   Rawls, Wendell, Jr. "Jury Choice Slow In Trial
          Of Klansmen." New York Times. July 14, 1980,
          p. 16.

6,133.   _____. "Lawmen Tied To Klan In
          Communists' Protest." New York Times. October 2,
          1981, p. A14.

6,134.   "Raymond D. Mills Arrested." Raleigh News & Observer.
          December 16, 1969, p. 9.

6,135.   Raynor, George. " 'Revival' Of Klan." Raleigh News
          & Observer. November 3, 1963.

6,136.   "Reaction To Verdict Is Varied." Charlotte Observer.
          November 19, 1980, p. 10A.

6,137.   "Real Achievement." Raleigh News & Observer.
          February 28, 1952.

6,138.   "Recording Indicates KKK's Racial Hatred."
          Wilmington Journal. May 7, 1981, p. 1.

6,139.   "Records Show Action Was Aimed At Klan." Raleigh
          News & Observer. July 22, 1967.

6,140.   "Regrettable Conduct." Durham Morning Herald.
          October 20, 1966.

6,141.   Reid, Milton A. "Klan-Style Justice." Norfolk
          Journal & Guide. November 19, 1980, p. 8.

6,142.   Reid, Robert H. "Klans 'Changing With The Times'."
          Durham Morning Herald. December 23, 1973.

6,143.   "Report From Greensboro: Reds, Whites, And Jews."
          Present Tense. Vol. 8, Winter, 1981, pp. 12-14.

6,144.   "Revolt Threatens Over Jones' Leadership." Raleigh
          News & Observer. April 4, 1967, p. 1.

6,145.   "Rhetoric Fuels Marchers." Greensboro Daily News.
          November 12, 1979.

6,146.   "Rights For Klan." Greensboro Daily News. March 29,
          1966.

6,147.   "Rights Group Helps Klan Aide In Fight To Regain
          His Job.' New York Times. July 20, 1971, p. 15.

6,148.   "Rights Of The KKK." Winston-Salem Journal. March
          26, 1966.

6,149.   "Rights Of The Klan." Winston-Salem Journal. March
          22, 1966.

6,150.   "Rights Of The Klan." Winston-Salem Journal. May 6,
          1966.

6,151.   " 'Rights Violated' Says Harnett KKK." Raleigh
          News & Observer. May 22, 1966.

6,152.   "Road Division Removes Signs Of Ku Klux Klan."
          Winston-Salem Journal. November 3, 1966.

6,153.   "Robed Klansman And Negro Youth Fight In Carolina."
New York Times. August 1, 1966, p. 13.

6,154.   "Robed Pickets Protest Movie." Raleigh News &
Observer. August 10, 1973, p. 26A.

6,155.   "Robes Show Rank." Raleigh News & Observer. May
23, 1965.

6,156.   "Robeson County Klan Trial Of Three Declared Mistrial." Durham Morning Herald. March 29, 1952, p. 1.

6,157.   "Robeson Klan Rally Held 'Grave' Danger." Durham
Morning Herald. March 17, 1966.

6,158.   "Rocky Mount: End Klan Picketing." Charlotte
Observer. March 25, 1966.

6,159.   "Role Of Bill Sampson In Anti-KKK Rally In N.C.
Discussed." Los Angeles Times. November 23, 1979,
Sect. 1A, p. 13.

6,160.   Rollins, Ray. "First KKK Rally In Lexington Quiet."
Winston-Salem Journal. July 15, 1966.

6,161.   _____. "He Dislikes Klan, Backs Its Rights."
Winston-Salem Journal. March 27, 1966, p. A6.

6,162.   _____. "Lexington Klansmen Expect KKK Officials
At Their Rally." Winston-Salem Journal. July 14,
1966.

6,163.   Ross, James. "Anderson, SBI Head Admits File On
KKK Barred To Committee." Greensboro Daily News.
July 28, 1966.

6,164.   _____. "Black Power: Negroes In State Reject
Separation." Greensboro Daily News. August 21,
1966.

6,165.   _____. "Did Klan Win In Rowan?" Greensboro
Daily News. November 16, 1966.

6,166.   _____. "N.C.'s Klan Will Not Endorse Candidate
Slate, Says Jones." Greensboro Daily News. May
28, 1966.

6,167.   "Rowan GOP Shuns Ku Klux Candidates." Greensboro
Daily News. April 30, 1966.

6,168.   "Rowan GOP Wants No Klan Candidates." Winston-
Salem Journal. April 30, 1966.

6,169.   "Rowan Klan Marches Without Invitation." Raleigh
News & Observer. December 4, 1968, p. 3.

6,170.   "Rowan Sheriff Denies Badge Not For Dragon."
          Raleigh News & Observer. September 29, 1968, p. 1.

6,171.   Rowan, Carl. "Death Of Participant In N.C. Anti-
          Klan Protest." Washington Post. November 8, 1979,
          p. 1C.

6,172.   _____. "KKK Greensboro Ambush And Blacks' Pro-
          gress." New Orleans Times Picayune. November 12,
          1979, p. 23.

6,173.   Ruark, Henry G. "Fear Klan Revival In The Carolinas."
          Christian Century. Vol. 75, February 26, 1958,
          pp. 257-258.

6,174.   "Said Vehicle Of Death, Destruction, Fear."
          Raleigh News & Observer. December 11, 1967, p. 1.

6,175.   "Sanford Warns Klan: Leave Church Alone." Raleigh
          News & Observer. July 12, 1964.

6,176.   Savage, Stuart. "Judge Fines Kluxers For 'Demon-
          strating'." Daily Reflector. March 28, 1966.

6,177.   "Say 'Never' To Klan Tactics." Charlotte Observer.
          August 8, 1966.

6,178.   "Say They Were Flogged By Klan." New York Times.
          February 18, 1952, p. 20.

6,179.   "Says Return Of KKK Is Progress." Daily Reflector.
          December 11, 1965.

6,180.   "SBI Denies Agent Had Kludd Fired." Raleigh News
          & Observer. June 16, 1967, p. 48.

6,181.   "SBI Denies Hiding Of Klan Data." Virginian Pilot.
          July 21, 1966.

6,182.   "SBI Denies Klan Data Suppressed." Raleigh News &
          Observer. July 21, 1966.

6,183.   "SBI Finds Crippled Youth Removed From Klan Rally."
          Greensboro Daily News. July 13, 1966.

6,184.   "SBI Is Asked To Open Files." Winston-Salem Journal.
          July 20, 1966.

6,185.   "SBI Lauded For Job." Raleigh News & Observer.
          October 18, 1966.

6,186.   "SBI Says Klan Facts Not Hidden." Greensboro Daily
          News. July 21, 1966.

6,187.   "SBI Surveillance Of Klan Booth Kept 'Incidents'
          Minor." Daily Reflector. October 17, 1966.

6,188. "SBI Turns Over Klan Materials." _New Bern Journal_."
July 21, 1966.

6,189. "The SBI's Klan Files." _Winston-Salem Journal_.
July 27, 1966.

6,190. "School Bus Idled By Fear Of Klan." _Daily Reflector_.
December 2, 1966.

6,191. Schlosser, Jim. "Klan In N.C. Appears To Have Hit
Hard Times." _Durham Sun_. October 24, 1974.

6,192. Scism, Jack. "Four Die In Klan-Leftist Shootout."
Greensboro Daily News. November 4, 1979, pp. A1, A6.

6,193. _____. "Funeral March Is Peaceful." _Greensboro
Daily News_. November 12, 1979.

6,194. "SCLC Prevented March On Klan." _Winston-Salem
Journal_. March 13, 1966.

6,195. "Scott Rejects Klan Invitation." _New York Times_.
August 10, 1957, p. 16.

6,196. "Scuffles Mark Start Of Trial In The Slayings Of 5
Leftists." _New York Times_. June 17, 1980, p. 12.

6,197. Scully, Malcolm. "A Craig Phillips Grapples Klansmen." _Charlotte Observer_. October 8, 1966.

6,198. "Seawell Apologizes About Klan Issue." _Winston-
Salem Journal_. May 5, 1966.

6,199. "Seawell Apologizes To Eure, Says Klan May Lose
Permit." _Charlotte Observer_. May 5, 1966, p. 6A.

6,200. "Seawell Blasts Klan Decision." _Fayetteville
Observer_. July 1, 1966.

6,201. "Seawell Charges SBI Men 'Locked Up' Klan Evidence."
Greensboro Daily News. July 19, 1966.

6,202. "Seawell Comments On Klan Legality." _New Bern Sun-
Journal_. July 19, 1966.

6,203. "Seawell Declares SBI Klan Files 'Withheld'."
Durham Morning Herald. July 19, 1966.

6,204. "Seawell Finds Plans Of Klan Bring Uproar." _New
Bern Sun-Journal_. July 7, 1966.

6,205. "Seawell Hints Move Possible Against Klan." _Durham
Morning Herald_. May 1, 1966.

6,206. "Seawell Labels Anderson's Klan Statement 'Evasive'."
Durham Morning Herald. July 23, 1966.

6,207.   "Seawell Mum To Him On Klan, Eure Says." Winston-Salem Journal. September 27, 1966.

6,208.   "Seawell Predicts Klan Will Step Up Activity." Greensboro Daily News. March 9, 1966.

6,209.   "Seawell Quits Elections Post." Winston-Salem Journal. July 29, 1966.

6,210.   "Seawell Reports Robeson County Uproar Over Klan." Daily Reflector. March 16, 1966.

6,211.   "Seawell Says Klan Reports Locked Up." Winston-Salem Journal. July 19, 1966.

6,212.   "Seawell Says SBI's Statement 'Evasive'." Greensboro Daily News. July 23, 1966.

6,213.   "Seawell Talks Here Of Klan-Lumbee Tiff." Winston-Salem Journal. April 16, 1966.

6,214.   "Self-Defense Argument Ridiculed At Klan Trial." New York Times. November 5, 1980, p. A14.

6,215.   "Set A Positive Example." Southern Exposure. Vol. 8, Summer, 1980, pp. 92-94.

6,216.   "700 Attend KKK Rally." Raleigh News & Observer. March 29, 1964.

6,217.   "700 Initiated In Military-Type Klan Ceremony." Durham Morning Herald. October 3, 1966.

6,218.   "700 Present For Klan Rites." Raleigh News & Observer. October 3, 1966.

6,219.   "7 Of 13 Defendants Offer No Contest As Whiteville Flogging Trials Open." Durham Morning Herald. May 7, 1952, p. 1.

6,220.   "7 Plead No Defense In Carolina Flogging." New York Times. May 7, 1952, p. 18.

6,221.   "7,000 Defy Ku Klux Klan In Greensboro, N.C." Pittsburgh Courier. February 16, 1980, p. 1.

6,222.   "Seven Units Of KKK Listed In Pitt County." Daily Reflector. October 20, 1965.

6,223.   Sexton, William. "Gastonia Editor Fights KKK Plan To Stage North Carolina Comeback." Asheville Citizen. April 29, 1949.

6,224.   "Sharing The Blame." Greensboro Daily News. November 11, 1979.

6,225.   "Sheet Drawn Slowly Over The Old KKK." Raleigh
          News & Observer. December 23, 1973, p. 14.

6,226.   "Sheriff Who Joined Klan Is Candidate." Charlotte
          Observer. April 7, 1966.

6,227.   "Sheriff Praises Ex-Klansman." New York Times.
          October 25, 1965, p. 32.

6,228.   "Sheriff's Officers." New York Times. February
          28, 1952, p. 28.

6,229.   Shires, William A. "Avoided Serious Confrontations."
          Daily Reflector. June 15, 1966.

6,230.   _____. "If Charge True, A Challenge Due."
          Daily Reflector. November 17, 1966.

6,231.   _____. "Law And Order Role Stressed." Daily
          Reflector. September 22, 1966.

6,232.   _____. "New KKK Likes Its Publicity, And, Like
          Old Klan, Its Due." Durham Morning Herald. August
          18, 1957.

6,233.   _____. "The Oath That Faces Challenge." Daily
          Reflector. November 18, 1966.

6,234.   _____. "One Topic Gets Governor Angry." Daily
          Reflector. October 30, 1966.

6,235.   _____. "Seawell Isn't One To Give Up." Daily
          Reflector. June 27, 1966.

6,236.   _____. "Seawell Speaks Now As Citizen." Daily
          Reflector. July 4, 1966.

6,237.   "Shooting At Anti-Klan Rally In Greensboro, N.C.,
          Discussed." New Orleans Times Picayune. November
          5, 1979, p. 1.

6,238.   "Shooting Victims Honored In Rites." New York Times.
          November 2, 1981, p. A17.

6,239.   "Shootout In Greensboro." Time. Vol. 114, November
          12, 1979, p. 31.

6,240.   "Shotgun In Raffle At A Klan Rally." New Bern Sun-
          Journal. August 22, 1966.

6,241.   "Shots Fired At House In Robeson." Charlotte
          Observer. March 21, 1966.

6,242.   "Showdown With Klan." Raleigh News & Observer.
          February 29, 1952.

6,243.   Shumaker, James. "The Rise And Fall Of The Ku
          Klux Klan." Durham Morning Herald. October 5,
          1952.

6,244.   Siceloff, Bruce. "Battle Lines Were Drawn And
          Death Paid A Visit." Raleigh News & Observer.
          November 4, 1979, pp. 1, 20.

6,245.   _____. "4,000 March In Greensboro Against
          Klan." Raleigh News & Observer. November 6, 1979.

6,246.   _____. "Klan Sign Toppled After 10 Years."
          Raleigh News & Observer. March 27, 1977.

6,247.   _____. "Party Had Felt It Was Ignored."
          Raleigh News & Observer. November 11, 1979.

6,248.   "Sickening Spectacle." Durham Morning Herald.
          August 17, 1966.

6,249.   "A Sign In The Night." Daily Reflector. March
          29, 1965.

6,250.   "Signing-Out Suds." Raleigh News & Observer.
          March 27, 1966.

6,251.   "6 Arrested In Alleged Nazi Revenge Plot In
          Greensboro, N.C." San Francisco Chronicle.
          March 3, 1981, p. 2.

6,252.   "Six Arrested In Bomb Plot." Washington Post.
          March 3, 1981, p. A4.

6,253.   "Six Facing Trial In Greensboro." Raleigh News &
          Observer. August 12, 1967, p. 3.

6,254.   "Six Indicted For Negro Intimidations." Raleigh
          News & Observer. September 12, 1967, p. 3.

6,255.   "6 Nazis And Followers Are Seized In Carolina In
          Plot To Bomb Town." New York Times. March 3,
          1981, p. B11.

6,256.   "6 Nazis Convicted And Sentenced For Plot To Blow
          Up Greensboro, N.C." New Orleans Times Picayune.
          September 19, 1981, p. 3.

6,257.   "6 Nazis Convicted In Plot To Bomb Greensboro."
          New York Times. September 19, 1981, p. 8.

6,258.   "16 Now Face Prosecution In Two Cases." Asheville
          Citizen. February 28, 1952.

6,259.   "Sketches Of The 6 Men Who Were Acquitted."
          Charlotte Observer. November 18, 1980, p. 6A.

6,260.   Slaughter, Jack. "Person Protesters Confer With
           Board Of Education." Durham Morning Herald.
           December 6, 1966, p. 12A.

6,261.   " 'Smear Sheets' Klan Label For Newspapers At
           Rally." Raleigh News & Observer. October 20,
           1956.

6,262.   Smith, Bill. "No Crackdown On Klan Planned."
           Chapel Hill Weekly. December 20, 1967.

6,263.   Smith, Jim. "Disabled Princeton Veteran Vows To
           Continue Battle Against Klan." Raleigh News &
           Observer. June 29, 1969.

6,264.   Snider, William D. "Is Greensboro's Image Dis-
           torted?" Greensboro Daily News. November 11. 1979.

6,265.   "Solicitor Studying Klan Actions." Raleigh News
           & Observer. August 20, 1951.

6,266.   "Solon Seeks Probe On N.C. Klan Charges." New
           Bern Sun-Journal. July 27, 1966.

6,267.   "Southern Organizing Committee Asks N.C. To Drop
           All KKK March Charges." Baltimore Afro-American.
           December 1, 1979, p. 6.

6,268.   "Southern Organizing Comm. Eyes Deaths At Greens-
           boro, N.C. Rally." Norfolk Journal & Guide.
           November 23, 1979, p. 3A.

6,269.   "Southern Studies Inst. Issues Report On Greens-
           boro, N.C. Deaths." Baltimore Afro-American.
           October 10, 1981, p. I.

6,270.   "Speaker Invitations 'Shock' Broughton." Charlotte
           Observer. April 2, 1966.

6,271.   "Special Danger In Robeson Justifies Court Injunc-
           tion." Charlotte Observer. March 19, 1966.

6,272.   "Special Grand Jury Confers With Two Flogging
           Victims." Durham Morning Herald. February 22,
           1952, p. 1.

6,273.   "Special Jury Panel Called In Flogging." New
           York Times. April 29, 1952, p. 22.

6,274.   "Speech Or Provocation?" Greensboro Daily News.
           November 13, 1979.

6,275.   "Spending Of Klan Funds Barred." Raleigh News &
           Observer. October 21, 1965.

6,276.   "Spotlight To Hit N.C. Klan Drive." Raleigh News
          & Observer. October 17, 1965.

6,277.   "A Sputtering Spark." Greensboro Daily News.
          August 5, 1966, p. 8.

6,278   Stark, Louis. "A.F. Of L. Moves In Carolina
          Strikes." New York Times. April 9, 1929, p. 17.

6,279.   "State Eyes Klan Rally At Maxton." Greensboro
          Daily News. March 16, 1966.

6,280.   "State Fair Improves With Years." Durham Morning
          Herald. October 6, 1966.

6,281.   "State Fair Rules Need Changing." Durham Morning
          Herald. October 28, 1966.

6,282.   "State Klan Chief Jones Charged With Perjury."
          Raleigh News & Observer. January 13, 1966.

6,283.   "State May Issue Warrants For Klan." New Bern Sun-
          Journal. August 9, 1966.

6,284.   "State Should Make Ku Klux Toe Line." Raleigh
          News & Observer. July 17, 1966.

6,285.   "State's Officials Look Bad In Dispute Over Klan
          Files." Charlotte Observer. July 28, 1966.

6,286.   "Statute Enacted By Negro Solon During Reconstruc-
          tion Saves North Carolina Kluxers." Black Dispatch.
          April 12, 1959.

6,287.   "Stay Out Of Robeson County Hodges Warns Klan;
          KKK Plans Another Rally." Pittsburgh Courier.
          February 8, 1958, p. B4.

6,288.   Stephens, Bob. "Temporary Tourist Attractions:
          Klan Rally." Chapel Hill Weekly. July 7, 1968.

6,289.   "Stevens Is Found Guilty In Columbus KKK Lashing."
          Durham Morning Herald. July 25, 1952, p. 6.

6,290.   Stingley, Jim. "Robeson Klan Rallies Are Ruled
          As Legal." Raleigh News & Observer. April 19,
          1966.

6,291.   Stites, Tom. "Four Shot To Death At Anti-Klan
          March." New York Times. November 4, 1979, pp. 1,
          45.

6,292.   "Stop It Where It Is!" Raleigh News & Observer.
          January 17, 1952.

6,293.   "Storm Troopers?" Daily Reflector. September 21,
          1964.

6,294.   " 'Street Walk' By Kluxers Saturday." Daily
          Reflector. May 24, 1965.

6,295.   "Strength Sinks Low In NC." Raleigh News & Observer.
          December 24, 1969, p. 1.

6,296.   "Strict Conditions Put On Klan Rally." Winston-
          Salem Journal. August 11, 1966.

6,297.   "Struggle To Get The Truth Out And To Secure
          Justice." Black Collegian. Vol. 12, October/
          November, 1981, p. 10.

6,298.   "Students Fail To Get Klan Charged." New Bern
          Sun-Journal. October 4, 1966.

6,299.   "Students Plan Wilkinson Talk Just Off Campus."
          New Bern Sun-Journal. March 2, 1966.

6,300.   Suber, Ron. "Greensboro Verdict Was 'License To
          Kill'." Florida Courier. December 6, 1980, pp. 1,
          11.

6,301.   "Sunday Klan Rally Attracts Hundreds." Raleigh News
          & Observer. April 17, 1966.

6,302.   "Surge In Membership Claimed By Klan." Durham Morn-
          ing Herald. September 23, 1966.

6,303.   "Suspects Held Without Bond In Murders At Anti-
          KKK Rally." New Orleans Times Picayune. November
          6, 1979, p. 4.

6,304.   Swofford, Stan. "Nazis As Well As Klansmen Had
          Role." Greensboro Daily News. November 5, 1979.

6,305.   "Tar Heel Rave." Charlotte Observer. October 26,
          1966.

6,306.   "Tar Heel Klansmen Meet In Salisbury." Raleigh
          News & Observer. September 1, 1963.

6,307.   "Tar Heels No. 1 For Klan." Raleigh News &
          Observer. October 24, 1965.

6,308.   Taylor, Benjamin. "Rights, Klan, Labor Cut Patrol
          Efficiency." Greensboro Daily News. September 17,
          1966.

6,309.   "Technical Error Foils KKK Papers." Durham Morning
          Herald. June 23, 1965.

6,310.   "Ten Face Hearing." Christian Science Monitor.
          February 18, 1952, p. 10.

6,311.   "10 Fair Bluff Ex-Klansmen Indicted; Robeson 11
Will Be Tried On March 7." Durham Morning Herald.
February 29, 1952, p. 1.

6,312.   "10 Klansmen Convicted In Night-Riding Terror; KKK
Chieftain Is Blamed." Durham Morning Herald.
May 14, 1952, p. 1.

6,313.   "10 Warrants Are Served On Alleged Ex-Klansmen."
Durham Morning Herald. June 26, 1952, p. 2.

6,314.   "Terrorism Hits Mt. Airy; 2 Buildings, Cross Fired."
Durham Morning Herald. March 3, 1952, p. 1.

6,315.   "Terrorism Laid To 12 In Carolina." New York Times.
July 19, 1967, pp. 1, 43.

6,316.   "Text Of Injunction." Winston-Salem Journal.
March 18, 1966.

6,317.   "There Are Many Smithfields And Many Souths."
Raleigh News & Observer. August 30, 1970, Sect.
4, p. 5.

6,318.   "The Third Of November." Southern Exposure. Vol.
9, Fall, 1981, pp. 55-67.

6,319.   "13 Are Held For Trial In Carolina Flogging." New
York Times. May 6, 1952, p. 40.

6,320.   "13 Ex-Klansmen Will Go On Trial." Raleigh News &
Observer. May 15, 1954.

6,321.   "13 Plead Not Guilty To Charges In Deaths Of Klan
Foes At Rally." New York Times. January 19, 1980,
p. 21.

6,322.   "34 Arrested In N.C. March For Communists Slain At
Rally." Houston Post. November 12, 1979, p. 7A.

6,323.   "3 Held In Alabama In Probe Of 1957 Violence."
New Orleans Times Picayune. February 22, 1976, p. 2.

6,324.   "Tight Security Set For Funerals Of Greensboro
Rally Victims." New Orleans Times Picayune.
November 11, 1979, p. 10.

6,325.   Thompson, Roy. "Barrier To Rally By Klan Removed."
Winston-Salem Journal. April 19, 1966.

6,326.   _____. "Court Orders Klan To Call Off Rally."
Winston-Salem Journal. March 18, 1966.

6,327.   _____. "Disenchanted Tar Heels Are Swelling
KKK." Winston-Salem Journal. June 30, 1965, pp. 1,
2.

6,328.   _____. "Klan Apparently Will Not Hold Its Rally In Robeson County." <u>Winston-Salem Journal</u>. March 25, 1966.

6,329.   _____. "Klan, Indians Set To Collide." <u>Winston-Salem Journal</u>. March 16, 1966.

6,330.   _____. "Klan Rally Set In Robeson." <u>Winston-Salem Journal</u>. March 9, 1966.

6,331.   _____. "Klan's Robeson Rally Plan Stirs Uneasiness And Fear." <u>Winston-Salem Journal</u>. March 10, 1966.

6,332.   _____. "Two Explosions Jolt Town's Racial Peace." <u>Winston-Salem Journal</u>. September 9, 1966.

6,333.   Thornton, Mary. "Study Cites Links Between Greensboro Police, Klan." <u>Washington Post</u>. October 3, 1981, p. A4.

6,334.   "Threats Oust Minister." <u>New York Times</u>. February 1, 1952, p. 23.

6,335.   "Three Appeal Case In Hyde." <u>Raleigh News & Observer</u>. October 14, 1969, p. 3.

6,336.   "Three Convicted Klansmen Begin 2-Year Sentences." <u>Durham Morning Herald</u>. May 28, 1952, p. 1.

6,337.   "3 Found Guilty Of Assault In Columbus Flogging Case." <u>Durham Morning Herald</u>. May 11, 1952, p. 1.

6,338.   "3 In Klan Sentenced In A Bombing Plot." <u>New York Times</u>. March 21, 1958, p. 44.

6,339.   "3 Klansmen Charged In Burnings." <u>Raleigh News & Observer</u>. April 8, 1967, p. 9.

6,340.   "3 Klansmen Say Won't Face Trial." <u>Raleigh News & Observer</u>. April 7, 1967, p. 8.

6,341.   "Three Men Arrested At Rally." <u>Raleigh News & Observer</u>. August 24, 1970, p. 3.

6,342.   "3 On Trial Identify Others In Flogging." <u>New York Times</u>. May 9, 1952, p. 33.

6,343.   "Three Suspects Post Bond In New Bern Bombing Case." <u>Raleigh News & Observer</u>. January 30, 1965.

6,344.   "To Be No Bullying By Klan At Rally." <u>New Bern Sun-Journal</u>. August 12, 1966.

6,345.   "To Raise $11,000 For Leader's Pay." <u>Raleigh News & Observer</u>. August 14, 1968, p. 11.

6,346.   "Tolerating Klan Activities." Durham Morning
         Herald. October 14, 1966.

6,347.   "Tom Hamilton Resigns Post As KKK Chief." Durham
         Morning Herald. October 22, 1952, p. 10.

6,348.   "Tragedy On The Fringe." Greensboro Daily News.
         November 11, 1979.

6,349.   "Trial Of 11 Former Klansmen Set May 12 In
         Wilmington Court." Durham Morning Herald. March
         28, 1952, p. 5.

6,350.   "Tragedy On The Fringe." New York Times. November
         6, 1979, p. 18.

6,351.   "Treatment At Klan Booth." Durham Morning Herald.
         October 22, 1966.

6,352.   "Trial Called A Sham." New York Times. November
         19, 1980, p. A24.

6,353.   "Trial Date On Dueling Charge Set." Winston-
         Salem Journal. March 30, 1966.

6,354.   "Trial Of Nazis And Klansmen Is Going To The Jury
         Today." New York Times. November 7, 1980, p. A12.

6,355.   "Trial Of 6 In KKK For Killing Of 5 Blacks In N.C.
         Continues." Houston Post. November 5, 1980, p. 6A.

6,356.   "Troops Deployed In Durham, N.C." New York Times.
         July 21, 1967, p. 35.

6,357.   "Troops On Vigil Today At Funeral Of Klan Foes."
         New York Times. November 11, 1979, p. 31.

6,358.   Troxler, Howard and David McKinnon. "5th Shootout
         Victim Dies; 14 Defendants Denied Bail." Raleigh
         News & Observer. November 6, 1979.

6,359.   "12 Charged In Racial Conspiracy." Raleigh News
         & Observer. July 19, 1967.

6,360.   "12 Facing Action In Klan Case." Raleigh News &
         Observer. August 30, 1967, p. 3.

6,361.   "12 Guilty In Flogging." New York Times. July
         24, 1952, p. 8.

6,362.   "12 Still Unsolved." Raleigh News & Observer.
         February 18, 1952.

6,363.   "28 Klan Leaders Named Defendants." Winston-Salem
         Journal. March 18, 1966.

6,364. "25 Accused By Jury In 4 Klan Floggings." New York Times. April 2, 1952, p. 36.

6,365. "25 Alleged Ex-Klansmen To Go On Trial Tomorrow." Durham Morning Herald. April 27, 1952, p. 1.

6,366. "25 Facing Trial In N.C. Flogging." Raleigh News & Observer. April 27, 1952.

6,367. "25 To Go On Trial In Flogging Case." New York Times. April 27, 1952, p. 73.

6,368. "2 Alleged Floggings In Brunswick County Under Investigation." Durham Morning Herald. March 1, 1952, Sect. 2, p. 1.

6,369. "Two Governors Warn Against Klan Violence." Asheville Citizen. August 29, 1951.

6,370. "2 Held For Trying To Burn North Carolina Church." New York Times. July 15, 1964, p. 16.

6,371. "2 Incidents In 1950's Almost Killed Ku Klux Klan In N.C." Winston-Salem Journal. October 28, 1965, p. 11.

6,372. "2 More KKK Members Arrested In Connection With N.C. Killings." Chicago Tribune. November 5, 1979, p. 2.

6,373. "2 More Surry Men Nabbed On Crossburning Charges." Durham Morning Herald. March 13, 1952, p. 11.

6,374. "200 Attend Klan Rally In Durham; Top Leaders Talk." Durham Morning Herald. November 30, 1966.

6,375. "2 Imprisoned In Cross Burning." New York Times. April 2, 1980, p. 14.

6,376. "2 In Klan Sentenced." New York Times. March 15, 1958, p. 38.

6,377. "Two Klan Members Get Order Forbidding Rally." Greensboro Daily News. March 22, 1966.

6,378. "Two Klansmen Are Sentenced Today." New Bern Sun-Journal. July 9, 1966.

6,379. "2 Klansmen Face Charges In Clash." New York Times. January 20, 1958, pp. 1, 14.

6,380. "2 Klansmen Get Terms." Raleigh News & Observer. March 11, 1967.

6,381. "2500 Expected At March For Persons Killed At Anti-Klan Rally." San Francisco Chronicle. November 9, 1979, p. 25.

6,382.   "2,000 Watch Klan Meeting." New York Times.
          November 26, 1951, p. 26.

6,383.   "Two Victims' Widows Interrupt Klansmen's Murder
          Trial." New York Times. August 5, 1980, p. A8.

6,384.   "12 Men On Trial In Anti-KKK Rally Shooting In
          Greensboro, N.C." New Orleans Times Picayune.
          November 7, 1979, p. 3.

6,385.   "UNC Students Heckle Klansman Off Stage." Raleigh
          News & Observer. January 18, 1975.

6,386.   "UNC To Ask Rule On Klan." Raleigh News & Observer.
          October 24, 1965.

6,387.   "Under The Dome." Raleigh News & Observer.
          June 10, 1966, p. 6.

6,388.   "Under The Dome." Raleigh News & Observer.   June
          12, 1966.

6,389.   "Under The Dome." Raleigh News & Observer.   July
          2, 1966.

6,390.   "Underground." Raleigh News & Observer.   February
          21, 1958.

6,391.   "The Unevolved Klansmen." Greensboro Daily News.
          October 17, 1966.

6,392.   "United Klans Slate Meeting." Raleigh News &
          Observer. June 25, 1970, p. 5.

6,393.   "Unions Rap Klan Booth At N.C. Fair." Raleigh
          News & Observer. November 2, 1966.

6,394.   " 'Un-Klannish' Klan Unit Is Disbanded By Grand
          Dragon." Durham Morning Herald. January 25,
          1952, p. 1.

6,395.   "Unkluxing The Klan." Asheville Citizen.   March 1,
          1952.

6,396.   "Unprepared For A Well Advertised Battle." Durham
          Morning Herald. January 20, 1958.

6,397.   Upton, Bob. "450 Klansmen Rally On Capitol Grounds."
          Raleigh News & Observer. July 11, 1966, p. 24.

6,398.   _____. "Klansmen Rally On Capitol Grounds."
          Raleigh News & Observer. July 11, 1966.

6,399.   "U.S. Agents Involvement In Klan Killings In N.C.
          Last Nov. Eyed." San Francisco Chronicle.   July
          15, 1980, p. 2.

6,400.   "U.S. Civil Rights Commission A.N.C. Unit May Probe Greensboro March." _Atlanta Daily World_. December 23, 1979, p. 2.

6,401.   "U.S. Court Jury Convicts Six Nazis In N.C. Bombing Plot." _Los Angeles Times_. September 19, 1981, p. 27.

6,402.   "U.S. Grand Jury Indicts 6 Nazis In Greensboro, N.C. Bomb Plot." _New Orleans Times Picayune_. March 3, 1981, Sect. 4, p. 14.

6,403.   "U.S. Justice Dept. Indicts KKK Members In Shootings." _New Orleans Times Picayune_. April 5, 1979, p. 5.

6,404.   "U.S. Moves For Swift Trial Of Accused Kidnap-Floggers." _Durham Morning Herald_. February 21, 1952, Sect. 2, p. 9.

6,405.   "U.S. Opposed Klan's Move." _Winston-Salem Journal Sentinel_. September 11, 1966.

6,406.   "U.S. To Probe 1979 Anti-Klan Rally That Left Five Dead." _Washington Post_. March 9, 1982, p. A2.

6,407.   "Valentine Backs Klan Ouster." _Greensboro Daily News_. October 28, 1966.

6,408.   Van Alstyne, William. "Joan Little And Greensboro Verdict." _Los Angeles Times_. December 14, 1980, Sect. 6, p. 5.

6,409.   "Verdict In Greensboro." _Progressive_. Vol. 45, January, 1981, pp. 9-10.

6,410.   "Verdict In N.C. Klan Shootings Noted." _San Francisco Chronicle_. July 23, 1980, p. 32.

6,411.   "Verdict In N.C.-KKK-Nazi Murder Trial." _Chicago Tribune_. November 20, 1980, Sect. 3, p. 1.

6,412.   "Victims Of Klan Violence In N.C. Hold Rally At San Francisco City Hall." _San Francisco Chronicle_. February 12, 1980, p. 32.

6,413.   "Vigilant Action." _Raleigh News & Observer_. May 24, 1952.

6,414.   "Violence Planned By Klan." _Raleigh News & Observer_. January 10, 1968, p. 1.

6,415.   "Voice From The Grave Tells All." _Greensboro Daily News_. May 24, 1970.

6,416.   "Voter Drive Spreads." _New York Times_. February 27, 1965, p. 10.

6,417.   Walls, Dwayne. "Is GOP Winner 'Klansville' Sheriff?"
          Charlotte Observer. November 15, 1966.

6,418.   "Wants FBI Probe Of Letter." Raleigh News &
          Observer. June 17, 1967, p. 11.

6,419.   "The War Whoop Sounds Again." New York Times.
          January 20, 1958, p. 22.

6,420.   "Warrants Drawn Linking Hamilton To N.C. Flogging."
          Durham Morning Herald. May 24, 1952, p. 1.

6,421.   "Watch Kept On Klan Booth." Durham Morning Herald.
          October 18, 1966, p. 3A.

6,422.   Watson, Robert. "The Other Side Of The Greensboro
          Shootout." Washington Post. March 2, 1980, pp.
          C1, C5.

6,423.   "Wave Of Floggings Laid To Klansmen." New York
          Times. January 20, 1952, p. 50.

6,424.   "We Stopped The Klan In Greensboro, N.C." IFCO
          News (Interreligious Foundation For Community
          Organization). Vol. 7, April, 1980, pp. 1, 4, 5, 11.

6,425.   "We, The United Klan Of America, Inc., Believe."
          Daily Reflector. November 19, 1965.

6,426.   "Wealthy N.C. Citizen Defies Ku Klux Klan."
          Pittsburgh Courier. September 29, 1923, p. 1.

6,427.   "Weapons Brought To Court In Klansmen's Murder
          Trial." New York Times. August 30, 1980, p. 30.

6,428.   Weaver, Bill Rhodes. "Bishop Shuns Klan And
          'Black Power'." Greensboro Daily News. September
          19, 1966.

6,429.   Weisbecker, Lee. "Greensboro Jury Starts Delibera-
          ting Klan Case Today." Charlotte Observer.
          November 7, 1980, p. B1.

6,430.   _____. "Klan, Nazi Witness Total 350."
          Charlotte Observer. June 24, 1980, p. B1.

6,431.   _____. "Klan Trial Jurors Still Deliberating."
          Charlotte Observer. November 11, 1980, p. B1.

6,432.   _____. "Marchers Protest Klan Acquittals In 3
          N.C. Cities." Charlotte Observer. November 21,
          1980, pp. C1, C2.

6,433.   _____. "Questions Linger After Acquittal Of
          Klansmen, Nazis." Charlotte Observer. November
          23, 1980, pp. A1, A11.

6,434.   Weisbecker, Lee. "6 Klansmen, Nazis Acquitted."
          Charlotte Observer. November 18, 1980, pp. A1, A6.

6,435.   Welch, William M. "What Happened In N.C.?" Forest
          City Courier. November 7, 1980, p. 3.

6,436.   Weronka, Bill. "Defendants Rejoice; Prosecutors
          Stunned." Forest City Daily Courier. November 18,
          1980, p. 7.

6,437.   West, Bernard. "Church Is Painted Despite Fire
          Threat, Klan Warning." Raleigh News & Observer.
          July 15, 1964.

6,438.   "What Hamilton Forgets." Raleigh News & Observer.
          May 30, 1952.

6,439.   "What's New About Klan? Nothing." Durham Morning
          Herald. June 24, 1964, Sect. A, p. 4.

6,440.   "When Carolina Indians Went On The Warpath."
          U.S. News & World Report. Vol. 44, January 31, 1958,
          pp. 14-15.

6,441.   "Where The Klan Spreads Terror." New York Times
          Magazine. June 6, 1965, Sect. 6, p. 22.

6,442.   "Which Infiltrated? Sheriff? Klan?" Raleigh News
          & Observer. October 27, 1965.

6,443.   Whitaker, Garland. "Klan Cross-Burning Draws
          Estimated 1,000 To Rally." Daily Reflector.
          September 28, 1964.

6,444.   _____. "Three Clergymen At Klan Rally Were
          Intimidated By Greenshirts, Searched." Daily
          Reflector. September 29, 1964.

6,445.   "White Jury Frees Klan Murderers." Burning Spear.
          December, 1980, p. 1.

6,446.   "Whites Fire Weapons Into Anti-Klan Rally In N.C.
          Killing 4." New Orleans Times Picayune. November
          4, 1979, p. 1.

6,447.   Whitley, William B. "Ku Klux Klan Leader States
          'Neither Gov. Scott, Police' Can Keep Klan Out Of
          State." Durham Morning Herald. December 13,
          1949.

6,448.   "Who Is Entitled To 'Protection'?" Raleigh News
          & Observer. January 28, 1958.

6,449.   "Wife Of Grand Dragon Charges 'Pre-Judging' By
          Party Official." Greensboro Daily News. April 19,
          1966.

6,450.   "Wife Of Klan Head Seeks Rowan Post." Greensboro
          Daily News. April 16, 1966.

6,451.   "Wife Of Klan's Dragon To Run For Rowan Office."
          Winston-Salem Journal. April 16, 1966.

6,452.   "Wife's Job Hurts Grocer's." Charlotte Observer.
          October 27, 1966, p. 8A.

6,453.   "Wilkinson Speech On Klan Hearings Set For Tuesday."
          Durham Morning Herald. February 26, 1966.

6,454.   "Will Defend Non-Klansmen: Granite Quarry." Raleigh
          News & Observer. August 25, 1967, p. 12.

6,455.   Williams, Oliver. "Burning Crosses, Threats Place
          Klan At Edge Of Law." Raleigh News & Observer.
          August 25, 1964.

6,456.   _____. "Cleaned-Up Klan Claims Comeback With
          Old Power." Raleigh News & Observer. June 21,
          1964.

6,457.   _____. "Klan Runs Students From State." Raleigh
          News & Observer. June 20, 1964.

6,458.   _____. "Leaders Promote Klan Extremism."
          Raleigh News & Observer. August 24, 1964.

6,459.   _____. "Rebirth Of Klan Counters Moderate
          Action In State." Raleigh News & Observer. August
          23, 1964.

6,460.   _____. "Threat Of Klan Brings Concern."
          Raleigh News & Observer. August 26, 1964.

6,461.   "Wilmington Chief Denies Joint Patrol With Ku
          Klux." Raleigh News & Observer. November 5,
          1971, p. 32.

6,462.   Wilson, Margaret. "King Blames The Negroes For
          Some Racial Wrongs." New Bern Sun-Journal.
          September 22, 1966.

6,463.   "Winston-Salem Rally Hears Wizard." Raleigh News
          & Observer. April 29, 1968, p. 3.

6,464.   "Witness From Klan Rally Tells Of Gunfire And
          Fights." New York Times. August 12, 1980, p. 12.

6,465.   "Witness Says 4 Defendants Fired Guns At Klan Rally."
          New York Times. September 4, 1980, p. A18.

6,466.   "Witness Says Klansmen Didn't Fire All Shots At
          Rally." New York Times. September 25, 1980, p.
          A25.

6,467.   "Witness Testifies About First Shot-At Fatal Rally."
         Washington Post. August 13, 1980, p. C2.

6,468.   "Wizard Boots Kludd, Pals." Raleigh News & Observer.
         April 5, 1967, p. 1.

6,469.   "Wizard Shelton Claims Klan To Become Major Voting
         Bloc." Daily Reflector. June 5, 1965.

6,470.   "Wizard To Skip Today's Hearing." Charlotte
         Observer. March 31, 1966.

6,471.   "Wizard Tries Hard To Rebuild Organization."
         Raleigh News & Observer. November 27, 1970, p. 10.

6,472.   Womble, Bill. "SBI Aids New Bern Blasts Probe."
         Raleigh News & Observer. January 26, 1965.

6,473.   _____. "Wilmington Paper Asks Sheriff's Ouster."
         Raleigh News & Observer. November 12, 1965.

6,474.   Wood, Ernie. "Old KKK House Will Be Park's Com-
         munity Center." Raleigh News & Observer. December
         26, 1972.

6,475.   Wood, John. "Acquittal Gives Hate Groups The
         Signal." Forest City Courier. November 19, 1980,
         p. 4A.

6,476.   Wood, Rob. "445 Klansmen March, Rally At N.C.
         Capital." Charlotte Observer. July 11, 1966.

6,477.   _____. "445 Of Klan In Parade In N.C. Capital."
         Virginian Pilot. July 11, 1966.

6,478.   _____. "Jones Says Klan Still Growing In N.C."
         Durham Morning Herald. April 3, 1966.

6,479.   _____. "Judge Delays Ruling On Klan's Injunc-
         tion." Greensboro Daily News. April 1, 1966.

6,480.   _____. "KKK Initiation Staged In Public."
         Daily Reflector. October 3, 1966.

6,481.   _____. "Klan Bidding To Smoke Peace Pipe With
         Lumbee Indians." Durham Morning Herald. March
         21, 1966.

6,482.   _____. "Klan Has Busy Weekend In East N.C."
         Raleigh News & Observer. June 7, 1965.

6,483.   _____. "Klan Hopes To Make Peace With Lumbees."
         Greensboro Daily News. March 21, 1966.

6,484.   _____. "Klan In Court Over Proposed Robeson
         Rally." New Bern Sun-Journal. March 31, 1966.

6,485.   . "Klan Rites Unite Two In Cornfield."
Raleigh News & Observer. May 23, 1965.

6,486.   . "The Klan Surges Back Into Open; Wedding
Tonight." Raleigh News & Observer. May 22, 1965.

6,487.   . "Klan To Braves: Let's Bury Hatchet."
Charlotte Observer. March 21, 1966.

6,488.   . "Klansmen Hold Raleigh Rally During
Sunday." New Bern Sun-Journal. July 11, 1966.

6,489.   . "Moore Labels Ku Klux Klan A Hate Group."
New Bern Sun-Journal. October 25, 1966.

6,490.   "The Work Of Criminals." Greensboro Daily News.
November 11, 1979.

6,491.   "Workers World Party Reps. Eye Violence In Greensboro, N.C." Norfolk Journal & Guide. November 9,
1979, p. 2A.

6,492.   Wright, Mark. "Jailer: Klansman Said He 'Got'
3 At Rally." Winston-Salem Sentinel. August 28,
1980, pp. 1-2.

6,493.   "Writes In Defense Of The Ku Klux Klan." News
Herald. June 1, 1922.

6,494.   "Yadkin County Cross Burnings Are Reported."
Durham Morning Herald. March 17, 1952, p. 1.

6,495.   Yancey, Noel. "Klansmen Chase Negroes From Rally
In Raleigh Park." Charlotte Observer. August 1,
1966.

6,496.   . "Moore Indicating Klan In N.C. Is
Small Minority." Raleigh News & Observer. October
28, 1965.

6,497.   . "Scuffle Marks Klan And King Rival
Meeting." New Bern Sun-Journal. August 1, 1966.

6,498.   Young, Perry. "Klan Linen Is Aired." Raleigh News
& Observer. December 14, 1965.

6,499.   . " 'People Say The Ku Klucks Is A Mean
Outfit...'." Chapel Hill Weekly. December 6,
1964.

6,500.   "Youth Is Charged In Sniping." Daily Reflector.
November 8, 1966.

6,501.   Zwerling, Philip. "Ku Klux Klan Trial In N.C."
Los Angeles Times. August 3, 1980, Sect. 4, p. 5.

33. NORTH DAKOTA

6,502.   "Klan Wins Dakota City Election." New York Times.
            April 8, 1926, p. 18.

6,503.   "Ku Klux Klan In South Dakota." Grand Forks
            Herald. January-February, 1923.

6,504.   "Ku Klux Klan In South Dakota." National Kourier.
            June, 1925.

34. OHIO

6,505.   "Accuses Race Ministers Of Working With Ku Klux."
            Pittsburgh Courier. October 13, 1923, p. 3.

6,506.   "Adjutant General Doubts Story." New York Times.
            March 27, 1928, p. 5.

6,507.   "Anti-Klan And Anti-Nazi Rally Held At Cleveland
            State University." Cleveland Call & Post. November
            17, 1979, p. 1A.

6,508.   "Anti-Klan Protest Ends Rally In Columbus, Ohio."
            Atlanta Daily World. July 7, 1977, p. 2.

6,509.   "Arrest Seventy-Five Klansmen At Funeral." New
            York Times. July 7, 1923, p. 4.

6,510.   "Attempted Cross-Burning In Hartwell Leaves Black
            Family Shocked, Helpless." Cincinnati Herald.
            June 20, 1981, pp. 1, 9.

6,511.   "Black Legion, KKK Chief Forms Cult Aimed At Race."
            Norfolk Journal & Guide. March 26, 1938, p. 3.

6,512.   Bohn, Frank. "The Ku Klux Klan Interpreted."
            American Journal of Sociology. Vol. 30, January,
            1925, pp. 385-407.

6,513.   "Bomb Is Exploded In Ohio Mayor's House." New
            York Times. October 30, 1924, p. 21.

6,514.   "Boy Kluxers Kidnap And Gag Youngster." Pittsburgh
            Courier. October 20, 1923, pp. 9-10.

6,515.   "Boys Playing 'Ku Klux Klan' Bind And Injure Ohio
            Child." New York Times. September 27, 1923, p. 1.

6,516.   "Brawl Erupts At Ohio KKK Rally." New Orleans
            Times Picayune. September 6, 1977, Sect. 4, p. 17.

6,517.   "Burn Crosses For Bryant." New York Times. August
            1, 1925, p. 2.

6,518.   "Charges Ohio Klan Created Terrorism." New York
          Times. March 27, 1928, p. 5.

6,519.   "Charge Negro Preachers Are Aiding Klan." New
          York Amsterdam News. October 10, 1923, p. 1.

6,520.   "City Cheers Arriving Troops." New York Times.
          November 2, 1924, p. 2.

6,521.   "Cleveland Klan Parade Forbidden. New York Times.
          June 23, 1926, p. 2.

6,522.   "Cleveland's Mayor Orders Ku Klux Out." Chicago
          Defender. September 10, 1921, p. 1.

6,523.   "Columbus, Ohio Ku Klux Klan Stages Protest."
          Chicago Tribune. July 5, 1977, p. 2.

6,524.   "Confrontation Between KKK And Opposition Group
          In Ohio Viewed." San Francisco Chronicle. July
          23, 1979, p. 2.

6,525.   "Court Voids Law On Urging Violence." New York
          Times. June 10, 1969, p. 24.

6,526.   "Crisis Deferred, Akron Believes." New York Times.
          September 26, 1936, p. 4.

6,527.   "Dale R. Reusch." New York Times. February 7, 1974,
          p. 46.

6,528.   "Demonstrators Disrupt Ku Klux Klan Rally In
          Columbus, Ohio." Washington Post. July 5, 1977,
          p. 3A.

6,529.   "Declares Ohio Has Klan Police." New York Times.
          November 13, 1924, p. 2.

6,530.   Duffus, R.L. "The Ku Klan In The Middle West."
          World's Work. Vol. 46, 1923, pp. 367-373.

6,531.   "Eight Injured In Fights Following Breakup Of KKK
          Rally In Ohio." Houston Post. September 6, 1977,
          p. 7A.

6,532.   "Ends Nile's Martial Law." New York Times. November
          6, 1924, p. 21.

6,533.   "Ex-CP Reporter Shocked By KKK Statehouse Rally."
          Cleveland Call & Post. July 16, 1977, p. 12B.

6,534.   "Ex-Nazi Links Klan Empress To Plots." New York
          Times. February 22, 1966, p. 16.

6,535.   "Fight Klan To The End, Says G.A.R. Leader."
          Pittsburgh Courier. July 7, 1923, p. 14.

6,536.   "Fighting Erupts At End Of KKK Rally In Columbus, Ohio." _Chicago Tribune_. September 6, 1977, p. 8.

6,537.   "Five Klan Mayors Join To Purify Ohio Cities." _New York Times_. November 10, 1923, p. 15.

6,538.   "Governor Assumes Chief Command." _New York Times_. November 2, 1924, p. 2.

6,539.   "Hamilton, Ohio, Police Quell Vandalism By Negro Youths." _New York Times_. March 7, 1968, p. 27.

6,540.   "Hearing Set For 72 Klansmen." _New York Times_. July 8, 1923, Sect. 2, p. 7.

6,541.   Hofmann, Paul. "Tensions In Cleveland Ghetto Forcing Store To Close." _New York Times_. April 10, 1967, p. 16.

6,542.   "Indict 104 In Niles Klan Fight Would Oust Mayor And Chief." _New York Times_. December 6, 1924, p. 1.

6,543.   "Induct 2,000 In The Klan." _New York Times_. June 19, 1921, p. 4.

6,544.   Jenkins, William D. "The Ku Klux Klan In Youngstown, Ohio: Moral Reform In The Twenties." _Historian_. November, 1978, pp. 76-93.

6,545.   "KKK Gets Undue Exposure." _Cleveland Call & Post_. July 16, 1977, p. 2B.

6,546.   "K.K.K. Produces Movie Thriller." _Pittsburgh Courier_. October 13, 1923, p. 3.

6,547.   "KKK Rally In Ohio." _National Observer_. June 7, 1965, p. 5.

6,548.   "KKK Supporters And Foes Trade Taunts Before KKK Rally In Ohio." _New Orleans Times Picayune_. July 23, 1979, p. 4.

6,549.   "KKK Tries To Give Midwest(Cleveland, Ohio) Its Flaming Cross Brand." _The Worker_. August 30, 1966, p. 1.

6,550.   "KKK Wizard Roughed Up At Rally." _Atlanta Daily World_. July 7, 1977, p. 2.

6,551.   "Klan And Foes Riot, Wound 12 In Niles, O.; Troops Hold Town." _New York Times_. November 2, 1924, pp. 1, 2.

6,552.   "Klan Beaten In Ohio." _New York Times_. August 14, 1924, p. 2.

6,553.   "Klan Calls 100,000 To Youngstown." New York
          Times. November 9, 1923, p. 4.

6,554.   "Klan Causes Church Panic." New York Times. April
          11, 1926, Sect. 2, p. 19.

6,555.   "Klan Chief Loses Verbal Battle To Black Anta-
          gonist." Cleveland Call & Post. July 16, 1977,
          p. 12B.

6,556.   "Klan Empress Boasts Her Home Was Members' Entry
          To Ohio." New York Times. February 15, 1966,
          p. 22.

6,557.   "Klan Greatest Meance To Better Relations Between
          Races, Says Woman Speaker." Pittsburgh Courier.
          December 29, 1923, p. 11.

6,558.   "Klan Issue Feared In Ohio Convention." New York
          Times. August 25, 1924, p. 2.

6,559.   "Klan Keeps Up Growth Over North." Chicago
          Defender. September 2, 1922, p. 1.

6,560.   "Klan Leader Says Order Fights 'Social Equality'
          For Negroes." Pittsburgh Courier. March 2, 1940,
          p. 4.

6,561.   "Klan Losing Fight In Ohio Primaries." New York
          Times. August 13, 1924, p. 1.

6,562.   "Klan Member Barred From Being On Jury." Pittsburgh
          Courier. October 20, 1923, p. 1.

6,563.   "Klan Movie Ban Taken To Court." People's Voice.
          October 25, 1947, p. 7.

6,564.   "Klan Parade Barred By Cleveland Official." Broad
          Ax. July 3, 1926, p. 2.

6,565.   "Klan Rally Ends In Skirmish." New York Times.
          September 6, 1977, p. 24.

6,566.   "Klan Riot Inquiry Starts At Niles." New York
          Times. November 3, 1924, pp. 1, 4.

6,567.   "Klan To Make Fight For Ohio Organizer." New
          York Times. February 16, 1923, p. 8.

6,568.   "Klan To Picket." New York Times. September 3,
          1966, p. 48.

6,569.   "Klan Wants Religion In Schools." New York Times.
          December 6, 1922, p. 4.

6,570.   "Klan's Rally Puts Ohio Aides On Alert." New York
         Times. July 4, 1966, p. 16.

6,571.   "Klansmen Fight Demonstrators In Columbus, Ga."
         Los Angeles Times. July 5, 1977, p. 9.

6,572.   "Klansman In Ohio Vows Book Fight." New York
         Times. April 3, 1967, p. 21.

6,573.   "Klansman Sentenced For Shooting." New York Times.
         April 11, 1925, p. 20.

6,574.   "Klansmen Abandon March In Ohio City." New York
         Times. August 22, 1923, p. 16.

6,575.   "Klansmen And Demonstrators Battle In Ohio."
         Washington Post. July 5, 1977, p. A3.

6,576.   "Klansmen Must Not Wear Masks - Reese." Pittsburgh
         Courier. October 27, 1923, p. 8.

6,577.   "Klansmen Rush To Ohio Riot Scene." New York Times.
         August 17, 1923, pp. 1, 2.

6,578.   "KKK Literature Being Distributed In Ohio Discussed."
         Cleveland Call & Post. October 17, 1981, p. 1A.

6,579.   "Ku Klux Klan Plans To Revolt Against Community."
         Christian Science Monitor. February 19, 1969, p. 12.

6,580.   "Ku Klux Klan Rally In Ohio Turns Into A Brawl."
         New Orleans Times Picayune. July 5, 1977, p. 5.

6,581.   "Ku Klux Klan Upsets Conviction Of Ohioan."
         Christian Science Monitor. June 11, 1969, p. 13.

6,582.   "Ku Klux Prosecutes Ohioans As Rioters." New York
         Times. October 31, 1923, p. 19.

6,583.   "Ku Klux Revenge Blamed For Injunction That Halts
         Betting At Columbus Races." New York Times.
         July 29, 1923, p. 1.

6,584.   "Ku Klux Women Battle." New York Times. January
         8, 1924, p. 25.

6,585.   "League Fights Klan." New York Times. December 12,
         1922, p. 3.

6,586.   Lee, Lucius E. "Klan Rally Was 'Marred'." Cleveland
         Call & Post. September 24, 1977, p. 11A.

6,587.   "Let The Klan Speak." Cleveland Call & Post.
         August 20, 1977, p. 2B.

6,588.   "Many Klan Meetings Held." New York Times. August 20, 1923, p. 2.

6,589.   Meier, August and Elliott Rudwick. "Early Boycotts Of Segregated Schools: The Case Of Springfield, Ohio, 1922-23." American Quarterly. Vol. 20, Winter, 1968, pp. 744-758.

6,590.   "More Than Ninety Seek Ohio Offices." New York Times. August 6, 1922, p. 5.

6,591.   "Move To Oust Klan Is Started In Ohio." Pittsburgh Courier. September 15, 1923, p. 1.

6,592.   "Negroes Form Klan." New York Times. March 22, 1924, p. 12.

6,593.   "Negro's Home Bombed." New York Times. May 26, 1953, p. 32.

6,594.   "Ohio City In Terror, Fearing Klan Clash." New York Times. November 1, 1924, p. 17.

6,595.   "Ohio Democrats Defeat Klan Faction." New York Times. August 26, 1924, p. 3.

6,596.   "Ohio Democrats Denounce The Ku Klux Klan, Putting Davis's Statement Into Their Platform." New York Times. August 27, 1924, p. 1.

6,597.   "Ohio Klan Charged With Plot To Dynamite Buildings." New York Times. February 11, 1966, p. 22.

6,598.   "Ohio Klan, Defiant, Threatens Niles." New York Times. November 4, 1924, p. 2.

6,599.   "Ohio Klan Leader Denies Charges In Cross-Burning." New York Times. August 8, 1964, p. 6.

6,600.   "Ohio Klan Rally Ends." New York Times. August 23, 1965, p. 18.

6,601.   "Ohio Klansman Describes Plot To Use Dynamite In A Civil War." New York Times. February 12, 1966, p. 56.

6,602.   "Ohio Klansmen Ask Protection." New York Amsterdam News. November 7, 1923, p. 3.

6,603.   "Ohio Mayor Raps Klux And Joins N.A.A.C.P." Chicago Defender. October 1, 1921, p. 1.

6,604.   "Ohioans Challenges KKK In Dragon's Lair." Afro-American. July 2, 1949, p. 3.

6,605.   "Ohioans To Fight Klan Secrecy." New York Times.
          August 21, 1923, p. 5.

6,606.   "Organize To Defeat Klan." New York Times.
          January 29, 1923, p. 17.

6,607.   Oulahan, Richard V. "Republican Trend Strong In
          Ohio." New York Times. October 25, 1928, p. 4.

6,608.   "People's Voice Uncovers KKK Plot In Ohio." People's
          Voice. October 18, 1947, p. 4.

6,609.   "Pledges The Klan To Religious Fight." New York
          Times. August 23, 1925, p. 22.

6,610.   "Police Chief Apologizes." New York Times. August
          21, 1923, p. 5.

6,611.   "Police Protect Klansmen." New York Times.
          November 11, 1923, p. 18.

6,612.   "Portsmouth (O.) Police Arrest 244 Parading Klans-
          men." New York Times. October 29, 1923, p. 1.

6,613.   "Protesters Disrupt Klan's Rally In Ohio." New
          York Times. July 5, 1977, p. 12.

6,614.   "Protesters In Ohio Leave Before Klan Rally Begins."
          New York Times. July 23, 1979, p. 12.

6,615.   "Protesters Storm 4th Of July KKK Rally On Ohio
          Capitol's Steps." Houston Post. July 5, 1977,
          p. 14A.

6,616.   "Racist Attitudes Of KKK And U.S. Rep. Ashbrook."
          Cleveland Call & Post. October 17, 1981, p. 8A.

6,617.   "Rally Provokes Riot In Ohio Capital." Cleveland
          Call & Post. July 9, 1977, p. 1.

6,618.   "A Remedy As Bad As The Disease." New York Times.
          August 23, 1923, p. 14.

6,619.   "Rep. Les Brown Condemns KKK In Ohio House Talk."
          Cleveland Call & Post. July 16, 1977, p. 12B.

6,620.   "The Riot At Niles." Outlook. Vol. 138, November
          12, 1924, p. 396.

6,621.   Scott, Lael. "Empress (Mrs. Eloise Whittle of
          Ohio) Of The Klan." New York Post. February 20,
          1966, p. 23.

6,622.   "Seize Arms In Klan Raid." New York Times.
          November 5, 1924, p. 20.

6,623.   "State Klan Leader's Statement." New York Times.
          November 3, 1924, p. 4.

6,624.   "Steubenville Klan Asks State Guard." New York
          Times. August 19, 1923, p. 2.

6,625.   Stuart, Reginald. "Impending Desegregation Brings
          Some Uneasiness To Ohio's Cities." New York Times.
          August 30, 1977, p. 10.

6,626.   "Sue Klan For $200,000." New York Times. July 11,
          1924, p. 15.

6,627.   "Taking Its Own Prescription." New York Times.
          August 18, 1923, p. 8.

6,628.   "Tear Bomb Prevents Riot." New York Times.
          January 19, 1925, p. 10.

6,629.   "Ten Plead Guilty In Niles Riot." New York Times.
          March 25, 1925, p. 34.

6,630.   "Toledo Bars Klan Parade." New York Times.
          October 12, 1937, p. 20.

6,631.   "29 Fined In Niles (Ohio) Klan Riot." New York
          Times. March 26, 1925, p. 10.

6,632.   "Veiled KKK Threats Sent To Health Dept."
          Cincinnati Herald. January 31, 1981, p. 1.

6,633.   "Will Fire On Klansmen." New York Times. October
          20, 1923, p. 17.

6,634.   Wilson, Shuara R. "Columbus Groups Denounce
          Greensboro Jury's Acquittal Of Klansmen, Nazis."
          Columbus Call & Post. November 22, 1980, p. 1.

6,635.   "Would Bar Firms Here From Other States." New
          York Times. April 1, 1923, Sect. 1, Part 2, p. 5.

35. OKLAHOMA

6,636.   "Affluent Teens In Oklahoma Form Branch Of Ku
          Klux Klan." New Orleans Times Picayune. January
          26, 1978, p. 2.

6,637.   "Aims To Strike All Secret Organizations." New
          York Times. November 25, 1923, p. 22.

6,638.   "All Oklahomans Called To Arms." New York Times.
          September 25, 1923, p. 1.

6,639.   "Anti-Klan Bill Goes To Gov. Trapp." New York
          Times. December 8, 1923, p. 15.

6,640.   "Anti-Klan Forces Unite." New York Times.
          December 2, 1923, p. 16.

6,641.   "Anti-Ku Klux Klan Society Is Organized In Oklahoma."
          New York Times. March 16, 1922, p. 19.

6,642.   "Bars Terrorism Of Tulsa Floggers." New York
          Times. September 7, 1923, p. 17.

6,643.   Blake, Aldrich. "Oklahoma's Klan-Fighting
          Governor." Nation. Vol. 117, October 3, 1923, p.
          353.

6,644.   Bliven, Bruce. "From The Oklahoma Front." New
          Republic. Vol. 36, October 17, 1923, pp. 202-205.

6,645.   Burbank, Garin. "Agrarian Radicals And Their
          Opponents: Political Conflict In Southern Oklahoma,
          1910-1924." Journal of American History. Vol. 58,
          June, 1971, pp. 5-23.

6,646.   "Calling The Ku Klux Klan 'The Worst Blight Ever
          Known In American History'." New York Times.
          September 16, 1923, p. 23.

6,647.   "Can The Ku Klux Klan Survive In Oklahoma?" Harlow's
          Weekly. Vol. 23, September 6, 1924, pp. 6-7.

6,648.   "Consider Anti-Klan Bill." New York Times.
          December 6, 1923, p. 3.

6,649.   "Constable Sent To Jail." New York Times. August
          28, 1923, p. 4.

6,650.   "Constitution Week In Oklahoma." Literary Digest.
          Vol. 79, October 13, 1923, pp. 12-13.

6,651.   "Cross-Burners Hit Newspaper." Washington Post.
          April 11, 1981, p. A7.

6,652.   "Defeats Anti-Klan Move." New York Times.
          November 27, 1923, p. 21.

6,653.   "Defendant May Ask If Juror Is A K.K.K." New York
          Times. January 4, 1925, Sect. 8, p. 2.

6,654.   "Demands Ousting Of Tulsa Officials." New York
          Times. September 13, 1923, p. 21.

6,655.   "Democracy Or Invisible Empire?" Current Opinion.
          Vol. 75, November, 1923, pp. 521-523.

6,656.   "Denies Walton's Charges." New York Times.
          September 19, 1923, p. 5.

6,657.   "Deputy Sheriff Accused In Floggings." New York
          Times. August 21, 1923, p. 5.

6,658.   Douglas, W.A.S. "Ku Klux." American Mecury. Vol.
          13, March 1928, pp. 272-279.

6,659.   "Dynamite Wrecks Fiery Klan Cross Near Tulsa, Okla."
          Pittsburgh Courier. September 29, 1923, p. 2.

6,660.   "Editorial Comment Of White Press On Walton-Cauffiel
          'Law And Order' Edict." Pittsburgh Courier.
          September 29, 1923, p. 14.

6,661.   "Evangelist Flanks Bible With Two Loaded Pistols."
          New York Times. October 8, 1922, Sect. 2, p. 1.

6,662.   "Foes Of Gov. Walton Take Steps To Rush Impeachment
          Move." New York Times. October 8, 1923, pp. 1, 2.

6,663.   Frost, Stanley. "Behind The White Hoods: The Re-
          generation Of Oklahoma." Outlook. Vol. 135,
          November 21, 1923, pp. 492-494.

6,664.   _____. "The Klan, The King, And A Revolution:
          The Regeneration Of Oklahoma." Outlook. Vol. 135,
          November 28, 1923, pp. 530-531.

6,665.   _____. "Night Riding Reformers: The Regeneration
          Of Oklahoma." Outlook. Vol. 135, November 14,
          1923, pp. 438-440.

6,666.   _____. "The Oklahoma Regicides Act." Outlook.
          Vol. 135, November 7, 1923, pp. 395-396.

6,667.   "Gov. Walton Offers To Resign Office." New York
          Times. October 10, 1923, p. 3.

6,668.   "Governor Dares Floggers." New York Times. Septem-
          ber 17, 1923, p. 2.

6,669.   "Governor Discusses Ownership." New York Times.
          September 16, 1923, p. 23.

6,670.   "Governor Lawton Of Oklahoma And The Ku Klux Klan."
          California Eagle. October 26, 1923, p. 10.

6,671.   "Governor Reported Ill At Home." New York Times.
          September 19, 1923, p. 5.

6,672.   "Gov. Walton's Justification." New York Times.
          September 8, 1923, p. 12.

6,673.   "Governor Walton Loses At Polls." Pittsburgh
          Courier. October 6, 1923, p. 16.

6,674.   "Guns Command Court And Capitol In Oklahoma City."
          New York Times. September 18, 1923, pp. 1, 3.

6,675.   Harlow, Victor E. "The Achievement Of The Klan."
          Harlow's Weekly. Vol. 23, June 19, 1924, p. 1.

6,676.   _____. "A New Place In The Klan." Harlow's
          Weekly. Vol. 23, December 6, 1924, p. 1.

6,677.   "Harreld Threatens War On Dry Agents." New York
          Times. October 9, 1925, p. 10.

6,678.   "He Can See Only One Mistake." New York Times.
          November 26, 1923, p. 16.

6,679.   "Jack, The Klan-Fighter In Oklahoma." Literary
          Digest. Vol. 79, October 20, 1923, pp. 38, 40, 42,
          44.

6,680.   "Klan Chief Accused Of Rioting." New York Times.
          September 22, 1923, p. 5.

6,681.   "Klan Crosses Light Up Oklahoma." New York Times.
          August 19, 1923, p. 2.

6,682.   "Governor And Mayor Attend Ku Klux Banquet In Oregon."
          New York Times. March 5, 1923, p. 1.

6,683.   "Klan Fight Causes Statewide Martial Law." Harlow's
          Weekly. Vol. 22, September 22, 1923, pp. 8-9.

6,684.   "Klan Head Asks Tulsa To Rally." Chicago Defender.
          August 20, 1921, p. 1.

6,685.   "The Klan In Oklahoma Attempts To Come Back."
          Harlow's Weekly. Vol. 30, September 24, 1931, pp.
          4-7.

6,686.   "The Klan In Retreat And Defeat." Independent.
          Vol. 113, August 30, 1924, pp. 114-115.

6,687.   "Klan Is Assailed By Ex-Gov. Walton." New York
          Times. May 31, 1924, p. 2.

6,688.   "Klan Judge Dismisses Case Against Walton." New
          York Times. April 19, 1924, p. 15.

6,689.   "Klan Jurymen Barred." New York Times. September
          28, 1921, p. 4.

6,690.   "Klan Leader To Start Chapter In Idabel, Okla."
          Pittsburgh Courier. February 2, 1980, p. 2.

6,691.   "Klan Leader To Visit Scene Of Oklahoma Race Riot."
          New York Times. January 24, 1980, p. 16.

6,692.   "Klan Paraders Kidnap An Oklahoma Editor." New
York Times. September 22, 1921, p. 3.

6,693.   "Klan Preacher Hints At Fight Against A 'Super-
Government'." New York Times. March 17, 1923, p. 15.

6,694.   "Klan Ticket Sweeps Tulsa." New York Times. April
2, 1924, p. 4.

6,695.   "Klan Ties Made Challenge Basis In Picking Jury."
Broad Ax. November 29, 1924, p. 2.

6,696.   "Klan To Fight Walton." New York Times. August 8,
1924, p. 2.

6,697.   "Klansmen Confess To Oklahoma Floggings." Pittsburgh
Courier. September 1, 1923, p. 13.

6,698.   "Klansmen Whip 4 Rum Runners." Chicago Defender.
August 26, 1922, p. 13.

6,699.   "Ku Klux Bars Bootleggers." New York Times.
December 23, 1921, p. 6.

6,700.   "Ku Klux 'Bomb' City From Air." Chicago Defender.
August 5, 1922, p. 1.

6,701.   "Ku Klux Klan Forms: Soviet Foe This Time." New
York Times. July 1, 1934, Sect. 4, p. 7.

6,702.   "KKK Plans To Demonstrate Against Protesting
Atheists In Oklahoma." New Orleans Times Picayune.
February 18, 1981, p. 5.

6,703.   "Ku Klux Foe Leading." New York Times. August 2,
1922, p. 2.

6,704.   "Ku Klux Issue In Oklahoma." New York Times.
August 1, 1922, p. 21.

6,705.   "Ku Klux Issue Up In Oklahoma Fight." New York
Times. July 31, 1922, p. 15.

6,706.   "Ku -Klux Jailed." New York Amsterdam News.
August 22, 1923, p. 7.

6,707.   "Ku Klux Klan In Oklahoma." Current Opinion.
Vol. 75, November, 1923, pp. 523-524.

6,708.   "Ku Klux Spray Notes; Women, Men Quit Town."
Chicago Defender. November 5, 1921, pp. 1-2.

6,709.   "Law Or Anarchy, Which?" Pittsburgh Courier.
September 22, 1923, pp. 14-15.

6,710.   "Legislators Defy Oklahoma Governor." New York
         Times. September 19, 1923, pp. 1, 5.

6,711.   "Machine Guns Back Walton In Fight Against Ku Klux
         Klan." Pittsburgh Courier. September 22, 1923, p.
         13.

6,712.   "Man States Hooded Mob Cut Off Ear." Pittsburgh
         Courier. September 29, 1923, pp. 1, 4.

6,713.   "Martial Law." New York Times. September 8, 1923,
         p. 15.

6,714.   "Martial Law In Oklahoma." New York Times.
         September 5, 1923, p. 14.

6,715.   "Martial Law In Oklahoma." Outlook. Vol. 135,
         September 26, 1923, pp. 133-134.

6,716.   "Martial Law Rules In Tulsa Streets." New York
         Times. August 15, 1923, p. 10.

6,717.   "Martial Law Widened After New Outrage." New York
         Times. September 1, 1923, p. 2.

6,718.   "Masked Floggers Of Tulsa." Literary Digest.
         Vol. 78, September 22, 1923, pp. 17-18.

6,719.   "Masked Kidnappers Routed In Oklahoma." New York
         Times. October 31, 1922, p. 1.

6,720.   "Masked Whippers Indicted." New York Times.
         February 28, 1923, p. 19.

6,721.   "May Put All State Under Martial Law." New York
         Times. September 8, 1923, p. 15.

6,722.   "Military Censor For Tulsa Tribune." New York
         Times. September 15, 1923, p. 17.

6,723.   "Military Released Three Prisoners." New York
         Times. September 21, 1923, p. 2.

6,724.   "Miners Scare Klansmen." New York Times. November
         3, 1924, p. 4.

6,725.   "Mob Law In Oklahoma." New York Amsterdam News.
         September 26, 1923, pp. 12-13.

6,726.   Nelson, Llewellyn. "The K.K.K. For Boredom."
         New Republic. Vol. 41, January 14, 1925, pp. 196-
         198.

6,727.   Neuringer, Sheldon. "Governor Walton's War On The
         Ku Klux Klan: An Episode In Oklahoma History,
         1923 To 1924." Chronicles Of Oklahoma. Vol. 45,
         Summer, 1967, pp. 153-179.

6,728.   "No Oklahoma Appeal To Coolidge." New York Times.
          September 19, 1923, p. 5.

6,729.   Oates, Stephen B. "Boom Oil! Oklahoma Strikes It
          Rich!" American West. Vol. 5, January, 1968,
          pp. 11-15, 64-66.

6,730.   "Okla. Youth Buried, KKK Recruiting Mission Fails."
          Jet. Vol. 57, February 21, 1980, p. 7.

6,731.   "Oklahoma Anti-Klan Gain." New York Times. Novem-
          ber 28, 1923, p. 20.

6,732.   "Oklahoma Democrats Give Walton Victory." New York
          Times. August 4, 1922, p. 6.

6,733.   "Oklahoma Governor Bars Klan." New York Times.
          August 4, 1922, p. 6.

6,734.   "Oklahoma House Bars Klan Exposure." New York
          Times. October 16, 1923, p. 23.

6,735.   "Oklahoma House Moves Promptly To Impeach Walton."
          New York Times. October 12, 1923, pp. 1, 3.

6,736.   "Oklahoma In Doubt As Hot Fight Rages." New York
          Times. September 24, 1924, p. 3.

6,737.   "Oklahoma Kingless, Not Klanless." Literary Digest.
          Vol. 79, December 8, 1923, pp. 9-11.

5,738.   "Oklahoma Klan Bars Masked Parades." New York
          Times. September 11, 1923, p. 19.

6,739.   "Oklahoma Whippings 2,500." New York Times. July
          1, 1923, p. 7.

6,740.   "Oklahoma's Klan War From Over The Border."
          Harlow's Weekly. Vol. 22, September 22, 1924, pp.
          4-5.

6,741.   "Oklahoma's Disgrace." Pittsburgh Courier.
          September 29, 1923, pp. 14-15.

6,742.   "Oklahoma's Uncivil Civil War." Literary Digest.
          Vol. 78, September 29, 1923, pp. 10-11

6,743.   "Order Martial Law In Tulsa, Oklahoma." New York
          Times. August 14, 1923, p. 5.

6,744.   "Post Guns To Stop Oklahoma Session." New York
          Times. September 22, 1923, pp. 1, 5.

6,745.   "Predicts Defeat Of Ex-Gov. Walton." New York
          Times. August 10, 1924, p. 30.

6,746.   "Predicts Klan Issue In Election." New York Times.
         September 24, 1923, p. 2.

6,747.   "Prevent Revealing Of Klan Membership." New York
         Times. November 29, 1923, p. 23.

6,748.   "Puts All Oklahoma Under Martial Law To Suppress
         Klan." New York Times. September 16, 1923, p. 1.

6,749.   "Raskob Opens Drive To End 'Whispering'." New
         York Times. September 22, 1928, p. 2.

6,750.   "Rush Preparation Of Walton Charges." New York
         Times. October 14, 1923, p. 5.

6,751.   "Says Klan Fights Smith In Oklahoma." New York
         Times. February 28, 1928, p. 3.

6,752.   "Says Klan Shames Tulsa." New York Times.
         September 17, 1923, p. 2.

6,753.   "Says Republicans Are Running Klan." New York
         Times. August 27, 1924, p. 3.

6,754.   "School In Oklahoma." Pittsburgh Courier.
         October 6, 1923, p. 16.

6,755.   "Secretary Weeks." New York Times. September 8,
         1923, p. 15.

6,756.   "Sees Plot Of Ku Klux Against Governor." New York
         Times. December 3, 1922, Sect. 1, Part 2, p. 5.

6,757.   "Situation In Tulsa Eased." New York Times.
         August 22, 1923, p. 16.

6,758.   "Six Arrested In Tulsa." New York Times. August
         17, 1923, p. 2.

6,759.   "69 Assure Session Of Oklahoma House." New York
         Times. September 21, 1923, p. 2.

6,760.   "Smith Assails Intolerance, Answers Foes On Record,
         Oklahoma Crowd Cheers." New York Times. September
         21, 1928, pp. 1, 2.

6,761.   "Southern Man Says 'To Hell With Ku Klux'."
         Chicago Defender. September 9, 1922, pp. 3-4.

6,762.   "Tests Martial Law Edict." New York Times. September
         19, 1923, p. 5.

6,763.   "To Indict 400 Klansmen." New York Times. October
         30, 1923, p. 22.

6,764.   "Troops Take Over Oklahoma Capitol; Displace Officials." New York Times. September 17, 1923, p. 1.

6,765.   "Tulsa Fighting Military Rule." New York Times. August 20, 1923, p. 2.

6,766.   "Tulsa Military Inquiry Halted." New York Times. August 19, 1923, p. 2.

6,767.   "Tulsa's 'Lash Reign' Blamed On Ku Klux Klan." Pittsburgh Courier. September 15, 1923, pp. 13-14.

6,768.   "University Of Oklahoma And The Ku Klux Klan." School And Society. Vol. 16, October 7, 1922, pp. 412-413.

6,769.   "Vote To Investigate Oklahoma Klan." New York Times. October 18, 1923, p. 23.

6,770.   Walton, J.C. "Oklahoma Governor Tells Why Violence Grips State." New York Times. August 26, 1923, Sect. 6, p. 13.

6,771.   "Walton Appeals To Federal Court." New York Times. November 7, 1923, p. 15.

6,772.   "Walton Calls Klan Anarchistic." New York Times. September 18, 1923, p. 3.

6,773.   "Walton Charges Plot By Klan To Oust Him." New York Times. October 28, 1923, p. 3.

6,774.   "Walton Denounces Bloodshed Threats." New York Times. September 23, 1923, Sect. 2, p. 1.

6,775.   "Walton Is Indicted; Klan Rouses Senate." New York Times. November 24, 1923, p. 1.

6,776.   "Walton Loses Move To Stop His Trial." New York Times. November 8, 1923, p. 3.

6,777.   "Walton Now Calls Anti-Klan Session." New York Times. October 7, 1923, p. 1.

6,778.   "Walton Trial Begins In Oklahoma Senate." New York Times. November 9, 1923, p. 4.

6,779.   "Will Use All Oklahoma Troops, Says Walton, If Needed To End Mob Violence And Flogging." New York Times. September 5, 1923, p. 19.

36. OREGON

6,780.   "Hall, Klan Candidate, Leads Gov. Olcott In Close Race In Oregon Primary." New York Times. May 21, 1922, p. 1.

6,781.   "Hall Leading In Oregon." New York Times. May 22, 1922, p. 3.

6,782.   "Hall Loses Oregon Lead." New York Times. May 23, 1922, p. 1.

6,783.   "Harding Disapproves Klan." New York Times. April 25, 1922, p. 21.

6,784.   Harvier, Ernest. "What The Klan Did In Oregon Elections." New York Times. December 3, 1922, Sect. 2, p. 8.

6,785.   Holman, Alfred. "Rail Isolation Retards Oregon's Business Rise." New York Times. December 2, 1924, Sect. 9, p. 10.

6,786.   Holsinger, M. Paul. "The Oregon School Controversy; 1922-25." Pacific Historical Review. Vol. 37, August, 1968, pp. 327-341.

6,787.   "KKK In Oregon." Capital (Salem) Journal. November 10, 1923, p. 1.

6,788.   "KKK In Oregon." Catholic Sentinel. February 10, 1921, p. 1.

6,789.   "KKK In Oregon." Catholic Sentinel. October 12, 1922, p. 1.

6,790.   "KKK In Oregon." Catholic Sentinel. November 16, 1922, p. 1.

6,791.   "KKK In Oregon." Catholic Sentinel. May 4, 1939, p. 1.

6,792.   "KKK In Oregon." Corvallis Gazette Times. January 10, 1923, p. 1.

6,793.   "KKK In Oregon." Cottage Grove Sentinel. January 19, 1923, p. 1.

6,794.   "KKK In Oregon." Dallas (Tex.) Observer. November 2, 1922, p. 1.

6,795.   "KKK In Oregon." Eugene Guard. November 6, 1922, p. 1.

6,796.   "KKK In Oregon." Eugene Register. October 24, 1924, p. 1.

6,797.   "KKK In Oregon." Fiery Cross. May 11, 1923, p. 1.

6,798.   "KKK In Oregon." Foster Road News. May, 1924, p. 1.

6,799.   "KKK In Oregon." <u>Grants Pass Spokesman</u>. April 26, 1924, p. 1.

6,800.   "KKK In Oregon." <u>Heppner Herald</u>. December 18, 1923, p. 1.

6,801.   "KKK In Oregon." <u>Hood River Glacier</u>. October 5, 1922, p. 1.

6,802.   "KKK In Oregon." <u>Klamath Falls Herald</u>. November 30, 1923, p. 1.

6,803.   "KKK In Oregon." <u>Klamath Falls Herald</u>. December 5, 1923, p. 1.

6,804.   "KKK In Oregon." <u>Marshfield News</u>. December 24, 1923, p. 1.

6,805.   "KKK In Oregon." <u>Marshfield Times</u>. November 5, 1923, p. 1.

6,806.   "KKK In Oregon." <u>Mc Minnville Register</u>. October 24, 1924, p. 1.

6,807.   "KKK In Oregon." <u>Medford Clarion</u>. May 23, 1922, p. 1.

6,808.   "KKK In Oregon." <u>Medford Tribune</u>. November 2, 1922, p. 1.

6,809.   "KKK In Oregon." <u>Milton Eagle</u>. March 26, 1925, p. 1.

6,810.   "KKK In Oregon." <u>Morning (Oregon City) Enterprise</u>. November 5, 1922, p. 1.

6,811.   "KKK In Oregon." <u>Morning (Portland) Oregonian</u>. August 2, 1922, p. 1.

6,812.   "KKK In Oregon." <u>Morning (Portland) Oregonian</u>. October 19, 1923, p. 1.

6,813.   "KKK In Oregon." <u>Morning (Portland) Oregonian</u>. May 14, 1924, p. 1.

6,814.   "KKK In Oregon." <u>Morning (Portland) Oregonian</u>. April 11, 1937, p. 1.

6,815.   "KKK In Oregon." <u>Myrtle Creek Mail</u>. October 10, 1924, p. 1.

6,816.   "KKK In Oregon." <u>Nation</u>. Vol. 113, 1923, pp. 233-234.

6,817.   "KKK In Oregon." <u>Nation</u>. Vol. 116, 1922, pp. 6, 325.

6,818.   "KKK In Oregon." National Kourier. April, 1925,
          p. 1.

6,819.   "KKK In Oregon." Newberg Graphic. May 1, 1924, p. 1.

6,820.   "KKK In Oregon." Oregon City Courier. August 24,
          1930, p. 1.

6,821.   "KKK In Oregon." Oregon (Salem) Statesmen.
          August 4, 1922, p. 1.

6,822.   "KKK In Oregon." Oregon (Portland) Voter.
          March 25, 1922, January 20, 1923, p. 1.

6,823.   "KKK In Oregon." Oregonian (Portland). April 11,
          1937, p. 1.

6,824.   "KKK In Oregon." Oregonian (Portland). April 18,
          1937, p. 1.

6,825.   "KKK In Oregon." Portland Telegram. March 12,
          1923, p. 1.

6,826.   "KKK In Oregon." Portland Telegram. May 5, 1923,
          p. 1.

6,827.   "KKK In Oregon." Riddle Enterprise. April 10,
          1924, p. 1.

6,828.   "KKK In Oregon." Roseburg Review. September 12,
          1923, p. 1.

6,829.   "KKK In Oregon." Spectator (Portland). January,
          1925, p. 1.

6,830.   "KKK In Oregon." St. Helens Columbian. December
          26, 1923, p. 1.

6,831.   "KKK In Oregon." Survey. Vol. 49, 1922, pp. 76-
          77.

6,832.   "KKK In Oregon." Tillamook Headlight. January
          4, 1924, p. 1.

6,833.   "KKK In Oregon." Western (Portland) American.
          May 9, 1924, p. 1.

6,834.   "KKK In Oregon." Weston Leader. November 30,
          1923, p. 1.

6,835.   "KKK In Oregon." Wheeler Reporter. June 26,
          1924, p. 1.

6,836.   "KKK In Oregon." Willamina Times. October 23,
          1924, p. 1.

6,837.   "Klan Candidate Carries Oregon." New York Times.
          November 8, 1922, p. 3.

6,838.   "Klan Fights School Board." New York Times.
          December 8, 1922, p. 19.

6,839.   "Klan Victories In Oregon And Texas." Literary
          Digest. Vol. 75, November 25, 1922.

6,840.   "Klan Wins Victory At Portland Polls." New York
          Times. September 11, 1923, p. 19.

6,841.   "Ku Klux Brand Woman." Chicago Defender. October
          29, 1921, p. 1.

6,842.   "Ku Klux Klan In Politics." Literary Digest.
          Vol. 73, June 10, 1922, p. 15.

6,843.   "Ku Klux Klan Rule In Oregon." New York Times.
          December 16, 1922, p. 14.

6,844.   "Move To Recall Oregon Governor." New York Times.
          October 15, 1923, p. 2.

6,845.   "The Oregon School Law." New York Times. August
          5, 1923, p. 4.

6,846.   "An Oregon Venture." New York Times. November 12,
          1922, Sect. 2, p. 6.

6,847.   "Rampages Of Ku Klux Klan On Pacific Coast." The
          Messenger. Vol. 4, June, 1922, pp. 419-420.

6,848.   Roberts, Waldo. "The Ku Kluxing Of Oregon."
          Outlook. Vol. 133, March 14, 1923, pp. 490-491.

6,849.   "Royal Riders Growing." New York Times. November
          30, 1922, p. 21.

6,850.   " 'Rout Klan Or Face Civil War'." New York
          Amsterdam News. December 20, 1922, p. 1.

6,851.   Toll, William. "Progress And Piety: The Ku Klux
          Klan And Social Change In Tillamook, Oregon."
          Pacific Northwest Quarterly. Vol. 69, April, 1978,
          pp. 75-85.

6,852.   Toy, Eckard V. Jr. "The Ku Klux Klan In Tillamook,
          Oregon." Pacific Northwest Quarterly. Vol. 53,
          April, 1962, pp. 60-64.

6,853.   Tyack, David B. "Perils Of Pluralism: The Back-
          ground Of The Pierce Case." American Historical
          Review. Vol. 74, October, 1968, pp. 74-98.

6,854. "Wiping Out Oregon's School Law." Literary Digest. Vol. 81, April 26, 1924, pp. 33-34.

37. PENNSYLVANIA

6,855. "Asserts Klan Rivals Back Law And Peace." New York Times. September 16, 1923, Sect. 1, Part 2, p. 5.

6,856. "Big Klan Meeting At Nazareth, Pa." New York Times. August 3, 1924, p. 17.

6,857. "Bishop Mc Connell Raps Klan As Anti-American." Pittsburgh Courier. October 27, 1923, p. 2.

6,858. "Bishop McConnell Rebukes Ku Klux." Pittsburgh Courier. October 20, 1923, p. 3.

6,859. "Bishop Ousts Klansmen." New York Times. October 9, 1923, p. 1.

6,860. "Blames Klan For Dynamite Blast." New York Times. April 26, 1922, p. 6.

6,861. "Bloody Klan Riot Probed." Pittsburgh Courier. September 1, 1923, p. 1.

6,862. "Branded By Masked Men." New York Times. September 16, 1922, p. 8.

6,863. "Burros Cremated In Pennsylvania." New York Times. November 3, 1965, p. 20.

6,864. "Charles Fred White Says Judge Lewis Is A 'Ku Kluxer'." Pittsburgh Courier. November 12, 1927, p. 12.

6,865. "Church Darkened When Ku Klux Visit Church." Pittsburgh Courier. May 17, 1924, p. 5.

6,866. "Churchmen Beat Up Klansmen; Drive Away Hooded Band." Pittsburgh Courier. April 7, 1923, p. 1.

6,867. "CIO In Pennsylvania Bans Red Officers." New York Times. April 26, 1947, p. 3.

6,868. "Clairton, Pa., Group Protests KKK Garb At School Basketball Game." Pittsburgh Courier. January 28, 1978, Sect. 2, p. 9.

6,869. Clarke, Susan. "Klan Dictates To Media Over Black Coverage." Pittsburgh Courier. November 1, 1980, pp. 1, 20.

6,870. " 'Come Prepared' Order For Klan Parade." New York Times. August 30, 1923, p. 4.

6,871.   "Commend Ban On Klan." New York Times. June 24, 1926, p. 33.

6,872.   " 'Convocation Of Love' Opposes Klan Rally." New York Times. October 27, 1980, p. A16.

6,873.   "Court Frees Klan Heads." New York Times. February 17, 1944, p. 11.

6,874.   "Decides Against Klan In Pennsylvania Case." New York Times. August 14, 1929, p. 25.

6,875.   "A Detail Of The Ku Klux Klan." New York Times. August 28, 1923, p. 19.

6,876.   "Driving The Point Home." Jet. Vol. 60, June 4, 1981, p. 45.

6,877.   "Electric Klan Cross On Stage With Heflin." New York Times. February 12, 1928, p. 26.

6,878.   "Ex-Members Ask Receiver For Klan." New York Times. July 14, 1927, p. 13.

6,879.   "Fiery Cross Rouses Guard." New York Times. August 27, 1922, p. 10.

6,880.   "Fooling Themselves." Pittsburgh Courier. October 20, 1923, p. 8.

6,881.   "Former Klan Cyclops Out For Smith." New York Times. September 16, 1928, p. 17.

6,882.   "Four Klansmen March." New York Times. June 12, 1966, p. 79.

6,883.   "Gardner Not A Member Of Ku Klux Klan." Pittsburgh Courier. September 8, 1923, p. 1.

6,884.   "Girl Faints In Church Choir As Klansmen March To Altar." New York Times. May 7, 1923, p. 17.

6,885.   Green, Ward. "Notes For A History Of The Klan." American Mercury. Vol. 5, 1925, pp. 240-243.

6,886.   "Harrisburg, Pa." Pittsburgh Courier. May 23, 1981, p. 1.

6,887.   "Heflin Guarded During Speech." Pittsburgh Courier. February 18, 1928, p. 12.

6,888.   "Heflin Speaks At Klan Meeting; Favors Hoover." Pittsburgh Courier. September 15, 1928, p. 3.

6,889.   "Hooded Men Shoot At Negro Boy Scouts." New York Times. July 9, 1924, p. 6.

6,890.   "Indicted For Klan Threat." New York Times.
          December 8, 1923, p. 11.

6,891.   Janson, Donald. "Leaders In Klan And Nazi Party
          Accused Of Rape." New York Times. July 7, 1979,
          p. 20.

6,892.   _____. "3 Who Suit Klan Tell Of Dissent." New
          York Times. May 30, 1971, p. 37.

6,893.   Jones, Robert. "Pittsburgh Thrills To Crusader's
          Story." New York Times. July 17, 1927, Sect. 2,
          p. 7.

6,894.   "Judicial Spanking For The Klan." Literary Digest.
          Vol. 97, April 28, 1928, pp. 8-9.

6,895.   "Kendrick Bars Klan At Sesquicentennial." New
          York Times. June 23, 1926, p. 3.

6,896.   "Keystone Klan Backs Roosevelt On Black." New
          York Times. September 19, 1937, p. 39.

6,897.   "KKK." Pittsburgh Courier. May 9, 1981, p. 1.

6,898.   "KKK In Pennsylvania." Literary Digest. Vol. 68,
          February 5, 1921, pp. 42, 45, 46.

6,899.   "KKK In Pennsylvania." Nation. Vol. 113, 1921,
          pp. 285-286.

6,900.   "Killing And Terror Laid To Klan Chiefs In
          Pittsburgh Trial." New York Times. April 10,
          1928, pp. 1, 16.

6,901.   "KKK Infiltration Of Police." Washington Post.
          October 15, 1980, p. A13.

6,902.   "KKK Infiltration Of Police Force Alleged By
          Harrisburg, Pa., Black." Washington Post. October
          14, 1980, p. A6.

6,903.   "KKK Looks To Pitt Steel Mills For New Membership."
          Jet. Vol. 57, February 28, 1980, p. 7.

6,904.   "Klan And Legion Clash." New York Times. November
          13, 1923, p. 7.

6,905.   "Klan As A Victim Of Mob Violence." Literary
          Digest. Vol. 78, September 8, 1923, pp. 12-13.

6,906.   "Klan Demands Dry Raids." New York Times.
          September 26, 1922, p. 6.

6,907.   "Klan Initiation Picture And Victims." Pittsburgh
          Courier. September 1, 1923, p. 1.

6,908.   "Klan Knights Put Out Of Church." Literary Digest.
         Vol. 77, May 5, 1923, pp. 37-38.

6,909.   "Klan Leader And 4 Others Released In Philadelphia."
         New York Times. October 13, 1966, p. 38.

6,910.   "Klan Leader Arrested." New York Times. October
         9, 1966, p. 65.

6,911.   "Klan Loses In Pittsburgh." New York Times.
         November 8, 1923, p. 3.

6,912.   "Klan Meets In Pa." Washington Star. October 27,
         1980, p. A1.

6,913.   "Klan Members Mass On Carnegie Hall." New York
         Times. August 27, 1923, pp. 1, 2.

6,914.   "Klan Offers Reward For Firebug." New York Times.
         August 16, 1925, Sect. 2, p. 3.

6,915.   "Klan Parade Forbidden." New York Times. August
         26, 1923, p. 13.

6,916.   "Klan Prescribes A Church." New York Times.
         March 7, 1932, p. 19.

6,917.   "Klan Puts 'K' On Man's Face." Chicago Defender.
         October 7, 1922, p. 13.

6,918.   "Klan Riot Inquiry Balked At Carnegie." New York
         Times. August 28, 1923, p. 19.

6,919.   "Klan Riots Quelled In Philadelphia." New York
         Amsterdam News. June 24, 1925, p. 3.

6,920.   "Klan Threat To Dry Chief." New York Times.
         June 20, 1922, p. 21.

6,921.   "Klan To Appeal Lost Suit." New York Times.
         July 7, 1928, p. 15.

6,922.   "Klan Trial Suspended By Disorder In Court." New
         York Times. June 11, 1924, p. 10.

6,923.   "Klan Warns Squire For Mixed Marriage." Pittsburgh
         Courier. August 11, 1923, p. 1.

6,924.   "Klan, White Robed With Revolvers In Hand, Flee
         When Police Appear." Pittsburgh Courier. November
         3, 1923, p. 12.

6,925.   "Klansman Is Slain, Many Are Injured, In Riot At
         Carnegie." New York Times. August 26, 1923, pp.
         1, 13.

6,926.   "Klansman Reports Shooting." New York Times.
          October 25, 1965, p. 24.

6,927.   "Klansmen." New York Times.   April 3, 1923, p. 7.

6,928.   "Klansmen Fight Retrial." New York Times.   July
          15, 1928, Sect. 2 & 3, p. 1.

6,929.   "Klansmen Freed Of Slaying At Lilly." New York
          Times.   June 15, 1924, p. 17.

6,930.   "Klansmen Parade At Lancaster Polls." New York
          Times.   November 7, 1923, p. 6.

6,931.   "Klansmen Treated Correctly." New York Times.
          April 3, 1923, p. 22.

6,932.   "Ku Klux Klan Un-American Says Pastor." Pittsburgh
          Courier.   April 14, 1923, pp. 1, 2.

6,933.   "Ku Klux Mob Rule Upheld By Minister." Pittsburgh
          Courier.   September 22, 1923, p. 3.

6,934.   "Legislature Attire?" Washington Afro-American.
          May 19, 1981, p. 1.

6,935.   Lowenfels, Walter.   "Pennsylvania GOP Coddles The
          Klan." Daily Worker.   September 22, 1946, Sect. 2,
          p. 7.

6,936.   _____.   "Philadelphia Civil Rights Congress
          Demands City Jail Klansmen." Daily Worker.   July
          3, 1952, p. 8.

6,937.   _____.   "Philadelphians Urge Mayor Act As KKK
          Parades." Daily Worker.   June 29, 1952, pp. 1, 8.

6,938.   "Lynching, Rioting, Murder Charged As Klan Factions
          War." Pittsburgh Courier.   August 13, 1927, pp.
          1, 8.

6,939.   "Mantle Club Is Accused." New York Times.
          December 7, 1941, p. 44.

6,940.   "Masons Outlaw Ku Klux." New York Times.   December
          28, 1922, p. 7.

6,941.   "Misuse Of $15,000,000 Charged Against Klan."
          New York Times.   October 20, 1927, p. 31.

6,942.   "Murdered By 'No One'." Pittsburgh Courier.
          October 6, 1923, p. 16.

6,943.   "Nazis Are Granted A Permit For A Rally In
          Philadelphia." New York Times.   February 21,
          1979, p. 12.

6,944.   "Negro Boys Burn Cross In Hoax." New York Times.
          August 3, 1946, p. 17.

6,945.   "New Anti-Klan Order Launched In Pa." New York
          Amsterdam News. August 22, 1923, p. 2.

6,946.   "9 Freed In Carnegie Riot." New York Times.
          September 21, 1923, p. 2.

6,947.   "No Philadelphia Klan Arrests Despite Mayor's
          Pledge." Daily Worker. July 17, 1952, p. 8.

6,948.   "Notes On People." New York Times. April 29,
          1978, p. 16.

6,949.   "Officials Probe Charges Of Klansmen Among Pa.
          Police." Jet. Vol. 59, November 13, 1980, p. 54.

6,950.   "Orders Acquittal At Klan Trial." New York Times.
          November 23, 1924, p. 21.

6,951.   "Pa. Klan Leader Talks About The Klan." Baltimore
          Afro-American. December 24, 1977, p. 8.

6,952.   "Pastor Turns Down Blood Money." Pittsburgh
          Courier. November 3, 1923, pp. 1, 10.

6,953.   "Penn Has No Room For Klan." Pittsburgh Courier.
          December 1, 1923, p. 2.

6,954.   "Philadelphia Klan Defiant." New York Times.
          December 2, 1922, p. 14.

6,955.   "Pittsburgh Church Puts Klansmen Out." New York
          Times. April 2, 1923, p. 1.

6,956.   "Pittsburgh Lawyer Unmasks And Drives Klansmen Out
          Of Church." New York Amsterdam News. April 4,
          1923, p. 1.

6,957.   "Pittsburgh NAACP And S.W. Pa. N.O.W. Reps. Decry
          KKK Activity." Pittsburgh Courier. December 8,
          1979, p. 1.

6,958.   "Pittsburgh Trial To Uncover Klan." New York
          Times. April 9, 1928, p. 23.

6,959.   "Rebukes Klansmen For Unamericanism." New York
          Times. April 9, 1923, p. 31.

6,960.   "Recruit For 'Klan' In North." New York Times.
          August 10, 1921, p. 2.

6,961.   " 'Red Knights' Form To Oppose Ku Klux." New York
          Times. September 7, 1923, p. 17.

6,962. "Robed Men Shoot Police." New York Times. July 4, 1924, p. 6.

6,963. "Seeks War On Klan In Pennsylvania." Cleveland Call & Post. April 5, 1947, p. 1.

6,964. "The Self Proclaimed Head." New York Times. March 2, 1974, p. 1.

6,965. "Sentenced For Lilly Riot." New York Times. July 2, 1924, p. 2.

6,966. Shepherd, William G. "How I Put Over The Klan." Collier's. Vol. 82, July 14, 1928, pp. 5-7, 32, 34-35.

6,967. _____. "Ku Klux Koin." Collier's. Vol. 28, July 21, 1928, pp. 8-9, 38-39.

6,968. "7 Pennsylvania Klansmen Plan March To Washington." New York Times. June 11, 1966, p. 15.

6,969. "Signs Order Against Klan." New York Times. August 7, 1927, Sect. 2, p. 11.

6,970. "600 Attend KKK Rally In Pennsylvania." Washington Star. October 27, 1980, p. A7.

6,971. "Station Allowed To Air Klansman And Nazi." New York Times. October 1, 1977, p. 8.

6,972. "Stolen F.B.I. Papers Described As Largely Of A Political Nature." New York Times. May 13, 1971, p. 18.

6,973. Ransom, Lou. "Klan Membership Probed In Harrisburg Police Force." Pittsburgh Courier. October 25, 1980, pp. 1, 5.

6,974. "Textile Workers Pledge New Drive." New York Times. May 19, 1939, p. 13.

6,975. "Thank God For A Man." Pittsburgh Courier. April 14, 1923, p. 16.

6,976. "Their Threats Came To Nothing." New York Times. July 3, 1924, p. 14.

6,977. "They Invited Trouble And It Came." New York Times. April 8, 1924, p. 18.

6,978. "Threats Of Ambushing." New York Times. August 28, 1923, p. 19.

6,979. "To Oust Klan Miners." New York Times. April 3, 1924, p. 2.

6,980.   "Town Forced By Klan Threat To Cancel Defense Parade." New York Times. September 13, 1924, p. 1.

6,981.   "Violence Breeds Violence." Washington Post. August 28, 1923.

6,982.   "Wants Klan Barred At Sesquicentennial." New York Times. June 22, 1926, p. 24.

6,983.   "Will Move To Oust Klan." New York Times. April 23, 1928, p. 14.

38.   RHODE ISLAND

6,984.   "Bars Klan From Armories." New York Times. June 8, 1924, p. 3.

6,985.   "Battalion Is Accused Of Being Klan Force." New York Times. March 18, 1928, p. 2.

6,986.   "KKK In Rhode Island." National Kourier. November 21, 1925, p. 1.

6,987.   "KKK In Rhode Island." Providence Evening Bulletin. June 9, 1924, p. 1.

6,988.   "KKK In Rhode Island." Providence Evening Bulletin. March 17, 1928, p. 1.

6,989.   "KKK In Rhode Island." Providence Evening Bulletin. March 29, 1928, p. 1.

6,990.   "KKK In Rhode Island." Fiery Cross. March, 1933.

6,991.   "Klan Boomed In School." New York Times. December 8, 1924, p. 11.

6,992.   "Klan Secrets Revealed." New York Times. March 30, 1928, p. 7.

6,993.   "Klan Troop Inquiry Looms In Providence." New York Times. March 20, 1928, p. 45.

6,994.   "Orders Inquiry On Klan." New York Times. March 24, 1928, p. 30.

6,995.   "Rhode Island Klan Rally." New York Times. July 27, 1924, p. 2.

6,996.   "Rhode Island Klansman Acquitted." New York Times. January 10, 1929, p. 5.

6,997.   "Says Klan Branded Him." New York Times. August 6, 1924, p. 17.

39. SOUTH CAROLINA

6,998.   "Angry Carolinians Beat Up 6 Kluxers." Afro-
           American. June 4, 1949, p. 1.

6,999.   "Anti-Klan Bill Defeated." New York Times.
           February 15, 1923, p. 20.

7,000.   "Ask Justice Department To Probe S.C. Klan."
           Norfolk Journal & Guide. December 23, 1939, p. 11.

7,001.   "Backfire: South Carolina's Myrtle Beach." Time.
           Vol. 56, September 11, 1950, pp. 26-27.

7,002.   "Baptist Group Sets KKK Fight." New York Times.
           November 28, 1948, p. 34.

7,003.   "Believe Ries Men Have Eye On Klan Leaders Of State."
           Pittsburgh Courier. February 17, 1940, p. 1.

7,004.   "Byrnes Backs Fight Against Night Riders." New
           York Times. January 22, 1951, p. 36.

7,005.   "Byrnes Hits Police In 2 Klan Beatings." New York
           Times. August 30, 1951, p. 16.

7,006.   "Byrnes Lumps The Klan, N.A.A.C.P. As Meance."
           New York Times. March 18, 1954, p. 32.

7,007.   "Byrnes Signs Klan Curb." New York Times. April
           12, 1951, p. 29.

7,008.   "Byrnes Warns Klan He'll Run His State." New York
           Times. November 18, 1950, p. 9.

7,009.   "Carolina Arrests In Beating Reach 7." New York
           Times. January 21, 1951, p. 59.

7,010.   "Carolina Governor Asks Law Against Klansmen."
           Pittsburgh Courier. March 23, 1940, p. 3.

7,011.   "Carolina Ku Klux Klan Claim Negro Federal Agent
           Probing South." Pittsburgh Courier. February 3,
           1940, p. 13.

7,012.   "Chief Arrested After Riot Fatalities." Christian
           Science Monitor. January 1, 1950, p. 11.

7,013.   "Colored Democrats To Be Purged, Says KKK Chief."
           Washington Afro-American. February 18, 1939, p. 8.

7,014.   "8 More Klansmen Jailed." New York Times.
           September 2, 1950, p. 17.

7,015.   "The Feel Of The Whip." Durham (N.C.) Morning
           Herald. October 5, 1952.

7,016.   "Five Hundred Robed Klansmen March Through Rain
          Drenched Streets In South Carolina City." Black
          Dispatch. February 26, 1949, p. 1.

7,017.   " 'Flight From Injustice' In South By Negro Pastor
          Related In Court." New York Times. November 26,
          1955, p. 9.

7,018.   "Four Klansmen Receive Prison Terms In Beating Of
          Negro In South Carolina." New York Times. January
          24, 1958, p. 12.

7,019.   "14 Of Klan Arrested In South Carolina." New York
          Times. November 2, 1951, p. 33.

7,020.   "G-Men Study Evidence Of KKK Threats In Vote Case."
          Norfolk Journal & Guide. September 9, 1939, pp.
          1, 10.

7,021.   "Governor Of S.C. Charges Klans Supported By Nazis."
          Pittsburgh Courier. July 5, 1941.

7,022.   "Greenville Klan To Hamper Registration." New
          York Amsterdam News. August 5, 1939, p. 20.

7,023.   "Greenville Lawyer Who Befriended Negroes Against
          Ku Klux Klan Kills Self." Pittsburgh Courier.
          April 6, 1940, p. 12.

7,024.   Hoffman, Edwin D. "The Genesis Of The Modern Move-
          ment For Equal Rights In South Carolina, 1930-1939."
          Journal of Negro History. Vol. 44, October, 1959,
          pp. 346-369.

7,025.   "Hold Dance After KKK Warning." Pittsburgh Courier.
          February 3, 1940, p. 2.

7,026.   "Inquiry Into Flogging On." New York Times.
          November 11, 1950, p. 7.

7,027.   "Integrated Class Quits In Carolina." New York
          Times. July 14, 1956, p. 13.

7,028.   "Judge In Klan Robe Killed In Gun Battle." New
          York Times. August 29, 1950, p. 28.

7,029.   "KKK Critic Taken For Ride In Night Clothes."
          Norfolk Journal & Guide. November 18, 1939, p. 10.

7,030.   "KKK Surges Back." Christian Science Monitor.
          May 2, 1957, p. 10.

7,031.   "Klan Abduct And Beat Up Four Brothers: Start New
          Reign Of Terrorism In South Carolina." Pittsburgh
          Courier. July 27, 1940, p. 20.

7,032.   "Klan Attacks Laid To Attempt To Get Lily-White
            Ballot." Norfolk Journal & Guide. October 21,
            1939, p. 1.

7,033.   "Klan Chief Arrested In Killing Of Officer." New
            York Times. September 1, 1950, p. 14.

7,034.   "Klan Demonstrates In 100 Autos." New York Times.
            May 14, 1950, p. 53.

7,035.   "Klan Denies Charges In Letter To Byrnes." New
            York Times. November 20, 1950, p. 18.

7,036.   "Klan Has Hard Time In South Carolina." New York
            Times. November 19, 1923, p. 17.

7,037.   "Klan Holds Rally In South Carolina." Washington
            Evening Star. August 19, 1963.

7,038.   "Klan Is Condemned." New York Times. August 23,
            1955, p. 20.

7,039.   " 'The Klan Is God'." Durham Morning Herald.
            October 5, 1953, p. 1.

7,040.   "Klan Leader And 9 Accused In Carolina Of A
            Robbery Plot." New York Times. September 18,
            1970, p. 13.

7,041.   "Klan Leader Complains: Birchers Are Integrated."
            Norfolk Journal & Guide. August 17, 1963, p. 2.

7,042.   "Klan Leader Defiant." New York Times. January
            7, 1966, p. 9.

7,043.   "Klan Leader Released." New York Times. December
            25, 1969, p. 58.

7,044.   "Klan N.A.A.C.P. To March." New York Times.
            September 6, 1969, p. 7.

7,045.   "Klan Official Arrested." New York Times. May 21,
            1951, p. 21.

7,046.   "Klan Plans Back Seat For Negro In Next Democratic
            Convention." Pittsburgh Courier. February 18,
            1939, p. 1.

7,047.   "Klan Probe Has South Carolinians Worried: Believe
            Dies Men Have Eye On Klan Leaders Of State."
            Pittsburgh Courier. February 17, 1940, p. 3.

7,048.   "Klan Revival Charged." New York Times. October
            21, 1955, p. 16.

7,049.   "Klan Reward Money Asked Returned." Christian
          Science Monitor. June 5, 1952, p. 11.

7,050.   "Klan Rides Again." Pittsburgh Courier. October
          7, 1939.

7,051.   "Klan Seeks Data Passer." New York Times. November
          24, 1967, p. 1.

7,052.   "Klan Seeks To Parade." New York Times. February
          8, 1948, p. 3.

7,053.   "Klan Threats To Voters." Crisis. Vol. 46,
          August, 1939, pp. 241-242.

7,054.   "Klan Warned By Byrnes." New York Times. January
          20, 1951, p. 19.

7,055.   "Klan Warned On Jail For Gunfire Threats." New
          York Times. September 4, 1950, p. 27.

7,056.   "Klan Wizard Reported Chosen." New York Times.
          February 6, 1952, p. 17.

7,057.   "Klansman On Parade." New York Times. March 1,
          1960, p. 20.

7,058.   "Klansman Seeks Hearing." New York Times. January
          28, 1958, p. 36.

7,059.   "Klansmen Blast 'Beatles-Johnson'." New Bern
          Sun-Journal. August 10, 1966.

7,060.   "Klansmen Burn Records Of Beatles." Winston-
          Salem Journal. August 11, 1966.

7,061.   "Klansmen Claim Being Whipped By 14 Negroes."
          Greensboro Daily News. April 20, 1966.

7,062.   "Klansmen Faces Charges." New York Times.
          September 19, 1950, p. 28.

7,063.   "Klansmen Hit Editor." New York Times. August
          14, 1955, p. 43.

7,064.   "Ku Klux Klan Acts In Outrages." Christian Science
          Monitor. February 10, 1951, p. 14.

7,065.   "Ku Klux Klan Threatens To Ride In South Carolina."
          Norfolk Journal & Guide. July 22, 1939, p. 3.

7,066.   "Marching, Too!" Pittsburgh Courier. August 31,
          1963, p. 4.

7,067.   "Masons Review Plea By Klansmen." Charlotte
          Observer. May 1, 1966, p. 1.

7,068.   "McNair Won't Intervene In Klan-Beating Case."
Charlotte Observer. April 21, 1966, p. 21A.

7,069.   "Move Seen To Stop Outrages By Klan." Christian
Science Monitor. November 21, 1950, p. 6.

7,070.   "Negro Quits Contest." New York Times. February
12, 1952, p. 28.

7,071.   "Negroes Register In Spite Of Klan." New York
Amsterdam News. August 19, 1939, p. 12.

7,072.   "Negroes, Whites Defy KKK In Charleston." Daily
Worker. May 23, 1950.

7,073.   "New Law Strips Masks From Klan." Christian
Science Monitor. April 20, 1951, p. 19.

7,074.   "Nightriders Beat Up Ill Farmer, 2 Sons." New
York Times. November 10, 1950, p. 16.

7,075.   "Permission To Parade Denied Ku Klux Klan." New
York Times. February 11, 1948, p. 29.

7,076.   Post, Louis F. "A 'Carpetbagger' In South
Carolina." Journal of Negro History. Vol. 10,
January, 1925, pp. 10-79.

7,077.   "Push Fight To Vote Despite Pressure Of Court,
Ku Klux." New York Amsterdam News. September 16,
1939, p. 1.

7,078.   "Race Violence Victim." Washington Post. March
15, 1960, p. A17.

7,079.   "Ready To Attack Klan On Vote Bars." New York
Amsterdam News. July 22, 1939, p. 1.

7,080.   "Salute To The South." New York Times. April 14,
1951, p. 14.

7,081.   "S.C. Hoodlum K.K.K. Again On Rampage." Chicago
Defender. April 20, 1940, p. 12.

7,082.   "School Building Set." Raleigh News & Observer.
August 23, 1971, p. 7.

7,083.   Shapiro, Herbert. "The Ku Klux Klan During Reconstruction: The South Carolina Episode." Journal
of Negro History. Vol. 49, January, 1964, pp. 35-
55.

7,084.   Simkins, Francis B. "The Ku Klux Klan In South
Carolina, 1868-1871." Journal of Negro History.
Vol. 12, October, 1927, pp. 606-647.

7,085.   "Six Arrested In Flogging." New York Times.
          January 4, 1957, p. 14.

7,086.   "6 Officers Cited For Klan Arrest." New York Times.
          November 5, 1951, p. 18.

7,087.   "Smash His Doors And Wait." Norfolk Journal &
          Guide. November 25, 1939, pp. 1, 10.

7,088.   "South Carolina Governor Denies Negro Investigator
          Probes Ku Klux Terrorisms." Black Dispatch.
          February 3, 1940, p. 1.

7,089.   "South Carolina Race War." New Republic. Vol. 123,
          September 11, 1950, pp. 8-9.

7,090.   "South Carolina Senate Votes To Unmask Klan."
          New York Times. March 8, 1951, p. 22.

7,091.   "South Carolina Whites Held For Flogging Mother."
          Pittsburgh Courier. May 17, 1924, p. 2.

7,092.   Spears, Charlie. "Nightraiders, Beware! G Men
          May Get You." Norfolk Journal & Guide. November
          4, 1939, p. 9.

7,093.   Stagg, J.C.A. "The Problem Of Klan Violence:
          The South Carolina Up-Country, 1868-1871."
          Journal of American Studies. Vol. 8, December,
          1974, p. 303-318.

7,094.   "Students Jeer Klan In South Carolina." New York
          Times. February 24, 1949, p. 15.

7,095.   Taylor, A.A. "The Negro In South Carolina:
          Opposition To The Reconstruction." Journal of
          Negro History. Vol. 9, July, 1924, pp. 442-468.

7,096.   Thomas, Dana-Ford. "Newsman Unmasks Klan At
          South Carolina Rally." Raleigh News & Observer.
          March 26, 1956.

7,097.   "Trouble At Charlie's Place." Newsweek. Vol. 36,
          September 11, 1950, pp. 36-37.

7,098.   "2 Held In Blasting Of Doctor's House." Washington
          Post. July 1, 1958.

7,099.   "United States Probes Kluxers In South Carolina."
          Pittsburgh Courier. February 10, 1940, p. 4.

7,100.   "U.S. Judge Hits Klan, NAACP As School Foes."
          Washington Evening Star. August 24, 1955, p. A18.

7,101.   "Unmasked Klansmen Bashful On Parade: South Carolina
Governor Bans Wearing Of Hoods In Public - Grand
Dragon Heckled While Speaking In Spartanburg,
S.C." Pittsburgh Courier. July 12, 1941, p. 2.

7,102.   "Which S.C. Klan Is The Klan?" Raleigh News &
Observer. March 2, 1972, p. 8.

7,103.   "Vigilance Vital To Avert Clashes." Christian
Science Monitor. September 27, 1951, p. 3.

7,104.   White, Walter F. "The Shambles Of South Carolina."
Crisis. Vol. 33, December, 1926, pp. 72-75.

7,105.   "Young Speaker." New York Times. July 30, 1956,
p. 9.

40.   SOUTH DAKOTA

7,106.   "KKK In South Dakota." Fiery Cross. May, 1923,
p. 1.

7,107.   "KKK In South Dakota." National Kourier. June,
1925, p. 1.

7,108.   Oulahan, Richard V. "Smith Sentiment Gains
Momentum In South Dakota." New York Times.
August 24, 1927, pp. 1, 12.

7,109.   Rambow, Charles. "The Ku Klux Klan In The 1920's:
A Concentration On The Black Hills." South
Dakota History. Vol. 4, Winter 1973, pp. 63-81.

7,110.   "South Dakota Klan Honors Bryant." New York Times.
August 8, 1925, p. 4.

41.   TENNESSEE

7,111.   Alexander, T.B. "Ku Kluxism In Tennessee, 1865-
1869: A Technique For The Overthrow Of Radical
Reconstruction." Tennessee Historical Quarterly.
Vol. 8, September, 1949, pp. 195-219.

7,112.   "Anderson Klan Rallies Near Clinton." Knoxville
Journal. June 26, 1978.

7,113.   "Appointee Is KKK Stand, Alexander Says." Knoxville
News-Sentinel. July 30, 1980, p. A5.

7,114.   "Arrests Of 3 Suspected KKK Members In Chattanooga,
Tenn. Viewed." San Francisco Chronicle. July 27,
1980, p. 10A.

7,115.   Beard, William E. "January 20 - The Mysterious Ku
Klux Klan." Nashville Banner. January 1921.

7,116.   "Beatings Reported." Christian Science Monitor.
          May 12, 1949, p. 19.

7,117.   "Black Ministers Help Calm Chattanooga, Tenn."
          Jet. Vol. 58, August 14, 1980, p. 6.

7,118.   "Black Ministers Patrol Riot-Stricken Area Of
          Tennessee." Los Angeles Times. July 26, 1980, p.
          17.

7,119.   "Blacks Relive KKK Incident." Pittsburgh Courier.
          May 9, 1981, p. 3.

7,120.   "Bomb Threat Checked At Meredith's Hospital."
          New York Times. June 7, 1966, p. 29.

7,121.   "Burning, Looting Follow Verdict In Klan Case."
          Washington Star. July 23, 1980, p. A1.

7,122.   Canady, Hoyt. "Black Leaders Helped Calm City."
          Knoxville News-Sentinel. July 28, 1980, pp. A1,
          A3.

7,123.   _____. "Joblessness Blamed In Part For
          Chattanooga Racial Violence." Knoxville News-
          Sentinel. July 27, 1980, pp. A1, A2.

7,124.   "Case Of Another Meddling." New York Times.
          May 28, 1925, p. 20.

7,125.   "Chattanooga Blacks Warned." Washington Post.
          August 2, 1980, p. A10.

7.126.   "Chattanooga Curfew Kept After Arrest Of 3
          Klansmen." New York Times. July 28, 1980, p. 12.

7,127.   "Chattanooga Extends Curfew, Firearm Ban."
          Washington Post. July 28, 1980, p. A10.

7,128.   "Chattanooga Is Relatively Quiet After Violence
          Over Klan Verdict." New York Times. July 24,
          1980, p. 12.

7,129.   "Chattanooga Klan Condemns Smith." New York Times.
          June 15, 1923, p. 2.

7,130.   "Chattanooga Mayor Extends Curfew Following KKK
          Arrests." Chicago Tribune. July 28, 1980, p. 8.

7,131.   "Chattanooga Mayor Lifts Curfew." Knoxville News-
          Sentinel. July 28, 1980, p. A1.

7,132.   "Chattanooga Officials Agree To Withdraw Police To
          Ease Rioting." Chicago Tribune. July 26, 1980,
          Sect. N1, p. 3.

7,133.   "Chattanooga Police Arrest Three Armed Klansmen."
          Washington Post. July 27, 1980, p. A2.

7,134.   "Chattanooga, Tenn. Police Seize 3 Klansmen As
          Tension Eases." Chicago Tribune. July 27, 1980,
          Sect. 2, p. 15.

7,135.   "Chattanooga Quiet For Now, But KKK Leader Vows
          Visit." Knoxville News-Sentinel. July 26, 1980,
          p. 1.

7,136.   "Chattanooga Race Riots Ease And Authorities Lift
          Curfew." Chicago Tribune. July 29, 1980, p. 6.

7,137.   "Chattanooga Seeks Ban." Christian Science Monitor.
          January 26, 1949, p. 2.

7,138.   "Chattanooga Still Calm As Police Resume Patrols."
          Knoxville News-Sentinel. July 29, 1980, p. A1.

7,139.   "Chattanooga Violence Flares Anew; 9 Officers
          Hurt." Knoxville News-Sentinel. July 25, 1980,
          pp. 1, 4.

7,140.   Chester, Tom and Carol Parks. "KKK Rally Draws
          Light Crowd." Knoxville Journal. August 30,
          1976, p. 1.

7,141.   "Could Have Cleared Victim Of 1915 Lynch Mob, Man
          Says." Washington Post. March 8, 1982, p. A8.

7,142.   "Curfew Lifted As Chattanooga Calms." Washington
          Post. July 29, 1980, p. A2.

7,143.   "Data On Klan Given By Memphis Paper." New York
          Times. November 1, 1965, p. 23.

7,144.   "Demonstrators March In Chattanooga Again."
          Washington Star. July 24, 1980, p. A5.

7,145.   "8 Policemen Injured In Chattanooga Racial Unrest."
          Chicago Tribune. July 25, 1980, p. 2.

7,146.   "Ex-Klansman And His Son Stand Trial In Winchester,
          Tennessee." Atlanta Daily World. September 4,
          1981, p. 1.

7,147.   "Ex-Klansman's Life Threatened." Washington Star.
          February 17, 1981, p. A5.

7,148.   "Ex-Member Claims Klan Abducted Him." Washington
          Star. February 15, 1981, p. A12.

7,149.   "Ex-Tenn. KKK Member Cites Klan Links To Drugs And
          Porn Dealings." San Francisco Chronicle. February
          17, 1981, p. 3.

7,150.   "FBI To Probe Shootings In Which Klansmen Were Acquitted In Tenn." Los Angeles Times. July 24, 1979, p. 23.

7,151.   "FBI To Probe Shooting Of Four Blacks In Tenn." Washington Post. July 24, 1980, p. A2.

7,152.   "Federal Civil Rights Suit Filed Against KKK In Chattanooga." New York Amsterdam News. November 21, 1981, p. 2.

7,153.   "Fed. Judge In Tenn. Rules On Jury Selections In KKK Bomb Case." New Orleans Times Picayune. November 8, 1981, p. 3.

7,154.   "Fear Of Ku Klux Causes Shooting." New York Amsterdam News. February 28, 1923, p. 1.

7,155.   "Fight F.D.R. Designee On Klan Record." New York Amsterdam News. July 15, 1939, p. 1.

7,156.   Fine, Benjamin. "Nashville Calls Warn 13 Negroes." New York Times. August 29, 1957, p. 25.

7,157.   "500 Attend Clinton Ku Klux Klan Rally." Knoxville News-Sentinel. June 25, 1978, p. 1.

7,158.   "4 Blacks Shot In Tennessee; Three Klansmen Arrested." New York Times. April 20, 1980, p. 26.

7,159.   Franklin, Ben A. "Chattanooga Mayor Lifts Curfew And Finds Hope In Recent Trouble." New York Times. July 29, 1980, p. 10.

7,160.   _____. "Chattanooga Turns To Civilian Patrols." New York Times. July 26, 1980, pp. 1, 6.

7,161.   _____. "Chattanooga's Mayor Meets Black Group On Grievances." New York Times. July 27, 1980, p. 20.

7,162.   "Held For Church Robbery." New York Times. August 21, 1924, p. 3.

7,163.   "Hours Of Curfew Reduced By Chattanooga Mayor." Washington Star. July 27, 1980, p. A8.

7,164.   "Investigative Journalist Tells Of Guns At Ku Klux Klan Meetings." Houston Post. December 15, 1980, p. 3A.

7,165.   Jackson, Alex. "A Ku Klux Incident Of 1869." Nashville Banner. October 20, 1935.

7,166.   "Jailed Klansman Freed After Only 3½ Months." Knoxville News-Sentinel. January 1, 1981, p. 5.

7,167.   "Journalist Says KKK Called To Be Prepared To
          'Kill' Infiltrators." Houston Post. December 13,
          1980, p. 28A.

7,168.   "Jury In Tenn. Returns Verdict Against 3 Klansmen."
          Los Angeles Times. July 23, 1980, p. 14.

7,169.   "KKK Holds Rally, Burns Cross Behind Clinton
          Center." Knoxville News-Sentinel. July 27, 1980,
          p. A1.

7,170.   "KKK Imperial Wizard Pays $100 In Fines To
          Manchester, Tenn." New Orleans Times Picayune.
          April 29, 1981, Sect. 7, p. 14.

7,171.   "KKK Member In Tenn. Released From Prison Under
          New Law." San Francisco Chronicle. January 2,
          1981, p. 2.

7,172.   "KKK Protest." Knoxville Journal. June 9, 1975,
          p. 1.

7,173.   "KKK Stages March In Manchester, Tenn. Despite
          Earlier Arrests." New Orleans Times Picayune.
          May 3, 1981, p. 46.

7,174.   "A Klan Backed Man In Tennessee Race." New York
          Times. October 12, 1966, p. 25.

7,175.   "Klan Blocked From Parade." Washington Post.
          December 8, 1980, p. A7.

7,176.   "Klan Chief Reportedly Bans Confrontation With
          Police." New York Times. June 18, 1981, p. A20.

7,177.   "Klan Blocked In Nashville." New York Times.
          December 8, 1980, p. 18.

7,178.   "Klan Charges Dropped." Washington Post. September
          16, 1980, p. A14.

7,179.   "Klan Chief Asserts Arnall Joined in '42." New
          York Times. September 4, 1946, p. 11.

7,180.   "Klan Foe Carried Memphis By 1,244." New York
          Times. November 10, 1923, p. 15.

7,181.   "Klan Incident Verified." New York Times. August
          14, 1946, p. 16.

7,182.   "Klan Is Defeated At Memphis Polls." New York
          Times. November 9, 1923, p. 3.

7,183.   "KKK Leader Arrested In Tenn. For Parading Without
          A Permit." San Francisco Chronicle. April 27,
          1981, p. 8.

7,184.   "Klan Leader Is Arrested." New York Times. April 27, 1981, p. B12.

7,185..   "Klan Leader Reportedly Informed For F.B.I." New York Times. August 31, 1981, p. A10.

7,186.   "Klan Members Sued For Personal Injuries." Southern Exposure. Vol. 10, January/February, 1982, p. 6.

7,187.   "Klan Ordered To Pay Five Black Women $535,000 Hurt In Shooting Spree." Jet. Vol. 62, March 22, 1982, p. 28.

7,188.   "Klan Leader Released From Jail." New York Times. April 29, 1981, p. 14.

7,189.   "Klan Losing Ground Among Tennesseans." New York Times. November 16, 1923, p. 19.

7,190.   "Klan Rally Draws Estimated 3,000." Knoxville Journal. May 6, 1974, p. 1.

7,191.   "Klan Scores Kasper." New York Times. March 17, 1957, p. 78.

7,192.   "Klan Shooting Testimony." Washington Star. July 20, 1980, p. A8.

7,193.   "Klan Shoots Women." Off Our Backs. Vol. 10, June, 1980, pp. 16-17.

7,194.   "Klan Surfaces In Knoxville Area." Knoxville News-Sentinel. July 24, 1978, p. 1.

7,195.   "Klan Team No Barrier." New York Times. August 16, 1957, p. 10.

7,196.   "Klan To Be At Parade." New York Times. December 7, 1980, p. 29.

7,197.   "Klan To Try Again For Permit." Knoxville News-Sentinel. August 18, 1980, p. A3.

7,198.   "Klan Torches Set Dixie Ablaze (Chattanooga, Tenn.)." Pittsburgh Courier. December 15, 1945, p. 3.

7,199.   "Klan Intervention On Schools Is Cited." New York Times. February 13, 1951, p. 23.

7,200.   "Klansman Convicted, 2 Freed In Wounding Of Black Women." Washington Post. July 23, 1980, p. A2.

7,201.   "Klansmen Held In Shooting." New York Times. April 21, 1980, p. 14.

7,202.   "Klansmen Visit Birthplace Of K.K.K. On Centennial."
          New York Times. December 25, 1965, p. 10.

7,203.   "Kluxer Rears His Ugly Head." New York Amsterdam
          News. October 26, 1946, p. 32.

7,204.   "Knights KKK Head Talks To Quiet Sale Creek Crowd."
          Knoxville Journal. June 25, 1979, p. 1.

7,205.   "Knoxville (Tenn.) KKK In Labor Day Picnic."
          Chicago Defender. September 6, 1947, p. 13.

7,206.   "Ku Klux Klan Fined." Washington Post. February
          28, 1982, p. A4.

7,207.   "KKK Group Charged In Plot To Bomb Tenn. Synagogue."
          San Francisco Chronicle. May 27, 1981, p. 5.

7,208.   "Ku Klux Klan Invade Church, Pray, Leave Gift."
          Christian Science Monitor. January 25, 1949, p. 7.

7,209.   "Ku Klux Klan Members Accused In Bombing Plot In
          Tennessee." Los Angeles Times. May 27, 1981, p. 4.

7,210.   "Ku Klux Klansman Arrested After Shooting of 4
          Blacks In Tenn." Houston Post. April 20, 1980,
          p. 16A.

7,211.   "Ku Klux Organizer Is Circularizing Churches In
          State, Rev. Wingfield Says." Knoxville News-
          Sentinel. September 4, 1946, p. 1.

7,212.   "Ku Klux Violence In Haywood County, Tennessee."
          American Missionary Magazine. Vol. 13, February,
          1869, pp. 40-42.

7,213.   "Lashing Of 7 Negroes Laid To Georgia Klan." New
          York Times. April 4, 1949, p. 18.

7,214.   Loggins, Kirk and Susan Thomas. " 'New' Klan
          Spread Fails To Mask Racism." The Tennessean.
          February 17, 1980, pp. A1, A16-A18.

7,215.   "Man Indicted In Activity." Christian Science
          Monitor. February 18, 1949, p. 6.

7,216.   "Manchester, Tenn. Okays KKK March Following Last
          Weeks Arrests." New Orleans Times Picayune. May
          2, 1981, p. 25.

7,217.   "Manchester, Tenn. Police Chief Arrests KKK
          Followers." New Orleans Times Picayune. April
          28, 1981, p. 5.

7,218.   "Mayor Imposes Curfew In Uneasy Chattanooga."
          Washington Post. July 25, 1980, p. A14.

7,219.   "Mayor Of Chattanooga Hit For Toting Pistol In
          Belt." Washington Post. July 26, 1980, p. A2.

7,220.   "Measure To Keep KKK Off School Grounds Passed."
          Jet. Vol. 59, November 20, 1980, p. 22.

7,221.   Mitchell, Enoch L. "The Role Of George Washington
          Gordon In The Ku Klux Klan." West Tennessee
          Historical Society Papers. 1947, pp. 73-80.

7,222.   "More Arrests Expected In Klan Plot." New York
          Times. May 27, 1981, p. A22.

7,223.   Morton, M.B. "Last Parade Of Ku Klux Klan."
          Nashville Banner. May 3, 1936.

7,224.   " 'Music Row' Gets Show: 15 Klansmen Seeking
          Cash." Washington Post. August 18, 1980, p. C3.

7,225.   "NAACP Aide Denounces Early Release Of KKK Member
          From Tenn. Jail." New Orleans Times Picayune.
          January 2, 1981, p. 8.

7,226.   "NAACP Establishes Chapter Near Ku Klux Klan Site."
          Jet. Vol. 59, January 8, 1981, p. 8.

7,227.   "Nashville Police Bar The KKK From Marching
          Behind Xmas Parade." San Francisco Chronicle.
          December 8, 1980, p. 10.

7,228.   "Negroes Defeat Klan Candidates In Chattanooga."
          The Messenger. Vol. 5, June, 1923, pp. 733-734.

7,229.   "Officials Lift Curfew In Chattanooga, Tenn."
          Washington Star. July 29, 1980, p. A5.

7,230.   Oulahan, Richard V. "Split In Tennessee On Smith's
          Religion." New York Times. September 26, 1928,
          p. 3.

7,231.   Phillips, Paul D. "White Reaction To The Freedmen's
          Bureau In Tennessee." Tennessee Historical
          Quarterly. Vol. 25, Spring, 1966, pp. 50-62.

7,232.   "Police In Nashville Halt Kasper Rally." New York
          Times. August 5, 1957, p. 9.

7,233.   "Police Withdraw, Citizen Patrols Move Into Area
          Hit By Violence." Washington Star. July 26, 1980,
          p. A5.

7,234.   Popham, John N. "Klan Chief Issue 'White Rule'
          Edict." New York Times. July 24, 1947, p. 22.

7,235.   _____. "Klan Extends Its Nocturnal Activities
          Fields Team In Tennessee Softball League." New
          York Times. May 1, 1957, p. 28.

7,236.   _____. "Tennessee Invokes Anti-KKK Statute Of 1869 to Indict Grocer For Gambling Club 'Raid'." New York Times. February 19, 1949, p. 30.

7,237.   Press, Robert M. "The Chattanooga Violence." Christian Science Monitor. July 25, 1980, p. 6.

7,238.   "Prohibiting Solicitations By Klan Ruled Illegal." Knoxville News-Sentinel. August 14, 1980, p. 2.

7,239.   "Pulaski, Tenn. Has Black Mayoral Candidate." New Orleans Times Picayune. October 25, 1973, p. 18C.

7,240.   "Reporter In Tenn. Begins Series On Infiltration Of Ku Klux Klan." Houston Post. December 8, 1980, p. 22A.

7,241.   "Reporter Joins KKK, Exposes Group's Acts." Washington Star. December 8, 1980, p. A4.

7,242.   "Samuel Green." New York Times. August 9, 1949, p. 27.

7,243.   Schappes, Morris U. "Murder In Tennessee, 1868." Jewish Life. February, 1950, pp. 13-15.

7,244.   "7 Policemen Shot As Racial Violence Erupts In Chattanooga." Washington Star. July 25, 1980, pp. A1, A4.

7,245.   "The South: Its Dark Side." American Missionary Magazine. Vol. 13, October, 1869, pp. 230-231.

7,246.   "Sues Klan Head For $25,000." New York Times. January 7, 1925, p. 18.

7,247.   "Tenn. Grand Jury Lets Klan Get Away Again." Pittsburgh Courier. October 11, 1947, p. 21.

7,248.   "Tennessee Klan Organizes: Extensive Drive To Sell White Supremacy." Pittsburgh Courier. March 23, 1946, pp. 1, 4.

7,249.   "Tenn. Judge Hits Klan." California Eagle. November 30, 1923, pp. 1, 2.

7,250.   "Tenn. Journalist Describes Ku Klux Klan Initiation Ceremony." Houston Post. December 11, 1980, p. 10B.

7,251.   "Tenn. Klansmen Charged In Gunning Down Black Women." Jet. Vol. 58, May 8, 1980, p. 6.

7,252.   "Tennessee Reporter's Double Life As Klansman Viewed." San Francisco Chronicle. December 8, 1980, p. 10.

7,253.   "Tenn. Reporter Tells Of Double Life In The Ku
Klux Klan." Los Angeles Times. December 8, 1980,
p. 5.

7,254.   "Tennessee Reporter Tells Of Joining Klan Groups."
New York Times. December 14, 1980, p. 71.

7,255.   "Tennessee Reporter Who Infiltrated The KKK."
San Francisco Chronicle. December 9, 1980, p. 1.

7,256.   "Threat To Negro Voters." New York Times. November
2, 1948, p. 31.

7,257.   "3 Are Arrested In Nashville In Synagogue Bombing
Plot." Washington Post. May 27, 1981, p. A2

7,258.   "3 Held In Nashville Plot To Bomb A Synagogue."
New York Times. May 26, 1981, p. A14.

7,259.   "3 Ku Klux Klansmen Held In Connection With
Shooting In Tenn." San Francisco Chronicle.
April 21, 1980, p. 2.

7,260.   "20 Of KKK Visit Church, 2 Women Fall In Faint."
New York Times. January 25, 1949, p. 11.

7,261.   "2 Former Klansmen Denied New Trial In Chattanooga."
Atlanta Daily World. July 12, 1981, p. 1.

7,262.   "2 Klansmen Acquitted, 3d Convicted In Tennessee."
New York Times. July 23, 1980, p. 10.

7,263.   "2 Klansmen And 1 Neo-Nazi Found Guilty In
Nashville Case." Bilalian News. December 11,
1981, p. 4.

7,264.   "2 Klansmen Freed, 1 Convicted On Reduced Charge."
Knoxville Journal. July 23, 1980, p. 3.   .

7,265.   "Urge Knoxville Outlaw Kluxers." Chicago Defender.
October 19, 1946, p. 9.

7,266.   "U.S. Ct. Reduces Bail For Klansman In Plot To
Bomb Tenn. Temple." Los Angeles Times. June 11,
1981, p. 16.

7,267.   "Violence Erupts After Jury Acquits Klansmen In
Chattanooga Shooting." Jet. Vol. 58, August 7,
1980, p. 8.

7,268.   Waldron, Martin. "A Klan Organizer Made Visit To
Ray." New York Times. October 3, 1968, p. 23.

7,269.   Walker, Hugh. "Ku Klux Klan, Born In Pulaski,
Nursed In Violence." The Tennessean. February
17, 1980, p. 16A, 17A.

7,270.   "Women Sue Klansmen." Washington Post. September 13, 1980, p. A9.

42. TEXAS

7,271.   "Accuses Klan Of Crimes." New York Times. July 26, 1921, p. 16.

7,272.   Alexander, Charles C. "Secrecy Bids For Power: The Ku Klux Klan In Texas Politics In The 1920's." Mid-America. Vol. 46, January, 1964, pp. 3-28.

7,273.   Allen, Lee N. "The Democratic Presidential Primary Election Of 1924 In Texas." Southwestern Historical Quarterly. Vol. 61, April, 1958, pp. 474-493.

7,274.   "Another Is Tarred By Mysterious Band." New York Times. July 24, 1921, p. 15.

7,275.   "Anti-Klan Candidate Shot In Texas Contest For Sheriff." New York Times. August 18, 1924, p. 15.

7,276.   "Anti-Klan Mayor Sails." New York Times. July 4, 1924, p. 14.

7,277.   "Anti Ku Klux Warn Texas Judge To Leave." Chicago Defender. August 6, 1921, p. 1.

7,278.   "Arrest In Texas Flogging." New York Times. January 20, 1923, p. 6.

7,279.   "Ask Ku Klux To Disband." New York Times. April 7, 1922, p. 10.

7,280.   "Asks Klan To Show Books." New York Times. July 1, 1923, p. 2.

7,281.   "Asks Mayfield Seat, Charges Klan Fraud." New York Times. February 23, 1923, pp. 1, 4.

7,282.   "Assails Klan, Riot Starts." New York Times. August 23, 1922, p. 32.

7,283.   "Banton Found Klan Negligible In Texas." New York Times. December 4, 1922, p. 24.

7,284.   "Beating Investigated." New York Times. March 9, 1960, p. 19.

7,285.   Bentley, Max. "A Texan Challenges The Klan." Collier's.Vol. 72, November 3, 1923, pp. 12, 22.

7,286.   "Black Candidate For Tex. Justice Of Peace Backed By KKK." New Orleans Times Picayune. April 28, 1974, p. 17.

7,287.   Bliss, David. "Antiwar Movement Attacks Links Of Houston Police To Ku Klux Klan." _Militant_. Vol. 34, November 27, 1970, p. 3.

7,288.   "Both Sides Predict Victory In Texas." _New York Times_. August 22, 1924, p. 3.

7,289.   "Boys Reported Learning To Shoot And Kill At A Klan Camp In Texas." _New York Times_. November 24, 1980, p. A21.

7,290.   "Brand Negro With Acid After Flogging Him." _New York Times_. April 3, 1921, p. 13.

7,291.   "Brothers Kidnapped And Beaten." _New York Times_. August 19, 1923, p. 1.

7,292.   "Burleson Wants Klan Read Out Of Party." _New York Times_. August 27, 1924, p. 3.

7,293.   Byrne, Kevin and Oliver Houghton. "Texas Klan Rally; Cow Pasture Politics." _Space City_. Vol. 3, August 31, 1971, p. 15.

7,294.   "Cheer 'Ma' Ferguson At Houston Meeting." _New York Times_. August 21, 1924, p. 3.

7,295.   "Choice Of Ku Klux Has Big Texas Lead." _New York Times_. August 27, 1922, p. 21.

7,296.   "City Officials Arrested." _New York Times_. April 26, 1923, p. 40.

7,297.   "Convict Claims Klan Runs Survival Camps." _Washington Star_. December 8, 1980, p. A4.

7,298.   "Count On El Paso For Mrs. Ferguson." _New York Times_. August 23, 1924, p. 3.

7,299.   Crowell, Evelyn Miller. "My Father And The Klan." _New Republic_. Vol. 114, July 1, 1946, pp. 930-931.

7,300.   "Davidson To Run In Texas In 1926." _New York Times_. September 4, 1924, p. 4.

7,301.   "Death In Texas Protested." _New York Times_. November 25, 1979, p. 44.

7,302.   "Defends Texas Congressmen." _New York Times_. December 31, 1922, p. 18.

7,303.   "Destroy The Klan, Culbersor Urges." _New York Times_. April 2, 1922, p. 14.

7,304.   Devine, Edward T. "The Klan In Texas." Survey.
           Vol. 48, April 1, 1922, pp. 10-11; May 13, 1922,
           pp. 251-253.

7,305.   _____. "More About The Klan." Survey. Vol.
           48, April 8, 1922, pp. 42-43; May 13, 1922, pp.
           251-253.

7,306.   "Dies After Ku Klux Parade." New York Times.
           October 6, 1921, p. 19.

7,307.   "Dies Probes Activity Of Negroes In Texas As
           Band, KKK Run State." Chicago Defender. August
           3, 1940, p. 1.

7,308.   "El Paso Bars Public Masked Gatherings." New
           York Times. September 17, 1921, p. 4.

7,309.   "Ex-Wizard Indicted Under Mann Law. New York
           Times. March 2, 1923, p. 6.

7,310.   "Exodus Follows Ku Klux Parade." New York
           Amsterdam News. November 29, 1922, p. 2.

7,311.   Fanning, Jerry and Andy Bustin. "KKK Grand Dragon
           Indicted In Houston." Militant. Vol. 35, September
           17, 1971, p. 24.

7,312.   "Farmer Lashed With Wet Rope." New York Times.
           August 19, 1923, p. 1.

7,313.   "Fed. Ct. Orders KKK And Texas Fishermen To Leave
           Viet Refugees Alone." New Orleans Times Picayune.
           May 15, 1981, Sect. 2, p. 10.

7,314.   "Ferguson As Chief Speaks For Wife, Calling Foes
           Liars." New York Times. November 28, 1925, pp.
           1, 2.

7,315.   "Ferguson Says Moody Seeks The Klan Vote." New
           York Times. March 28, 1926, p. 18.

7,316.   "Fishing Town In Texas Tells The Klan To Stay
           Away." New York Times. November 22, 1979, p.
           A17.

7,317.   "Flogs Two Texas Negroes." New York Times. October
           22, 1921, p. 14.

7,318.   "Forces Negroes To Work." New York Times.
           September 6, 1921, p. 17.

7,319.   "Gov. Neff Deplores Klan Parade Fight." New York
           Times. October 4, 1921, p. 5.

7,320.   "Grand Jury To Act On Ku Klux Clash." New York
           Times. October 3, 1921, p. 1.

7,321.   "Guerrilla Training By Texas Ku Klux Klansmen
           Discussed." San Francisco Chronicle. August 10,
           1980, p. 5B.

7,322.   "Harding Starts Belated Battle To Crush Klux."
           Chicago Defender. October 21, 1922, pp. 3-4.

7,323.   "Hearing On KKK Harassment Suit Against Viet
           Fishermen Begins." San Francisco Chronicle.
           May 13, 1981, p. 6.

7,324.   "Houston Chronicle Reports KKK Member Teaching
           Scouts." San Francisco Chronicle. November 24,
           1980, p. 5.

7,325.   "Houston Dock Owner Testifies In Alleged KKK
           Refugee Harassment." New Orleans Times Picayune.
           May 12, 1981, p. 6.

7,326.   "Houston Explorer Post Denied Boy Scout Charter Over
           Gun Training." Houston Post. November 27, 1980, p.
           21B.

7,327.   "Houston Socialist Candidate Debates Klan Leader."
           Militant. Vol. 35, June 18, 1971, pp. 12-14.

7,328.   "In Texas, Too." Chicago Defender. August 6,
           1921, p. 16.

7,329.   "Indict 26 For Texas Whippings." New York Times.
           May 6, 1923, Sect. 2, p. 1.

7,330.   "Intimidation Of Oil Men Charged." New York Times.
           February 23, 1923, p. 4.

7,331.   "The Invisible Empire." Dallas Morning News.
           September 10, 1921, p. 1.

7,332.   "Is O'Daniel A Klansman?" Pittsburgh Courier.
           February 11, 1939, p. 2.

7,333.   "Jails Ku Klux Witness." New York Times. April
           9, 1922, pp. 2.

7,334.   "Jimmie Johnson Elected Grand Dragon On KKK In
           Texas." Washington Post. July 10, 1974, p. 3A.

7,335.   "Justice Backed To Wall By Texas Ku Klux Klan."
           Chicago Defender. March 25, 1922, p. 1.

7,336.   "K. Of C. Challenges Klan." New York Times.
           January 22, 1923, p. 14.

7,337.   "K.K.K." New York Times. December 21, 1921, p. 15.

7,338.   "KKK Aide Reportedly Taught Scouts And C.A.P.
           Cadets Warfare In Tex." Chicago Tribune. November
           24, 1980, p. 2.

7,339.   "KKK Allows Texas TV Crew And Students To Film
           Paramilitary Session." New Orleans Times Picayune.
           February 5, 1981, Sect. 5, p. 10.

7,340.   "KKK Claims Credit For 30 Alien Arrests Along
           Border." Los Angeles Times. October 26, 1977,
           p. 36.

7,341.   "KKK Pickets Tex. Funeral Home Over Funeral
           Refusal." San Francisco Chronicle. January 1,
           1980, p. 14.

7,342.   "KKK To End Border Patrols In Favor Of Watching
           Fields For Aliens." Los Angeles Times. October
           29, 1977, p. 23.

7,343.   "Klan Activism Stirs Houston." Washington Post.
           June 20, 1971, p. 3B.

7,344.   "Klan Advisor, Trains Scouts And Cadets To Kill
           Blacks." Cincinnati (Ohio) Herald. November
           29, 1980, p. 3.

7,345.   "Klan Backs Norris, Says Texas Dragon." New York
           Times. July 24, 1926, p. 9.

7,346.   "Klan Calls 150,000 To Meet In Dallas." New York
           Times. October 15, 1923, p. 1.

7,347.   "Klan Candidate Is Beaten." New York Times.
           January 1, 1923, p. 7.

7,348.   "Klan Criticizes Gov. Smith." New York Times.
           June 21, 1926, p. 14.

7,349.   "Klan Entrant Leads In Texas Primary." New York
           Times. July 27, 1924, p. 2.

7,350.   "Klan Flowers Judge's Grave." Chicago Defender.
           May 13, 1922, pp. 20-21.

7,351.   "Klan Hall Is Burned; Call Fire Incendiary."
           New York Times. November 7, 1924, p. 3.

7,352.   "Klan Head, Free, Vows New Drive On Negroes."
           New York Times. November 18, 1969, p. 29.

7,353.   "Klan Head's Bond Raised." New York Times.
           March 6, 1923, p. 24.

7,354.   "The Klan In Texas." New York Times. August 19, 1924, p. 14.

7,355.   "Klan In Texas State House." New York Times. April 28, 1923, p. 21.

7,356.   "Klan In Texas Threatens Newspaper And Civic Leader; Both Defy Hooded Order." Norfolk Journal & Guide. February 15, 1939, p. 4.

7,357.   "Klan Is Denounced In Texas." New York Times. September 3, 1924, p. 2.

7,358.   "Klan Leader To Leave Prison." New York Times. November 14, 1969, p. 20.

7,359.   "Klan Protests Refugees." Washington Post. October 18, 1980, p. A10.

7,360.   "Klan Rally At Johnson City." New York Times. April 15, 1966, p. 78.

7,361.   "Klan Sets Rally In Texas." New York Times. February 23, 1966, p. 26.

7,362.   "Klan Shifts LBJ Ranch Rally." New York Times. April 22, 1966, p. 38.

7,363.   "Klan-Tied Scouts Lose Charter." Florida Star. December 6-12, 1980, p. 1.

7,364.   "Klan Training Site Shut." Washington Star. December 6, 1980, p. A4.

7,365.   "Klan Wanes In Texas." New York Times. July 1, 1923, p. 20.

7,366.   "Klanism Ended In Texas." New York Times. January 20, 1925, p. 20.

7,367.   "Klan's Removal To Texas Hurts Garner." New York Amsterdam News. May 13, 1939, p. 14.

7,368.   "Klansman Announces He'll Run For Senate." Chicago Defender. March 11, 1922, p. 3.

7,369.   "Klansman Denied Parole." New York Times. August 8, 1969, p. 13.

7,370.   "Klansman Instructs Teenagers In Murder." New York Daily World. November 25, 1980, p. 2.

7,371.   "Klansman Whitens Name." New York Times. January 16, 1975, p. 32.

7,372.   "Klansmen Battle In A Texas Town."   Chicago
          Defender.   October 8, 1921, p. 1.

7,373.   "Klansmen Bilked By Promise Of Lead Poisoning."
          Washington Afro-American.   February 18, 1939,
          p. 2.

7,374.   "Klansmen Dip Texan In Hot Tar."   Chicago Defender.
          February 18, 1922, p. 3.

7,375.   "Klansmen Must Surrender Jobs."   The Messenger.
          Vol. 4, April, 1922, pp. 387-388.

7,376.   "Klansmen Parade In Dallas."   New York Times.
          November 4, 1975, p. 45.

7,377.   "Klansmen Use Whips On Texans."   Chicago Defender.
          December 10, 1921, pp. 1, 2.

7,378.   "Klansmen vs. Vietnamese."   Washington Post.
          February 15, 1981, p. All.

7,379.   "Klansmen's Dragon Resigns His Post."   New Bern
          Sun-Journal.   March 14, 1966, p. 1.

7,380.   "Ku Klux Bid For Senator."   New York Times.
          August 20, 1922, Sect. 7, p. 3.

7,381.   "Ku Klux Burn Initials In Bellboy's Forehead."
          Chicago Defender.   April 9, 1921, p. 3.

7,382.   "Ku Klux Initiates 700 In Texas."   New York Times.
          February 4, 1922, p. 8.

7,383.   "Ku Klux Klan."   Dallas Morning News.   September
          6, 1921, September 8, 1921, September 9, 1921;
          September 15, 1921; April 23, 1922.

7,384.   "Ku Klux Klan Border Patrol."   Los Angeles Times.
          October 23, 1977, Sect. 7, p. 4.

7,385.   "Ku Klux Klan's Border Patrol."   New Orleans Times
          Picayune.   October 27, 1977, p. 20.

7,386.   "Ku Klux Klan Border Patrol - Interlandi Cartoon."
          Los Angeles Times.   October 25, 1977, Sect. 2, p. 7.

7,387.   "Ku Klux Klan Candidate Leading In Texas; Most
          Big Cities And Counties Carried By Them."   New York
          Times.   July 24, 1922, p. 1.

7,388.   "Ku Klux Klan Group Patrols Border Looking For
          Aliens."   New Orleans Times Picayune.   October
          26, 1977, p. 12.

7,389.   "Ku Klux Klan Members Hold Rallies In Texas And
           Arkansas." New Orleans Times Picayune. June 18,
           1979, p. 2.

7,390.   "Ku Klux Klan Members Plan Border Patrol To Curb
           Alien Influx." Los Angeles Times. October 18,
           1977, Sect. 2, p. 2.

7,391.   "Ku Klux Klan Patrols To Help Stem Tide Of Illegal
           Aliens." New Orleans Times Picayune. October 20,
           1977, p. 20.

7,392.   "Ku Klux Klan's Welcome To Aliens - Interlandi
           Cartoon." Los Angeles Times. November 3, 1977,
           Sect. 2, p. 5.

7,393.   "Ku Klux Sheriff Ousted." New York Times. June
           10, 1922, p. 26.

7,394.   "Ku Klux Terror Runs Riot; Scores Flogged."
           Chicago Defender. July 30, 1921, pp. 1, 2.

7,395.   "The Ku Klux Victory In Texas." Literary Digest.
           Vol. 74, August 5, 1922, pp. 14-15.

7,396.   "Ku Klux Violence To Teachers In The South."
           American Missionary Magazine. Vol. 18, September,
           1874, pp. 208-209.

7,397.   "Ku Kluxism Shows Its Quality." New York Times.
           October 4, 1921, p. 14.

7,398.   "Liberals Ask Texas U. To Let Klansman Speak."
           New York Times. January 19, 1966, p. 7.

7,399.   "Links Mayfield With Klan." New York Times.
           January 23, 1924, p. 21.

7,400.   " 'Ma' Ferguson And 'Dan' Moody To Battle." New
           York Times. April 4, 1926, Sect. 9, p. 3.

7,401.   "Ma Ferguson And The K.K.K." New Statesman.
           Vol. 23, October 4, 1924, pp. 728-729.

7,402.   " 'Ma' Ferguson, From Texas Home, Tells News Of
           Victory." New York Times. August 25, 1924, p. 2.

7,403.   " 'Ma' Ferguson Routs Klan In Texas; Majority Of
           100,000 Now Indicted." New York Times. August
           24, 1924, p. 1.

7,404.   " 'Ma' Ferguson Sees Texas Free Of Klan; Her Lead
           Now 77,801." New York Times. August 25, 1924,
           pp. 1, 2.

7.405.   " 'Ma' Ferguson Signs Act Prohibiting Masks In
          Texas." New York Times. March 10, 1925, p. 1.

7.406.   " 'Ma' Ferguson Tells Of Plans To Oust Klan."
          New York Times. August 31, 1924, Sect. 8, p. 3.

7.407.   " 'Ma' Ferguson's Rise Blocks Texas Klan." New
          York Times. January 19, 1925, p. 5.

7.408.   "Masked Floggers Kill One, Lacerate Three."
          New York Times. March 22, 1922, p. 2.

7.409.   "Masked Men Flog Woman And Caller." New York
          Times. January 14, 1923, p. 3.

7,410.   "Masked Men Tar And Feather Texan." New York
          Times. September 28, 1921, p. 4.

7,411.   "Mayfield Case In Doubt." New York Times.
          February 24, 1923, p. 12.

7,412.   "Mayfield Denies Big Klan Fund." New York Times.
          January 10, 1923, p. 2.

7,413.   "Mayfied Denounces Charges As Infamous." New
          York Times. March 6, 1923, p. 24.

7,414.   "Mayfield Says He Is Not Worried." New York Times.
          February 23, 1923, p. 4.

7,415.   "Mayor Named Wrong Man." New York Times. December
          21, 1922, p. 6.

7.416.   "Moody Denies He Is A Klansman." New York Times.
          May 5, 1926, p. 20.

7,417.   "Moody Scores In Texas Vote." New York Times.
          November 6, 1924, p. 3.

7,418.   "More Jailings Predicted." New York Times.
          October 30, 1965, p. 12.

7,419.   "More Texas Klansmen Indicted." Militant. Vol.
          35, June 25, 1971, p. 5.

7,420.   "Mrs. Ferguson Attacks Klan." New York Times.
          August 25, 1924, p. 2.

7,421.   "Mrs. Ferguson Second To Klan's Man In Texas;
          May Run Off In Final Primary For Governor."
          New York Times. July 28, 1924, p. 1.

7,422.   "Negro Is Beaten By White Youths." New York Times.
          March 8, 1960, p. 23.

7,423.   "Negro Says 3 Whites Beat, Cut KKK On Him."
          Washington Post. March 9, 1960, p. A2.

7,424.   "Nine Texans Seek Seat In The Senate." New York
          Times. July 16, 1922, Sect. 2, p. 3.

7,425.   "No Quarter Shown In Texas Klan Fight." New York
          Times. August 20, 1924, p. 17.

7,426.   "19 Alleged Klansmen Arrested In A Murder." New
          York Times. December 17, 1921, p. 10.

7,427.   "No Border Clashes Reported." New York Times.
          October 30, 1977, p. 16.

7,428.   "100,000 Suit Against Klan Filed In Texas."
          Pittsburgh Courier. September 1, 1923, p. 1.

7,429.   "Oust Klux Cop; 10,000 Protest." Chicago Defender.
          June 24, 1922, p. 13.

7,430.   "Oust The Klan From Congress." The Messenger.
          Vol. 6, February, 1924, pp. 38-39.

7,431.   "Ousting Texas Klansmen." New York Times. March
          29, 1923, p. 11.

7,432.   "Owner Closes Texas Camp Used By KKK For Para-
          military Training." Houston Post. December 6,
          1980, p. 9A.

7,433.   "Paramilitary Actions Irk Neighbors Of Texas
          Camp." New York Times. November 30, 1980, p. 67.

7,434.   "Paramilitary Camp Is Closed By Owner." New York
          Times. December 6, 1980, p. 8.

7,435.   "Pardons Texas Klansman." New York Times. October
          19, 1926, p. 31.

7,436.   "Plan Fusion To Beat Klan." New York Times.
          September 13, 1922, p. 4.

7,437.   "Police Sought." New York Times. September 19,
          1956, p. 20.

7,438.   "Posse Fights Klan In Lorena, Texas, Streets;
          Sheriff Wounded By Paraders, 8 Others Hurt." New
          York Times. October 2, 1921, p. 1.

7,439.   "Press Coverage Of Ku Klux Klan 'Border Patrol'
          Viewed." Los Angeles Times. October 27, 1977,
          p. 3.

7,440.   "Race Problem In Texas." The Freeman. Vol. 5,
           August 30, 1922, pp. 578-579.

7,441.   "Race Problem In Texas." The Freeman. Vol. 5,
           September 20, 1922, pp. 42-43.

7,442.   "Rebuke To Ku Klux Seen In Texas Vote." New
           York Times. August 29, 1922, p. 4.

7,443.   "Reports Of Revival Checked." Christian Science
           Monitor. August 15, 1955, p. 11.

7,444.   "Result Hangs On Turnout Of Voters." New York
           Times. August 23, 1924, p. 3.

7,445.   Ring, Harry. "Houston Election Campaign Puts
           Socialists On The Map." Militant. Vol. 35,
           December 24, 1971, pp. 12-13.

7,446.   "Riot At Texas Klan Parade." New York Times.
           July 25, 1927, p. 19.

7,447.   "Runs As Foe Of Ku Klux." New York Times. March
           23, 1922, p. 10.

7,448.   "San Diego Mayor Wilson Objects To Ku Klux Klan
           Border Tour." Los Angeles Times. October 19,
           1977, p. 2.

7,449.   "Says Klan Spent $25,000 In Texas." New York Times.
           May 21, 1924, p. 2.

7,450.   "Says Klan Suppresses Him." New York Times.
           July 6, 1924, p. 5.

7,451.   "Says 'Ma' Ferguson Will Be Nominated." New York
           Times. August 21, 1924, p. 3.

7,452.   "Scott Nelson." New York Times. April 27, 1974,
           p. 15.

7,453.   "Scout Post Is Denied Charter." New York Times.
           November 27, 1980, p. A22.

7.454.   "Scouts Lose Charter In Klan Camp Furor."
           Washington Star. November 27, 1980, p. A10.

7,455.   "Seadrift, Texas, Residents Ask Ku Klux Klan To
           Stay Out Of City." Houston Post. November 22,
           1979, p. 11B.

7,456.   "Secret Ku Klux Klan Training Camp In Texas
           Disclosed." Los Angeles Times. September 10,
           1980, Sect. IA, p. 10.

7,457.   "See Danger Ahead If Ku Klux Thrive." Chicago
          Defender. August 13, 1921, p. 2.

7,458.   "See Woman Winning Against Texas Klan For State
          Governor." New York Times. August 17, 1924,
          pp. 1, 21.

7,459.   "750 Attend Klan Rally For Fishermen In Texas."
          New York Times. February 15, 1981, p. 36.

7,460.   "75,000 Klansmen Gather In Dallas To Impress
          Nation." New York Times. October 25, 1923, pp.
          1, 3,

7,461.   Singer, Stu. "Armed Klansmen Threaten Socialists."
          Militant. Vol. 39, March 7, 1975, p. 28.

7,462.   "6 Judges, 2 Cities Warn Klan In Texas." New
          York Times. October 5, 1921, p. 18.

7,463.   "6 More Accused In Texas." New York Times.
          December 23, 1921, p. 9.

7,464.   "Six Unmasked Men Whip And Tar Texan." New York
          Times. April 3, 1923, p. 7.

7,465.   Sonnichsen, C. L. And M. G. McKinney. "El Paso --
          From War To Depression." Southwestern Historical
          Quarterly. Vol. 74, January, 1971, pp. 357-371.

7,466.   Stevens, William K. "Klan Inflames Gulf Fishing
          Fight Between Whites And Vietnamese." New York
          Times. April 25, 1981, p. 1.

7,467.   "Stop Harassing Viets, Judge Tells The KKK."
          Washington Post. May 15, 1981, p. A20.

7,468.   Sullivan, Mark. "Midsummer Politics And Primaries."
          World's Work. Vol. 44, July, 1922, pp. 296-302.

7,469.   "Tar And Feather Grocer." New York Times.
          February 23, 1922, p. 10.

7,470.   "Tarring At Terrell Denied By Editor." New York
          Times. April 11, 1928, p. 14.

7,471.   "Tears Off Ku Klux Mask, Is Badly Beaten."
          Chicago Defender. July 15, 1922, p. 3.

7,472.   "Tells Of Klan Outrages." New York Times. May
          14, 1924, p. 2.

7,473.   "Testing The Klan's Strength." Chicago Defender.
          August 26, 1922, p. 12.

7,474.   "Texan Plank Names Klan." New York Times. September 4, 1924, p. 5.

7,475.   "Texas Policeman Testifies At Trial On Alleged Refugee Harassment." New Orleans Times Picayune. May 14, 1981, p. 2.

7,476.   "Texans To Put Klan Before The Senate As National Issue." New York Times. October 27, 1923, pp. 1, 5.

7,477.   "Texas Bars Ku Klux Query, 69-54." New York Times. July 28, 1921, p. 13.

7,478.   "Texas Civil Liberties Union Hits Corrections Suit Against Groups." Houston Post. January 22, 1980, p. 2A.

7,479.   "Texans Denounce Klan." New York Times. August 14, 1924, p. 2.

7,480.   "Texas Governor Roused By Disorders." New York Times. August 19, 1923, p. 1.

7,481.   "Texas KKK Claims Mexican Border Watch For Illegal Aliens Success." Houston Post. October 31, 1977, p. 6A.

7,482.   "Texas Klan Chiefs Deny Burnings." New York Times. April 11, 1928, p. 14.

7,483.   "Texas Klan Concedes Nomination Of Smith." New York Times. May 29, 1928, p. 4.

7,484.   "Texas Klan Elects New Head." New York Times. March 14, 1966, p. 37.

7,485.   "Texas Klan Leaders Becoming Anxious." New York Times. August 19, 1924, p. 5.

7.486.   "Texas Klans Secede." New York Times. June 24, 1923, p. 17.

7.487.   "Texas Klansmen Ban Underwood." New York Times. October 26, 1923, p. 19.

7.488.   "Texas Ranger Captain." New York Times. August 17, 1923, p. 2.

7,489.   "Texas Republicans Denounce Ku Klux." New York Times. August 10, 1922, p. 6.

7,490.   "Texas Senate Commends Parker." New York Times. January 17, 1923, p. 8.

7,491.   "Texas Votes Today In Fight On Klan." New York Times. August 23, 1924, pp. 1, 3.

7,492.   "Texas War On Klan Enters Final Phase." New York
           Times. August 18, 1924, p. 15.

7,493.   "Third KKK Camp To Open In State." Houston Informer.
           December 6, 1980, p. 1.

7,494.   Thompson, Sid. "Alleged Klansman Is Governor In
           Texas." New York Amsterdam News. September 7,
           1946, p. 5.

7,495.   "3 Anti-KKK Groups In Texas Seek Probe Of Explorer
           Camp." Houston Post. November 26, 1980, p. 10A.

7,496.   "Threatened By Klan, Vietnamese In Texas Ask FBI
           Protection." Washington Star. April 22, 1981,
           p. A10.

7,497.   "To Ask Texas Klan Inquiry." New York Times.
           July 10, 1921, p. 1.

7,498.   "To Guard Texas Initiation." New York Times.
           September 22, 1923, p. 5.

7,499.   "Trailing Floggers In Texas." New York Times.
           August 21, 1923, p. 5.

7,500.   "True Mrs. Ferguson Revealed In Home." New York
           Times. August 26, 1924, p. 2.

7,501.   "Unpunished Murder Starts Texas Fight On Klan's
           Outrages." New York Times. October 28, 1923,
           pp. 1, 3.

7,502.   "U.S. Dst. Judge Denies Restraining Order On KKK
           Border Watch." Los Angeles Times. October 28, 1977,
           p. 3.

7,503.   "U.S. Judge Enjoins Texas KKK From Harassing Viet
           Fishermen." Bilalian News. July 31, 1981, p. 7.

7,504.   "U.S. District Ct. Orders KKK To Stay Away From
           Fishing Refugees." San Francisco Chronicle.
           May 15, 1981, p. 28.

7,505.   "Videotapes Of Klan Leader Shown At Shrimper
           Hearing." New York Times. May 13, 1981, p. A18.

7.506.   "Viet Fishermen Sue Klan." Washington Post.
           April 17, 1981, p. All.

7.507.   "Vigilante Groups Warned Against Border Actions."
           New York Times. October 29, 1977, p. 8.

7;508.   Waldron, Martin. "Liberals Accuse Houston's Police."
           New York Times. November 3, 1970, p. 56.

7,509.   Waldron, Martin. "2 Bombings Laid To 4 In Houston."
          New York Times. June 12, 1971, p. 35.

7,510.   "Wanted To Mutilate Texas Editor." New York
          Amsterdam News. April 8, 1925, p. 2.

7,511.   "Wants Floggers Indicted." New York Times.
          January 16, 1923, p. 13.

7,512.   "Wants Klan Paper To Live." New York Times.
          December 23, 1922, p. 2.

7,513.   "Welcome Ku Klux." Chicago Defender. September
          24, 1921, p. 3.

7,514.   "Winrod States His Views." New York Times.
          March 2, 1937, p. 10.

7,515.   "Wizard Is Defiant To Foes Of Ku Klux." New York
          Times. December 8, 1922, p. 19.

7,516.   "Woman Governor Or Klan: A Texas Choice." New
          York Times. August 3, 1924, Sect. 8, p. 3.

43. UTAH

7,517.   King, Wayne. "Prosecution And Defense Rest In Utah
          Trial Involving Deaths Of 2 Blacks. New York
          Times. March 3, 1981, p. A14.

7,518.   Papikolas, Helen Zeese. "The Greeks Of Carbon
          Country (KKK in Utah)." Utah Historical Quarterly.
          Vol. 22, No. 2, April 1954, p. 163.

7,519.   _____. "Tragedy And Hate." Utah Historical
          Quarterly. Vol. 38, No. 2, Spring, 1970, pp. 176-
          181.

7,520.   "Santa Is 'Unmasked' On Protest Of Klan." New
          York Times. December 24, 1925, p. 5.

7,521.   "What Ku Klux Klan Stands For." News Advocate.
          July 16, 1922,.

7,522.   "What Ku Klux Klan Stands For." News Advocate.
          November 16, 1922.

7,523.   "What Ku Klux Klan Stands For." News Advocate.
          August 17(?), 1923.

44. VERMONT

7,524.   "Involve A Klansman In Cathedral Robbery." New
          York Times. August 17, 1924, Sect. 2, p. 1.

7,525.   "Klansman Admits Theft." New York Times. November 7, 1924, p. 14.

7,526.   "Klansman Admits Theft." The Messenger. Vol. 6, December, 1924, p. 373.

7,527.   "Vermont Klansmen Sent To Prison." New York Times. November 19, 1924, p. 18.

45.   VIRGINIA

7,528.   "Anti-KKK Demonstrators Disrupt KKK Rally In Va. Beach." Bilalian News. October 26, 1979, p. 3.

7,529.   "Ask Bar Of Ku Klux In Virginia." New York Times. April 15, 1921, p. 9.

7,530.   Barker, Karlyn. "A Resurgence Of The Klan: Symbol Of Racism Exploits New Tensions." Washington Post. June 2, 1980, pp. A1, A2.

7,531.   Boodman, Sandra G. "Swastika Mars Federal Official's Lawn." Washington Post. August 5, 1980, p. A12.

7,532.   "Boycott Of Stores By 4 Rights Groups Is Upheld By Court." New York Times. June 6, 1967, p. 37.

7,533.   "Cross Burned Behind House Of Va. Chief." Greensboro Daily News. December 12, 1966, p. A7.

7,534.   "Cross-Burners To Be Sought." New York Times. December 15, 1966, p. 36.

7,535   "Cross Burns Near Mansion." New York Times. December 11, 1966, p.

7,536.   Dewar, Helen. "Klan's Virginia Drive Considered Minor Irritant." Washington Post. September 21, 1965.

7,537.   Early, Tracy. "Klan Kludd: To Be Or Not To Be." Christian Century. Vol. 84, February 22, 1967, pp. 236-237.

7,538.   "Election Plot Laid To Virginia Klan." New York Times. November 2, 1925, p. 6.

7.539.   "Ends Suit To Upset Radio Allocation." New York Times. August 3, 1927, p. 28.

7.540.   "Fires From Window, Kills Masked Man." New York Times. August 26, 1927, p. 19.

7,541.   "Five Are Arrested At Richmond In Two Illegal Cross Burnings." New York Times. January 2, 1967, p. 22.

7,542. "5 Lose MP Jobs For Klan Membership." Washington
        Post. November 14, 1980, p. A32.

7,543. "4 Sailors Guilty Over Klan Rally." New York Times.
        October 21, 1979, p. 31.

7,544. "Goodwin Reaffirms Opposition." Christian Science
        Monitor. February 1, 1967, p. 6.

7,545   "Governor Will Combat Virginia Cross Burning."
        New York Times. December 8, 1966, p. 39.

7,546. "Journal & Guide And Anti-KKK Rally In Va. Beach."
        Norfolk Journal & Guide. October 19, 1979, p. 8A.

7,547. Kennedy, Stetson. "Virginia Kluxer Plots To Seize
        Leadership." Afro-American. October 1, 1949, p.
        20.

7,548. "KKK Fading." Christian Science Monitor. September
        22, 1967, p. 1.

7,549. "KKK Holds Rally In Virginia To Recruit Navy
        Population." Baltimore Afro-American. October 13,
        1979, p. 1.

7,550. "KKK & Anti-KKK Forces Clash In Virginia Beach,
        Virginia." Norfolk Journal & Guide. October 12,
        1979, p. 1A.

7,551. "KKK Makes An Offer." Durham Morning Herald.
        October 11, 1966, p. 1.

7,552. "KKK Solicitations Irk Va.'s Black Leaders."
        Pittsburgh Courier. May 2, 1981, pp. 1, 3.

7,553. "KKK Vandalism Plagues Army Man In Va." Baltimore
        Afro-American. July 16, 1977, p. 15.

7,554. "KKK Wizard Attacks Carter And Praises Reagan In
        N. Va. Visit." San Francisco Chronicle. October
        27, 1980, p. 22.

7,555. "Klan Breaks Up Virginia Family In Short Order."
        Chicago Defender. April 8, 1922, pp. 3-4.

7,556. "Klan Charges FBI Agents With Assault." Winston-
        Salem Journal. November 30, 1966.

7,557. "Klan Charges 2 FBI Agents." Greensboro Daily
        News. November 30, 1966, p. 1.

7,558. "Klan Jeers Hopewell Negro Protest." Washington
        Post. August 7, 1966.

7,559. "Klan Meeting Sept. 3." New York Times. August 27, 1960, p. 7.

7,560. "Klan Member Cancels Rally In Va., Cites 'Harassment'." Washington Star. March 5, 1981, p. B5.

7,561. "Klan Offers To Reconstruct Negro Church Hit By Blast." New York Times. October 11, 1966, p. 39.

7,562. "Klan Radio Station Seek 50,000 Watts." New York Times. October 9, 1927, p. 6.

7,563. "Klan Raid Cabaret." Pittsburgh Courier. August 25, 1923, p. 9.

7,564. "Klan Resurgency Arouses Virginia." New York Times. December 11, 1966, p. 49.

7,565. "Klan Session Is Set." New York Times. August 21, 1960, p. 95.

7,566   "Klan To 'Serenade' Glass." New York Times. May 29, 1927, p. 6.

7,567. "Klan Power Said Increasing." New Burn Sun Journal. October 15, 1966, p. 1.

7,568. "Klansman Assails 'Judas' Preachers." New York Times. September 5, 1960, p. 21.

7,569. "Klansmen Ousted From MP Posts." Washington Star. November 14, 1980, p. B1.

7,570. "Ku Klux Klan Given Permit For Va. Rally." Washington Star. February 27, 1981, p. B3.

7,571. "Ku Klux Klan Holds Rally In Virginia." Washington Post. October 6, 1979, p. 3C.

7,572. "Ku Klux Klan Threatens Arlington Librarian." Library Journal. Vol. 87, May 15, 1962, pp. 1866-1867.

7,573. "Ku Kluxers' Spectacles Are Smoked." Chicago Defender. February 4, 1922, p. 1, part 2.

7,574. "Library Panel Rejects Display Of Klan Paper." Washington Star. March 26, 1981, p. B4.

7,575. "NAACP Marches Against Richmond Police Brutality, KKK Watches." San Francisco Chronicle. August 24, 1980, p. 7B.

7,576. Nachman, Bill. "KKK Solicitations Anger Black Leaders." Norfolk Journal & Guide. April 15, 1981, p. 1.

7,577.   "Negro Protest In Virginia Is Jeered By Klansmen."
          New York Times. August 7, 1966, p. 47.

7,578.   Nordheimer, Jon. "To Ku Klux Klan, Year Was Trying."
          New York Times. September 8, 1969, p. 19.

7,579.   "Norfolk Council Rejects Resolution Condemning
          Ku Klux Klan." Washington Post. October 11, 1979,
          p. 6A.

7,580.   "Norfolk Council's Defeat Of Anti-KKK Resolution."
          Norfolk Journal & Guide. October 19, 1979, p. 8A.

7,581.   "Opposition Voiced On Ku Klux Klan." New Bern
          Sun Journal. September 29, 1966, p. 1.

7,582.   "Organizer Of Klan Passes Away At 91." New York
          Amsterdam News. October 5, 1935, p. 2.

7,583.   "Organizing The KKK In Virginia." Richmond Times-
          Dispatch. August 9, 1952, p. 1.

7,584.   Oulahan, Richard V. "Anti-Smith Sheets Deluge
          Virginia." New York Times. September 19, 1928,
          p. 2.

7,585.   Preston, Alex R. "Negroes In Virginia Defy Klan,
          Hold Rally With Police On Guard." Washington
          Evening Star. October 3, 1965.

7,586.   "Purcell Wins In Virginia." New York Times.
          November 5, 1925, p. 8.

7,587.   "Radio Board Seeks Klan Air Programs." New York
          Times. October 28, 1927, p. 18.

7,588.   "Rebuffs Senator Heflin." New York Times.
          September 16, 1928, p. 5.

7,589.   "Refuse Klan Gift." Pittsburgh Courier. October
          29, 1927, p. 4.

7,590.   "Says Communists Were Guilty Of Klan Activities
          In Norfolk, Va." Pittsburgh Courier. September
          3, 1938, p. 12.

7,591.   " 'Smash The Klan' Forces To Demonstrate At KKK
          Rally In Virginia." Norfolk Journal & Guide.
          October 5, 1979, p. 1A.

7,592.   "Swastika Burned Into McLean Lawn Of AFT Bureau
          Head." Washington Star. August 4, 1980, p. A5.

7,593.   "10 Richmond, Virginia Residents Offer Their Views
          Of KKK." Baltimore Afro-American. July 11, 1981,
          p. 14.

7,594.   "Threatens Gov. Byrd." New York Times. June 8, 1928, p. 12.

7,595.   "Three Klansmen Are Caught Posting Signs." Winston-Salem Journal. March 24, 1966.

7,596.   "Three Klansmen Put To Rout By Race Man." Pittsburgh Courier. September 8, 1923, p. 11.

7,597.   "21 Seized In Virginia." New York Times. July 26, 1967, p. 19.

7,598.   "Va. ACLU Dir. Eyes Navy Ban On Servicemen Going To KKK Rally." Chicago Defender. October 11, 1979, p. 5.

7,599.   "Va. ACLU Opposes Navy Telling Sailors Not To Go To KKK Rally." Atlanta Daily World. October 11, 1979, p. 1.

7,600.   "Virginia KKK Bars Newsmen." New York Times. July 18, 1967, p. 24.

7,601.   "Virginia Klan Loses Bid To Arrest U.S. Judge." New York Times. September 5, 1970, p. 9.

7,602.   "Virginia Klan Tells Gov. Godwin Police 'Harass' Members." New York Times. January 19, 1967, p. 71.

7,603.   "Virginians Make KKK Scram." New York Daily World. March 6, 1981, p. 2.

7,604.   "Virginia Newspapers Coverage Of Ku Klux Klan Rally." Norfolk Journal & Guide. October 12, 1979, p. 6A.

7,605.   "Who's Afraid." Washington Afro-American. May 5, 1981, p. 1.

46. WASHINGTON

7,606.   "Ku Klux Commend Pastor." New York Times. March 11, 1922, p. 3.

47. WEST VIRGINIA

7,607.   "Body Exhumed For Clue." New York Times. April 13, 1923, p. 28.

7,608.   "Charleston, W. Va. Preacher Hiding Due To Terrorism By KKK." New Orleans Times Picayune. January 1, 1981, p. 5.

7,609.   "Doctor On Trial In W. Va.; Has K.K.K. On Jury." Pittsburgh Courier. July 14, 1923, pp. 2,3.

7,610.   Franklin, Ben A. "Evidence Grows That Byrd Will
           Get High Court Seat." New York Times. October
           11, 1971, pp. 1, 25.

7,611.   Graham, Fred P. "McGovern Would Oppose Byrd;
           Rules Out 'A Racist' For Court." New York Times.
           October 12, 1971, pp. 1, 15.

7,612.   "Hooded Mob's Warning Sends 100 West Virginians
           In Flight." New York Times. May 21, 1924, p. 1.

7,613.   "Hoods Banned In W. Va. City To Restrain KKK."
           Jet. Vol. 59, September 25, 1980, p. 5.

7,614.   "KKK Grows In W. Va. As Job Problems Worsen."
           Jet. Vol. 57, March 6, 1980, p. 5.

7,615.   "Klan Boast Derided." New York Times. September
           23, 1923, Sect. 2, p. 1.

7,616.   "Klan Holds Rally In Textbook Fight." New York
           Times. February 16, 1975, p. 26.

7,617.   "Klan Leader In W. Virginia Files For Vice
           President." New York Times. February 9, 1976,
           p. 21.

7,618.   "Klan Preacher Is Jailed." New York Times.
           October 28, 1924, p. 38.

7,619.   "Klan Threatens Johnson." New York Times. August
           24, 1923, p. 11.

7,620.   "Klansmen Act As Pallbearers At Funeral Of A
           Negro Miner." New York Times. August 26, 1925,
           p. 21.

7,621.   "Labor Vote Split In West Virginia." New York
           Times. October 14, 1924, p. 3.

7,622.   "Mrs. Rose Robinson." New York Times. April 26,
           1923, p. 8.

7,623.   "Pastor Says He's In Hiding After Ku Klux Klan
           Threats." New York Times. January 1, 1981, p. A5.

7,624.   "Peyser Assails Law Agents Over Minister-Klan
           Case." New York Times. January 15, 1981, p. A18.

7,625.   "Refuses Charter To Ku Klux Klan." New York Times.
           October 7, 1921, p. 36.

7,626.   "Rev. Michael Curry And Wife Ella, Discuss Flight
           From KKK In W. Va." San Francisco Chronicle.
           February 8, 1981, p. 4.

7,627.   "Seven Men Arrested In Klan Shooting." New York
          Times. August 9, 1924, p. 2.

7,628.   Sherrill, Robert. "The Embodiment Of Poor White
          Power." New York Times Magazine. February 28,
          1971, Sect. 6, pp. 9, 48-53.

7,629.   "The Judge Denounces Ku Klux." New York Times.
          November 22, 1922, p. 23.

7,630.   "Threat Against W. Va. Families Is Laid To Klan."
          Pittsburgh Courier. October 27, 1923, p. 1.

7,631.   "Told Klan Secrets; Found Shot Dead." New York
          Amsterdam News. April 11, 1923, p. 3.

7,632.   "Two Churches Refuse Ku Klux Klan Gift." Pittsburgh
          Courier. May 10, 1924, p. 3.

7,633.   "U.S. Rep. Peyser Releases W. Va. Minister's
          Deposition On KKK." New Orleans Times Picayune.
          January 15, 1981, p. 4.

7,634.   "W. Va. City, To Restrain Klan, Makes It Illegal
          To Wear Hood." Washington Post. August 31,
          1980, p. C3.

7,635.   "West Virginia Minister And Wife Find Refuge From
          Klan Terror." New York Times. January 12, 1981,
          p. A14.

7,636.   "West Virginia Political Club Forces Candidates
          To Give Attitude On Negro." Pittsburgh Courier.
          May 10, 1924, pp. 14-15.

48.   WISCONSIN

7,637.   Berger, Victor L. "The Klan." Pittsburgh Courier.
          October 27, 1923, pp. 1, 16.

7,638.   "Breaks Up Klan Meeting." New York Times.
          February 28, 1924, p. 8.

7,639.   "Convict Six In Klan Riot." New York Times.
          November 2, 1926, p. 8.

7,640.   "Convicted On Either Supposition." New York Times.
          October 20, 1922, p. 16.

7,641.   Goldberg, Robert A. "The Ku Klux Klan In Madison,
          1922-1927." Wisconsin Magazine of History.
          Vol. 58, Autumn, 1974, pp. 31, 44.

7,642.   "Klan Barred From Wisconsin." New York Times.
          April 23, 1925, p. 2.

7,643. "Klan Defies Gov. Blaine; Orders Night Rally Held."
        New York Times. September 8, 1924, pp. 17.

7,644. "Klan Incorporation Refused By Wisconsin." Broad
        Ax. May 2, 1925, p. 2.

7,645. "Klan Threat In Wisconsin." New York Times.
        January 4, 1923, p. 21.

7,646. Kraemer, Lynn. "Wisconsin And The KKK." Wisconsin
        Then And Now. Vol. 15, April, 1969, pp. 1, 3.

7,647. "Ku Klux Threaten To Kill Milwaukee Lawyer."
        Chicago Defender. May 28, 1921, pp. 1, 2.

7,648. "Rights Protest Stirs Wisconsin." New York Times.
        August 28, 1966, p. 52.

7,649. "Sentenced For Attack On Klan Tent Meeting."
        New York Times. November 4, 1926, p. 3.

7,650. "Shotgun Blast Hits Home Of Wisconsin Klan Chief."
        New York Times. October 9, 1966, p. 65.

7,651. "Stanback To Speak On Rise Of KKK." Milwaukee
        Community Journal. October 29 - November 5, 1980,
        p. 7.

7,652. "Starts Klan Inquiry." New York Times. September
        25, 1921, p. 14.

7,653. "3 In Midwest Klans Seized In Bombings." New
        York Times. September 27, 1966, p. 32.

7.654. "War On Klan Begun By Governor Blaine." New
        York Times. September 6, 1924, p. 26.

7,655. "Wisconsin Charter Of Klan Is Revoked." New
        York Times. December 11, 1946, p. 3.

7,656. "Wisconsin Home Of Klan Leader Hit By Shotgun
        Blast." Durham Morning Herald. October 9, 1966.

7,657. "Wisconsin Sues KKK For Charter." Philadelphia
        Tribune. November 5, 1946, p. 1.

7.658. "Wisconsin Klansman Quits." New York Times.
        April 26, 1966, p. 22.

7,659. "Won't Bar Ku Klux Klan." New York Times.
        August 28, 1921, p. 16.

49. DISTRICT OF COLUMBIA

7,660. "Bars Anti-Klan Demonstration Where Klan Meets
        In Capital." New York Times. July 8, 1925, p. 1.

7,661.   "Big Ku Klux Rites Planned In Capital." New York
          Times. September 11, 1926, p. 3.

7,662.   "Check Klan Parades In Washington." Chicago
          Defender. April 1, 1922, p. 3.

7,663.   "Commissioners Decline To Cancel Klan Parade."
          New York Amsterdam News. July 8, 1925, p. 10.

7,664.   "A Cross Flames Beyond." New York Daily News.
          January 25, 1938, p. 1.

7,665.   "Cross Is Set Ablaze At Warren's Home." New York
          Times. July 15, 1956, pp. 1, 37.

7,666.   "Deny There Were Ku Klux In White House." New
          York Amsterdam News. September 26, 1923, p. 7.

7,667.   "Ex-Goblin Sues Ku Klux." New York Times.
          December 13, 1921, p. 40.

7,668.   "Ex Chief Opposes Klan Parade Plan." New York
          Times. June 28, 1925, p. 7.

7,669.   Folliard, Edward T. "These Marchers In Washington
          Wore Hoods." Washington Post. April 18, 1965,
          p. E2.

7,670.   "40,000 Klansmen Parade In Washington As 200,000
          Spectators Look On Quietly; Called Order's Biggest
          Demonstration." New York Times. August 9, 1925,
          p. 1.

7,671.   "Great Klan Host To Visit Capital." New York
          Times. August 6, 1925, p. 1.

7,672.   "He Could Decide The Matter." New York Times.
          July 4, 1925, p. 10.

7,673.   "He Must Do More Than Refuse." New York Times.
          June 26, 1925, p. 16.

7,674.   "Inquiry Demanded On Klan In Capital." New York
          Times. November 25, 1922, p. 3.

7,675.   "Kapital Klan Kapers." New York Amsterdam News.
          July 8, 1925, p. 1.

7,676.   "Klan Masses Near Capital." New York Times.
          June 2, 1923, p. 13.

7,677.   "Klan Moves Headquarters To Nation's Capital."
          New York Amsterdam News. May 13, 1925, pp. 12-13.

7,678.   "The Klan Parade." Opportunity. Vol. 3, September,
1925, pp. 279-280.

7,679.   "Klan Parade Fails To Worry Capital." New York
Times. August 7, 1925, p. 3.

7,680.   "Klan Parade May Lead To Riots." New York Amsterdam
News. July 1, 1925, p. 3.

7,681.   "Klan Parade Protested." New York Times. September
5, 1926, p. 3.

7,682.   "Klan Ranks Thinner In Capital Parade." New York
Times. September 14, 1926, pp. 1, 3.

7,683.   "Klan Spirit Will Rule, Says Wizard." New York
Amsterdam News. January 3, 1923, p. 10.

7,684.   "Klan To Establish National Headquarters Near
Large Catholic Church In Washington." New York
Times. February 13, 1928, p. 1.

7,685.   "Klan To Parade In Washington." New York Times.
August 26, 1926, p. 6.

7.686.   "Klan To Use High Power." New York Times.
November 23, 1927, p. 19.

7,687.   "The Klan Walks In Washington." Literary Digest.
Vol. 86, August 22, 1925, pp. 7, 8.

7,688.   "Klan's Big Rally Ends With Oratory." New York
Times. August 10, 1925, p. 26.

7,689.   McQueen, Michel. "Network Takes Aim At KKK."
Washington Post. February 5, 1981, pp. DC 1, 6.

7,690.   Merritt, Dixon. "Klan On Parade." Outlook.
Vol. 140, August 19, 1925, pp. 553-554.

7,691.   "Mundt-Nixon Foes Talk Of Besieging Capital
Tomorrow." New York Times. June 1, 1948, pp. 1, 21.

7,692.   "Negro Women Protest." New York Times. August 9,
1925, p. 2.

7,693.   "Negroes, Klan Rally Here." Washington Evening
Star. June 27, 1966, p. 1.

7,694.   "Only 5,000 Klansmen To March On Aug. 8." New
York Times. July 31, 1925, p. 2.

7,695.   "Professed Ku Klux Scares Parents; Attacks Girl."
Chicago Defender. September 16, 1922, pp. 2, 3.

7,696.   "Protest Klan Parade." New York Times. June 27,
          1925, p. 15.

7,697.   "Protest On Parade Places Klan Issue Before Presi-
          dent." New York Times. July 3, 1925, pp. 1, 2.

7,698.   "Say Klan Operates In A University." New York
          Times. April 5, 1923, p. 21.

7,699.   "Says Klan Is Ready To Defend Mexico." New York
          Times. September 15, 1926, p. 27.

7,700.   "75,000 Of Klan To March Today In Washington; Auto
          Vanguard Precedes Trains Due At Dawn." New York
          Times. September 13, 1926, p. 2.

7,701.   Shannon, William V. "Mr. Nixon's Revenge."
          New York Times. October 12, 1971, p. 43.

7,702.   "20,000 Klansmen Reach Washington; 50,000 Expected."
          New York Times. August 8, 1925, pp. 1, 5.

7,703.   "Wants Burns Inquiry Concerning Ku Klux." New York
          Times. November 26, 1922, p. 20.

7,704.   "Washington Authorizes Klan Parade." New York
          Times. June 18, 1925, p. 6.

7,705.   "Well-Laid Plans Repudiated." New York Times.
          July 31, 1925, p. 14.

7,706.   "Will Ask Coolidge To Review The Klan." New York
          Times. June 25, 1925, p. 6.

7,707.   Woolever, Harry E. "Shall The Ku Klux Klan Parade
          In The Nation's Capital?" Southwest Christian
          Advocate. July 30, 1925, pp. 601-602.

2. HUGO BLACK AND THE KU KLUX KLAN

A Selected List

7,708   Berman, Daniel M. "Hugo L. Black: The Early Years."
          Catholic University of America Law Review. Vol. 8,
          May 1959, pp. 103-116.

7,709.   "Black: A Klan Member On The Supreme Court? New
          Evidence Comes To Light." Newsweek. Vol. 10,
          September 20, 1937, pp. 9-12.

7,710.   "Black Admits He Joined The Klan; Quit, Then Ig-
          nored 'Unsolicited' Card; Cites Record As Liberal
          In Senate." New York Times. October 2, 1937, pp.
          1, 2.

7,711.   "Black Is Still Silent In His London Retreat."
          New York Times. September 16, 1937, p. 14.

7,712.   "Black Leaves London After Refusing Replies; Goes To
          Country When Reporters Find Him." New York
          Times. September 15, 1937, p. 3.

7,713.   "Black Ouster Now Is Held Impossible." New York
          Times. September 14, 1937, p. 18.

7,714.   "Black Quoted As Crediting Klan For His Victory In
          Senate Fight." New York Times. September 15,
          1937, p. 2.

7,715.   "Black Resignation Put To Roosevelt." New York
          Times. October 3, 1937, p. 3.

7,716.   "Both Roosevelt And Black Are Silent On Klan
          Story." New York Times. September 14, 1937, p. 1.

7,717.   "Justice Black Backed By KKK." Mobile (Ala.)
          Register. April 15, 1926, p. 1.

7,718.   "Justice Black Is Recorded As Still A Member Of
          Klan." New York Times. September 13, 1937, pp. 1,
          3.

7,719.   "Justice Black's Speech." New York Times. October
          2, 1937, pp. 1, 3.

7,720.   "Klansman Black?" Commonweal. Vol. 26, September
          24, 1937, pp. 483-484.

7,721.   "Lists Jobs Given By Black." New York Times.
          September 16, 1937, p. 14.

7,722.   "Moore Says Black Should Explain." New York Times.
          September 15, 1937, p. 2.

7,723.   "A New Justice Robes Himself." New York World-
          Telegram. October 4, 1937.

7,724.   "No Place For Fanatics." Collier's. Vol. 100.
          October 23, 1937, pp. 74-75.

7,725.   Porter, Russell B. "In Klan, Then Out, Gov. Graves
          Avers." New York Times. September 14, 1937, p. 18.

7,726.   _____. "Alabama Aware Of Black's Ties." New
          York Times. September 13, 1937, p. 3.

7,727.   "Re-Entry Of Black Into Klan Described In Its
          'Archives'." New York Times. September 14, 1937,
          pp. 1, 18.

7,728.   "Talent Rewarded: Mr. Justice Black." Catholic
          World. Vol. 146, November, 1937, pp. 129-134.

7,729.   Van Der Veer, Virginia. "Hugo Black And The K.K.K."
          American Heritage. Vol. 19, April, 1968, pp. 60-64,
          108-111.

3. POLITICS

A Selected List

7,730.   "Advises Klan On Voting." New York Times.
          September 2, 1924, p. 3.

7,731.   "AFL - CIO Support Jewish Veterans." New York Times.
          November 30, 1946, p. 10.

7,732.   "Against League Plank." New York Times. June 23,
          1924, p. 3.

7,733.   "Alleges Klan Deal To Support Reed." New York
          Times. June 3, 1928, p. 2.

7,734.   " 'American Party' Asks Klan Aid In Election."
          New York Times. June 5, 1924, p. 3.

7,735.   " 'American' Party Names Candidates." New York
          Times. June 4, 1924, p. 23.

7,736.   "Anti-Defamation League Expresses 'Deep Concern'."
          (Fort Pierce, Fla.) Chronicle. November 20, 1980,

7,737.   "Anti-Klan Men Lost By 4.30 Vote Margin." New York
          Times. June 30, 1929, pp. 1, 6.

7,738.   "Anti-Klan Outburst, Hour Of Cheers For M'Adoo
          Stir Convention." New York Times. June 26, 1924,
          pp. 1, 23.

7,739.   "Anti-Klan Plank Gets Ohio Backing." New York
          Times. June 24, 1924, p. 2.

7,740.   "Anti-Klan Plank Pushed Forward To Eliminate
          M'Adoo; He Fights Back, Assailing City Papers And
          Wall Street; More Booms Arrive In Town With Incoming
          Delegates." New York Times. June 23, 1924, pp. 1, 3.

7,741.   "Anti-Klan Plank That Won And Amendment That Was
          Lost." New York Times. June 29, 1924, p. 1.

7,742.   "Anti-Smith Group Revealed In A Suit." New York
          Times. June 20, 1928, p. 7.

7,743.   "Attacks Coolidge Talk." New York Times. September
          27, 1924, p. 3.

7,744.   "Backs Smith's Charges." New York Times. October
           31, 1928, p. 2.

7,745.   "Birch Chief Parries Query On Johnson." New York
           Times. September 7, 1964, p. 20.

7,746.   "Brings Anti-Klan Plank." New York Times. June 22,
           1924, p. 9.

7,747.   "Broome Regulars Win." New York Times. September
           28, 1925, p. 40.

7,748.   "Bryant Will Be Asked His Stand On The Klan." New
           York Times. June 22, 1924, p. 5.

7,749.   Buckley, William F. Jr. "The Klan And The Candi-
           dates." Washington Star. September 23, 1980, p.
           A4.

7,750.   Burner, David B. "The Democratic Party In The
           Election Of 1924." Mid-America. Vol. 46, April
           1964, pp. 92-113.

7,751.   "Bush Says Reagan Made Mistake In Remarks About
           The Ku Klux Klan." San Francisco Chronicle.
           September 4, 1980, p. 11.

7,752.   "Calls For Stand On Klan." New York Times.
           October 25, 1928, p. 3.

7,753.   "Calls Klan 'Smith's Alibi'." New York Times.
           November 1, 1928, p. 16.

7,754.   "Calls On Negroes To Back LaFollette." New York
           Times. October 7, 1924, p. 7.

7,755.   "Candidates Ignore Klan." New York Times. April
           23, 1928, p. 12.

7,756.   Carroll, Maurice. "Calls To Violence Scored By
           Buckley." New York Times. October 31, 1970,
           p. 13.

7,757.   "Carter Vows To Help 'Root Out' Killers Of Blacks."
           Los Angeles Times. October 24, 1980, p. 14.

7,758.   "Carter's Retreat On Racism Charge." Chicago
           Tribune. September 19, 1980, p. 2.

7,759.   "Casting Out The Klan." Independent. Vol. 113,
           September 13, 1924, p. 141.

7,760.   "Charges Plot To Link Republicans To Klan." New
           York Times. October 31, 1928, p. 2.

7,761.   "The Claim-All Klan." _New York Times_. August 9, 1924, p. 10.

7,762.   "Clarke Says Klan 'Put Mayfield Over'." _New York Times_. May 29, 1924, p. 2.

7,763.   Clines, Francis X. "Carter Suggests Turn To Racism In Reagan Views." _New York Times_. September 17, 1980, p. B10.

7,764.   _____. "A Cold Slows Conservative." _New York Times_. October 29, 1970, p. 49.

7,765.   "Color Urges Klan Plank." _New York Times_. June 28, 1924, p. 2.

7,766.   "Communists Report Gitlow Missing In Arizona; Tells Of Legion And Klan Threat To Candidate." _New York Times_. October 13, 1928, p. 17.

7,767.   "Convention, By One Vote, Defeats Plank Naming Klan, Bryan, In Bitter Debate, Pleading For Party Unity, Proposal For League Referendum Wins, Despite Baker." _New York Times_. June 29, 1924, pp. 1, 2.

7,768.   "Convention Here Faces Klan Fight." _New York Times_. June 12, 1924, p. 7.

7,769.   "Coolidge And The Klan." _New York Times_. September 21, 1924, Sect. 7, p. 12.

7,770.   "Coolidge Discusses Campaign Policies With Gen. Davis." _New York Times_. August 26, 1924, pp. 1, 2.

7,771.   "Coolidge Opposes Aims Of Klan, Says Slemp, In Reply To Questionnaire From New York." _New York Times_. September 3, 1924, p. 1.

7,772.   "Coolidge Speech Directed At Klan; 'Keynote' For 1926." _New York Times_. October 8, 1925, pp. 1, 8.

7,773.   "Coolidge Studies Ku Klux Klan Issue." _New York Times_. August 27, 1924, pp. 1, 2.

7,774.   "Coolidge To Confer With Dawes Today; May Discuss Klan." _New York Times_. August 25, 1924, p. 1.

7,775.   "Coolidge Will Act On Klan Challenge." _New York Times_. August 24, 1924, pp. 1, 3.

7,776.   "A Courageous Platform." _New York Times_. June 25, 1924, p. 22.

7,777.   "Criticizes Klan Plank." _New York Times_. June 30, 1924, p. 6.

7,778.   "Curtis Never Klansman He Notifies World." Pitts-
          burgh Courier. September 15, 1928, p. 3.

7,779.   "Dark Horses Are Encouraged By Anti-Klan Outburst."
          New York Times. June 26, 1924, p. 3.

7,780.   "Davis Again Scores The Ku Klux Klan." New York
          Times. October 17, 1924, pp. 1, 2.

7,781.   "Davis Asks Coolidge To State Position On Corrup-
          tion Issue." New York Times. October 28, 1924,
          pp. 1, 3.

7,782.   "Davis Assails Klan, Fall And 'Oil Fraud' In
          Denver Speeches." New York Times. September 12,
          1924, pp. 1, 2.

7,783.   "Davis Declares Honesty The Issue; Indicts Re-
          publicans And Executive; Promises Fight Without
          Kid Gloves." New York Times. August 12, 1924,
          pp. 1, 2.

7,784.   "Davis Denounces Klan In Politics." New York
          Times. October 24, 1924, p. 3.

7,785.   Davis, Elmer. "Gloom Doubts Klan Will Be Sensi-
          tive." New York Times. June 30, 1924, p. 3.

7,786.   "Davis No Klansman And Never Will Be." New York
          Times. August 8, 1924, p. 1.

7,787.   "Declare Klan Fight Has Not Hurt Party." New York
          Times. June 30, 1924, p. 3.

7,788.   "Declares Harrison Heads Klan Group." New York
          Times. June 18, 1924, p. 2.

7,789.   "Decline In Nonviolent Civil Rights Tradition In
          South Viewed." Los Angeles Times. June 17,
          1979, p. 1.

7,790.   "The Deeper Causes." New York Times. July 5,
          1924, p. 12.

7,791.   "Defeats Of Klan Cheer Politicians In Washington."
          New York Times. November 5, 1925, pp. 1, 8.

7,792.   "Delegations Bring Plans And Hopes." New York
          Times. June 23, 1924, p. 4.

7,793.   "The Democratic Platform." New York Times. July
          2, 1924, p. 18.

7,794.   "Democrats Discuss An Anti-Klan Plank." New York
          Times. November 20, 1923, p. 21.

7,795.   "Democrats Elated By Reports In West." New York
          Times. September 4, 1924, pp. 1, 3.

7,796.   "Democrats Face Two Big Issues." New York Times.
          May 19, 1924, p. 19.

7,797.   "Denies Political Expenses." New York Times.
          October 18, 1928, p. 10.

7,798.   "Dewey And The Klan Defeat Wilkie." People's
          Voice. April 15, 1944, p. 17.

7,799.   "Drives Shaped Against Klan." Christian Science
          Monitor. January 13, 1951, p. 8.

7,800.   "Expected Outbreaks Over Klan Planks." New York
          Times. June 29, 1924, p. 8.

7,801.   "Fight Waged To Rout KKK." Christian Science
          Monitor. September 15, 1950, p. 10.

7,802.   "590 Delegates Reported Pledged To A Plank De-
          nouncing The Klan." New York Times. June 23,
          1924, pp. 1, 3.

7,803.   "First M'Adoo Interview." New York Times. June
          22, 1924, pp. 1, 2.

7,804.   " 'Freedom's Missionaries'." New York Times.
          August 3, 1964, p. 24.

7,805.   Frost, Stanley. "Klan's ½ of 1 Percent Victory."
          Outlook. Vol. 137, July 9, 1924, pp. 384-387.

7,806.   _____. "Masked Politics Of The Klan." World's
          Work. Vol. 55, February, 1928, pp. 399, 407.

7,807.   "Galleries Fuddled By League And Klan." New York
          Times. June 29, 1924, p. 11.

7,808.   "Garvey's Klan Parley Revealed By Imperial Giant
          Of Ku Klux Klan." New York Amsterdam News.
          February 14, 1923, p. 7.

7,809.   "Garrett Assails Republican Record." New York
          Times. February 23, 1922, p. 32.

7,810.   "Gitlow Safe In Texas; He Denies Kidnapping."
          New York Times. October 15, 1928, p. 28.

7,811.   Hagerty, James A. "Dewey Sees Racism On Alabama
          Ticket." New York Times. October 9, 1952, p. 14.

7,812.   _____. "Drive Is Started Against Robinson."
          New York Times. June 29, 1928, pp. 1, 10.

7,813.   Harris, Julian. "Roosevelt Speech Resented In South." New York Times. October 16, 1927, Sect. 8, p. 2.

7,814.   "Harris Attacks GOP Platform On KKK Backing." Washington Star. August 7, 1980, p. A3.

7,815.   "Harris Blasts Reagan On Backing By Klan." Washington Post. August 7, 1980, p. A7.

7,816.   "Harrison Rebuffs Klan." New York Times. August 27, 1927, p. 14.

7,817.   " 'Have M'Adoo Stopped,' Foes Assert." New York Times. June 21, 1924, pp. 1, 2.

7,818.   "Heflin Fails To Back Up Charges Against Smith; Got Pay For 'Lecture'." New York Times. June 1, 1928, pp. 1, 4.

7,819.   "Heflin Sees Smith Easily Defeated." New York Times. May 31, 1928, p. 3.

7,820.   "Heflin Tells Klan Smith Cannot Win." New York Times. July 2, 1927, p. 10.

7,821.   "Henry Ford Listening To Klan Says Weitz." New York Times. September 18, 1923, p. 3.

7,822.   Herbers, John. "Robert Byrd Considered For Supreme Court Seat." New York Times. October 1, 1971, pp. 1, 73.

7,823.   "H.W. Evans Attacks Smith For The Klan." New York Times. September 22, 1928, p. 5.

7,824.   "Ignores Curry Letter." New York Times. June 10, 1924, p. 9.

7,825.   "In Doubtful Company." New York Times. August 28, 1928, p. 22.

7,826.   Ingraham, Joseph C. "President Decries 'Evil Propaganda' In Election." New York Times. October 18, 1960, p. 26.

7,827.   "The Irish To The Rescue." New York Times. August 15, 1925, p. 10.

7,828.   "An Irrepressible Conflict." New York Times. June 30, 1924, p. 14.

7,829.   "John M. Bailey." New York Times. July 26, 1964, p. 38.

7,830.   "Johnston's Speech Naming Underwood." New York Times. June 26, 1924, p. 6.

7,831.   Kenworthy, E.W. "Democrats Fear Losses In South." New York Times. August 4, 1964, pp. 1, 14.

7,832.   _____. "Goldwater Gains In Drive For Unity." New York Times. July 30, 1964, pp. 1, 11.

7,833.   "Keynote At Hartford Arraigns The Klan." New York Times. September 18, 1924, p. 6.

7,834.   "K.K.K. Kaputt." New York Times. October 8, 1926, p. 22.

7,835.   "KKK Leader David Duke To Enter N.C. Presidential Primary." New Orleans Times Picayune. May 20, 1979, p. 3.

7,836.   "KKK May Launch Third Party To Split Labor." Chicago Defender. October 26, 1946, p. 2.

7,837.   "Klan Advised How To Vote." New York Times. November 5, 1924, p. 6.

7,838.   "Klan And Dry Issues To Bring First Test Of Strength Between Smith And M'Adoo; Boom For Davis In Capital And Chicago." New York Times. June 20, 1924, p. 2.

7,839.   "Klan And League Contests Begin Before Committee." New York Times. June 25, 1924, p. 1.

7,840.   "Klan And The Bottle." Nation. Vol. 117, November 21, 1923, pp. 570-572.

7,841.   "The Klan And The Campaign." Christian Science Monitor. August 26, 1980, pp. 24-25.

7,842.   "Klan And The Candidates." Literary Digest. Vol. 82, September 6, 1924, pp. 10-11.

7,843.   "The Klan And The Democrats." Literary Digest. Vol. 81, June 14, 1924, pp. 12-13.

7,844.   "Klan Answers Underwood." New York Times. May 15, 1924, p. 3.

7,845.   "The Klan As A Campaign Issue." New York Amsterdam News. February 28, 1923, p. 12.

7,846.   "Klan At Bay." Current Opinion. Vol. 77, October, 1924, pp. 419-422.

7,847.   "Klan Bans Smith, Underwood, Ford As 1924 Nominees." New York Times. November 4, 1923, pp. 1, 3.

7,849.   "Klan Chief Critical Of McGovern." Raleigh News
          & Observer. July 17, 1972, p. 5.

7,850.   "Klan Delegates Sad Despite Victory." New York
          Times. June 30, 1924, p. 3.

7,851.   "Klan Denounces LaFollette Aims." New York Times.
          August 11, 1924, p. 2.

7,852.   "Klan Dominating In 3 Southwest States." New York
          Times. November 1, 1923, pp. 1, 3.

7,853.   "The Klan Enters The Campaign." Literary Digest.
          Vol. 82, July 12, 1924, pp. 9-10.

7,854.   "Klan Fight Stirs The 'Dark Horses'." New York
          Times. June 29, 1924, pp. 1, 9.

7,855.   "Klan Head Assails Smith." New York Times. June
          16, 1927, p. 16.

7,856.   "Klan Head Attacks Smith." New York Times.
          August 7, 1927, Sect. 2, p. 8.

7.857.   "Klan Head Reveals Plan To Fight Smith." New York
          Times. December 23, 1927, p. 12.

7,858.   "Klan In Politics: Force Or Farce?" U.S. News &
          World Report. Vol. 89, September 15, 1980, p. 13.

7.859.   "Klan In Southwest Faces Another Test. New York
          Times. August 11, 1924, p. 2.

7.860.   "The Klan Issue." Nation. Vol. 231, September
          15, 1980, p. 10.

7,861.   "Klan Issue Overshadows All On Eve Of Balloting;
          Plank Splits Platform Makers, M'Adoo Wins On
          League, Last Nominees Are In, Underwood And Davis
          Stronger." New York Times. June 28, 1924, pp.
          1, 2, 3.

7,862.   "Klan Issue Rises And Is Bothering Both Big Parties."
          New York Times. May 14, 1924, pp. 1, 2.

7,863.   "Klan Joins Fight On World Court." New York Times.
          November 7, 1925, pp. 1, 2.

7,864.   "Klan Leader Calls Attack By Democrats An 'Honor'."
          New York Times. August 25, 1964, p. 23.

7,865.   "Klan Leaders Call Plank Battle Won." New York
          Times. June 26, 1924, p. 7.

7,866.   "Klan Letter On Nominees." New York Times.
          November 4, 1924, p. 2.

7,867.   "Klan Membership Denied." New York Times.
October 9, 1947, p. 16.

7,868.   "Klan Out For Watson; Senator Disavows It." New
York Times. June 10, 1924, p. 3.

7,869.   "Klan Paper Boosts Hoover." Pittsburgh Courier.
September 8, 1928, p. 3.

7,870.   "Klan Planning To Run A Presidential Ticket."
New York Times. September 3, 1974, p. 70.

7,871.   "The Klan Repudiated." New York Times. August
8, 1964, p. 18.

7,872.   "Klan Revived To War On Smith, Says Hawes." New
York Times. October 6, 1928, p. 2.

7,873.   "Klan Seeks Role As A Voting Bloc." New York
Times. July 25, 1965, p. 38.

7,874.   "Klan Seeks To Test Jersey Candidates." New York
Times. April 22, 1928, p. 13.

7,875.   "Klan Sees Smith A Nominee." New York Times.
November 14, 1927, p. 3.

7,876.   "Klan-Senator Tieup Charged." Chicago Defender.
October 26, 1946, p. 2.

7,877.   "Klan Strongly Opposes Harding World Court Plan."
New York Times. July 1, 1923, p. 1.

7,878.   "Klan Sworn Against Smith." New York Times.
June 13, 1927, p. 21.

7,879.   "Klan Threatens Anti-Smith Bolt." New York Times.
December 31, 1927, pp. 1, 13.

7,880.   "Klan To Back Goldwater Despite His Repudiation."
New York Times. August 14, 1964, p. 8.

7,881.   "Klan Victories And Defeats." Literary Digest.
Vol. 83, November 22, 1924, p. 16.

7,882.   "Klan Victory Laid To Split In Foes." New York
Times. June 30, 1924, p. 2.

7,883.   "Klan Votes Compared With First Ballot." New
York Times. July 1, 1924, p. 3.

7,884.   "Klan Will Not Parade At Inauguration - Evans."
Pittsburgh Courier. January 19, 1929, p. 1.

7,885.   "The Klan's Political Role." Literary Digest.
Vol. 79, November 24, 1923, pp. 13-14.

7,886. "Klansman Sees End Of Klan In Politics." New York
Times. August 28, 1924, p. 2.

7,887. "Klansmen To Enter 1980 Presidential Primaries;
Membership Grows In U.S." Jet. Vol. 56, June 21,
1979, p. 5.

7,888. "Klansmen Prepare For Bitter Fight." New York
Times. June 23, 1924, p. 3.

7,889. "Klansmen Won Some, Lost Other Elections." New
York Times. April 5, 1923, p. 1.

7,890. "The Ku Klux In Politics." Literary Digest.
Vol. 73, June 10, 1922, p. 15.

7,891. "Ku Klux Klan And The Election." Christian
Century. Vol. 41, November 20, 1924, pp. 1496-
1497.

7,892. "Ku Klux Klan And The Next Election." World's
Work. Vol. 46, October, 1923, pp. 573-575.

7,893. "Ku Klux Klan Endorses George S. Brown For
President." New Orleans Times Picayune. February
19, 1975, Sect. 3, p. 15.

7,894. "Ku Klux Klan Is Not The Real Problem." Pittsburgh
Courier. November 1, 1980, pp. 1, 2.

7,895. "La Follette Replies To Questions Of Jews." New
York Times. September 16, 1924, p. 2.

7,896. "Law And Order And Incidently The Klan Issue."
New York Times. June 30, 1929, p. 5.

7,897. "Leaders Said To Have Released Delegates On Klan
Issue." New York Times. June 27, 1924, p. 1.

7,898. "League Comes To The Front For Democratic Action,
Rivaling The Klan Issue In The Late Maneuvering."
New York Times. June 24, 1924, pp. 1, 2.

7,899. "Legion Accused Of Gitlow Kidnapping; Communists
Hear Candidate Is In Nogales." New York Times.
October 14, 1928, p. 18.

7,900. Lewis, Anthony. "A Nice Guy Contest?" New York
Times. September 22, 1980, p. 27.

7,901. "Libel Suit Left Standing." New York Times.
February 25, 1969, p. 24.

7,902. "M'Adoo Defies 'Enemies'." New York Times. June
30, 1924, pp. 1, 2.

7,903.   "M'Adoo Forces Lose In The First Test Vote, 513 to
559; Leaders Said To Have Released Delegates On
Klan Issue; Outsiders Help Stage 73 - Minute Uproar For Smith." New York Times. June 27, 1924,
pp. 1, 3, 5.

7,904.   "M'Adoo Men Gave No Orders On Klan." New York
Times. June 29, 1924, p. 5.

7,905.   "Makers Of Platform In Morning Prayer." New York
Times. June 29, 1924, pp. 1, 7.

7,906.   "Mann Contradicts Smith Statement." New York
Times. September 22, 1928, p. 2.

7,907.   Marteen, Alpheus. "ADL Deplores Thousands Of
Votes Going To KKKluxers." Westchester County
(N.Y.) Press. November 20, 1980, p. 1.

7,908.   Mazo, Earl. "Goldwater View Is 'Frightening' To
Rockefeller." New York Times. July 18, 1964,
pp. 1, 46.

7,909.   "Mellon And Butler Defend Oil Silence; Hays Under
Hot Fire." New York Times. March 14, 1928, pp.
1, 16, 17.

7,910.   "Menace Of Ku Klux Worries The South." New York
Times. June 27, 1924, p. 5.

7,911.   " 'Mississippi Kid' Is Back." New York Times.
June 29, 1924, p. 13.

7,912.   "Missourians Bring A Factional Fight." New York
Times. June 22, 1924, p. 2.

7,913.   Mohr, Charles. "Goldwater Bars Klan Aid, Confers
With Eisenhower." New York Times. August 7,
1964, p. 1.

7,914.   _____. "Goldwater, In A Unity Bid, Rejects
Extremists Aid; Eisenhower Is 'Satisfied'."
New York Times. August 13, 1964, pp. 1, 17.

7,915.   "Morgenthau Asserts Klan Is The Issue." New York
Times. November 5, 1928, p. 9.

7,916.   "Mr. Heflin's Boomerang." Pittsburgh Courier.
July 12, 1930, editorial page.

7,917.   "Mrs. Harris Quotes Klan In Its Backing Of Reagan."
New York Times. August 7, 1980, p. B7.

7,918.   "Mrs. King Calls The Klan 'Comfortable' With
Reagan." New York Times. September 30, 1980, p.
A20.

7,919.   Myers, William S.   "Know Nothing And Ku Klux Klan."
          North American Review. Vol. 219, January, 1924,
          pp. 1, 7.

7,920.   "Negroes Are Disappointed." New York Times. June
          30, 1924, p. 4.

7,921.   "Negroes Ask A Klan Plank." New York Times. June
          24, 1924, p. 3.

7,922.   "Negroes Ask CoolidgeFor Statement On Klan."
          Broad Ax. June 7, 1924, p. 1.

7,923.   "Northern Leaders Confer With Davis On Party
          Chances." New York Times. July 25, 1924, pp. 1,
          3.

7,924.   "Not A Religious Issue." New York Times. July
          1, 1924, p. 20.

7,925.   "Now Klansmen Threaten The President." New York
          Times. August 18, 1923, p. 8.

7,926.   "Oklahoma Klan Loses." New York Times. June 24,
          1924, p. 3.

7,927.   Oulahan, Richard V. "Battle Lines Are Formed."
          New York Times. June 23, 1924, pp. 1, 2.

7,928.   _____. "Clean-Up Demand Grown In Indiana."
          New York Times. April 15, 1928, p. 16.

7,929.   _____. "Klan Feeling Still Keen." New York
          Times. June 30, 1924, pp. 1, 2.

7,930.   _____. "Tense Feeling On Ku Klux." New York
          Times. June 29, 1924, pp. 1, 7.

7,931.   "Owen Says Klan Didn't Win." New York Times.
          June 30, 1924, p. 4.

7,932.   "Platform Drafted After Long Siege." New York
          Times. June 12, 1924, pp. 1, 3.

7,933.   "Platform Drafters Hotly Debate Anti-Klan Plank."
          New York Times. June 11, 1924, p. 1.

7,934.   "Platform Pleases Texans." New York Times. June
          30, 1924, p. 3.

7,935.   "Plea For Negro Vote." New York Times. October
          27, 1924, p. 3.

7,936.   "Political Power Of Klan Dissipated." New York
          Times. February 5, 1928, Sect. 2, p. 1.

7,937.   "Predict Klan Row Will Injure Party." New York
          Times. June 29, 1924, pp. 1, 7.

7.938.   "Press Views On League And Klan Planks." New
          York Times. June 30, 1924, p. 4.

7,939.   "Questions And Answers - Racism In Campaign."
          New York Times. September 19, 1980, p. B5.

7,940.   Randolph, A. Philip. "The Election In Retrospect."
          The Messenger. Vol. 6, December, 1924, pp. 369-
          371, 390.

7,941.   "Reagan Answers Charges On Remark Made Concerning
          Carter And Klan." Los Angeles Times. September
          3, 1980, p. 1.

7,942.   "Reagan's Apology For Remark About KKK." Chicago
          Tribune. September 3, 1980, p. 2.

7,943.   "Reagan Campaign Renews Charge Of Carter 'Smear'."
          New York Times. September 2, 1980, p. 7.

7,944.   "Reagan Klan Remarks Stir Dispute." Washington
          Star. September 2, 1980, p. A3.

7,945.   "Reagan's Remark About Carter And The KKK -
          Stayskal Cartoon." Chicago Tribune. September
          7, 1980, Sect. 2, p. 4.

7,946.   "Reagan's Remarks About The Ku Klux Klan - Letters."
          Los Angeles Times. September 10, 1980, Sect. 2,
          p. 4.

7,947.   "Reagan's Statements During Campaign - Conrad Car-
          toon." Los Angeles Times. September 4, 1980, Sect.
          2, p. 11.

7,948.   Reed, Roy. "Carter Sweep In South Is In Doubt
          As Two States Lean Toward Ford." New York Times.
          October 29, 1976, p. 18.

7,949.   "Reed Puts Wheeler Under Sharp Fire." New York
          Times. June 18, 1926, pp. 1, 2.

7,950.   "Religious Prescription." New York Times. June
          22, 1924, Sect. 2, p. 4.

7,951.   "Report That Smith May Quit Is Denied." New York
          Times. June 29, 1924, p. 5.

7,952.   "A Republican Swap." New York Times. November
          5, 1928, p.22.

7,953.   "Republicans Assailed By Vassar President." New
          York Times. October 19, 1924, p. 29.

7,954.   "Repudiates Klan Meeting." New York Times.
         October 30, 1928, p. 4.

7,955.   "Reverses Of Klan Surprise Capital." New York
         Times. September 16, 1926, p. 3.

7,956.   Rogers, Will. "Platform Makers Prayer Impresses
         Will Rogers, Who Says It's A Bit Late." New
         York Times. June 29, 1924, p. 5.

7,957.   "Ronald Reagan Blames Carter For Controversy Over
         His Klan Remark." San Francisco Chronicle.
         September 3, 1980, p. 1.

7,958.   "Roosevelt Assails Big Primary Funds." New York
         Times. September 10, 1926, p. 5.

7,959.   "Roosevelt Spurns Klan Endorsement." New York
         Times. November 30, 1923, p. 3.

7,960.   Rosenthal, Harry F. "Reagan Apologizes For Klan
         Remark." Winston-Salem Journal. September 3,
         1980, p. 1.

7,961.   "Says Democrats Are Inconsistent." New York
         Times. June 30, 1924, p. 3.

7,962.   "Says Klan Quit Politics." New York Times. March
         13, 1926, p. 10.

7,963.   "Says Negroes Back Davis." New York Times.
         October 28, 1924, p. 3.

7,964.   "Scores Republican Prohibition Attitude." New
         York Times. November 4, 1928, p. 2.

7,965.   "Sets Heflin Talk At $125." New York Times.
         June 2, 1928, p. 19.

7,966.   "Shades Of K.K.K. Appear In G.O.P. Propaganda."
         The Muncie (Indiana) Post Democrat. September
         22, 1944, p. 1.

7,967.   "Shavers Sees Klan As Issue 'In Spots'." New
         York Times. July 29, 1924, p. 2.

7,968.   Smith, Robert B. "Klan Spooks In Congress."
         Independent. Vol. 116, June 19, 1926, pp. 718-
         719.

7,969.   Smith, Terence. "Carter Says He Isn't Terming
         Reagan Racist." New York Times. September 19,
         1980, p. B4.

7,970.   "Smith And M'Adoo Managers Predict Swift Victory
          With Balloting For President Beginning Today;
          Klan Fight Hurts Ralston; Antis Lost By 4.30
          Votes." New York Times. June 30, 1924, pp. 1, 2.

7,971.   "Smith And Moody Fail To Meet Here." New York
          Times. June 29, 1927, p. 27.

7,972.   "Smith Men Reject Two Compromises." New York Times.
          June 28, 1924, p. 5.

7,973.   "Smith Stands On Platform." New York Times.
          June 30, 1924, pp. 1, 2.

7,974.   "Socialists Demand Nationalized Mines." New York
          Times. May 23, 1923, p. 23.

7,975.   "Socialists Says Dawes Wants Fascism Here." New
          York Times. August 30, 1924, p. 3.

7,976.   "Socialists Scrap Soap Box Oratory." New York
          Times. May 22, 1923, p. 21.

7,977.   "Some Other City Elections." New York Times.
          November 5, 1925, p. 22.

7,978.   Speers, L.C. "An Elder Statesman Takes Stock Of
          America." New York Times. September 11, 1927,
          Sect. 9, p. 3.

7,979.   _____. "Klan Shadow Falls On Nation's
          Politics." New York Times. November 18, 1923,
          Sect. 9, p. 3.

7,980.   "Straw Votes Catch Interest Of West." New York
          Times. October 19, 1924, Sect. 2, pp. 1, 2.

7,981.   "Support Not Wanted." New York Times. October
          26, 1927, p. 28.

7,982.   "Text Of Bryan's Daybreak Prayer." New York
          Times. June 30, 1924, p. 4.

7,983.   "Text Of Democratic Party Platform's Domestic
          Section As Approved By Committee." New York
          Times. August 25, 1964, p. 24.

7,984.   "Text Of Klan Debate." New York Times. June 29,
          1924, pp. 1, 6.

7,985.   "Text Of The Proposed Anti-Klan Plank Which Will
          Be Urged On Resolutions Committee." New York Times.
          June 23, 1924, p. 1.

7,986.   "3d Party Backers In United Meeting." New York
          Times. August 5, 1924, p. 2.

7,987.   "This Might Elect Him." New York Times. January
          2, 1928, p. 30.

7,988.   "Tom Heflin's Great Task." New York Times.
          October 29, 1923, p. 14.

7,989.   "Two Delegations Split Over Klan." New York Times.
          June 28, 1924, p. 2.

7,990.   "2 Party Chairmen Revive Charges Of Campaign
          Racism." New York Times. September 24, 1980,
          p. A26.

7,991.   "Two Reagan Campaign Aides." New York Times.
          September 4, 1980, p. B11.

7,992.   "Underwood Assails Klan." New York Times.
          October 28, 1923, p. 3.

7,993.   "U.S. Official Attacks Reagan And Ku Klux Klan's
          Endorsement Of Him." San Francisco Chronicle.
          August 7, 1980, p. 8.

7,994.   "U.S. Presidential Election And Ku Klux Klan."
          Christian Science Monitor. August 26, 1980, p. 24.

7,995.   "Underwood Issues A Klan Ultimatum." New York
          Times. June 24, 1924, p. 3.

7,996.   "Victories By Klan Feature Election." New York
          Times. November 6, 1924, pp. 1, 3.

7,997.   "Vote By States On Plank Condemning Ku Klux Klan."
          New York Times. June 29, 1924, p. 1.

7,998.   Waldron, Martin. "Citrus Growers Backing Wallace."
          New York Times. October 6, 1968, p. 74.

7,999.   "Wants All Funds Listed." New York Times.
          November 3, 1928, p. 4.

8,000.   "Wants Dry Funds Sifted By Sargent." New York
          Times. October 24, 1928, p. 3.

8,001.   "Wants Republicans To Denounce Klan." New York
          Times. December 11, 1923, p. 13.

8,002.   Weisman, Steven R. "Bush Assails Carter on 'Ugly
          Insinuations' Of Racism." New York Times.
          September 18, 1980, p. B10.

8,003.   Wicker, Tom. "Democratic Convention Opened;
          Humphrey Gaining For 2d Place; Klan, Birchers, Reds
          Condemned." New York Times. August 25, 1964,
          pp. 1, 22.

8,004.   Wicklein, John. "Rockefeller Hails Kennedy's '60 Bid As U.S. Milestone." New York Times. November 12, 1959, p. 1.

8,005.   "Willis And Smith Predicted By Means." New York Times. September 4, 1927, p. 10.

8,006.   "Woman Explains Shift In Klan Vote." New York Times. June 30, 1924, pp. 1, 3.

8,007.   "Woman Klan Head Opposes Smith." New York Times. July 11, 1927, p. 23.

8,008.   "Won't Investigate Wille Brandt Talks." New York Times. October 6, 1928, p. 2.

8,009.   "Won't Reject Klan Backing." New York Times. August 3, 1964, p. 10.

8,010.   "World Out For Smith." New York Times. June 23, 1924, p. 3.

8,011.   "Would Bar Klan As Political Issue." New York Times. November 23, 1924, p. 14.

8,012.   "You're Another." New Republic. Vol. 183, September 27, 1980, p. 7.

4. COUNTRIES

A. AUSTRALIA

8,013.   "Nazi Group In Australia Linked To Ku Klux Klan." New York Times. February 22, 1960, p. 5.

B. CANADA

8,014.   "Activities Of The Ku Klux Klan In Saskatchewan." Queen's Quarterly (Canada). Vol. 35, Autumn, 1928, pp. 592-609.

8,015.   "Blame Church Fires On Klan In Canada." New York Times. December 6, 1922, p. 4.

8,016.   Calderwood, William. "The Decline Of The Progressive Party In Saskatchewan, 1925-1930." Saskatchewan History. Vol. 21, Autumn, 1968, pp. 81-99.

8,017.   Calderwood, William. "Religious Reactions To The
            Ku Klux Klan In Saskatchewan." Saskatchewan
            History. Vol. 26, Autumn, 1973, pp. 103-114.

8,018.   "Calls On Hibernians To Fight The Ku Klux; Deery
            Sees American Liberty In Danger." New York Times.
            July 19, 1923, p. 17.

8,019.   "Canada Ousts Klan Agent." New York Times.
            July 17, 1928, p. 33.

8,020.   "Canada To War On Ku Klux Is Reported." Pittsburgh
            Courier. January 20, 1923, p. 1.

8,021.   "Canadian KKK Members Barred From Entering U.S.
            For Rally In N.Y." San Francisco Chronicle.
            January 9, 1981, p. 2.

8,022.   "Canadian Province Turns To The Klan." New
            York Times. July 8, 1928, Sect. 3, p. 7.

8,023.   "Canada's 'Keep-out' To Klanism." Literary
            Digest. Vol. 76, February 3, 1923, pp. 20-21.

8,024.   "Canadian Paper Dares Ku Klux To Move A Peg."
            Chicago Defender. April 1, 1922, p. 1.

8,025.   "Charter For 'Klan' Refused By Ontario." New
            York Times. February 25, 1925, p. 5.

8,026.   "Guards On Quebec Church." New York Times.
            February 16, 1923, p. 2.

8,027.   "Guilty Of Church Blast." New York Times.
            October 15, 1926, p. 18.

8,028.   Harewood, John. "Media In Love With KKK."
            Contrast (Toronto). October 3, 1980, p. 7.

8,029.   "Hear Klan Organizers In Canada." New York Times.
            May 4, 1924, Sect. 2, p. 7.

8,030.   "Held In Church Bombing." New York Times.
            June 23, 1926, p. 30.

8,031.   "Hibernians Are Urged To Wage War On Ku Klux."
            Pittsburgh Courier. July 28, 1923, p. 1.

8,032.   "How Do We Handle The Klan." Contrast (Toronto).
            October 3, 1980, p. 6.

8,033.   "Immigration Issue In Western Canada." New York
            Times. June 2, 1929, Sect. 3, p. 2.

8,034.   James, Royson. "KKK Given Forum In High School
            History Class." Contrast (Canada). March 13,
            1981, pp. 1, 3.

8,035.   "Keep KKK Out Of Schools." Contrast (Canada).
          March 13, 1981, p. 6.

8,036.   "KKK In Canada." Winston-Salem Sentinel. August
          29, 1980, p. 30.

8,037,   "KKK Link In Plot Called 'Baffling'." Contrast.
          May 1, 1981, p. 1.

8,038.   "Klan Leader Held In Plot." Washington Post.
          February 11, 1982, p. A26.

8,039.   "Klan Leader, In Britain, Hints Subsidiary There."
          New York Times. April 22, 1965, p. 21.

8,040.   "Klan Openly Entering Canada Encounters Official
          Inquiry." New York Times. February 17, 1925, p. 1.

8,041.   "Klan Organizer Ordered Deported." Pittsburgh
          Courier. August 4, 1928, p. 2.

8,042.   "Klan Threatens Calgary." New York Times.
          April 14, 1923, p. 8.

8,043.   "Klan Recruiting Probed In Toronto." Washington
          Star. October 18, 1980, p. A2.

8,044.   "Klansmen In Ontario." New York Times. May 4,
          1930, Sect. 3, p. 4.

8,045.   "Ku Klux Klan; Attempts To Establish Ku Klux Klan
          In Canada." Canadian Forum. Vol. 10, April,
          1930, p. 233.

8,046.   "The Ku Klux Klan In Saskatchewan." Queen's
          Quarterly. Vol. 35, August, 1928, pp. 592-602.

8,047.   "Ku Klux Klan Trails Bullock; Invades Canada."
          Chicago Defender. March 25, 1922, p. 1.

8,048.   "Ku Klux Kanada." MacLeans. Vol. 90, April 4,
          1977, p. 70-71.

8,049.   Malcolm, Andrew H. "Toronto Paper Details Intrigue
          To Invade Dominica." New York Times. May 17, 1981,
          p. 4.

8,050.   "Police Say Prisoner Dynamited Church." New York
          Times. June 22, 1926, p. 25.

8,051.   Smith, Philip G. "Same Problems, New Faces."
          Dollars And Sense. Vol. 6, February/March, 1981,
          pp. 45, 49.

C. CHILE

8,052.   " 'Klan' Group Seized In Chile." New York Times.
           May 25, 1958, p. 3.

D. CUBA

8,053.   "Cubans Here Assail Gen. Garcia's Junta." New
           York Times. April 2, 1924, p. 32.

E. DOMINICA

8,054.   "Alleged Backer Of 'Invasion' Of Dominica Kills
           Himself." New York Times. June 23, 1981, p. A14.

8,055.   "Arrest Of Dominican Coup Conspirators In
           Louisiana." New Orleans Times Picayune. May 2,
           1981, p. 16.

8,056.   "Ten Arrested In New Orleans Over Alleged Plot
           Against Dominica." San Francisco Chronicle.
           April 29, 1981, p. 16.

8,057.   "Attempted KKK Takeover Unifies Dominican Resi-
           dents." The Voice. July 12, 1981, p. 1.

8,058.   "Bizarre Plot To Invade Dominica From U.S.
           Discussed." Los Angeles Times. August 3, 1981,
           p. 1.

8,059.   "Dominica Beefs Up Police And Tightens Immigration
           Since Coup Bid." New Orleans Times Picayune.
           June 27, 1981, p. 18.

8,060.   "Dominica Coup Plot Described To Court." New
           York Times. June 18, 1981, p. A9.

8,061.   "Dominica Plot Defendant Claims Coup Bid Was To
           Benefit U.S." New Orleans Times Picayune.
           June 9, 1981, p. 13.

8,062.   "Ex-KKK Leader Ties Atty's Suicide To Dominica
           Coup Figure's Lie." New Orleans Times Picayune.
           June 23, 1981, p. 9.

8,063.   "Fed. Grand Jury Charges 10 In Connection With
           Dominican Coup Bid." New Orleans Times Picayune.
           May 8, 1981, p. 1.

8,064.   "Fed. Official Says KKK Subpoenas Not Tied To
           Dominica Coup Bid." New Orleans Times Picayune.
           May 5, 1981, Sect. 2, p. 4.

8,065.   "KKK Plotted Invasion." Pittsburgh Courier. May
          16, 1981, pp. 1, 2.

8,066.   "Klansman Tied To Dominica Coup Claims He's A
          Military Adviser." New Orleans Times Picayune.
          June 10, 1981, p. 23.

8,067.   "Klansmen Guilty." Birmingham Times. June 25-27,
          1981, p. 1.

8,068.   "Klansmen Are Among 10 Indicted In Plot On
          Caribbean Island Nation." New York Times. May 8,
          1981, p. A16.

8,069.   "KKK Leader Convicted In Dominica Plot Claims
          Bond Is Too High." New Orleans Times Picayune.
          July 25, 1981, p. 22.

8,070.   "Mercenaries Granted Immunity In Dominica Plot
          Probe." New Orleans Times Picayune. August 6,
          1981, p. 16.

8,071.   Thomas, Jo. "Dominica Unsettled In Wake Of
          Thwarted Invasion." New York Times. June 7,
          1981, p. 32.

8,072.   "3 Of 10 Arrested In Aborted Dominica Plot Tied To
          Neo-Nazi Organs." New Orleans Times Picayune.
          May 1, 1981, p. 25.

8,073.   "3 Men Charged In Caribbean Island Plot Linked
          To Ku Klux Klan." New Orleans Times Picayune.
          April 29, 1981, p. 1.

8,074.   "2 Guilty In New Orleans For Plot On Dominica
          Invasion." New York Times. June 21, 1981, p. 22.

                    F.   FRANCE

8,075.   "Birth Of A Nation Again Banned In Paris, Must Cut
          Out K.K.K. And Negro Scenes." Pittsburgh Courier.
          October 20, 1923, p. 1.

                    G.   GERMANY

8,076.   "Bare German 'Klan' As Foe Of Republic." New
          York Times. September 11, 1925, p. 5.

8,077.   "Berlin Juvenile Klan Proves Den Of Thieves."
          New York Times. October 9, 1925, p. 2.

8,078.   Clark, Conrad. "Harassing Negro GIs In Germany."
          New York Amsterdam News. April 17, 1965, pp. 1,
          3, 4.

8,079.   "Germany Checks Efforts To Form 'Klan' There; Club
          Is Raided; Two Americans Arrested." New York
          Times. September 10, 1925, p. 1.

8,080.   "Germany To Deport Alleged Klansman." New York
          Times. September 21, 1925, p. 8.

8,081.   Griggs, Lee. "Klan Seeks Backers In West Germany."
          Washington Star. June 21, 1981, p. D16.

8,082.   "KKK Activity Reported In West Germany." Bilalian
          News. September 11, 1981, p. 23.

8,083.   "Klan In AF Bases In Germany." Washington Post.
          June 17, 1981, p. A20.

8,084.   "Klan Reported In Lithuania, Aiming At Catholic
          Church." New York Times. July 15, 1928, Sect.
          2 & 3, p. 2.

8,085.   "Klan Sets Up Branches On Air Force Bases." Jet.
          Vol. 60, July 9, 1981, p. 38.

8,086.   "Ku Klux Klan In Germany." Living Age. Vol. 327,
          October 17, 1925, p. 128.

8,087.   "No K.K.K. Found In Augsburg." New York Times.
          April 7, 1960, p. 8.

8,088.   "Officer In Germany Denies U.S. Base Has Klan
          Unit." New York Times. June 3, 1970, p. 8.

8,089.   "Our Klan Crosses The Ocean." New York Times.
          September 11, 1925, p. 22.

                    H.   GREAT BRITAIN

8,090.   Allan, William. "KKK Cross Burned At Home Of
          Indian In English Town." The Worker. June 15,
          1965.

8,091.   "Britain Serves Deportation Order On Klan Leader
          David Duke." New Orleans Times Picayune. March
          14, 1978, p. 16.

8,092.   "Britain To Deport American Ku Klux Klan Leader,
          Bill Wilkinson." New Orleans Times Picayune.
          March 20, 1978, p. 8.

8,093.   "British Activity Discounted." Christian Science
           Monitor. June 30, 1965, p. 7.

8,094.   "British Immigration Officials Send KKK Leader
           Back To U.S." Chicago Tribune. March 21, 1978,
           p. 14.

8,095.   "British Immigration Ousts La. Ku Klux Klan
           Leader." Washington Post. March 21, 1978, p. 8A.

8,096.   "British KKK Investigated." New York Times. May
           14, 1947, p. 18.

8,097.   "British Consul Arrives." New York Times. May 15,
           1957, p. 14.

8,098.   "British To Expel Ku Klux Klan Leader David Duke."
           New Orleans Times Picayune. March 8, 1978, p. 2.

8,099.   "Butler Plays Down KKK Role." Christian Science
           Monitor. May 3, 1957, p. 1.

8,100.   "Claim American GIs KKK Are Playing Key Roles,
           Inciting British Racists." Pittsburgh Courier.
           September 13, 1958, p. 3.

8,101.   "Cross Burned In Britain Again." New York Times.
           June 15, 1965, p. 31.

8,102.   "England Started The Klan." New York Times.
           April 11, 1926, Sect. 2, p. 8.

8,103.   Farnsworth, Clyde H. " 'Klan' In Britain Preaches
           Hatred." New York Times. June 14, 1965, p. 39.

8,104.   Flynn, Laurie and Paul Greengrass. "The Klan's
           Latest Method Of Propagating Its Gospel - TV."
           Listener. Vol. 105, April 16, 1981, p. 497.

8,105.   "KKK Chief Leaves Britain." Baltimore Afro-
           American. April 8, 1978, p. 6.

8,106.   "KKK Wizard Expelled." Christian Science Monitor.
           March 9, 1978, p. 2.

8,107.   "Klan Emperor Wires Lloyd George Support." New
           York Times. October 24, 1923, p. 5.

8,108.   "The Klan - Ye Shall Have Always." Pulse. Vol. 5,
           November, 1947, p. 8.

8,109.   "Klansman Expelled." Christian Science Monitor.
           March 15, 1978, p. 2.

8,110.   "Ku Klux Klan Case In Britain." Christian Science
           Monitor. September 15, 1965, p. 3.

8,111.   "Ku Klux Klan Director Slips Into England Despite
          Ban." New Orleans Times Picayune. March 4, 1978,
          p. 9.

8,112.   "Ku Klux Klan Forms Branch In Britain." New York
          Times. April 30, 1957, p. 7.

8,113.   "Ku Klux Klan Leader From La. Continues To Evade
          British Police." New Orleans Times Picayune.
          March 13, 1978, p. 9.

8,114.   "The Ku Klux Klan In Great Britain Discussed."
          New Orleans Times Picayune. April 16, 1978,
          p. 36.

8,115.   "Ku Klux Klan Leader Holds News Conference In
          Britain." New Orleans Times Picayune. March 5,
          1978, p. 2.

8,116.   "Ku Klux Klansman Bill Wilkinson Detained In
          Britain." Chicago Tribune. March 20, 1978,
          p. 18.

8,117.   "La. KKK Leader Urges British To Watch Ports For
          Non-Whites." New Orleans Times Picayune. March
          7, 1978, Sect. 2, p. 4.

8,118.   "La. Moves To Recall Convicted KKK Leader From
          Great Britain." New Orleans Times Picayune.
          March 16, 1978, p. 8.

8,119.   "London's View Of The Klan Row." Literary Digest.
          Vol. 77, May 19, 1923, p. 20.

8,120.   "Pub Owner Disrupts British Klan Session." New
          York Times. June 13, 1965, p. 2.

8,121.   "Self Styled Ku Klux Klanners In Britain." New
          York Times. July 4, 1965, Sect. 4, p. 2.

8,122.   "The Strange Invasion." Newsweek. Vol. 49,
          May 13, 1957, p. 58.

I.   ITALY

8,123.   Cortesi, Arnaldo. "Truman Assailed By Reds Of
          Italy." New York Times. October 9, 1947, p. 16.

8,124.   "Italian Fasciti Is Not Like U.S. Ku Klux Klan."
          Chicago Defender. October 7, 1922, p. 3.

8,125.   "Song About America Is Censored In Italy." New
          York Times. June 24, 1971, p. 36.

8,126.   "Unita Prints Klan Denial." <u>New York Times</u>.
          October 10, 1947, p. 4.

J. MEXICO

8,127.   "Allege Klan Persecution." <u>New York Times</u>.
          October 6, 1922, p. 28.

K. NEW ZEALAND

8,128.   "Report 1,000 In New Zealand Klan." <u>New York
          Times</u>. August 28, 1923, p. 19.

L. PANAMA

8,129.   "Panama Denies Barring Klan." <u>New York Times</u>.
          September 14, 1926, p. 3.

M. RUSSIA

8,130.   Darnton, John. "Prague's Hard Line Strains Ties
          To U.S." <u>New York Times</u>. November 23, 1979, p.
          A10.

8,131.   "Russia Denounces Klan." <u>New York Times</u>. December
          6, 1946, p. 16.

N. SWEDEN

8,132.   "Neo-Nazi Leader In Sweden Called Texas Klan
          Member." <u>New York Times</u>. May 14, 1965, p. 6.

O. EUROPE

8,133.   " 'Hooded Men' Held Power In Europe." <u>New York
          Times</u>. September 19, 1937, p. 22.

8,134.   "The Klan In Europe." <u>New York Times</u>. July 29,
          1922, p. 6.

8,135.   "Klan Stretches Forth Wings To Conquer Europe."
          <u>Chicago Defender</u>. August 12, 1922, p. 2.

8,136.   Yerkey, Gary. "Links Between Fascist Groups In U.S., Europe?" <u>Christian Science Monitor</u>. November 25, 1980, p. 9.

5. GENERAL

8,137.   Abbott, Robert S. "Ku Klux Made Possible By Bigotry And Cowardice Of American White Man." Chicago Defender. September 2, 1922, p. 1.

8,138.   "Absorbing Volume About Ku Klux Klan." Knoxville News-Sentinel. April 16, 1939.

8,139.   "Accuse Klan Chief Of Irregularities." New York Times. October 30, 1923, p. 22.

8,140.   "Accuses Brower Again." New York Times. October 3, 1937, p. 3.

8,141.   The ACLU And Free Speech." Washington Post. December 28, 1977, p. A18.

8,142.   "A.C.L.U. And The Klan: 'Consider The Consequences'." New York Times. May 13, 1977, p. 26.

8,143.   "ACLU Attacked For Defending Rightist Organizations." Washington Post. July 30, 1981, p. 7A.

9,144.   A.C.L.U. Calls Klan Obnoxious But Defends Its Right To Organize." New York Times. October 10, 1976, p. 19.

9,145.   "ACLU Defense Of Nazi Party And Ku Klux Klan." Washington Post. January 4, 1978, p. 14A.

9,146.   "ACLU Rift With Jewish Member's Over Nazi Groups." Washington Post. December 28, 1977, p. 18A.

9,147.   "A.C.L.U. To Support Klan Chief In Contempt Of Congress Plea." New York Times. September 6, 1966, p. 34.

8,148.   "Adam Clayton Powell, Jr. Endorses Plan To Ban
          KKK." People's Voice. November 13, 1943, p. 15.

8,149.   "Addenda." Washington Post. March 13, 1981, p.
          A16.

8,150.   "ADL Report On KKK - Letter." Chicago Defender.
          December 27, 1979, p. 9.

8,151.   "ADL Report On Ku Klux Klan." Michigan Chronicle.
          December 15, 1979, p. 8A.

8,152.   "AFL Boss Silent On KKK; Says Reds Workers' Foe."
          Chicago Defender. September 21, 1946, p. 12.

8,153.   "AFL Charges Klan Kidnapped Negro." New York
          Times. June 15, 1946, p. 10.

8,154.   "The A.F. Of L.'s Convention." The Messenger.
          Vol. 6, December, 1924, p. 374.

8,155.   "AFL - CIO Support Jewish Veterans." New York
          Times. November 30, 1946, p. 10.

8,156.   "AFSC Deplores KKK." Christian Century. Vol.
          98, October 14, 1981, pp. 1016-1017.

8,157.   Aikman, Duncan. "Prairie Fire." American
          Mercury. Vol. 6, October, 1925, pp. 209-214.

8,158.   "Ain't Nothing You Can Do But Join The Klan."
          Esquire. Vol. 93, March, 1980, pp. 27-37.

8,159.   "Aldermen Condemn Klan As 'Lawless'." New York
          Times. October 12, 1921, p. 5.

8,160.   Alexander, Charles C. "Kleagles And Cash: The Ku
          Klux Klan As A Business Organization, 1915-1930."
          Business History Review. Vol. 39, Autumn, 1965,
          pp. 348-367.

8,161.   "All Reservations Of Court's Friends Win In The
          Senate." New York Times. January 27, 1926, p. 1.

8,162.   "Alleged KKK 'Ire' At Black U.S. Postal Workers."
          Norfolk Journal & Guide. December 7, 1979, p. 9.

8,163.   Allen, Devere. "Substitutes For Brotherhood."
          The World Tomorrow. Vol. 7, March, 1924, pp. 74-
          76.

8,164.   Allen, Frederick L. "KKK." Literary Digest.
          Vol. 124, October 9, 1937, pp. 15-17.

8,165.   Allen, Ward. "A Note On The Origin Of The Ku
          Klux Klan." Tennessee Historical Quarterly.
          Vol. 23, June, 1964, p. 182.

8,166.   American Friends Service Committee. "Ku Klux Klan."
           Cleveland Call & Post. October 24, 1981, p. 8A.

8,167.   "American Friends Committee On KKK - Letter."
           Chicago Defender. October 3, 1981, p. 16.

8,168.   "American Hits U.S. In Prague." New York Times.
           October 10, 1950, p. 20.

8,169.   "America's Greatest Institution: The Ku Klux Klan."
           The Messenger. Vol. 8, April, 1926, pp. 124-125.

8,170.   "American Legion Hits At Klansmen." New York Times.
           May 21, 1923, p. 15.

8,171.   "The American Legion - Our National Ku Klux Klan."
           The Messenger. Vol. 2, February, 1920, p. 4.

8,172.   "American Legion Censures Klan." New York Amsterdam
           News. October 24, 1923, p. 7.

8,173.   "The American Unity League Is Planning To Wage A
           Nationwide Fight Against The Ku Klux Klan."
           Broad Ax. August 19, 1922,.

8,174.   "And The Gun Lobby Still Prevails." New York Times.
           December 30, 1980, p. A10.

8,175.   "And These Are The Children Of God." Collier's.
           Vol. 124, August 6, 1949, p. 74.

8,176.   "Anderson's Alliance To Link Protestants." New
           York Times. June 27, 1925, p. 15.

8,177.   "Answers Klan Leader." New York Times. October 30,
           1923, p. 19.

8,178.   "Anti-Defamation League Of B'Nai B'rith Says KKK
           Is Growing." Chicago Tribune. November 27, 1977,
           p. 36.

8,179.   "Anti-Defamation League Releases Report On Ku Klux
           Klan." Atlanta Daily World. November 20, 1979, p. 1.

8,180.   "Anti-Defamation League Report On Ku Klux Klan."
           Chicago Defender. December 1, 1979, p. 6.

8,181.   "Anti-Japanese Act Speakers' Target." New York
           Times. September 22, 1924, p. 19.

8,182.   "Anti-Klan Bills Urged." New York Times. March
           9, 1952, p. 19.

8,183.   "Anti-Klan Group Calls For Action Against KKK And
           Nazis." San Francisco Chronicle. February 2,
           1981, p. 38.

8,184. "Anti-Klan Group Plans Action Against Racism."
        New York Times. February 2, 1981, p. A12.

8,185. "Anti-Klan Network." Cleveland Call & Post.
        November 24, 1979, p. 9A.

8,186. "Anti-Klan Bill Feared For Effect On Lawful."
        Greensboro Daily News. July 22, 1966.

8,187. "Anti-Klan Bill Defended." Virginian Pilot.
        July 28, 1966.

8.188. "Anti-Klan Call To Negro." New York Times. May
        13, 1924, p. 23.

8,189. "Anti-Klan Forces Win By One Vote." New York Times.
        September 25, 1924, pp. 1, 2.

8,190. "Anti-Klan Lobbying Scheduled In Wash." Indianapo-
        lis Recorder. May 2, 1981, p. 1.

8,191. "Anti-Klan Measure Attacked Anew As House Unit Winds
        Up Hearings." Durham Morning Herald. July 23,
        1966.

8,192. "Anti-Klan Network Seeks More Government Input."
        Pittsburgh Courier. May 23, 1981, pp. 1, 2.

8,193. "Anti-Klan Network Plans 'Spring Offensive'."
        SCLC Magazine. Vol. 10, March/April, 1981, pp.
        48-50.

8,194. "Anti-Klan Network Is To Fight Rise of KKK." Capital
        (D.C.) Spotlight. May 14, 1981, p. 1.

8,195. "Anti-Red Activity Found On The Wane." New York
        Times. June 23, 1924, p. 22.

8,196. "Any Link To Klan Denied By Brower." New York
        Times. October 2, 1937, p. 2.

8,197. "Appeal For Justice For Klan Victims." New York
        Amsterdam News. February 27, 1982, p. 3.

8,198. "Appeals Court Upholds Conviction Of Klansman."
        New York Times. August 15, 1968, p. 44.

8,199. Aptheker, Herbert. "Why Nazis And The KKK Should
        Be Banned." Daily World. January 15, 1981,
        pp. 12, 13.

8,200. "Archbishop Hayes Denounces Ku Klux." New York
        Times. October 17, 1921, p. 8.

8,201.   Arnall, Ellis. "My Battle Against The Klan."
          Coronet. Vol. 20, No. 6, October, 1946,
          pp. 3-8.

8,202.   "Aroused South Pushes To Crush Klan." Christian
          Science Monitor. June 29, 1949, p. 3.

8,203.   "Arrests By FBI Praised In South." New York Times.
          December 7, 1964, p. 39.

8,204.   "Ask Coolidge To Bar Klan." New York Times.
          August 27, 1923, p. 2.

8,205.   "Ask Dies To Investigate Klan Rumor." Norfolk
          Journal & Guide. February 25, 1939, p. 9.

8,206.   "Ask Move On Race Stress." New York Times.
          November 4, 1943, p. 25.

8,207.   Askari, Nyewusi. "White Power, Klan Activity
          Increasing In Nation." Portland Observer.
          November 20, 1980, pp. 1, 2.

8,208.   "Asks House Group Study Propaganda." New York
          Times. January 24, 1946, p. 15.

8,209.   "Asks House Klan Inquiry." New York Times.
          December 7, 1922, p. 7.

8,210.   "Asserts Law Bars Black." New York Times.
          October 3, 1937, p. 3.

8,211.   "Asserts 'Whispers' Call Willkie Nazi." New York
          Times. September 29, 1940, p. 39.

8,212.   "An Attack Gave It Importance." New York Times.
          May 28, 1925, p. 20.

8,213.   "Attack... The FBI vs. The Ku Klux Klan - CBS
          Reviewed." Washington Post. February 21, 1975,
          p. 14B.

8,214.   "Attacks Follow Defense Of Klan." New York Times.
          June 7, 1926, p. 2.

8,215.   "Attacks Klan At Negro Meeting." New York Times.
          September 15, 1925, p. 13.

8,216.   "Attacks Legion As Foe Of Freedom." New York Times.
          May 16, 1927, p. 12.

8,217.   "Attorney General Alert To Black Muslim Moves."
          New York Times. July 3, 1963, p. 10.

8,218.   "Attorney General Clark Denounces Ku Klux Klan."
          New York Herald Tribune. May 14, 1946.

8,219.   "Attorney General Daugherty And The Ku Klux."
           The Messenger. Vol. 4, October, 1922, p. 498.

8,220.   "Author Discusses Research For Book On Ku Klux
           Klan." Houston Post. October 29, 1978, p. 18AA.

8,221.   "Authoritative Only For The Timid." New York
           Times. October 14, 1924, p. 22.

8,222.   "Authority On The Klan: Donald Thomas Appell."
           New York Times. October 29, 1965, p. 28.

8,223.   "Awakening America's Conscience." USA Today.
           Vol. 109, June, 1981, p. 5.

8,224.   Babcock, Charles R. "Booklet On Klan Attacked For
           Cast Given U.S. Society." Washington Post.
           December 2, 1981, p. A22.

8,225.   "Backlash Boosts Klan Membership." Knoxville News-
           Sentinel. January 19, 1967, p. 1.

8,226.   Bachr, Harry W. Jr. "Out Of The Reconstruction
           Days Comes A Law Now Serving U.S. In Way Creators
           Never Foresaw." New York Herald Tribune. May 29,
           1938.

8,227.   "Backlash Fuels Klan's New Growth." News American.
           December 7, 1980, pp. 17A-18A.

8,228.   Bagnall, Robert W. "The Spirit Of The Ku Klux
           Klan." Opportunity. Vol. 1, September, 1923, pp.
           265-267.

8,229.   _____. "The Three False Gods Of Civilization."
           The Messenger. Vol. 5, August, 1923, pp. 789-791.

8,230.   Baldwin, Roger N. "Haters Among Us." Saturday
           Review Of Literature. Vol. 48, June 19, 1965,
           p. 36.

8,231.   "Ball Urges Curb On Union Powers." New York Times.
           May 19, 1946, p. 9.

8,232.   "Ban The Klan." Jet. Vol. 59, October 2, 1980,
           p. 5.

8,233.   Bancroft, Griffing. "Facts On KKK Suppressed 6
           Years By House Un-American Activities Group."
           PM. June 16, 1947.

8,234.   "Bankhead Hits At Black Critics." New York Times.
           September 15, 1937, p. 2.

8,235.   Barron, John. "The FBI's Secret War Against The
Ku Klux Klan." Reader's Digest. Vol. 88, January,
1966, pp. 87-92.

8,236.   Bassett, T.R. "Say HUAC Probe Of KKK Will Hit
Rights Groups." The Worker. April 20, 1965, p. 8.

8,237.   Batten, James K. "Jury Convicts Klan's Leader Of
Contempt." Charlotte Observer. September 15, 1966.

8,238.   _____. "Verdict Due Today For KKK Leader."
Charlotte Observer. September 14, 1966.

8,239.   Beal, Frances M. "Let's Unite To Stamp Out The
Klan." Black Scholar. Vol. 11, March/April,
1980, pp. 2-9.

8,240.   Beazell, W.P. "The Rise Of The Ku Klux Klan."
The World Tomorrow. Vol. 7, March, 1924, pp. 71-
73.

8,241.   Belair, Felix, Jr. "Kefauver Cites Smear Campaign."
New York Times. August 31, 1960, p. 19.

8,242.   _____." "President Denies U.S. Imperialism In
Marshall Plan." New York Times. October 10,
1947, pp. 1, 4.

8,243.   "Belgian League For Human Rights Pres. Sees Int'l.
Fascism Links." Christian Science Monitor.
November 25, 1980, p. 9.

8,244.   Bell, Edward P. "Israel Zangwill On The Ku Klux
Klan." Landmark. Vol. 6, June, 1924, pp. 441-
418.

8,245.   "Benson Forsees Successor To Klan." New York
Times. November 12, 1924, p. 6.

8,246.   Bentz, Thomas Orrin." We Can Stop The Klan."
C.R.J. Reporter. Summer, 1980, pp. 30-32.

8,247.   Berger, Victor L. "Berger Defends His War Record;
Sees New Fascist: In Ku Klux Klan." New York
Times. December 3, 1922, Sect. 9, p. 3.

8,248.   "Bernstein Attacks Klan." New York Times.
September 4, 1924, p. 5.

8,249.   Berry, Abrer W. "There's $ Sign On Klan Robes:
Senator Would Overthrow NAACP." Daily Worker.
October 30, 1955, pp. 2, 13.

8,250.   Besal, Dorothy. "Reasonable Racism." Community.
Vol. 24, May, 1965, p. 3.

8,251.   "Beware - Spooks On The Rise." Scoop U.S.A.
          October 31, 1980, p. 1.

8,252.   "Bid For Negro Vote Made By Democrats." New
          York Times. August 27, 1924, pp. 1, 2.

8,253.   "Big Navy Men Seek To Put Peace Pact In Second
          Place." New York Times. December 16, 1928, pp.
          1, 2.

8,254.   Bigart, Homer. "Klan's Founder, In 1866, Stressed
          Humaneness." New York Times. March 27, 1965,
          p. 11.

8,255.   "Bigotry Incarnate." New York Times. March 10,
          1980, p. 19.

8,256.   "Bill On Klan Will Get Hearing." Winston-Salem
          Journal. March 20, 1966.

8,257.   "The Bird And The Beast." New York Times.
          September 29, 1933, p. 18.

8,258.   " 'A Bit Surprising' To Bulow." New York Times.
          September 16, 1937, p. 14.

8,259.   "Black Jailer And Imprisoned Ku Klux Klan - Stayskal
          Cartoon." Los Angeles Times. November 11, 1979,
          Sect. 5, p. 5.

8,260.   "Black Lawyer Challenges Right Of KKK To Exist."
          Jet. Vol. 58, August 21, 1980, p. 4.

8,261.   "Black Leaders And Foreign vs. Domestic Issues -
          Letter." Michigan Chronicle. November 24, 1979,
          p. 10A.

8,262.   "Black Leaders Score Rise Of Hate Groups."
          Washington Post. May 6, 1981, p. A15.

8,263.   "Black Panthers In The K.K.K." New York Times.
          September 27, 1970, Sect. 4, p. 14.

8,264.   "Black Police Group Asks For FBI Probe On Klan."
          Jet. Vol. 56, July 12, 1979, p. 7.

8,265.   "Blacks Remembering 'Jim Crow' Of 1950's."
          Michigan Chronicle. November 3, 1979, p. 9A.

8,266.   Blair, William M. "Obstructing Peace Hit By
          Eisenhower." New York Times. September 4, 1946,
          p. 2.

8,267.   "Blames Catholics For Mexican Rows." New York
          Times. March 10, 1927, p. 5.

8,268.   "Blessing In Bigotry Seen." New York Times.
          July 8, 1927, p. 18.

8,269.   "B'nai B'rith Calls On Fed. To End Klan Terrorism."
          Milwaukee Community Journal. Oct. 29-November 5,
          1980, pp. 3, 18.

8,270.   "B'nai B'rith Releases Report On Ku Klux Klan."
          New York Amsterdam News. November 24, 1979, p. 5.

8,271.   "B'nai B'rith Releases Study Of Ku Klux Klan."
          Baltimore Afro-American. November 24, 1979, p. 6.

8,272.   "B'nai B'rith Study Shows Increase In KKK Violence
          And Strength." New Orleans Times Picayune.
          November 15, 1979, p. 22.

8,273.   "Bond With Wizard." Washington Star. December
          5, 1980, p. A2.

8,274.   "Both Leave The Klan Unexplained." New York Times.
          June 5, 1925, p. 16.

8,275.   Bracker, Milton. "Segregation Conflict: Role
          Of The 'Councils'." New York Times. February
          26, 1956, Sect. 4, p. 9.

8,276.   Braden, Anne. "A Klan Revival." The Review.
          Vol. 1, January, 1981, pp. 14-16.

8,277.   _____. "Lessons From A History Of Struggle."
          Southern Exposure. Vol. 8, Summer, 1980, pp.
          56-61.

3,278.   Braden, George. "The Ku Klux Klan: An Apology."
          Southern Bivouac. Vol. 4, September, 1885,
          pp. 103-109.

8,279.   Bradley, P. "Psycho-Analyzing The Ku Klux Klan."
          American Review. Vol. 2, November-December, 1924,
          pp. 683-686.

3,280.   "Branch Rickey Defies Klan." New York Age.
          January 22, 1949, p. 12.

3,281.   "Break The Klan Now." New York Times. August 26,
          1924, p. 10.

8,282.   "Bridges Recalls Hearing Demand." New York Times.
          September 15, 1937, p. 2.

8,283.   Brier, Royce. "Nightshirt Knights." Forum.
          Vol. 106, July, 1946, pp. 54-55.

8.284.   Brisbane, Frances. "... 'This Terrible Under-
          current In Our Society'." New York Times.
          December 2, 1977, Sect. 21, p. 26.

8,285. "B'rith Abraham To Fight Ku Klux." New York Times.
        November 23, 1922, p. 23.

8,286. "Broadside Of Klan Suits." New York Times.
        December 6, 1921, p. 5.

8,287. Brooks, Fred. "Criminal Violence Escalates Against
        Minorities." Criminal Justice Issues. Vol. 6,
        June, 1981, pp. 1-2.

8,288. "Broughton Chosen As Leader Of Elks." New York
        Times. July 10, 1946, p. 24.

8,289. Broun, Heywood. "It Seems To Me." New York World.
        December 23, 1925.

8,290. _____. "Up Pops The Wizard." New Republic.
        Vol. 99, June 21, 1939, pp. 186-187.

8,291. Brown, Francis. "The Violent Story Of The Klan."
        New York Times Book Review. April 23, 1939, pp.
        4-5.

8,292. Brown, Les. "7 PBS Stations Reject Klansman And
        Nazi Interview." New York Times. October 8, 1977,
        p. 48.

8,293. _____. "Two PSB Programs Creating Problems."
        New York Times. September 27, 1977, p. 78.

8,294. _____. "WNET Rejects Black Program." New
        York Times. November 24, 1977, p. C20.

8,295. "Brown Assails Klan 'Bigotry'." New York Times.
        September 14, 1937, p. 18.

8,296. Brown, William G. "The Ku Klux Movement."
        Atlantic Monthly. Vol. 87, May, 1901,
        pp. 634-644.

8,297. "Bryan May Discuss Klan." New York Times. August
        26, 1924, p. 2.

8,298. Buchwald, Art. "FBI Infiltration Of Ku Klux Klan."
        Washington Post. December 9, 1975, p. 1C.

8,299. _____. "The Shoes Below The Sheets, Or
        Creating Chaos In The Klan." Washington Post.
        December 9, 1978, p. C1.

8,300. "Bund, Klan Linked At Sedition Trial." New York
        Times. July 18, 1944, p. 32.

8,301. "Burke Tries To Phone Black." New York Times.
        September 16, 1937, p. 14.

8,302.   "Burnings At Stake At Behest Of Evans Told At Klan
          Trial." New York Times. April 11, 1928, pp. 1, 14.

8,303.   " 'Burning Cross' Is Daring Expose Of Ku Klux Klan."
          Pulse. Vol. 5, November, 1947, pp. 14-15.

8,304.   "Burns Gets Orders To Trail Ku Klux." New York
          Times. September 25, 1921, p. 14.

8,305.   "Bury It." New York Amsterdam News. August 29,
          1923, p. 12.

8,306.   "Buying And Selling The Ku Klux Klan." New York
          Times. February 14, 1924, p. 16.

8,307.   "Cal. Atty. Gen. Warns Ku Klux Klan Making Gains
          In State." Los Angeles Times. September 30,
          1980, p. 3.

8,308.   Calbreath, Dean. "Kovering The Klan." Columbia
          Journalism Review. Vol. 19, March/April, 1981,
          pp. 42-45.

8,309.   "Call Truman Lax On Klan." New York Times.
          August 19, 1946, p. 29.

8,310.   Callaway, E.E. "Notes On A Kleagle." American
          Mercury. Vol. 43, February, 1938, pp. 248-249.

8,311.   "Calls Klan Congress To Reform The Order." New
          York Times. January 3, 1924, p. 3.

8,312.   "Calls Klan Misguided." New York Times. January
          25, 1926, p. 23.

8,313.   "Calls Ku Klux Klan Practically Bankrupt." New
          York Times. December 15, 1921, p. 12.

8,314.   "Calls Letter On Klan Attempt At Publicity." New
          York Times. December 29, 1923, p. 6.

8,315.   "Calls Rivals 'Frantic'." New York Times.
          October 28, 1944, p. 30.

8,316.   Campbell, Will. "Clean Up The Botulism."
          Southern Exposure. Vol. 8, Summer, 1980, p. 99.

8,317.   Canby, Vincent. "Film: 2 Documentaries On Cities
          And The Klan." New York Times. September 29,
          1981, p. C6.

8,318.   "Can't Be Intimidated, Negro Leaders Warn." New
          York Times. January 20, 1952, p. 50.

8,319.   "Carolinas Strike At Klan Violence." New York
          Times. August 29, 1951, p. 34.

8,320.   Carter, Everett. "Cultural History Written With
          Lightening: The Significance Of The Birth Of A
          Nation." _American Quarterly_. Vol. 12, Fall, 1960,
          pp. 347-357.

8,321.   "Carter Orders Justice Dept. To Use FBI To Probe
          KKK Activity." _Atlanta Daily World_. November 8,
          1979, p. 1.

8,322.   Carter, Ulish. "Ku Klux Klan Is Not The Real
          Problem." _Florida Courier_. November 8, 1980,
          pp. 1, 3.

8,323.   "Carter Urges Klan Probe After Talks With Blacks."
          Jet. Vol. 57, November 22, 1979, p. 8.

8,324.   Catchpole, Terry. "Operation Contempts; HUAC vs.
          KKK." _National Review_. Vol. 18, February 22,
          1966, p. 152.

8,325.   Catledge, Turner. " 'Propaganda' Seen." _New York
          Times_. March 2, 1937, p. 1.

8,326.   "Catholics Protest Black." _New York Times_.
          October 5, 1937, p. 20.

8,327.   "Catholics Warned To Encourage Klan." _New York
          Times_. December 6, 1943, p. 18.

8,328.   "Caucasian Crusade." _Outlook_. Vol. 155, August
          6, 1930, p. 539.

8,329.   "Chain Letters Are Indicated." _New York Times_.
          March 9, 1937, p. 15.

8,330.   "A Challenge." _New York Times_. August 24, 1924,
          Sect. 2, p. 4.

8,331.   Chalmers, David. "The Rise And Fall Of The
          Invisible Empire Of The Ku Klux Klan." _Contemporary
          Review_. Vol. 237, August, 1980, pp. 57-64.

8,332.   "Changing Values." _Forbes_. Vol. 120, September
          15, 1977, pp. 241-248.

8,333.   "Charges Murder Within The Klan." _New York Times_.
          February 25, 1924, p. 17.

8,334.   "Charges Klan Head Is Taking Tribute." _New York
          Times_. July 17, 1922, p. 13.

8,335.   Chestnut, J. Le Count. "Klux Chief Winces At Big
          Inquiry." _Chicago Defender_. October 15, 1921,
          p. 3.

8,336.   Chestnut, J. Le Count. "U.S. Drops Ku Klux Probe."
           Chicago Defender. October 22, 1921, p. 1.

8,337.   "Chief Faces Trial." Christian Science Monitor.
           October 27, 1951, p. 8.

8,338.   "Chiefs Of KKK Limit Their Pleas Of Guilty."
           Durham Morning Herald. November 19, 1966.

8,339.   "Choice Of Black Roosevelt Secret." New York
           Times. October 2, 1937, p. 3.

8,340.   "Choose M'Naugher Presbyterian Head." New York
           Times. September 23, 1921, p. 15.

8,341.   " 'Christ Versus Ku Klux' - His Subject." New
           York Amsterdam News. December 20, 1922, p. 1.

8,342.   "Church Unit Assails U.S. Justice System." New
           York Times. November 11, 1979, p. 4.

8,343.   "Church Urges Members To Struggle Against KKK."
           Jet. Vol. 60, April 2, 1981, p. 36.

8,344.   "Churches Vow KKK Offensive." National Catholic
           Reporter. Vol. 16, December 28, 1979, p. 1.

8,345.   "Churchmen Favor The World Court." New York Times.
           October 23, 1923, p. 21.

8,346.   "Citizen's Councils Vie With Klans." Christian
           Science Monitor. July 10, 1957, p. 3.

8,347.   "Civil Rights Activist Andrew Young Address
           Psychiatry Conv. In New Orleans." New Orleans
           Times Picayune. May 14, 1981, p. 16.

8,348.   "Civil Rights Law." New York Times. June 12,
           1979, p. 13.

8,349.   "Civil Rights Leaders Discuss Klan And Racial
           Tension Rise." Norfolk Journal & Guide. August
           27, 1980, pp. 1, 2.

8,350.   "Civil Rights Leaders Testify To U.S. House
           Com. On Violence." New Orleans Times Picayune.
           June 4, 1981, Sect. 6, p. 3.

8,351.   "Civil Rights Reunion: Challenge To Complacency."
           Christian Science Monitor. November 6, 1979, p. 24.

8,352.   "Clark Would Not Have Voted." New York Times.
           September 16, 1937, p. 14.

8,353.   "Clarke Quits Post As Head Of Ku Klux." New York
           Times. October 5, 1922, p. 10.

8,354.   "Clergy Give Thanks For New Peace Hope." New York
          Times. November 25, 1921, p. 17.

8,355.   Coates, Paul V. "Will Klan 'Ride Again' - To Thwart
          High Courts?" Pittsburgh Courier. October 9,
          1954, p. 11.

8,356.   Cohen, Stanley. "The Assault On Victorianism In
          The Twentieth Century." American Quarterly.
          Vol. 27, December, 1975, pp. 604-625.

8,357.   "Col. Simmons Begins Defense Of The Klan." New
          York Times. March 19, 1922, p. 18.

8,358.   "Colby Pays Tribute To Jews In War." New York
          Times. May 21, 1923, p. 11.

8,359.   Cole, Nancy. "How FBI Aided Klan Terrorists."
          Militant. Vol. 39, December 12, 1975, p. 3.

8,360.   _____. "Informer Reveals FBI's Role In Ku Klux
          Klan Attacks." Intercontinental Press. Vol. 13,
          December 15, 1975, pp. 758-759.

8,361.   "College 'Convention' Assails Intolerance."
          New York Times. May 19, 1928, p. 14.

8,362.   "Colonel Simmons, And $146,500 From K.K.K. To
          K.F.S." Literary Digest. Vol. 80, March 8,
          1924, pp. 36, 38, 40.

8,363.   "College Students Shun Extremists." New York
          Times. February 7, 1971, p. 54.

8,364.   "Columbus Orator Attacks The Klan." New York
          Times. October 13, 1924, p. 17.

8,365.   Commager, Henry S. "Does The Klan Ride To Its
          Death? Scholastic. Vol. 49, October 7, 1946,
          pp. 7-8.

8,366.   "Comment Of Press Is Critical Of Justice Black."
          New York Times. October 2, 1937, p. 2.

8,367.   "Committee Against Racism Campaigns Against Ku
          Klux Klan And Nazis." Washington Post. March 9,
          1978, p. 1C.

8,368.   "Communists Opposed." New York Times. November
          11, 1946, p. 22.

8,369.   "Complete The Picture." New York Amsterdam News.
          May 13, 1925, p. 16.

8,370.   "Compulsory Laws For Schools Scored." New York
          Times. May 6, 1925, p. 22.

8,371.   "Condemns Divorce, Masons And Klan." New York
          Times. November 13, 1922, p. 6.

8,372.   "Condemn Religious Issue." New York Times.
          August 19, 1924, p. 30.

8,373.   "Congress Asked By A.D.A. To Refuse Contempt
          Step." New York Times. January 23, 1966, p. 58.

8,374.   "Congress Inquiry In Ku Klux Is Off." New York
          Times. October 18, 1921, p. 6.

8,375.   "Congress vs. Extremists." American Legion
          Magazine. Vol. 82, January 1967, pp. 12-14.

8,376.   "Congressional Black Caucus Calls For National
          Outcry Against Klan Activiyy." United Church
          Of Christ Commission News. Vol. 9, January-
          February, 1980, p. 3.

8,377.   "Congressional Inquiries." Criminal Justice
          Issues. Vol. 6, June, 1981, pp. 2-8.

8,378.   Conklin, William R. "Eisenhower Sets Parleys
          On Policy." New York Times. November 17, 1952,
          p. 18.

8,379.   Conroy, Thomas M. "The Ku Klux Klan And The
          American Clergy." Ecclesiastical Review.
          Vol. 70, January, 1924, pp. 47-59.

8,380.   "Conspiracy Of Klan To Control Whole Nation
          Exposed By Rigid Investigation." Pittsburgh
          Courier. November 3, 1923, p. 16.

8,381.   "Conversions Were Impossible." New York Times.
          December 20, 1922, p. 18.

8,382.   "Conviction Of Klan Leader Upheld By Appeals
          Court." New York Times. August 16, 1968, p. 13.

8,383.   Cook, Samuel D. "Political Movements And Organi-
          zations." Journal of Politics. Vol. 26, February
          1, 1964, pp. 130-153.

8,384.   "Coolidge Demands Tolerance For All As Basis For
          Peace At Home And Abroad; Attacks Propaganda By
          Army Officers." New York Times. October 7, 1925,
          pp. 1, 2.

8,385.   "Copeland Presses Attack On Black In City Campaign."
          New York Times. September 14, 1937, p. 1.

8,386.   "Corliss Lamont Accused By House." New York Times.
          June 27, 1946, p. 4.

8,387.   Corrigan, Richard. "Defiance Voiced By Klan
          Wizard." Washington Post. January 8, 1966.

8,388.   "A Counterattack Takes Hold." News American.
          December 7, 1980, pp.17A-18A.

8,389.   "Counters A Klan Order." New York Times. April
          1, 1923, Sect. 1, Part 2, p. 5.

8,390.   "Court Delays Klan Head Trial." Greensboro Daily
          News. October 5, 1966.

8,391.   "Court Permits Klan Leader To Avoid Stay In Negro
          Jail." New York Times. February 4, 1969, p. 29.

8,392.   "Court Reworks Calendar; Delays Klan Trials."
          Charlotte Observer. October 5, 1966.

8,393.   Coy, Harold. "Catholics, Jews, Negroes, Labor...:
          The Klan Hates Them All." Equality. 1940, pp.
          55-61.

8,394   . "The Klan Hates Them All." Equality.
          Vol. 2, April, 1940, pp. 9-14.

8,395.   Crawford, Kenneth. "Kurtains For The Klan."
          Newsweek. Vol. 66, December 13, 1965, pp. 34-35.

8,396.   Crewdson, John M. "Ex-Operative Says He Worked
          For F.B.I. To Disrupt Political Activities Up To
          '74." New York Times. February 24, 1975, p. 36.

8,397.   . "Saxbe Says Top Officials Had Some
          Knowledge Of F.B.I.'s Drive To Disrupt Various
          Political Groups." New York Times. November 19,
          1974, p. 27.

8,398.   Crews, Harry. "The Buttondown Terror Of David
          Duke." Playboy. Vol. 27, February, 1980, pp. 102-
          108.

8,399.   Cripps, Thomas R. "The Reaction Of The Negro To
          The Motion Picture 'Birth Of A Nation'." The
          Historian. Vol. 25, May, 1963, pp. 344-362.

8,400.   Crockett, Phyllis. "Ku Klux Klan." Dollars &
          Sense. Vol. 6, June/July, 1980, pp. 94, 96-99.

8,401.   "Curley Laughs At Klan." New York Times.
          December 30, 1922, p. 26.

8,402.   "Current Events Classroom - HUAC Hearings On KKK."
          National Observer. October 25, 1965, p. 5.

8,403.   "Current Events Classroom - Ku Klux Klan."
          National Observer. July 27, 1964, p. 5.

8,404.   "Current Events Classroom - Ku Klux Klan." National
          Observer. September 10, 1962, p. 5.

8,405.   "Curriculum On KKK Now Available." International
          Books For Children. Vol. 12, No. 4-5, 1981,
          pp. 32-33.

8,406.   Curry, Brack. "Klan Probe On In Seven States;
          U.S. May Broaden Its Inquiry." Washington
          Evening Star. August 19, 1946.

8,407.   Dabney, Dick. "Mean Talk, Mean Times."
          Washingtonian. Vol. 16, January, 1981, pp. 88-91,
          110-111.

8,408.   "Dangerous Klan Tactics." New York Times. April
          11, 1926, Sect. 2, p. 8.

8,409.   Daniels, Jonathan. "K.K.K. Versus U.S.O."
          Nation. Vol. 153, November 8, 1941, pp. 456-457.

8,410.   "Dark Days In Weird Week." Time. Vol. 86,
          October 29, 1965, pp. 29-30.

8,411.   "Data On Un-Americanism." New York Times.
          February 18, 1952, p. 18.

8,412.   "Daugherty Endorses Inquiry." New York Times.
          October 5, 1921, p. 18.

8,413.   "Daugherty Orders Ku Klux Inquiry." New York Times.
          September 21, 1921, p. 19.

8,414.   "Daugherty To Call Ku Klux Leaders." New York
          Times. September 23, 1921, p. 18.

8,415.   "David Duke, Grand Wizard Of Knights Of KKK, Tours
          New England." Chicago Defender. December 10,
          1979, p. 5.

8,416.   "David Duke, Grand Wizard Of Knights Of KKK, Enters
          Presidential Race." Bilalian News. December 28,
          1979, p. 4.

8,417.   "David Duke Requests Equal Time To Present Other
          Side Of Roots." New Orleans Times Picayune.
          March 5, 1977, Sect. 2, p. 2.

8,418.   "Davis Assails Klan, Fall And 'Oil Fraud' In
          Denver Speeches." New York Times. September 12,
          1924, pp. 1, 2.

8,419.   "Davis Denounces Ku Klux Klan By Name; Challenges
          Coolidge To Do Likewise And Take That Issue Out
          Of Campaign." New York Times. August 23, 1924,
          p. 1.

8,420.　"Davis Will Answer Coolidge On Stump; First Speech Friday." New York Times. August 16, 1924, p. 1.

8,421.　"Davis Wins Praise For Attacking Klan." New York Times. August 24, 1924, pp. 1, 3.

8,422.　"DC Catholic Archbishop Baum Tells Of Concern Over Ku Klux Klan." Washington Post. April 15, 1977, p. 6E.

8,423.　Deaton, Ron. "Klan Revival: Work Of D. Duke." Progressive. Vol. 39, June, 1975, p. 29.

8,424.　"Declares Publicity Is Way To End Klan." New York Times. April 15, 1923, p. 16.

8,425.　"Dedicated Klansman: Robert M. Shelton, Jr." New York Times. October 19, 1965, p. 28.

8,426.　"The Deep South." New York Times. November 28, 1948, Sect. 4, p. 6.

8,427.　"Defender Digs Up History Of Ku Klux Klan." Chicago Defender. September 24, 1921, p. 2.

8,428.　"Defends 'Women Of Klan'." New York Times. November 7, 1923, p. 15.

8,429.　"A Defense Of The Ku Klux Klan." Literary Digest. Vol. 76, January 20, 1923, pp. 18-19.

8,430.　"Defers Klan Inquiry." New York Times. October 7, 1921, p. 8.

8,431.　Degler, Carl N. "A Century Of The Klan: A Review Article." Journal of Southern History. Vol. 31, November, 1965, pp. 435-443.

8,432.　Delaney, Paul. "U.S. To Study Race Issues Among Troops In Europe." New York Times. August 31, 1970, p. 3.

8,433.　"Delay On Loyalty Post." New York Times. June 28, 1955, p. 12.

8,434.　"Demands Black Resign." New York Times. October 5, 1937, p. 20.

8,435.　"Democrats Hit Klan In New Hampshire." New York Times. September 27, 1924, p. 3.

8,436.　"Denial By Ku Klux Klan." New York Times. August 8, 1921, p. 3.

8,437.　"Denies Catholic-Klan Link." New York Times. March 9, 1928, p. 27.

8,438.   "Denies Grant Precedent Applies." New York Times.
          November 28, 1922, p. 23.

8,439.   "Denies He Belongs To Anti-Klan Body." New York
          Times. November 13, 1923, p. 22.

8,440.   "Denies New Fight On Klan." New York Times.
          August 29, 1924, p. 3.

8,441.   "Deposed Goblins Say Klan Is Broken." New York
          Times. December 3, 1921, p. 7.

8,442.   De Silver, Albert. "The Ku Klux Klan: 'Soul Of
          Chivalry'." Nation. Vol. 113, September 14, 1921,
          pp. 285-186.

8,443.   Desmond, Shaw. "K.K.K.: The Strongest Secret
          Society On Earth." Wide World Magazine. Vol. 47,
          September, 1921, pp. 355-365.

8,444.   "Dewey's Victory Seen By Brownell." New York Times.
          October 28, 1944, p. 8.

8,445.   "Dies Again Urged To Probe K.K. Klan." New York
          Amsterdam News. June 24, 1939, p. 2.

8,446.   "Dies Committee Members Agree To Probe K.K.K."
          New York Amsterdam News. June 3, 1939, p. 2.

8,447.   "Did Grant Break The Old Klan." New York Times.
          August 31, 1924, Sect. 8, p. 10.

8,448.   "A Difference With A Distinction." New York Times.
          January 24, 1923, p. 12.

8,449.   "Discontinue Klan, Negro Press Stories." Pittsburgh
          Courier. October 13, 1928, p. 9.

8,450.   "Diverse Groups Merge Efforts To Combat Revival
          Of Ku Klux Klan." Los Angeles Times. December 8,
          1980, p. 1.

8,451.   "Dissension In The Klan." Pittsburgh Courier.
          November 19, 1927, editorial page.

8,452.   "Dixon Condemns Klan." New York Times. August 5,
          1924, p. 18.

8,453.   "Don't Judge South By Its KKK And Bilbo." New
          York Amsterdam News. August 31, 1946, p. 9.

8,454.   Douglas, Lloyd C. "Patriotism Of Hatred."
          Christian Century. Vol. 40, October 25, 1923,
          pp. 1371-1374.

8,455.   "Dr. Mims Disputed On Klan." New York Times.
          December 19, 1926, Sect. 8, p. 12.

8,456.   Drebinger, John. "Dodgers Answer Klan Challenge."
          New York Times. January 15, 1949, p. 12.

8,457.   "Dressed To Hate." New York Times. December 17,
          1980, p. A34.

8,458.   "Drive To Expose Klan." U.S. News & World Report.
          Vol. 58, April 12, 1965, p. 69.

8,459.   "Dry Law Breakers Likened To 'Reds'." New York
          Times. February 11, 1923, Sect. 2, p. 1.

8,460.   Du Bois, W.E.B. "The Shape Of Fear." North
          American Review. Vol. 223, June-August, 1926,
          pp. 291-303.

8,461.   Duffus, Robert L. "Ancestry And End Of The Ku
          Klux Klan." World's Work. Vol. 46, September,
          1923, pp. 527-536.

8,462.   _____. "Counter-mining The Ku Klux Klan."
          World's Work. Vol. 46, July, 1923, pp. 275-
          284.

8,463.   _____. "The Ku Klux Klan In The Middle West."
          World's Work. Vol. 46, August, 1923, pp. 363-372.

8,464.   _____. "Salesmen (KKK) Of Hate." World's
          Work. Vol. 42, October, 1923, pp. 461-469.

8,465.   Dunning, Frederick A. "Ku Klux Fulfills The
          Scripture." Christian Century. Vol. 41,
          September 18, 1924, pp. 1205-1207.

8,466.   Dykeman, Wilma and James Stokely. "The Klan
          Tries A Comeback: In The Wake Of Desegregation."
          Commentary. Vol. 29, January, 1960, pp. 45-51.

8,467.   Eastland, Terry. "The Communists And The Klan."
          Commentary. Vol. 69, May, 1980, pp. 65-67.

8,468.   Editorials. "Sheets And Swastikas." New York
          Amsterdam News. November 22, 1980, p. 16.

8,469.   "Education Group Offers Teachers' Guide On Klan."
          New York Times. July 3, 1981, p. A6.

8,470.   "Education-Weapon Against Bigotry." Christian
          Science Monitor. December 22, 1978, p. 22.

8,471.   "Educators Publish Guide To Fight Racism, Klan."
          Jet. Vol. 60, July 30, 1981, p. 23.

8,472.   "Efforts By The Ku Klux Klan To Change Its Image."
           Los Angeles Times. January 29, 1979, p. 1.

8,473.   Egan, Cy. "How 36G Tip Killed Klanswoman." New
           York Post. February 13, 1970, p. 3.

8,474.   "18 Governors Said To Be Klansmen." New York
           Amsterdam News. August 29, 1923, p. 3.

8,475.   "1871 Rights Law Revived By Court." New York
           Times. June 8, 1971, p. 15.

8,476.   "1872: Visitor From Hell; Excerpts From Congres-
           sional Hearings On The KKK." Southern Exposure.
           Vol. 8, Summer, 1980, pp. 62-63.

8,477.   "Emancipation Credited To The Klan." New York
           Times. July 25, 1924, p. 12.

8,478.   "Embers Smolder." Christian Science Monitor.
           July 6, 1957, p. 5.

8,479.   "Emperor Hiram." New York Times. December 24,
           1927, p. 14.

8,480.   "End Of Hearings On The Klan." America. Vol. 114,
           March 12, 1966, p. 343.

8,481.   "Enough Of Ku Kluxism." Chicago Defender.
           August 27, 1921, p. 16.

8,482.   "Episcopalians Assail Ku Klux." The Messenger.
           Vol. 4, October, 1922, pp. 497-498.

8,483.   Eringer, Robert. "The Force Of Willis Carto."
           Mother Jones. April, 1981, p. 6.

8,484.   "Especially For The Ku Klux Klan." Chicago
           Defender. August 27, 1921, p. 16.

8,485.   "Ethical Culturists Hear Klan Analyzed." New York
           Times. November 3, 1924, p. 2.

8,486.   Evans, Hiram W. "The Klan: Defender Of Americanism."
           Forum. Vol. 74, December, 1925, pp. 801-814.

8,487.   _____. "The Klan's Fight For Americanism."
           North American Review. March-April-May, 1926,
           pp. 33-63.

8,488.   Evans, Margaret. "Like A Thief." New Republic.
           Vol. 28, August 31, 1921, pp. 16-17.

8,489.   Evans, Rowland and Robert Novak. "Inside Report:
           The Klan Boomerang." New York Herald Tribune.
           May 26, 1965.

8,490. "Evans Assails Smith And Catholic Church." New York Times. November 28, 1926, p. 16.

8,491. "Even The Klan Has Rights." Nation. Vol. 115, December 13, 1922, p. 654.

8,492. "Ex-Chief Of Florida Offers To Aid House Panel." New York Times. April 8, 1965, p. 21.

8,493. "Ex-FBI Agent Describes Ku Klux Klan Activities To Senate." New Orleans Times Picayune. December 3, 1975, p. 2.

8,494. "Ex-Goblin Accused Of Embezzling Funds." New York Times. December 10, 1921, p. 15.

8,495. "Ex-Klan Leader Released From Prison." New Orleans Times Picayune. March 22, 1976, p. 1.

8,496. "Ex-Operative Charges F.B.I. Failed To Bar Klan Violence." New York Times. December 1, 1975, p. 62.

8,497. "Expects Black To Stay." New York Times. October 2, 1937, p. 2.

8,498. "Expects Coolidge To Speak On Klan." New York Times. August 25, 1924, p. 2.

8,499. "Exploiters Of Hate Wise Calls Ku Klux." New York Times. October 10, 1921, p. 4.

8,500. "Extent Of KKK Activity In U.S. Navy." Bilalian News. October 19, 1979, p. 26.

8,501. "Extent Of KKK Activity Within Ranks Of U.S. Navy Discussed." Baltimore Afro-American. October 6, 1979, p. 1.

8,502. "Extremists Active In '72, Gray Asserts." New York Times. January 26, 1973, p. 77.

8,503. "Extremists Scored By Church Women." New York Times. October 9, 1964, p. 24.

8,504. "Evans Says Black Is Not In The Klan." New York Times. September 14, 1937, p. 19.

8,505. "The Face Of The Klan." CRJ Reporter. Summer, 1981, p. 21.

8,506. "The Fading Klan." New York Times. February 6, 1928, p. 18.

8,507. "Farley Cites Perils, Urges Strong Nation." New York Times. February 16, 1947, p. 5.

8,508.   "Farrand Marvels At Our Intolerance." New York
          Times. October 12, 1925, p. 13.

8,509.   "FBI Acts On Klan In Seven States." New York Times.
          August 1, 1946, p. 14.

8,510.   "FBI's Closer Watch On The Ku Klux Klan Viewed."
          San Francisco Chronicle. June 10, 1979, p. 30.

8,511.   "FBI Document Reveals KKK Wizard Acted As FBI
          Informant." New Orleans Times Picayune. August
          30, 1981, p. 1.

8,512.   "FBI Efforts To Discredit Extremists Under Hoover
          Viewed." Washington Post. March 8, 1974, p. 1A.

8,513.   "FBI Efforts To Harass KKK Noted." New Orleans
          Times Picayune. August 16, 1975, p. 2.

8,514.   "F.B.I. Embassy Break-Ins Put At One-A-Month
          Rate." New York Times. July 21, 1975, p. 27.

8,515.   "FBI Failed To Protect 'Freedom Riders' In 1961."
          Christian Science Monitor. February 19, 1980, p. 2.

8,516.   "FBI Harrassed Ku Klux Klan In 1960s, Documents
          Show." Miami Herald. August 16, 1975.

8,517.   "FBI Keeping Watchful Eye On Klans In Seven States."
          Afro American. August 6, 1946.

8,518.   "FBI Releases Documents On Leaks To Klan On
          Freedom Riders In 1961." Washington Post.
          August 20, 1978, p. 3A.

8,519.   "Federal Court Bars Suit To Oust Klan." New York
          Times. April 12, 1928, pp. 1, 17.

8,520.   "Federal Jury Indicts Seven Klan Leaders."
          Charlotte Observer. March 4, 1966.

8,521.   "Federal Jury Picked For Klansman's Trial."
          Greensboro Daily News. September 13, 1966.

8,522.   "Federal Law To Disband Ku Klux." Chicago
          Defender. September 24, 1921, p. 1.

8,523.   "Federation Spurs 'One Big Union'." New York
          Times. June 17, 1921, p. 15.

8,524.   "Fighting For Tolerance." New York Times.
          November 13, 1923, p. 20.

8,525.   "Find Preachers And Detectives Among Ku Klux."
          Chicago Defender. May 13, 1922, p. 1.

8,526.   Fitzgerald, John E. "Catholic Women And The
          Klan." New York Times. July 22, 1975.

8,527.   Fleming, Walter L. "Perscript Of Ku Klux Klan."
          Publications Of The Southern History Association.
          Vol. 7, September, 1903, pp. 327-348.

8,528.   "Foes Of Klan Fight 'Birth Of A Nation'." New
          York Times. December 3, 1922, Sect. 1, Part 2,
          p. 5.

8,529.   "Foes See Klan Impeding Growth Of A 'New South'."
          New York Times. August 19, 1979, p. 12.

8,530.   Footlick, Jerrold K. and Anthony Marro. "G-Men
          And Klansmen." Newsweek. Vol. 86, August 25,
          1975, pp. 74-75.

8,531.   "For And Against The Ku Klux Klan." Literary
          Digest. Vol. 70, September 28, 1921, pp. 34, 36,
          38, 40.

8,532.   "For Broader Klan Inquiry." New York Times.
          October 8, 1921, p. 4.

8,533.   "For Group Discussion." The World Tomorrow.
          Vol. 7, March, 1924, p. 98.

8,534.   "For Him There Are No Mysteries." New York Times.
          December 14, 1922, p. 20.

8,535.   "Forced Labor In U.S. Reported To U.N. Unit."
          New York Times. November 8, 1952, p. 3.

8,536.   "Ford Denies Praising Klan; Says He Gave No
          Interview." New York Times. August 28, 1924,
          p. 19.

8,537.   "Ford Is Charged With Backing Klan." New York
          Times. May 29, 1923, p. 2.

8,538.   "Form National Body To Fight The Klan." New York
          Times. November 12, 1923, pp. 1, 8.

8,539.   "Former Agent Interviewed By L.A. Times On FBI
          And KKK." New Orleans Times Picayune. November
          30, 1975, p. 2.

8,540.   "Former Leader Now Denounces The Klan." New
          York Times. December 28, 1923, pp. 1, 5.

8,541.   "Forms Rival To Klan As Mystic Kingdom." New
          York Times. July 16, 1924, p. 6.

8,542.   "14 Arrested By F.B.I. In Klan Floggings In
           Carolinas In 3d Round-Up In 18 Months." New York
           Times. November 17, 1953, p. 18.

8,543.   "14 Members Charged." Christian Science Monitor.
           March 29, 1966, p. 2.

8,544.   Frankel, Glenn. "Guerrilla-Style Training Of
           KKK Alleged In 7 States." Washington Post.
           October 24, 1980, p. A29.

8,545.   Franklin, Ben A. "Katzenbach Sees Klan Bill
           Merit." New York Times. July 21, 1966, p. 18.

8,546.   "Frederic March And Wife Defend 16 Accused Of
           Contempt Of Congress." New York Times. June 26,
           1947, p. 1.

8,547.   "Freedom To Be Vile." Washington Post. January
           14, 1978, p. A14.

8,548.   "From 1922 To 1925." New York Times. October 3,
           1937, Sect. 4, p. 8.

8,549.   "From The Kreed Of Klanishness." World Tomorrow.
           Vol. 7, March, 1924, pp. 76-77.

8,550.   Frost, Stanley. "Klan Restates Its Case." Outlook.
           Vol. 138, October 15, 1924, pp. 244-245.

8,551.   Fry, Henry P. "Why Did Congress Fail To Suppress
           Ku Klux?" Chicago Defender. January 14, 1922,
           p. 3, part 2.

8,552.   "G-Men Checking Klan Activities In 7 States."
           PM. August 1, 1946.

8,553.   "Ga. Sen. Bond Sees KKK As Serious Threat To
           U.S. Peace." San Francisco Chronicle. April 29,
           1981, p. 54.

8,554.   "Gains By Democrats Are Seen By Ewing." New York
           Times. February 3, 1946, p. 32.

8,555.   Gallman, Vanessa. "1979-1980: Klan Confrontations."
           Southern Exposure. Vol. 8, Summer, 1980, pp. 76-
           78.

8,556.   _____. "The Continuing Saga Of The KKK."
           Southern Changes. Vol. 2, September, 1979, pp.
           18-21.

8,557.   "Gallup Poll On Attitudes Toward The Ku Klux
           Klan." Houston Post. November 8, 1979, p. 3C.

8,558.   "Gallup Poll On Opinion Of Ku Klux Klan." New
           Orleans Times Picayune. November 8, 1979, Sect.
           4, p. 16.

8,559.   "Gambling On HUAC." Commonweal. Vol. 82, April
           16, 1965, p. 101.

8,560.   "Garvey's Klan Parley Revealed By Imperial Giant
           Of Ku Klux." New York Amsterdam News. February
           14, 1923, p. 7.

8,561.   Gardner, Virginia. "Klansmen Crusade For Dewey."
           New Masses. Vol. 53, No. 5, October 31, 1944,
           pp. 3-8, 16.

8,562.   _____. "Fellow-Travelers Of The Klan." New
           Masses. Vol. 54, No. 3, June 25, 1946, pp. 20-21.

8,563.   Garson, Robert A. "Political Fundamentalism And
           Popular Democracy In The 1920's." South Atlantic
           Quarterly. Vol. 76, Spring, 1977, pp. 219-233.

8,564.   Gates, Harvey. "We Can't Afford To Let The Klan
           Intimidate Our Children." Atlanta Voice. July 4,
           1981, p. 4.

8,565.   "Gets Ku Klux Evidence." New York Times. October
           11, 1921, p. 4.

8,566.   Gibbs, C.R. "How The Ku Klux Klan Changes With
           The Times." Sepia. Vol. 29, June, 1980, pp. 24-
           25.

8,567.   "Girl Secret Agent Tells Pelley 'Plot'." New York
           Times. April 3, 1940, p. 4.

8,568.   "Gives Federal Jury A Hint On Ku Klux." New York
           Times. September 14, 1921, p. 9.

8,569.   Glass, Roger. "Increased Klan Violence May Only Be
           The Tip Of The Iceberg." Washington Afro-American.
           December 13, 1980, pp. 1, 5.

8,570.   _____. "KKK Leader Ejected At Capitol."
           Washington Afro-American. December 13, 1980, pp.
           1, 5.

8,571.   "Glass Says Black Will Not Quit Post." New York
           Times. September 19, 1937, p. 39.

8,572.   " 'God Don't Like Ugly': The Klan Rises In The
           New South." Encore. Vol. 8, October 15, 1979,
           pp. 12-16.

8,573.   "Goblins Try To Oust Kleagle Clarke." New York
           Times. December 2, 1921, p. 8.

8,574.   Gohdges, Clarence. "The Ku Klux Klan And The
          Classics." Georgia Review. Vol. 7, Spring, 1953,
          pp. 18-24.

8,575.   Goldenweiser, Alexander. "Prehistoric K.K.K."
          The World Tomorrow. Vol. 7, March, 1924, pp. 81-
          82.

8,576.   "Gompers Assails Red Plot In Labor." New York
          Times. October 2, 1923, p. 9.

8,577.   Goodman, Walter. "How Should Public TV Handle The
          Inflammatory?" New York Times. December 11, 1977,
          Sect. 2, p. 39.

8,578.   _____. "H.U.A.C. Meets The K.K.K." New York
          Times Magazine. December 5, 1965, pp. 48, 142-
          146.

8,579.   "GOP Senator Speaks Out Against Ignoring Klan."
          Jet. Vol. 60, July 23, 1981, p. 7.

8,580.   "Government Says Klan Entitled To Equal Time."
          Greensboro Daily News. July 31, 1966.

8,581.   "Government Sifts Reports Bund Is Busy And
          Collaborates With The Ku Klux Klan." New York
          Times. October 2, 1946, p. 13.

8,582.   "Governors Assail Work Of Klansmen." New York
          Times. December 15, 1922, p. 9.

8,583.   "Governors Discuss Curbing Of Ku Klux." New York
          Times. December 17, 1922, p. 9.

8,584.   "Governors To Discuss Liquor And Ku Klux." New
          York Times. December 14, 1922, p. 24.

8,585.   Graham, Fred. "Communist Party Again On Trial."
          New York Times. November 7, 1965, Sect. 4, p. 10.

8,586.   _____. "The Contempt Issue Overtakes The Klan."
          New York Times. September 18, 1966, Sect. 4, p. 7.

8,587.   _____. "High Court Backs U.S. Prosecutions In
          Rights Deaths." New York Times. March 29, 1966,
          pp. 1, 23.

8,588.   _____. "Klan Case May Go To U.S. Jury Soon."
          New York Times. September 14, 1966, p. 39.

8,589.   Graham, Fred P. "Klan Leader Is Convicted Of
Contempt Of Congress." New York Times. September
15, 1966, pp. 1, 24.

8,590.   "Grand Drag; Investigation By House Committee On
Un-American Activities." Reporter. Vol. 33,
November 18, 1965, pp. 10, 12, 14.

8,591.   Grant, George S. "Garveyism And The Ku Klux Klan."
The Messenger. Vol. 5, October, 1923, pp. 835-836,
842.

8,592.   Grauer, Stuart. "War Of Cliche's At A Flaming
Cross." New York Times. October 7, Sect. 21,
p. 20.

8,593.   Greene, Ward. "Notes For A History Of The Klan."
American Mercury. Vol. 5, June, 1925, pp. 240-
243.

8,594.   Gregory, Dick. "And I Ain't Just Whistlin' Dixie."
Ebony. Vol. 26, August, 1971, pp. 149-150.

8,595.   Grizzard, Vernon. "Fraternity And Brotherhood...
Police And The Klan." Kudzu. Vol. 3, September,
1970, pp. 8-9.

8,596.   "Group Criticizes NEA's Use Of Classroom Kit On
KKK." Houston Post. October 24, 1981, p. 28D.

8,597.   "Group Records Klan Data." Washington Star.
December 11, 1980, p. A3.

8,598.   "Group Seeks Legislation To Outlaw KKK Terrorist
Training Camps." Buffalo Challenger. March 4,
1981, p. 1.

8,599.   "Groups Urge Probe In Klan Victim's Deaths."
New York Amsterdam News. April 3, 1982, p. 3.

8,600.   "Growing Bigotry Feared." New York Times. June
29, 1946, p. 18.

8,601.   "Growth Of The Klan." New York Times. June 9,
1925, p. 20.

8,602.   "Growth Reported." Christian Science Monitor.
February 3, 1967, p. 2.

8.603.   Hall, Grover C. "We Southerners." Scribner's
Magazine. Vol. 83, January, 1928, pp. 82-88.

8,604.   Halloran, Richard. "Army Spied On 18,000 Civilians
In 2-Year Operation." New York Times. January
18, 1971, p. 1.

8,605.   "Halt Klan Probe!" _The Messenger_. Vol. 3, November, 1921, p. 273.

8,606.   "Hannegan Denounces Klan Charge." _New York Times_. October 27, 1944, p. 14.

8,607.   "Harding Approves Ku Klux Inquiry." _New York Times_. September 22, 1921, p. 3.

8,608.   "Harding Deplores Growth Of Factions And Strikes At Klan." _New York Times_. May 18, 1923, pp. 1, 8.

8,609.   "Harding Is Urged To Suppress Klan." _New York Times_. November 28, 1922, p. 23.

8,610.   "Harding Rebukes Menacing Groups; Hit At Klan Seen." _New York Times_. June 6, 1923, pp. 1, 2.

8,611.   Hare, Nathan. "Passing Of The Jim Crow Vigilantes." _Negro History Bulletin_. Vol. 24, May, 1961, pp. 181-182, 184.

8,612.   Harris, Julian. "Klan Power Wanes In Parts Of South." _New York Times_. November 6, 1927, Sect. 3, p. 2.

8,613.   _____. "Observations From Times Watch-Towers." _New York Times_. January 8, 1928, Sect. 3, pp. 1, 2.

8,614.   _____. "Smith Threats Laid Largely To Clergy." _New York Times_. July 15, 1928, Sect. 2 & 3, p. 6.

8,615.   _____. "South Again Turns To Flogging Cases." _New York Times_. November 27, 1927, Sect. 3, pp. 1, 2.

8,616.   Harris, Louis. "Whites Is South Against Klan By 3-1." _New York Post_. January 17, 1966.

8,617.   Harris, Ronald and D. Michael Cheers. "Ku Klux Klan: Robed Racists Are Active From Coast To Coast." _Ebony_. Vol. 34, October, 1979, pp. 164-165.

8,618.   Hart, Reese. "Klan Held Illegal Under 1953 Law." _Winston Salem Journal_. June 20, 1966, p. 1.

8,619.   Hartt, Rollin L. "The New Negro." _Independent_. Vol. 105, January 15, 1921, pp. 59-60.

8,620.   Hatch, Richard W. " 'Kick-Em'Out' Krew In Klan Konstitution." _Raleigh News & Observer_. June 10, 1967.

8,621.   Hatcher, George. "Klan Now Facing Heavier Attacks." _New York Times_. December 4, 1949, Sect. 4, p. 11.

8,622. "Hate Movements Viewed As Peril." New York Times. February 14, 1943, p. 17.

8,623. "Hate The KKK And Not The PLO?" Washington Star. August 18, 1980, p. A8.

8,624. Hayden, Wes. "Contempt Trials Of Four In N.C. Klan Leaders Are Postponed." Durham Morning Herald. July 20, 1966.

8,625. _____. "Hearings Open Today On Bill To Curb Activities Of Klan." Durham Morning Herald. July 20, 1966.

8,626. _____. "Klansmen Bid For Dismissal." Durham Morning Herald. April 9, 1966.

8,627. Haynes, George E. "How Shall We Meet The Klan?" The World Tomorrow. Vol. 7, March, 1924, pp. 85-86.

8,628. "Head Of Quarreling Racists Complains Of Coup By Klan." New York Times. August 26, 1964, p. 35.

8,629. "Hearings Begin Today." New York Times. October 17, 1965, p. 77.

8,630. "Hearings On Klan Bill End." Winston-Salem Journal. July 23, 1966.

8,631. "Hearings On Klan To Resume." Winston Salem Journal. July 17, 1966.

8,632. "Hears Klan Will Take Jewish War Veterans." New York Times. August 8, 1924, p. 2.

8,633. Hedrick, Travis. "White Supremacy Chief Aim Of Klan." People's Voice. June 1, 1946, p. 9.

8,634. "Heflin Is Rebuked By Borah In Senate." New York Times. April 25, 1929, p. 1.

8,635. "Henry Ford Defends Klan As A Body Of Patriots." New York Times. August 27, 1924, p. 1.

8,636. Herbers, John. "Fund Misuse Laid To Klan Leaders." New York Times. October 21, 1965, pp. 1, 28.

8,637. _____. "House To Get Bill Curbing The Klan." New York Times. June 12, 1966, p. 79.

8,638. _____. "House Unit Votes Contempt Action For 7 Klan Chiefs." New York Times. January 7, 1966, pp. 1, 9.

8,639. _____. "Inquiry Reported To Damage Klan." New York Times. February 10, 1966, p. 41.

8,640. Herbers, John. "Johnson Rebukes Rioters As Destroyers Of Rights." New York Times. August 21, 1965, pp. 1, 8.

8,641. _____. "Johnson's Panel On Rights Urges A Vast Program." New York Times. May 25, 1966, pp. 1, 28.

8,642. _____. "Klan Chief Calls President A 'Liar'." New York Times. March 27, 1965, pp. 1, 11.

8,643. _____. "Klan Data Called Surprise To Many." New York Times. October 31, 1965, p. 85.

8,644. _____. "Klan Head Balks At 73 Questions As Inquiry Opens." New York Times. October 20, 1965, pp. 1, 28.

8,645. _____. "Klan Inquiry Opening Tomorrow In House Likely To Run 13 Weeks." New York Times. October 18, 1965, p. 24.

8,646. _____. "Klan Jobs Called Bonanza For Two." New York Times. October 22, 1965, pp. 1, 33.

8,647. _____. "Klan Loss Is Laid To House Hearings." New York Times. February 21, 1966, p. 45.

8,648. _____. "Klan Witness Resigns On Stand; 2d Tells Of Threats." New York Times. October 23, 1965, pp. 1, 21.

8,649. _____. "Law Professors Score House Contempt Action." New York Times. February 7, 1966, p. 21.

8,650. _____. "Offshoot Of Klan Is Called Violent." New York Times. November 2, 1965, pp. 1, 20.

8,651. _____. "Klan To Organize Its Own Towns As Havens From Desegregation." New York Times. March 23, 1964, pp. 1, 16.

8,652. _____. "Plan To Control Klan Is Stalled." New York Times. June 10, 1965, p. 70.

8,653. _____. "Shelton Indicted With Six Others." New York Times. March 4, 1966, p. 17.

8,654. _____. "South Is Aroused Against Floggings." New York Times. July 17, 1927, Sect. 2, p. 7.

8,655. _____. "South Making Headway In Fight Against Klan." New York Times. August 28, 1949, Sect. 4, p. 7.

8,656.   Herbers, John. "Training In Arms Charged To Klan."
          New York Times. October 29, 1965, p. 28.

8,657.   "Herring Is Now Against Him." New York Times.
          September 14, 1937, p. 18.

8,658.   Herring, Hubert C. "Ku Klux To The Rescue."
          New Republic. Vol. 34, May 23, 1923, pp. 341-342.

8,659.   Herring, Mary W. "The Why Of The Ku Klux." New
          Republic. Vol. 33, February 7, 1923, p. 289.

8,660.   " 'Hey! Don't Mob The KKK!' - M. Paul." The
          Westchester County Press. April 9, 1981, p. 1.

8,661.   "Hibernians Extol Smith." New York Times.
          August 21, 1928, p. 2.

8,662.   "Hibernians Hear Quota Law Attacked." New York
          Times. July 23, 1925, p. 2.

8,663.   "High Court Refuses Plea By Genovese." New York
          Times. January 14, 1969, p. 22.

8,664.   "High Court Ruling Weighed In South." New York
          Times. June 11, 1950, Sect. 4, p. 10.

8,665.   Hinton, Harold B. "Klan In South Keeps Under
          Cover." New York Times. September 1, 1946,
          Sect. 4, p. 4.

8,666.   _____. "Unions Drive In South At Slow But Sure
          Pace." New York Times. June 30, 1946, Sect. 4,
          p. 10.

8,667.   "Hints Klan-Bund Link." New York Times. August
          31, 1946, p. 28.

8,668.   "His Defiance Has Its Significance." New York
          Times. January 24, 1924, p. 16.

8,669.   "His Object Attained Successfully." New York
          Times. June 7, 1923, p. 18.

8,670.   "His Stand Again Is Stated." New York Times.
          October 25, 1924, p. 14.

8,671.   "History Of Klan And Its Effect On U.S. Race
          Relations." Chicago Tribune. September 6, 1976,
          p. 5.

8,672.   "The History Of The Ku Klux Klan: Rule By Terror."
          American History Illustrated. Vol. 14, January,
          1980, pp. 8-15.

8,673.   Hitchcock, James. "American Problems." Catholic World. Vol. 206, February, 1968, p. 232.

8,674.   Hixson, Fred. "Southern States Move To Put Curbs On Klan." New York Times. April 10, 1949, Sect. 4, p. 9.

8,675.   Hofmann, Paul. "Radicals Scored As Gun Curb Foes." New York Times. June 26, 1968, p. 21.

8,676.   "Hooded Horsemen Gallop Out Of The Past In A Sudden Revival Of The KKK." Life. Vol. 58, April 23, 1965, pp. 28-35.

8,677.   "The Hooded Knights Revive Rule By Terror In The 'Twenties'." American History Illustrated. Vol. 14, February, 1980, pp. 28-36.

8,678.   "Hooded Witness: FBI Stooped To Illegal, Immoral Acts." Christian Science Monitor. December 3, 1975, p. 3.

8,679.   "Hoods Off The Klan." Economist. Vol. 217, October 23, 1965, pp. 386-387.

8,680.   Hooks, Benjamin. "KKK 'Manual For Murder' Stirs U.S." Chicago Defender. April 18, 1981, p. 18.

8,681.   "Hoover Finds Peril In New Left." New York Times. May 19, 1968, pp. 1, 25.

8,682.   "Hoover Says Reds Use Black Power." New York Times. January 6, 1968, pp. 1, 59.

8.683.   Horne, Gerald C. "Affirmative Action: The Ku Klux Klan, The Media And The Police." St. Paul Recorder. October 23, 1980, pp. 1, 8.

8,684.   _____. "The KKK Menace." Sacramento Observer. November 6-12, 1980, pp. B1, B4.

8,685.   Horrock, Nicholas M. "F.B.I. Releascd Most Files On Its Programs To Disrupt Dissident Groups." New York Times. November 22, 1977, p. 26.

8,686.   "House Committee Sets New Round Of Klan Hearings." Durham Morning Herald. July 17, 1966.

8,687.   "House Group Plans Inquiry Of Klan." New York Times. May 27, 1946, p. 24.

8,688.   "House Hearings On Klan Due To Resume Next Week." New York Times. December 29, 1965, p. 18.

8,689.   "House Inquiry Into Klan Resumes Today In Capital." New York Times. October 25, 1965, p. 24.

8,690.   "House Panel Backs Anti-Klan Measure But Keeps It
         Quiet." New York Times. October 22, 1966, p. 36.

8,691.   "House Panel Hears Witness On Klan." New York
         Times. July 22, 1965, p. 17.

8,692.   "House Panel Report Says Klan Is Still A Terrorist
         Conspiracy." New York Times. December 11, 1967,
         p. 31.

8,693.   "House Unit Accuses Terror Use." Christian
         Science Monitor. December 20, 1967, p. 3.

8,694.   "House Unit Approval Of Klan Bill Revealed."
         Durham Morning Herald. October 22, 1966.

8,695.   "House Unit Calls Klan Terroristic." Greensboro
         Daily News. October 25, 1966.

8,696.   "House Wets Attack Fund For Dry Army." New York
         Times. June 27, 1927, p. 20.

8,697.   "Houston's Views On Klan." New York Times. June
         28, 1924, p. 2.

8,698.   "How FBI Infiltrated KKK." Christian Science
         Monitor. December 21, 1977, p. 11.

8,699.   "How The Klans Are Organized." New York Times.
         September 13, 1981, Sect. 11, p. 17.

8,700.   "How To Make A Wizard Talk; Citations For Con-
         tempt Of Congress." Time. Vol. 87, January 14,
         1966, p. 21B.

8,701.   "How Many Members." Christian Science Monitor.
         November 12, 1968, p. 5.

8,702.   "How The First Ku Klux Klan Was Organized In The
         South." New York Herald Tribune. December 18,
         1922, p. 1.

8,703.   "How To Explain The Klan." New York Times. July
         7, 1924, p. 14.

8,704.   Howe, Elizabeth M. "Ku Klux Uniform." Buffalo
         Historical Society Publications. Vol. 25, 1921,
         pp. 9-41.

8,705.   "HUAC Calls Klan A Band Of Terrorists." Charlotte
         Observer. October 25, 1966.

8,706.   "HUAC Concludes Klan Probe." Greensboro Daily
          News. February 25, 1966.

8,707.   "HUAC Holds Hearings On Ku Klux Klan Activities."
          National Observer. October 25, 1965, p. 3.

8,708.   "HUAC Told Klan Bill Not Needed." Charlotte
          Observer. July 23, 1966.

8,709.   "HUAC vs. The KKK." Senior Scholastic. Vol. 88,
          March 11, 1966, pp. 16-17.

8,710.   "HUAC Versus The Klan." Reporter. Vol. 32,
          April 22, 1965, pp. 9-10.

8,711.   "HUAC Will Hold 2nd Klan Hearing." Charlotte
          Observer. July 17, 1966.

8,712.   Hughan, Jessie Wallace. "An Antidote For Preju-
          dice." The World Tomorrow. Vol. 7, March, 1924,
          p. 95.

8,713.   Hughes, Langston. "Little Klanny." New York Post.
          July 30, 1965, p. 30.

8,714.   Hunter, Marjorie. "Liberties Union Protests Plan
          To Investigate Klan." New York Times. February
          16, 1965, p. 17.

8,715.   Hyer, Marjorie. "Rise Of KKK Is Linked To Mideast
          Bids." Washington Post. October 18, 1980, p. B12.

8,716.   "Hyland Adds Pinchot To Presidency List; Foresees
          A Revolt." New York Times. December 10, 1922,
          pp. 1, 6.

8,717.   "Hylan Asks Harding To Stop Klan Paper." New York
          Times. December 21, 1922, pp. 1, 6.

8,718.   "Immigration Chief Says KKK May Not Hold Aliens."
          New Orleans Times Picayune. July 22, 1978, p. 14.

8,719.   "The Imperial Emperor Of The KKK Meets The Press."
          American Mercury. Vol. 69, November, 1949, pp. 529-
          538.

8,720.   "Imperial Kloncilium Brands Charges Against Klan
          Officers 'Absurd, False And Malicious'."
          Imperial Night-Hawk. June 27, 1923, pp. 1-2, 8.

8,721.   "Imperial Lawlessness." Outlook. Vol. 129,
          September 14, 1921, p. 46.

8,722.   "Imperial Wizard And His Klan." Literary Digest.
          Vol. 68, February 5, 1921, pp. 40-46.

8,723.   "Imperial Wizard Praises The Klan." New York Times.
          September 25, 1924, p. 25.

8,724.   "Imperial Wizard Banishes Five Grand Dragons From
          Klan." Washington Post. October 12, 1975, p. 1A.

8,725.   "Imperial Wizard, Robert Shelton, Interviewed."
          New Orleans Times Picayune. September 28, 1977,
          p. 10.

8,726.   "Imperial Wizard Tearlach MacPhearson Interviewed."
          Washington Post. August 20, 1972, p. 13G.

8,727.   "In An Eddy Of Oblivion." New York Times.
          November 2, 1923, p. 16.

8,728.   "In Defense Of Liberty." Current. January, 1980,
          pp. 34-51.

8,729.   "Increase In Violent Activities By Ku Klux Klan
          Factions Viewed." San Francisco Chronicle.
          April 8, 1979, p. 4.

8,730.   "Indict Imperial Wizard Clarke For Fraud Through
          Mails In Conduct Of Ku Klux Klan." New York Times.
          October 6, 1922, p. 1.

8,731.   "Informer Scores F.B.I. On Violence." New York
          Times. December 3, 1975, p. 23.

8,732.   "Insult To The White Race." New York Amsterdam
          News. December 27, 1922, p. 8.

8,733.   "Interesting Facts About Ku Klux Klan." The
          Messenger. Vol. 3, March, 1921, pp. 194-195.

8,734.   "Interreligious Foundation For Community Organiza-
          tions To Hold Anti-KKK Conference." Norfolk
          Journal & Guide. November 16, 1979, p. 3A.

8,735.   "Interview With SCLC National Pres. J. Lowery."
          Chicago Defender. December 4, 1979, p. 4.

8,736.   "The Instrusive Issue." New York Times.
          September 4, 1924, p. 18.

8,737.   "Investigating K.K.K. In U.S. Navy." New York
          Amsterdam News. November 7, 1923, p. 8.

8,738.   "Investigating Klan." New York Times. April 4,
          1965, Sect. 4, p. 11.

8,739.   "Investigating The Klans." New Republic. Vol.
          152, April 10, 1965, pp. 5-6.

8,740.   "Investigating The Ku Klux Klan." The Crisis.
          Vol. 72, May, 1965, pp. 279-280.

8,741.   "Investigation By Congress Of Ku Klux Klan."
          New York Times. September 16, 1921, p. 12.

8,742.   "Invisible Empire In The Spotlight." Current
          Opinion. Vol. 71, November, 1921, pp. 561-564.

8,743.   "Invisible Government." Outlook. Vol. 132,
          December 13, 1922, p. 643.

8,744.   Irwin, Theodore. "The Klan Kicks Up Again."
          American Mercury. Vol. 50, August, 1940, pp.
          470-476.

8,745.   "Is The Ku Klux Klan Returning?" The Messenger.
          Vol. 4, February, 1922, pp. 356-357.

8,746.   "Is The Ku Klux Un-American; Pro And Con, Mostly
          Con!" Forum. Vol. 75, February, 1926, pp. 305-308.

8,747.   "It Was No Party For Grant." New York Times.
          December 26, 1923, p. 14.

8,748.   "It's Leap Year Folks!" Pittsburgh Courier.
          March 3, 1928, editorial page.

8,749.   "It's Not So, Say Justice Dept. Heads, FBI Does Not
          Ask Aid Of KKK." Afro American. September 24,
          1924, p. 1.

8,750.   Jackson, Charles O. "William J. Simmons: A Career
          In Ku Kluxism." Georgia Historical Quarterly.
          Vol. 50, December, 1966, pp. 351-365.

8,751.   "James Haygood and Will Hazelton Speak In Atlanta
          About KKK." Atlanta Daily World. November 30,
          1979, p. 1.

8,752.   Jaworski, Leon. "Knights Of The Invisible
          Empire." Crisis. Vol. 88, No. 6, July, 1981,
          pp. 274-276.

8,753.   "J.D. Culbertson Sees Decline In WCC And Klan
          Activities." Afro American. December 29, 1956,
          p. 5.

8,754.   Jenness, Linda. "Not In The Name Of Feminism."
          Militant. Vol. 39, June 27, 1975, p. 11.

8,755.   "Jersey, Georgia Trade Klan Data." New York
          Times. August 10, 1946, p. 15.

8,756.   "Jews Denounce Klan." New York Times. November
           27, 1922, p. 2.

8,757.   "Jews Expose KKK Paramilitary Activities."
           Precint-Reporter. November 13, 1980, p. 1.

8.758.   "Jews See New Era In Arms Conference." New York
           Times. October 4, 1921, p. 9.

8,759.   "Jews State Stand On Vital Questions." New York
           Times. January 27, 1923, p. 4.

8,760.   Johnson, Gerald W. "The Ku-Kluxer." American
           Mercury. Vol. 1, February, 1924, pp. 207-211.

8,761.   _____. "The Battling South." Scribner's
           Magazine. March, 1926, pp. 302-307.

8,762.   Johnson, Guy B. "The Race Philosophy Of The Ku
           Klux Klan." Opportunity. Vol. 1, September, 1923,
           pp. 268-270.

8,763.   _____. "A Sociological Interpretation Of The
           New Ku Klux Movement." Social Forces. Vol. 1,
           March, 1923, pp. 440-444.

8,764.   Johnson, Linda. "New KKK Drawing Students; Schools
           Must Combat Influence." The Observer (Chicago).
           May 30, 1981, p. 1.

8,765.   Johnson, Thomas A. "Rights Leaders Troubled By
           Prospects Of Leftist Gains Among Blacks." New
           York Times. November 19, 1979, p. 38.

8,766.   Johnson, Tom. "Dixie Jew." New Masses. Vol. 12,
           July 24, 1934, pp. 21-22.

8,767.   Johnston, Ernie. "KKK In The 1950'a." New York
           Amsterdam News. November 10, 1979, p. 29.

8,768.   Johnston, Frank, Jr. "Religious And Racial
           Prejudice In The United States." Current History.
           Vol. 20, July, 1924, pp. 573-578.

8,769.   "Joke That Became A Terror." Illustrated World.
           Vol. 33, March, 1920, p. 110.

8,770.   Jones, Paul. "The Ku Klux Goes Calling." New
           Republic. Vol. 85, January 8, 1936, p. 251.

8,771.   _____. "What Brotherhood Demands." The World
           Tomorrow. Vol. 7, March, 1924, pp. 82-83.

8,772.   "Judge Throws Klan Out Of His Court." New York
           Times. April 14, 1928, p. 8.

8,773.   "Judicial Candidate Got Ku Klux Threat." New
York Times. December 7, 1922, p. 7.

8,774.   "Junior Chamber Picks Louis, Bolte, Beirne Among
Ten Leading Young Men Of The Year." New York
Times. January 20, 1947, p. 11.

8,775.   "Jury Chosen For Contempt Trial Of Klan Chief
Shelton." Durham Morning Herald. September 13,
1966.

8,776.   "Just Social Order Held Vital To Jews." New
York Times. September 18, 1933, p. 12.

8,777.   " 'Justice' By Violence." World Tomorrow. Vol. 7,
March, 1924, pp. 78-79.

8,778.   "Justice Dept. Releases Review Of KKK Activity In
Fiscal 1979." Los Angeles Sentinel. November 8,
1979, p. 10B.

8,779.   "Justice Dept. Reports On KKK Activity In Fiscal
1979." Atlanta Daily World. October 19, 1979,
p. 1.

8,780.   "Justice Dept. Study Says Violent Faction Of KKK
'Bears Watching'." Houston Post. November 24,
1980, p. 5A.

8,781.   "Justice Urges Scrutiny Of KKK Group." Washington
Star. November 25, 1980, p. A4.

8,782.   "K Of C. Names Tobin Supreme Director." New York
Times. August 7, 1924, p. 17.

8,783.   Kantor, Louis. "How Grant Broke Old Ku Klux."
New York Times. August 17, 1924, Sect. 8, p. 4.

8,784.   Katz, William Loren. "The People vs. The Klan
In Mass Combat." Freedomways. 2nd quarter,
1980, pp. 96-100.

8,785.   "Katzenbach Critizes Anti-KKK Legislation."
Durham Morning Herald. July 21, 1966.

8,786.   Kelly, Michael. "Ku Klux Klan." Washington Post.
November 4, 1978, p. 19A.

8,787.   Kennedy, Stetson. "Does The FBI Actually Ask
Aid Of KKK In Dixie?" Afro-American. September
24, 1949, pp. 1, 2.

8,788.   _____. "How Negroes Can Beat The Kluxers."
Pittsburgh Courier. February 8, 1958, pp. 2, 8.

8,789.   Kennedy, Stetson. "KKK vs. Labor: A Sampler."
          Southern Exposure. Vol. 8, Summer, 1980, p. 61.

8,790.   _____. "Klan Invades Southern Union Get A
          Stranglehold On Some." Daily Compass. February 7,
          1950, p. 1.

8,791.   _____. "The Ku Klux Klan." New Republic.
          Vol. 114, July 1, 1946, pp. 928-930.

8,792.   Kent, Frank R. "Ku Klux Klan In America."
          Spectator. Vol. 130, February 17, 1923, pp. 279-
          280.

8,793.   Keresey, John McPike. "How Shall We Meet The
          Klan?" The World Tomorrow. Vol. 7, March, 1924,
          p. 86.

8,794.   "Keynote At Hartford Arraigns The Klan." New York
          Times. September 18, 1924, p. 6.

8,795.   Khalifah, H.K. "Educating The Black Masses."
          Norfolk Journal & Guide. August 19, 1981, p. 6.

8,796.   King, Wayne. "The Klan Has More Crosses To Bear
          Than Burn." New York Times. July 30, 1978,
          Sect. 4, p. 5.

8,797.   _____. "Leader Says Klan, Not Black, Wrote
          'Attack' Book." New York Times. February 20,
          1978, p. 12.

8,798.   _____. "More Than A Dozen Ku Klux Klan Factions
          Compete For Membership And Feud Over Predominance."
          New York Times. July 11, 1977, p. 14.

8,799.   _____. "Violent Klan Group Gaining Members."
          New York Times. March 15, 1979, p. 18.

8,800.   "K.K.K." The Messenger. Vol. 5, February, 1923,
          p. 594.

8,801.   "The K.K.K." The Messenger. Vol. 8, November,
          1926, p. 345.

8,802.   "The K.K.K." New Republic. Vol. 28, September
          21, 1921, pp. 88-89.

8,803.   "K.K.K." Opportunity. Vol. 2, June, 1924, p. 191.

8,804.   "KKK Activity Across America." Atlanta Daily
          World. November 9, 1979, p. 4.

8,805.   "KKK Activities And Affirmative Action." Norfolk
          Journal & Guide. October 26, 1979, p. 1A.

8,806.   "The K.K.K. Again." Chicago Defender. September
          17, 1921, p. 16.

8,807.   "K.K.K. Again." New York Times. February 24,
          1952, Sect. 4, p. 2.

8,808.   "KKK Began 'Loyalty' Query Un-Americans Now Use."
          Daily Worker. April 14, 1950.

8,809.   "The KKK Can Be Cured." Afro-American. May 28,
          1949, p. 4.

8,810.   "KKK Chiefs Plan To Repeal Civil Rights Act."
          Chicago Tribune. November 17, 1980, p. 1.

8,811.   "KKK Chief Tells Group To Stop Run-Ins With
          Police." Jet. Vol. 60, July 9, 1981, p. 6.

8,812.   "KKK And Children." Cleveland Call & Post.
          June 13, 1981, p. 6.

8,813.   "KKK Feeding Off Hard Times, Says NAACP Head."
          Jet. Vol. 56, September 13, 1979, p. 7.

8,814.   "The KKK Goes Military." Newsweek. Vol. 96,
          October 6, 1980, p. 52.

8,815.   "KKK Group Advocates All-Out Racial Warfare."
          Michigan Chronicle. December 6, 1980, p. 3.

8,816.   "KKK Head Shelton Guilty Of Contempt." Greensboro
          Daily News. September 15, 1966.

8,817.   "KKK Imperial Wizard Expelled From U.S. Con-
          gressional Hearing." San Francisco Chronicle.
          December 10, 1980, p. 28.

8,818.   "K.K.K. In Court." Chicago Defender. January 7,
          1922, p. 16.

8.819.   "KKK In National Comeback; Strikes From Coast To
          Coast." Los Angeles Sentinel. April 25, 1946.

8,820.   "KKK Klavern Advocates Race War." Louisiana
          Weekly. December 6, 1980, pp. 1, 5.

8,821.   "KKK - Letter." Los Angeles Sentinel. December
          6, 1979, p. 6A.

8,822.   "KKK - Like Activity Across U.S." Baltimore Afro-
          American. October 27, 1979, p. 4.

8,823.   "The KKK's Lingering Stain." American Federa-
          tionist. Vol. 88, August, 1981, pp. 20-24.

8,824.   "KKK Member Teaching Scouts How To Kill - Stayskal
           Cartoon." <u>Chicago Tribune</u>. November 28, 1980,
           Sect. 3, p. 2.

8,825.   "KKK Out To Knock Off NAACP." <u>Pittsburg Courier</u>.
           January 11, 1958, p. 2.

8,826.   "KKK Reported Rising In South." <u>Raleigh News &
           Observer</u>. August 26, 1955.

8,827.   "KKK - The Invisible Empire - Focus On The Klan."
           <u>Christian Science Monitor</u>. September 28, 1965,
           p. 6.

8,828.   "KKK Teachings To Children At Camps Highlighted."
           <u>Los Angeles Times</u>. October 1, 1981, Sect. 1C,
           p. 1.

8,829.   "KKK Threatens Whitney Young." <u>New York Amsterdam
           News</u>. April 17, 1965, p. 1.

8,830.   "KKK Training Young Children In Guerrilla Warfare
           Tactics." <u>San Francisco Chronicle</u>. December 1,
           1980, p. 10.

8,831.   "KKK Wizard Appears On TV Talk Show With Ga.
           State Sen. J. Bond." <u>San Francisco Chronicle</u>.
           December 5, 1980, p. 8.

8,832.   "KKK's View Of U.S. Government - Interlandi Cartoon."
           <u>Los Angeles Times</u>. August 27, 1981, Sect. 2, p. 11.

8,833.   "Klan Crosses Viewed As Warning To Reds." <u>New
           York Times</u>. July 27, 1951, p. 26.

8,834.   "Klan Dissolves But Subject To Revival." <u>Pulse</u>.
           Vol. 2, July, 1944, p. 14.

8,835.   "Klan Drive Is Seen As A Fight On C.I.O." <u>New
           York Times</u>. October 31, 1937, Sect. 5, p. 6.

8,836.   "Klan Fading - Or Are They?" <u>Christian Science
           Monitor</u>. May 5, 1977, p. 3.

8,837.   "Klan Founder Asks Restraining Order." <u>Pittsburgh
           Courier</u>. April 7, 1923, p. 1.

8,838.   "Klan Has 'New' Plan To Resettle Negroes."
           <u>Winston-Salem Journal</u>. June 30, 1965.

8,839.   "Klan Is Major Topic For Black History Month."
           <u>Jet</u>. Vol. 59, February 26, 1981, p. 30.

8,840.   "Klan Inspires Anti-Marriage Bills - NAACP."
           <u>Philadelphia Tribune</u>. March 5, 1927.

8,841.   "Klan Is Condemned." New York Times. August 23,
          1955, p. 20.

8,842.   "Klan Is Suppressed In Both Carolinas." New York
          Times. September 3, 1950, p. 41.

8,843.   "Klan Leader Adamant." New York Times. January
          12, 1957, p. 38.

8,844.   "Klan Leader Begins Drive In Northeast." New
          York Times. December 8, 1979, p. 26.

8,845.   "Klan Leader, Followers Arrested In Tennessee;
          More Face Charges In Texas." Jet. Vol. 60,
          May 21, 1981, p. 8.

8,846.   "Klan Leaders Ordered To Reveal Their Identies."
          Jet. Vol. 62, March 8, 1982, p. 5.

8,847.   "Klan Leader's Offer To Sell His Group To Rival
          Faction Revealed." Los Angeles Times. July 22,
          1979, p. 5.

8,848.   "Klan Opens New Attack On Negro." Pittsburgh
          Courier. September 10, 1949, p. 1.

8,849.   "Klandestine." Los Angeles Times Book Review.
          May 2, 1976, p. 13.

8,850.   "Klan's Listing As Subversive Costs Ex-Kluxer
          U.S. Job." Afro-American. May 21, 1949, p. 3.

8,851.   Kritzer, Oscar J. "The Revival Of The K.K.K."
          Congress Weekly. May 17, 1946, pp. 12-13.

8,852.   "The Ku Klux Are Riding Again." The Crisis.
          Vol. 17, March, 1919, pp. 229-231.

8,853.   "The Ku Klux Kids." Rolling Stone. June 11,
          1981, pp. 22-24.

8,854.   "Ku Klux Klan Activity." Norfolk Journal & Guide.
          November 9, 1979, p. 8A.

8,855.   "Ku Klux Klan Activity Across The U.S." Chicago
          Defender. November 13, 1979, p. 6A.

8,856.   "Ku Klux Klan Activities." Los Angeles Sentinel.
          November 8, 1979, p. 1A.

8,857.   "Ku Klux Klan Barred From Employment." Christian
          Science Monitor. October 22, 1951, p. 10.

8,858.   "Ku Klux Klan And Civil Rights Struggle In U.S."
          Christian Science Monitor. November 6, 1979,
          p. 24.

8,859.   "Ku Klux Klan And Firearms - Cartoon." Los Angeles Times. December 16, 1980, Sect. 2, p. 7.

8,860.   "Ku Klux Klan begins Drive For Teen-Age Members." New Orleans Times Picayune. September 4, 1972, p. 6.

8,861.   "Ku Klux Klan Decides To Take Off Its Masks; Wizard Says Hood Are Gone Forever." Pittsburgh Courier. April 27, 1940, p. 2.

8,862.   "Ku Klux Klan Grand Wizard, David Duke, Quits To Form Own Group." Los Angeles Times. July 25, 1980, p. 15.

8,863.   "Ku Klux Klan Growth Reported." Christian Science Monitor. September 29, 1966, p. 3.

8,864.   "Ku Klux Klan Has New Enemy In Big Power Concentrations." Washington Post. April 27, 1972, p. 11G.

8,865.   "Ku Klux Klan - Interlandi Cartoon." Los Angeles Times. June 21, 1979, Sect. 2, p. 7.

8,866.   "The Ku Klux Klan Is Making Notes On Pornographic Movies And The Potential Sex Criminals That Attend Them." National Observer. April 17, 1973, p. 6.

8.867.   "Ku Klux Klan Lawyer Found Guilty Of Evading Taxes." New Orleans Times Picayune. May 15, 1977, p. 12.

8,868.   "Ku Klux Klan Leader Comments On Increased Membership." Washington Post. November 20, 1977, p. 16A.

8,869.   "Ku Klux Klan - Letter." New Orleans Times Picayune. May 21, 1976, p. 16.

8,870.   "Ku Klux Klan - Marlette Cartoon." Washington Post. November 10, 1979, p. 23A.

8,871.   "The Ku Klux Klan Movement." American Mercury. May, 1901, pp. 634-644.

8,872.   "Ku Klux Klan - Oliphant Cartoon." San Francisco Chronicle. November 18, 1979, p. 1.

8,873.   "Ku Klux Klan On The Way Back." U.S. News And World Report. Vol. 57, October 19, 1964, pp. 51-52.

8,874.   "Ku Klux Klan Opens Ranks To Women And Catholics In National Drive." Los Angeles Times. November 6, 1980, Sect. 1A, p. 8.

8,875.   "Ku Klux Klan Organization's Founding." Atlanta
          Daily World. November 20, 1979, p. 3; December
          4, 1979, p. 8.

8,876.   "Ku Klux Klan Scored By Amer. Party Dir. At News
          Conf." New Orleans Times Picayune. August 24,
          1972, Sect. 4, p. 16.

8,877.   "Ku Klux Klan Seek $50 Million In Suit Against
          Klan." New Orleans Times Picayune. August 27,
          1977, Sect. 3, p. 4.

8,878.   "Ku Klux Klan Seek To Spread Propaganda Via
          Radio." Broad Ax. July 11, 1925, p. 2.

8,879.   "Ku Klux Klan Stages National Recruiting Drive."
          New Orleans Times Picayune. August 26, 1979,
          p. 6.

8,880.   "Ku Klux Klan Starts Drive To Recruit Teenage
          Members." Los Angeles Times. September 4, 1972,
          p. 9.

8,881.   "Ku Klux Klan Stops Gilpin's Tour Of South."
          Chicago Defender. January 28, 1922, p. 1.

8,882.   "Ku Klux Klan To Challenge UMW Ban Of KKK Members."
          New Orleans Times Picayune. April 7, 1975, p. 6.

8,883.   "Ku Klux Klan Tokens." Antiques Journal. Vol.
          36, October, 1981, p. 48.

8,884.   "Ku Klux Klan Tries To Catch On In Midwest."
          Christian Science Monitor. June 23, 1966, p. 1.

8,885.   "Ku Klux Klan Tries To Ride Again." Christian
          Science Monitor. September 17, 1955, p. 5.

8,886.   "Ku Kluxers Flood North With Notes." Chicago
          Defender. June 3, 1922, p. 1.

8,887.   "Ku Klux Klan Uses Lie Detector Tests To Spot
          Informers." Washington Post. September 13,
          1972, p. 26A.

8,888.   "Ku Klux Klan Viewed." San Francisco Chronicle.
          August 18, 1979, p. 4.

8,889.   "Ku Klux Klan - Wright Cartoon." Washington Post.
          August 18, 1979, p. 13A.

8,890.   "Ku Klux Klan Youth Camps." Bilalian News.
          August 7, 1981, p. 7.

8,891.   "Ku Klux Menace To The North." New York Times.
          July 6, 1923, p. 12.

8,892.   "Klan Leader Surrenders." New York Times. May
          25, 1952, p. 43.

8,893.   "Klan Letter Reveals Revival In Midwest." New
          York Times. October 2, 1927, p. 3.

8,894.   "Klan Of 6 States Merge In National Group; Masked
          Delegates Vote To Ban All Masks." New York Times.
          August 24, 1949, p. 16.

8,895.   "Klans Reach Agreement." New York Times. November
          23, 1949, p. 16.

8,896.   "Klan Resurgence A Big Threat: Union Official."
          Jet. Vol. 59, February 19, 1981, p. 29.

8,897.   "The Klan Reviewed." Chicago Tribune. November
          5, 1978, Sect. 7, p. 12.

8,898.   "Klan, SCLC Promise Summer Will Be 'Hot' And Long
          In The South." Jet. Vol. 56, June 28, 1979, p. 5.

8,899.   "Klan Victories In Oregon And Texas." Literary
          Digest. Vol. 75, November 25, 1922, p. 12.

8,900.   "The Klan's Archnemisis Speaks: 'Kind Treatments
          Whip A Devil'." Encore. Vol. 8, October 15, 1979,
          pp. 14-15.

8,901.   "Klan Violence Becomes Nat'l Problem: Vivian."
          Jet. Vol. 58, April 24, 1980, p. 6.

8,902.   "Klan Writes A Violent New Chapter." U.S. News
          & World Report. Vol. 87, November 19, 1979, p. 59.

8,903.   "Klan's Rural Power Assayed By Schary." New York
          Times. June 14, 1965, p. 39.

8,904.   "Klansmen Stirring, Seek New Members." New York
          Times. July 30, 1956, p. 9.

8,905.   "The Klansman." Christian Science Monitor.
          February 7, 1968, p. 21.

8,906.   "The Klansman: This Flop Stars Richard Burton,
          Lee Marvin And O.J. Simpson." Christian Science
          Monitor. January 15, 1975, p. 9.

8,907.   "Kluxers On The Prowl." Newsweek. Vol. 34,
          July 11, 1949, pp. 21-22.

8,908.   "Kluxery Seeps Up In South's Piedmont." Christian
          Science Monitor. July 9, 1957, p. 3.

8,909.   "KKK Resurgence." The Crisis. Vol. 88, June,
          1981, p. 252.

8,910.   "The KKK, The Media And The Police." _Arizona Informant_. November 19, 1980, pp. 1, 8.

8,911.   "K.K.K. Philosophy." _Opportunity_. Vol. 2, January, 1924, p. 30.

8,912.   "KKK Wizard Was FBI Informant, Paper Says." _Jet_. Vol. 61, September 24, 1981, p. 10.

8,913.   "K. Of C. Convention Challenges Klan." _New York Times_. August 8, 1923, p. 23.

8,914.   "Klan A Governors' Theme." _New York Times_. December 5, 1922, p. 3.

8,915.   "Klan Active Against Court." _New York Times_. January 10, 1926, p. 17.

8,916.   "Klan Allegiance Oath." _New York Times_. October 2, 1937, p. 3.

8,917.   "Klan And Clarke Part." _New York Times_. February 24, 1923, p. 4.

8,918.   "The Klan As A Menace." _New York Times_. February 28, 1923, p. 16.

8,919.   "The Klan As A National Problem." _Literary Digest_. Vol. 75, December 2, 1922, pp. 12-13.

8,920.   "The Klan As A 'Tangent'." _New York Times_. August 29, 1924, p. 10.

8,921.   "Klan As An Issue." _Outlook_. Vol. 138, September 3, 1924, pp. 5-6.

8,922.   "The Klan - As It Was And Is: An Aftermath Of Civil War That Was Reborn In World Conflict." _New York Herald Tribune_. September 19, 1937, p. 3.

8,923.   "Klan As Symptom." _Christian Century_. Vol. 84, November 22, 1967, p. 1484.

8,924.   "Klan Atrocities Bared." _Pittsburgh Courier_. April 14, 1928, pp. 1, 4.

8,925.   "Klan Attacks Rule On Mixed Marriage." _New York Times_. April 16, 1927, p. 32.

8,926.   "Klan Audit Reports Gains." _New York Times_. June 18, 1924, p. 21.

8,927.   "Klan Ban To Be Asked." _Greensboro Daily News_. July 17, 1966.

8,928.   "Klan Bill Could Cover Unions And Fraternities."
          Virginian Pilot. July 23, 1966.

8,929.   "Klan Bill Termed 'Fraud'." _Durham Morning Herald_.
          July 22, 1966.

8,930.   "The Klan Bipartisan." _New York Times_. July 31,
          1924, p. 12.

8,931.   "Klan Called Status Symbol." _New York Times_.
          September 6, 1959, p. 76.

8,932.   "Klan Candidate Notified." _New York Times_.
          July 5, 1924, p. 6.

8,933.   "Klan Case Await Decision On Shelton." _Raleigh
          News & Observer_. December 9, 1966.

8,934.   "Klan Chaplain Called FBI Spy." _Durham Morning
          Herald_. December 11, 1975.

8,935.   "Klan Chief Is Convicted Of Contempt." _Durham
          Morning Herald_. September 15, 1966.

8,936.   "Klan Chief On The Road, Seeking To Regain Power."
          New York Times. November 28, 1970, p. 55.

8,937.   "Klan Chief Writes Of Ku Klux Aims." _New York
          Times_. March 8, 1926, p. 2.

8,938.   "Klan Chiefs Plead Guilty." _Raleigh News &
          Observer_. November 24, 1966.

8,939.   "Klan Denounced As Hearings End." _New York Times_.
          February 25, 1966, p. 17.

8,940.   "Klan Disbands As National Body; Claimed 5,000,000
          Roll In 1920s." _New York Times_. June 5, 1944,
          p. 21.

8,941.   "Klan Doffs Mask And Changes Name." _New York Times_.
          February 23, 1928, pp. 1, 2.

8,942.   "Klan Dragons Go On Trial Today." _Greensboro
          Daily News_. November 18, 1966.

8,943.   "Klan Drive Attacked." _New York Times_. May 24,
          1961, p. 22.

8,944.   "Klan - Dry Bloc Fails To Halt Redistricting."
          Pittsburgh Courier. May 25, 1929, p. 3.

8,945.   "Klan Emperor Endorses Appeal." _New York Times_.
          December 28, 1923, p. 5.

8,946.   "Klan Emperor Hits Wizard As 'Hiding'." New York
          Times. November 9, 1923, p. 4.

8,947.   "Klan 'Exiles' Bereft Of Stephenson Aid." New
          York Times. April 13, 1928, p. 27.

8,948.   "Klan Goes In For Face-Lifting." Literary Digest.
          Vol. 96, March 10, 1928, pp. 15-16.

8,949.   "Klan Got Trademarks For 30 Newspapers." New York
          Times. August 31, 1925, p. 17.

8,950.   " 'Klan Has Filthy Hands,' Says Judge." Pittsburgh
          Courier. April 21, 1928, p. 3.

8,951.   "Klan Has Strength In Thirteen States." New York
          Times. September 4, 1924, p. 4.

8,952.   "Klan Head Assails C.I.O." New York Times. July
          12, 1937, p. 4.

8,953.   "Klan Head Seeks Willis Testimony." Greensboro
          Daily News. September 11, 1966.

8,954.   "Klan Hearing." New York Times. October 26,
          1965, p. 44.

8,955.   "Klan Image." New York Times Magazine. July 26,
          1964, Sect. 6, pp. 4, 14.

8,956.   "The Klan In Court." Pittsburgh Courier. April
          21, 1928, editorial page.

8,957.   "Klan In House?" Milwaukee Community Journal.
          October 26-November 5, 1980, p. 5.

8,958.   "The Klan In Texas And Maine." The Messenger.
          Vol. 6, October, 1924, p. 312.

8,959.   "Klan Inquiry Is Suspended." New York Times.
          November 10, 1965, p. 7.

8,960.   "Klan Investigation." New York Times. October
          24, 1965, Sect. 4, p. 11.

8,961.   "Klan Investigation Panel To Include 4 Southerners."
          New York Times. May 14, 1965, p. 19.

8,962.   "Klan Investigation Urged." New York Times.
          June 4, 1947, p. 25.

8.963.   "Klan Is All 'Bluff' Declares Founder." New
          York Times. September 23, 1937, p. 7.

8,964.   "Klan Is Assailed In House Hearing." New York
          Times. October 12, 1921, p. 5.

8,965.   "Klan Is Dead; Long Live The —?" Christian
          Century. Vol. 45, March 8, 1928, pp. 306-307.

8,966.   "Klan Is Denounced As Foe Of Liberty." New York
          Times. July 5, 1924, p. 6.

8,967.   "Klan Is Denounced By Chairman Pell." New York
          Times. August 15, 1924, p. 4.

8,968.   "Klan Is Denounced By 'The Klansman'." New York
          Times. January 23, 1923, p. 23.

8,969.   "Klan Is Discussed By Mgr. M'Mahon." New York
          Times. November 13, 1923, p. 8.

8,970.   "The Klan Is Everywhere." The Scope. February
          13, 1981, p. 1.

8,971.   "Klan Is Major Topic For Black History Month."
          Jet. Vol. 59, February 26, 1981, p. 30.

8,972.   "Klan Is Urged To Unite To Combat Rights Act."
          New York Times. July 25, 1964, p. 9.

8,973.   "Klan Issue Raised On Apportionment." New York
          Times. December 16, 1928, p. 19.

8,974.   "Klan Leader Gets Prison Term For Failure To
          Produce Records." New York Times. October 15,
          1966, p. 14.

8,975.   "Klan Leaders Ask Johnson Meeting." New York Times.
          March 29, 1965, p. 28.

8,976.   "Klan Leaders In Pleas Of Guilty." New Bern Sun
          Journal. November 18, 1966.

8,977.   "Klan Leader Ousted From Hearing On Hill."
          Washington Post. December 10, 1980, p. A12.

8.978.   "Klan Leaders Plan Campaign." Washington Evening
          Star. July 10, 1963.

8,979.   "Klan Leaders Trial Is Deferred." New York Times.
          June 14, 1966, p. 26.

8,980.   "Klan Lets The Wizard Keep On 'Strutting'." New
          York Times. September 16, 1926, p. 10.

8,981.   "Klan; Liberty League Urged On Historians."
          New York Times. September 26, 1937, p. 39.

8,982.   "Klan Loses To Magazine." New York Times.
          November 6, 1923, p. 5.

8,983.   "Klan Makes Simmons Emperor For Life." New York Times. November 29, 1922, p. 2.

8,984.   "Klan Membership Seen On Increase." New York Times. September 22, 1966, p. 54.

8,985.   "Klan Motorcade Leaves Capital; To Tour 2 States." Durham Morning Herald. July 17, 1966.

8,986.   "Klan Not Open To Jews." New York Times. August 31, 1924, p. 6.

8,987.   "Klan Now Degrading Childhood." Pittsburgh Courier. January 8, 1949, p. 3.

8,988.   "Klan Officials Will Be Tried In Washington." Winston Salem Journal. November 15, 1966.

8,989.   "Klan On Stand." New York Times. October 24, 1965, Sect. 4, p. 1.

8,990.   "Klan On The Pan." Senior Scholastic. Vol. 86, April 15, 1965, p. 27.

8,991.   "Klan Ousts Clarke From Official Post." New York Times. March 7, 1923, p. 1.

8,992.   "Klan Poses Paramilitary Threat-Training 'Killers' In 7 States." Louisiana Weekly. November 8, 1980, pp. 1, 8.

8,993.   "Klan Power On Wane, Report Says." New York Amsterdam News. April 15, 1925, p. 2.

8,994.   "Klan Praises Mrs. Grow." New York Times. December 2, 1922, p. 14.

8,995.   "Klan Protests 'Aliens'." New York Times. August 2, 1937, p. 4.

8,996.   "The Klan Rears Its Head Again." Literary Digest. Vol. 118, July 21, 1934, p. 19.

8,997.   "Klan Rebirth Seen As Peace Meance." New York Times. October 3, 1937, Sect. 2, p. 10.

8.998.   "Klan Receivership Plea Is Waived." New York Times. October 28, 1928, p. 25.

8,999.   "Klan Recruitment Efforts Increase." Interracial Books For Children. Vol. 12, #4-5, 1981, p. 32.

9,000.   "Klan Re-elects Shelton." New York Times. September 5, 1967, p. 40.

9,001.   "Klan Resurgence Aimed At Young." Pittsburgh
         Courier. May 30, 1981, p. 1.

9,002.   "Klan, Retirement, TV Focus Of Resolutions Passed
         By Educators." Washington Star. July 6, 1980, p.
         A7.

9,003.   "Klan Returns To Secrecy." New York Times. August
         28, 1925, p. 16.

9,004.   "Klan Revives." Commonweal. Vol. 65, October 12,
         1956, p. 38.

9,005.   "Klan Rise Is Detailed By Hoover." Washington
         Post. July 5, 1966.

9,006.   "Klan Seeks U.S. Protection For Rallies."
         Atlanta Daily World. July 10, 1977, p. 2.

9,007.   "The Klan Sheds Its Hood." New Republic. Vol.
         45, February 10, 1926, pp. 310-311.

9,008.   "Klan Story Denied By Truman Again." New York
         Times. November 1, 1944, p. 40.

9,009.   "Klan Story False, Truman Declares." New York
         Times. October 27, 1944, p. 14.

9,010.   "Klan Terrorism Will Escalate By Spring. Jet.
         Vol. 60, March 26, 1981, p. 38.

9,011.   "The Klan To Be Issue Next Year." Pittsburgh
         Courier. December 15, 1923, p. 16.

9,012.   "Klan To Let Catholics And Immigrants Join."
         New York Times. December 16, 1974, p. 67.

9,013.   "Klan To 'Stay' Legal." New York Times. October
         1, 1956, p. 18.

9,014.   "Klan Unit Set For Race War." Scoop U.S.A.
         November 28, 1980, pp. 1, 16.

9,015.   "The Klan Unmasks." Pittsburgh Courier. March 3,
         1928, editorial page.

9,016.   "Klan, U.S. Nazi Hit By Speaker." Charlotte
         Observer. October 6, 1966, p. 7A.

9,017.   "Klan Uses An Alias To Bar Consequences As Sub-
         versive, AVC Head Charges." New York Times.
         December 26, 1948, p. 46.

9,018.   "Klan Using Bond Slogan, Treasury Chief Is Told."
         New York Times. October 17, 1941, p. 15.

9,019.   "Klan Will Sweep Colleges, She Says." New York Times. November 1, 1923, p. 18.

9,020.   "Klan Wins Point In Court." New York Times. September 1, 1923, p. 5.

9,021.   "Klan Wizard Declines Debate With Rabbi." New York Times. October 30, 1923, p. 22.

9,022.   "Klans Assets In July Totaled $1,087,373." New York Times. November 1, 1923, p. 3.

9,023.   "Klan's Challenge And The Reply." Literary Digest. Vol. 79, November 17, 1923, pp. 32-33.

9,024.   "Klan's Challenge Quickly Taken Up." New York Times. October 26, 1923, p. 19.

9,025.   "Klan's Imperial Wizard Denies Contempt Of Congress Charge." New York Times. January 8, 1966, p. 22.

9,026.   "The Klan's Invisible Empire Is Fading." New York Times. February 21, 1926, Sect. 8, pp. 1, 15.

9,027.   "Klan's New Krisis." Christianity Today. Vol. 10, November 19, 1965, pp. 42-43.

9,028.   "Klan's Right To Exist Challenged." New York Times. August 5, 1980, p. A8.

9,029.   "Klansman Fought Kosher Products." New York Times. February 16, 1966, p. 46.

9,030.   "Klansman Shelton Draws Year, Fine's Appeal Is Planned." Durham Morning Herald. October 15, 1966.

9,031.   "Klansman Summons Head Of House Unit." New York Times. June 15, 1966, p. 23.

9,032.   "Klansman Tosses Hood Into Political Ring." Knoxville Journal. May 21, 1969.

9,033.   "The Klansman's Secret; New York Times. Story." Time. Vol. 86, November 12, 1965, p. 54.

9,034.   "The Klansmen." Newsweek. Vol. 84, December 16, 1974, pp. 16-16A.

9,035.   "Klansmen Bid For Dismissal.: Durham Morning Herald. April 9, 1966.

9,036.   "Klansmen Called Traitors By Wise." New York Times. February 3, 1924, Sect. 2, p. 1.

9,037.   "Klansmen 'Citizens' Not Members Of Invisible
         Empire." New York Amsterdam News. May 20, 1925,
         p. 3.

9,038.   "Klansmen Cut Capers Everywhere." Chicago Defender.
         March 18, 1922, p. 1.

9,039.   "Klansmen In Revolt Establish New Order." New York
         Times. February 27, 1924, p. 8.

9,040.   "Klansmen In Revolt, To Form A New Order." New
         York Times. December 5, 1921, p. 18.

9,041.   "Klansmen Punished In Contempt Case." New York
         Times. March 15, 1969, p. 34.

9,042.   "Klashing In." Newsweek. Vol. 66, November 1,
         1965, pp. 34-35.

9,043.   "Kleagle Asks Arrest Of 3 Grand Goblins." New York
         Times. December 4, 1921, p. 18.

9,044.   Kleber, Louis C. "Ku Klux Klan." History Today.
         Vol. 21, August, 1971, pp. 567-574.

9,045.   Klemesrud, Judy.   "Women In Ku Klux Klan Move Into
         The Male Power Structure." New York Times. May
         22, 1975, p. 44.

9,046.   "Kluxer Says Klan Is Negros' Friend." New York
         Amsterdam News. August 15, 1923, p. 7.

9,047.   "The Kluxers Merge." Pittsburgh Courier.
         September 3, 1949, p. 19.

9,048.   "Knew Black Facts, Borah Now Says." New York Times.
         October 2, 1937, p. 2.

9,049.   "The Koo Koo Klan Again." The Messenger. Vol. 4,
         September, 1922, pp. 489-490.

9,050.   "The Ku Klux Act Upheld." New York Times.
         November 21, 1928, p. 28.

9,051.   "Ku Klux Catholics." Pittsburgh Courier. May 28,
         1927, editorial page.

9,052.   "Ku Klux Certain To Be Political Issue In 1924."
         Pittsburgh Courier. October 6, 1923, p. 10.

9,053.   "Ku Klux Chief Says Klan Does Not Kill." New York
         Times. December 26, 1922, p. 3.

9,054.   "Ku Klux Condemned By The Religious Press."
         Literary Digest. Vol. 71, October 1, 1921, pp. 30-
         31.

9,055.   "Ku Klux Considers Women Auxilaries." New York
Times. November 30, 1922, p. 21.

9,056.   "Ku Klux Declares Against Gov. Smith." New York
Times. April 27, 1924, p. 2.

9,057.   "Ku Klux Defeat Pleases Thomas." New York Times.
August 25, 1924, p. 2.

9,058.   "Ku Klux Denounced By Justice Gannon." New York
Times. September 17, 1921, p. 4.

9,059.   "Ku Klux Denounced From Many Pulpits." New York
Times. December 1, 1922, p. 2.

9,060.   "Ku Klux Klan." American Federationist. Vol. 30,
November, 1923, p. 919.

9,061.   "Ku Klux Klan." Catholic World. Vol. 116,
January, 1923, pp. 433-443.

9,062.   "The Ku Klux Klan." Century. Vol. 28, August,
1884, pp. 948-950.

9,063.   "The Ku Klux Klan." The Messenger. Vol. 5,
January, 1923, p. 564.

9,064.   "The Ku Klux Klan." New York Times Book Review.
November 6, 1932, p. 21.

9,065.   "Ku Klux Klan." New York World. October 25,
1923.

9.066.   "The Ku Klux Klan - A Threat To America." Chicago
Defender. December 7, 1946, p. 14.

9,067.   "Ku Klux Klan Again." Outlook. Vol. 129,
September 21, 1921, p. 79.

9,068.   "The Ku Klux Klan Again." New Republic. Vol.
114, June 10, 1946, p. 822.

9,069.   "Ku Klux Klan Can Claim Equal Times." Charlotte
Observer. July 31, 1966.

9,070.   "Ku Klux Klan Celebrates." New York Times. May 5,
1921, p. 4.

9,071.   "The Ku Klux Klan - How To Fight It." The
Messenger. Vol. 3, November, 1921, pp. 276-277.

9,072.   "Ku Klux Klan In Row Over Women." New York Amsterdam News. April 4, 1923, p. 7.

9,073.   "Ku Klux Klan Membership Up." Pittsburgh Courier.
April 29, 1978, p. 1.

9,074.   "Ku Klux Klan Names Colescott New Chief." New
          York Times. June 11, 1939, p. 47.

9,075.   "Ku Klux Klan On The Downgrade." Christian Century.
          Vol. 40, September 13, 1923, pp. 1158-1160.

9,076.   "Ku Klux Klan Ousts Simmons And Clarke." New York
          Times. January 12, 1924, p. 1.

9,077.   "Ku Klux Klan Recruits From Elementary And High
          Schools." New Crusader. May 30, 1981, pp. 1, 3.

9,078.   "Ku Klux Klan: Re-emergence Of The 'Haters'."
          New York Times. April 30, 1977, p. 24.

9,079.   "Ku Klux Klan Seeks Catholics As Members." New
          York Times. April 24, 1957, p. 35.

9,080.   "Ku Klux Klan Seizing The Government." The
          Messenger. Vol. 4, December, 1922, pp. 537-538.

9,081.   "Ku Klux Klan Slowly Dying; Loses Five Lives Out
          Of Nine." Chicago Defender. May 6, 1922, p. 14.

9,082.   "Ku Klux Klan: The Violent History Of A Hooded
          Society." Senior Scholastic. Vol. 87, December
          2, 1965, pp. 5-8.

9,083.   "Ku Klux Klan Tries For A Comeback." U.S. News And
          World Report. Vol. 78, June 23, 1975, pp. 32-34.

9,084.   "Ku Klux Klan - Unmasked." Time. Vol. 11, March
          5, 1928, pp. 10-11.

9,085.   "Ku Klux Klan Uprising: Klan Recruits Kids."
          Buckeye Review. May 29, 1981, pp. 1, 5.

9,086.   "Ku Klux Klan Wants Negroes To Join." The Messenger.
          Vol. 7, April, 1925, pp. 156-157.

9,087.   "Ku Klux Klansmen." New York Times. May 28, 1971,
          p. 13.

9,088.   "Ku Klux Kourts." The Messenger. Vol. 6,
          December, 1929, p. 373.

9,089.   "Ku Klux Letters Assail Dr. Butler." New York
          Times. February 25, 1924, p. 17.

9,090.   "Ku Klux Loses Suit." New York Times. August 10,
          1923, p. 10.

9,091.   "Ku Klux Must Go, Says Dr. Straton." New York
          Times. December 4, 1922, p. 4.

9,092.   "Ku Klux Offers Reward." New York Times.
          January 18, 1921, p. 6.

9,093.   "The Ku Klux, Past And Present." New York
          Amsterdam News. June 30, 1923, p. 12.

9,094.   "Ku Klux Revive 'Birth Of A Nation'." New York
          Amsterdam News. December 6, 1922, p. 1.

9,095.   "The Ku Klux Trial." American Missionary Magazine.
          Vol. 16, February, 1872, pp. 39-40.

9,096.   "Ku Kluxers Everywhere, Says Doctor." Chicago
          Defender. April 15, 1922, p. 1.

9,097.   "Labor Drops Issue Of Road Ownership." New York
          Times. June 21, 1922, p. 28.

9,098.   "LaFollette Scores The Ku Klux Klan." New York
          Times. August 9, 1924, p. 1.

9,099.   Langford, David L. "A Self-Made Wizard Spreads The
          Racist Word To Eager Ears." Atlantic City Press.
          December 30, 1980.

9,100.   _____. "A 'Wizard' Sees Race War Ahead."
          Atlantic City Press. December 31, 1980.

9,101.   _____. "Who Is Behind The Hood?" Atlantic
          City Press. December 31, 1980.

9,102.   "Law Officers Exhorted." New York Times. March
          27, 1965, p. 11.

9,103.   "Lawless Outbreaks Involve 4 States; Lashings
          Increase." New York Times. August 19, 1923, p. 1.

9,104.   Lawrence, David. "Un-American Activities."
          Greensboro Daily News. August 20, 1966.

9,105.   "Lawyer Questioned At Inquiry On Klan." New York
          Times. January 17, 1929, p. 16.

9,106.   "Lawyer Starts Fight On Black." New York Times.
          September 17, 1937, p. 12.

9,107.   Lay, Wilfrid. "Psychoanalyzing The Klan." The
          World Tomorrow. Vol. 7, March, 1924, pp. 79-80.

9,108.   "Leave For Simmons; Clarke To Run Klan." New York
          Times. June 10, 1922, p. 26.

9,109.   Lee, Kendrick. "Ku Klux Klan." Editorial Research
          Report. Vol. 2, July 10, 1946, pp. 449-464.

9,110.   "Legal And Registered Weapons Of Ku Klux Klan
          Members." Chicago Tribune. March 20, 1979,
          Sect. 3, p. 2.

9,111.   "Legion And Klan." New York Times. October 20,
          1923, p. 14.

9,112.   "Legion Approves Mild Klan Censure." New York
          Times. October 19, 1923, p. 7.

9,113.   "Legion Deadlocked On Bonus Question." New York
          Times. October 18, 1923, p. 3.

9,114.   "Legion's Head Hits Klan." New York Times.
          August 10, 1924, p. 3.

9,115.   Leiferman, Henry P. "Klan Youth Corps Teaches
          Military Drill, Bigotry Cheap." Nashville Banner.
          April 24, 1968.

9,116.   Lerner, Max. "The Passing Of The Klansman." PM.
          May 24, 1945.

9,117.   "Let The Klan Die." New York Times. November
          20, 1923, p. 18.

9,118.   "Letters - KKK." Interracial Books For Children
          Bulletin. Vol. 11, #6, 1980, p. 22.

9,119.   "Letters To The Editor." New York Times Book
          Review. October 16, 1932, p. 26.

9,120.   Leubsdorf, Carl P. "Katzenbach's Testimony Due
          On Klan Today." New Bern Sun-Journal. July 20,
          1966.

9,121.   _____. "Klan Inquiry Not Resulting In House
          Bill." New Bern Sun-Journal. September 24, 1966.

9,122.   Leviero, Anthony. "Byrnes 'Failed Miserably,'
          Truman Is Quoted As Saying." New York Times.
          September 27, 1950, pp. 1, 23.

9,123.   Levey, Stanley. "Steel Union Bars Reds And
          Facists." New York Times. September 25, 1954, p. 1.

9,124.   Lewis, Anthony. "Hoover And King Discuss Dispute."
          New York Times. December 2, 1964, pp. 1, 32.

9,125.   "Liberties Union Scores Klan Bill." New York Times.
          July 23, 1966, p. 7.

9,126.   Lingeman, Richard R. "Annals Of The Ku Klux Klan."
          New York Times. May 8, 1971, p. 27.

9,127.   "Link To Klan Denied." New York Times. May 11,
          1955, p. 26.

9,128.   Lipset, Seymour M. "An Anatomy Of The Klan."
          Commentary. Vol. 40, October, 1965, pp. 74-83.

9,129.   "Liquor Storm Stirs The House All Day; Drys Repel
          Attack." New York Times. December 8, 1922
          pp. 1, 3.

9,130.   Lisagor, Peter. "LBJ And The Klan." New York
          Post. March 28, 1965.

9,131.   "Local Issues Big In This Campaign." New York
          Times. October 22, 1922, Sect. 2, p. 1.

9,132.   "Locals Take Stock." Christian Science Monitor.
          November 4, 1965, p. 1.

9,133.   Loftis, Randy L. "Has The KKK Duped The Press?"
          The Civil Rights Quarterly Perspectives. Vol. 12,
          Fall, 1980 - Winter, 1981, pp. 14-15.

9,134.   Loggins, Kirk and Susan Thomas. "The Meance
          Returns." Southern Exposure. Vol. 8, Summer,
          1980, pp. 50-54.

9,135.   "Lonergan Submits Choice To Black." New York
          Times. September 19, 1937, p. 39.

9,136.   Long, Margaret. "The Imperial Wizard Explains The
          Klan." New York Times Book Review. July 5, 1964,
          Sect. 6, pp. 8, 25-26.

9,137.   " 'Long, Hot Summer' Flaring In The South?" U.S.
          News And World Report. Vol. 86, June 25, 1979, p.
          12.

9,138.   "A Long White Summer For KKK Kids." Life. Vol.
          2, August, 1979, pp. 108-109.

9,139.   "A Look At The Ku Klux Klan Today." Chicago
          Tribune. September 24, 1978, p. 14.

9,140.   Lovejoy, Gordon W. "In Brotherhood Week: A Look
          At The South." New York Times Magazine.
          February 17, 1957, Sect. 6, pp. 13, 50, 52, 54, 56.

9,141.   Lowther, William. "Bigots In Bedsheets."
          MacLeans. January 8 1979, pp. 6-7.

9,142.   Lowry, Edward G. "A Great Doubt In The Middle
          West." New York Times. October 13, 1924, p. 16.

9,143.   MacDonald, William. "Ku Kluxism, A Product Of
          The American Mind." New York Times Magazine.
          March 16, 1924, Sect. 3, p. 3.

9,144. Maeroff, Gene I. "Klan's Critics Split On Educa-
        tional Response." New York Times. October 25,
        1981, p. 25.

9,145. "Mahoney Assails Black." New York Times.
        October 2, 1937, p. 2.

9,146. "Mahoney Attacks Copeland On Klan." New York
        Times. September 15, 1937, p. 3.

9,147. "Mail From J. Edgar Hoover And The Ku Klux Klan."
        Washington Post. August 22, 1975, p. 24A.

9,148. "Major KKK Faction Modifies Membership Tradition."
        New Orleans Times Picayune. December 16, 1974,
        p. 5.

9,149. "Many In South See Cool To Klan." New York Times.
        September 6, 1946, p. 23.

9,150. "Many Klanswomen Quit. New York Times. March 13,
        1927, p. 13.

9,151. Marable, Manning. "Klan Violence Against Black
        People." North Shore (Evanston, Ill.) Examiner.
        May 29, 1981, p. 5.

9,152. "Mark Of The Beast: Special Section On The Ku
        Klux Klan." Southern Exposure. Vol. 8, Summer,
        1980, pp. 49-100.

9,153. Marro, Anthony. "Rising Concern Over Informers
        Being Voiced By Legal Officials." New York Times.
        July 23, 1978, pp. 1, 10.

9,154. "Masons And The Ku Klux." New York Times.
        September 2, 1923, Sect. 7, p. 10.

9,155. "Masons Strike Out To Hasten Klan's Demise."
        Chicago Defender. July 8,1922, p. 9.

9,156. "Mason-Dixon Scribes Uphold Ku Klux Klan."
        Chicago Defender. August 6, 1921, p. 3.

9,157. Martin, Harold H. "The Truth About The Klan
        Today." Saturday Evening Post. Vol. 222,
        October 22, 1949, pp. 17-18, 122-126.

9,158. Martin, Phillip W.D. "For A New Push On Civil
        Rights." Christian Science Monitor. January 8,
        1981, p. 23.

9,159. "A Matter Of History." Chicago Defender.
        September 24, 1921, p. 16.

9,160.   "M'Adoo Punctures Klan Note Canard." New York
          Times. January 23, 1924, p. 21.

9,161.   "May Launch TV Campaign Reader Writes Extremists.
          Christian Science Monitor. July 25, 1970, p. E3.

9,162.   McFarland, Richard. "Resurgence Of KKK And
          Nazism Condemned By Church Council." Atlanta
          Daily World. May 14, 1978, p. 1.

9,163.   McGill, Ralph. " 'God Made A Mistake'." Winston-
          Salem Journal. April 18, 1966.

9,164.   _____. "Therapy For Justice In The South."
          Washington Evening Star. December 25, 1965, p. A-5.

9,165.   McKee, Don. "Klan Claims Membership Gain." Twin
          City Sentinel. July 17, 1964.

9,166.   McNeilly, John S. "Enforcement Act Of 1871 and
          Ku Klux Klan." Mississippi Historical Society.
          Vol. 9, November, 1906, pp. 109-171.

9,167.   _____. "Reconstruction And The Ku Klux."
          Confederate Veteran. Vol. 30, March, 1922,
          pp. 96-97.

9,168.   "M'Reynolds Wary On Black's Status." New York
          Times. October 2, 1937, p. 3.

9,169.   McWhiney, H. Grady, and Francis F. Simkins.
          "Ghostly Legend Of The Ku Klux Klan." The Negro
          History Bulletin. Vol. 14, February 1951, pp.
          109-112.

9,170.   "Measure To Keep KKK Off School Grounds Passed."
          Jet. Vol. 59, November 20, 1980, p. 22.

9,171.   Mecklin, John M. "Ku Klux Klan And The Democratic
          Tradition." American Review. Vol. 2, May, 1924,
          pp. 241-251.

9,172.   "Meeting Of The Nat'l Knights Of The Ku Klux Klan
          Described." Chicago Tribune. September 6, 1976,
          p. 1.

9,173.   Mellard, James M. "Racism, Formula, And Popular
          Fiction." Journal Of Popular Culture. Vol. 5,
          Summer, 1971, pp. 10-37.

9,174.   "Members Of The Ku Klux Klan." New York Times.
          September 8, 1923, p. 15.

9,175.   "Membership In The American Facist: Disclaimed."
          The Messenger. Vol. 4, November 1, 1922, pp. 518-
          519.

9,176.   "Menace Of Ku Klux Worries The South." New York
           Times. June 27, 1924, p. 5.

9,177.   Merz, Charles. "The New Ku Klux Klan." Indepen-
           dent. Vol. 118, February 12, 1927, pp. 179-180,
           196.

9,178.   "The Messenger Editors." The Messenger. Vol. 3,
           March, 1921, p. 194.

9,179.   "Methodist Global Ministries Board Takes Stand On
           Key Issues." Michigan Chronicle. October 27,
           1979, p. 3A.

9,180.   "Methodists Defeat Assault On Klan." New York
           Times. April 21, 1925, p. 19.

9,181.   "Methodists Turn Against Stokes." New York Times.
           March 8, 1924, p. 26.

9,182.   "Michigan Rep. Collins Offers Bill On Paramilitary
           Camps." Bilalian News. September 11, 1981, p. 23.

9,183.   Miller, Robert M. "Note On The Relationship
           Between The Protestant Churches And The Revived
           Ku Klux Klan." Journal Of Southern History.
           Vol. 22, August, 1956, pp. 355-368.

9,184.   . "The Social Attitudes Of The American
           Methodists, 1919-1920." Religion In Life.
           Vol. 28, Spring, 1958, pp. 185-198.

9,185.   Mills, Joshua E. "Juvenile Journalism."
           Columbia Journalism Review. Vol. 19, January/
           February, 1981, p. 14; The Civil Rights Quarterly
           Perspectives, Vol. 13, Spring, 1981, p. 45.

9,186.   "Mine-Workers Politics." New York Times.
           February 1, 1924, p. 16.

9,187.   "Miner Insurgents Vote Lewis Down." New York
           Times. January 30, 1924, p. 21.

9,188.   "Miners In Uproar, Fight Lewis's Rule." New York
           Times. January 31, 1924, p. 19.

9,189.   "Miners Vote Down Klan Ban Repeal." New York
           Times. February 2, 1924, p. 3.

9,190.   "Miss Davis's Klan Book." New York Times.
           May 21, 1925, p. 6.

9,191.   Mitchell, Louis D. "Klan Today." The Crisis.
           Vol. 85, February, 1978, pp. 48-53, 56.

9,192.   "Mixup Derails House Group's Probe Of Klan."
           Washington Evening Star. November 10, 1965.

9,193.   "Mob Violence And The Ku Klux Klan." The Messenger.
           Vol. 3, September, 1921, pp. 244-246.

9,194.   Mockler, William E. "Source Of Ku Klux." Names.
           Vol. 3, March, 1955, pp. 14-18.

9,195.   Mohr, Charles. "Johnson Opens Fight On Klan
           After F.B.I. Seizes 4 Members In Alabama Murder
           Of Woman." New York Times. March 27, 1965,
           pp. 1, 11.

9,196.   "Moore Says Dawes Straddled On Klan." New York
           Times. August 25, 1924, p. 2.

9.197.   Moose, Ruth. "Decent Klansmen." New York Times.
           March 10, 1980, p. 19

9,198.   Morris, John D. "Full Investigation Of Klan Voted
           By House Committee." New York Times. March 31,
           1965, pp. 1, 19.

9.199.   _____. "Inquiry Into Klan Studied In House."
           New York Times. February 13, 1965, p. 17.

9,200.   "Morse Hints Doubt On Hate Note At U.N." New
           York Times. December 14, 1960, p. 44.

9,201.   "Move To Curb Ku Klux." New York Times. August
           12, 1922, p. 20.

9,202.   "Mr. Borah's Explanation." New York Times.
           October 3, 1937, Sect. 4, p. 8.

9,203.   Muhammad, Elijah. Message To The Blackman In
           America. Chicago: Muhammad Mosque Of Islam No. 2,
           1965. "Answer To Christian Knights of The Ku
           Klux Klan." pp. 330-341.

9,204.   Mullen, Kevin. "From Klan Hood To Mantle."
           Reader's Scope. May, 1945, pp. 29-32.

9,205.   Murray, David. "(Martin Luther) King Set Up
           Special Panel To Probe Klan." New York Post.
           March 31, 1965, p. 5.

9,206.   "Mu Sigma Denounces Klan." New York Times.
           December 27, 1922, p. 2.

9,207.   "Murder Within The Law." New York Amsterdam News.
           3 January, 1923, p. 1; 10 January, 1923, p. 1;
           17 January, 1923, p. 1; 24 January, 1923, p. 1;
           31 January, 1923, p. 1; 7 February, 1923, p. 1;
           21 February, 1923, p. 3; 28 February, 1923, p. 3;
           7 March, 1923, p. 1; 14 March, 1923, p. 17;

11 April, 1923, p. 12.

9,208.   Murphy, Robert J. "The South Fights Bombing."
          Look. Vol. 23, January 6, 1959, pp. 13-17.

9,209.   Muscatine, Alison. "Rights Leader Calls Thurmond
          Plan 'Odious'." Washington Star. December 1,
          1980.

9,210.   "Mussolini Joins The Klan." Pittsburgh Courier.
          October 6, 1928, Editorial page.

9,211.   Myers, Lisa. "President Backs Off 'Racism'."
          Washington Star. September 19, 1980, pp. A1, A4.

9,212.   Myers, William Starr. "The Ku Klux Klan Of
          Today." North American Review. Vol. 223, June-
          August, 1926, pp. 304-309.

9,213.   "NAACP Convention Delegates Warned Of KKK Threat."
          Atlanta Daily World. July 7, 1981, p. 1.

9,214.   "NAACP Declares Non-Violent War On The Klan."
          Arizona Informant. April 29, 1981, p. 1.

9,215.   "NAACP Executive Director Hooks On The Ku Klux
          Klan - Letter." Baltimore Afro-American.
          December 15, 1979, p. 4.

9,216.   "NAACP Leader Hooks Interviewed On 'Face The
          Nation'." San Francisco Chronicle. July 7, 1980,
          p. 2.

9,217.   "NAACP Official Eyes ADL Criticism Of NEA View
          Of KKK." New York Amsterdam News. November 7,
          1981, p. 3.

9,218.   "N.A.A.C.P. Opposes Bill To Curb Klan." New York
          Times. July 22, 1966, p. 34.

9,219.   "NAACP Opposes Klan Bill." Winston-Salem Journal.
          July 22, 1966, p. 1.

9,220.   "NAACP Pledges Fight For Anti-Bias Rider And Hits
          Ike's KKK Choice." Freedom. May-June, 1955,
          p. 5.

9,221.   "N.A.A.C.P. Was First To Learn Of Klan Perfidy."
          Chicago Defender. October 15, 1921, p. 2.

9,222.   "The Nation And The Klan." The Messenger. Vol.
          6, March, 1924, pp. 69-70.

9,223.   "National Affairs-Ku Klux Klan." Time. Vol. 4,
          August 18, 1924, pp. 3-4.

9,224.   "National Churches Council Views KKK And Racial Justice Issues." Atlanta Daily World. November 8, 1979, p. 2.

9,225.   "National Council Of Churches Condemns Resurgence Of The KKK And Nazism." Atlanta Daily World. May 14, 1978, p. 1.

9,226.   "Nat'l Council Of Churches Eyes Resurgence Of KKK." Bilalian News. November 30, 1979, p. 5.

9,227.   "Nat'l Dir. Of Knights Of KKK Comments On His Arrest." New Orleans Times Picayune. September 13, 1976, p. 12.

9,228.   "National Education Association Prepares Curriculum Guide On KKK." Bilalian News. July 10, 1981, p. 4.

9,229.   "A National Plot To Kill Blacks." U.S. News And World Report. Vol. 87, November 3, 1980, p. 7.

9,230.   "Nations Defends Klan." New York Times. August 31, 1924, p. 3.

9,231.   "Navy Announces Remedial Education And Anti-Racist Programs." Washington Post. August 30, 1979, p. 7A.

9,232.   "Navy Confirms Klan Inquiry On 2 Ships In Atlantic Fleet." New York Times. July 1, 1979, p. 17.

9,233.   "Navy Cracks Down On 'Racist Activity'." New York Times. August 30, 1979, p. A16.

9,234.   "Nazis Likened To Klan." New York Times. March 30, 1933, p. 13.

9,235.   "Nazis, The Ku Klux Klan And Free Speech." Washington Post. January 14, 1978, p. A14.

9,236.   "NBA Immediate Past President Drafts Legislation To Ban KKK Violence." National Bar Bulletin. Vol. 13, February, 1981, p. 1.

9,237.   "NEA Releases Curriculum Guide On Ku Klux Klan." Baltimore Afro-American. July 11, 1981, p. 3.

9,238.   "Need For Support For Anti-KKK Activities." Los Angeles Sentinel. November 22, 1979, p. 6A.

9,239.   "The Negro And The Klan." New York Times. September 7, 1924, Sect. 7, p. 10.

9,240.   "Negro Conference Resists Dixie Bans." New York Times. March 22, 1948, p. 24.

9,241.   "Negro Duties And Rights." The Freeman. Vol. 4,
          September 21, 1921, pp. 26-27.

9,242.   "Negro Leader For Davis." New York Times.
          September 15, 1924, p. 2.

9,243.   "Negro Legislators." The Messenger. Vol. 3,
          October, 1921, pp. 260-261.

9,244.   "The Negro Question." Kourier Magazine. Vol. 3,
          May, 1927, pp. 29-32.

9,245.   "Negroes Ask Klan Quiz." New York Times. March
          26, 1940, p. 10.

9,246.   "Negroes Blame Klan For Race Troubles." New York
          Times. September 21, 1925, p. 10.

9,247.   "Negroes Defend Black." New York Times. October
          2, 1937, p. 3.

9,248.   "Negroes Denounce Black." New York Times.
          September 19, 1937, p. 39.

9,249.   "Negroes Protest Against Watson." New York Times.
          May 15, 1924, p. 3.

9,250.   "Negroes Threaten To Bolt On Klan." New York
          Times. September 17, 1924, p. 2.

9,251.   "Neither Klan Nor Colony." New York Times.
          July 28, 1924, p. 10.

9,252.   Nelson, Jack. "FBI Ex-Informant Tells Actions
          Of Klan." Washington Post. December 1, 1978,
          p. C6.

9,253.   _____. "FBI Knew About -- But Didn't Stop --
          Violence By Klan, Informant Says." Miami Herald.
          November 30, 1975, pp. 1A, 19A.

9,254.   "The New Crusaders." Opportunity. Vol. 2, August,
          1924, pp. 227-228.

9,255.   "The New Face Of Anti-Semitism." Los Angeles.
          Vol. 26, June, 1981, pp. 192-200.

9,256.   " 'New' KKK Drawing Students: Schools Must Combat
          Influence." Vibration. #68, July-September, 1981,
          p. 8.

9,257.   "The New Klan." Chicago Defender. March 11, 1978,
          p. 6.

9,258.   "The New Klan." Michigan Chronicle. March 25,
          1978, p. 8.

9,259.   " 'New' Klan Gets Into Marketing Its Memorabilia
In A Big Way." _Charlotte Observer_. December 25,
1980, p. 32A.

9,260.   "New Klan Group Faces An Inquiry." _New York Times_.
January 13, 1929, p. 17.

9,261.   "New Klan Hearings Set." _New York Times_. July 14,
1966, p. 3.

9,262.   "_The New Klan: Heritage Of Hate_: Documentaries
Pose Questions." _Christian Science Monitor_.
November 16, 1978, p. 16.

9,263.   "_The New Klan, Heritage Of Hate_, TV Documentary,
Reviewed." _New Orleans Times Picayune_. November
19, 1978, TV Section, p. 24.

9,264.   "New KKK Might Include Catholics." _Raleigh News &
Observer_. November 21, 1969, p. 8.

9,265.   "New Klan Organized." _New York Times_. March 1,
1960, p. 18.

9,266.   "New Klan Organized." _New York Times_. October 25,
1955, p. 38.

9,267.   "New Marketing Of Various KKK Articles." _Chicago
Tribune_. December 18, 1980, p. 1.

9,268.   "New National Klan Formed By Old Group's Dissidents."
New York Times. October 14, 1975, p. 15.

9,269.   "Newly Resurgent Ku Klux Klan Exploits Racial
Tensions In American Schools." _NEA Reporter_.
Vol. 20, June, 1981, pp. 8-9.

9,270.   "News Item - 'South Hit By Heavy Snow'." _Pittsburgh
Courier_. January 14, 1928, Editorial page.

9,271.   "Next Step: Button-Down Robes." _Time_. Vol. 83,
May 1, 1964, pp. 23-24.

9,272.   "1953 Pulitzer Prize Won By Hemingway And 'Picnic'."
New York Times. May 5, 1953, pp. 1, 24.

9,273.   "1971 FBI Plot Against Ku Klux Klan Revealed."
Washington Post. April 16, 1976, p. 1.

9,274.   "No Hint By Black Of Details Of Talk Over Radio
Tonight." _New York Times_. October 1, 1937,
pp. 1, 11.

9,275.   "No, The Klan Didn't Grow And Thrive 'On Its Social
Conscience'." _New York Times_. March 24, 1980,
p. 23.

9,276.   "Northeast Klansmen Quit Bill Wilkinson's Invisible
          Empire." New Orleans Times Picayune. January 25,
          1981, Sect. 7, p. 12.

9,277.   "Now On The Other Foot." New York Times. August
          28, 1924, p. 16.

9,278.   "N.O.W. Takes Several Actions During Last Hours
          Of Nat'l Convention." Los Angeles Times. June 16,
          1980, Sect. 2, p. 1.

9,279.   "N.Y. UL Concerned About KKK Activity In Northeast
          U.S." New York Amsterdam News. December 29, 1979,
          p. 5.

9,280.   "Observer: The Klan Plays With Dynamite." New York
          Times. May 13, 1965, p. 36.

9,281.   "Obstacles Block South In Curbing Klan." Christian
          Science Monitor. October 12, 1950, p. 3.

9,282.   "O'Connell Assails Dawes." New York Times. August
          27, 1924, p. 3.

9,283.   O'Connor, John J. "Genesis Of Atomic Bomb And
          Klan's Recruiting." New York Times. September
          19, 1980, p. C27.

9,284.   _____. "TV: First Of Two Balanchine Programs."
          New York Times. December 14, 1977, p. C24.

9,285.   "Odd Fellows Ignore Complaint Of Klan." New York
          Times. August 20, 1924, p. 17.

9,286.   "Odd Fellows Plan Fight On The Klan." New York
          Times. August 19, 1924, p. 7.

9,287.   "Odd Fellows Reject Attack On The Klan." New York
          Times. August 22, 1924, p. 3.

9,288.   "Of All The Wrongs You've Done To Me." Pittsburgh
          Courier. March 12, 1927, p. B8.

9,289.   "Offers To Defend Klan." New York Times.
          September 10, 1923, p. 19.

9,290.   "Official War Dept. Document Nails All Color, Race,
          Blood, Jim-Crow, Anti-Semitics, KKK Lies." In Fact.
          August 26, 1946, pp. 104-107.

9,291.   Olsen, Otto H. "The Ku Klux Klan: A Study Of
          Reconstruction Politics And Propaganda." North
          Carolina Historical Review. Vol. 39, July, 1962,
          pp. 340-362.

9,292.   "111 Years Of KKKronology." Southern Exposure.
          Vol. 8, Summer, 1980, pp. 58-59.

9,293.   "$1,000,000 Centre For Jews Is Opened." New York
          Times. January 1, 1923, p. 16.

9,294.   "An Open Letter To America On The Ku Klux Klan."
          The Messenger. Vol. 2, December, 1920, pp. 166-
          168.

9,295.   "Opposes A Female Klan." New York Times.
          November 6, 1923, p. 5.

9,296.   "Opposition Curbs New Rise." Christian Science
          Monitor. February 5, 1949, p. 18.

9,297.   "Opposition To KKK Comeback Grows." Bilalian News.
          July 29, p. 7.

9,298.   "Orders Klan Secrets Kept." New York Times.
          June 23, 1923, p. 13.

9,299.   "Oscar Underwood's Great Service." World's Work.
          Vol. 48, July, 1924, pp. 242-243.

9,300.   Oulahan, Richard V. "Closure Wins, 68-26,
          Assuring Victory For World Court." New York Times.
          January 26, 1926, p. 2.

9,301.   _____. "Congress Pressed For Education Bill."
          New York Times. March 10, 1926, p. 4.

9,302.   "Our Own Secret Fascisti." Nation. Vol. 115,
          November 15, 1922, pp. 514-515.

9,303.   Owen, Chandler. "Opinion." Pittsburgh Courier.
          November 3, 1923, p. 16.

9,304.   Owens, John W. "Does The Senate Fear The Ku Klux
          Klan?" New Republic. Vol. 37, December 26, 1923,
          pp. 113-114.

9,305.   "Pastor Says Klan Plans World Drive." New York
          Times. November 27, 1922, pp. 1, 2.

9,306.   "A Pathetic Appeal To Klansmen." New York Times.
          September 12, 1924, p. 20.

9,307.   Pattangall, William R. "Is The Ku Klux Un-
          American?" Forum. Vol. 74, September, 1925,
          pp. 321-332.

9,308.   Patterson, Pat. "The Resurgence Of The Klan."
          Crisis. Vol. 88, March, 1981, p. 57.

9,309.   Patton, R.A.   "A Ku Klux Klan Reign Of Terror."
          Current History. Vol. 28, April, 1928, pp. 51-55.

9,310.   Payne, George H.   "Does The Ku Klux Need The Jew?"
          Forum.   Vol. 74, December, 1925, pp. 915-917.

9,311.   Pear, Robert.   "Justice Dept. Restricts Subpoenas
          For Reporters And Phone Records." New York Times.
          November 13, 1980, p. A30.

9,312.   Pearson, Drew.   "Klan Out To 'Get' Pearson Spy."
          Washington Post.   December 18, 1944.

9,313.   _____. "Klansman Up North." New York Post.
          November 2, 1965.

9,314.   _____. "Klan Grows In North." New York Post.
          July 2, 1966.

9,315.   _____. "Spotlight On The Klan." New York Post.
          October 20, 1965.

9,316.   "Pending Bills To Curb Immigration Assailed As
          Putting Iron Curtain About United States." New
          York Times.   February 20, 1952, p. 13.

9,317.   "Pentagon Official Reports 'A New Racism' In
          Military." New York Times.   July 24, 1979, p. 10.

9,318.   Percy, Leroy.   "The Modern Ku Klux Klan." Atlantic
          Monthly.   Vol. 130, July, 1922, pp. 122-128.

9,319.   Perlmutter, Emanuel.   "Powell Attacks Clergy Of
          South." New York Times.   September 26, 1960, p. 28.

9,320.   "Pershing And Dawes Hit Reds And Klan." New York
          Times.   December 7, 1922, p. 21.

9,321.   Pfister, Joe.   "Book Review - The Klan By Patsy
          Sims." Southern Exposure.   Vol. 8, Summer, 1980,
          pp. 101-102.

9,322.   Phillips, Cabell.   "Funds Voted For Study Of Klan
          By Un-American Activities Unit." New York Times.
          April 15, 1965, p. 18.

9,323.   "Pink Ballots For The Ku Klux Klan." Outlook.
          Vol. 137, June 25, 1924, pp. 306-309.

9,324.   "Pity The Jews And The Catholics." Chicago
          Defender.   September 3, 1921, pp. 16-17.

9,325.   "Plans A Movement For Nation's Youth." New York
          Times.   December 30, 1923, p. 3.

9,326.   "Political Night Riders Invade State Campaigns."
           New York Times. June 18, 1922, Sect. 7, p. 1.

9,327.   "Political Power Claimed." New York Times.
           September 6, 1964, p. 34.

9,328.   " 'Politics' Asserts Logan." New York Times.
           September 14, 1937, p. 18.

9,329.   Popham, John N. "Aroused South Takes Steps
           Against New Klan Violence." New York Times.
           June 26, 1949, Sect. 4, p. 10.

9,330.   _____. "Klan In Latest Phase Is A Censor Of
           Morals." New York Times. February 24, 1952,
           Sect. 4, p. 10.

9,331.   _____. "Organized Resistance To Racial Laws
           Grows." New York Times. December 2, 1956, Sect.
           4, p. 9.

9,332.   _____. "South Makes Head-Way In Fight On The
           Klan." New York Times. July 24, 1949, Sect. 4,
           p. 8.

9,333.   Porter, Russell B. "Evans Denies Klan Had Life
           Members." New York Times. September 15, 1937,
           p. 3.

9,334.   _____. "Klan, Shorn Of Power, Seeking To Re-
           gain It." New York Times. September 19, 1937,
           Sect. 4, p. 6.

9,335.   _____. "Roosevelt Misses Black Broadcast."
           New York Times. October 2, 1937, pp. 1, 5.

9,336.   "Potentate To Potentate Speaks." New York Times.
           September 16, 1926, p. 26.

9,337.   "Powerful Aid For The Klan." The Crisis. Vol.
           46, August, 1939, pp. 241-242.

9,338.   Powledge, Fred. "Ruling On Sit-ins May Free
           3,000, Mostly In The South." New York Times.
           December 15, 1964, p. 1.

9,339.   "Pr. George's City Group Reacts To Increasing
           Racism." Washington Post. June 24, 1977, p. 19B.

9,340.   "Praises Klan Principles." New York Times.
           December 21, 1925, p. 24.

9,341.   "Preacher Praises Klan." New York Times. April
           30, 1923, p. 17.

9,342.   "Predict Coolidge Will Sweep State." New York
           Times. September 11, 1924, p. 3.

9,343.   Preece, Harold. "The Klan Declares War." New
           Masses. Vol. 57, No. 3, October 16, 1945, pp. 3-7.

9,344.   _____. "Klan 'Murder, Inc.' In Dixie." The
           Crisis. Vol. 53, October, 1946, pp. 299-301.

9,345.   _____. "The Klan's 'Revolution Of The Right'."
           Crisis. Vol. 53, July, 1946, pp. 202-203, 219-
           220.

9,346.   "Prelates Assails Klan And Masons." New York
           Times. November 23, 1922, p. 23.

9,347.   "The President At Omaha." New York Times.
           October 7, 1925, p. 26.

9,348.   "President Coolidge Refuses To Comment On Davis's
           Attack On The Ku Klux Klan." New York Times.
           August 23, 1924, p. 1.

9,349.   "President's Speech On Danger Of Rioting." New
           York Times. August 21, 1965, p. 8.

9,350.   Preslar, Lloyd. "Seven Klansmen Indicted."
           Winston-Salem Journal. March 4, 1966, p. 1.

9,351.   _____. "Jury Due To Get Klansman's Case."
           Winston-Salem Journal. September 14, 1966.

9,352.   _____. "Klan Contempt Trials Delayed In-
           definitely." Winston-Salem Journal. October
           4, 1966.

9,353.   _____. "Klan Trial Jurymen Selected." Winston-
           Salem Journal. September 13, 1966.

9,354.   _____. "3 Klansmen Plead Guilty Conditionally."
           Winston-Salem Journal. November 15, 1966.

9,355.   Press, Robert M. "Klan Activity On Increase."
           Christian Science Monitor. June 10, 1981, p. 5.

9,356.   _____. "A Smaller Ku Klux Klan Exploiting
           White Frustration." Christian Science Monitor.
           June 8, 1979, p. 4.

9,357.   _____. "Some U.S. Religious Militants Adopt
           Trappings Of Real War." Christian Science Monitor.
           March 24, 1981, p. 15.

9,358.   _____. "South Facing New Era Of Racial Tension."
           Christian Science Monitor. June 26, 1979, p. 7.

9,359.   Press, Robert M.   "Southern Towns Silent As Ku
           Klux Klan Rumbles." Christian Science Monitor.
           March 25, 1981, p. 4.

9,360.   "The Press As Unwitting Ally To The Klan."
           American Federationist. Vol. 88, August, 1981,
           pp. 22-23.

9,361.   Price, Ben. "Ku Klux Klan Almost A Joke In New
           South." Washington Post. April 17, 1949.

9,362.   Price, Charles E. "Tough Times For The Klan."
           Atlanta Daily World. July 7, 1977, p. 4.

9,363.   Price, William A. "HUAC Skirts Issue Of Klan
           Violence." National Guardian. November 6, 1965,
           p. 8.

9,364.   "Pro-Klan Journal Buys Radio Station." New York
           Times. July 27, 1927, p. 26.

9,365.   "A Problem Hard To Solve." New York Times.
           December 6, 1922, p. 18.

9,366.   "Progress By Blacks Said Spurring Membership In
           KKK." New Orleans Times Picayune. November 18,
           1979, p. 37.

9,367.   "Prosecutors May Well Be Puzzled." New York Times.
           December 7, 1922, p. 18.

9,368.   "Protestants Disowning The Ku Klux." Literary
           Digest. Vol. 75, November 25, 1922, pp. 33-34.

9,369.   "Public Backing Extremist Due To Hard Times -
           Interlandi Cartoon." Los Angeles Times. June
           11, 1980, Sect. 2, p. 7.

9,370.   "Pulitzer Prize For 1922 Awarded." New York Times.
           May 14, 1923, p. 14.

9,371.   "Puts Klan At 1,450,000." New York Times.
           February 14, 1923, p. 3.

9,372.   "Puts Klan Into Speakership." New York Times.
           December 30, 1922, p. 26.

9,373.   "Quaint Customs And Methods Of The Ku Klux Klan."
           Literary Digest. Vol. 74, August 5, 1922, pp. 44-
           52.

9,374.   "Quinn Denies Charge." New York Times. November
           16, 1923, p. 19.

9,375.   "Rabbi Calls Klan 'Vile And Monstrous'." New York
          Times. November 30, 1922, p. 21.

9,376.   "Rabbi Calls Klan Pirates." New York Times.
          January 8, 1923, p. 4.

9,377.   "Race Author Writes On 'Ku Klux Spirit'."
          Pittsburgh Courier. June 30, 1923, p. 1.

9,378.   "Racism In The U.S. Military Viewed." San
          Francisco Chronicle. October 21, 1979, p. 35.

9,379.   "Racist And Demeaning Names And Euphemism."
          Chicago Defender. November 17, 1979, p. 14B.

9,380.   "Racist Hate Note Sent To U.N. Aides." New York
          Times. November 29, 1960, p. 4.

9,381.   Randolph, A. Philip. "The Political Situation And
          The Negro: Coolidge, Davis Or LaFollette." The
          Messenger. Vol. 6, October, 1924, pp. 325-328,
          330.

9,382.   Raskin, A.H. "Murray Demands Pay Rise, Price
          Cut." New York Times. May 13, 1950, p. 2.

9,383.   Rawls, Jr., Wendell. "Civil Rights Advocates
          Upset At Rise In Klan-Style Harassment." New York
          Times. August 20, 1981, p. A23.

9,384.   "Reaction To Klan. New York Times Magazine.
          July 26, 1964, Sect. 6, p. 4.

9,385.   "Ready To Show K.C. Roster." New York Times.
          December 2, 1922, p. 14.

9,386.   "Reagan Wins Endorsement Of A Major Klan Group."
          New York Times. July 31, 1980, p. B10.

9,387.   "Real Menace Of The Klan." New York Times.
          June 4, 1925, p. 18.

9,388.   "Recent Ku Klux Klan Activity In Southern U.S.
          Discussed." Christian Science Monitor. June 8,
          1979, p. 4.

9,389.   "Recent Racial Tension In Southern U.S. Discussed."
          Christian Science Monitor. June 26, 1979, p. 7.

9,390.   "Reconstruction And The Ku Klux." New York Times.
          December 17, 1922, Sect. 2, p. 6.

9,391.   "Reforming The Informing Business." New York
          Times. July 26, 1978, p. 20.

9,392.   Reich, Frances. "The Klan Rides Hitler." Jewish
          Survey. Vol. 2, June 1942, pp. 4-6.

9,393.   "The Reign Of The Tar Bucket." Literary Digest.
          Vol. 70, August 27, 1921, pp. 12-13.

9,394.   "Reply To Ku Klux Charge." New York Times.
          January 31, 1921, p. 8.

9,395.   "Report Klan Growth Up 50% Over Last Four Years."
          Jet. Vol. 57, January 3, 1980, p. 14.

9,396.   "Report 'Vigorous' Klan Recruitment Of 10-Year-
          Olds In Public Schools." North Shore (Evanston,
          Ill.) Examiner. May 29, 1981, p. 1.

9,397.   "Reports Speech Affecting Mail." New York Times.
          March 7, 1937, p. 2.

9,398.   "Republicans Plan A Short Session." New York Times.
          January 14, 1925, p. 23.

9,399.   "The Republican State Convention." New York Times.
          September 24, 1924, p. 18.

9,400.   "Republicans Debate Policy On Klan." New York
          Times. August 24, 1924, p. 3.

9,401.   "Resignations Are Forecast." New York Times.
          October 31, 1965, p. 85.

9,402.   Resner, Lawrence. "CIO Drive In South Pushed By
          Bittner." New York Times. May 17, 1946, p. 10.

9,403.   "Resolution On KKK At Synod 12." Criminal Justice
          Issues. Vol. 6, June, 1981, p. 11.

9,404.   "Resurgence Of Ku Klux Klan." Chicago Defender.
          July 11, 1981, p. 19.

9,405.   "Resurgence Of Ku Klux Klan Activity Across U.S."
          Chicago Defender. November 24, 1979, p. 14B.

9,406.   "Resurgence Of KKK Activity Across U.S." Atlanta
          Daily World. November 30, 1979, p. 6.

9,407.   "Resurgence Of Ku Klux Klan Discussed." Washington
          Post. November 13, 1979, p. 8A.

9,408.   "Resurgence Of Ku Klux Klan In The South, Dis-
          cussed." Chicago Tribune. October 26, 1980, p. 1.

9,409.   "The Return Of The KKK." Present Tense. Vol. 6,
          Summer, 1979, p. 14-15.

9,410.   "Returning Senators Are Silent On Black." New
          York Times. October 2, 1937, p. 3.

9,411.   "Review Of The Press." Pittsburgh Courier.
          January 20, 1923.

9,412.   "Revised And Amended Prescript Of The Order Of
          The... (i.e., Ku Klux Klan)." American Historical
          Society Quarterly. Vol. 5, January, 1900, pp. 3-26.

9,413.   "Revival Of Klan Feared After War." New York
          Times. November 10, 1944, p. 21.

9,414.   Riccio, Bill and Bill Wilkinson. "The Klan
          Speaks." Southern Exposure. Vol. 8, Summer,
          1980, pp. 88-90.

9,415.   "Ridding Society Of Menace." Christian Science
          Monitor. June 27, 1949, p. E2.

9,416.   "Rights Of Nazis And KKK Members." Los Angeles
          Times. May 9, 1978, Sect. 2, p. 8.

9,417.   "Rigorous Military Training In 5 States By Ku
          Klux Klan Noted." San Francisco Chronicle.
          October 24, 1980, p. 25.

9,418.   Riley, Clayton. "Macho Imagery Versus Human
          Rights." Crisis. Vol. 88, March, 1981, p. 64-
          69.

9,419.   Riley, Rochelle. "Board Seeks To Ban Klan."
          The National Bar Bulletin. Vol. 12, April-June,
          1980, p. 2.

9,420.   "The Rise Of The Klan." Crisis. Vol. 88, March,
          1981, pp. 62-69.

9,421.   "The Rise And Fall Of The K.K.K." New Republic.
          Vol. 53, November 30, 1927, pp. 33-34.

9,422.   "Rise And Fall Of The Ku Klux Klan." Outlook.
          Vol. 138, October 15, 1924, pp. 237-238.

9,423.   "Robert Guillaume Hopes To Film Movie On Klan."
          Jet. Vol. 61, September 24, 1981, p. 58.

9,424.   "Robert Shelton Says KKK Will Sue FBI." New
          Orleans Times Picayune. August 13, 1977, p. 10.

9,425.   Roberts, Dick. "HUAC Probe Of Klan: Way Paved
          For Attack On SNCC." Militant. April 26, 1965.

9,426.   Robertson, Nan. "The Invisible Empire: A Guided
          Tour." New York Times. October 20, 1965, pp. 1,
          29.

9,427.   Robinson, Douglas. "Hoover Asks Vigil Over Ex-
          tremists." New York Times. December 13, 1964,
          p. 79.

9,428.   Robinson, Steve and Jed Horne. "A Virulent Ku
          Klux Klan Rearms." Life. Vol. 4, June, 1981,
          pp. 32-40.

9,429.   Rogers, Joel A. "The Ku Klux Klan: A Menace Or
          A Promise?" The Messenger. Vol. 5, March, 1923,
          pp. 626-629; April, 1923, pp. 662-663, 675-678;
          June, 1923, pp. 738-40; August, 1923, pp. 785, 795;
          October, 1923, pp. 833-835.

9,430.   "Roosevelt Aides Irked." New York Times. Septem-
          ber 14, 1937, p. 18.

9,431.   "Roosevelt Named Black Unaware Of Link To Klan."
          New York Times. September 15, 1937, pp. 1, 2.

9,432.   "Roosevelt Named Both The Justices." New York
          Times. June 11, 1946, p. 2.

9,433.   "Roosevelt Sees Smith As A Czar." New York Times.
          October 28, 1924, p. 1.

9,434.   Rosenberg, Harold. "The Art World: Liberation
          From Detachment." New Yorker. Vol. 46, November
          7, 1970, p. 136, 138, 141.

9,435.   Rork, C.M. "A Defense Of The Klan." New Republic.
          Vol. 37, December 5, 1923, p. 44-45.

9,436.   Rowan, Carl T. "The Klan And Black Progress."
          Washington Evening Star. November 12, 1979, p. A9.

9,437.   _____. "Outrage Over Resurgence Of Ku Klux
          Klan Violence." Houston Post. November 11, 1979,
          p. 23.

9,438.   "Rules Ku Klux Acts Are States' Cases." New York
          Times. December 5, 1922, p. 3.

9,439.   "Russian Says Klan Rises." New York Times.
          April 15, 1946, p. 14.

9,440.   Rustin, Bayard. "KKK: Delusions Of Grandeur."
          Norfolk Journal & Guide. May 26, 1978, p. 8;
          Los Angeles Times. May 18, 1978, p. 7.

9,441.   "Same Old HUAC." Nation. Vol. 201, November 1,
          1965, pp. 290-291.

9,442.   "Saxbe To Disclose A Study Of Secret Hoover
          Tactics." New York TImes. November 16, 1974, p. 23.

9,443.   "Saying Less." New York Times. August 16, 1924, p. 10.

9,444.   "Says American Party Will Seek Klan Aid." New York Times. August 26, 1924, p. 2.

9,445.   "Says Bund Seeks To Unite Fascists." New York Times. October 6, 1938, p. 11.

9,446.   "Says Evans Instigated Killing Of Klan's Foe." New York Times. April 3, 1928, p. 2.

9,447.   "Says Klan Is U.S. Problem." New York Times. December 26, 1922, p. 3.

9,448.   "Says Klan Training Killers." Carolinian (Raleigh). November 6, 1980, pp. 1, 2.

9,449.   "Says Klan's Scout Got Anti-Klan Money." New York Times. June 29, 1924, p. 9.

9,450.   "Says Masons Oppose Klan." New York Times. December 31, 1922, p. 18.

9,451.   "Says Negroes Shun Subversive Groups." New York Times. October 9, 1946, p. 24.

9,452.   "Says New Yorkers Prefer Cleopatra." New York Times. October 22, 1923, p. 8.

9,453.   "Says Simmons Sold His Rights In Klan." New York Times. February 13, 1924, p. 5.

9,454.   "The Secrecy Of The Klan." New York Times. September 14, 1924, Sect. 8, p. 12.

9,455.   "Says There Is No Evidence." New York Times. September 16, 1937, p. 14.

9,456.   Schaefer, Richard T. "Ku Klux Klan: Continuity And Change." Phylon. Vol. 32, Summer, 1971, pp. 143-157.

9,457.   "A School Girl On The Klan." New York Times. December 13, 1922, p. 20.

9,458.   "SCLC And KKK Activity - Letter." Baltimore Afro-American. October 27, 1979, p. 4.

9,459.   "SCLC Endorses NEA's Curriculum On KKK." Atlanta Daily World. December 3, 1981, p. 1.

9,460.   "Scoggin On U.S. Klan Indictments." New Bern Sun Journal. March 4, 1966.

9,461.   "Scores Of Crosses Are Set Afire Over Four-State
          Area In South." New York Times. March 27, 1960,
          pp. 74.

9,462.   "Scores Truman Avowals." New York Times. October
          24, 1944, p. 15.

9,463.   Scott, Martin J. "Catholics And The Ku Klux Klan."
          North American Review. Vol. 223, June, 1926, pp.
          268-281.

9,464.   "Secret Agents In KKK Report Growth In North."
          New York Age. December 11, 1948, p. 2.

9,465.   "Sees America Head Of A United Jewry." New York
          Times. April 22, 1925, p. 24.

9,466.   "Sees Bid For Klan Vote." New York Times. October
          18, 1924, p. 2.

9,467.   "Sees Jews 'Goats' In Drive On Reds." New York
          Times. October 22, 1946, p. 17.

9,468.   "Sees Klan Defense In Dawe's Attack." New York
          Times. August 24, 1924, p. 3.

9,469.   "Sees Klan Power Growing In West." New York Times.
          December 11, 1926, p. 2.

9,470.   "Sees Less Mob Violence." New York Times. February
          8, 1925, Sect. 9, p. 6.

9,471.   "Sees Our Liberties Slowly Vanishing." New York
          Times. July 26, 1927, p. 8.

9,472.   "Senate Group Won By Prof. Edgerton." New York
          Times. December 5, 1937, p. 39.

9,473.   "Senators Demand Black Tell Status." New York
          Times. September 15, 1937, p. 2.

9,474.   "Senators Pass Lie In Bitter Debate." New York
          Times. February 25, 1927, pp. 1, 6.

9,475.   "Senators Receive Books Of The Klan." New York
          Times. May 15, 1924, p. 3.

9,476.   "Senators Will Visit Chicago To Inquire Into
          Illinois Funds." New York Times. June 28, 1926,
          p. 1.

9,477.   Sendor, Elizabeth. "When Terror Rode At Night."
          Senior Scholastic. Vol. 111, February 8, 1979,
          pp. 17-19.

9,478.   "7 Klan Heads Deny Guilt In U.S. Court In Contempt
          Cases." New York Times. March 12, 1966, p. 24.

9,479.   "7 Klan Leaders Cited By House." New York Times.
          February 3, 1966, pp. 1, 2.

9,480.   "7 Klan Leaders Indicted For Contempt." Durham
          Morning Herald. March 4, 1966, p. 5A.

9,481.   "7 Klansmen Are Handed Indictments." Greensboro
          Daily News. March 4, 1966, p. 1.

9,482.   "Seven Southern Governors Defy Mob Violence."
          Pittsburgh Courier. July 26, 1930, p. 8.

9,483.   "Several Church Leaders View 'Resurgence' Of KKK
          Activity." Atlanta Daily World. November 6, 1979,
          p. 1.

9,484.   "Shadow Of Ku Klux Klan Grows Larger In Congress
          And Nation." New York Times. December 10, 1922,
          Sect. 9, p. 6.

9,485.   Shanker, Albert. "How Not To Teach About The KKK:
          NEA Materials Come Up Short." New York Times.
          November 1, 1981, p. E9.

9,486.   Shankman, Arnold. "Julian Harris And The Ku Klux
          Klan." Mississippi Quarterly. Vol. 28, No. 2,
          1975, pp. 147-169.

9,487.   "Sharp Rise Noted In Klan's Rosters In Last 6
          Months." New York Times. October 14, 1965, p. 40.

9,488.   "Shed A Tear For The Klan." Nation. Vol. 119,
          October 9, 1924, pp. 351-352.

9,489.   Shepard, Robert. "Lowery Criticizes Justice
          Department." New York Recorder. May 9, 1981, p. 2.

9,490.   Sherrill, Robert. "Expose Of Tedium, Terror And
          Fiscal Tricks At HUAC." New South. Vol. 21,
          Winter, 1966, pp. 57-63.

9,491.   "Shooting At The Klan But Wounding The Negro."
          Christian Century. Vol. 82, September 22, 1965,
          p. 1149.

9,492.   "A Short War But Successful." New York Times.
          September 27, 1921, p. 18.

9,493.   Silverman, Joseph. "The Ku Klux Klan A Paradox."
          North American Review. Vol. 223, June-August, 1926,
          pp. 282-291.

9,494.   "Simmons Defies Klan 'Muckrakers'." New York Times.
          December 8, 1921, p. 9.

9,495.   "Simmons Depicts Klan As Crumbling." New York
         Times. August 19, 1923, p. 2.

9,496.   "Simmons, In Affidavit, Attacks Klan Leaders."
         New York Times. April 8, 1928, p. 24.

9,497.   Sitton, Claude. "Ku Klux Klan Is Riding Again."
         New York Times. September 16, 1962, Sect. 4, p. 6.

9,498.   Skinner, R. Dana. "Is The Ku Klux Klan Katholik?
         Independent. Vol. 111, November 24, 1923, pp. 242-
         243.

9,499.   Smith, Baxter. "The Resurgence Of The KKK." The
         Black Scholar. Vol. 12, January-February, 1981,
         p. 25-30.

9,500.   "Smith Denounces Coolidge's Silence On Ku Klux
         Klan." New York Times. October 19, 1924, pp. 1, 3.

9,501.   "Snake-Pit." Newsweek. Vol. 67, January 24,
         1966, pp. 29-30.

9,502.   "Socialists Assail The Klan By Name." New York
         Times. July 9, 1924, p. 6.

9,503.   "Socialists Condemn The Klan." New York Times.
         July 10, 1924, p. 20.

9,504.   "Solemn But Undignified Penguins." Nation. Vol.
         116, January 3, 1923, pp. 6-7.

9,505.   " 'Sorry Thing' To Johnson." New York Times.
         October 3, 1937, p. 3.

9,506.   "Southern Editor Discusses The Ku Klux Klan In
         April Current History. New York Times. March 25,
         1928, Sect. 2, p. 3.

9,507.   "Southern Editor Holds Klan Responsible For Rights
         Deaths." New York Times. February 21, 1966, p. 44.

9,508.   "Sparkman Decries 'Smear' By Dewey." New York
         Times. October 23, 1952, p. 16.

9,509.   "Spectators Swear They Saw Klan Give A Life Member-
         ship To Black." New York Times. September 18,
         1937, p. 17.

9,510.   Spiegel, Irving. "Civil Rights Gains Are Stressed
         At Session Of B'nai B'rith Unit." New York Times.
         October 25, 1952, p. 12.

9,511.   Spiegel, Irving. "Medical Schools Take More Jews."
          New York Times. January 13, 1961, p. 32.

9,512.   _____. "U.S. To Intensify Civil Rights Drive."
          New York Times. September 5, 1953, p. 5.

9,513.   _____. "Zionist Sees Rise In Anti-Semitism."
          New York Times. August 29, 1966, pp. 1, 15.

9,514.   "Spinks Severs All Klan Links." New York Times.
          September 18, 1950, p. 30.

9,515.   "State Dept. Stops Paying For Women's Year Mail."
          New York Times. November 24, 1977, p. B4.

9,516.   "State G.O.P. Faces Ku Klux Klan Issue." New York
          Times. September 4, 1924, p. 4.

9,517.   "Shanley Is Criticized." New York Times. March 23,
          1957, p. 39.

9,518.   "The 'Sheeted Jenks' Of The Ku Klux Klan." Nation.
          Vol. 169, July 2, 1949, pp. 2-4.

9,519.   Shepherd, William G. "How I Put Over The Klan."
          Colliers. Vol. 81, July 14, 1928, pp. 5-7; July 21,
          1928, pp. 8-9; July 28, 1928, pp. 8-9.

9,520.   Sherrill, Robert. "A Look Inside The Invisible
          Empire." New South. Vol. 23, Spring, 1968, pp. 4-
          30.

9,521.   Shields, Art. "KKK-Bund 'Marriage' Photos Shown
          Jury." Daily Worker. July 18, 1944, p. 2.

9,522.   "Shows Jones, Klan At Odds." Twin City Sentinel.
          October 25, 1965, p. 1.

9,523.   Shuler, Rev. A.C. "The Klan And Its Purpose."
          Southern Gospel. September-October, 1949, pp. 2-3.

9,524.   Simpson, Cynthia. "Ku Klux Klan." Cleveland Call
          And Post. December 19, 1981, p. 17A.

9,525.   Smith, Baxter. "The Resurgence Of The KKK."
          Black Scholar. Vol. 12, No. 1, January-February,
          1981, pp. 25-30.

9,526.   "South Organizing Comm. Wants Carter And N.C.
          Governor To Act Against KKK." Norfolk Journal &
          Guide. November 16, 1979, p. 14B.

9,527.   "Southern Branches Of N.A.A.C.P. Not Terrified By
          K.K.K., Says R.W. Bagnall." New York Amsterdam
          News. June 13, 1923, pp. 1-8.

9,528.   "Southern Judges Condemn The Klan." New York Times.
          October 12, 1927, p. 17.

9,529.   "Southern Poverty Law Center Sets Up Group To
          Monitor KKK." Houston Post. December 11, 1980,
          p. 11B.

9,530.   Spiegel, Irving. "Negroes Called Victors In
          South." New York Times. June 5, 1961, p. 20.

9,531.   _____. "Revival Of Klan Held Ineffective."
          New York Times. April 7, 1958, p. 23.

9,532.   "Spurn Klan 'Bribes' Baptist Aide Urges." New York
          Times. January 29, 1949, p. 14.

9,533.   Stagg, J.C.A. "The Problem Of Klan Violence: The
          South Carolina Up-Country, 1868-1871." Journal Of
          American Studies. Vol. 8, 1974, pp. 303-318.

9,534.   "State Dept. Cuts Int'l. Women's Year Commissions
          Mail Funds Over Article." Washington Post.
          November 24, 1977, p. 21A.

9,535.   "State Socialists Denounce Klan; Back LaFollette."
          New York Times. July 27, 1924, p. 1.

9,536.   "States Urged To Outlaw KKK Camps." Buckeye (Ohio)
          Review. February 20, 1981, pp. 1, 5.

9,537.   "Status Of Three Klansmen Awaits Shelton's Trial."
          Durham Morning Herald. December 9, 1966, p. 4C.

9,538.   Stokely, James and Wilma Dykeman. "The Klan Makes
          A Comeback: In The Wake Of Desegregation."
          Commentary. Vol. 29, No. 1, 1960, pp. 45-51.

9,539.   Stern, Laurence. "Klan Sex Lives Called Target."
          Washington Post. December 3, 1975, p. A4.

9,540.   Stockbridge, Frank Parker. "The Ku Klux Klan
          Revival." Current History. Vol. 14, April, 1921,
          pp. 19-25.

9,541.   "Stockpiling Of Weapons By Ku Klux Klan, Other Orgs."
          Houston Post. December 11, 1980, p. 2B.

9,542.   Stokes, Dillard. "U.S. Opens Campaign To Smash
          Klan Before It Regains Power." Washington Post.
          August 1, 1946.

9,543.   "Straton's Talk Is A Surprise." New York Herald
          Tribune. December 11, 1922.

9,544.   "Strength Of The KKK." Pittsburgh Courier.
          November 17, 1979, p. 6.

9,545.   Suall, Irwin. "The Ku Klux Klan Malady Lingers On."
          The Civil Rights Quarterly Perspectives. Vol. 12,
          Fall, 1980 - Winter, 1981, pp. 11-15.

9,546.   "Such Services Ignored By Klansmen." New York Times.
          October 27, 1924, p. 8.

9,547.   "Sues Klan For $500,000." New York Times. June 29,
          1924, Sect. 2, p. 2.

9,548.   "Suggested To Mr. Dies." New York Times. November
          5, 1939, Sect. 4, p. 9.

9,549.   "A Surprising Vitality Is Shown." New York Times.
          September 14, 1922, p. 20.

9,550.   "Survey Shows Klan Active In 14 States." PM.
          September 9, 1946, p. 1.

9,551.   "A Survey Of The Klan." New York Times. February
          21, 1926, Sect. 2, p. 8.

9,552.   "Suspension Of Klan Investigation Is Said To Bar
          'Significant' Data." New York Times. November 11,
          1965, p. 31.

9,553.   "Support Of U.S. State Dept. Nominee Lefever-
          Conrad Cartoon." Los Angeles Times. June 5, 1981,
          Sect. 2, p. 7.

9,554.   "Survey Shows Declining Strength." Christian
          Science Monitor. April 10, 1950, p. 2.

9,555.   "Survivalists Preparation For The Future." New
          Orleans Times Picayune. March 12, 1981, Sect. 7,
          p. 4.

9,556.   Sweeney, Charles. "The Great Bigotry Merger."
          Nation. Vol. 115, July 5, 1922, pp. 8-10.

9,557.   Tannenbaum, Frank. "Books To Cure Clannishness."
          The World Tomorrow. Vol. 7, March, 1924, p. 94.

9,558.   _____. "The Ku Klux Klan: Its Social Origin
          In The South." Century. Vol. 105, April, 1923,
          pp. 873-882.

9,559.   "Tarheels Among 7 Klansmen To Face Contempt
          Charges." Durham Morning Herald. March 12, 1966,
          p. 1.

9,560.   "Tax Deductions Disallowed." New York Times.
          August 9, 1961, p. 24.

9,561.   Taylor, Alva W. "Klan Seen Trying For A Comeback."
          Christian Century. Vol. 67, February 1, 1950,
          pp. 148, 150.

9,562.   "Teachers Group Fighting KKK." Watts (Calif.) Star Review. June 5, 1981, p. 1.

9,563.   "Teachers' Group Plans To Issue Anti-Klan Guide." Jet. Vol. 60, June 11, 1981, p. 14.

9,564.   "Teachers To Fight Against Klan's Recruitment Of School Children." Washington Star. May 24, 1981, p. A7.

9,565.   "Teaching Aids Designated To Fight Klans' Student Recruiting." New York Times. July 12, 1981, p. 24.

9,566.   "Tells Jews To Fight Foes." New York Times. October 27, 1923, p. 2.

9,567.   "Tells K. Of C. To Defend Catholic Schools." New York Times. January 2, 1923, p. 17.

9,568.   "Tells Of Klan Outrages." New York Times. May 14, 1924, p. 2.

9,569.   "Tells Of Night Rides Of Klan In Southland." Chicago Defender. September 24, 1921, p. 3.

9,570.   "Tells Only Half The Truth." New York Times. December 29, 1923, p. 12.

9,571.   "Tempo Article On Patsy Sims Research On The KKK." Chicago Tribune. November 13, 1978, Sect. 3, p. 1.

9,572.   "10 States To Fight Klan." New York Times. January 4, 1947, p. 8.

9,573.   "Texas KKK Calls Rally To Back LBJ On Viet." The Worker. October 31, 1965.

9,574.   "The New Klan, PBS, Reviewed." Washington Post. November 18, 1978, p. 1B.

9,575.   "The 'Boy Scout' Boot Camp." Newsweek. Vol. 96, December 15, 1980, p. 32.

9,576.   "These Holidays Are Tough On '100%' Americans." Pittsburgh Courier. December 2, 1927, editorial page.

9,577.   "This Fight Will Be Short." New York Times. September 10, 1921, p. 10.

9,578.   Thomas, Jo. "Documents Show F.B.I. Harassed Puerto Rican Separatist Parties." New York Times. November 22, 1977, p. 26.

9,579.   Thomas, Robert McG., Jr. "Influence Of Klan Is Doubted In Study." New York Times. November 11, 1979, p. 31.

9,580.   Thompson, Jerry.   "Children In Robes Of Hate ... It Made Me Want To Cry." The Tennesean. December 15, 1980.

9,581.   _____. "I Was Living Double Life, But Was I The Only One." The Tennesean. December 14, 1980.

9,582.   _____. "Klan 'Naturalization' A Long, Scary Wait." The Tennesean. December 10, 1980.

9,583.   _____. "Klan 'Naturalization' Baptism ... A 'Silly, Stupid' Ceremony." The Tennesean. December 11, 1980.

9,584.   _____. " 'President Carter Saw Red ... And Then He Called Me A Coward'." The Tennesean. December 12, 1980.

9,585.   _____. "Reporter Finds KKK A Growing Danger." The Tennesean. December 7, 1980.

9,586.   _____. "Reporter Survives Sudden KKK Quiz." The Tennesean. December 8, 1980.

9,587.   _____. "The Warning Was Clear: No Mercy For Spies." The Tennesean. December 13, 1980.

9,588.   Thompson, Roy. "Differing Views On Violence Split KKK." Winston-Salem Journal. July 3, 1965, pp. 1, 8.

9,589.   _____. "Hatchet Being Sharpened For KKK." Winston-Salem Journal. July 1, 1965, pp. 1, 16.

9,590.   _____. "The Klan Today: A New Conservative Group." Winston-Salem Journal. July 4, 1965, pp. A1, A14.

9,591.   "Threat To Bomb Movies." New York Times. January 18, 1923, p. 9.

9,592.   "3 Klan Chiefs Plead Guilty To Contempt In Inquiry By House." New York Times. November 19, 1966, p. 22.

9,593.   "3 KKK Factions Arming Themselves For 'Inevitable' Race War." Chicago Tribune. December 8, 1980, p. 10.

9,594.   "Three Klan Face Court." Raleigh News And Observer. November 18, 1966, p. 1.

9,595.   "3 Klansmen Enter Pleas Of Guilty." Greensboro Daily News. November 19, 1966, p. 1.

9,596.   "3 Negroes On Jury For Contempt Trial Of A Klan
          Leader." New York Times. September 13, 1966, p. 27.

9,597.   "Three Negroes On Klan Trial Jury." Charlotte
          Observer. September 13, 1966, p. 3A.

9,598.   "Three States Elect Governors Today." New York
          Times. November 6, 1923, p. 3.

9,599.   "To Curb Ku Klux Klan Terrorism." The AFL-CIO
          News. April 3, 1965.

9,600.   "To Defend Ku Klux Klan." New York Times. March 9,
          1922, p. 19.

9,601.   "To Meet On Klan Monday." New York Times. August
          9, 1946, p. 7.

9,602.   "To Start Congress Ku Klux Hearings." New York
          Times. October 2, 1921, p. 16.

9.603.   "To What The President's Silence Gives Consent."
          New York Times. October 20, 1924, p. 16.

9,604.   "Tolerance In A Democracy." New York Times. July
          17, 1946, p. 22.

9,605.   "Topics Of The Times." New York Times. December
          15, 1940, Sect. 4, p. 8.

9,606.   "Treated Just As They Treat Others." New York
          Times. September 20, 1924, p. 14.

9,607.   Trelease, Allen W. "The Lives And Times Of The
          Ku Klux Klan." Greensboro Daily News. February 3,
          1980.

9,608.   _____. "White Terror." New Republic. Vol.
          165, July 17, 1971, p. 30.

9,609.   "Tremors Of Bigotry That Worry America." U.S. News
          And World Report. Vol. 91, July 13, 1981, pp. 48-
          49.

9,610.   Trent, William P. "A New South's View Of Re-
          construction." Sewanee Review. Vol. 9, January,
          1901, pp. 13-29.

9,611.   "Tries To Bring Klan Into The Campaign." New York
          Times. June 21, 1932, p. 8.

9.612.   "Truman Klan Link Charged And Denied." New York
          Times. October 27, 1952, p. 20.

9,613.   Truzzi, Marcello.   "The 100% American Songbag:
          Conservative Folksongs In America." Western
          Folklore. Vol. 28, January, 1969, pp. 27-40.

9,614.   "Tumulty Assails Georgia Governor." New York
          Times. October 21, 1924, p. 8.

9,615.   "24 In House Ask Shift Of Ku Klux Klan Inquiry."
          New York Times. April 10, 1965, p. 16.

9,616.   "Two Federal Laws Cited." New York Times.
          September 6, 1964, p. 34.

9,617.   "Two Ku Klux Klans." New York Times. June 10,
          1923, Sect. 7, p. 5.

9,618.   "Two Novelties Confront The Klansmen." New York
          Times. September 18, 1924, p. 20.

9,619.   "Two States Forbid Masks." New York Times. April
          10, 1923, p. 26.

9,620.   "TV Cameraman Removed From U.S. House Hearing On
          Violence And KKK." San Francisco Chronicle.
          March 5, 1981, p. 15.

9,621.   "A Typical Member Of The Klan." New York Times.
          November 7, 1923, p. 16.

9,622.   "The Ultimate White Sale." Mother Jones. Vol. 4,
          April, 1979, p. 8.

9,623.   " 'Un-American' H.U.A.C." New York Times. December
          26, 1965, Sect. 6, p. 23.

9,624.   "Uncle Henry On The Klan Komplex." Collier's.
          Vol. 72, January 27, 1923, pp. 15-16.

9,625.   "Underwood Assails Klan As Traitorous." New York
          Times. November 12, 1923, p. 8.

9,626.   "Underwood Wants Party To Fight Klan." New York
          Times. January 23, 1924, p. 21.

9,627.   Underwood, Oscar W. "Underwood Sees Klan As Chief
          Issue." New York Times. June 8, 1924, Sect. 8,
          p. 4.

9,628. "Union Asked To Bar Klansmen." New York Times.
        March 30, 1965, p. 26.

9,629. "Unitarians Condemn Stirring Of Bigotry." New
        York Times. September 15, 1923, p. 5.

9,630. "United Against Ku Kluxism." The Messenger.
        Vol. 5, August, 1923, pp. 781-782.

9,631. "United Front Against Ku Klux Menace." The
        Messenger. Vol. 4, September, 1922, pp. 478-479.

9,632. "United Mine Workers Response." Christian Science
        Monitor. October 22, 1975, p. 31.

9,633. "United Methodist Magazine Devotes One Issue To
        KKK." Atlanta Daily World. August 30, 1981, p. 1.

9,634. "Unlikely Members Of The KKK." Washington Post
        Parade. December 27, 1981, p. 13.

9,635. "Unmasked." New York Times. April 21, 1940,
        Sect. 4, p. 2.

9,636. "Unmasking The Ku Klux Klan." New York Amsterdam
        News. May 30, 1923, p. 12.

9,637. "Unraveling Secrets Of The Hooded Klan." U.S.
        News And World Report. Vol. 59, November 1, 1965,
        pp. 12-13.

9,638. "Unsheeting The Klan." Newsweek. Vol. 65, April
        12, 1965, pp. 29-30.

9,639. "Unteaching Racism." Black Enterprise. Vol. 12,
        March 1982, p. 17.

9,640. "Untermyer Assails Klan." New York Times. January
        7, 1923, p. 21.

9,641. "Untermyer Assails Klan As Cowardly." New York
        Times. December 25, 1922, p. 3.

9,642. "Upsurge Of KKK Activity In U.S." New York Amster-
        dam News. November 10, 1979, p. 22.

9,643. "Upsurge Of KKK Activity Across The U.S." Michigan
        Chronicle. November 10, 1979, p. 8A.

9,644. "Upsurge Of Ku Klux Klan Activity Across U.S."
        Chicago Defender. October 30, 1979, p. 12.

9,645. "Upsurge Of KKK Activity In 1979 Analyzed In
        Depth." Chicago Defender. October 22, 1979, p. 6.

9,646. "Urges Catholic Action Against The Klan." New York
        Times. August 16, 1924, p. 6.

9,647. "Urge Committee To Probe K.K.K." New York
        Amsterdam News. September 10, 1938, p. 1.

9,648. "U.S. Aid Sought To Halt Violence." Christian
        Science Monitor. November 10, 1950, p. 1.

9,649. "U.S. Anarchy Threatened By Ku Klux." Chicago
        Defender. August 20, 1921, p. 3.

9,650. "U.S. Attorney General Starts Probe Of Ku Klux
        Klan." Chicago Defender. October 1, 1921, p. 3.

9,651. "U.S. Civil Rights Comm. Told Ku Klux Klan On
        Upswing In South." Houston Post. September 11,
        1979, p. 6D.

9,652. "U.S. Congressional Hearing On Racial Violence
        Interrupted." Los Angeles Times. December 10,
        1980, p. 4.

9,653. "U.S. District Attorney Sees Danger In Ku Klux."
        Chicago Defender. October 8, 1921, p.2.

9,654. "U.S. Jury Calls Klan 'Cancerous Growth'." New
        York Times. March 26, 1953, p. 35.

9,655. "U.S. Starts Ku Klux Probe." Chicago Defender.
        September 3, 1921, p. 1.

9,656. "U.S. Rep. Collins On Ku Klux Klan Activity."
        Baltimore Afro-American. November 17, 1979, p. 4.

9,657. "U.S. Rep. P. Mitchell Scores American Apathy On
        Hate Groups." San Francisco Chronicle. May 6,
        1981, p. 10.

9,658. "U.S. Rep. Mitchell Wants Curbs On KKK And Nazis
        Enforced." Baltimore Afro-American. August 29,
        1981, p. 6.

9,659. "U.S. Report Calls Violent KKK Groups A Serious
        Threat." San Francisco Chronicle. November 24,
        1980, p. 5.

9,660. "U.S. Reports Show Govt. Knew Of KKK Informer's
        Crimes In 1960's." Chicago Tribune. February 17,
        1980, Sect. 3, p. 16.

9,661. "U.S. Teacher Group To Fight A Klan Drive For
        Students." Christian Science Monitor. May 20,
        1981, p. 2.

9,662. "Vandenberg For Action." New York Times. September
        14, 1937, p. 18.

9,663. "The Various Shady Lives Of The Ku Klux Klan."
        Time. Vol. 85, April 9, 1965, pp. 24-25.

9,664.   Verlie, Leslie. "The Klan Rides The South Again."
          Collier's. Vol. 122, October 9, 1948, pp. 13-15,
          74-75.

9,665.   "Veterans Asked To Oppose Ku Klux." New York
          Times. September 28, 1921, p. 4.

9,666.   "Veteran's Bureau Silent About Klan." New York
          Times. October 11, 1942, p. 17.

9,667.   "Vets Oppose Klan." Atlanta Constitution. June 6,
          1946, p. 1.

9,668.   "Vile Bodies." Economist. Vol. 264, July 9,
          1977, pp. 36-37.

9,669.   "Violence In South Laid To K.K.K. Unit." New York
          Times. February 11, 1957, p. 21.

9,670.   "The Violent Rebirth Of The Ku Klux Klan."
          Reader's Digest. Vol. 118, March, 1981, pp. 118-121.

9,671.   "Violence Will Kill Ku Klux, Says Allen." New York
          Times. December 14, 1922, p. 24.

9,672.   "A Virulent Klan Rearms." Life. Vol. 4, June,
          1981, pp. 32-39.

9,673.   "Vote To Confirm K.K.K. Candidate." New York
          Amsterdam News. January 28, 1925, p. 15.

9,674.   Wald, Kenneth D. "The Visible Empire: The Ku
          Klux Klan As An Electoral Movement." Journal
          Of Interdisciplinary History. Vol. 11, Autumn,
          1980, pp. 217-234.

9,675.   Wald, Matthew L. "Meriden Resents Image Caused
          By Klan Clashes." New York Times. July 18,
          1981, p. 26.

9,676.   Waldron, Martin. "Militants Stockpile Illegal
          Guns Across The U.S." New York Times. December 28,
          1969, p. 42.

9,677.   "Walker Says He Will Reply Later." New York Times.
          October 21, 1924, p. 8.

9,678.   Wallace, Irving, et al. "Unlikely Members
          (President Harry Truman, Chief Justice Edward D.
          White, Supreme Justice Hugo Black, Gutzon Borglum,
          Jockey Mary Bacon) Of The Ku Klux Klan." Parade.
          December 27. 1981, p. 13.

9,679.   Wallace, Robert. "Freedom To Jim Crow: Part II:
          Background Of Segregation." Life. Vol. 41,
          September 10, 1956, pp. 96-108.

9,680.   Walsh, Robert K.   "Further Crackdowns Hinted By Klan
          Contempt Charges." Washington Evening Star.
          January 7, 1966.

9,681.   "Walsh Asks Black To Repudiate Klan." New York
          Times. September 16, 1937, p. 14.

9,682.   "Walsh Recalls 'Rush'." New York Times. September
          14, 1937, p. 18.

9,683.   "Walsh Says Klan Threatens Parties." New York Times.
          November 22, 1922, p. 23.

9,684.   "Want Aliens Admitted." New York Times. November
          19, 1923, p. 3.

9,685.   "Want 5,000,000 Signers For Kill Ku Klux Klan Drive."
          People's Voice. August 4, 1943, p. 4.

9,686.   Warnecke, Nancy, Kirk Loggins And Susan Thomas.
          " 'Just Like The Scouts': The Klan Youth Corps."
          Southern Exposure. Vol. 8, Summer, 1980, pp. 91-92.

9,687.   "Warns At Columbia Of 'Klan Mentality'." New York
          Times. June 3, 1929, p. 5.

9,688.   Warwick, Loy. "Father's Private Miracle." Coronet.
          Vol. 45, August, 1958, pp. 19-23.

9,689.   "Watch KKK, Workers Told." Florida Courier.
          February 14, 1981, pp. 1, 3.

9,690.   "Wayne State Univ. Organization On Facist Movements -
          Letter." Michigan Chronicle. December 15, 1979,
          p. 4D.

9,691.   "The Week - KKK." Nation. Vol. 6, April 9, 1968,
          p. 283.

9,692.   "Week's Votes In The House." New York Times.
          February 7, 1966, p. 18.

9,693.   " 'We're The Future Klan'." NEA Reporter. Vol.
          20, June, 1981, p. 9.

9,694.   "W.H. Moses." The Messenger. Vol. 3, October,
          1921, pp. 264-266.

9,695.   "What Is Wrong With The Klan? Nation. Vol. 118,
          June 18, 1924, pp. 698-699.

9,696.   "What The Sit-Ins Are Stirring Up." U.S. News And
          World Report. Vol. 48, April 18, 1960, pp. 52-54,
          56.

9,697.   "What This Klan Has Done." New York Times.
          October 23, 1924, p. 20.

9 698.   "Wheeler Assails The Klan." New York Times.
          September 3, 1924, p. 2.

9,699.   "When And Where Did The Ku Klux Klan Originate?"
          Twin City Sentinel. January 6, 1967.

9,700.   "When Terror Rode At Night." Senior Scholastic.
          Vol. 111, February 8, 1979, pp. 17-19.

9,701.   "Where Does The Contempt Lie?" New York Times.
          February 8, 1966, p. 38.

9,702.   "Where The Klan Fails." New York Times. November
          1, 1923, p. 20.

9,703.   "White Accuses Byrnes." New York Times. March 22,
          1954, p. 19.

9,704.   White, Arthur Corning. "An American Fascismo."
          The Forum. Vol. 72, November, 1924, pp. 636-642.

9,705.   "White Asserts Black Was And Is Klansman." New
          York Times. September 15, 1937, p. 3.

9,706.   "White Band To Preserve White Supremacy In America."
          New York World. November 11, 1930.

9,707.   "White Editor Describes South As Crime Breeder."
          Chicago Defender. August 20, 1921, p. 3.

9,708.   "White House Orders Inquiry." New York Times.
          November 6, 1979, p. A16.

9,709.   " 'White Knight Or False Prophet'? New York Times
          Magazine. August 22, 1948, Sect. 6, p. 34.

9,710.   "White Labor Leaders Aroused By Rise Of Ku Klux."
          Chicago Defender. August 27, 1921, p. 3.

9,711.   "White Supremacy Shaky." Pittsburgh Courier.
          October 20, 1923, p. 8.

9,712.   White, Walter F. "Reviving The Ku Klux Klan."
          Forum. Vol. 65, April, 1921, pp. 426-434.

9,713.   "Whitewashing White Racists: Junior Scholastic And
          The KKK." Interracial Books For Children.
          Vol. 11, #5, 1980, pp. 3-6, 21.

9,714.   White, William Allen. "Annihilate The Klan!"
          Nation. Vol. 120, January 7, 1925, p. 7.

9,715.   White, William Allen.   "Patience And Publicity."
          The World Tomorrow.   Vol. 7, March, 1924, p. 87.

9,716.   "Why Men Join The Klan."   New York Times.   November
          5, 1924, p. 18.

9,717.   "Why People Join The Ku Klux."   New York Times.
          December 12, 1922, p. 18.

9,718.   "Why They Join The Klan."   New Republic.   Vol. 36,
          November 21, 1923, pp. 321-322.

9,719.   Wicker, Tom.   "New Approach By KKK For Black
          Supression."   Chicago Tribune.   March 22, 1979,
          Sect. 3, p. 4.

9,720.   _____.   "President Seeks Stiffer Klan Law."
          New York Times.   March 30, 1965, pp. 1, 26.

9,721.   Wiggins, David.   "Has Klan's Voice Changed With
          David Ernest Duke?"   Kernersville (N.C.) News.
          October 19, 1978, pp. 1, 3.

9,722.   Wilayton, Phil.   "Fighting The Klan In The Military."
          Southern Changes.   Vol. 2, January, 1980, pp. 8-11.

9,723.   "Wilkins Column Eyes The ACLU And Hate Groups."
          Baltimore Afro-American.   June 10, 1978, p. 4.

9,724.   Wilkins, Roy.   "The Klan's Battle Plan."   New
          York Post.   January 30, 1966.

9,725.   "Will Answer Tumulty."   New York Times.   October
          22, 1924, p. 8.

9,726.   Williams, Dennis A. and Lea Donosky.   "The Great
          White Hope."   Newsweek.   Vol. 90, November 14, 1977,
          pp. 45-46.

9,727.   _____, Eleanor Clift and William Schmidt.
          "Klan Also Rises."   Newsweek.   Vol. 87, January 12,
          1976, pp. 33-34.

9,728.   Williams, Donald F.   "Protest Under The Cross:
          The Ku Klux Klan Presents Its Case To The Public,
          1960."   The Southern Speech Journal.   Vol. 27,
          Fall, 1961, pp. 43-55.

9,729.   "Willis Comments On Klan Proposal."   New Bern Sun
          Journal.   October 22, 1966.

9,730.   Wilson, D.L.   "The Ku Klux Klan: Its Origin,
          Growth, And Disbandment."   Century.   Vol. 28,
          July, 1884, pp. 398-410.

9,731.   Wilson, Margaret. "Dragon's Wife 'Doesn't Hate,'
Syble Jones Heads A KKK Auxiliary." Twin City
Sentinel. September 21, 1965, p. 1.

9,732.   "Wins Right To Word 'Klan'." New York Times.
April 1, 1926, p. 11.

9,733.   "Wizard At A Klorero With Black Pictured Revenge
On Underwood." New York Times. September 17,
1937, p. 12.

9,734.   "Wizard Collapses Defending Ku Klux." New York
Times. October 14, 1921, pp. 1, 3.

9,735.   "Wizard In Vigorous Defence Of Ku Klux." New
York Times. October 13, 1921, pp. 1, 9.

9,736.   "Wizard Of Ku Klux Klan, Bobby Shelton, Interviewed." Los Angeles Times. February 10, 1974,
p. 12.

9,737.   "Wizard Too Ill To Appear." New York Times.
October 15, 1921, p. 17.

9,738.   "Wizard Who Revived Klan Joins Friend Hitler In
Death." Afro-American. June 12, 1945.

9,739.   "Wizards And Witches." The Worker. October 3,
1965.

9,740.   "Wm. Green Silent On Black's Speech." New York
Times. October 3, 1937, p. 3.

9,741.   Wolf, Horace J. "How Shall We Meet The Klan?"
World Tomorrow. Vol. 7, March, 1924, p. 85.

9,742.   "Woman Organizer Defends Ku Klux." New York Times.
September 12, 1921, p. 15.

9,743.   "Women Win Suit Against Klan." New York Amsterdam
News. March 6, 1982, p. 3.

9,744.   Wood, Lewis. "Black Hastened Details Of Taking
Double Oath." New York Times. September 17, 1937,
pp. 1, 12.

9,745.   _____. "Black Took Oath As Court Justice
Secretly Aug. 19." New York Times. September 16,
1937, pp. 1, 14.

9,746.   _____. "Byrnes Advocates Blockade Of China."
New York Times. January 17, 1951, pp. 1, 3.

9,747.   _____. "90 Groups, Schools Named On U.S. List
As Being Disloyal." New York Times. December 5,
1947, pp. 1, 18.

9,748.   Woodward, C. Vann. "White Terror." New York
         Times' Book Review. May 23, 1971, Sect. 7,
         pp. 5, 28.

9,749.   Wooten, James T. "Klan Leader Vows New White
         Supremacy Drive." New York Times. November 30,
         1969, p. 78.

9,750.   Workman, W.D., Jr. "Klan Again On The March."
         New York Times. December 3, 1950, Sect. 4, p. 10.

9,751.   "World Court Vote Faces Long Delay; Tax Bill Deal
         Fails." New York Times. January 22, 1926, pp. 1, 9.

9,752.   "World Crisis- Powell Cartoon." Washington Post.
         November 17, 1979, p. 15A.

9,753.   "Writers, Officials Ignore Race Bias." New York
         Times. January 16, 1949, Sect. 5, p. 3.

9,754.   "Wrong Reasons Given For Right Doing." New York
         Times. December 5, 1921, p. 16.

9,755.   "Xenophobia." New York Times. January 9, 1923,
         p. 22.

9,756.   Yaffe, Richard A. "N.Y. Outlaws Klan; 1100 Names
         To FBI." PM. July 30, 1946, p. 30.

9,757.   Zander, James W. Vander. "The Klan Revival."
         American Journal Of Sociology. Vol. 65, March,
         1960, pp. 456-462.

Appendixes

A
Archival and Manuscript Collections

A SELECTED LIST

STATES

1. ALABAMA

Beittel, Adam D., Papers. Historical Collections, Library, Talladega College

2. ARKANSAS

Remmel, Harmon L., Papers and Letters. Special Collections, Library, University of Arkansas

3. CALIFORNIA

Ku Klux Klan Miscellaneous Materials. Special Collection, Oviatt Library, California State University, Northridge

Jones, Herbert C., Papers. Special Collections, Library, Stanford University.

Project South. Transcripts. University Archives, Library, Stanford University

4. COLORADO

Carr, Ralph L., Papers. Colorado State Archives and Record Service.

Downing, Warwick W., Papers. State Historical
Society of Colorado.

Doyle, Edward Lawrence, Papers. Western History
Department, Denver Public Library.

Fairall, Herbert, Papers. Western History Department, Denver Public Library.

Gunter, Julius, Papers. State Historical Society
of Colorado.

Hurwitz, Benjamin M., Papers. Western History
Department, Denver Public Library.

Johnson, Arthur C., Papers. Western Historical
Collection, University of Colorado Library.

Keating, Edward, Papers. Western Historical
Collection, University of Colorado Library.

Ku Klux Klan Collection. Special Collections,
Colorado College Library.

Ku Klux Klan Collection. State Historical Society
of Colorado.

Ku Klux Klan Collection. Western History Department, Denver Public Library.

Lindsey, Benjamin B., Papers. State Historical
Society of Colorado.

Morley, Clarence, Papers. Colorado State Archives
and Record Service.

Norlin, George, Papers. Western Historical Collection, University of Colorado Library.

O'Donnell, Thomas J., Papers. Western Historical
Collection, University of Colorado Library.

Ownbey, James, Papers. Western Historical Collection, University of Colorado Library.

Rockwell, Robert, Papers. Western Historical
Collection, University of Colorado Library.

Shafroth, John Franklin, Collection. State
Historical Society of Colorado.

Stapleton, Benjamin F., Collection. State
Historical Society of Colorado.

Sweet, William E., Papers. Colorado State
Archives and Record Service.

Taylor, Edward T., Papers. State Historical
Society of Colorado.

U.S. Works Progress Administration Papers. Western
History Department, Denver Public Library.

Work, Hubert, Papers. Colorado State Archives
and Record Service.

5. GEORGIA

American Jewish Committee. Papers. Southern
Region, Atlanta, Georgia.

Anti-Defamation League of Bnai B'rith. Southern
Eastern Regional Office, Atlanta, Georgia

Dobbins, John S. Papers. Special Collections,
Robert W. Woodruff Library for Advanced Studies,
Emory University.

Harris, Julian L. Papers. Special Collections,
Robert W. Woodruff Library for Advanced Studies,
Emory University.

Ku Klux Klan. Miscellaneous materials. Department
of Archives and History, State of Georgia.

McGill, Ralph. Papers. Special Collections,
Robert W. Woodruff Library for Advanced Studies,
Emory University

Slaughly, Henry P. Papers. Atlanta University
Library.

Stephens, Alexander H. Papers. Special Collections, Robert W. Woodruff Library for Advanced
Studies, Emory University.

Woodruff Library for Advanced Studies, Emory
University.

6. ILLINOIS

Allen, John W. Papers. Special Collections,
Morris Library, Southern Illinois University.

Angle, Paul M. Bloody Williamson papers. Manuscript Department, Chicago Historical Society.

Birger, Charles. Papers. Special Collections,
Morris Library, Southern Illinois University.

Campbell, Lewis E. Papers. Special Collections,
Morris Library, Southern Illinois University.

Edwards, Clark. Papers. Special Collections,
Morris Library, Southern Illinois University.

French, George H. Papers. Special Collections,
Morris Library, Southern Illinois University.

Ku Klux Klan. Pamphlet Collection, University
of Illinois, Chicago, Illinois.

Ku Klux Klan. Miscellaneous materials. Special
Collections, Morris Library, Southern Illinois
University.

Ku Klux Klan Papers. Manuscript Department,
Chicago Historical Society.

Paisley, Oldham. Papers. Special Collections,
Morris Library, Southern Illinois University.

Pamphlet Collection, University of Illinois.

Raines, Edgar F. Papers. Special Collections,
Morris Library, Southern Illinois University.

7. INDIANA

Ku Klux Klan. Papers. Wabash Carnegie Public
Library.

Ku Klux Klan. Three Warning Notes. Ball State
University, Special Collection Library.

8. KANSAS

Kansas West Conference of the United Methodist
Church Collection, Archives and History Library,
Southwestern College.

9. LOUISIANA

American Missionary Association. Archives,
Amistad Research Center, Dillard University.

Debaillon, Paul, and Family. Papers. Southwestern
Archives and Manuscripts Collection, Center for
Louisiana Studies, University of Southwestern
Louisiana.

Parker, John M. Papers. Southwestern Archives and
Manuscripts Collection, Center for Louisiana
Studies, University of Southwestern Louisiana.

10. MARYLAND

Bond, Hugh Lennox. Papers. Maryland Historical
Society.

Buchanan, Robert C. Papers. Maryland Historical
Society.

11. MASSACHUSETTS

Ku Klux Klan. Papers. College Library, Harvard
University.

12. MICHIGAN

Glenn, Andrew W., and Family. Papers. Division
of Archives and Manuscripts, Minnesota Historical
Society.

Hale, William D., and Family. Papers. Division
of Archives and Manuscripts, Minnesota Historical
Society.

Jewish Community Relations Council of Minnesota.
Papers. Division of Archives and Manuscripts,
Minnesota Historical Society.

Lutheran Church. Missouri Synod. Michigan
Schools Committee. Papers. Michigan Historical
Collections, Bentley Historical Library, Univer-
sity of Michigan.

13. MISSISSIPPI

Carvett, E.D. Papers. Mitchell Memorial Library,
Mississippi State University.

Swann-Cavett Family. Papers. Mitchell Memorial
Library, Mississippi.

14. MISSOURI

Atwood, Frank E. Papers. Western Historical
Manuscript Collection/State Historical Society
of Missouri Manuscripts, Ellis Library, University
of Missouri.

Barnes, Charles M. Papers. Western Historical
Manuscript Collection/State Historical Society of
Missouri Manuscripts, Ellis Library, University
of Missouri.

Decker, Perl D. Papers. Western Historical
Manuscript Collection/State Historical Society
of Missouri Manuscripts, Ellis Library, University
of Missouri.

Dorsey Family. Papers. Manuscript Department, Missouri Historical Society.

Goltra, Edward F. Papers. Manuscript Department, Missouri Historical Society.

Harrington, George R. Papers. Manuscript Department. Missouri Historical Society.

Hickman Family. Papers. Western Historical Manuscript Collection/State Historical Society of Missouri Manuscripts, Ellis Library, University of Missouri.

Hyde, Arthur M. Papers. Western Historical Manuscript Collection/State Historical Society of Missouri Manuscripts, Ellis Library, University of Missouri.

Ku Klux Klan. Papers. Manuscript Department, Missouri Historical Society.

Larwill, William C., and Sons. Papers. Western Historical Manuscript Collection/State Historical Society of Missouri Manuscripts, Ellis Library, University of Missouri.

Mitchell, Ewing Y., Jr. Papers. Western Historical Manuscript Collection/State Historical Society of Missouri Manuscripts, Ellis Library, University of Missouri.

Smith, Luther R. Papers. Manuscript Department, Missouri Historical Society.

Stevens, Walter V. Scrapbooks. Western Historical Manuscript Collection/State Historical Society of Missouri Manuscripts, Ellis Library, University of Missouri.

15. NEW YORK

Banta, Edwin P. Papers. Manuscripts and Archives Division, New York Public Library.

Bruce, John E. Papers. Schomburg Center for Research in Black Culture, New York Public Library.

Fleming, Walter L. Historical Collections. Manuscripts and Archives Division, New York Public Library.

Kennedy, Stetson. Papers. Schomburg Center for Research in Black Culture, New York Public Library.

National Negro Congress. Records. Schomburg
Center for Research in Black Culture, New York
Public Library.

Pickens, William. Papers. Schomburg Center for
Research in Black Culture, New York Public Library.

Slavery and Abolition Collection. Miscellaneous
materials. Schomburg Center for Research in
Black Culture, New York Public Library.

16. NORTH CAROLINA

Adams, Crawford C. Papers. Manuscript Department,
Perkins Library, Duke University.

Aglionby, Frances Y. Papers. Manuscript Department, Perkins Library, Duke University.

Ames Family. Papers. Manuscript Department,
Perkins Library, Duke University

Archbell, Lillie V. Papers. Southern Historical
Collection, Wilson Library, University of North
Carolina.

Bagley, Dudley W. Papers. Southern Historical
Collection, Wilson Library, University of North
Carolina.

Bailey, Josiah W. Papers. Manuscript Department,
Perkins Library, Duke University.

Ball, William W. Papers. Manuscript Department,
Perkins Library, Duke University.

Belknap, William Worth. Papers. Perkins Library,
Duke University.

Bernard, George S. Papers. Manuscript Department,
Perkins Library, Duke University.

Boardman, James Locke. Papers. Manuscript
Department, Perkins Library, Duke University.

Bowen, Reuben D. Papers. Manuscript Department,
Perkins Library, Duke University.

Brenson, Eugene C. Papers. Southern Historical
Collection, Wilson Library, University of North
Carolina.

Brotherton, William H. Papers. Perkins Library,
Duke University.

Bryan Family. Books and papers. Southern Historical Collection, Wilson Library, University of North Carolina.

Bryant, John E. Papers. Manuscript Department, Perkins Library, Duke University.

Chamberlain, G. Hope. Papers. Manuscript Department, Perkins Library, Duke University.

Civil War and Reconstruction. Papers. Division of Archives and History, North Carolina Department of Cultural Resources.

Confederate Veteran Papers. Perkins Library, Duke University.

Congress of Industrial Organizations. Organizing Committee. Papers. Manuscript Department, Perkins Library, Duke University.

Dixon, Thomas Jr. Papers. Dover Library, Gardner-Webb College.

Edwards, Fredrick C. Papers. Manuscript Department, Perkins Library, Duke University.

Ellington, L.S. Papers. Manuscript Department, Perkins Library, Duke University.

Fox, John. Papers. Manuscript Department, Perkins Library, Duke University.

Fraser, Fredrick. Letters. Manuscript Department, Perkins Library, Duke University.

Fuller-Thomas Family. Papers. Manuscript Department, Perkins Library, Duke University.

Georgia, State of. Miscellaneous Papers. Manuscript Department, Perkins Library, Duke University.

Gardner, Paris C. Papers. Manuscript Department, Perkins Library, Duke University.

Gould, John M. Papers. Manuscript Department, Perkins Library, Duke University.

Hamilton, James R. Papers. Southern Historical Collection, Wilson Library, University of North Carolina.

Hayne, Paul H. Papers. Manuscript Department, Perkins Library, Duke University

Hedrick, Benjamin S. Papers. Manuscript Department, Perkins Library, Duke University.

Hemphill Family. Papers. Manuscript Department, Perkins Library, Duke University.

Hoke, William A. Papers. Southern Historical Collection, Wilson Library, University of North Carolina.

Holden, William W. Papers. Division of Archives and History, North Carolina Department of Cultural Resources.

_____. Papers. Manuscript Department, Perkins Library, Duke University.

_____. Papers. Southern Historical Collection, Wilson Library, University of North Carolina.

Howell, Robert P. Memoirs. Southern Historical Collection, Wilson Library, University of North Carolina.

Johnston, John W. Papers. Manuscript Department, Perkins Library, Duke University.

Jones, Charles E. Papers. Manuscript Department, Perkins Library, Duke University.

Kilgo, John C. Papers. Archives, Perkins Library, Duke University.

Kinyoun, John H. Papers. Manuscript Department, Perkins Library, Duke University.

Keitt, Ellison S. Papers. Manuscripts Division, South Caroliniana Library, University of South Carolina.

Ku Klux Klan. Papers. Manuscript Department, Perkins Library, Duke University.

Lipscomb Family. Papers. Southern Historical Collection, Wilson Library, University of North Carolina.

London, Issac S. Papers. Division of Archives and History, North Carolina Department of Cultural Resources.

Martin, Sue A. Papers. Manuscript Department, Perkins Library, Duke University.

Matton, William G. Papers. Manuscript Department, Perkins Library, Duke University.

Mason, Lucy R. Papers. Manuscript Department,
Perkins Library, Duke University.

Mencken, Henry L. Papers. Manuscript Department,
Perkins Library, Duke University.

Nash Family. Papers. Southern Historical Collection, Wilson Library, University of North Carolina.

Nunn, Romulus A. Papers. Manuscript Department,
Perkins Library, Duke Library

North Carolina. Miscellaneous papers. Manuscript
Department, Perkins Library, Duke University.

Pearson, Richmond M. Papers. Southern Historical
Collection, Wilson Library, University of North
Carolina.

Potts Family. Papers. Manuscript Department,
Perkins Library, Duke University.

Rice, James H., Jr. Papers. Manuscript Department,
Perkins Library, Duke University.

Robins, Marmaduke S. Papers. Southern Historical
Collection, Wilson Library, University of North
Carolina.

Robinson, W.D. Papers. Southern Historical Collection, Wilson Library, University of North
Carolina.

Ruffins, Thomas. Papers. Perkins Library, Duke
University.

Russell, Daniel L. Papers. Southern Historical
Collection, Wilson Library, University of North
Carolina.

Scarborough Family. Papers. Manuscript Department, Perkins Library, Duke University.

Schenck, David. Papers. Southern Historical
Collection, Wilson Library, University of North
Carolina.

Shotwell, Nathan. Papers. Southern Historical
Collection, Wilson Library, University of North
Carolina.

Simms, Robert N. Papers. Manuscript Department,
Perkins Library, Duke University.

Simpson, William D. Papers. Manuscript Department,
Perkins Library, Duke University.

Slattery, Harry. Papers. Manuscript Department, Perkins Library, Duke University.

Socialist Party of America. Papers. Manuscript Department, Perkins Library, Duke University.

Thomas, Ella G. Journals. Manuscript Department, Perkins Library, Duke University.

Warmouth, Henry C. Papers. Southern Historical Collection, Wilson Library, University of North Carolina.

Underwood, Oscar W. Papers. Southern Historical Collection, Wilson Library University of North Carolina.

17. OHIO

Ku Klux Klan Papers. Library, Ohio Historical Society.

18. OKLAHOMA

Division of Manuscripts. Uncataloged collection. Western History Collections, Monnet Hall, University of Oklahoma.

Hinkel, John W. Papers. Western Historical Collection, Monnet Hall, University of Oklahoma.

Johnston, Henry S. Collection. Western Historical Collection, Monnet Hall, University of Oklahoma.

Ku Klux Klan Woman's Organization. Collection. Western Historical Collection, Monnet Hall, University of Oklahoma.

Peterson, H.C. Collection. Western Historical Collection, Monnet Hall, University of Oklahoma.

Walton, Jack C. Collection. Western Historical Collection, Monnet Hall, University of Oklahoma.

Weaver, Carlton. Collection. Western Historical Collection, Monnet Hall, University of Oklahoma.

Weldon, Bettie. Collection. Western Historical Collection, Monnet Hall, University.

19. OREGON

Estes, George. Papers. Library, Oregon Historical Society.

Ku Klux Klan Records.   Oregon Collection, Library,
University of Oregon.

Olcott, Ben W. Papers.   Oregon Collection, Library,
University of Oregon.

20. PENNSYLVANIA

Negro Materials.   Lancaster County Historical
Society Library, Lancaster, Pennsylvania.

21. RHODE ISLAND

Ku Klux Klan.   Papers.   Rhode Island Historical
Society Library, Providence, Rhode Island.

22. SOUTH CAROLINA

Bratton Family.   Papers.   Manuscripts Division,
South Caroliniana Library, University of South
Carolina.

23. TENNESSEE

Christian Advocate.   Files.   Library, Methodist
Publishing House.

Elliott, Collins D.   Papers.   Manuscript Section,
Tennessee State Library and Archives.

Johnson, Charles S.   Papers.   Fisk University
Library.

Race Relations Information Center Library, Nashville.

Tennessee Historical Society.   Miscellaneous
collection.   Manuscripts Section, Tennessee State
Library and Archives.

24. TEXAS

Biggers, Don H.   Papers.   Southwest Collection,
Library, Texas Tech University.

Colquitt, Oscar B.   Papers.   University of Texas
Archives,   Austin, Texas.

Ku Klux Klan.   Records.   Texas Collection, Moody
Memorial Library, Baylor University.

Ku Klux Klan. Materials. Special Collections, Library, Texas A&M University.

Love, Thomas B. Paper. Dallas Historical Society Archives, Dallas, Texas.

Teagarden, William B. Papers. Barker Texas History Center, Lamar Library, University of Texas.

25. VIRGINIA

Akerman, Amos T. Letterbooks. Manuscripts Department, Alderman Library, University of Virginia.

26. WASHINGTON, D. C.

Craig, Calvin. Interview. Ralph J. Bunche Oral History Collection, Howard University, MSRC.

The writer is the Grand Dragon of the Georgia KKK. He discuses the principles and programs of the Klan.

Cranford, Raymond. Interview. Ralph J. Bunche Oral History Collection, Howard University, MSRC.

Foulke, William D. Papers. Manuscript Division, Library of Congress.

National Association for the Advancement of Colored People. Records. Manuscript Division, Library of Congress.

27. WEST VIRGINIA

Davis, William P. Collection. West Virginia Collection, Library, West Virginia University.

Glassworkers' Oral History. West Virginia Collection, Library, West Virginia University.

Ku Klux Klan. Manuscripts. West Virginia Collection, Library, West Virginia University.

Mullen Family. Papers. West Virginia Collection, Library, West Virginia University.

Ogden Family. Papers. West Virginia Collection, Library, West Virginia University.

Smith, Clarence E. Papers. West Virginia Collection, Library, West Virginia University.

28. WISCONSIN

Contemporary Social Action Collection.   State
Historical Society of Wisconsin.

B
Ku Klux Klan Publications

A SELECTED LIST

Knights of Damon. <u>Life Insurance Plan For Its Member</u>.
   <u>G. M. Rosser, State Deputy For South Carolina</u>. Columbus,
   S. C.: Knights of Damon, n.d. 8pp. (Located at Duke University, Durham, N.C.).

Ku Klux Klan. <u>Dawn: The Herald Of A New And Better Day</u>.
   (Organ of the Ku Klux Klan of Illinois). Vols. 1-2;
   October 21, 1922 - February 9, 1924. Microfilmed by the
   Library of Congress Photoduplication Service, 1966.

<u>The Imperial Night-Hawk</u>.(Organ of the Ku Klux Klan). Atlanta:
   Knights of the Ku Klux Klan. Vols. 1-2, No. 34; March 28,
   1923 - November 19, 1924. Microfilmed by the New York
   Public Library, 1966.

<u>Ku Klux Kaleidoscope</u> (Goldsboro, N.C.) (Weekly newspaper).
   June 19 (Vol. 1, No. 13), July 10, 17, August 7, 21, 28,
   October 16, 1869. Located at the University of North
   Carolina at Chapel Hill.

<u>The Kourier: The Magazine of Americanism</u>. (Organ of the
   Knights of the Ku Klux Klan of Atlanta). Vols. 1-4, No.
   11; Vol. 4, No 12; Vol. 7, No. 10. April 1929- May, 1930.
   Microfilmed by the Library of Congress Photoduplication
   Service, 1969.

C
Estimated Membership of the Ku Klux Klan

FOR THE YEAR 1925*

Alabama......................115,910

Arizona.......................5,001

Arkansas....................150,000

California..................350,000

Colorado....................126,930

Connecticut..................65,590

Delaware.....................20,000

District of Columbia.........15,133

Florida.....................391,040

Georgia.....................156,010

Idaho........................30,000

Illinois....................300,324

Indiana.....................200,000

Iowa........................350,031

Kansas......................150,000

Kentucky....................441,560

Louisiana....................50,000

*Washington Post. November 2, 1930, p. 14. Reprinted with permission.

Maine...................150,041

Maryland................53,190

Massachusetts........... 130,780

Michigan................875,130

Minnesota...............65,000

Mississippi.............93,040

Missouri................175,000

Montana.................40,000

Nebraska................352,110

Nevada..................1,003

New Hampshire...........75,000

New Jersey..............720,220

New Mexico..............5,311

New York................300,429

North Carolina..........129,410

North Dakota............50,000

Ohio....................400,000

Oklahoma................239,550

Oregon..................150,000

Pennsylvania............300,000

Rhode Island............21,321

South Carolina..........200,641

South Dakota............54,329

Tennessee...............163,980

Texas...................450,000

Utah....................20,000

Vermont.................80,301

Virginia................169,630

```
Washington..................150,000
West Virginia.............. 75,903
Wisconsin...................220,850
Wyoming.................... 24,989
                Total:  8,904,887
```

D
Organizations and Groups
Concerned with
Ku Klux Klan Activities

A SELECTED LIST

American Jewish Committee
165 East 56th Street
New York, N.Y. 10022
Founded in 1906

American Jewish Congress
15 E. 84th Street
New York, N.Y. 10028
Founded in 1918

Anti-Defamation League of B'nai B'rith
823 United Nations Plaza
New York, N.Y.   10017
Founded in 1913

Commission For Racial Justice
105 Madison Avenue
New York, N.Y.   10016
Founded in 1963

Congress of Racial Equality
1916-38 Park Avenue
New York, N.Y.   10037
Founded in 1942

Greensboro Justice Fund
853 Broadway, Room 1912
New York, N.Y.   10003
Founded in 1980

John Brown Anti-Klan Committee
P.O. Box 7239
Chicago, Ill.   60680
Founded ca. 1981?

Joint Center For Political Studies
1301 Pennsylvania Ave., N. W.
Washington, D. C.   20005
Founded in 1970

Klanwatch
1001 S. Hull St.
Montgomery, Alabama   36101
Founded in 1980

National Anti-Klan Network
P.O. Box 10500
Atlanta, Ga.   30310
Founded in 1979

National Association For The Advancement
   of Colored People (NAACP)
1790 Broadway
New York, N. Y.   10019
Founded in 1909

NAACP Legal Defense and Educational Fund
Ten Columbus Circle
New York, N. Y.   10019
Founded in 1939

National Black United Front
415 Atlantic Avenue
Brooklyn, New York   11217
Founded in 1980

National Catholic Conference For Interracial
   Justice
1200 Varnum St., N. E.
Washington, D. C.   20017
Founded in 1960

National Education Association
1201 16th St., N. W.
Washington, D. C.   20036
Founded in 1857

National Urban League
500 East 62nd St.
New York, N. Y.   10021
Founded in 1910

Operation PUSH
930 E. 50th St.
Chicago, Illinois   60615
Founded in 1971

Sojourner Truth Organization
P.O. Box 8493
Chicago, Ill.   60680
Founded ca. 1981?

Southern Christian Leadership Conference
334 Auburn Avenue, N. E.
Atlanta, Ga.   30312
Founded in 1957

Southern Poverty Law Center
1001 S. Hull St.
Montgomery, Alabama   36101
Founded in 1971

Southern Regional Council
75 Marietta St., N. W.
Atlanta, Ga.   30303
Founded in 1918

United Church of Christ
Commission For Racial Justice
105 Madison Avenue
Suite 1112
New York, N. Y.   10016
Founded in 1967

E
A Klansman's Creed

THE CREED

I believe in God and the tenets of the Christian religion and that a godless nation can not long prosper.

I believe that a church that is not grounded on the principles of morality and justice is a mockery to God and to man.

I believe that a church that does not have the welfare of the common people at heart is unworthy.

I believe in the eternal separation of Church and State

I hold no allegiance to any foreign government, emperor, king, pope or any other foreign, political or religious power.

I hold my allegiance to the Stars and Stripes next to my allegiance to God alone.

I believe in just laws and liberty.

I believe in the upholding of the Constitution of these United States.

I believe that our Free Public School is the cornerstone of good government and that those who are seeking to destroy it are enemies of our Republic and are unworthy of citizenship.

I believe in freedom of speech.

I believe in free press uncontrolled by political parties or by religious sects.

I believe in law and order.

I believe in the protection of our pure woman-hood.

I do not believe in mob violence, but I do believe that laws should be enacted to prevent the causes of mob violence.

I believe in a closer relationship of capital and labor.

I believe in the prevention of unwarranted strikes by foreign labor agitators.

I believe in the limitation of foreign immigration.

I am a native-born American citizen and I believe my rights in this country are superior to those of foreigners.

Author Index

About the Compilers

LENWOOD G. DAVIS, Associate Professor of History at Winston-Salem State University, North Carolina, is a noted Black historian and internationally known bibliographer.

JANET SIMS-WOOD, a librarian at Howard University, is a bibliographer and compiler of Black history.